Preface

I have great pleasure in placing this book before the aspirants of Staff Selection Commission's Combined Graduate Level, Combined Higher Secondary Level, Central Police Organization and other exams. This book has been compiled to meet the growing demands and requirements of the SSC aspirants appearing not only for SSC exams but also for Bank and other Competitive exams conducted by Central and State Governments.

Although this book has been compiled with the prime intention of providing all the Previous Years Vocabularies asked in SSC Exams till date but I thought it would be injustice not to include some other important English vocabulary words which are frequently used and asked. Therefore, this book has been compiled comprehensively, so that students can use it even for other exams and most importantly for gradual self-learning and improvement of English Vocabulary.

I welcome comments and suggestions from the readers of this book. (WhatsApp at 9999 121 127 – Message Only)

All the Best. ☺

Nikhil Gupta

INDEX

SECTION: I
(SSC Previous Papers + Practice MCQs)

PART A: ONE WORD SUBSTITUTIONS

PART B: IDIOMS / PHRASES

PART C: SYNONYMS / ANTONYMS

PART D: SPELLING

BLACKBOOK

of

ENGLISH

VOCABULARY

SSC Vocabulary Updated till February 2023

SSC द्वारा पूछे गए शब्दावली का संकलन
(फरवरी 2023 तक अपडेटेड)

<u>How to check Genuineness of BlackBooks</u>

1. Make sure there is a **3D HOLOGRAM** on the cover of book.
2. You will see a **Unique Serial No**. at the bottom of Hologram, note it down (e.g. For the hologram present at right side Serial no is "BBXXXXXXXX".
3. **Scan the QR code** using any QR scanning app available on Google Play Store.
4. Write the Hologram Serial No. (**Numbers only** without BB Prefix) in the form and if its duplicate you will receive a message.

First Edition : -

Version 1.0 : July 2019
Version 1.1 : July 2019 (Reprint)
Version 1.2 : November 2019
Version 1.3 : November 2019 (Reprint)

Second Edition : -

Version 2.0 : August 2020
Version 2.1 : February 2021
Version 2.2 : February 2021 (Reprint)
Version 2.3 : January 2022
Version 2.4 – 2.6 : January 2022 (Reprint with minor updates)
Version 2.7 : March 2023 *(Current Edition)*
Printed on : 25th June 2023 (BN: HT0623)

Price : ₹ 399 /-

Co-Edited by : **Ashish Gupta**
Published by : **Gupta EduTech**
For Distributorship : Contact us at **support@qmaths.in**
WhatsApp at **9999 121 127 (Message Only)**

Your constructive feedback and suggestions are most important and our team will be highly obliged if you message/mail us your feedback or suggestions at support@qmaths.in.

Join Us:

 Telegram  Facebook  Twitter  Instagram  YouTube

https://bit.ly/Qm_tele   https://bit.ly/Qm_fb   https://bit.ly/Qm_Tw   https://bit.ly/Qm_insta   https://bit.ly/Qm_YT

<h1 align="center">SECTION: II</h1>

PART E: THE HINDU VOCABULARY

<h1 align="center">SECTION: III</h1>

PART F: SPECIAL WORDS

<h1 align="center">APPENDIX</h1>

HOW TO USE THIS BOOK

First of all, I want to tell you that it is not expected to rote each and every vocabulary given in this book, do not try to mug up all the words without thinking. This book has been divided into several parts, which serves distinct objectives. Therefore, you need to refer and learn vocabulary according to your needs and requirements of the examination.

One of the main objectives of compiling this book was to provide all Vocabularies asked by SSC till the very date for upcoming SSC Exams. Hence, I have added all the new vocabulary asked in SSC exams till **February 2023**.

SECTION - I:

This is very essential part, as an SSC aspirant, you need to cover this part compulsorily. Almost **80 to 85 %** questions asked in SSC exams are from this part only. Recently in 2021 SSC Conducted CGL, CHSL, CPO, GD Constable, Stenographer, Selection Post, and MTS etc. exams and it was found that more than 80% of the OWS were repeated and had been asked from previous years.

- Chapters A1, B1, C1, C2, C6 and D1 gives you **MASTER LIST of all Vocabularies** asked in SSC exams in alphabetical manner.

- Chapters A2, B2, C3, C7 and D2 is for **last minute revision**, which includes most repeated vocabularies and have been asked repetitively in SSC exams. This list has been sorted based on number of times a vocabulary has been asked.

- Chapters A3, B3, C4, C8 and D3 includes recent vocabulary asked by TCS Vender. This is for quick revision and helps students to know and understand the type and pattern of vocabs asked by TCS.

- Chapters A3, B3, C4, C9 and D4 is practice section and includes 30 or 20 short **MCQs Practice Sets** in each topic to gauge your learning. This is mandatory part for SSC aspirants and includes recently asked MCQs of SSC.

Topics	Unique Words	Total Words
OWS	1638	3024
Idioms	1580	3058
Combo	604	2093
Synonyms	1339	1701
Antonyms	1267	1693
Spelling	3749	6322
The Hindu	1077	1077
Special	2600	2600
Root Words	870	870
Vocab asked in Recent Exams (2023)	995	995
Grand Total	15719	23433

Symbols used:

SN: Serial Number

#R: Number of times a word has been repeated (asked) in SSC Exams

// : Alternate Phrases used to ask same word substitution

/ : used with either of the words

PoS: Parts of Speech

N.: Noun

V.: Verb

Adj.: Adjective

Adv.: Adverb

SECTION - II:

This section contains vocabularies which are frequently used in The Hindu Newspaper. It is often seen that many of these vocabularies appear in one exam or other. Moreover, it contains some legal or technical words which you are expected to know as an educated person. A good knowledge of this part not only increases your vocabulary but it will help you to read faster. Yes, you will read the Hindu much faster and this will serve a boon for your Reading Comprehension (Passage, Cloze Tests etc) part of Competitive exams.

SECTION - III:

This section contains a list of special technical vocabularies which are frequently asked in SSC and other competitive examinations. These terms are technical and you need to pay little attention in this section. It may be noted that though some of the vocabularies are more frequent, some are rarely asked. It is advisable to use selective reading if you have time constraint. Do not attempt to mug up all the vocabulary (in one go).

APPENDIX: (PART G)

This part is very useful to understand etymology. It is known that once you learn the meaning of a root word it would be very easy to learn similar words and even to guess the words in exam when you have not studied it. This part is again for self-learning and improvement of English vocabulary understanding and its etymology and learning should be gradual.

PART - A

(ONE WORD SUBSTITUTIONS)

One word substitution refers to a single word which describes the given definition or property. In OWS questions, a phrase will be given and you will be asked to choose One Word for this phrase from the 4 options provided in the question.

All the "**One Word Substitutions**" provided in this chapter have been asked in SSC exams and compiled here for faster revision. *You should understand that sometimes options are not an exact match and students have to choose from the best available options out of the given 4 options in the question.*

SN	Phrases	One Word (#R)	PoS	Hindi
1	Become less intense or widespread	Abate	(V.)	कम या मंद कर देना
2	A place where animals are slaughtered for consumption as food	**Abattoir (3)**	(N.)	कसाईखाना
3	The superior of a monastery	Abbot	(N.)	मठ का प्रमुख
4	To reduce to a shorter form intended to stand for the whole	**Abbreviation (4)**	(N.)	किसी शब्द या वाक्यांश संक्षिप्त रूप
5	To give up one's authority or throne	**Abdicate (6)**	(V.)	अपना पद (या दावा) छोड़ देना
6	Act of giving up the throne	**Abdication (2)**	(N.)	अपने अधिकार अथवा पद का त्याग करने की क्रिया
7	Deviation from the right course	Aberration	(N.)	असामान्यता
8	The act of washing oneself	Ablution	(N.)	हाथ या शरीर को धोने/साफ करने की क्रिया
9	Formally put an end to a system, practice, or institution	**Abolish (3)**	(V.)	किसी रिवाज या स्थापित नियम का अंत करना
10	Existing in a land from the earliest times or from before the arrival of colonists	Aboriginal	(Adj.)	किसी देश के मूल निवासी
11	The inhabitants living from earliest times in a country // The original inhabitants/natives of a country	**Aborigines (3)**	(N.)	किसी देश के मूल निवासी
12	To shorten a piece of writing without losing the sense	Abridge	(V.)	छोटा कर देना
13	A shortened version of a larger work	Abridgement	(N.)	संक्षिप्त करने की क्रिया
14	Cancel or do away with (a law or agreement)	Abrogate	(V.)	निरस्त या रद्द कर देना
15	Formal forgiveness of a person's sins	Absolution	(N.)	पापमुक्ति
16	Wildly unreasonable, illogical or ridiculous	Absurd	(Adj.)	बेतुका
17	To increase the speed	**Accelerate (2)**	(V.)	गति बढ़ाना
18	Any award, honour or laudatory notice	Accolade	(N.)	पुरस्कार/सम्मान
19	A person who helps another to commit a crime or to do something morally wrong // A partner in crime	**Accomplice (8)**	(N.)	सह-अपराधी
20	Be harmonious or consistent with	Accord	(V.)	अनुरूप होना
21	A person whose profession is to keep accounts	Accountant	(N.)	मुनीम/लेखपाल
22	Sharp and direct	Acerbic	(Adj.)	कड़वा स्वभाव
23	The scientific study of sound	**Acoustics (5)**	(N.)	ध्वनि-विज्ञान

SN	Phrases	One Word (#R)	PoS	Hindi
24	To decide and state officially in court that somebody is not guilty of a crime	**Acquit (3)**	(V.)	बरी (दोषमुक्त) कर देना
25	One who performs daring gymnastic feats // An entertainer who performs difficult physical feats	**Acrobat (3)**	(N.)	हवाई करतब करने वाला
26	An abbreviation formed from the initial letters of other words and pronounced as a word	**Acronym (4)**	(N.)	शब्दों के पहले अक्षरों से बना शब्द
27	Fear of great heights	Acrophobia	(N.)	ऊँचाई का डर
28	To do something // to behave in a particular way // to perform a part in a play / film / function	Act	(V.)	कार्य करना
29	Make a machine active or operative	Activate	(V.)	सक्रिय करना
30	The ability to make good judgments and take quick decisions // Sharpness and accuracy of judgement	**Acumen (2)**	(N.)	कुशाग्र बुद्धि
31	A person who is physically dependent on a substance / harmful drugs	**Addict (2)**	(N.)	नशेडी
32	Believe in and follow the practices of	Adhere	(V.)	पालन करना
33	The period between the beginning of puberty and adulthood	**Adolescence (4)**	(N.)	किशोरावस्था
34	An extremely beautiful young man	Adonis	(N.)	खूबसूरत नौजवान
35	Make impure by adding inferior substances	Adulterate	(V.)	मिलावट करना
36	A person who supports or speaks in favour of something	Advocate	(N.)	वकील / अधिवक्ता
37	Growing / existing / living in air	**Aerial (2)**	(Adj.)	हवाई
38	Concerned with beauty or the appreciation of beauty	**Aesthetic (3)**	(Adj.)	सौन्दर्यबोधी
39	A list of items to be discussed at a meeting	**Agenda (4)**	(N.)	कार्यसूची
40	Always ready to attack or quarrel // One who is hostile and violent	Aggressive	(Adj.)	आक्रामक
41	One who is not sure about God's existence	**Agnostic (2)**	(N.)	ईश्वर के बारे में संशयवादी व्यक्ति
42	Extreme mental or physical suffering	**Agony (2)**	(N.)	कष्ट
43	A blank book for keeping a collection of photographs, stamps or pictures.	Album	(N.)	चित्र संग्रह की किताब
44	Fear of pain.	Algophobia	(N.)	शरीर में कष्ट होने का डर
45	A person belonging to a foreign country // different from what you are used to // A fictional being from another world	**Alien (4)**	(N.)	अजनबी
46	An allowance made to a wife by her husband, when they are legally separated.	**Alimony (4)**	(N.)	परित्यक्ता पत्नी के लिये गुजारा भत्ता

SN	Phrases	One Word (#R)	PoS	Hindi
47	A story, play, picture, etc. In which each character / event is a symbol representing an idea / a quality, such as truth, evil, death, etc.	**Allegory (2)**	(N.)	नीति कथा
48	Words that begin with the same letter, syllable or sound // Repetition of an initial sound in two or more words of a line	**Alliteration (3)**	(N.)	अनुप्रास अलंकार
49	Soil deposited by flowing water	Alluvium	(N.)	पानी के बहाव द्वारा बिछाई गयी मिटटी
50	The school or college in which one has been educated	Alma Mater	(N.)	जहाँ शिक्षा पाई वह संस्था
51	Mountain climbing	Alpinism	(N.)	पर्वतारोहण
52	A table or flat surface where offerings are made to a deity	Altar	(N.)	वह स्थान जहाँ भगवान पर चढ़ाने वाली सामग्रियाँ रखी जाती है
53	Instrument that measures the altitude of the land surface	Altimeter	(N.)	ऊँचाई नापने का यंत्र
54	The height above sea level	**Altitude (2)**	(N.)	ऊंचाई
55	Someone who makes charitable donations intended to increase human wellbeing	**Altruist (9)**	(N.)	परोपकारी
56	A former student of a school, college or university	Alumnus	(N.)	भूतपूर्व छात्र
57	One who plays for pleasure rather than as a profession // A person who is neither well experienced nor professional // A non-professional who is inept at a particular activity	**Amateur (9)**	(N.)	शौक़ीन व्यक्ति
58	Fear of riding in a car	Amaxophobia	(N.)	वाहनों का डर
59	A diplomatic representative in another country	Ambassador	(N.)	राजदूत
60	Able to use the left hand and right hand equally well	**Ambidextrous (11)**	(N.)	उभयहस्त (दोनों हाथों से समान रूप से काम करने वाला)
61	Capable of being understood in either of two or more possible senses, and therefore not definite.	**Ambiguous (4)**	(Adj.)	संदिग्धार्थी / अस्पष्ट
62	Having or showing both good and bad feelings	Ambivalent	(Adj.)	उभयभावी (किसी चीज़ के बारे में दोहरे मनोभाव वाला)
63	One who has the qualities like shyness and openness at the same time	Ambivert	(N.)	अन्तर्मुखी और बहिमुखी दोनों प्रतिभा बराबर
64	Walk or move at a slow, relaxed pace // To walk aimlessly	**Amble (2)**	(V.)	धीमी गति में चलना

SN	Phrases	One Word (#R)	PoS	Hindi
65	Make (something bad or unsatisfactory) better	Ameliorate	(V.)	बेहतर बनाने के लिए सुधार करना
66	Readily reacting to suggestions and influences // willing to be guided or controlled	Amenable	(Adj.)	आज्ञाकारी
67	Someone who is friendly and good natured	Amicable	(Adj.)	मैत्रीपूर्ण/सौहार्दपूर्ण
68	A partial or total loss of memory	**Amnesia (5)**	(N.)	भूलने की बीमारी
69	An official pardon // the formal act of liberating someone	**Amnesty (4)**	(N.)	राज-क्षमा
70	Not following any moral rules and not caring about right / wrong	**Amoral (2)**	(Adj.)	नीतिहीन
71	Animal that can live both on land and in water	**Amphibians (7)**	(N.)	उभयचर जन्तु (वह जानवर जो जल और स्थल दोनों में रह सकता है)
72	A person who has had one or more limbs removed	Amputee	(N.)	अपंग, छिन्नांग
73	Comparison between things that have similar features	Analogy	(N.)	समानता
74	Detailed examination of something complex	Analysis	(N.)	विश्लेषण
75	A person who believes that laws and governments are not necessary // A person who believes in or tries to bring about a state of lawlessness	**Anarchist (4)**	(N.)	अराजकतावादी
76	A situation in a country, an organization, etc. In which there is no government, order / control	**Anarchy (8)**	(N.)	अराजकता
77	The branch of science concerned with the bodily structure of humans, animals, and other living organisms	Anatomy	(N.)	शरीर रचना विज्ञान
78	A person who presents a radio / television programme	**Anchor (4)**	(N.)	समाचार उद्घोषक
79	Belonging to long past	**Ancient (2)**	(Adj.)	प्राचीन
80	A short, interesting or amusing story about a real person or an event	**Anecdote (3)**	(N.)	लघुकथा
81	A medical specialist who administers drugs for relieving pain during surgery	**Anesthetist (2)**	(N.)	बेहोशी लाने वाला
82	Like a weak old woman	Anile	(N.)	कमजोर वृद्ध महिला के समान
83	A strong dislike / hostility	**Animosity (2)**	(N.)	घृणा
84	To destroy completely	Annihilate	(V.)	विनाश करना
85	The date on which an event happened in some previous year	**Anniversary (4)**	(N.)	सालगिरह

SN	Phrases	One Word (#R)	PoS	Hindi
86	A fixed sum paid annually	Annuity	(N.)	वार्षिक भत्ता
87	Whose names are not known // An unknown author.	**Anonymous (5)**	(Adj.)	बेनाम/गुमनाम
88	Obsessive desire to lose weight by refusing to eat	Anorexia	(N.)	वजन कम करने के लिए भोजन त्याग की तीव्र इच्छा
89	A collection of poems, stories, etc. That have been written by different people and published together in a book // a collection of poems	**Anthology (2)**	(N.)	साहित्यिक संग्रह
90	The study of human race, especially of its origin, development, customs and beliefs	**Anthropology (3)**	(N.)	मानव विज्ञान
91	Look forward to	Anticipate	(V.)	आशा रखना
92	A medicine to nullify the effect of poison	**Antidote (5)**	(N.)	विष नाशक
93	Strong dislike between two persons // A deep-seated feeling of aversion	**Antipathy (4)**	(N.)	घृणा, चिढ़
94	One who studies antique things	Antiquarian	(N.)	पुरातात्विक
95	The exact opposite	Antithesis	(N.)	विपरीत/प्रतिवाद
96	Words which are opposite in meaning	Antonym	(N.)	विलोम शब्द
97	A policy that segregates people on the basis of race // Policy of racial discrimination	**Apartheid (3)**	(N.)	रंगभेद
98	A set of rooms forming one residence in a building	Apartment	(N.)	किसी इमारत में कमरों का समूह (फ्लैट)
99	Showing or feeling no interest, enthusiasm, or concern	**Apathetic (2)**	(Adj.)	उदासीन/भावहीन
100	The feeling of not being interested in or enthusiastic	**Apathy (3)**	(N.)	उदासीनता
101	Loss of speech due to medical problem	Aphasia	(N.)	मस्तिष्क क्षति के कारण समझने या अभिव्यक्त करने की क्षमता का न होना
102	A place where bees are kept	**Apiary (4)**	(N.)	मधुमक्खियों के पालने का स्थान
103	To express regret for something that one has done wrong	Apologize	(V.)	क्षमा मांगना
104	The state of having rejected your religious beliefs or your political party or a cause	Apostasy	(N.)	स्वधर्मत्याग
105	A pioneer of a reform movement	Apostle	(N.)	धर्म प्रचारक
106	Causing shock or dismay	Appalling	(Adj.)	भयावह
107	Be appropriate or applicable	Appertain	(V.)	सम्बन्ध रखना
108	A person who formally requests something, especially a job	Applicant	(N.)	आवेदक

SN	Phrases	One Word (#R)	PoS	Hindi
109	Estimation of a thing's worth	Appraisal	(N.)	मूल्यांकन
110	To rise in value	Appreciate	(V.)	मूल्य बढ़ाना
111	A person who works for an expert to learn a trade	**Apprentice (3)**	(N.)	शिक्षार्थी
112	Being afraid of water or being near water	Aquaphobia	(N.)	जल का भय
113	A glass tank where fish and water plants are kept	**Aquarium (6)**	(N.)	मछलीघर
114	Animals and plants growing or living in, or near water	**Aquatic (6)**	(Adj.)	जलीय
115	Suitable for growing crops	Arable	(Adj.)	कृषि योग्य
116	Based on chance rather than on reason or a plan	Arbitrary	(Adj.)	मनमाना
117	A person who is chosen to settle a disagreement // a person appointed by two parties to resolve a dispute	**Arbitrator (3)**	(N.)	पंच/माध्यस्थ
118	One who studies human antiquities	Archaeologist	(N.)	पुरातत्व विज्ञानी
119	The study of human history and prehistory through the excavation of sites	**Archaeology (6)**	(N.)	पुरातत्त्व
120	No longer in use.	Archaic	(Adj.)	प्राचीन
121	A large body of water with many islands	**Archipelago (4)**	(N.)	द्वीपसमूह
122	The place where public, government or historical records are kept	**Archive (6)**	(N.)	अभिलेखागार
123	Zeal; burning enthusiasm; passion	Ardour	(N.)	तत्परता
124	A place where fights take place // A place or scene of activity, debate, or conflict	**Arena (2)**	(N.)	अखाड़ा
125	A government by the nobles / government by person of highest social order	**Aristocracy (4)**	(N.)	श्रेष्ठ जनों के द्वारा राज्य शासन
126	A military structure where arms and ammunition and other military equipment are stored	**Arsenal (5)**	(N.)	शस्त्रागार
127	Deliberately and maliciously set something (buildings usually) on fire	**Arson (2)**	(N.)	आग लगाना
128	A criminal who illegally sets fire to property	Arsonist	(N.)	आगजनी करने वाला
129	Fear of fire	Arsonphobia	(N.)	आग से डर
130	Good at expressing ideas / feelings clearly in words // Having or showing the ability to speak fluently and coherently	**Articulate (3)**	(Adj.)	सुस्पष्ट
131	One who practice one of the fine arts	**Artist (2)**	(N.)	कलाकार
132	One who denies oneself ordinary bodily pleasures	**Ascetic (4)**	(N.)	तपस्वी
133	Regard something as being due to a cause	Ascribe	(V.)	श्रेय देना/उत्तरदायी ठहराना

SN	Phrases	One Word (#R)	PoS	Hindi
134	Nations that do not trust each other / look upon each other.	Askance	(Adj.)	शक या अविश्वास के साथ देखना
135	A person who physically attacks another	Assailant	(N.)	आक्रमणकारी
136	To agree to a request / an idea / a suggestion	Assent	(V.)	स्वीकृति
137	The quality of being politely firm and demanding	Assertive	(Adj.)	दबंग, हठ धर्मी
138	One who tells future from the stars	Astrologer	(N.)	ज्योतिषी
139	A person who is trained to travel in space	**Astronaut (3)**	(N.)	अन्तरिक्ष यात्री
140	The scientific study of celestial bodies like sun, moon, stars, planets, etc.	**Astronomy (4)**	(N.)	खगोल शास्त्र
141	Place that provides refuge // a hospital where people who were mentally ill could be cared for, often for a long time	**Asylum (3)**	(N.)	शरणस्थल, अस्पताल
142	One who doesn't believe in the existence of God	**Atheist (8)**	(N.)	नास्तिक
143	An action of making amends for a wrong or injury	Atonement	(N.)	प्रायश्चित
144	That can be heard clearly	**Audible (2)**	(Adj.)	सुनाई देने योग्य
145	An official inspection of a company's, or individual's, accounts	Audit	(N.)	लेखा परीक्षा / हिसाब किताब की जांच
146	One who makes an official examination of accounts/financial records	**Auditor (5)**	(N.)	हिसाब किताब की जांच करने वाला
147	A building where an audience sits	**Auditorium (2)**	(N.)	सभागार
148	Made or done in the traditional or original way // Something that is genuine	**Authentic (2)**	(Adj.)	प्रामाणिक
149	The life history of a person written by himself	**Autobiography (7)**	(N.)	आत्मकथा
150	A system of government of a country in which one person has complete power	Autocracy	(N.)	तानाशाही
151	A ruler who has complete power	Autocrat	(N.)	तानाशाह
152	A self-governing country or region	**Autonomy (2)**	(N.)	स्वशासन
153	An official examination of a dead body by a doctor in order to discover the cause of death	Autopsy	(N.)	शव परीक्षण
154	A mass of snow, ice and rocks falling rapidly down a mountainside.	Avalanche	(N.)	पहाड़ से तेजी से गिरता हुआ बर्फ का ढेर
155	The group, especially in the arts, regarded as being the most experimental	Avant-Garde	(Adj.)	अपने क्षेत्र में अग्रणी
156	Insatiable desire for wealth	**Avarice (2)**	(N.)	लोभ
157	Having an extreme desire for wealth	Avaricious	(Adj.)	लालची
158	A place where birds are kept	**Aviary (11)**	(N.)	पक्षीशाल / चिड़ियाघर

SN	Phrases	One Word (#R)	PoS	Hindi
159	Killing of birds	**Avicide (2)**	(N.)	पक्षियों को मारना
160	Keen interest or enthusiasm	Avidity	(N.)	उत्सुकता
161	To keep away from	Avoid	(V.)	दूर रहना
162	A rule / principle that most people believe to be true	Axiom	(N.)	सिद्धांत
163	A man who remains unmarried	Bachelor	(N.)	अविवाहित
164	A place where bread and cakes are made	Bakery	(N.)	ऐसी जगह जहाँ रोटी और केक बनाया जाता है
165	A man having no hair on the scalp	**Bald (2)**	(Adj.)	गंजा
166	Senseless talk or writing	Balderdash	(N.)	बकवास
167	A large bundle bound for storage or transport	**Bale (4)**	(N.)	गट्ठा
168	Poem in short stanzas narrating a popular story	Ballad	(N.)	गाथागीत
169	Using (an idea, term, or name) frequently in casual talk	Bandying	(V.)	सविस्तार वर्णन करना
170	One who is unable to pay his debts	**Bankrupt (3)**	(N.)	दिवालिया
171	An instrument used for measuring atmospheric pressure	**Barometer (3)**	(N.)	वायु-दाब-मापक
172	Place given to soldiers to live in	**Barracks (3)**	(N.)	सैनिकों के लिए बने घर
173	A wooden drum in which beer or oil is stored	**Barrel (2)**	(N.)	पीपा
174	Revel in and make the most of something pleasing	Bask	(V.)	आनंद लेना
175	A group of guns or missile launchers operated together at one place	Battery	(N.)	तोपों का समूह जो एक साथ चलाये जाते हैं
176	A person who is fond of fighting	Bellicose	(Adj.)	लड़ाकू
177	The sound made by a crocodile	Bellow	(V.)	मगरमच्छ की आवाज
178	One who helps people by giving them money or other aid	**Benefactor (3)**	(N.)	धन आदि से सहायता करने वाला
179	A person who gains as a results of something	Beneficiary	(N.)	लाभार्थी
180	Deprived of or lacking of something	Bereft	(Adj.)	अभाव से दुःखी
181	Any soft drink except water	Beverage	(N.)	पेय पदार्थ
182	A group of girls / boys / birds etc	**Bevy (2)**	(N.)	झुंड
183	A list of the books referred to in a scholarly work	**Bibliography (3)**	(N.)	संदर्भ-ग्रंथसूची
184	Preoccupation with the acquisition and possession of books	Bibliomania	(N.)	किताबों के लिए पागलपन
185	One who is a great lover of books	**Bibliophile (6)**	(N.)	पुस्तक प्रेमी

SN	Phrases	One Word (#R)	PoS	Hindi
186	200th anniversary.	Bicentennial	(N.)	दो सौ साल का
187	Happening every second year	**Biennial (2)**	(N.)	द्विवार्षिक
188	A person who is intolerant towards those holding different opinions	**Bigot (3)**	(N.)	कट्टर व्यक्ति
189	A person who can speak only two languages	**Bilingual (5)**	(Adj.)	द्विभाषिक
190	Twice a month	Bimonthly	(Adj.)	त्रैमासिक
191	Capable of being decomposed by biological agents, especially bacteria	Biodegradable	(Adj.)	प्राकृतिक तरीके से सड़नशील
192	The story of a person's life written by somebody else	**Biography (2)**	(N.)	जीवनी
193	Study of living organisms	Biology	(N.)	जीव विज्ञान
194	The removal of tissue from the body of somebody who is ill and its examination in order to find out more about the disease	Biopsy	(N.)	जीवित ऊतकों की जांच
195	Very strange or unusual	Bizarre	(Adj.)	विचित्र
196	Words uttered impiously about God // The act of speaking irreverently about sacred things.	**Blasphemy (5)**	(N.)	ईश्वर की निंदा
197	The sound made by sheep	**Bleat (3)**	(V.)	मिमियाना / भेड़ बकरी या बछड़े की आवाज
198	A person of South African Dutch descent	Boer	(N.)	डच या डच वंशीय
199	One who does not follow the usual rules of social life // An unconventional style of living	**Bohemian (3)**	(Adj.)	रूढ़िमुक्त
200	Subject (someone) to a continuous flow of questions, criticisms or information	Bombard	(V.)	बौछार करना
201	Using high-sounding words but with little meaning	Bombastic	(Adj.)	बड़े बड़े शब्दों वाला
202	Dwarf varieties of trees and shrubs grown in pots	Bonsai	(N.)	उथले बर्तन में उगी झाड़ी का किस्म
203	A sum of money added to a person's wages as a reward for good performance.	Bonus	(N.)	अधिलाभ / पारितोषिक
204	An avid book reader // One who reads a lot	**Bookworm (2)**	(N.)	किताबी कीड़ा
205	A hunting weapon which comes back, used by Australian Aborigines	Boomerang	(N.)	एक किस्म का मुड़ा हुआ बाण जो फेंकने वाले के पास लौट आता हैं
206	To take something on loan with the intention of returning it	Borrow	(V.)	उधार लेना
207	One who is well-versed in the knowledge of plants	Botanist	(N.)	वनस्पति-विज्ञानी
208	The scientific study of plants and their structure	**Botany (6)**	(N.)	वनस्पति विज्ञान

SN	Phrases	One Word (#R)	PoS	Hindi
209	A narrow or busy section of road where the traffic often gets slower and stops	Bottleneck	(N.)	रास्ते का संकीर्ण भाग
210	A broad road bordered with trees	Boulevard	(N.)	मुख्य मार्ग
211	An arrangement of flowers that is usually given as a present	**Bouquet (7)**	(N.)	गुलदस्ता
212	Belonging to middle class.	Bourgeois	(N.)	मध्य वर्ग
213	A shop that sells women's clothes and jewellery	Boutique	(N.)	महिलाओं का वस्त्रालय
214	Affecting or relating to cows // Pertaining to cattle	**Bovine (2)**	(Adj.)	गाय से संबंधित
215	A shady place under trees	**Bower (2)**	(N.)	पेड़ों के नीचे का छायादार स्थान
216	An act of breaking or failing to observe a law	Breach	(V.)	नियम तोड़ना
217	A factory where beer is made	Brewery	(N.)	शराब की भट्ठी
218	Leather straps put around a horse's head to control it	Bridle	(N.)	लगाम
219	Member of a band of robbers	**Brigand (2)**	(N.)	डाकू
220	Hard but easily broken // liable to break easily	**Brittle (6)**	(Adj.)	भंगुर/आसानी से टूटने योग्य
221	The young of an animal cared for at one time // A family of young birds	**Brood (2)**	(N.)	किसी जीव का बच्चा
222	A meal that is usually taken late in the morning that combines a late breakfast and an early lunch	Brunch	(N.)	नाश्ते और खाने को साथ खाना
223	A woman with dark brown hair	**Brunette (2)**	(N.)	गहरे भूरे बाल वाली स्त्री
224	An itemized summary of estimated expenses for a given period along with proposals for financing them	Budgeting	(N.)	बजट
225	Gold and silver before using for manufacturing ornaments	Bullion	(N.)	सोने चाँदी की ईंट
226	A collection of sticks	Bundle	(N.)	गट्ठा
227	A large single detached house with single or double story	Bungalow	(N.)	बंगला/कोठी
228	Carry out a task clumsily or incompetently	Bungle	(V.)	गड़बड़ करना
229	A government run by officials in a state	**Bureaucracy (4)**	(N.)	नौकरशाही
230	A person who enters a building illegally in order to steal	Burglar	(N.)	सेंधमार
231	Hole excavated by an animal as dwelling	**Burrow (4)**	(N.)	बिल
232	The sound made by bees	Buzz	(V.)	भनभनाहट
233	Place where cows are sheltered	Byre	(N.)	गोशाला

SN	Phrases	One Word (#R)	PoS	Hindi
234	A group of things that have been hidden in some place	Cache	(N.)	गुप्त भंडार
235	One who is bad in spellings	Cacographer	(N.)	अशुद्ध वर्तनी वाला
236	Harsh or discordant sound // Loud confusing disagreeable sounds // An incongruous or chaotic mixture	**Cacophony (3)**	(N.)	कोलाहल
237	The young one of a cow	Calf	(N.)	बछड़ा
238	A person who is skilled at producing beautiful handwriting	**Calligrapher (4)**	(N.)	सुलेखक
239	The art of beautiful handwriting	**Calligraphy (4)**	(N.)	सुलेख
240	A man devoid of kind feeling and sympathy.	Callous	(Adj.)	कठोर हृदय
241	That which makes it difficult to recognize the presence or real nature of something	Camouflage	(N.)	छलावरण
242	A person who eats human flesh	**Cannibal (8)**	(N.)	नरभक्षक
243	Love for dogs	**Canophilia (2)**	(N.)	कुत्ते से प्यार
244	House or shelter of a gipsy // A group of people, especially traders or pilgrims, travelling together across a desert	**Caravan (6)**	(N.)	काफिला
245	The dead body of an animal	**Carcass (2)**	(N.)	पशु शव
246	Something which is considered to be very important	**Cardinal (2)**	(N.)	मुख्य/प्रधान
247	A doctor who specializes in the study or treatment of heart diseases	**Cardiologist (5)**	(N.)	हृदय रोग विशेषज्ञ
248	The study of the heart and its action and disease	Cardiology	(N.)	हृदय विज्ञान
249	A picture of a person or a thing drawn in such a highly exaggerated manner as to cause laughter	**Caricature (2)**	(N.)	व्यंग्य-चित्र
250	Animals that eat meat	**Carnivorous (4)**	(N.)	मांसभक्षी
251	Song which is sung in a church by a group of singers	Carol	(N.)	ईसाईयों का भजन
252	A person who draws or makes maps	**Cartographer (10)**	(N.)	मानचित्रकार
253	The art or process of drawing or making maps	**Cartography (4)**	(N.)	मानचित्रकारी
254	An amusing drawing about politics / events in the news	Cartoon	(N.)	व्यंगचित्र
255	A place where gambling games are played	**Casino (2)**	(N.)	जुआखाना
256	A large, deep pot used both in the oven and as a serving vessel.	Casserole	(N.)	हाँडी (एक तरह का बरतन)
257	A list or collection of books or informative graphics	**Catalogue (6)**	(N.)	सूची
258	An event causing great and sudden damage or suffering	Catastrophe	(N.)	तबाही

SN	Phrases	One Word (#R)	PoS	Hindi
259	Causing great damage or suffering	Catastrophic	(Adj.)	विनाशकारी
260	A large, deep, metal pot used for cooking over open fire	Cauldron	(N.)	हंडा, कडाही
261	Soldiers who fight on horseback	Cavalry	(N.)	घुड़सवार सेना
262	The sound of a crow	Caw	(N.)	कौवे की कांव-कांव
263	A time when enemies agree to stop fighting	Ceasefire	(N.)	युद्ध विराम
264	The state of being unmarried by choice	**Celibacy (3)**	(N.)	ब्रह्मचर्य
265	Underground place for storing wine or other provisions	**Cellar (2)**	(N.)	तहख़ाना
266	A large burial ground	**Cemetery (2)**	(N.)	कब्रिस्तान
267	A person who is a 100 years old or more	**Centenarian (3)**	(N.)	सौ वर्ष का
268	The 100th anniversary of an event	Centennial	(N.)	सौ साल का
269	Anything tending to move away from centre	Centrifugal	(Adj.)	अपकेन्द्री
270	Something that is related to the brain or the intellect	Cerebral	(Adj.)	दिमागी
271	Art of designing or writing on wax	Cerography	(N.)	मोम पर नक्काशी का काम करना
272	Rub a part of the body to restore warmth or sensation	Chafe	(V.)	रगड़कर गरमाना
273	Vexation for humiliation or disappointment	Chagrin	(N.)	विफलता, निराशा की वजह से शर्मिंदगी महसूस होना
274	A child who is believed to have been secretly left in exchange for another	Changeling	(N.)	बदला हुआ बच्चा
275	A small building / room used for christian worship in a school, prison, large private house, etc.	**Chapel (3)**	(N.)	छोटा गिरजा घर
276	Compelling attractiveness or charm that can inspire or influence others	Charisma	(N.)	आकर्षण
277	Exercising a compelling charm which inspires devotion in others	**Charismatic (2)**	(Adj.)	आकर्षक
278	A person falsely claiming to have a special knowledge or skill	**Charlatan (2)**	(N.)	ढोंगी
279	Run after in order to catch or catch up with	Chase	(V.)	पीछा करना
280	A deep fissure in the earth's surface	Chasm	(N.)	गहरी खाई
281	The base frame of car or other wheel vehicle	Chassis	(N.)	ढाँचा
282	A person employed to drive a private or hired car	**Chauffeur (9)**	(N.)	मोटर-चालक
283	Palm reading	Chiromancy	(N.)	हस्तरेखा विद्या
284	A group of singers in a church	**Choir (3)**	(N.)	गायक-मंडली
285	A routine task, especially a household one	Chore	(N.)	दैनिक काम

SN	Phrases	One Word (#R)	PoS	Hindi
286	One who plans the steps and moves in a dance	**Choreographer (5)**	(N.)	नृत्य-निर्देशक
287	A disease persisting for a long time or recurring again and again	Chronic	(Adj.)	दीर्घ/स्थायी
288	A factual written account of important or historical events in the order of their occurrence.	Chronicle	(N.)	कालक्रम से अभिलेखन
289	An arrangement of events or dates in the order of their occurrence	**Chronology (9)**	(N.)	कालक्रम
290	An instrument for measuring time accurately in spite of motion or variations in temperature, humidity, and air pressure.	Chronometer	(N.)	बिलकुल ठीक समय बतानेवाली घड़ी
291	Rude in a mean-spirited and surly way	Churlish	(Adj.)	अभद्र
292	Extreme self-confidence or audacity	Chutzpah	(N.)	दुस्साहस
293	The use of many words where only a few are necessary	**Circumlocution (3)**	(N.)	शब्द-बाहुल्य
294	Clues available at a scene	Circumstantial	(Adj.)	पारिस्थितिक
295	A fortress typically one on high ground above a city	Citadel	(N.)	किला/गढ़
296	Climb or move with difficulty or a lot of effort, typically using one's hands and feet	Clamber	(V.)	हाथ पैर के बल कठिनाई से चढ़ना
297	Making a loud and confused noise	Clamorous	(Adj.)	कोलाहलपूर्ण
298	A loud appeal or demand	Clamour	(N.)	कोलाहल/शोर
299	An extreme fear of being in a small confined place	**Claustrophobia (9)**	(N.)	छोटे जगह में होने का अत्यधिक डर
300	All the customers of a business	**Clientele (2)**	(N.)	ग्राहक गण
301	A room in a public building where outdoor clothes or luggage may be left	Cloakroom	(N.)	सामान कक्ष
302	The sound made by a hen	Cluck	(V.)	मुर्गी की आवाज
303	Land beside a sea	Coast	(N.)	समुद्र तट
304	A spider's home	Cobweb	(N.)	मकड़ी का जाला
305	A small compartment in an aircraft for the pilot	Cockpit	(N.)	वायु-यान में चालक-कक्ष
306	A drink usually made from a mixture of one or more alcoholic drinks	Cocktail	(N.)	मिश्रित शराब
307	An instruction that is added later to a will, usually to change a part of it	Codicil	(N.)	वसीयतनामे के बाद का परिवर्तन पत्र
308	Use of force or threats to get someone to agree to something	**Coercion (3)**	(N.)	जोर जबरदस्ती
309	A strongbox or small chest for holding valuables	Coffer	(N.)	तिजोरी
310	A collection of slaves	Coffle	(N.)	गुलामों का काफिला

SN	Phrases	One Word (#R)	PoS	Hindi
311	A remarkable concurrence of events or circumstances without apparent causal connection	Coincidence	(N.)	संयोग
312	A person that one work with at the same place, in a profession or a business	**Colleague (5)**	(N.)	सहकर्मी
313	Mutual discourse	**Colloquy (2)**	(N.)	वार्तालाप
314	A gigantic statue	Colossus	(N.)	विशाल मूर्ति
315	To keep a great person or event in people's memory	Commemorate	(V.)	स्मरण करना
316	Money given to agent on sales	Commission	(N.)	दलाली
317	To have a strong feeling of sympathy with a desire to help.	Compassion	(N.)	दया / अनुकम्पा
318	People who belong to the same country	Compatriots	(N.)	स्वदेशवासी
319	A person who introduces the performers or contestants in a variety show	**Compere (2)**	(N.)	कार्यक्रम–उद्घोषक
320	Satisfied, with no desire to change or improve	Complacent	(Adj.)	आत्मसंतुष्ट
321	To make perfect or complete	Complement	(N.)	पूरक
322	A remark that expresses approval or admiration	Compliment	(N.)	प्रशंसा
323	One who sets type for books, newspapers, etc.	Compositor	(N.)	अक्षरयोजक
324	Having too much pride in yourself and what you do	Conceited	(Adj.)	अभिमानी
325	Capable of being imagined or grasped mentally	Conceivable	(Adj.)	कल्पनीय
326	Having a common centre, as circles or spheres	Concentric	(Adj.)	संकेन्द्री
327	Living together of a man and woman without being married to each other	Concubinage	(N.)	बिना विवाह के साथ रहना
328	An apartment building in which each apartment is owned separately by the people living in it, but also containing shared areas.	Condominium	(N.)	फ्लैट की तरह का घर
329	Forgive or pardon some wrongdoing or an offence	Condone	(V.)	माफ़ करना
330	A company or person that makes or sells sweets or chocolate	**Confectioner (2)**	(N.)	मिठाई बेचने वाला
331	To own up to something as true	Confess	(V.)	कबूल करना
332	An arrangement of parts or elements in a particular form or figure	Configuration	(N.)	एक विशेष आकृति में तत्वों की व्यवस्था
333	To officially take something away from somebody	Confiscate	(V.)	जब्त करना
334	Combustibles – flammable	Conflagrant	(Adj.)	जलता हुआ
335	Place where two or more rivers meet	Confluence	(N.)	संगम
336	Pertaining to an individual from birth	Congenital	(Adj.)	जन्मजात
337	A corporation made up of a number of different companies that operate in diversified fields	Conglomerate	(N.)	कॉम्पनियों का समूह

SN	Phrases	One Word (#R)	PoS	Hindi
338	An assembly of worshippers // A group of people who have come together in a religious building for worship and prayer	**Congregation (5)**	(N.)	धार्मिक सभा
339	An opinion or conclusion formed on the basis of incomplete information	Conjecture	(N.)	निराधार कल्पना
340	A man who knows a lot about things like food, music and art	**Connoisseur (4)**	(N.)	विशेषज्ञ, पारखी
341	Feeling inside you which tells you what is right and what is wrong	Conscience	(N.)	जमीर, अन्तरात्मा
342	One who does one's work thoroughly and seriously	**Conscientious (2)**	(Adj.)	कर्तव्यनिष्ठ
343	A careful preservation and protection of wildlife is the need of the hour.	Conservation	(N.)	प्राकृतिक संरक्षण
344	Opposed to great or sudden change.	Conservative	(N.)	रूढ़िवादी, अपरिवर्तनवादी
345	Comfort someone at a time of grief or disappointment	Console	(V.)	सांत्वना देना
346	A group of stars that forms a shape in the sky and has a name	**Constellation (8)**	(N.)	नक्षत्र
347	State of anxiety or dismay causing mental confusion	Consternation	(N.)	घबराहट
348	Imposed a restriction on	Constrained	(Adj.)	विवश किया हुआ
349	Extremely skilled	Consummate	(Adj.)	उत्कृष्ट
350	Easily spread from one person to another (disease) // A disease which spreads with contact	**Contagious (3)**	(Adj.)	संक्रामक
351	Something made impure by exposure to polluting substances	Contaminated	(Adj.)	दूषित
352	Belonging to the same time // A person living in the same age with another	**Contemporary (13)**	(Adj.)	समकालीन
353	Someone who is satisfied with life is general	Contented	(Adj.)	संतुष्ट
354	Touching along the side or boundary	Contiguous	(Adj.)	निकटवर्ती
355	An event that may / may not happen	Contingency	(N.)	आकस्मिकता
356	Prohibited by law or treaty from being imported or exported	Contraband	(N.)	वर्जित सामग्री
357	A man who is recovering from illness.	**Convalescent (4)**	(N.)	बीमारी से ठीक होना
358	A place where nuns live and work	**Convent (2)**	(N.)	मठ
359	A group of vehicles travelling together, typically one accompanied by armed troops	Convoy	(N.)	काफ़िला
360	Ceremony of crowning a king	**Coronation (2)**	(N.)	राज तिलक करना
361	To confirm with the help of evidence	**Corroborate (2)**	(V.)	पुष्टि करना
362	A funeral procession	Cortege	(N.)	शव-यात्रा

SN	Phrases	One Word (#R)	PoS	Hindi
363	Science of the constitution of the whole universe	**Cosmography (2)**	(N.)	विश्वरचना
364	A person who regards the whole world as his country // One who is a citizen not of a country but of the world	**Cosmopolitan (5)**	(Adj.)	समस्त संसार का
365	Made in imitation so as to be passed off fraudulently as genuine	Counterfeit	(N.)	जाली
366	A stanza having two lines in verse	Couplet	(N.)	द्विपदी दोहा
367	A person who takes care of cattle	Cowherd	(N.)	ग्वाला
368	That can be believed or trusted	**Credible (3)**	(Adj.)	विश्वसनीय
369	A person who readily believes others easily	**Credulous (4)**	(Adj.)	भोला-भाला
370	A system of religious belief; a faith	Creed	(N.)	संप्रदाय
371	A place where a dead person's body is burnt.	Crematorium	(N.)	शवदाहगृह
372	Turning point of danger / disease	Crisis	(N.)	संकट
373	A principle or standard by which anything is or can be judged	Criterion	(N.)	मापदंड
374	One who finds nothing good in anything	Critic	(N.)	आलोचक
375	A group of people	Crowd	(N.)	भीड़
376	Break or fall apart into small fragments in the process of deterioration	Crumble	(V.)	चूर चूर होना
377	A dynamic campaign for political, social or religious change	Crusade	(N.)	धर्मयुद्ध
378	Having or forming a hard outer layer	Crusted	(N.)	पपड़ीदार
379	A device for deciphering codes and ciphers	Cryptograph	(N.)	कूट-लेखन
380	The study of secret writing and coded language or words	Cryptography	(N.)	गुप्तलेखन
381	A style of cooking food, characteristic of a particular country or region	Cuisine	(N.)	भोजन
382	Guilty of the crime	Culpable	(Adj.)	अपराधिक
383	All the arts, beliefs and social institutions etc. Characteristic of a race	Culture	(N.)	संस्कृति
384	A person in charge of a museum	**Curator (5)**	(N.)	संग्रहालय अध्यक्ष
385	Signal under martial law for people to remain indoors	Curfew	(N.)	निषेधाज्ञा
386	A strong desire to know or learn something	Curiosity	(N.)	जिज्ञासा
387	The system of money used in a particular country	Currency	(N.)	मुद्रा
388	The expression of a wish that misfortune or doom befall a person	Curse	(V.)	कोसना
389	One who sneers at the aims and beliefs of his fellow men. // A person who believes that only selfishness motivates human actions	**Cynic (2)**	(N.)	निंदक, मानवद्वेषी

SN	Phrases	One Word (#R)	PoS	Hindi
390	Extreme fear of dogs	Cynophobia	(N.)	कुत्ते से असाधारण भय
391	Centre of attraction	**Cynosure (2)**	(N.)	आकर्षण-बिन्दु
392	A secret or disguised way of writing	Cypher	(N.)	गुप्त लिखावट
393	Dealing with cells	Cytology	(N.)	कोशिका विज्ञान
394	A situation when no progress is possible	Deadlock	(N.)	गतिरोध
395	A period of ten years	**Decade (3)**	(N.)	दशक
396	Act of injuring another's reputation by any slanderous communication	**Defamation (2)**	(N.)	मानहानि
397	To injure one's reputation	Defame	(V.)	बदनाम करना
398	To protect from harm or danger	Defend	(V.)	बचाव करना
399	Open refusal to obey orders	Defiance	(N.)	अवज्ञा
400	A shortage of vitamins, minerals, etc. Needed for good health	Deficiency	(N.)	पोषक तत्वों की कमी
401	To give one's authority to another	**Delegate (2)**	(V.)	प्रतिनिधि
402	Slow and careful movement or thought	Deliberation	(N.)	सोच समझ कर
403	An omission of duty	Delinquency	(N.)	कर्तव्य में चूक
404	A young person tending to commit crime, particularly minor crime.	Delinquent	(Adj.)	अपराधी
405	Become liquid, typically during decomposition	Deliquesce	(V.)	पिघलना / गलना
406	A disturbed state of mind caused by an illness	Delirium	(N.)	ज्वर में उत्पन्न मस्तिष्क विभ्रम
407	A political leader appealing to popular desires and prejudices	Demagogue	(N.)	जनोत्तेजक नेता
408	A system of government in which all the people of a country can vote to elect their representatives	**Democracy (3)**	(N.)	जनतंत्र
409	The study of population and its dynamics	**Demography (5)**	(N.)	जनसांख्यिकी
410	A lions' home	Den	(N.)	माँद
411	Take away or alter the natural qualities of	Denature	(V.)	विकृत करना
412	Criticize unfairly	Denigrate	(V.)	बदनाम करना
413	Portray in words	Depict	(V.)	शब्दों में वर्णन करना
414	Person who gives written testimony for use in a law court	Deponent	(N.)	गवाह
415	Morally corrupt	Depraved	(Adj.)	भ्रष्ट
416	To feel and express strong disapproval	Deprecate	(V.)	विरोध करना
417	To become less valuable over a period of time	Depreciate	(V.)	मूल्य कम करना
418	Unable to think clearly because of a mental illness	Deranged	(Adj.)	विक्षिप्त / पागल
419	A person without a home, a job or property	**Derelict (2)**	(Adj.)	आवारा व्यक्ति
420	Failing to discharge one's duty	Dereliction	(N.)	कर्तव्य का त्याग

SN	Phrases	One Word (#R)	PoS	Hindi
421	To laugh at something in a cruel way	Deride	(V.)	उपहास करना
422	A doctor who studies and treats skin diseases	**Dermatologist (3)**	(N.)	त्वचा विशेषज्ञ
423	The scientific study of skin diseases	**Dermatology (5)**	(N.)	त्वचाविज्ञान
424	The abandonment of one's country or cause	Desertion	(N.)	परित्याग
425	A person without money, food and other things necessary for life	Destitute	(Adj.)	बदहाली
426	One who investigates and solves crimes	**Detective (2)**	(N.)	जासूस
427	The action of discouraging an action or event through instilling doubt or fear of the consequences	Deterrence	(N.)	रुकावट डालना
428	Showing a skilful use of underhand tactics to achieve goals	Devious	(Adj.)	धूर्त
429	Skilful with your hands	Dexterous	(Adj.)	निपुण
430	Determine the nature of the disease	Diagnose	(V.)	रोग पहचानना
431	The process of deciding the nature of a disease by examination	Diagnosis	(N.)	रोग की पहचान
432	A particular form of a language which is peculiar to a specific region	Dialect	(N.)	बोली
433	Bitter and violent attack in words	Diatribe	(N.)	आक्षेप
434	A ruler with total power over a country, typically one who has obtained control by force	**Dictator (2)**	(N.)	तानाशाह
435	Giving orders in a manner that permits no refusal	Dictatorial	(Adj.)	तानाशाही
436	A book giving meaning of various words	Dictionary	(N.)	शब्दकोश
437	Spread over a wide area or between a large number of people	Diffuse	(Adj.)	फैला हुआ
438	A situation requiring a choice between equally undesirable alternatives or confusions	Dilemma	(N.)	दुविधा
439	A dabbler in the art and literature	**Dilettante (2)**	(N.)	मस्तमौला
440	Showing care and effort in your work / duties	Diligent	(Adj.)	मेहनती
441	Irresistible craving for alcoholic drinks	**Dipsomania (2)**	(N.)	शराब की लत
442	A book of names and addresses	Directory	(N.)	नाम और पते की पुस्तक
443	A song sung in the past at a funeral or for a dead person	**Dirge (2)**	(N.)	शोकगीत
444	An act that has disastrous consequences	Disaster	(N.)	आपदा
445	A heavy round plate of metal thrown by an athlete	Discus	(N.)	चक्का फेंक प्रतियोगिता
446	The state of being deprived of a right or privilege, especially the right to vote.	Disenfranchisement	(N.)	मताधिकार से वंचित करना
447	An act that makes feel morally bad or ashamed.	Disgraceful	(Adj.)	शर्मनाक

SN	Phrases	One Word (#R)	PoS	Hindi
448	Change the appearance to deceive or to hide the identity	**Disguise (2)**	(V.)	भेष बदलना
449	Break up into small parts as the result of impact or decay	**Disintegrate (2)**	(V.)	विघटित हो जाना
450	Causing a mood of gloom and depression	Dismal	(Adj.)	निराशपूर्ण
451	To throw an event into confusion or disorder	Disrupt	(V.)	तितर बितर करना
452	A range of different things	Diversity	(N.)	विविधता
453	One thing that can be divided	Divisible	(Adj.)	भाज्य
454	Country treated as permanent home by an individual	Domicile	(N.)	मूल निवास
455	An area of land that is controlled by a ruler	Dominion	(N.)	अधिराज्य
456	Not active or growing	Dormant	(Adj.)	निष्क्रिय
457	A large bedroom for a number of people in a school or institution	**Dormitory (4)**	(N.)	शयनागार
458	Situated on back	Dorsal	(Adj.)	सतहीय
459	A heavy fall of rain that often starts suddenly	Downpour	(N.)	मूसलधार बारिश
460	A game in which no one wins	**Draw (5)**	(V.)	अनिर्णित करना
461	The nest of a squirrel, typically in the form of a mass of twigs in a tree	Drey	(N.)	गिलहरी का घोंसला
462	Light rain falling in small drops	Drizzle	(V.)	बूंदा बांदी होना
463	Mania for travel	Dromomania	(N.)	यात्रा की धुन
464	Dry weather with no rainfall	Drought	(N.)	सूखा
465	A herd or flock of animals being driven in a body	**Drove (2)**	(N.)	झुंड
466	(A metal) that can be made into a thin wire	Ductile	(Adj.)	तन्य
467	A contest between two people to settle a point of honour	Duel	(N.)	द्वंद युद्ध
468	One who can't speak	**Dumb (2)**	(Adj.)	गूंगा
469	Something that is strong and lasts a long time without breaking or becoming weaker.	Durable	(Adj.)	टिकाऊ
470	A person, animal or plant much below the usual height	Dwarf	(N.)	बौना आदमी
471	A wall built to prevent the sea or a river from flooding an area	Dyke	(N.)	बांध
472	Succession of rulers belonging to one family.	Dynasty	(N.)	राजवंश
473	A disorder that involve difficulty in reading, interpret words	Dyslexia	(N.)	अक्षरों को पढ़ने में कठिनाई होने वाला मानसिक रोग
474	One who listens secretly to private conversation	**Eavesdropper (3)**	(N.)	छिपकर बातें सुनने वाला
475	A man with abnormal habits	**Eccentric (3)**	(Adj.)	विचित्र

SN	Phrases	One Word (#R)	PoS	Hindi
476	Repetition of a sound caused by reflection of sound waves.	**Echo (2)**	(N.)	प्रतिध्वनि
477	One who studies and cares about environment	Ecologist	(N.)	पर्यावरण विज्ञानशास्री
478	Study of the interaction of people with their environment	**Ecology (3)**	(N.)	पर्यावरण विज्ञान
479	Careful in the spending of money, time, etc.	Economical	(Adj.)	किफ़ायती
480	A thing fit to be eaten	**Edible (5)**	(Adj.)	खाद्य
481	Instruct or improve someone morally or intellectually.	Edify	(V.)	उपदेश देना
482	To prepare written material for publication by correcting or modifying it	Edit	(V.)	संपादन करना
483	Rub or wipe out	Efface	(V.)	मिटाना
484	A change which is the result of an act or some cause	Effect	(N.)	प्रभाव
485	Man behaving more like a woman than as a man	**Effeminate (4)**	(Adj.)	नारी जैसा
486	Favouring social equality	Egalitarian	(Adj.)	समानाधिकारवादी
487	One who is preoccupied with his own interests	**Egoist (3)**	(N.)	आत्महितैषी
488	A person who talks too much of himself // A person who speaks always in praise of himself // A person who is excessively conceited and self-absorbed	**Egotist (4)**	(N.)	अहंवादी
489	All the people in a country or area who are entitled to vote in an election	**Electorate (2)**	(N.)	मतदाता
490	A poem that express lament for the dead	**Elegy (4)**	(N.)	शोकगीत
491	A small mischievous fairy	**Elf (3)**	(N.)	शरारती परी
492	The art of effective speaking // Public oratory skills	**Elocution (2)**	(N.)	वाककला
493	To run away secretly with a romantic partner	**Elope (2)**	(V.)	भाग जाना
494	Fluent or persuasive in speaking or writing	Eloquent	(Adj.)	सुवक्ता
495	Make perfectly clear	Elucidate	(V.)	स्पष्ट करना
496	A paradise with perfect bliss.	Elysium	(N.)	स्वर्ग
497	To free from restraint	Emancipate	(V.)	बंधनमुक्त करना
498	The act of setting free from bondage of any kind	Emancipation	(N.)	मुक्ति
499	Fix an object firmly and deeply in a surrounding mass	Embed	(V.)	अंतःस्थापित करना
500	A small piece of burning or glowing coal or wood in a dying fire	Ember	(N.)	अंगार
501	Steal or misappropriate money	Embezzle	(V.)	गबन करना
502	An act of misappropriation of money	**Embezzlement (4)**	(N.)	गबन

SN	Phrases	One Word (#R)	PoS	Hindi
503	Be an expression of or give a tangible or visible form to an idea, quality, or feeling	Embody	(V.)	मूर्त रूप देना
504	One who is honourably discharged from service	Emeritus	(Adj.)	अवकाश प्राप्त
505	Medicine that causes vomiting	Emetic	(N.)	वमनकारी औषध
506	A person who leaves his country to live in another	**Emigrant (8)**	(N.)	देशत्यागी
507	One who goes for a secret official mission	Emissary	(N.)	गुप्तचर
508	The ability to understand another person's feelings, experience, etc.	**Empathy (3)**	(N.)	संवेदना
509	One who employs	Employer	(N.)	काम देनेवाला
510	A reference work (often in several volumes) containing articles on various topics (often arranged in alphabetical order) dealing with the entire range of human knowledge or with some particular specialty	**Encyclopedia (3)**	(N.)	विश्वकोश
511	Try hard to do or achieve something	Endeavour	(V.)	प्रयत्न
512	Regularly found in a particular place or among a particular group of people and difficult to get rid of // a disease that is prevalent in a particular area and is difficult to get rid of	**Endemic (2)**	(Adj.)	स्थानिक
513	To sweep over something so as to surround it completely	Engulf	(V.)	निगल जाना
514	A state of mental weariness from lack of occupation	Ennui	(N.)	ग्लानि
515	Preserve a right, tradition, or idea in a form that ensures it will be protected and respected	Enshrine	(V.)	प्रतिष्ठापित करना
516	A scientist who studies insects	**Entomologist (2)**	(N.)	कीटविज्ञानी
517	The scientific study of worms and insects	**Entomology (7)**	(N.)	कीटविज्ञान
518	Likely to arouse envy	Enviable	(Adj.)	ईर्ष्या के योग्य
519	Lasting for a very short time	**Ephemeral (5)**	(Adj.)	क्षणिक
520	Long poem based on a noble theme	Epic	(N.)	महाकाव्य
521	Devoted to pleasure and enjoy yourself	Epicurean	(Adj.)	भोगवादी
522	Widespread outbreak of a disease which affects large populations at the same time	**Epidemic (3)**	(N.)	महामारी
523	A disease causing a person to fall unconscious involuntarily	Epilepsy	(N.)	मिर्गी
524	A short speech at the end of a play	**Epilogue (5)**	(N.)	उपसंहार
525	A verse letter	Epistle	(N.)	काव्यपत्र
526	An inscription on a tombstone in the memory of the person who has died	**Epitaph (12)**	(N.)	समाधि-लेख
527	A person or thing that is a perfect example of a particular quality or type	Epitome	(N.)	साक्षात् उदाहरण

SN	Phrases	One Word (#R)	PoS	Hindi
528	Imaginary line dividing Earth into northern and southern hemispheres	Equator	(N.)	भूमध्य रेखा
529	A state of perfect balance	**Equilibrium (3)**	(N.)	समतुल्यता
530	The dates when days and nights are of equal length	**Equinox (2)**	(N.)	जब दिन और रात समान लंबाई के हो
531	Which can be rooted out	Eradicable	(Adj.)	उन्मूलनीय
532	Rub out writing	Erase	(V.)	मिटाना
533	Excessive desire to work.	Ergomania	(N.)	काम करने की अत्यधिक इच्छा
534	A lover of work	Ergophile	(N.)	काम का प्रेमी
535	A mistake in a book	Erratum	(N.)	किताब में अशुद्धि
536	Profound scholarly knowledge	Erudition	(N.)	पांडित्य
537	One who accompanies somebody to protect him	**Escort (2)**	(N.)	मार्गरक्षी
538	The condition of being honoured (esteemed or respected or well regarded)	Esteem	(N.)	आदर
539	Something which lasts forever	**Eternal (3)**	(Adj.)	अनंत
540	Infinite or unending time	Eternity	(N.)	अनंतकाल
541	The philosophical study of moral values and rules	Ethics	(N.)	आचार विचार
542	Science of the races of mankind	**Ethnology (2)**	(N.)	मानव जाति विज्ञान
543	Make pale by excluding light	Etiolate	(V.)	पीला करना
544	The customary code of polite behaviour in society	**Etiquette (2)**	(N.)	शिष्टाचार
545	The study of the origin and history of words	**Etymology (2)**	(N.)	शब्दों के उद्गम का शास्त्र
546	A science of race, culture and human development	Eugenics	(N.)	मनुष्यों की सन्तति सुधार का अध्ययन
547	Praise highly in speech or writing	Eulogise	(V.)	प्रशंसा करना
548	A formal expression of praise for someone who has died.	**Eulogy (3)**	(N.)	प्रशंसा भाषण
549	Substitution of a mild for a very blunt expression	**Euphemism (2)**	(N.)	कठोर बात को कोमल रीति से कहना
550	Feelings of great happiness and excitement	Euphoria	(N.)	परम सुख बोध
551	Bringing about gentle and painless death from incurable disease	**Euthanasia (4)**	(N.)	इच्छामृत्यु
552	Soon passing out or of a short duration	Evanescent	(Adj.)	क्षणिक
553	Expel someone from a property, especially with the support of the law	Evict	(V.)	बेदखल करना
554	To develop gradually	Evolved	(V.)	विकसित

SN	Phrases	One Word (#R)	PoS	Hindi
555	Represent something as larger, better or worse than it really is	Exaggerate	(V.)	बढा चढा कर कहना
556	A person who is examined	Examinee	(N.)	परीक्षार्थी
557	A short piece of writing, music, film, etc. Taken from a longer whole	Excerpt	(N.)	अंश
558	A short journey for pleasure	Excursion	(N.)	पर्यटन
559	Critical explanation or interpretation of a text, especially of scripture	Exegesis	(N.)	व्याख्या
560	An urgent need or demand	Exigency	(N.)	तत्कालिक आवश्यकता
561	A poll taken of voters leaving the voting place that is usually used for predicting the winners.	Exit Poll	(N.)	निर्गम मत सर्वेक्षण
562	A situation in which many people leave a place at the same time	Exodus	(N.)	कूच
563	To free somebody from all blame	**Exonerate (7)**	(V.)	दोषमुक्त करना
564	Extremely high.	Exorbitant	(Adj.)	अत्यधिक
565	A large open area of land, water or sky	Expanse	(N.)	विस्तार
566	A person who lives outside his native country	Expatriate	(N.)	निर्वासित
567	A journey undertaken by a group of people with a particular purpose, especially that of exploration or research	Expedition	(N.)	अभियान
568	Officially make a student leave a school for ever	Expel	(V.)	निकाल बाहर करना
569	To make atonement for one's sins	**Expiate (2)**	(V.)	प्रायश्चित करना
570	To come to an end	Expire	(V.)	समाप्त होना
571	To remove an objectionable part from a book.	Expurgate	(V.)	छाँटना
572	A speech or a presentation made without previous preparation.	**Extempore (7)**	(Adj.)	बिना तैयारी के
573	Stop something from burning	Extinguish	(V.)	बुझाना
574	Obtaining something, usually money, by using force or threat	Extortion	(N.)	जबरन वसूली
575	To send back a criminal or an unwanted person to the country of his / her origin	Extradite	(V.)	भागे हुए अपराधी को अधिकारी को सौंपना
576	A person who wastes his money on luxury	**Extravagant (4)**	(Adj.)	फिजूल खर्च
577	A lively and confident person who enjoys being with other people // one who is outgoing	**Extrovert (3)**	(N.)	बहिर्मुखी
578	A short story with a moral, usually with animals as characters	**Fable (3)**	(N.)	कल्पित कहानी
579	Performing adroitly and without effort	Facile	(Adj.)	सहज
580	An exact copy of handwriting or a picture produced by a machine	Facsimile	(N.)	प्रतिच्छाया

SN	Phrases	One Word (#R)	PoS	Hindi
581	A small organised dissenting group within a larger one	Faction	(N.)	गुट
582	A thing that is not genuine	Fake	(Adj.)	नकली
583	One who is subject to failure or to committing mistakes	Fallible	(Adj.)	पतनशील
584	Farmland ploughed and harrowed but left for a period without being sown in order to restore its fertility	Fallow	(N.)	परती भूमि
585	A lack of food during a long period of time in a region	Famine	(N.)	अकाल
586	A person motivated by irrational enthusiasm	**Fanatic (3)**	(N.)	कट्टरपंथी
587	Marked by extreme enthusiasm	Fanatical	(Adj.)	कट्टरता
588	A pleasant situation that you imagine but that is unlikely to happen	**Fantasy (2)**	(V.)	कोरी कल्पना
589	One who is difficult to please	**Fastidious (7)**	(Adj.)	ढीठ, हठी
590	Causing or ending in death	**Fatal (5)**	(Adj.)	घातक
591	The belief that events are decided by fate and that you cannot control them	**Fatalism (3)**	(N.)	भाग्यवाद
592	One who believes in fate	**Fatalist (4)**	(N.)	भाग्यवादी
593	The animals living in an area or in a particular period of history	**Fauna (2)**	(N.)	पशुवर्ग
594	That is possible and likely to be achieved	**Feasible (2)**	(Adj.)	संभव
595	Ceremony to formally congratulate success.	Felicitating	(N.)	बधाई देना
596	Well chosen or suited to the circumstances	Felicitous	(Adj.)	परम सुखी
597	Relating to or involved in crime	Felonious	(Adj.)	अपराधी
598	One who believes in giving equal opportunity to women in all fields	**Feminist (2)**	(N.)	नारीवादी
599	A boat or ship for conveying passengers and goods, especially over a relatively short distance and as a regular service	Ferry	(N.)	नौका
600	Relating to a festival	Festal	(Adj.)	उत्सव संबंधी
601	Bitter quarrel over a long period of time	Feud	(N.)	शत्रुता
602	Changing frequently	Fickle	(Adj.)	चंचल
603	As opposed to reality imagined not real	Fictitious	(Adj.)	काल्पनिक
604	Something that is imagined but does not exist	Figment	(N.)	मनगढ़ंत
605	Killing of one's own child	Filicide	(N.)	पुत्र-हत्या
606	A strong interest in something or someone	Fixation	(N.)	किसी से गहरा लगाव
607	A person who attracts attention with a flashy style	Flamboyant	(N.)	भड़कीला
608	A group of ships sailing together	**Fleet (3)**	(N.)	जहाजों का बेड़ा
609	Which can easily be carved without breaking	Flexible	(Adj.)	लचीला
610	A quick, sudden movement	Flick	(N.)	झटका

SN	Phrases	One Word (#R)	PoS	Hindi
611	Shine with a bright but brief or irregular light	Flicker	(V.)	झिलमिलाना
612	Unwelcome aspect of a situation	Flip Side	(N.)	अवांछित पहलू
613	A group of birds of one kind	**Flock (2)**	(N.)	झुण्ड
614	The plants and vegetation of a particular region	**Flora (4)**	(N.)	वनस्पति
615	A person who sells and arranges cut flowers	**Florist (7)**	(N.)	फूलवाला
616	To struggle helplessly	**Flounder (2)**	(V.)	घबरा जाना
617	Accidental good fortune	**Fluke (2)**	(N.)	अकस्मात सफलता
618	Continuous movement and change	Flux	(N.)	प्रवाह
619	Go or come after a person or thing proceeding ahead	Follow	(V.)	पीछा करना
620	Chief of a group of workmen	Foreman	(N.)	अधिकर्मी
621	Ability to see what might happen in the future	Foresight	(N.)	दूरदर्शिता
622	Be deprived of property or a right or privilege as a penalty for wrongdoing	Forfeited	(Adj.)	जब्त कर लिया
623	Move ahead or forward steadily and gradually	Forge	(V.)	लगातार आगे बढना
624	Falsification of documents etc.	**Forgery (2)**	(N.)	जालसाजी
625	Direct and outspoken	Forthright	(Adv.)	स्पष्टवादी
626	A period of two weeks	**Fortnight (2)**	(N.)	दो सप्ताह
627	Something that is to your advantage but happened by chance	Fortuitous	(Adj.)	भाग्यशाली
628	The hard remains of a prehistoric animal or planet that are found inside a rock	Fossil	(Adj.)	जीवाव␣शेष
629	An abandoned child of unknown parents who is found by some- body.	Foundling	(N.)	परित्यक्त शिशु
630	An entrance hall in a building used by the public, especially a hotel or theatre	**Foyer (3)**	(N.)	बराम्दा
631	Something which gets broken easily	**Fragile (4)**	(Adj.)	भंगुर
632	Weakness and poor health	Frailty	(N.)	कमज़ोरी
633	Constitutional right to cast vote	Franchise	(N.)	मताधिकार
634	An act of murdering one's brother	**Fratricide (3)**	(N.)	भ्रातृहत्या
635	An act of deceiving somebody in order to make money	**Fraud (2)**	(N.)	धोखा
636	Causing or affected by anxiety or stress	Fraught	(Adj.)	व्याकुल
637	The feeling of being upset or annoyed as a result of being unable to change or achieve something.	Frustration	(N.)	निराशा
638	One who runs away from justice or the law	**Fugitive (5)**	(N.)	भगोड़ा
639	Doing something awkwardly or in a clumsy manner	Fumbling	(Adj.)	गड़बड़ करना
640	One who walks on ropes	Funambulist	(N.)	रस्सी पर चलनेवाला नट

SN	Phrases	One Word (#R)	PoS	Hindi
641	Simple, fast-spreading plant without flowers or leaves, which can often cause disease	Fungus	(N.)	फफूँदी
642	Hair of animals, which is soft and used for making wool	Fur	(N.)	रोआँ
643	The main body of an aircraft	Fuselage	(N.)	हवाई जहाज़ का ढांचा
644	A brave, nobleminded or chivalrous man	Gallant	(Adj.)	वीर
645	Causing annoyance or resentment	Galling	(Adj.)	कष्टकर
646	To express in an unclear way	Garbled	(Adj.)	अस्पष्ट
647	Talks a lot to explain something very trivial	Garrulous	(Adj.)	बातूनी
648	The art and practice of cooking and eating good food	Gastronomy	(N.)	पाक कला
649	Chief or Commander of army	General	(N.)	सेनाध्यक्ष
650	Science of heredity	**Genetics (3)**	(N.)	आनुवंशिकी
651	The murder of a whole race or a group of people	**Genocide (6)**	(N.)	जातिसंहार
652	Really coming from its stated, advertised or reputed source	Genuine	(Adj.)	असली
653	A person who studies the Earth and the materials of which it is made	**Geologist (2)**	(N.)	भूवैज्ञानिक
654	The study of earth, including the origin and history of the rocks and soil of which the earth is made	**Geology (3)**	(N.)	भूगर्भशास्त्र
655	The branch of medical science which deals with the problems of the old	Geriatrics	(N.)	वृद्धावस्था चिकित्साशास्त्र
656	A state governed by old people	Gerontocracy	(N.)	वृद्ध-शासन
657	Study of the various aspects of aging	Gerontology	(N.)	वृद्धावस्था
658	A movement of part of the body to express an idea or feeling	**Gesture (2)**	(N.)	इशारा
659	In a threatening manner	Ghastly	(Adv.)	ख़ौफ़नाक रूप से
660	A part of the city especially the slum area	Ghetto	(N.)	बस्ती
661	Inflammation of gums	Gingivitis	(N.)	मसूड़े की सूजन
662	An extremely large mass of ice which moves very slowly, often down a mountain valley	**Glacier (2)**	(N.)	हिमनदी
663	A person who repairs broken window-glasses	Glazier	(N.)	कांच का काम करनेवाला
664	A list of technical / special words, especially those in a particular text, explaining their meanings	Glossary	(N.)	शब्दकोश
665	To look at someone in an angry or threatening way	Glower	(V.)	घूर कर देखना
666	One who eats too much	**Glutton (5)**	(N.)	खाऊ, पेटू
667	To bite like a rat	Gnaw	(V.)	कुतरना

SN	Phrases	One Word (#R)	PoS	Hindi
668	Who loves good food and knows a lot about it // Connoisseur of food	**Gourmet (3)**	(N.)	खाद्य पारखी
669	Writing or drawings scribbled, scratched, or sprayed illicitly on a wall or other surface in a public place	**Graffiti (4)**	(N.)	दीवार चित्रण
670	A piece of a living tissue or plant that is transplanted surgically	Graft	(N.)	रिश्वत
671	A building where grain is stored	**Granary (2)**	(N.)	धान्यागार
672	Costing nothing.	Gratis	(Adv.)	निशुल्क
673	A room or building, for the preservation of plants	Green House	(N.)	पौधा-घर
674	An animal that lives in groups // Tending to associate with others of one's kind	**Gregarious (8)**	(Adj.)	झुण्ड में रहनेवाला
675	The sound a bear makes	Growl	(N.)	भालू के गुर्राने की आवाज
676	The sound made by a camel	Grunt	(N.)	ऊँट की गुगुराहट की आवाज़
677	One who is easily deceived	**Gullible (8)**	(Adj.)	आसानी से धोखा खानेवाला
678	Eat or drink food quickly and in large amounts	Gulp	(V.)	निगल जाना
679	A strong blast of wind.	Gust	(N.)	हवा का झोंका
680	A room filled with equipment for games and physical exercise.	Gymnasium	(N.)	व्यायामशाला
681	One who treats female ailments	Gynaecologist	(N.)	स्त्रीरोग विशेषज्ञ
682	Science of blood	Haematology	(N.)	रुधिरविज्ञान
683	A perception without objective reality	**Hallucination (3)**	(N.)	माया
684	A drug which makes one see things that are not really there.	Hallucinogen	(N.)	विभ्रामक दवा
685	A very small village	**Hamlet (3)**	(N.)	छोटा गांव
686	Come in the way of	Hamper	(V.)	रोकना
687	Activities such as sewing and making cloth that use skill with your hands and artistic ability to make things	Handicraft	(N.)	हस्तशिल्प
688	A building in which aircraft are housed	**Hangar (4)**	(N.)	विमानशाला
689	A lengthy and aggressive speech addressed to a large assembly.	**Harangue (2)**	(N.)	प्रभावशाली भाषण
690	Trouble and annoy continually	Harass	(V.)	परेशान करना
691	Somebody that foretells the coming of something	Harbinger	(N.)	सन्देशवाहक
692	A place of shelter for ships	Harbour	(N.)	बंदरगाह
693	A spear used for hunting large fish	Harpoon	(N.)	मत्स्य भाला
694	Acutely distressing	Harrowing	(Adj.)	खौफ़नाक

SN	Phrases	One Word (#R)	PoS	Hindi
695	Irritating inconvenience	Hassle	(V.)	परेशान करना
696	Number of fishes getting caught	Haul	(N.)	जाल में फँसी हुई मछलियों की संख्या
697	A transport vehicle for conveying the coffin at a funeral	**Hearse (3)**	(N.)	शवयान
698	In an enthusiastic way	Heartily	(Adv.)	उत्साह से
699	Making one feel very sad	Heart-Wrenching	(Adj.)	दुखी करने वाला
700	Interrupt (a public speaker) with derisive or aggressive comments or abuse	Heckle	(V.)	प्रश्नों से तंग करना
701	One who believes that gaining pleasure is the most important thing in life	Hedonist	(N.)	सुखवादी
702	Pay attention	Heed	(V.)	सावधान रहना
703	Person who is the natural successor to ancestral property	Heir	(N.)	वारिस
704	Preferring or attracted to sunlight	**Heliophilous (2)**	(Adj.)	सूर्यभिमुख
705	The therapeutic use of sunlight	Heliotherapy	(N.)	सूर्य चिकित्सा
706	A seven-sided figure	Heptagon	(N.)	सप्तभुज
707	Place for collection of dried plant specimens	**Herbarium (2)**	(N.)	वनस्पति संग्रहालय
708	Animal that feeds on plants	**Herbivorous (2)**	(N.)	शाकाहारी
709	A group of cattle or sheep	**Herd (3)**	(N.)	झुंड
710	A belief or an opinion that is against the principle of a particular religion. // Opinion contrary to accepted doctrines	**Heresy (2)**	(N.)	विधर्म
711	Things of different nature	**Heterogeneous (2)**	(Adj.)	विविध
712	Allowing or assisting to discover	Heuristic	(Adj.)	खोज करने मे सहायक
713	A geometrical figure with six sides	Hexagon	(N.)	षट्भुज
714	To spend winter in a dormant state	Hibernate	(V.)	शीतनिद्रा में होना
715	Condition of sleep during certain parts of the year	Hibernation	(N.)	शीतनिद्रा
716	A person claiming to be superior in culture and intellect to others	Highbrow	(Adj.)	बुद्धिमान
717	An act of violence to take control of a plane	**Hijack (2)**	(V.)	विमान का अपहरण
718	Parts of a country behind the coast or a river bank.	Hinterland	(N.)	आंतरिक इलाके
719	The sound made by a snake	Hiss	(N.)	साँप की फुफकारी आवाज़
720	Very dramatic	Histrionic	(Adj.)	नाटकीय
721	To secretly store more than what is allowed	Hoard	(V.)	खजाना
722	Destruction or slaughter on a mass scale	Holocaust	(N.)	विध्वंस
723	Killing of a person by another	**Homicide (3)**	(N.)	मानव हत्या

SN	Phrases	One Word (#R)	PoS	Hindi
724	All (things or people) of the same or similar kind or nature	**Homogeneous (3)**	(Adj.)	सजातीय
725	Things which are of the same kind and of the same dimensions	Homogenous	(Adj.)	एक समान
726	Words that are spelt and pronounced in the same way but have different meanings	Homonyms	(N.)	समोच्चारित भिन्नार्थक शब्द
727	A mass of wax cells built by honey bees to store honey	Honeycomb	(N.)	शहद का छत्ता
728	A payment given for professional services that are rendered nominally without charge	Honorarium	(N.)	मानदेय
729	Holding an office without receiving a pay	**Honorary (5)**	(Adj.)	माननीय
730	The cry of an owl	**Hoot (2)**	(N.)	उल्लू की बोली
731	A large group of people	**Horde (4)**	(N.)	भीड़
732	The line where the land and sky seems to meet	**Horizon (5)**	(N.)	क्षितिज
733	Something that is extremely unpleasant	Horrendous	(Adj.)	भयानक
734	The study of growing garden plants	**Horticulture (4)**	(N.)	उद्यान-विज्ञान
735	One who studies the art of gardening	Horticulturist	(N.)	बाग़बानी करनेवाला
736	Friendly and welcoming to visitors.	Hospitable	(Adj.)	सत्कार करने वाला
737	Receiving guests warmly	Hospitality	(N.)	अतिथि सत्कार
738	Someone taken a prisoner to fulfil demands	Hostage	(N.)	बंधक
739	A woman who entertains guests	Hostess	(N.)	सत्कारिणी
740	One who loses temper very soon	Hot-Headed	(Adj.)	उग्र स्वभाव का
741	Annoyed or irritated and quick to take offence at petty things	Huffy	(Adj.)	झुंझलाया हुआ
742	The organic component of soil, formed by the decomposition of leaves and other plant material	Humus	(N.)	सड़ी पत्तियों की मिट्टी
743	Assembly or parliament in which no party has got clear majority.	Hung	(Adj.)	लटका हुआ
744	In a quick manner.	Hurriedly	(Adv.)	हड़बड़ी में
745	A box or cage for rabbits or small animals	**Hutch (4)**	(N.)	छोटे जानवरों के रहने का घर
746	The science of surveying and charting bodies of water	Hydrography	(N.)	जलराशि विज्ञान
747	Extreme fear of water	**Hydrophobia (6)**	(N.)	पानी से भय
748	A song or music in praise of God	**Hymn (2)**	(N.)	स्तुति का गीत
749	An exaggerated statement not to be taken seriously or literally	Hyperbole	(N.)	अतिशयोक्ति
750	Excessive preoccupation with one's health	Hypochondria	(N.)	रोगभ्रम
751	A person who suffers from an imaginary illness // A person who is abnormally anxious about his health	**Hypochondriac (7)**	(N.)	रोगभ्रमी

SN	Phrases	One Word (#R)	PoS	Hindi
752	A person pretending to be somebody he isn't	**Hypocrite (7)**	(N.)	पाखंडी
753	A tentative theory about the natural world	Hypothesis	(N.)	परिकल्पना
754	One who destroys images or attacks popular beliefs // A person who criticises traditional beliefs and customs	**Iconoclast (9)**	(N.)	रिवाज़ तोड़नेवाला
755	A person's peculiar habit	**Idiosyncrasy (2)**	(N.)	अनोखापन
756	A mode of behavior or way of thought peculiar to an individual (not sub- or abnormal in any way)	Idiosyncratic	(Adj.)	विशेष स्वभाव का
757	An image of a God used for worship	**Idol (2)**	(N.)	प्रतिमा/मूर्ति
758	The practice of worshipping statues as gods	**Idolatry (2)**	(N.)	मूर्ति पूजा
759	Extremely happy, peaceful, or picturesque	Idyllic	(Adj.)	शांतिपूर्ण
760	A small round house / shelter built from blocks of hard snow by the inuit people of northern n. America	**Igloo (2)**	(N.)	हिम-कुटी
761	Not to pay attention to someone or something	Ignore	(N.)	नज़रअंदाज़ करना
762	Handwriting which is difficult or impossible to read	**Illegible (10)**	(Adj.)	अपठनीय
763	That which is unlawful	**Illicit (2)**	(Adj.)	अवैध
764	A person who cannot read or write	**Illiterate (5)**	(Adj.)	निरक्षर
765	To brighten up with lights	**Illuminate (2)**	(V.)	प्रकाश करना
766	Pictures given in a book for the purpose of explaining things	**Illustration (2)**	(N.)	चित्रण
767	Existing only in the mind	Imaginary	(Adj.)	काल्पनिक
768	A very complex situation	Imbroglio	(N.)	उलझन
769	Something which can be copied	Imitable	(Adj.)	अनुकरणीय
770	The action of using someone or something as a model	Imitation	(N.)	नकल/अनुकरण
771	A foreigner who settles in a country. // A person coming to a foreign land to settle there.	**Immigrant (3)**	(N.)	अप्रवासी
772	That which cannot be moved	Immobile	(Adj.)	अचल
773	Matter which is against moral values	Immoral	(Adj.)	अनैतिक
774	Resistant to a particular infection	**Immune (2)**	(Adj.)	प्रतिरक्षित
775	Protection or exemption from something, especially an obligation or penalty	Immunity	(N.)	प्रतिरोधक क्षमता
776	Transfix or pierce with a sharp instrument	Impale	(V.)	छेदना
777	Not supporting any side in an argument	Impartial	(Adj.)	निष्पक्ष
778	The policy of extending a country's empire and influence	Imperialism	(N.)	साम्राज्यवाद
779	Not allowing fluid to pass-through. // A person who remains unmoved and unaffected by other people's opinions, suggestions	**Impervious (2)**	(Adj.)	अभेद्य

SN	Phrases	One Word (#R)	PoS	Hindi
780	A person who dishonestly pretends to be somebody else	**Imposter (3)**	(N.)	बहुरूपिया
781	Strong and impossible to defeat / change // that which cannot be taken by force	**Impregnable (2)**	(Adj.)	अभेद्य
782	Made or done without previous preparation	Impromptu	(Adj.)	बिना तैयारी के
783	Make better	Improve	(V.)	बेहतर बनाना
784	One who is too careless to plan for the future	Improvident	(Adj.)	लापरवाह
785	Shamelessly rude	Impudent	(Adj.)	बेहूदा
786	Without risk of punishment	**Impunity (2)**	(N.)	दण्ड मुक्ति
787	Incapable of being approached	**Inaccessible (4)**	(Adj.)	दुर्गम
788	Not endowed with life / lifeless objects	**Inanimate (2)**	(Adj.)	अचेतन
789	Unable to speak distinctly or express oneself clearly	**Inarticulate (2)**	(Adj.)	व्यक्त करने में असमर्थ
790	Something that cannot be heard	**Inaudible (9)**	(Adj.)	अश्राव्य
791	A deity or spirit embodied in human form	Incarnate	(Adj.)	अवतार लिया हुआ
792	Motive or incitement to action	**Incentive (2)**	(N.)	प्रोत्साहन
793	Lack of civic-mindedness or of patriotism	**Incivism (2)**	(N.)	देशद्रोह
794	Travelling under a name other than one's own	Incognito	(Adj.)	गुम रूप से
795	Something that is expressed in a confusing way	Incoherent	(Adj.)	असंगत
796	Something that is difficult to understand	**Incomprehensible (3)**	(Adj.)	समझ से बाहर
797	One who cannot be corrected // One who is beyond reform	**Incorrigible (11)**	(Adj.)	असंशोधनीय
798	That which cannot be believed	**Incredible (5)**	(Adj.)	अविश्वसनीय
799	Owing money to someone	Indebted	(Adj.)	ऋणी
800	Incapable of feeling tired or exhausted	**Indefatigable (5)**	(Adj.)	न थकनेवाला
801	That which cannot be effaced	**Indelible (2)**	(Adj.)	स्थायी
802	Extreme or indefinite to be adequately described.	Indescribable	(Adj.)	अवर्णनीय
803	Originating or occurring naturally in the place or country where found // native	Indigenous	(Adj.)	स्वदेशी
804	Anger about an unfair situation or about someone's unfair behaviour	**Indignation (2)**	(N.)	अन्याय देखकर क्रोधित होना
805	A person who is absolutely necessary for someone or something	Indispensable	(Adj.)	अपरिहार्य
806	One who works very hard	Industrious	(Adj.)	मेहनती
807	Not fit to eat	**Inedible (2)**	(Adj.)	अखाद्य
808	That cannot be expressed in words	**Ineffable (3)**	(Adj.)	अवर्णनीय
809	Someone not fit to be chosen	**Ineligible (2)**	(Adj.)	अयोग्य
810	Showing a lack of skill	Ineptness	(Adj.)	अयोग्यता
811	Unable to act	Inert	(Adj.)	अक्रिय

SN	Phrases	One Word (#R)	PoS	Hindi
812	Something that cannot be avoided // Certain to happen	**Inevitable (12)**	(Adj.)	अटल
813	Not to be moved by entreaty	Inexorable	(Adj.)	हठी
814	That which cannot be put out	Inextinguishable	(Adj.)	जिसे बुझाया न जा सके
815	One who cannot make mistake	**Infallible (10)**	(Adj.)	अचूक
816	Murder of an infant	**Infanticide (3)**	(N.)	शिशु हत्या
817	Not limited by number	**Infinite (2)**	(Adj.)	अनंत
818	A place in a large institution for the care of those who are ill.	**Infirmary (2)**	(N.)	अस्पताल
819	That can burn / catches fire easily	**Inflammable (5)**	(Adj.)	ज्वलनशील
820	A cluster of flowers on a branch	Inflorescence	(N.)	पुष्पगुच्छ
821	The money, property, etc. That you receive from somebody when he dies	Inheritance	(N.)	विरासत
822	Causing no harm	Innocuous	(Adj.)	अहानिकर
823	An indirect reference	Innuendo	(N.)	इशारा (गलत भावना से)
824	Treat with a vaccine, usually by injection to promote immunity against a disease	Inoculate	(V.)	टीका लगाना
825	One who is very curious to know things and asks questions	Inquisitive	(Adj.)	जिज्ञासु
826	That which cannot be satisfied	**Insatiable (5)**	(Adj.)	लालची
827	Write or carve words on stone or paper	Inscribe	(V.)	अंकित करना
828	Words carved on a stone or monument	Inscription	(N.)	शिलालेख
829	A problem that is so difficult that it cannot be answered	Insoluble	(Adj.)	अघुलनशील
830	Being unable to pay one's debt	**Insolvent (4)**	(Adj.)	दिवालिया
831	The condition of being unable to sleep over a period of time	**Insomnia (5)**	(N.)	अनिद्रा
832	Covered with a material or substance in order to stop heat, sound etc. From entering or escaping	Insulated	(Adj.)	विद्युत-रोधित
833	Rebellious or opposing the authority	Insurgent	(N.)	विद्रोही
834	That which cannot be perceived by touch	Intangible	(Adj.)	अस्पृश्य
835	Combine to form a whole	Integrate	(V.)	संघटित करना
836	The quality of being honest and having strong moral principles.	**Integrity (3)**	(N.)	अखंडता
837	One who interferes in the affairs of others, often for selfish reasons	Interloper	(N.)	घुसपैठिया
838	Interval between two events	**Interlude (2)**	(N.)	मध्यांतर कार्यक्रम

SN	Phrases	One Word (#R)	PoS	Hindi
839	One who intervenes between two or more parties to settle differences	**Intermediary (2)**	(Adj.)	मध्यस्थ
840	The act of burying a dead person	Interment	(N.)	दफ़न
841	Continuing for a very long time	Interminable	(Adj.)	अनंतकालीन
842	The act of confining someone in a prison	Internment	(N.)	नजरबंदी
843	Estimate the value of	Interpolate	(V.)	अनुमान लगाना
844	Place or insert between one thing and another	Interpose	(V.)	घुसाना
845	The period between two reigns	**Interregnum (2)**	(N.)	दो शासनों के बीच का काल
846	To prevent or alter a result or course of events	Intervene	(V.)	हस्तक्षेप करना
847	One who dies without a will	**Intestate (5)**	(Adj.)	बिन वसीयत मरा हुआ
848	Force someone through fear to do or not to do something	Intimidate	(V.)	धमकाना
849	The examination or observation of one's own mental and emotional processes	**Introspection (2)**	(N.)	आत्म निरीक्षण
850	A quiet person who is more interested in his own thoughts and feelings than in spending time with other people	**Introvert (5)**	(N.)	अन्तर्मुखी व्यक्ति
851	A person who enters without any invitation	Intruder	(N.)	घुसपैठिया
852	Overflow or fill an area with excess water, as in a flood	Inundate	(V.)	डुबोना
853	A person weak and disabled by illness	Invalid	(N.)	लंबे समय से बीमार व्यक्ति
854	A detailed list of things in a place	Inventory	(N.)	वस्तु सूची
855	An animal lacking a backbone	Invertebrates	(N.)	अकशेरुकी
856	An official examination of the facts about a situation, crime, etc.	Investigation	(N.)	जाँच पड़ताल
857	A person who supervises during an examination	**Invigilator (6)**	(N.)	निरीक्षक
858	Refresh and revive	**Invigorate (2)**	(V.)	बलवर्धन करना
859	That which cannot be conquered	**Invincible (3)**	(Adj.)	अजेय
860	Call upon God or any other power (like law) etc. For help or protection	Invocation	(N.)	आह्वान
861	Easily provoked	Irascible	(Adj.)	चिड़चिड़ा
862	A statement which cannot be contradicted	Irrefutable	(Adj.)	अखंडनीय
863	Showing a lack of respect for people or things that are generally taken seriously	Irreverent	(Adj.)	अपमान जनक
864	That which cannot be called back	**Irrevocable (6)**	(Adj.)	अटल
865	To supply land with water by artificial means	Irrigate	(V.)	सींचना
866	A piece of land entirely surrounded by water	Island	(N.)	द्वीप

SN	Phrases	One Word (#R)	PoS	Hindi
867	A small island	Islet	(N.)	छोटा द्वीप
868	Far away from other places	Isolated	(Adj.)	अलग किया हुआ
869	A narrow stretch of land connecting two large bodies of land	Isthmus	(N.)	भूमि की एक संकरी पट्टी जो दो बड़े भभागों को जोड़ती है
870	Travelling from place to place, especially to find work	**Itinerant (2)**	(Adj.)	भ्रमणकारी
871	A plan of a journey, including the route and the places that you visit	**Itinerary (6)**	(N.)	यात्रा कार्यक्रम
872	One who takes care of a building	Janitor	(N.)	चौकीदार
873	Special words and phrases used by particular groups of people, especially in their work	Jargon	(N.)	विशिष्ट शब्दावली
874	A short journey that you make for pleasure	Jaunt	(N.)	मनोरंजन की यात्रा
875	Having or expressing a lively, cheerful, and self-confident manner	Jauntily	(Adv.)	मनोरंजन से
876	To cross streets on foot carelessly	Jaywalk	(N.)	रास्ता पार करने में लापरवाह होना
877	Extreme form of patriotism	Jingoism	(N.)	कट्टर राष्ट्रवाद
878	A person or thing that brings bad luck	Jinx	(N.)	मनहूस
879	Something which brings bad luck	Jinxed	(V.)	मनहूस
880	A person who rides in horse races, especially as a profession	**Jockey (2)**	(N.)	घुड़दौड़ का घुड़सवार
881	The work of collecting and writing news, stories for newspapers, magazines, radio or television	Journalism	(N.)	पत्रकारिता
882	A person who writes for newspapers and magazines	Journalist	(N.)	पत्रकार
883	The act of traveling from one place to another	Journey	(N.)	यात्रा
884	Merry, convivial, hearty and good humoured	Jovial	(Adj.)	उल्लासपूर्ण
885	A person in a court who has the authority to decide how criminals should be punished or to make legal decisions	Judge	(N.)	न्यायाधीश
886	The part of a country's government responsible for its legal system	Judiciary	(N.)	न्यायतंत्र
887	A military or political group that rules a country after taking power by force	Junta	(N.)	सत्ताधारी सेना
888	The science or philosophy of law	Jurisprudence	(N.)	न्यायशास्त्र
889	A group of members of the public who listen to the facts of a case in a court and decide whether or not somebody is guilty of a crime	**Jury (2)**	(N.)	न्यायपीठ
890	Connected with young people who are not yet adults	Juvenile	(Adj.)	किशोर

SN	Phrases	One Word (#R)	PoS	Hindi
891	Placing different things in order to create an interesting effect	**Juxtapose (3)**	(V.)	पास-पास रखना
892	Small shelter for dog	**Kennel (2)**	(N.)	कुत्ता-घर
893	The inner soft part of a seed, fruit or nut	**Kernel (2)**	(N.)	गिरी/दाना
894	A person with strong desire to steal.	**Kleptomania (6)**	(N.)	चोरी करने की बीमारी
895	A natural skill at doing something	**Knack (2)**	(N.)	कौशल
896	The sound of the funeral bell	Knell	(N.)	शोक सूचक घंटे की ध्वनि
897	A deep cut or tear in skin or flesh	Laceration	(N.)	घाव
898	Two lengths of rope, bamboo or wood with rungs used for climbing up and down walls, sides of ships etc.	**Ladder (2)**	(N.)	सीढ़ी
899	A place where wild animals live	Lair	(N.)	माँद
900	The young one of a sheep	Lamb	(N.)	मेमना
901	A room or large cupboard for storing food	Larder	(N.)	खाद्य भण्डार रखने की जगह
902	Denoting the second or second mentioned of two people or things	Latter	(Adj.)	बाद वाला
903	Worthy of high praise	Laudable	(Adj.)	प्रशंसनीय
904	A place where clothes are washed and pressed	Laundry	(N.)	धोबीघर
905	Honour given for some achievement	Laurel	(N.)	प्रतिष्ठा
906	A medicine that softens the bowels	Laxative	(Adj.)	पेट साफ करने वाली
907	Unwilling to work or use energy	Lazy	(Adj.)	आलसी
908	A legal agreement that allows someone to use a building or land for a period of time, usually in return for rent	Lease	(N.)	पट्टा
909	A sly look that is lustful	Leer	(N.)	बुरी नज़र से देखना
910	The property left to someone by a will	**Legacy (2)**	(N.)	विरासत
911	That which is lawful	Legal	(Adj.)	क़ानूनी
912	A person who writes and edits dictionaries	**Lexicographer (7)**	(N.)	शब्दकोश के लेखक
913	The activity of writing dictionaries	Lexicography	(N.)	शब्दकोश निर्माण
914	A list of words on a particular subject or in a language in alphabetical order	Lexicon	(N.)	शब्दकोश
915	Responsible according to law	Liable	(Adj.)	उत्तरदायी
916	A person who strongly believes that people should have the freedom to do and think as they like	Libertarian	(N.)	मुक्तिवादी
917	A strong band of tissues in the body that connects bones and supports organs and keeps them in position	**Ligaments (2)**	(N.)	जोड़

SN	Phrases	One Word (#R)	PoS	Hindi
918	Eating mud	**Limivorous (2)**	(Adj.)	मिट्टी खाने वाला
919	To stay longer than necessary	Linger	(V.)	विलंबित करना
920	A person who knows several foreign languages well // a person who studies languages	Linguist	(N.)	बहुभाषाविद्
921	One who can read and write	Literate	(Adj.)	साक्षर
922	One who talks a lot	**Loquacious (3)**	(Adj.)	बातूनी
923	Easy to understand	Lucid	(Adj.)	सुस्पष्ट
924	Profitable, yielding financial gain	Lucrative	(Adj.)	लाभकारी
925	A soft gentle song sung to make a child go to sleep	**Lullaby (2)**	(N.)	निद्रा गीत
926	A person as a source of intellectual light or moral inspiration	Luminary	(N.)	महान विद्वान
927	Related to the moon	**Lunar (3)**	(Adj.)	चन्द्र संबंधी
928	One who is mentally not sound	Lunatic	(Adj.)	पागल
929	A sudden unsteady movement; a stagger	Lurch	(N.)	झटका
930	A girl or young woman, especially an unmarried one	Maiden	(N.)	अविवाहिता
931	The first public speech delivered by a person	**Maiden-Speech (2)**	(N.)	प्रथम भाषण
932	Cause to continue; keep up; preserve (a state of affairs, an activity etc)	Maintain	(V.)	बनाए रखना
933	Usage of an incorrect word in place of the one which is similar in pronunciation	Malapropism	(N.)	ध्वनि में समानता वाले शब्द का गलत प्रयोग
934	Hatred	Malevolence	(N.)	द्वेष
935	Easy to shape in any desired form	Malleable	(Adj.)	लचीला
936	Insufficient feeding or nourishing	Malnutrition	(N.)	कुपोषण
937	Animals which suckle their young	Mammals	(N.)	स्तनपायी
938	In a way that is clear or obvious to the eye or mind	Manifestly	(Adv.)	साफ़ तौर पर
939	A written statement in which a group of people, especially a political party, explains their beliefs and says what they will do if they win an election	Manifesto	(N.)	घोषणापत्र
940	A dummy used to display clothes in a shop window	Mannequin	(N.)	पुतला
941	An underhand device resorted to in order to justify misconduct	Manoeuvre	(N.)	पैंतरेबाज़ी
942	An instrument used for measuring the pressure of liquids and gases	Manometer	(N.)	दबाव नापने का यंत्र
943	A large impressive house	**Mansion (2)**	(N.)	हवेली

SN	Phrases	One Word (#R)	PoS	Hindi
944	A copy of a book, piece of music, etc. Before it has been printed // A paper written by hand	**Manuscript (6)**	(N.)	हस्तलिपि
945	Animals living in the sea only	Marine	(N.)	समुद्री
946	Relating to soldiers or war	Martial	(Adj.)	युद्ध संबंधी
947	Someone who is killed fighting for the cause of religion or faith.	**Martyr (4)**	(N.)	शहीद
948	Someone who obtains pleasure from receiving punishment	Masochist	(N.)	पीड़ा सुखभोगी
949	A person skilled in cutting, dressing, and laying stone in buildings.	**Mason (3)**	(N.)	राजमिस्त्री
950	One for whom money is the most important thing	Materialistic	(Adj.)	भौतिकवादी
951	A cinema show held in the afternoon	**Matinee (5)**	(N.)	अपराह्न का फिल्म
952	Woman who is the head of the family	Matriarch	(N.)	मातृ सत्ता
953	The killing of one's mother	**Matricide (3)**	(N.)	मातृहत्या
954	The state of being married	Matrimony	(N.)	विवाह
955	A stately or impressive building housing a tomb or group of tombs	**Mausoleum (2)**	(N.)	मक़बरा
956	An established principle of practical wisdom // a short statement of a general truth or rule of conduct	**Maxim (2)**	(N.)	कहावत
957	An area of grassland where animals graze	**Meadow (2)**	(N.)	चारागाह
958	To try to settle a dispute between two other parties	Mediate	(V.)	मध्यस्थता करना
959	Belonging to the middle ages	Medieval	(Adj.)	मध्यकालीन
960	Of only average standard	Mediocre	(Adj.)	औसत दर्जे का
961	A musical composition made up of a series of songs or short pieces	Medley	(N.)	गीत समूह
962	Feeling or expressing pensive sadness	Melancholic	(Adj.)	उदासी की अवस्था
963	A sound that is pleasing to hear	**Melodious (2)**	(Adj.)	मधुर
964	Something that serves as a reminder	**Memento (2)**	(N.)	यादगार निशानी
965	A person or thing that is likely to cause harm	Menace	(N.)	हानिकारक
966	Someone working or acting merely for money or other rewards // A soldier who fights for the sake of money	**Mercenary (8)**	(N.)	किराये का सैनिक
967	The scientific study of metals and their uses	Metallurgy	(N.)	धातु विज्ञान
968	A change in the form or nature of something	Metamorphosis	(N.)	कायांतरण
969	Paying careful attention to every detail	**Meticulous (3)**	(Adj.)	अतिसावधान
970	Fear of small things	Microphobia	(N.)	छोटी चीजों से डर
971	An instrument used in scientific study for making very small things look larger so that you may examine them carefully	Microscope	(N.)	सूक्ष्मदर्शी

SN	Phrases	One Word (#R)	PoS	Hindi
972	A traveller who moves from one region or country to another	**Migrant (4)**	(N.)	प्रवासी
973	Movement of people or animals from one area to another	Migration	(N.)	प्रवास
974	A period of one thousand years	**Millennium (2)**	(N.)	हज़ार वर्ष
975	Imitate someone's action or words in order to entertain or ridicule	Mimic	(V.)	नकल उतारना
976	Taking heed or care; being conscious	Mindful	(Adj.)	होशियार
977	A place where money is coined by authority of the government	**Mint (7)**	(N.)	टकसाल
978	A person who hates and avoids other people	**Misanthrope (5)**	(N.)	मानवद्वेषी
979	A general contempt towards mankind	Misanthropy	(N.)	मानव से घृणा
980	Unfairly take something belonging to another for one's use	Misappropriate	(V.)	गबन करना
981	A person who loves money and hates spending it	**Miser (3)**	(N.)	कंजूस
982	An unforseen happening which creates some damage	Mishap	(N.)	दुर्घटना
983	A word or a name that is inappropriate for a person or thing	Misnomer	(N.)	नाम का गलत प्रयोग
984	A person who dislikes women	**Misogynist (6)**	(N.)	स्त्री द्वेषी
985	One who hates reason, argument, or enlightenment	Misologist	(N.)	तर्क वितर्क से नफ़रत करने वाला
986	A hater of new things	Misoneist	(N.)	नई चीजों से नफ़रत करने वाला
987	Helping you to remember something	Mnemonic	(Adj.)	स्मृति सहायक
988	A large crowd of people, especially one that may become violent / cause trouble	Mob	(N.)	भीड़
989	A particular method of working	Modus Operandi	(N.)	कार्य-प्रणाली
990	Lasting for a very short time	Momentary	(Adj.)	क्षणिक
991	Very important or serious	**Momentous (2)**	(Adj.)	सब से अहम
992	A supreme ruler	**Monarch (2)**	(N.)	सम्राट
993	A system of government by a king / a queen	**Monarchy (5)**	(N.)	राज-तंत्र
994	A building where monks live as a community	**Monastery (2)**	(N.)	मठ
995	A warning of impending danger	Monition	(N.)	चेतावनी
996	A person who practices one spouse at a time	Monogamist	(N.)	एक विवाहवादी
997	The practice of marrying one person at a time	**Monogamy (2)**	(N.)	एक विवाह प्रथा
998	Obsession with one particular thing	Monomania	(N.)	एक ही बात की धुन
999	The complete control of trade in particular goods or the supply of a particular service	Monopoly	(N.)	एकाधिकार
1000	A person who believes that there is only one god	Monotheist	(N.)	एकेश्वरवादी

SN	Phrases	One Word (#R)	PoS	Hindi
1001	Lacking in variety and interest	Monotonous	(Adj.)	नीरस
1002	A building which is constructed to keep alive one's memory	Monument	(N.)	स्मारक
1003	To secure a boat by attaching it to an anchor	Moor	(V.)	लंगर डालना
1004	Customs and habits of a particular group	Mores	(N.)	रीति रिवाज
1005	A place where dead bodies are kept for identification	Morgue	(N.)	मुर्दा घर
1006	The state of being subject to death	Mortality	(N.)	नश्वरता
1007	A legal agreement by which a bank lends you money to buy a house	Mortgage	(N.)	गिरवी
1008	A place for keeping dead bodies before burial or cremation	**Mortuary (4)**	(N.)	शवगृह
1009	Art consisting of a design made of small pieces of coloured stone / glass	Mosaic	(N.)	रंगीन पत्थर या कांच के टुकड़ो से बना कलात्मक रचना
1010	Mark with spots or smears of colour	Mottle	(N.)	चितकबरा
1011	Wrap or cover for warmth	Muffle	(V.)	ओढ़ना
1012	Consisting of many things or parts	Multitudinous	(Adj.)	बहुसंख्यक
1013	A body of a human / an animal that has been preserved by treating it with special oils and wrapping it in cloth	Mummy	(N.)	पुराना परिरक्षित शव
1014	Ordinary and dull	**Mundane (2)**	(Adj.)	साधारण
1015	A place where antiques are kept	**Museum (2)**	(N.)	संग्रहालय
1016	The act of refusing to obey the orders of somebody in authority, especially by soldiers / sailors	**Mutiny (2)**	(N.)	बगावत करना
1017	Lacking foresight or intellectual insight	Myopic	(Adj.)	अदूरदर्शी
1018	Something that is hidden	Mystery	(N.)	रहस्य
1019	Fear of telling lies	Mythophobia	(N.)	झूठ बोलने का डर
1020	Showing a lack of experience, wisdom or judgment	Naive	(Adj.)	अनुभवहीन
1021	A person or thing that has the same name as another	**Namesake (4)**	(N.)	हमनाम
1022	The habit of admiring yourself too much, especially your appearance	Narcissism	(N.)	अहंकार
1023	A person who admires himself / herself too much, especially his appearance	**Narcissist (3)**	(N.)	आत्ममोही
1024	A highly unpleasant, annoying, objectionable sound.	Nasty	(Adj.)	बहुत खराब
1025	Connected with the place you were born // a person, animal or plant belonging originally to a place	**Native (3)**	(Adj.)	मूल निवासी

SN	Phrases	One Word (#R)	PoS	Hindi
1026	Guide the course of a ship especially by using instruments or maps	**Navigate (2)**	(V.)	मार्ग निर्देशन करना
1027	Fluid secreted by flowers which is collected by bees for making honey	Nectar	(N.)	पुष्प रस
1028	So small or unimportant as to be not worth considering	Negligible	(Adj.)	नगण्य
1029	One who mediates in a deal or complex situation	Negotiator	(N.)	मध्यस्थ
1030	Sound of horses	**Neigh (2)**	(N.)	हिनहिनाहट
1031	Group of people living together in the same locality	Neighbourhood	(N.)	अड़ोस - पड़ोस
1032	Deserved and unavoidable punishment for wrong doing // Downfall that satisfies natural justice	**Nemesis (2)**	(N.)	अपरिहार्य दंड
1033	A new word coined by an author	Neologism	(N.)	नवनिर्मित शब्द
1034	A person who has recently started an activity	Neophyte	(N.)	नौसिखिया
1035	Giving undue favours to one's own kith and kin.	**Nepotism (6)**	(N.)	भाई-भतीजावाद
1036	A doctor who studies and treats diseases of nerves	Neurologist	(N.)	स्नायु विज्ञानी
1037	The study of nerves	Neurology	(N.)	स्नायु विज्ञान
1038	Scientific study of the nervous system and brain	Neuroscience	(N.)	तंत्रिका विज्ञान
1039	A hollow space in a wall for a statue or ornament	Niche	(N.)	दीवार पर छोटी सी गुहा
1040	The rejection of all religious and moral principles, in the belief that life is meaningless	Nihilism	(N.)	शून्यवाद
1041	A transcendent state in which there is neither suffering, desire, nor sense of self	Nirvana	(N.)	मोक्ष
1042	Occurring at night	Nocturnal	(Adj.)	रात में होने वाली
1043	People of no fixed abode	**Nomads (2)**	(N.)	ख़ानाबदोश
1044	A system of naming things	Nomenclature	(N.)	नाम पद्धति
1045	An unimportant person	Nonentity	(N.)	तुच्छ व्यक्ति
1046	Delusion of suffering from a disease	Nosomania	(N.)	बीमारी से पीड़ित होने का भ्रम
1047	Sentimental longing for a period in the past	**Nostalgia (7)**	(N.)	अतीत की घटनाओं की यादें
1048	Well-known for being bad // A person of evil reputation	**Notorious (8)**	(Adj.)	कुख्यात
1049	The quality of being new and original	Novelty	(N.)	नवीनता
1050	A person who is new to a profession without training or experience in a skill or subject	**Novice (3)**	(N.)	नौसिखिया

SN	Phrases	One Word (#R)	PoS	Hindi
1051	To reduce to nothing	Null	(V.)	शून्य
1052	One who studies the occult meanings of numbers and their supposed influence on human life	Numerologist	(N.)	अंक ज्योतिषि
1053	The study or collection of coins	Numismatics	(N.)	मुद्राशास्त्र
1054	A person who collects coins	**Numismatist (6)**	(N.)	मुद्राशास्त्री
1055	A place where young plants / trees are grown for sale / for planting somewhere else	Nursery	(N.)	पौधा-घर
1056	An extreme fear of darkness	Nyctophobia	(N.)	अँधेरे का डर
1057	A fertile tract in a desert (where the water table approaches the surface)	Oasis	(N.)	मरुस्थल के बीच हरित भूमि
1058	A notice of a person's death	**Obituary (5)**	(N.)	शोक सन्देश
1059	Not clear	Obscure	(Adj.)	अस्पष्ट
1060	A place where astronomical observations are made	Observatory	(N.)	वेधशाला
1061	Passing out of use	Obsolescent	(Adj.)	अप्रचलित
1062	Something no longer in use	**Obsolete (13)**	(Adj.)	अप्रचलित
1063	Relating to the countries of the west	**Occidental (3)**	(Adj.)	पश्चिमवासी
1064	A geometrical figure with eight sides	**Octagon (4)**	(N.)	अष्टभुज
1065	One who is eighty years old	Octogenarian	(N.)	अस्सी साल का बुढ़ा
1066	Eight armed sea creature	Octopus	(N.)	अष्टभुज समुद्रीय जीव
1067	A person who attends to the diseases of the eye is an	Oculist	(N.)	नेत्र-विशेषज्ञ
1068	Obsession for wine	**Oenomania (2)**	(N.)	मादक पेय के लिए एक असामान्य और अतृप्त लालसा
1069	Not quite coinciding with a central position	Off-Centre	(N.)	विकेन्द्र
1070	Government or rule by a small group of people	**Oligarchy (5)**	(N.)	अल्पतंत्र
1071	Suggesting that something unpleasant is likely to happen	**Ominous (2)**	(Adj.)	अशुभसूचक
1072	A volume containing several books previously published separately	Omnibus	(N.)	बहुग्रंथ
1073	One who is all powerful	**Omnipotent (5)**	(Adj.)	सर्वशक्तिमान
1074	Present everywhere	**Omnipresent (2)**	(Adj.)	सर्वव्यापक
1075	One who knows everything	**Omniscient (11)**	(Adj.)	सर्वज्ञानी
1076	An animal or person that eats a variety of food of both plant and animal origin.	Omnivore	(N.)	सर्वाहारी
1077	One who eats both vegetables and meat	**Omnivorous (4)**	(N.)	सर्व-भक्षक
1078	That through which light cannot pass	**Opaque (7)**	(Adj.)	अपारदर्शी
1079	Study of snakes	**Ophiology (2)**	(N.)	सांपों का अध्ययन

SN	Phrases	One Word (#R)	PoS	Hindi
1080	Fear of snakes	Ophiophobia	(N.)	सांप का डर
1081	A doctor who specializes in the diseases of the eyes	**Ophthalmologist (3)**	(N.)	नेत्र-विशेषज्ञ
1082	To be dogmatic in one's opinions.	Opinionated	(Adj.)	हठधर्मी
1083	Public disgrace arising from shameful conduct	Opprobrium	(N.)	अपमान
1084	One who see bright side of things	**Optimist (7)**	(N.)	आशावादी
1085	A musical work that has been created // An artistic work, especially one on a large scale	Opus	(N.)	संगीत रचना
1086	A formal speech, especially one given on a ceremonial occasion	Oration	(N.)	भाषण
1087	A proficient public speaker	**Orator (2)**	(N.)	वक्ता
1088	A piece of land / garden, in which fruit trees are grown	**Orchard (5)**	(N.)	फलोद्यान
1089	A large body of people playing various musical instruments.	Orchestra	(N.)	वादक समूह
1090	The arrangement or disposition of people or things in relation to each other according to a particular sequence, pattern, or method	Order	(N.)	क्रम
1091	Something like an opening, particularly one in the body such as a nostril	Orifice	(N.)	छिद्र
1092	A person who studies birds	**Ornithologist (2)**	(N.)	पक्षी विज्ञानी
1093	The scientific study of birds	**Ornithology (2)**	(N.)	पक्षीविज्ञान
1094	A child whose parents are dead	Orphan	(N.)	अनाथ
1095	A public institution for the care and protection of children without parents.	**Orphanage (2)**	(N.)	अनाथालय
1096	One who holds established opinions	Orthodox	(Adj.)	रूढ़िवादी
1097	The area of medicine that treats illnesses of bones	Orthopaedics	(N.)	हड्डी रोग
1098	Doctor who deals with bone problems	**Orthopaedist (4)**	(N.)	हड्डियों का डॉक्टर
1099	A person who looks after horses at an inn	Ostler	(N.)	घोड़ों की देखभाल करने वाला
1100	To banish or turn out of society and fellowship	Ostracise	(V.)	निष्कासित करना
1101	Be more successful than someone	Outdo	(V.)	आगे बढ़ना
1102	Looking or sounding foreign, bizarre, strange, unfamiliar	Outlandish	(Adj.)	विदेशी
1103	A person who has broken the law, especially one who remains at large or is a fugitive.	Outlaw	(N.)	नियमविरोधी
1104	Involvement with or influence in the community.	Outreach	(V.)	पहुँच
1105	Fail to notice; ignore; condone (an offence etc.)	Overlook	(V.)	अनदेखी करना
1106	Pertaining to sheep	Ovine	(N.)	भेड़ के समान
1107	Belief that war and violence are unjustified	**Pacifism (2)**	(N.)	शांतिवाद

SN	Phrases	One Word (#R)	PoS	Hindi
1108	A person who opposes war or use of military force.	**Pacifist (4)**	(N.)	शांतिवादी
1109	A group of wolves	Pack	(N.)	भेड़ियों का झुंड
1110	A set of 52 playing cards	Pack	(N.)	ताश की गड्डी
1111	A doctor who treats children diseases	**Paediatrician (2)**	(N.)	बच्चों का चिकित्सक
1112	A word that reads the same backwards as forwards	Palindrome	(N.)	ऐसा शब्द जो आगे और पीछे दोनों तरफ से एक जैसा हो
1113	Make something less severe.	Palliation	(N.)	कम गंभीर बनाना
1114	Thing that can be felt or touched	Palpable	(Adj.)	स्पर्शनीय
1115	A solution for all difficulties or diseases	**Panacea (15)**	(N.)	रामबाण इलाज
1116	Widespread occurrence of an infectious disease crossing international boundaries	Pandemic	(N.)	महामारी
1117	Wild and noisy disorder	Pandemonium	(N.)	कोलाहल
1118	Gratify an immoral or distasteful desire	Pander	(V.)	नीच कार्य में सहायता देनेवाला
1119	Sudden uncontrollable fear or anxiety, often causing wildly unthinking behaviour	Panic	(N.)	आतंक, भगदड़
1120	Wide, uninterrupted view	Panorama	(N.)	चित्रमाला
1121	Breathe hard and with difficulty	Pant	(V.)	हाँफ़ना
1122	The belief that God is in everything, including nature	**Pantheism (4)**	(N.)	सर्वेश्वरवाद
1123	A temple dedicated to all the gods	Pantheon	(N.)	सर्वदेवालय
1124	A small room in a big house, hotel, ship etc. Where glasses, dishes, spoons, food etc. Are kept.	**Pantry (2)**	(N.)	रसोई भंडार
1125	Story told to illustrate a moral or spiritual truth	**Parable (3)**	(N.)	नीति कथा
1126	One who lives/survives on others/other lives.	**Parasite (3)**	(N.)	परजीवी
1127	A method of boiling briefly to cook food slightly	Parboil	(V.)	अधूरा पकाना
1128	Having a limited or narrow outlook or scope	Parochial	(Adj.)	सीमित
1129	Permission that is given to a prisoner to leave prison before the end of his sentence on condition that he behaves well	Parole	(N.)	पैरोल
1130	The crime of killing your father, mother or a close relative	Parricide	(N.)	पितृघातक
1131	One who has suddenly gained new wealth, power or prestige	**Parvenu (2)**	(N.)	नयी नयी दौलत
1132	Sole right to make and sell some invention	Patent	(N.)	एकस्व अधिकार
1133	The scientific study of diseases	**Pathology (3)**	(N.)	रोग विज्ञान
1134	A system of society or government in which men hold the power and women are largely excluded from it	Patriarchy	(N.)	पितृसत्ता

SN	Phrases	One Word (#R)	PoS	Hindi
1135	Murdering his own father	Patricide	(N.)	पितृहत्या
1136	Relationship between father and child that continues in a family with each generation	Patrilineal	(Adj.)	पितृवंशीय
1137	Property that is given to somebody when his father dies	**Patrimony (3)**	(N.)	पैतृक संपत्ति
1138	A person who loves, supports and defends his country	**Patriot (5)**	(N.)	देश-भक्त
1139	To go around an area to keep a watch	Patrol	(V.)	गश्त लगाना
1140	One who has no money	**Pauper (2)**	(N.)	कंगाल
1141	Concerning or consisting of money.	Pecuniary	(Adj.)	धन-संबंधी
1142	The method and practice of teaching	Pedagogy	(N.)	शिक्षा शास्त्र
1143	A person who insists on adherence to formal rules or literary meaning	**Pedant (3)**	(N.)	रूढ़िवादी
1144	A style in which a writer makes display of his knowledge	Pedantic	(Adj.)	रूढ़िवादी
1145	A person who walks on foot and not travelling in a vehicle	**Pedestrian (6)**	(N.)	पैदल यात्री
1146	Branch of medicine concerned with children and their illness	Pediatrics	(N.)	बाल चिकित्सा
1147	A punishment imposed for breaking a law, rule, or contract.	Penalty	(N.)	जुर्माना
1148	A special fondness or liking for	**Penchant (2)**	(N.)	विशेष रुचि
1149	A small ornament which hangs down especially from a necklace	Pendant	(N.)	लटकन
1150	A large mass of land projecting into a body of water	Peninsula	(N.)	प्रायद्वीप
1151	Deep in thought	Pensive	(Adj.)	चिंताग्रस्त
1152	Something that happens often or that lasts for a long time	Perennial	(Adj.)	चिरस्थायी
1153	Continuing for a long period of time without interruption	**Perpetual (2)**	(Adj.)	लगातार
1154	An incidental benefit awarded for certain types of employment	Perquisite	(N.)	रिआयत
1155	Subject someone to hostility and ill-treatment, especially because of their race or political or religious beliefs	Persecute	(V.)	अत्याचार करना
1156	Constant effort to achieve something.	**Perseverance (3)**	(N.)	दृढ़ता
1157	A person employed in armed forces	Personnel	(N.)	कार्मिक
1158	The action of examining with care or reading carefully	Perusal	(N.)	अवलोकन
1159	A person who always expects bad things to happen or something not to be successful	**Pessimist (3)**	(N.)	निराशावादी
1160	Killing of pests	**Pesticide (2)**	(N.)	कीटनाशक

SN	Phrases	One Word (#R)	PoS	Hindi
1161	That which is morally dangerous	Pestiferous	(Adj.)	विनाशक
1162	Stick with a thick end used in a mortar for pounding	Pestle	(N.)	मूसल
1163	Decrease or fade gradually before coming to an end	Peter	(V.)	धीरे धीरे समाप्त हो जाना
1164	A long wooden seat with a back for people to sit on in a church	Pew	(N.)	गिरज़ाघर का बेंच
1165	A person who always runs after women	Philanderer	(N.)	इश्कबाज़
1166	One who loves all mankind // Someone who freely gives money and help to people who need it	**Philanthropist (7)**	(N.)	जन हितैषी
1167	The love of man or mankind	Philanthropy	(N.)	मानव प्रेम
1168	A person who collects or studies stamps	**Philatelist (7)**	(N.)	डाक के टिकट का संग्रहक
1169	The collection and study of postage stamps	Philately	(N.)	टिकट संग्रह करना
1170	One who does not care for literature or art.	**Philistine (4)**	(N.)	अशिक्षित
1171	The study of languages	Philology	(N.)	भाषाशास्त्र
1172	One who loves wisdom and hence pursues it	Philosopher	(N.)	दार्शनिक
1173	Intense and unreasoned fear or dislike	**Phobia (2)**	(N.)	भय
1174	The study and classification of sounds	**Phonetics (3)**	(N.)	ध्वनि-विज्ञान
1175	A doctor, who is a specialist in general medicine and not surgery	Physician	(N.)	चिकित्सक
1176	A study of the human body	Physiology	(N.)	शरीरविज्ञान
1177	Treatment by means of exercise and massage.	Physiotherapy	(N.)	भौतिक चिकित्सा
1178	A large number of things placed one on top of another	Pile	(N.)	ढेर
1179	The act of stealing something in small quantities	Pilferage	(N.)	छोटी चोरी
1180	A seat for a passenger on a bicycle or motorbike	Pillion	(N.)	पीछे की सीट
1181	One who does something for the first time	**Pioneer (2)**	(N.)	प्रथम अन्वेषक
1182	A person who attacks and robs ships at sea	**Pirate (2)**	(N.)	समुद्री डाकू
1183	One who lives on fish	Piscivorous	(Adj.)	मत्स्यभक्षी
1184	Make someone less angry or hostile	Placate	(V.)	शांत करना
1185	Not easily excited or upset	Placid	(Adj.)	शांत
1186	Take and use the thoughts, inventions, etc. Of another person as one's own	**Plagiarise (2)**	(N.)	साहित्यिक चोरी
1187	Stealing of ideas or writings of someone else	**Plagiarism (3)**	(N.)	साहित्यिक चोरी
1188	One who copies from other writers	**Plagiarist (3)**	(N.)	साहित्यिक चोर
1189	Person who files a suit.	Plaintiff	(N.)	अर्ज़ीदार
1190	Flat metal or Porcelain plate fixed on a wall as an ornament or memorial.	Plaque	(N.)	प्लेट को दीवार में सजाना

SN	Phrases	One Word (#R)	PoS	Hindi
1191	Seeming reasonable	Plausible	(Adj.)	संभाव्य
1192	A decision made by public voting.	Plebiscite	(N.)	जनमत-संग्रह
1193	A solemn promise or undertaking	**Pledge (2)**	(N.)	प्रतिज्ञा करना
1194	The state of being full or complete	Plenitude	(N.)	प्रचुरता
1195	Capable of bending easily without breaking	Pliable	(Adj.)	लचीला
1196	One who repairs leaking water pipes	Plumber	(N.)	नलसाज
1197	Government by the richest people of a country	**Plutocracy (3)**	(N.)	धनिक तन्त्र
1198	A speaker's platform	Podium	(N.)	मंच
1199	Evoking a keen sense of sadness or regret	Poignant	(Adj.)	मार्मिक
1200	Something that is pertaining to controversy	Polemical	(Adj.)	विवादात्मक
1201	The science or art of political government	Politics	(N.)	राजनीति शास्त्र
1202	The custom of having more than one husband at the same time	**Polyandry (2)**	(N.)	बहुपति प्रथा
1203	A person having more than one wife at the same time	Polygamist	(N.)	बहुपत्नीवादी
1204	The custom of having more than one husband or wife at the same time	**Polygamy (2)**	(N.)	बहुविवाह
1205	A person who knows and is able to use several languages.	**Polyglot (7)**	(N.)	बहुभाषी
1206	A flat shape with at least three straight sides and three angles, and usually five or more	Polygon	(N.)	बहुभुज
1207	One who believes in a plurality of gods	Polytheist	(N.)	बहुदेववादी
1208	Full of people	Populous	(Adj.)	घनी आबादी वाला
1209	A place where ships load and unload goods	Port	(N.)	बंदरगाह
1210	Something that can be carried easily	**Portable (3)**	(N.)	आसानी से साथ ले जाने योग्य
1211	A collection of drawings, documents, etc. That represent a person's, especially an artist's, work	Portfolio	(N.)	पेटिका
1212	Occurring or coming into existence after a person's death	**Posthumous (3)**	(Adj.)	मरणोपरांत
1213	A child born after the death of its father	Posthumous Child	(N.)	पिता के मरणोपरांत पैदा हुआ बच्चा
1214	A medical examination of a dead body	**Postmortem (3)**	(N.)	शवपरीक्षा
1215	Delay an event to a later date or time	Postpone	(V.)	स्थगित करना
1216	A note appended to a letter after the signature	**Postscript (2)**	(N.)	उपसंहार
1217	Safe to drink (water)	**Potable (5)**	(Adj.)	पीने योग्य
1218	A liquid with healing, magical, or poisonous properties	Potion	(N.)	पेय औषधि
1219	A mixture of dried flowers and leaves used for making a room smell	Potpourri	(N.)	सुगंधित मिश्रण

SN	Phrases	One Word (#R)	PoS	Hindi
1220	One who values practicality	Pragmatist	(N.)	व्यवहारवादी
1221	A previous case that might serve as an example or guide in subsequent situations	Precedent	(N.)	मिसाल
1222	A very steep or overhanging rock face or cliff on a mountain	Precipice	(N.)	खड़ी चट्टान
1223	An animal that lives by killing and eating other animals	**Predator (4)**	(N.)	परजीवी
1224	Something that precedes and indicates the approach of something / someone	Predecessor	(N.)	पूर्वज
1225	We are expecting a good monsoon this year	Predicting	(V.)	पूर्वानुमान करना
1226	An introduction to a book, especially one that explains the author's aims	Preface	(N.)	प्रस्तावना
1227	To be biased against	Prejudiced	(Adj.)	पक्षपातपूर्ण
1228	An action or event that happens before another important one and forms an introduction to it	Prelude	(N.)	प्रस्तावना
1229	The first public performance of a musical or theatrical work or the first showing of a film	**Premiere (2)**	(N.)	प्रथम प्रदर्शन
1230	A strong feeling that something is about to happen, especially something unpleasant	**Premonition (2)**	(N.)	पूर्वाभास
1231	To get ready	Prepare	(V.)	तैयार करना
1232	Feint	Pretended Attack	(V.)	छल,भुलावा
1233	To make evasive or misleading statement	**Prevaricate (2)**	(V.)	छल कपट करना
1234	A group of Lions	**Pride (2)**	(N.)	शेरों का समूह
1235	Right or advantage available to a person	Privilege	(N.)	विशेषाधिकार
1236	A person working on a trial period	Probationer	(N.)	काम सीखने के लिये नियुक्त
1237	Put off for a future time	**Procrastinate (2)**	(V.)	टालना
1238	The art of delaying	**Procrastination (2)**	(N.)	टालमटोल
1239	A person, especially a young one, with exceptional abilities	Prodigy	(N.)	विलक्षण प्रतिभासंपन्न व्यक्ति
1240	A high degree of skill	Proficiency	(N.)	निपुणता
1241	General view of a person's character	Profile	(N.)	बाह्य रूपरेखा
1242	Recklessly extravagant or wasteful in the use of resources	Profligate	(Adj.)	अतिअपव्ययी
1243	Working-class people regarded collectively	Proletariat	(N.)	श्रमिक वर्ग
1244	Rapid increase in the number or amount of something	Proliferation	(N.)	प्रसार, फैलाव
1245	An introduction to a literary work	**Prologue (3)**	(N.)	प्रस्तावना
1246	Continuing for a long time	Prolonged	(V.)	दीर्घकालीन
1247	A piece of wood, metal, etc. Used for supporting something or keeping it in position	Prop	(N.)	टेक, सहारा

SN	Phrases	One Word (#R)	PoS	Hindi
1248	A person sent by god to teach the people and give them messages from god	Prophet	(N.)	पैगम्बर (ईश्वरदूत)
1249	The action of driving or pushing forwards	Propulsion	(N.)	संचालक शक्ति
1250	A person who has been converted to another religious or political belief	Proselyte	(N.)	धर्मांतरित व्यक्ति
1251	Central character in a story or play	**Protagonist (3)**	(N.)	नायक
1252	A system of fixed rules and formal behaviour used at official meetings	**Protocol (2)**	(N.)	नियमों की प्रणाली
1253	The first design of something from which other forms are copied or developed	**Prototype (2)**	(N.)	नमूना
1254	Food for farm animals	Provender	(N.)	चारा
1255	Concern for one's own area or region at the expense of national or supranational unity	Provincialism	(N.)	प्रांतीयता
1256	A person who moves stealthily about or loiters near a place with a view to committing a crime	Prowler	(N.)	शिकार की खोज में घूमने वाला
1257	One who studies election trends by means of opinion polls.	**Psephologist (3)**	(N.)	चुनाव विश्लेषक
1258	The study of how people vote in elections	**Psephology (3)**	(N.)	चुनाव विश्लेषण
1259	A fictitious name especially one assumed by an author	**Pseudonym (5)**	(N.)	उपनाम
1260	A scientist trained in psychology	Psychologist	(N.)	मनोविज्ञानी
1261	The scientific study of the mind and how it influences behaviour	**Psychology (5)**	(N.)	मनोविज्ञान
1262	Careful in performing duties	**Punctilious (2)**	(Adj.)	अति शिष्टाचारी
1263	A person who gambles, places a bet, or makes a risky investment	Punter	(N.)	जुआरी
1264	To run after	Pursue	(V.)	पीछे लगे रहना
1265	Decay of organic matter producing a fetid smell	Putrefy	(V.)	सड़ना
1266	An obsessive desire to set fire to things	Pyromania	(N.)	आग लगाने का पागलपन
1267	Sound made by ducks	Quack	(V.)	बत्तख की आवाज
1268	A court or open space usually rectangular and enclosed by a building	Quadrangle	(N.)	चतुर्भुजाकार
1269	Any creature with four feet	**Quadruped (3)**	(N.)	चौपाया
1270	Reject as invalid, especially by legal procedure	Quash	(V.)	रद्द करना
1271	A shake or tremble in a person's voice	Quaver	(V.)	थरथराना
1272	Search for something	**Quest (2)**	(N.)	खोज
1273	A feather used as a pen	Quill	(N.)	पंख की कलम
1274	An event which happens once in five years	Quinquennial	(Adj.)	पंचवार्षिक
1275	To the utmost or most absolute extent or degree	Quite	(Adv.)	पूरी तौर से

SN	Phrases	One Word (#R)	PoS	Hindi
1276	A person preoccupied with an unrealistically optimistic approach to life	**Quixotic (2)**	(Adj.)	ख्याली
1277	A person who is good at telling stories in an interesting and amusing way	**Raconteur (2)**	(N.)	मज़ेदार कहानियाँ सुनाने वाला
1278	The act of spreading outward from a central source	Radiation	(N.)	विकिरण
1279	A person who advocates complete political or social change	Radical	(N.)	उग्र सुधारवादी
1280	Medical doctors who specialise in diagnosing diseases using X-rays, CT scans and ultrasound	**Radiologist (3)**	(N.)	विकिरण चिकित्सक
1281	The science dealing with x-rays and other high-energy radiation, especially for the diagnosis and treatment of disease.	Radiology	(N.)	विकिरण चिकित्सा विज्ञान
1282	Having a stale smell or taste	Rancid	(Adj.)	बासी
1283	Characterized by bitterness or resentment	Rancorous	(Adj.)	शत्रुतापूर्ण
1284	To free prisoner on payment	**Ransom (2)**	(N.)	फिरौती
1285	Greedy for money	Rapacious	(Adj.)	अति लोभी
1286	Reduction in tax or debt	Rebate	(N.)	छूट
1287	To take back, withdraw or renounce	Recant	(V.)	मुकर जाना
1288	A hollow object used to contain something.	Receptacle	(N.)	पात्र
1289	One who receives something	Recipient	(N.)	प्राप्तकर्ता
1290	Give and receive mutually	Reciprocate	(V.)	विनिमय करना
1291	A person who withdraws from the world to live in seclusion and often in solitude	**Recluse (4)**	(N.)	वैरागी
1292	Adjust or make right; correct, amend	Rectify	(V.)	सुधारना
1293	When something moves in a straight line	Rectilineal	(Adj.)	सीधा
1294	A process involving too much official formality	**Red-Tapism (3)**	(N.)	लाल फीताशाही
1295	That which is no longer useful	**Redundant (2)**	(Adj.)	अनावश्यक
1296	An act when people vote in order to make a decision about a particular subject or policy rather than voting for a person	**Referendum (2)**	(N.)	जनमत संग्रह
1297	An involuntary action under a stimulus is described	Reflex	(N.)	अनैच्छिक क्रिया
1298	The system which is observed to do progress	Reformism	(N.)	संशोधनवाद
1299	A person who has been forced to leave his country / home, because there is a war or for political, religious or social reasons	Refugee	(N.)	शरणार्थी
1300	Dress with medals, ribbons worn at official ceremony // symbols of royalty	**Regalia (2)**	(N.)	पदक, तमग़ा
1301	The act of killing a king	**Regicide (2)**	(N.)	राज-हत्या

SN	Phrases	One Word (#R)	PoS	Hindi
1302	Restore (someone) to health or normal life after imprisonment, addiction, or illness	Rehabilitate	(V.)	पूर्व दशा में लाना
1303	Younger looking skin.	Rejuvenated	(V.)	फिर से जवान बना देना
1304	Fall back or sink again (into a worse state after an improvement)	Relapse	(V.)	पूर्व दशा में आ जाना
1305	A deceased holy person's remains or belongings kept for reverence	Relic	(N.)	अवशेष
1306	Send back a criminal into custody for further investigation	Remand	(V.)	जेल वापसी
1307	To brought back to mind	Reminded	(V.)	याद दिलाया
1308	A characteristic of one thing that is suggestive of another	Reminiscence	(N.)	संस्मरण
1309	Having a feeling of guilt	Remorse	(N.)	पश्चाताप
1310	Amount paid to a man for his labour	Remuneration	(N.)	पारिश्रमिक
1311	Artistic, musical or dramatic interpretation	Rendition	(N.)	प्रस्तुतिकरण
1312	One who deserts his principles or party	Renegade	(N.)	पाखण्डी
1313	Restore something to better condition	Renovate	(V.)	नवीनीकरण करना
1314	The return of someone to his own country	**Repatriation (3)**	(N.)	स्वदेश लौटना
1315	Atonement for one's sins	Repentance	(N.)	पछतावा
1316	Fill up again	Replenish	(V.)	फिर से भरना
1317	An exact or a very close copy (of something)	Replica	(N.)	नक़ल
1318	Postponing or remitting punishment	Reprieve	(N.)	दण्डविराम
1319	Vertebrate animals that crawl on the ground	Reptiles	(N.)	सरीसृप
1320	Causing a strong dislike	Repulsive	(Adj.)	घिनौना
1321	Someone who is silent or uncommunicative in speech	Reserved	(Adj.)	अमिलनसार / संकोची
1322	A large natural or artificial lake used as a source of water supply	Reservoir	(N.)	जलाशय
1323	To become a strong person in spite of many difficulties.	**Resilient (2)**	(Adj.)	लचीला
1324	The process by means of which plants and animals breathe.	Respiration	(N.)	श्वसन
1325	Postponement or delay permitted in the suffering of a penalty or the discharge of an obligation.	Respite	(N.)	मोहलत
1326	Return the same sort of attack / give tit for tat	**Retaliate (2)**	(V.)	बदला लेना
1327	A person very reserved in speech	**Reticent (4)**	(Adj.)	अल्पभाषी
1328	Go back over the same route that one has just taken	Retrace	(V.)	दोहराना
1329	Withdraw from a forward position in battle	Retreat	(V.)	पीछे हटना

SN	Phrases	One Word (#R)	PoS	Hindi
1330	Action of reviewing past events in one's life	**Retrospection (3)**	(N.)	पश्चावलोकन
1331	To renovate or improve	Revamp	(V.)	मरम्मत करना
1332	A tune that is played to wake soldiers in the morning	Reveille	(N.)	जगाने का बिगुल
1333	Take great pleasure.	Revel	(V.)	आनंद लेना
1334	Feeling or showing deep and solemn respect	Reverent	(Adj.)	श्रद्धापूर्ण ढंग से
1335	Criticize in an abusive or angrily insulting manner	Revile	(V.)	गाली देना
1336	Meaningless language with an exaggerated style intended to impress. // The art of effective or persuasive speaking or writing	**Rhetoric (2)**	(N.)	शब्दाडम्बर
1337	A specialist in diseases of the nose	Rhinologist	(N.)	नाक के रोगों में विशेषज्ञ
1338	Scale used for measuring the strength of an earthquake	Richter	(N.)	भूकंप की ताकत मापने का स्केल
1339	Full of criticism and mockery	Ridicule	(V.)	उपहास
1340	One who has fixed opinions and beliefs // Hard and difficult to bend	**Rigid (2)**	(Adj.)	दृढ़ / कठोर
1341	Solemn religious acts	Rites	(N.)	संस्कार
1342	Circular building or hall with a dome	Rotunda	(N.)	गोल-घर
1343	The broken parts of objects found in an ancient site	Ruins	(N.)	खंडहर
1344	Move with urgent haste	Rush	(V.)	जल्दबाज़ी करना
1345	Deliberately destroy something for military advantage	**Sabotage (2)**	(N.)	तोड़-फोड़
1346	Violation of something holy or sacred	**Sacrilege (6)**	(N.)	अपवित्रीकरण
1347	Deriving pleasure from inflicting pain	Sadistic	(Adj.)	परपीड़न-कामुक
1348	The quality of being particularly noticeable	Salience	(N.)	विशेषता
1349	The firing of many guns at the same time to mark an occasion	Salvo	(N.)	फौजी सलामी
1350	One who helps a person in need	**Samaritan (3)**	(N.)	नेक आदमी
1351	The clandestine copying and distribution of literature banned by the state	Samizdat	(N.)	प्रतिबंधित साहित्य की नकल और वितरण
1352	A place of good climate for invalids	**Sanatorium (2)**	(N.)	आरोग्य निवास
1353	The state or quality of being holy	**Sanctity (2)**	(N.)	पवित्रता
1354	A protected place for birds and animals // A nature reserve for birds or animals	**Sanctuary (4)**	(N.)	अभयारण्य
1355	A battle or anything involving or causing much bloodshed	Sanguinary	(Adj.)	रक्तपातपूर्ण
1356	Optimistic in an apparently difficult situation	Sanguine	(Adj.)	आशावादी

SN	Phrases	One Word (#R)	PoS	Hindi
1357	The use of irony to mock or convey contempt	Sarcasm	(N.)	ताना
1358	Full of criticism and mockery	**Satire (2)**	(N.)	हास्य व्यंग्य
1359	Taste good food or drink and enjoy it to the full	Savouring	(V.)	स्वाद लेना
1360	A sheath for the blade of a sword	Scabbard	(N.)	म्यान
1361	Tale that brings bad reputation to somebody	Scandal	(N.)	कलंकपूर्ण कृत्य
1362	Barely sufficient or adequate	Scant	(Adj.)	अपर्याप्त
1363	A person who is blamed for the wrong doings of others	**Scapegoat (3)**	(N.)	बलि का बकरा
1364	The state of being in short supply.	Scarcity	(N.)	अभाव
1365	A person who is forgetful and unable to concentrate or think clearly	Scatterbrain	(N.)	अस्थिर व्यक्ति
1366	Search for and collect anything usable from discarded waste	Scavenge	(V.)	कूड़े में उपयोगी चीज ढूंढना
1367	Someone who habitually doubts accepted beliefs	**Sceptic (2)**	(N.)	संदेहवादी
1368	An ornamented staff carried by rulers on ceremonial occasions as a symbol of sovereignty	Sceptre	(N.)	राजाधिकार
1369	A plan of what is to be done and when	Schedule	(N.)	समय सारणी
1370	A grant or payment to support a student's education	Scholarship	(N.)	छात्रवृत्ति
1371	A group of fish	School	(N.)	मछलियों का झुंड
1372	A vivacious and lively experience	Scintillating	(Adj.)	बहुत शानदार
1373	A set of twenty	Score	(N.)	बीस का एक सेट
1374	A loud, harsh, piercing cry	Screech	(N.)	फटा आवाज़
1375	Small room where dishes are washed	Scullery	(N.)	बर्तन माँजने की जगह
1376	Making or spreading scandalous claims about someone with the intention of damaging their reputation / Severely abusive writing in journals	**Scurrilous (2)**	(Adj.)	अभद्र
1377	Government not connected with religious or spiritual matters	**Secular (4)**	(Adj.)	धर्म निरपेक्ष
1378	A drug or other substance that induces sleep	Sedative	(N.)	शांतिकर औषधि
1379	Marked by care and persistent effort	Sedulous	(Adj.)	परिश्रमी
1380	An instrument for detecting an earthquake	Seismograph	(N.)	भूकंप-सूचक यंत्र
1381	The scientific study of earthquakes	**Seismology (2)**	(N.)	भूकंप विज्ञान
1382	Take hold of forcibly or suddenly	Seize	(V.)	ज़ब्त करना
1383	Rarely; not often	Seldom	(Adv.)	कभी कभार
1384	That which is arranged by conferring or discussing	Seminar	(N.)	संगोष्ठी
1385	Aware of and able to understand other people and their feelings	**Sensitive (2)**	(Adj.)	संवेदनशील

SN	Phrases	One Word (#R)	PoS	Hindi
1386	A person between the ages of 70 and 79	Septuagenarian	(N.)	सत्तर वर्ष की अवस्था का मनुष्य
1387	A place of burial	Sepulchre	(N.)	क़ब्र
1388	The occurrence and development of events by chance in a happy or beneficial way	**Serendipity (3)**	(N.)	आकस्मिक लाभ
1389	Repeatedly committing the same offence and typically following a characteristic, predictable behaviour pattern	Serial	(Adj.)	अनुक्रमिक
1390	Rearing of silk worm	**Sericulture (3)**	(N.)	रेशम कीट-पालन
1391	To cut something into two pieces	Sever	(V.)	काटकर अलग करना
1392	A person between the ages of 60 and 69	Sexagenarian	(N.)	साठ वर्ष का
1393	A vertical passageway into a mine	Shaft	(N.)	ऊर्ध्वाधर मार्ग
1394	A close-fitting cover for a sword or knife // Cover for the blade of a weapon or a tool	**Sheath (5)**	(N.)	म्यान
1395	A large number of fish swimming together.	**Shoal (6)**	(N.)	मछलियों का समुदाय
1396	Fragments from an exploded artillery shell, mine, or bomb	Shrapnel	(N.)	बम का टुकड़ा
1397	Showing astute powers of judgement; clever and judicious	Shrewd	(Adj.)	चतुर
1398	A short rest or sleep taken after lunch	Siesta	(N.)	दोपहर का आराम
1399	The dark shape and outline of something visible against a bright background	Silhouette	(N.)	छाया-आकृति
1400	A figure of speech by which a thing is spoken of as being that which it only resembles	Simile	(N.)	उपमा
1401	Happening or being done at exactly the same time	Simultaneous	(Adj.)	समक्षणिक
1402	An office with high salary but no work	**Sinecure (4)**	(N.)	आराम की नौकरी
1403	An internal or external framework of bones	**Skeleton (2)**	(N.)	कंकाल
1404	Reduce or decrease in speed or intensity	Slacken	(V.)	धीमा पड़ जाना
1405	Have saliva dripping copiously from the mouth	Slobber	(V.)	लार टपकाना
1406	A given space, time or position	Slot	(N.)	निर्धारित समय
1407	Kill someone by covering their nose and mouth so that they suffocate	Smother	(V.)	गला घोंटकर मारना
1408	A person regarded as arrogant and annoying	Snob	(N.)	घमंडी
1409	The study and classification of human societies	Sociology	(N.)	नागरिक शास्त्र
1410	A brief or short stay at a place	**Sojourn (2)**	(N.)	थोड़े दिन का निवास
1411	A very delicate flaw or mistake which is not expected from the person making it	Solecism	(N.)	अशिष्टता
1412	One who talks to oneself	Soliloquist	(N.)	अपने आप से बातें करने वाला
1413	A speech made to oneself	**Soliloquy (3)**	(N.)	आत्मभाषण

SN	Phrases	One Word (#R)	PoS	Hindi
1414	The state of being alone, especially when you find this pleasant	Solitude	(N.)	एकांत
1415	Being able to pay one's debt	Solvent	(Adj.)	अपने ऋण चुकाने में समर्थ
1416	Walking in sleep	**Somnambulism (2)**	(N.)	नींद में चलना
1417	Someone who walks about in sleep	**Somnambulist (6)**	(N.)	नींद में चलने वाला
1418	One who talks in sleep	**Somniloquist (3)**	(N.)	नींद में बोलने वाला
1419	The act or habit of talking in one's sleep	Somniloquy	(N.)	नींद में बोलने वाला
1420	A fourteen-line poem	**Sonnet (2)**	(N.)	चौदह लाइन की कविता
1421	A drug or other substance that induces sleep	**Soporific (2)**	(N.)	नींद लाने वाला
1422	A type of magic in which spirits, especially evil ones, are used to make things happen	Sorcery	(N.)	जादू-टोना
1423	The murder of one's sister	**Sororicide (2)**	(N.)	बहन की हत्या
1424	Something kept as a reminder of an event	**Souvenir (3)**	(N.)	निशानी
1425	Sudden involuntary muscular contraction	Spasm	(N.)	ऐंठन
1426	A small amount of something that shows what the rest of it is like	Specimen	(N.)	नमूना
1427	The forming of a theory or conjecture without firm evidence	Speculation	(N.)	परिकल्पना
1428	Study of caves	Speleology	(N.)	गुहा विज्ञान
1429	One who spends money recklessly	Spendthrift	(N.)	खर्चीला
1430	An old unmarried woman	Spinster	(N.)	अधेड़ अविवाहिता
1431	One who speaks on behalf of others	**Spokesman (2)**	(N.)	प्रवक्ता
1432	One who speaks for others	Spokesperson	(N.)	प्रवक्ता
1433	Performed or occurring as a result of a sudden impulse	Spontaneous	(Adj.)	स्वतः
1434	Ccurring at irregular intervals in time	Sporadic	(N.)	छिटपुट
1435	Not being what it purports to be	Spurious	(Adj.)	जाली
1436	To walk unsteadily as if about to fall	Stagger	(V.)	लड़खड़ाना
1437	A sudden rush of a large number of frightened people or animals.	Stampede	(N.)	आकस्मिक भगदड़
1438	An upright bar, post, or frame forming a support or barrier	Stanchion	(N.)	स्तंभ
1439	A computer printout sent out by a bank regarding debits and credits in your account	Statement	(N.)	विवरण पत्र
1440	An attractively tall, graceful, and dignified woman	Statuesque	(Adj.)	सुडौल
1441	Written law of a legislative body	**Statute (2)**	(N.)	क़ानून
1442	Not able to produce children	Sterile	(Adj.)	बाँझ

SN	Phrases	One Word (#R)	PoS	Hindi
1443	One who loads and uploads ships	**Stevedore (2)**	(N.)	जहाजी कुली
1444	A person who can endure pain or hardship without showing his feelings /complaining	**Stoic (12)**	(N.)	सहनशील व्यक्ति
1445	Indifference to pleasure and pain	**Stoicism (3)**	(N.)	सहनशीलता
1446	One who hides away on a ship to obtain a free passage	Stowaway	(N.)	छिपकर यात्रा करने वाला
1447	A government by the military class	**Stratocracy (3)**	(N.)	सैन्य वर्ग द्वारा सरकार
1448	Showing a dislike of anything improper.	Strict	(Adj.)	कड़क, सख्त
1449	Angry or bitter disagreement over fundamental issues	Strife	(N.)	विवाद
1450	Speaking with a stammer or lisp.	Stuttering	(V.)	हकलाना
1451	A place where pigs are kept	Sty	(N.)	सुअर को रखने की जगह
1452	Too willing to obey other people	Subservient	(Adj.)	अनुसेवी
1453	Bare minimum needed for survival	Subsistence	(N.)	जीवन निर्वाह
1454	So delicate or precise as to be difficult to analyse or describe	Subtle	(Adj.)	सूक्ष्म
1455	Having juicy or fleshy and thick tissues	Succulent	(Adj.)	रसीला
1456	The right to vote in political elections	Suffrage	(N.)	मताधिकार
1457	The action of killing oneself intentionally	**Suicide (3)**	(N.)	आत्महत्या
1458	A set of rooms specially in a hotel for the use of one person or his family	Suite	(N.)	होटल का कमरा
1459	A brief account of a subject	Summary	(N.)	सारांश
1460	Splendid and expensive-looking	Sumptuous	(Adj.)	आलीशान
1461	Only on the surface of something	Superficial	(Adj.)	ऊपरी
1462	Of the highest quality	Superlative	(Adj.)	श्रेष्ठतासूचक
1463	Speed greater than that of sound	Supersonic	(Adj.)	पराध्वनिक
1464	The belief that particular events happen in a way that cannot be explained by reason / science	Superstition	(N.)	अंधविश्वास
1465	Ask or beg for something earnestly or humbly	Supplicate	(V.)	विनती करना
1466	Move suddenly and powerfully forward or upward	Surge	(N.)	लहर
1467	Having something more than required	Surplus	(N.)	अधिकता
1468	To give up completely or agree to forgo, especially in favour of another	Surrender	(N.)	आत्मसमर्पण
1469	Kept secret, especially because it would not be approved of	Surreptitious	(Adj.)	छल से किया हुआ
1470	A person's last performance	**Swan Song (2)**	(N.)	अंतिम प्रदर्शन
1471	A collection of bees	Swarm	(N.)	मधुमक्खियों का झुंड
1472	An edged, bladed weapon that is longer than a knife	Sword	(N.)	तलवार

SN	Phrases	One Word (#R)	PoS	Hindi
1473	A part of a word that can be pronounced separately	Syllable	(N.)	शब्दांश
1474	Reasoning method involving two statements from which a conclusion is reached	Syllogism	(N.)	न्यायवाक्य
1475	Traditionally in sonata form	Symphony	(N.)	स्वर की समता
1476	A building where the jews meet for religious worship and teaching	**Synagogue (2)**	(N.)	यहूदियो का आराधनालय
1477	Words of the same meanings	**Synonyms (2)**	(N.)	समानार्थक शब्द
1478	Made of artificial substance or material	Synthetic	(N.)	कृत्रिम
1479	Showing poor taste and quality	Tacky	(Adj.)	खराब स्वाद और गुणवत्ता वाला
1480	Of or connected with the sense of touch	**Tactile (2)**	(Adj.)	स्पर्श योग्य
1481	A rough, violent, troublesome person	Tartar	(N.)	चिडचिडा मनुष्य
1482	Indelible mark on the skin made by inserting pigment into the skin	Tattoo	(V.)	गोदना
1483	A statement in which you say the same thing twice in different words	Tautology	(N.)	अलग-अलग शब्दों में दो बार एक ही बात कहना
1484	A person who preserves skin of animals	**Taxidermist (2)**	(N.)	चर्म प्रसाधक
1485	The art of cleaning and preserving animal skins	**Taxidermy (2)**	(N.)	चर्म प्रसाधन
1486	Science regarding principles of classification	Taxonomy	(N.)	वर्गीकरण
1487	The application of scientific knowledge for practical purposes	Technology	(N.)	तकनीकी
1488	A person who never takes alcoholic drinks	**Teetotaller (6)**	(N.)	पूर्णतया मद्यत्यागी
1489	Power of reading thought of others	**Telepathy (2)**	(N.)	दूर संवेदन
1490	A violent windstorm	**Tempest (2)**	(N.)	तूफ़ान
1491	Lasting only for a very short while	Temporary	(Adj.)	अस्थायी
1492	Holding on to something or keeping an opinion with determination	Tenacious	(Adj.)	दृढ़/अटल
1493	Station at the end of a route	Terminus	(N.)	अंतिम स्टेशन
1494	A written statement about someone's character, usually provided by an employer	**Testimonial (2)**	(N.)	प्रशंसा पत्र
1495	One who believes in the existence of a god or gods	Theist	(N.)	आस्तिक
1496	Government of a country by religious leaders	Theocracy	(N.)	धर्मशास्त्र
1497	One who studies God and religion	Theologian	(N.)	धर्मशास्त्री
1498	Relating to the study of the nature of god and religious belief	Theological	(Adj.)	आध्यात्मविद्या सम्बन्धी
1499	The study of the nature of god and religious beliefs	**Theology (3)**	(N.)	धर्मशास्त्र

SN	Phrases	One Word (#R)	PoS	Hindi
1500	Religious madness (wherein the patient think he is the deity)	Theomania	(N.)	धर्मोन्माद – धर्म के नाम पर अशांति फैलाने वाला
1501	Relating to the healing of diseases	Therapeutic	(Adj.)	चिकित्सा सम्बन्धी
1502	An instrument for measuring body temperature	Thermometer	(N.)	तापमापी
1503	Complete with regard to every detail.	Thorough	(Adj.)	संपूर्ण
1504	A busy, main road for public use	Thoroughfare	(N.)	सार्वजनिक मार्ग
1505	Showing a lack of courage or confidence	Timid	(Adj.)	कायर
1506	Something that is very small/little	Tiny	(Adj.)	बहुत छोटा
1507	A long, angry speech of criticism or accusation	Tirade	(N.)	कड़ी निंदा
1508	Existing only in name	Titular	(Adj.)	नाममात्र का
1509	A young child just beginning to walk	Toddler	(N.)	नन्हा बच्चा
1510	A strong and fast moving stream of water	**Torrent (3)**	(N.)	प्रचंड धारा
1511	Full of twists and turns	Tortuous	(Adj.)	घुमावदार
1512	A system of government in which only one political party is allowed to function	**Totalitarianism (2)**	(N.)	सर्वसत्तावाद
1513	Something that is poisonous or unhealthy	Toxic	(Adj.)	विषैला
1514	A person who works against his country	Traitor	(N.)	गद्दार
1515	Free from disturbance	Tranquil	(Adj.)	शांतचित्त
1516	Beyond or above the range of normal or physical human experience	Transcendent	(Adj.)	सर्वोत्कृष्ट
1517	An apparatus for reducing or increasing the voltage of an alternating current.	Transformer	(N.)	परिवर्तक
1518	Someone who violates a law or command	Transgressor	(N.)	उल्लंघन करने वाला
1519	Lasting for only a short time	Transient	(N.)	क्षणिक
1520	A portable radio set	Transistor	(N.)	ले जाने योग्य रेडियो
1521	That which lasts for a short time	**Transitory (2)**	(Adj.)	क्षणसाथी
1522	Change in form, nature, or substance	Transmute	(V.)	बदल देना
1523	Relating to speeds close to that of sound	Transonic	(N.)	लगभग हवा में ध्वनि के बराबर गति
1524	Allowing you to see through it (glass etc.)	Transparent	(Adj.)	पारदर्शक
1525	To move back and forth or sideways	Traverse	(V.)	पर्वत पर तिरछे चढ़ना
1526	Distorted representation of something	Travesty	(N.)	उपहासात्मक रचना
1527	The crime of betraying one's country	Treason	(N.)	देशद्रोह
1528	Shaking movement of the ground	Tremor	(N.)	भूकंप के झटके
1529	Those who pass through this gate without permission will be prosecuted.	**Trespassers (2)**	(N.)	अनधिकार प्रवेश करने वाला
1530	Stream flowing into another big river	Tributary	(N.)	सहायक नदी
1531	Happening every three years	**Triennial (3)**	(Adj.)	त्रैवार्षिक
1532	A set of three related works by the same author	**Trilogy (2)**	(N.)	तीन रचनाओं का सेट
1533	A stand having three legs	Tripod	(N.)	तिपाई
1534	A group of three powerful people	Triumvirate	(N.)	तिकड़ी

SN	Phrases	One Word (#R)	PoS	Hindi
1535	Not important or serious // not worth considering // obvious and dull	**Trivial (2)**	(Adj.)	तुच्छ
1536	An award for success in war / hunting // something given as a token of victory	Trophy	(N.)	विजय चिन्ह
1537	A group of artists, dancers or acrobats	Troupe	(N.)	मण्डली
1538	A student who idly or without excuse absents himself/hersef from school	**Truant (3)**	(N.)	गैर हाजिर रहने वाला
1539	An agreement between enemies or opponents to stop fighting, arguing, etc., for a certain period of time	Truce	(N.)	युद्धविराम संधि
1540	Defiantly aggressive	Truculent	(Adj.)	लड़ाकू
1541	An obviously true or hackneyed statement	Truism	(N.)	सामान्य सत्य
1542	The sound made by an elephant	**Trumpet (2)**	(V.)	हाथी का चिंघाड़ना
1543	An extremely large wave in the sea caused by an earthquake	Tsunami	(N.)	भूकंप तरंग
1544	One who changes sides	**Turncoat (3)**	(N.)	दलबदलू
1545	Protection of or authority over someone	Tutelage	(N.)	संरक्षण
1546	Two children born together	Twins	(N.)	जुड़वा
1547	A cruel and oppressive ruler	Tyrant	(N.)	तानाशाह
1548	One who is new to a profession	Tyro	(N.)	नौसिखिया
1549	By everyone in a particular group	**Unanimously (2)**	(Adv.)	सर्वसम्मति से
1550	To put two and two together	Understand	(V.)	अर्थ समझना
1551	That can't be captured	Ungrippable	(Adj.)	जिसपर कब्जा नहीं किया जा सकता
1552	Not having knowledge or experience of a particular subject or activity	Uninitiated	(Adj.)	अदीक्षित
1553	Found all over the world	**Universal (4)**	(Adj.)	सार्वभौमिक
1554	Not knowable	Unknowable	(Adj.)	अज्ञात
1555	Something never done or known before	Unprecedented	(Adj.)	अभूतपूर्व
1556	Having no moral principles	Unscrupulous	(Adj.)	अनैतिक
1557	Something that cannot be handled easily	Unwieldy	(Adj.)	दुष्कर
1558	Rapid or sudden rise	Upsurge	(N.)	चढ़ाव
1559	The upward force that a fluid exerts on a body floating in it	Upthrust	(N.)	तरल में तैरते हुए शरीर पर ऊपर की ओर का बल
1560	A large vase that usually has a pedestal or feet	Urn	(N.)	कलश
1561	A person who shows people their seats	Usher	(N.)	प्रवेश कराने वाला
1562	One who lends money on high rates of interest	**Usurer (5)**	(N.)	सूदखोर
1563	The practice of taking exorbitant or excessive interest on the money lent	Usury	(N.)	सूदखोरी

SN	Phrases	One Word (#R)	PoS	Hindi
1564	An imagined society where everything is perfect and everyone is happy // A place of ideal perfection especially in laws, government, and social conditions	**Utopia (10)**	(N.)	आदर्श राज्य
1565	An imaginary ideal society free of poverty and suffering.	Utopian	(Adj.)	आदर्शवादी
1566	One extremely fond of one's wife	Uxorious	(Adj.)	जोरू का गुलाम
1567	A person who wanders from place to place without a home or job.	Vagabond	(N.)	खानाबदोश
1568	A person without a settled home or regular work who wanders from place to place and lives by begging.	Vagrant	(N.)	खानाबदोश
1569	Having or showing an excessively high opinion of one's appearance, abilities, or worth	Vain	(Adj.)	अहंकारी
1570	A person who is unduly anxious about his/her health	Valetudinarian	(N.)	बीमारी की अत्यधिक चिंता करने वाला
1571	A low area of land between hills	Valley	(N.)	घाटी
1572	One who damages public property	**Vandal (2)**	(N.)	उपद्रवी
1573	Killer of prophet	**Vaticide (2)**	(N.)	पैगंबर का हत्यारा
1574	One who eats no animal flesh	**Vegetarian (2)**	(N.)	शाकाहारी
1575	Showing strong feeling	Vehement	(Adj.)	उग्र
1576	The speed of something in a particular direction	**Velocity (2)**	(N.)	वेग
1577	Committing murder in revenge	Vendetta	(N.)	प्रतिशोध
1578	A person who is greatly respected because of wisdom	Venerable	(Adj.)	सम्मानित
1579	Regard with great respect	Venerate	(V.)	सम्मानित करना
1580	Seeking to harm someone in return for a perceived injury.	Vengeful	(Adj.)	प्रतिहिंसक
1581	A slight fault that can be forgiven.	Venial	(Adj.)	मामूली गलती
1582	One who has the art of speaking in such a way that the sound seems to come from another person / place.	**Ventriloquist (2)**	(N.)	तरह तरह की आवाज़ें निकाल सकने वाला
1583	A new project or business activity involving some risk	Venture	(N.)	उपक्रम
1584	Conformity to facts	Veracity	(N.)	सच्चाई
1585	In exactly the same words as were used originally	**Verbatim (5)**	(Adj.)	शब्द प्रति शब्द
1586	The use of too many words or of more difficult words than are needed to express an idea	Verbiage	(N.)	शब्दाडंबर
1587	Using or containing more words than are needed.	Verbosity	(N.)	शब्दाडंबर

SN	Phrases	One Word (#R)	PoS	Hindi
1588	A decision that is made by a jury in a court	Verdict	(N.)	फ़ैसला
1589	Someone having many skills	**Versatile (6)**	(Adj.)	सर्वगुण सम्पन्न
1590	An animal with a spinal cord	Vertebrate	(N.)	कशेरुकी जंतु
1591	Evening prayer in church	**Vespers (2)**	(N.)	गिरजाघर में सायंकाल की प्रार्थना
1592	A person who is long experienced or practiced in an activity	**Veteran (6)**	(N.)	अनुभवी
1593	The area near or surrounding a particular place	Vicinity	(N.)	आस-पास
1594	Person who portrays bad character roles in cinema	Villain	(N.)	खलनायक
1595	To show or state that someone or something is not guilty of something // Proved to be right in court	**Vindicate (2)**	(V.)	निर्दोष ठहराना
1596	One who is determined to take full revenge for wrongs done to him.	Vindictive	(Adj.)	प्रतिशोधी
1597	A person highly skilled in music	**Virtuoso (2)**	(N.)	कला प्रवीण व्यक्ति
1598	Of a disease or poison extremely severe or harmful in its effects	Virulent	(Adj.)	विषैला
1599	One who can think about the future with imagination and wisdom	Visionary	(Adj.)	काल्पनिक
1600	The cultivation of grapevines.	**Viticulture (2)**	(N.)	अंगूर की खेती
1601	Having a lively, attractive personality.	Vivacious	(Adj.)	फुर्तीला, जोश पूर्ण
1602	A substance easily evaporated at normal temperatures.	Volatile	(Adj.)	परिवर्तनशील
1603	The faculty or power of using one's will.	Volition	(N.)	इच्छा शक्ति
1604	A group of arrows	Volley	(N.)	तीर की बौछार
1605	Of one's own free will	**Voluntary (2)**	(Adj.)	स्वयंसेवी
1606	One who offers his service of his own freewill	**Volunteer (4)**	(N.)	स्वयं सेवक
1607	One who is greedy	Voracious	(Adj.)	लालची
1608	A long sea journey	Voyage	(N.)	समुद्री यात्रा
1609	Exposed to the possibility of being attacked or harmed, either physically or emotionally	**Vulnerable (2)**	(Adj.)	असुरक्षित
1610	A jocular person who is full of amusing anecdotes	Wag	(N.)	मसखरा
1611	A raised passageway in a building	Walkway	(N.)	पैदल रास्ता
1612	Walk or move in a leisurely or aimless way	Wander	(V.)	भटकना
1613	A place where clothes are kept	**Wardrobe (3)**	(N.)	अलमारी
1614	A steep descent of water of a stream or river	Waterfall	(N.)	झरना
1615	A list of passengers and luggage	Waybill	(N.)	यात्री की सूची
1616	Feeling or showing extreme tiredness	Weary	(V.)	थका माँदा
1617	To take someone somewhere suddenly and quickly	Whisk	(V.)	फुर्ती से ले जाना

SN	Phrases	One Word (#R)	PoS	Hindi
1618	Speak in a very low tone	Whisper	(V.)	फुसफुसा कर बोलना
1619	Reduce something in size, amount, or extent by a gradual series of steps	Whittle	(V.)	तराशना
1620	Someone who buys and sells goods in large amounts to shops and businesses	Wholesaler	(N.)	थोक व्यापारी
1621	A woman whose husband is dead especially one who has not remarried	Widow	(N.)	विधवा
1622	A man whose wife is dead	Widower	(N.)	विधुर
1623	Done deliberately, although the person doing it knows that it is wrong	Wilfully	(Adv.)	जान-बूझकर
1624	A plant, leaf, or flower becoming limp	Wilt	(V.)	मुरझाना
1625	An unexpected piece of good fortune	Windfall	(N.)	अप्रत्याशित लाभ
1626	To separate husk from the grain	Winnow	(V.)	फटकना
1627	The practice of magic	Witchery	(V.)	जादू-टोना
1628	Great sorrow or distress	Woe	(N.)	शोक
1629	To dispute angrily	Wrangle	(V.)	क्रोध से झगड़ना
1630	A decorative ring of flowers and leaves	**Wreath (4)**	(N.)	पुष्पांजलि
1631	The remains of something that has been badly damaged	Wreckage	(N.)	मलबे
1632	To move along with quick, short twistings	Wriggle	(N.)	छटपटाना
1633	Fear of foreigners	Xenophobia	(N.)	विदेशी लोगों का डर
1634	A feeling of intense longing for something	Yearning	(N.)	ललक
1635	A wooden object used for connecting animals that are pulling a vehicle	Yoke	(N.)	घोडागाडी में घोड़ों को जोड़ने वाली लकड़ी
1636	A person who is fanatical and uncompromising in pursuit of their religious, political, or other ideals	**Zealot (3)**	(N.)	कट्टरपंथी
1637	The highest point	Zenith	(N.)	शीर्ष बिंदु
1638	The scientific study of the behaviour, structure, physiology, classification and distribution of animals	Zoology	(N.)	जीव विज्ञान

*Total **1638** OWS asked **3024** times.*

SN	Phrases	One Word (#R)	PoS	Hindi
1	A solution for all difficulties or diseases	Panacea (15)	(N.)	रामबाण इलाज
2	Belonging to the same time // A person living in the same age with another	Contemporary (13)	(Adj.)	समकालीन
3	Something no longer in use	Obsolete (13)	(Adj.)	अप्रचलित
4	An inscription on a tombstone in the memory of the person who has died	Epitaph (12)	(N.)	समाधि-लेख
5	Something that cannot be avoided // Certain to happen	Inevitable (12)	(Adj.)	अटल
6	A person who can endure pain or hardship without showing his feelings /complaining	Stoic (12)	(N.)	सहनशील व्यक्ति
7	Able to use the left hand and right hand equally well	Ambidextrous (11)	(N.)	उभयहस्त (दोनों हाथों से समान रूप से काम करने वाला)
8	A place where birds are kept	Aviary (11)	(N.)	पक्षीशाल / चिड़ियाघर
9	One who cannot be corrected // One who is beyond reform	Incorrigible (11)	(Adj.)	असंशोधनीय
10	One who knows everything	Omniscient (11)	(Adj.)	सर्वज्ञानी
11	A person who draws or makes maps	Cartographer (10)	(N.)	मानचित्रकार
12	Handwriting which is difficult or impossible to read	Illegible (10)	(Adj.)	अपठनीय
13	One who cannot make mistake	Infallible (10)	(Adj.)	अचूक
14	An imagined society where everything is perfect and everyone is happy // A place of ideal perfection especially in laws, government, and social conditions	Utopia (10)	(N.)	आदर्श राज्य
15	Someone who makes charitable donations intended to increase human wellbeing	Altruist (9)	(N.)	परोपकारी
16	One who plays for pleasure rather than as a profession // A person who is neither well experienced nor professional // A non-professional who is inept at a particular activity	Amateur (9)	(N.)	शौक़ीन व्यक्ति
17	A person employed to drive a private or hired car	Chauffeur (9)	(N.)	मोटर-चालक
18	An arrangement of events or dates in the order of their occurrence	Chronology (9)	(N.)	कालक्रम
19	An extreme fear of being in a small confined place	Claustrophobia (9)	(N.)	छोटे जगह में होने का अत्यधिक डर
20	One who destroys images or attacks popular beliefs // A person who criticises traditional beliefs and customs	Iconoclast (9)	(N.)	रिवाज़ तोड़नेवाला
21	Something that cannot be heard	Inaudible (9)	(Adj.)	अश्राव्य

22	A person who helps another to commit a crime or to do something morally wrong // A partner in crime	Accomplice (8)	(N.)	सह-अपराधी
23	A situation in a country, an organization, etc. In which there is no government, order / control	Anarchy (8)	(N.)	अराजकता
24	One who doesn't believe in the existence of God	Atheist (8)	(N.)	नास्तिक
25	A person who eats human flesh	Cannibal (8)	(N.)	नरभक्षक
26	A group of stars that forms a shape in the sky and has a name	Constellation (8)	(N.)	नक्षत्र
27	A person who leaves his country to live in another	Emigrant (8)	(N.)	देशत्यागी
28	An animal that lives in groups // Tending to associate with others of one's kind	Gregarious (8)	(Adj.)	झुण्ड में रहनेवाला
29	One who is easily deceived	Gullible (8)	(Adj.)	आसानी से धोखा खानेवाला
30	Someone working or acting merely for money or other rewards // A soldier who fights for the sake of money	Mercenary (8)	(N.)	किराये का सैनिक
31	Well-known for being bad // A person of evil reputation	Notorious (8)	(Adj.)	कुख्यात
32	Animal that can live both on land and in water	Amphibians (7)	(N.)	उभयचर जन्तु (वह जानवर जो जल और स्थल दोनों में रह सकता है)
33	The life history of a person written by himself	Autobiography (7)	(N.)	आत्मकथा
34	An arrangement of flowers that is usually given as a present	Bouquet (7)	(N.)	गुलदस्ता
35	The scientific study of worms and insects	Entomology (7)	(N.)	कीटविज्ञान
36	To free somebody from all blame	Exonerate (7)	(V.)	दोषमुक्त करना
37	A speech or a presentation made without previous preparation.	Extempore (7)	(Adj.)	बिना तैयारी के
38	One who is difficult to please	Fastidious (7)	(Adj.)	ढीठ, हठी
39	A person who sells and arranges cut flowers	Florist (7)	(N.)	फूलवाला
40	A person who suffers from an imaginary illness // A person who is abnormally anxious about his health	Hypochondriac (7)	(N.)	रोगभ्रमी
41	A person pretending to be somebody he isn't	Hypocrite (7)	(N.)	पाखंडी
42	A person who writes and edits dictionaries	Lexicographer (7)	(N.)	शब्दकोश के लेखक
43	A place where money is coined by authority of the government	Mint (7)	(N.)	टकसाल
44	Sentimental longing for a period in the past	Nostalgia (7)	(N.)	अतीत की घटनाओं की यादें

45	That through which light cannot pass	Opaque (7)	(Adj.)	अपारदर्शी
46	One who see bright side of things	Optimist (7)	(N.)	आशावादी
47	One who loves all mankind // Someone who freely gives money and help to people who need it	Philanthropist (7)	(N.)	जन हितैषी
48	A person who collects or studies stamps	Philatelist (7)	(N.)	डाक के टिकट का संग्रहक
49	A person who knows and is able to use several languages.	Polyglot (7)	(N.)	बहुभाषी
50	To give up one's authority or throne	Abdicate (6)	(V.)	अपना पद (या दावा) छोड़ देना
51	A glass tank where fish and water plants are kept	Aquarium (6)	(N.)	मछलीघर
52	Animals and plants growing or living in, or near water	Aquatic (6)	(Adj.)	जलीय
53	The study of human history and prehistory through the excavation of sites	Archaeology (6)	(N.)	पुरातत्त्व
54	The place where public, government or historical records are kept	Archive (6)	(N.)	अभिलेखागार
55	One who is a great lover of books	Bibliophile (6)	(N.)	पुस्तक प्रेमी
56	The scientific study of plants and their structure	Botany (6)	(N.)	वनस्पति विज्ञान
57	Hard but easily broken // liable to break easily	Brittle (6)	(Adj.)	भंगुर / आसानी से टूटने योग्य
58	House or shelter of a gipsy // A group of people, especially traders or pilgrims, travelling together across a desert	Caravan (6)	(N.)	काफिला
59	A list or collection of books or informative graphics	Catalogue (6)	(N.)	सूची
60	The murder of a whole race or a group of people	Genocide (6)	(N.)	जातिसंहार
61	Extreme fear of water	Hydrophobia (6)	(N.)	पानी से भय
62	A person who supervises during an examination	Invigilator (6)	(N.)	निरीक्षक
63	That which cannot be called back	Irrevocable (6)	(Adj.)	अटल
64	A plan of a journey, including the route and the places that you visit	Itinerary (6)	(N.)	यात्रा कार्यक्रम
65	A person with strong desire to steal.	Kleptomania (6)	(N.)	चोरी करने की बीमारी
66	A copy of a book, piece of music, etc. Before it has been printed // A paper written by hand	Manuscript (6)	(N.)	हस्तलिपि
67	A person who dislikes women	Misogynist (6)	(N.)	स्त्री द्वेषी
68	Giving undue favours to one's own kith and kin.	Nepotism (6)	(N.)	भाई-भतीजावाद

69	A person who collects coins	Numismatist (6)	(N.)	मुद्राशास्त्री
70	A person who walks on foot and not travelling in a vehicle	Pedestrian (6)	(N.)	पैदल यात्री
71	Violation of something holy or sacred	Sacrilege (6)	(N.)	अपवित्रीकरण
72	A large number of fish swimming together.	Shoal (6)	(N.)	मछलियों का समुदाय
73	Someone who walks about in sleep	Somnambulist (6)	(N.)	नींद में चलने वाला
74	A person who never takes alcoholic drinks	Teetotaller (6)	(N.)	पूर्णतया मद्यत्यागी
75	Someone having many skills	Versatile (6)	(Adj.)	सर्वगुण सम्पन्न
76	A person who is long experienced or practiced in an activity	Veteran (6)	(N.)	अनुभवी
77	The scientific study of sound	Acoustics (5)	(N.)	ध्वनि-विज्ञान
78	A partial or total loss of memory	Amnesia (5)	(N.)	भूलने की बीमारी
79	Whose names are not known // An unknown author.	Anonymous (5)	(Adj.)	बेनाम/गुमनाम
80	A medicine to nullify the effect of poison	Antidote (5)	(N.)	विष नाशक
81	A military structure where arms and ammunition and other military equipment are stored	Arsenal (5)	(N.)	शस्त्रागार
82	One who makes an official examination of accounts/financial records	Auditor (5)	(N.)	हिसाब किताब की जांच करने वाला
83	A person who can speak only two languages	Bilingual (5)	(Adj.)	द्विभाषिक
84	Words uttered impiously about God // The act of speaking irreverently about sacred things.	Blasphemy (5)	(N.)	ईश्वर की निंदा
85	A doctor who specializes in the study or treatment of heart diseases	Cardiologist (5)	(N.)	हृदय रोग विशेषज्ञ
86	One who plans the steps and moves in a dance	Choreographer (5)	(N.)	नृत्य-निर्देशक
87	A person that one work with at the same place, in a profession or a business	Colleague (5)	(N.)	सहकर्मी
88	An assembly of worshippers // A group of people who have come together in a religious building for worship and prayer	Congregation (5)	(N.)	धार्मिक सभा
89	A person who regards the whole world as his country // One who is a citizen not of a country but of the world	Cosmopolitan (5)	(Adj.)	समस्त संसार का
90	A person in charge of a museum	Curator (5)	(N.)	संग्रहालय अध्यक्ष
91	The study of population and its dynamics	Demography (5)	(N.)	जनसांख्यिकी
92	The scientific study of skin diseases	Dermatology (5)	(N.)	त्वचाविज्ञान
93	A game in which no one wins	Draw (5)	(V.)	अनिर्णित करना
94	A thing fit to be eaten	Edible (5)	(Adj.)	खाद्य
95	Lasting for a very short time	Ephemeral (5)	(Adj.)	क्षणिक
96	A short speech at the end of a play	Epilogue (5)	(N.)	उपसंहार
97	Causing or ending in death	Fatal (5)	(Adj.)	घातक

98	One who runs away from justice or the law	Fugitive (5)	(N.)	भगोड़ा
99	One who eats too much	Glutton (5)	(N.)	खाऊ, पेटू
100	Holding an office without receiving a pay	Honorary (5)	(Adj.)	माननीय
101	The line when the land and sky seems to meet	Horizon (5)	(N.)	क्षितिज
102	A person who cannot read or write	Illiterate (5)	(Adj.)	निरक्षर
103	That which cannot be believed	Incredible (5)	(Adj.)	अविश्वसनीय
104	Incapable of feeling tired or exhausted	Indefatigable (5)	(Adj.)	न थकनेवाला
105	That can burn / catches fire easily	Inflammable (5)	(Adj.)	ज्वलनशील
106	That which cannot be satisfied	Insatiable (5)	(Adj.)	लालची
107	The condition of being unable to sleep over a period of time	Insomnia (5)	(N.)	अनिद्रा
108	One who dies without a will	Intestate (5)	(Adj.)	बिन वसीयत मरा हुआ
109	A quiet person who is more interested in his own thoughts and feelings than in spending time with other people	Introvert (5)	(N.)	अन्तर्मुखी व्यक्ति
110	A cinema show held in the afternoon	Matinee (5)	(N.)	अपराह्न का फिल्म
111	A person who hates and avoids other people	Misanthrope (5)	(N.)	मानवद्वेषी
112	A system of government by a king / a queen	Monarchy (5)	(N.)	राज-तंत्र
113	A notice of a person's death	Obituary (5)	(N.)	शोक सन्देश
114	Government or rule by a small group of people	Oligarchy (5)	(N.)	अल्पतंत्र
115	One who is all powerful	Omnipotent (5)	(Adj.)	सर्वशक्तिमान
116	A piece of land / garden, in which fruit trees are grown	Orchard (5)	(N.)	फलोद्यान
117	A person who loves, supports and defends his country	Patriot (5)	(N.)	देश-भक्त
118	Safe to drink (water)	Potable (5)	(Adj.)	पीने योग्य
119	A fictitious name especially one assumed by an author	Pseudonym (5)	(N.)	उपनाम
120	The scientific study of the mind and how it influences behaviour	Psychology (5)	(N.)	मनोविज्ञान
121	A close-fitting cover for a sword or knife // Cover for the blade of a weapon or a tool	Sheath (5)	(N.)	म्यान
122	One who lends money on high rates of interest	Usurer (5)	(N.)	सूदखोर
123	In exactly the same words as were used originally	Verbatim (5)	(Adj.)	शब्द प्रति शब्द
124	To reduce to a shorter form intended to stand for the whole	Abbreviation (4)	(N.)	किसी शब्द या वाक्यांश संक्षिप्त रूप
125	An abbreviation formed from the initial letters of other words and pronounced as a word	Acronym (4)	(N.)	शब्दों के पहले अक्षरों से बना शब्द
126	The period between the beginning of puberty and adulthood	Adolescence (4)	(N.)	किशोरावस्था

127	A list of items to be discussed at a meeting	Agenda (4)	(N.)	कार्यसूची
128	A person belonging to a foreign country // different from what you are used to // A fictional being from another world	Alien (4)	(N.)	अजनबी
129	An allowance made to a wife by her husband, when they are legally separated.	Alimony (4)	(N.)	परित्यक्ता पत्नी के लिये गुजारा भत्ता
130	Capable of being understood in either of two or more possible senses, and therefore not definite.	Ambiguous (4)	(Adj.)	संदिग्धार्थी / अस्पष्ट
131	An official pardon // the formal act of liberating someone	Amnesty (4)	(N.)	राज-क्षमा
132	A person who believes that laws and governments are not necessary // A person who believes in or tries to bring about a state of lawlessness	Anarchist (4)	(N.)	अराजकतावादी
133	A person who presents a radio / television programme	Anchor (4)	(N.)	समाचार उद्घोषक
134	The date on which an event happened in some previous year	Anniversary (4)	(N.)	सालगिरह
135	Strong dislike between two persons // A deep-seated feeling of aversion	Antipathy (4)	(N.)	घृणा, चिढ़
136	A place where bees are kept	Apiary (4)	(N.)	मधुमक्खियों के पालने का स्थान
137	A large body of water with many islands	Archipelago (4)	(N.)	द्वीपसमूह
138	A government by the nobles / government by person of highest social order	Aristocracy (4)	(N.)	श्रेष्ठ जनों के द्वारा राज्य शासन
139	One who denies oneself ordinary bodily pleasures	Ascetic (4)	(N.)	तपस्वी
140	The scientific study of celestial bodies like sun, moon, stars, planets, etc.	Astronomy (4)	(N.)	खगोल शास्त्र
141	A large bundle bound for storage or transport	Bale (4)	(N.)	गट्ठा
142	A government run by officials in a state	Bureaucracy (4)	(N.)	नौकरशाही
143	Hole excavated by an animal as dwelling	Burrow (4)	(N.)	बिल
144	A person who is skilled at producing beautiful handwriting	Calligrapher (4)	(N.)	सुलेखक
145	The art of beautiful handwriting	Calligraphy (4)	(N.)	सुलेख
146	Animals that eat meat	Carnivorous (4)	(N.)	मांसभक्षी
147	The art or process of drawing or making maps	Cartography (4)	(N.)	मानचित्रकारी
148	A man who knows a lot about things like food, music and art	Connoisseur (4)	(N.)	विशेषज्ञ, पारखी
149	A man who is recovering from illness.	Convalescent (4)	(N.)	बीमारी से ठीक होना
150	A person who readily believes others easily	Credulous (4)	(Adj.)	भोला-भाला

151	A large bedroom for a number of people in a school or institution	Dormitory (4)	(N.)	शयनागार
152	Man behaving more like a woman than as a man	Effeminate (4)	(Adj.)	नारी जैसा
153	A person who talks too much of himself // A person who speaks always in praise of himself // A person who is excessively conceited and self-absorbed	Egotist (4)	(N.)	अहंवादी
154	A poem that express lament for the dead	Elegy (4)	(N.)	शोकगीत
155	An act of misappropriation of money	Embezzlement (4)	(N.)	गबन
156	Bringing about gentle and painless death from incurable disease	Euthanasia (4)	(N.)	इच्छामृत्यु
157	A person who wastes his money on luxury	Extravagant (4)	(Adj.)	फ़िज़ूल ख़र्च
158	One who believes in fate	Fatalist (4)	(N.)	भाग्यवादी
159	The plants and vegetation of a particular region	Flora (4)	(N.)	वनस्पति
160	Something which gets broken easily	Fragile (4)	(Adj.)	भंगुर
161	Writing or drawings scribbled, scratched, or sprayed illicitly on a wall or other surface in a public place	Graffiti (4)	(N.)	दीवार चित्रण
162	A building in which aircraft are housed	Hangar (4)	(N.)	विमानशाला
163	A large group of people	Horde (4)	(N.)	भीड़
164	The study of growing garden plants	Horticulture (4)	(N.)	उद्यान-विज्ञान
165	A box or cage for rabbits or small animals	Hutch (4)	(N.)	छोटे जानवरों के रहने का घर
166	Incapable of being approached	Inaccessible (4)	(Adj.)	दुर्गम
167	Being unable to pay one's debt	Insolvent (4)	(Adj.)	दिवालिया
168	Someone who is killed fighting for the cause of religion or faith.	Martyr (4)	(N.)	शहीद
169	A traveller who moves from one region or country to another	Migrant (4)	(N.)	प्रवासी
170	A place for keeping dead bodies before burial or cremation	Mortuary (4)	(N.)	शवगृह
171	A person or thing that has the same name as another	Namesake (4)	(N.)	हमनाम
172	A geometrical figure with eight sides	Octagon (4)	(N.)	अष्टभुज
173	One who eats both vegetables and meat	Omnivorous (4)	(N.)	सर्व-भक्षक
174	Doctor who deals with bone problems	Orthopaedist (4)	(N.)	हड्डियों का डॉक्टर
175	A person who opposes war or use of military force.	Pacifist (4)	(N.)	शांतिवादी
176	The belief that God is in everything, including nature	Pantheism (4)	(N.)	सर्वेश्वरवाद
177	One who does not care for literature or art.	Philistine (4)	(N.)	अशिक्षित

178	An animal that lives by killing and eating other animals	Predator (4)	(N.)	परजीवी
179	A person who withdraws from the world to live in seclusion and often in solitude	Recluse (4)	(N.)	वैरागी
180	A person very reserved in speech	Reticent (4)	(Adj.)	अल्पभाषी
181	A protected place for birds and animals // A nature reserve for birds or animals	Sanctuary (4)	(N.)	अभयारण्य
182	Government not connected with religious or spiritual matters	Secular (4)	(Adj.)	धर्म निरपेक्ष
183	An office with high salary but no work	Sinecure (4)	(N.)	आराम की नौकरी
184	Found all over the world	Universal (4)	(Adj.)	सार्वभौमिक
185	One who offers his service of his own freewill	Volunteer (4)	(N.)	स्वयं सेवक
186	A decorative ring of flowers and leaves	Wreath (4)	(N.)	पुष्पांजलि
187	A place where animals are slaughtered for consumption as food	Abattoir (3)	(N.)	कसाईखाना
188	Formally put an end to a system, practice, or institution	Abolish (3)	(V.)	किसी रिवाज या स्थापित नियम का अंत करना
189	The inhabitants living from earliest times in a country // The original inhabitants/natives of a country	Aborigines (3)	(N.)	किसी देश के मूल निवासी
190	To decide and state officially in court that somebody is not guilty of a crime	Acquit (3)	(V.)	बरी (दोषमुक्त) कर देना
191	One who performs daring gymnastic feats // An entertainer who performs difficult physical feats	Acrobat (3)	(N.)	हवाई करतब करने वाला
192	Concerned with beauty or the appreciation of beauty	Aesthetic (3)	(Adj.)	सौन्दर्यबोधी
193	Words that begin with the same letter, syllable or sound // Repetition of an initial sound in two or more words of a line	Alliteration (3)	(N.)	अनुप्रास अलंकार
194	A short, interesting or amusing story about a real person or an event	Anecdote (3)	(N.)	लघुकथा
195	The study of human race, especially of its origin, development, customs and beliefs	Anthropology (3)	(N.)	मानव विज्ञान
196	A policy that segregates people on the basis of race // Policy of racial discrimination	Apartheid (3)	(N.)	रंगभेद
197	The feeling of not being interested in or enthusiastic	Apathy (3)	(N.)	उदासीनता
198	A person who works for an expert to learn a trade	Apprentice (3)	(N.)	शिक्षार्थी
199	A person who is chosen to settle a disagreement // a person appointed by two parties to resolve a dispute	Arbitrator (3)	(N.)	पंच/माध्यस्थ
200	Good at expressing ideas / feelings clearly in words // Having or showing the ability to speak fluently and coherently	Articulate (3)	(Adj.)	सुस्पष्ट

Total **200** *OWS asked* **1121** *times.*

SN	Many Word (SSC CGL Tier 1 2022)	One Word
1	A piece of a living tissue or plant that is transplanted surgically	Graft
2	Feeling or showing extreme tiredness	Weary
3	A person in love with himself	Narcissist
4	Giving the worrying impression that something bad is going to happen	Ominous
5	Plants of a particular region	Flora
6	A shortened version of a larger work	Abridgement
7	man supervising the exam	Invigilator
8	Adjust or make right; correct, amend	Rectify
9	Having or showing an excessively high opinion of one's appearance, abilities, or worth	Vain
10	The date when both, day and night are of approximately equal length	Equinox
11	One who has the ability to do many different things	Versatile
12	A speech made without preparation	Extempore
13	One who mediates in a deal or complex situation	Negotiator
14	A loud appeal or demand	Clamour
15	The study of languages	Philology
16	Sharp and direct	Acerbic
17	series of stars	Constellation
18	One who does something not professionally but for pleasure	Amateur
19	A person having significant experience in an occupation	Veteran
20	The act of washing oneself	Ablutions
21	A very expensive and elaborately built tomb	Mausoleum
22	A place where coins and medals are made.	Mint
23	An excessively intense desire for returning to past or lost conditions	Nostalgia
24	The act of killing one's mother	Matricide
25	small shelter for my dog	Kennel
26	Existing in a land from the earliest times or from before the arrival of colonists	Aboriginal
27	An eccentric manner of living	Bohemian
28	The property left to someone by a will	Legacy
29	A small island	Islet
30	A group of stars having a particular shape	Constellation
31	A huge building with a spacious area to house aircrafts.	Hangar
32	Allowance given to a wife from her husband on separation	Alimony
33	Formal forgiveness of a person's sins	Absolution
34	Holding on to something or keeping an opinion with determination	Tenacious
35	A perfectionist	Meticulous
36	Fail to notice; ignore; condone (an offence etc.)	Overlook
37	A room where dead bodies are kept until burial	Mortuary
38	The action of damaging the good reputation of someone	Defamation
39	An exaggerated statement not to be taken seriously or literally	Hyperbole
40	Cancel or do away with (a law or agreement)	Abrogate

41	To keep postponing doing a task later because you're lazy	Procrastinate
42	A battle or anything involving or causing much bloodshed	Sanguinary
43	Something which is worth believing	Credible
44	Strong hostility	Animosity
45	Murder of an infant	Infanticide
46	One who loves humanity or believes in universal brotherhood	Philanthropist
47	who loves good food and knows a lot about it.	Gourmet
48	One who can speak two languages	Bilingual
49	to give up completely or agree to forgo, especially in favour of another	Surrender
50	Something that is capable of being accomplished	Feasible
51	The scientific study of plants and their structure	Botany
52	man who drew maps.	Cartographer
53	One who runs away from law	Fugitive
54	Words that begin with the same letter, syllable or sound	Alliteration
55	not to be affected by the pleasures and pains of life.	Stoic
56	Having a feeling of guilt	Remorse
57	A person who criticises traditional beliefs and customs	Iconoclast
58	A poll taken of voters leaving the voting place that is usually used for predicting the winners.	Exit Poll
59	A formal statement testifying to someone's character and qualifications	Testimonial
60	Something that is very small/little	Tiny
61	Making of a false document with a false signature	Forgery
62	A list or collection of books or informative graphics	Catalogue

SN	Many Word (SSC CGL Tier 2 2021)	One Word
1	A book or set of books giving information on many subjects or on	Encyclopedia
2	a case for keeping a sword	Sheath
3	a doctor who specializes in heart diseases	Cardiologist
4	a large single detached house with single or double story	Bungalow
5	an animal or person that eats a variety of food of both plant and animal origin.	Omnivore
6	one who is all powerful	Omnipotent
7	one who lives on others	Parasite
8	one who speaks for others	Spokesperson
9	one who talks to oneself	Soliloquist
10	person who moves from one place to another, with intentions of finding work and settling, permanently or temporarily, at a new location	Migrant
11	symbols of royalty	Regalia

SN	Many Word (SSC CHSL Tier 1 2021)	One Word
1	Zeal; burning enthusiasm; passion	Ardour
2	someone who was only interested in the amount of money that he could get from a situation	Mercenary
3	the scientific study of sound	Acoustics
4	connoisseur of food	Gourmet
5	knows everything and has unlimited knowledge	Omniscient
6	The action of examining with care or reading carefully	Perusal
7	pretending to be what he is not	Hypocrite
8	A short text written on tombstone	Epitaph
9	a report giving the news of the death and details about the life of the deceased	Obituary
10	A pause between the acts of a play	Interlude
11	An instrument for detecting an earthquake	Seismograph
12	Fall back or sink again (into a worse state after an improvement)	Relapse
13	Looking or sounding foreign, bizarre, strange, unfamiliar	Outlandish
14	unable to pay his debts	Bankrupt
15	A person who leaves his/her own country to live in another country permanently	Emigrant
16	One thing that can be divided	Divisible
17	Unselfish interest in the welfare of others	Altruism
18	Unable to speak distinctly or express oneself clearly	Inarticulate
19	A small organised dissenting group within a larger one	Faction
20	inexperienced at this job	Novice
21	The study of population and its dynamics	Demography
22	speaks many languages	Polyglot
23	One who is well-versed in the knowledge of plants	Botanist
24	Eternal; lasting forever or indefinitely	Perpetual
25	wastes his money on luxurious objects	Extravagant
26	An outlook that is influenced by people from all over the world	Cosmopolitan
27	naturally able to eat both, plants and flesh	Omnivorous
28	helping other people willingly without expecting any payment for her services	Volunteer
29	The state of being full or complete	Plenitude
30	A remedy to counteract the effects of poison	Antidote
31	One who gives money or help to another person or cause	Benefactor
32	The love of man or mankind	Philanthropy
33	whose names are not known	Anonymous
34	One who loves the company of others	Gregarious
35	One who believes in the existence of a god or gods	Theist
36	someone who draws maps	Cartographer
37	Someone who is shy and spends time alone rather than being with others	Introvert
38	To dispute angrily	Wrangle
39	has many skills	Versatile

40	Direct and outspoken	Forthright
41	Allowing or assisting to discover	Heuristic
42	area where animals are slaughtered for the market	Abattoir
43	to renovate or improve	Revamp
44	Lasting for a very short period of time	Ephemeral
45	A journey undertaken by a group of people with a particular purpose, especially that of exploration or research	Expedition
46	A sudden unsteady movement; a stagger	Lurch
47	Reject as invalid, especially by legal procedure	Quash
48	Merry, convivial, hearty and good humoured	Jovial
49	Something that is pertaining to controversy	Polemical
50	A person as a source of intellectual light or moral inspiration	Luminary
51	living in the same time period	Contemporaries
52	Something that will cure all illnesses	Panacea
53	situation of no organisation and control due to the lack of an effective government	Anarchy
54	Strong taste or liking for something	Penchant
55	An omission of duty	Delinquency
56	The art of beautiful handwriting	Calligraphy
57	The work inscribed on the tomb in the memory of the person	Epitaph
58	Take and use the thoughts, inventions, etc. of another person as one's own	Plagiarise
59	One who makes an active effort to promote human welfare	Philanthropist
60	A person who loves and collects books	Bibliophile
61	The activity of writing dictionaries	Lexicography
62	One who is well versed in many languages	Polyglot
63	Easily provoked	Irascible
64	one who makes an active effort to promote human welfare	Philanthropist
65	has come to a different country from his own country for settling	Immigrant
66	knows many languages	Polyglot
67	A word that has the same or nearly the same meaning as another word in the same language	Synonym
68	number of fishes getting caught	Haul

SN	Many Word (SSC MTS Tier 1 2021)	One Word
1	The expression of a wish that misfortune or doom befall a person	Curse
2	A place for ammunition and weapons	Arsenal
3	Property left to someone by a will	Legacy
4	One who is unable to pay his debts	Bankrupt
5	One who does not tire easily	Indefatigable
6	A person who looks at the bright side of things	Optimist
7	Climb or move with difficulty or a lot of effort, typically using one's hands and feet	Clamber
8	A keeper or custodian of a museum	Curator

9	Any award, honour or laudatory notice	Accolade
10	Something happening in three years	Triennial
11	Story of an individual written by himself	Autobiography
12	A person exhibiting excessive worry about one's health	Hypochondriac
13	One who feeds on human flesh	Cannibal
14	A person who believes in or tries to bring about a state of lawlessness	Anarchist
15	One who believes in fate	Fatalist
16	The collection and study of postage stamps	Philately
17	A person who sells flowers	Florist
18	A disturbed state of mind caused by an illness	Delirium
19	One who collects coins	Numismatist
20	A large bundle bound for storage or transport	Bale
21	Made in imitation so as to be passed off fraudulently as genuine	Counterfeit
22	Killing one self	Suicide
23	An imaginary name assumed by an author	Pseudonym
24	The study of human mind and behaviour	Psychology
25	One who studies insect life	Entomologist
26	Of or relating to the moon	Lunar
27	A system of government by the wealthy class	Plutocracy
28	One who has a long experience of any occupation	Veteran
29	An agreement between enemies or opponents to stop fighting, arguing, etc., for a certain period of time	Truce
30	One who knows all	Omniscient
31	One who runs away from justice or a dangerous situation	Fugitive
32	Having or forming a hard outer layer	Crusted
33	The study of the heart and its action and disease	Cardiology
34	Incapable of making mistakes or being wrong	Infallible
35	Someone working or acting merely for money or other rewards	Mercenary
36	A non-professional who is inept at a particular activity	Amateur
37	Having a common centre, as circles or spheres	Concentric
38	One who can use either hand with ease	Ambidextrous
39	Existing or happening in the same time period	Contemporary
40	A room in a public building where outdoor clothes or luggage may be left	Cloakroom
41	A place for breeding and keeping birds	Aviary
42	The action of using someone or something as a model	Imitation
43	A game in which no one wins	Draw
44	One who is outspoken and outgoing	Extrovert
45	Someone who is silent or uncommunicative in speech	Reserved
46	A place where bees are kept	Apiary
47	One who does a thing for pleasure and not as a profession	Amateur
48	Incapable of making mistakes or being wrong	Infallible
49	Someone working or acting merely for money or other rewards	Mercenary
50	Government by king or queen	Monarchy

51	Violation or misuse of what is regarded as sacred	Sacrilege
52	Occurring after the death of the said person	Posthumous
53	A place where dead bodies are kept for identification	Morgue
54	Feelings of great happiness and excitement	Euphoria
55	In exactly the same words as were used originally	Verbatim
56	The life history of a person written by himself	Autobiography
57	An unconventional style of living	Bohemian
58	One who dislikes art and culture	Philistine
59	An abbreviation formed from the initial letters of other words and pronounced as a word	Acronym
60	An unlikely chance or occurrence, especially a piece of good luck	Fluke
61	Make (something bad or unsatisfactory) better	Ameliorate
62	An afternoon performance in a theatre or cinema	Matinee
63	An ability to find ways and directions	Navigate
64	A person who produces beautiful handwriting	Calligrapher
65	A state of perfect balance	Equilibrium
66	A collection of selected writings of various authors	Anthology
67	A short story with a moral	Parable
68	A place for storing grain	Granary
69	A group of fish	School
70	The science or art of political government	Politics
71	A book or paper written by hand	Manuscript
72	One who dies for a noble cause	Martyr
73	A place where government records are kept	Archive
74	A book that contains information on various subjects	Encyclopaedia
75	A thing or substance that is liable to catch fire easily	Inflammable
76	A group of guns or missile launchers operated together at one place	Battery
77	One who hates mankind	Misanthrope
78	Someone who attacks cherished ideas or traditional institutions	Iconoclast
79	One who collects stamps	Philatelist
80	Deliberately and maliciously set something (buildings usually) on fire	Arson
81	A cage for small animals	Hutch
82	One who is not sure about God's existence	Agnostic
83	The study of different skin diseases	Dermatology
84	One who is hostile and violent	Aggressive
85	Not fit to eat	Inedible
86	A large group of people, especially the nomadic	Horde
87	An action of making amends for a wrong or injury	Atonement
88	Animals that live in water	Aquatic
89	That which can be easily broken	Fragile
90	Weakness and poor health	Frailty
91	To own up to something as true	Confess
92	A person incapable of making mistakes	Infallible
93	A sound that is pleasing to hear	Melodious

94	A person who makes maps	Cartographer

SN	Many Word (SSC CPO Paper 1 2022)	One Word
1	Showing astute powers of judgement; clever and judicious	Shrewd
2	One who does a thing for pleasure and not as a profession	Amateur
3	A place for storage of arms and ammunition	Arsenal
4	Evoking a keen sense of sadness or regret	Poignant
5	Profitable, yielding financial gain	Lucrative
6	One who takes a dark view of things	Pessimist
7	Cause to continue; keep up; preserve (a state of affairs, an activity etc)	Maintain
8	A person who introduces the performers or contestants in a variety show	Compere
9	Taking heed or care; being conscious	Mindful
10	The scientific study of worms and insects	Entomology
11	The quality of being honest and having strong moral principles	Integrity
12	The one who makes maps and charts	Cartographer
13	The scientific study of the behaviour, structure, physiology, classification and distribution of animals	Zoology
14	Honour given for some achievement	Laurel
15	Killing of a person by another	Homicide
16	fast moving water	Torrent
17	Treat with a vaccine, usually by injection to promote immunity against a disease	Inoculate
18	One who knows all things	Omniscient
19	A group of worshippers	Congregation
20	Someone who is reserved and shy	Introvert
21	A happy development or happening of events by chance.	Serendipity
22	To become a strong person in spite of many difficulties.	Resilient
23	A large group of people	Horde
24	Person living at the same time	Contemporary
25	One who believes in his fate	Fatalist
26	Take hold of forcibly or suddenly	Seize
27	Someone who does not believe that God exists	Atheist
28	The arrangement of events or dates in the order of their occurrence	Chronology
29	Rarely; not often	Seldom
30	So delicate or precise as to be difficult to analyse or describe	Subtle
31	A person who regards the whole world as his country	Cosmopolitan
32	Try hard to do or achieve something	Endeavour
33	Rapid or sudden rise	Upsurge
34	person hired to drive our car	Chauffeur
35	One who is bad in spellings	Cacographer
36	Hatred	Malevolence
37	The main character in a story.	Protagonist

| 38 | A letter, poem etc. whose author is unknown. | Anonymous |

SN	Many Word (SSC CPO Paper 2 2020)	One Word
1	Branch of science that studies structure, classification and genetics of plants	botany
2	One who talks in sleep	somniloquist
3	An entrance hall in a building used by the public, especially a hotel or theatre	foyer
4	One who is beyond reform	incorrigible
5	A person skilled in cutting, dressing, and laying stone in buildings.	mason
6	A doctor who attends to bone problems	orthopaedist
7	One who is violently against established traditions and beliefs	iconoclast
8	A traveller who moves from one region or country to another	migrant
9	A small mischievous fairy	elf
10	An arrangement of flowers that is usually given as a present	bouquet

SN	Many Word (SSC GD Constable 2021)	One Word
1	Brighten with light	Illuminate
2	A vehicle used to carry a dead body	Hearse
3	Subject (someone to a continuous flow of questions, criticisms or information	Bombard
4	A place where antiques are kept	Museum
5	Person who is not an expert in a field of art or music	Amateur
6	Dwarf varieties of trees and shrubs grown in pots	Bonsai
7	Move faster	Accelerate
8	A partner in crime	Accomplice
9	Fluid secreted by flowers which is collected by bees for making honey	Nectar
10	Group of people moving together in a company for security, especially for crossing deserts	Caravan
11	A kind of decision on which one cannot go back	Irrevocable
12	Strong deep dislike	Antipathy
13	Something that cannot be avoided	Inevitable
14	Woman who is the head of the family	Matriarch
15	A steep descent of water of a stream or river	waterfall
16	Impossible to believe	Incredible
17	An event causing great and sudden damage or suffering	Catastrophe
18	The sound made by a snake	Hiss
19	Something that cannot be handled easily	Unwieldy
20	Study of living organisms	Biology
21	The science of surveying and charting bodies of water	Hydrography
22	Dead body of an animal	Carcass
23	The branch of science which deals with celestial bodies like stars, planets and natural objects in space	Astronomy
24	An imaginary ideal society free of poverty and suffering	Utopia

25	Causing a mood of gloom and depression	Dismal
26	Science of heredity	Genetics
27	A hole or tunnel dug by a small animal to live in	Burrow
28	One who disbelieves the existence of God	Atheist
29	One who supervises in an examination hall	Invigilator
30	Pictures given in a book for the purpose of explaining things	Illustration
31	Group of stars	Constellation
32	Ordinary and dull	Mundane
33	The practice of having more than one husband or wife at the same time	Polygamy
34	A deep-seated feeling of aversion	Antipathy
35	Not easily excited or upset	Placid
36	Animals living in the sea only	Marine
37	The practice of persuading someone to do something by using force or threats	Coercion
38	Something that is quickly and easily set on fire and burned	Inflammable
39	A geometrical figure with six sides	Hexagon
40	Mark or substance that is impossible to remove	Indelible
41	A thing no longer in use	Obsolete
42	Afternoon show of a film or play	Matinee
43	The sound an elephant makes	Trumpet
44	A person who walks in his/her sleep	Somnambulist
45	Shortened form of a word or phrase	Abbreviation
46	An animal that preys on other animals	Predator
47	The doctor who specialises in the study or treatment of heart diseases and heart abnormalities	Cardiologist
48	A disease which affects large populations at the same time	Epidemic
49	Study of insects	Entomology
50	A person who tends to be hopeful and confident about the future or the success of something	Optimist
51	Written law passed by a law-making body	Statute
52	A four-footed animal	Quadruped
53	An edged, bladed weapon that is longer than a knife	Sword
54	Detailed examination of something complex	Analysis
55	Sound reflected back as in mountains	Echo
56	Represent something as larger, better or worse than it really is	Exaggerate
57	the sound made by a crocodile	Bellow
58	Relating to a festival	Festal
59	One who treats female ailments	Gynaecologist
60	Belonging to very distant past and no longer in existence	Ancient
61	One who has fixed opinions and beliefs	Rigid
62	A person who physically attacks another	Assailant
63	Life history of a person written by someone else	Biography
64	Move with urgent haste	Rush
65	A strongbox or small chest for holding valuables	Coffer

66	A person who arranges and sells cut flowers	Florist
67	A small ornament which hangs down especially from a necklace	Pendant
68	A list of books available in a library	Catalogue
69	Run after in order to catch or catch up with	Chase
70	A period of ten years	Decade
71	Twice a month	Bimonthly
72	Song which is sung in a church by a group of singers	Carol
73	A type of substance or material that burns very quickly	Inflammable
74	A plan or route to be followed on a journey	Itinerary
75	A person who never drinks alcohol.	Teetotaller
76	First show of a film or theatre	Premiere
77	Matter which is against moral values	Immoral
78	Make a machine active or operative	Activate
79	A condition in which one is unable to sleep over a period of time	Insomnia
80	Ability to see what might happen in the future	Foresight
81	A person who walks, especially in an area where vehicles go	Pedestrian
82	Sound made by ducks	Quack
83	The system of money used in a particular country	Currency
84	Shortened form of a word	Abbreviation
85	A system of government in which most of the important decisions are taken by state officials rather than by elected representatives.	Bureaucracy
86	A building where monks live as a community	Monastery
87	A collection of sticks	Bundle
88	A means of altering one's appearance to conceal one's identity	Disguise
89	To reduce to a shorter form intended to stand for the whole	Abbreviate
90	An area where fruit trees are grown	Orchard
91	A solemn promise	Pledge
92	Sound made by a horse	Neigh
93	Person who is the natural successor to ancestral property	Heir
94	A piece of land where fruit trees are grown	Orchard
95	That which is lawful	Legal
96	A volume containing several books previously published separately	Omnibus
97	One who examines a company's financial records	Auditor
98	A person who knows everything	Omniscient
99	Anything that leads to death	Fatal
100	A person who supervises during an examination	Invigilator
101	Many fish swimming together	Shoal
102	One who collects coins	Numismatist
103	Hair of animals, which is soft and used for making wool	Fur
104	Break or fall apart into small fragments in the process of deterioration	Crumble
105	A large number of fish swimming together	Shoal
106	Delay an event to a later date or time	Postpone
107	An outgoing, socially confident person	Extrovert

108	A study of the human body	Physiology
109	Release someone from a duty or obligation	Exonerate
110	An object through which we cannot see at all	Opaque
111	Imitate someone's action or words in order to entertain or ridicule	Mimic
112	One who can use either hand easily	Ambidextrous
113	Something that can be carried easily	Portable
114	A piece of land entirely surrounded by water	Island
115	Eskimo's house that is made of ice blocks	Igloo
116	Certain to happen	Inevitable
117	Unable to act	Inert
118	A person who is excessively conceited and self-absorbed	Egotist
119	Words carved on a stone or monument	Inscription
120	Comparison between things that have similar features	Analogy
121	A spider's home	Cobweb
122	One who travels on foot	Pedestrian
123	A cage for keeping rabbits	Hutch
124	Fluent or persuasive in speaking or writing	Eloquent
125	Something that can be carried easily	Portable
126	Handwritten book	Manuscript
127	That through which light cannot pass	Opaque
128	One who has unlimited power	Omnipotent
129	Belonging to the middle ages	Medieval
130	A group of stars which form a pattern and have a name	Constellation
131	A line at which the earth's surface and the sky appear to meet	Horizon
132	A large group of people	Horde
133	A medical practitioner specialising in children and their diseases	Paediatrician
134	Person who sells and arranges cut flowers	Florist
135	Light rain falling in small drops	Drizzle
136	A medicine used to nullify the effect of poison	Antidote
137	A place where wild animals are kept in their natural environment	Sanctuary
138	An imaginary place where everything is perfect	utopia
139	Natural skill at doing something	Knack
140	A person who investigates and solves crimes	Detective
141	A place where money is coined	Mint
142	A remedy for all diseases	Panacea
143	The sound made by bees	Buzz
144	Lack of feeling	Apathy
145	A person who takes care of cattle	Cowherd
146	The action of killing oneself intentionally	Suicide
147	Someone who buys and sells goods in large amounts to shops and businesses	Wholesaler
148	The branch of biology that deals with the relations of organisms to one another and to their physical surroundings.	Ecology
149	One who cannot be changed or reformed	Incorrigible

150	A person who helps willingly without being paid for it	Volunteer
151	Go back over the same route that one has just taken	Retrace
152	A short interesting or amusing story	Anecdote
153	Fit to be eaten	Edible
154	A large cage, building or enclosure for keeping birds in	Aviary
155	A system of society or government in which men hold the power and women are largely excluded from it	Patriarchy
156	The art of effective speaking	Elocution
157	Not to pay attention to someone or something	Ignore
158	A change which is the result of an act or some cause	Effect
159	A recurrent urge to steal	Kleptomania
160	The sound a bear makes	Growl
161	A person who loves, supports and defends his country	Patriot
162	The state of being married	Matrimony
163	A game that no one wins	Draw
164	Not having knowledge or experience of a particular subject or activity	Uninitiated
165	A person who loves his/her country and, if necessary, will fight for it	Patriot
166	Become less intense or widespread	Abate
167	Person who portrays bad character roles in cinema	Villain
168	The sound of owls	Hoot
169	A large number of things placed one on top of another	Pile
170	Able to be harmed easily	Vulnerable
171	One who has keen interest in good food	Gourmet
172	Declare someone not guilty	Acquit
173	A place where birds are kept	Aviary
174	Able to be eaten	Edible
175	Owing money to someone	Indebted
176	A dummy used to display clothes in a shop window	Mannequin
177	The sound made by an elephant	Trumpet
178	To give up a throne voluntarily	Abdicate
179	A list of sources used when writing a scholarly article	Bibliography
180	One who makes an eloquent public speech	Orator
181	Go or come after a person or thing proceeding ahead	Follow
182	Connected with the sense of touch	Tactile
183	Giving orders in a manner that permits no refusal	Dictatorial
184	Study of diseases	Pathology
185	Disease that spreads by physical touch and contact	Contagious
186	Land beside a sea	Coast
187	Well-known for bad qualities or deeds	Notorious
188	Things which are of the same kind and of the same dimensions	Homogeneous

SN	Many Word (SSC Selection Post 2022 - 10th Level)	One Word
1	reminder of the place	Souvenir
2	The inner soft part of a seed, fruit or nut	Kernel
3	An official inspection of a company's, or individual's, accounts	Audit
4	An arrangement of flowers that is usually given as present.	Bouquet
5	safe to drink	Potable
6	something that lasts only for a short time	Ephemeral
7	The arrangement of events or dates in the order of their occurrence	Chronology
8	the men living in the same age	Contemporaries
9	make perfectly clear	Elucidate
10	A herd of cattle or animals driven in a body.	Drove
11	Delay in doing something to a later time	Procrastination
12	A large group of people	Horde
13	A funeral procession	Cortege
14	Widespread occurrence of an infectious disease crossing international boundaries	Pandemic
15	A meal that is usually taken late in the morning that combines a late breakfast and an early lunch	Brunch
16	absence of Government	Anarchy

SN	Many Word (SSC Selection Post 2022 - 12th Level)	One Word
1	One who loves wisdom and hence pursues it	Philosopher
2	One who is extravagantly romantic, chivalrous and impractical.	Quixotic
3	The killing of a whole race	Genocide
4	A highly unpleasant, annoying, objectionable sound.	Nasty

SN	Many Word (SSC Selection Post 2022 - Grad. Level)	One Word
1	To the utmost or most absolute extent or degree	Quite
2	Easy to understand	Lucid
3	The supervising person during an examination	Invigilator
4	An arrangement of parts or elements in a particular form or figure	Configuration
5	Short accounts of real and interesting incidents	Anecdotes
	Really coming from its stated, advertised or reputed source	Genuine

SN	Many Word (SSC Delhi Police Constable 2022)	One Word
1	Younger looking skin.	Rejuvenated
2	A disorder that involve difficulty in reading, interpret words	Dyslexia
3	Piece of enclosed land planted with fruit trees.	Orchard
4	One who loves to speak	Loquacious
5	Great sorrow or distress	Woe
6	A paper written by hand	Manuscript
7	The study of secret writing and coded language or words	Cryptography
8	Extremely high.	Exorbitant
9	Not quite coinciding with a central position	Off-Centre
10	Changing frequently	Fickle
11	Public oratory skills	Elocution

12	Using (an idea, term, or name) frequently in casual talk	Bandying
13	A person who is unsure about God's existence	Agnostic
14	Extreme physical or mental sufferings	Agony
15	Something which can be copied	Imitable
16	Mark with spots or smears of colour	Mottle
17	Causing or affected by anxiety or stress	Fraught
18	In a quick manner.	Hurriedly
19	A room filled with equipment for games and physical exercise.	Gymnasium
20	A group of things that have been hidden in some place	Cache
21	A soldier who fights for the sake of money	Mercenary
22	Fill up again	Replenish
23	Performed or occurring as a result of a sudden impulse	Spontaneous
24	Something that is modern or existing in the prevailing times	Contemporary
25	Ceremony to formally congratulate success.	Felicitating
26	Involvement with or influence in the community.	Outreach
27	Unable to pay his debts.	Insolvent
28	One who has the qualities like shyness and openness at the same time	Ambivert
29	Science of speech sounds	Phonetics
30	Someone who is friendly and good natured	Amicable
31	Study of the various aspects of aging	Gerontology
32	the art or practice of garden cultivation and management	Horticulture
33	Indifferent to the pains and pleasures of life.	Stoic
34	Having or showing the ability to speak fluently and coherently	Articulate
35	Lack of order in a country	Anarchy
36	An unknown author.	Anonymous
37	A community that is smaller than a village.	Hamlet
38	The quality of being new and original	Novelty
39	One who walks in sleep	Somnambulist
40	Extreme form of patriotism	Jingoism
41	Certain to happen	Inevitable
42	The act of killing a king	Regicide
43	Showing a lack of experience, wisdom or judgment	Naïve
44	Concerning or consisting of money.	Pecuniary
45	One who is very curious to know things and asks questions	Inquisitive
46	Feeling or showing deep and solemn respect	Reverent
47	Well known for bad qualities	Notorious
48	Religious madness (wherein the patient think he is the deity)	Theomania
49	One who knows everything and has infinite understanding	Omniscient
50	One who knows everything	Omniscient
51	Sentimental longing	Nostalgia
52	A range of different things	Diversity
53	A place of burial	Sepulchre
54	Denoting the second or second mentioned of two people or things	Latter
55	Repetition of a sound caused by reflection of sound waves.	Echo

56	Proved to be right in court	Vindicated
57	Small shelter for dog	Kennel
58	One who is capable of using both hands	Ambidextrous
59	Walk or move in a leisurely or aimless way	Wander
60	Study of statistics of population	Demography
61	One who is violently against established beliefs and traditions	Iconoclast
62	No longer in use.	Archaic
63	Government by military class	Stratocracy
64	To take own life.	Suicide

SN	Many Word (SSC IMD SA 2022)	One Word
1	A person who loves himself the most	Narcissist
2	Something that is suitable for drinking	Potable
3	A general contempt towards mankind	Misanthropy
4	The money paid as divorce settlement	Alimony
5	Relating to the countries belonging to the west of the world	Occidental
6	A group of houses in a village	Hamlet
7	A person who is skilled at producing beautiful handwriting	Calligrapher
8	A person who can use both his/her hands easily	Ambidextrous
9	Writing which cannot be read	Illegible
10	The imaginary line where the earth and sky seem to meet	Horizon
11	One who lends money at very high rates of interest	Usurer
12	Past events presented in order of sequence	Chronology
13	The killing of a group of people in a deliberate manner	Genocide
14	A very complex situation	Imbroglio
15	One who is the in-charge of a museum	Curator
16	A place for ammunition and weapons	Arsenal
17	A word or a name that is inappropriate for a person or thing	Misnomer
18	A place where bees are kept	Apiary
19	Something that happens often or that lasts for a long time	Perennial
20	A group of artists, dancers or acrobats	Troupe
21	Study of the change in number of births, deaths, diseases etc in a community over a period of time	Demography
22	That cannot be avoided in any circumstance	Inevitable
23	Words that are spelt and pronounced in the same way but have different meanings	Homonyms
24	Obtaining something, usually money, by using force or threat	Extortion
25	Something that is related to the brain or the intellect	Cerebral
26	The inhabitants living from earliest times in a country	Aborigines
27	An imaginary society free from crimes and poverty	Utopia
28	A doctrine that equates trod with the focus forces of the universe.	Pantheism
29	Someone who is reserved and shy.	Introvert

PRACTICE SET 01 (OWS)

1 A person belonging to a foreign country

(a) Native   (b) Resident
(c) Alien   (d) Inhabitant

2 Something that cannot be avoided

(a) Indelible   (b) Infallible
(c) Inevitable   (d) Invincible

3 A group of singers in a church

(a) Band   (b) Host
(c) Choir   (d) Troop

4 One who does not tire easily

(a) Inevitable   (b) Indefatigable
(c) Indelible   (d) Infallible

5 Impossible or extremely difficult to understand

(a) Inaudible   (b) Incomprehensible
(c) Incompatible   (d) Inevitable

6 A type of dome-shaped shelter built from blocks of solid snow

(a) Chalet   (b) Wigwam
(c) Hut   (d) Igloo

7 That which cannot be taken by force

(a) Impregnable   (b) Inapprehensible
(c) Inaccessible   (d) Immutable

8 A large impressive house

(a) Mansion   (b) Shack
(c) Cabin   (d) Fort

9 A rabbit's dwelling.

(a) Lair   (b) Den
(c) Sty   (d) Burrow

10 A sound that cannot be heard

(a) Inevitable   (b) Incomprehensible
(c) Inaudible   (d) Illegible

Keys: 1-c, 2-c, 3-c, 4-b, 5-b, 6-d, 7-a, 8-a, 9-d, 10-c

PRACTICE SET 02 (OWS)

1 A person, animal or plant much below the usual height

(a) Creature   (b) Witch
(c) Wizard   (d) Dwarf

2 A student who idly or without excuse absents himself/herself from school

(a) Vagrant   (b) Itinerant
(c) Migrant   (d) Truant

3 A person, animal or plant belonging originally to a place

(a) Occupant   (b) Alien
(c) Native   (d) Resident

4 A person without a settled home or regular work who wanders from place to place and lives by begging.

(a) Vagrant   (b) Truant
(c) Itinerant   (d) Migrant

5 A state of perfect balance

(a) Equinox   (b) Equivalent
(c) Equilibrium   (d) Equilateral

6 A person who draws or produces maps

(a) Calligrapher   (b) Cartographer
(c) Lexicographer   (d) Choreographer

7 An enclosure to keep the birds in

(a) Stable   (b) Apiary
(c) Sanctuary   (d) Aviary

8 An inscription on a tombstone written in memory of the deceased

(a) Slab   (b) Basilica
(c) Epitaph   (d) Pillar

9 Someone who believes that people cannot change the way events will happen

(a) Seer   (b) Prophet
(c) Fanatic   (d) Fatalist

10 Persons living at the same time

(a) Contemporaries   (b) Cosmopolitans
(c) Compatriots   (d) Colleagues

Keys: 1-d, 2-d, 3-c, 4-a, 5-c, 6-b, 7-d, 8-c, 9-d, 10-a

PRACTICE SET 03 (OWS)

1 Rapid increase in the number or amount of something

(a) Proliferation (b) Promotion
(c) Propensity (d) Paucity

2 Living in air

(a) Heavenly (b) Feathery
(c) Aerial (d) Visual

3 An instrument used for measuring atmospheric pressure

(a) Thermometer (b) Voltmeter
(c) Altimeter (d) Barometer

4 The study of human history and prehistory through the excavation of sites

(a) Archaeology (b) Psephology
(c) Anthropology (d) Geology

5 A person who can speak only two languages

(a) Monolingual (b) Multilingual
(c) Linguist (d) Bilingual

6 Guide the course of a ship especially by using instruments or maps

(a) Anchor (b) Sail
(c) Travel (d) Navigate

7 A remedy for all diseases

(a) Panacea (b) Antibiotic
(c) Antidote (d) Patent

8 That which cannot be heard

(a) Inaudible (b) Invisible
(c) Incorrigible (d) Incredible

9 One whose hobby is stamp collection

(a) Phonologist (b) Philanthropist
(c) Philatelist (d) Panegyrist

10 One who is in charge of a museum or art gallery

(a) Monitor (b) Curator
(c) Instructor (d) Collector

Keys: 1-a, 2-c, 3-d, 4-a, 5-d, 6-d, 7-a, 8-a, 9-c, 10-b

PRACTICE SET 04 (OWS)

1 A person appointed by two parties to resolve a dispute

(a) Arbitrator (b) Valuer
(c) Auditor (d) Broker

2 A family of young animals

(a) Nest (b) Clutch
(c) Offspring (d) Brood

3 A large, deep, metal pot used for cooking over open fire

(a) Barrel (b) Skillet
(c) Cauldron (d) Kettle

4 An arrangement of flowers that is usually given as a present

(a) Garland (b) Bouquet
(c) Wreath (d) Bundle

5 A large, deep pot used both in the oven and as a serving vessel.

(a) Casserole (b) Cauldron
(c) Skillet (d) Sauce-Pan

6 Flowers or leaves woven together in a circle for placing on a coffin or a grave

(a) Bunch (b) Wreath
(c) Bouquet (d) Garland

7 A trade that is prohibited by law

(a) Illicit (b) Incredible
(c) Illusive (d) Inapt

8 To give up the throne

(a) Consign (b) Abdicate
(c) Usurp (d) Bequeath

9 One who embraces voluntary death for the sake of one's country

(a) Martyr (b) Diplomat
(c) Fanatic (d) Patriot

10 One who is indifferent to art and culture

(a) Philanderer (b) Cynic
(c) Philistine (d) Scientist

Keys: 1-a, 2-d, 3-c, 4-b, 5-a, 6-b, 7-a, 8-b, 9-a, 10-c

PRACTICE SET 05 (OWS)

1 One who is difficult to please

(a) Feminist   (b) Fastidious
(c) Fatalist   (d) Fanatic

2 Something that catches fire easily

(a) Inflammable   (b) Inflatable
(c) Incredible   (d) Infallible

3 The state of remaining unmarried

(a) Monogamy   (b) Polygamy
(c) Feminism   (d) Celibacy

4 An office with high salary but no work

(a) Honorary   (b) Sinecure
(c) Autocracy   (d) Bureaucracy

5 One who is indifferent to pleasure or pain

(a) Wise   (b) Brave
(c) Stoic   (d) Temperate

6 A previous case that might serve as an example or guide in subsequent situations

(a) Precedent   (b) Predecessor
(c) President   (d) Precursor

7 One who walks on foot

(a) Pauper   (b) Pediatrician
(c) Pedestrian   (d) Protagonist

8 An official pardon

(a) Regicide   (b) Redemption
(c) Amnesty   (d) Amnesia

9 That which cannot be seen through

(a) Transparent   (b) Invisible
(c) Magical   (d) Opaque

10 Willing to be guided or controlled

(a) Adorable   (b) Adamant
(c) Amenable   (d) Abominable

PRACTICE SET 06 (OWS)

1 Something which cannot be understood

(a) Infallible   (b) Illegible
(c) Inexplicable   (d) Incomprehensible

2 Something which is fit to be eaten

(a) Edible   (b) Unpalatable
(c) Tasty   (d) Delicious

3 One who helps a person in need

(a) Mercenary   (b) Veteran
(c) Samaritan   (d) Collaborator

4 Sole right to make and sell some invention

(a) Copyright   (b) Inheritance
(c) Heirloom   (d) Patent

5 A fictitious name used by an author

(a) Homonym   (b) Alibi
(c) Pseudonym   (d) Anonymous

6 A place for storing guns and military equipment

(a) Apiary   (b) Arsenal
(c) Archive   (d) Aviary

7 One who is a great lover of books

(a) Bibliophile   (b) Pedophile
(c) Xenophile   (d) Hemophile

8 A place where fruit trees are grown

(a) Garden   (b) Plantation
(c) Orchard   (d) Farm

9 The act of looking back on past time

(a) Retrospection   (b) Inspection
(c) Introspection   (d) Circumspection

10 That which cannot be satisfied

(a) Incredible   (b) Insatiable
(c) Improbable   (d) Impossible

Keys: 1-b, 2-a, 3-d, 4-b, 5-c, 6-a, 7-c, 8-c, 9-d, 10-c

Keys: 1-d, 2-a, 3-c, 4-d, 5-c, 6-b, 7-a, 8-c, 9-a, 10-b

PRACTICE SET 07 (OWS)

1 People who enjoy social company
   - (a) Gregarious
   - (b) Unanimous
   - (c) Gorgeous
   - (d) Herbivorous

2 One who eats too much
   - (a) Overweight
   - (b) Glutton
   - (c) Corpulent
   - (d) Obese

3 A word formed from the initial letters of other words and pronounced as a word
   - (a) Ellipsis
   - (b) Precise
   - (c) Epitome
   - (d) Acronym

4 A short statement of a general truth or rule of conduct
   - (a) Instance
   - (b) Illustration
   - (c) Maxim
   - (d) Parable

5 The art of cleaning and preserving animal skins
   - (a) Taxonomy
   - (b) Taxidermy
   - (c) Etymology
   - (d) Dermatology

6 One who makes and sells sweets and pastries
   - (a) Cobbler
   - (b) Confectioner
   - (c) Barber
   - (d) Grocer

7 A person who is skilled at writing beautifully
   - (a) Painter
   - (b) Artist
   - (c) Calligrapher
   - (d) Cartoonist

8 The statistical study of the population
   - (a) Demography
   - (b) Sociology
   - (c) Psychology
   - (d) Anthropology

9 Place for collection of dried plant specimens
   - (a) Green house
   - (b) Nursery
   - (c) Warehouse
   - (d) Herbarium

10 A group of stars found close together
   - (a) Concoction
   - (b) Conflagration
   - (c) Confederation
   - (d) Constellation

PRACTICE SET 08 (OWS)

1 That which cannot be corrected
   - (a) Impregnable
   - (b) Immolation
   - (c) Incorrigible
   - (d) Ineligible

2 A person who is blamed for the wrong doings of others
   - (a) Bursar
   - (b) Captor
   - (c) Phlegmatic
   - (d) Scapegoat

3 The act of speaking irreverently about sacred things
   - (a) Atheist
   - (b) Blasphemy
   - (c) Bellicose
   - (d) Defection

4 A person who talks too much of himself
   - (a) Egoist
   - (b) Elite
   - (c) Emetic
   - (d) Egotist

5 Take away or alter the natural qualities of
   - (a) Denature
   - (b) Unadulterated
   - (c) Authentic
   - (d) Limpid

6 Decay of organic matter producing a fetid smell
   - (a) Putrefy
   - (b) Crisp
   - (c) Neoteric
   - (d) Virgin

7 Diminish in value over a period of time
   - (a) Escalate
   - (b) Augment
   - (c) Aggrandise
   - (d) Depreciate

8 Not able to produce children
   - (a) Gravid
   - (b) Hebetic
   - (c) Fecund
   - (d) Sterile

9 A funeral poem
   - (a) Elegy
   - (b) Pandemonium
   - (c) Parody
   - (d) Sonnet

10 One who walks in sleep
   - (a) Drover
   - (b) Fastidious
   - (c) Numismatist
   - (d) Somnambulist

Keys: 1-a, 2-b, 3-d, 4-c, 5-b, 6-b, 7-c, 8-a, 9-d, 10-d

Keys: 1-c, 2-d, 3-b, 4-d, 5-a, 6-a, 7-d, 8-d, 9-a, 10-d

PRACTICE SET 09 (OWS)

1 A person or thing that has the same name as another
  (a) Pseudonym   (b) Namesake
  (c) Relative   (d) Successor

2 Able to adapt to many different functions or activities
  (a) Expert   (b) Versatile
  (c) Surrogate   (d) Deputy

3 One who treats skin diseases
  (a) Radiologist   (b) Geologist
  (c) Cardiologist   (d) Dermatologist

4 The original inhabitants of a country
  (a) Immigrants   (b) Aborigines
  (c) Residents   (d) Slaves

5 A person who sells and arranges cut flowers
  (a) Nutritionist   (b) Agriculturist
  (c) Florist   (d) Botanist

6 One who draws or produces maps
  (a) Cartographer   (b) Photographer
  (c) Designer   (d) Draftsman

7 A game in which no one wins
  (a) Conquest   (b) Draw
  (c) Triumph   (d) Feat

8 A strong and fast moving stream of water
  (a) Rivulet   (b) Creek
  (c) Torrent   (d) Trickle

9 People living at the same time
  (a) Comrades   (b) Cosmopolitans
  (c) Friends   (d) Contemporaries

10 One who can use both hands efficiently
  (a) Ambivalent   (b) Skillful
  (c) Genius   (d) Ambidextrous

Keys: 1-b, 2-b, 3-d, 4-b, 5-c, 6-a, 7-b, 8-c, 9-d, 10-d

PRACTICE SET 10 (OWS)

1 One skilled in telling stories
  (a) Ventral   (b) Fanatic
  (c) Raconteur   (d) Tyro

2 Fear of Fire
  (a) Arsonphobia   (b) Astraphobia
  (c) Astrophobia   (d) Arrhenphobia

3 One who is honourably discharged from service
  (a) Belligerent   (b) Emeritus
  (c) Truant   (d) Mercenary

4 A perception without objective reality
  (a) Cynicism   (b) Hallucination
  (c) Illusion   (d) Optimism

5 A man devoid of kind feeling and sympathy
  (a) Callous   (b) Credulous
  (c) Gullible   (d) Bohemian

6 One who eats too much
  (a) Impostor   (b) Glutton
  (c) Hypochondriac   (d) Intestate

7 A roundabout way of speaking
  (a) Centipede   (b) Circumlocution
  (c) Coercion   (d) Concentric

8 An old unmarried woman
  (a) Masochist   (b) Septuagenarian
  (c) Sniper   (d) Spinster

9 One who is determined to take full revenge for wrongs done to him
  (a) Enmity   (b) Nigger
  (c) Pedantic   (d) Vindictive

10 Just punishment for wrong doing
  (a) Dandy   (b) Nemesis
  (c) Prodigy   (d) Wagon

Keys: 1-c, 2-a, 3-b, 4-b, 5-a, 6-b, 7-b, 8-d, 9-d, 10-b

PRACTICE SET 11 (OWS)

1 A strong blast of wind
(a) Implosion   (b) Trickle
(c) Gust   (d) Mantle

2 Phobia of dogs

(a) Orophobia   (b) Cynophobia

(c) Batrachophobia   (d) Phemophobia

3 One who is new to a profession

(a) Nuance   (b) Pun
(c) Tyro   (d) Vandal

4 A speech or a presentation made without previous preparation
(a) Euphemism   (b) Obituary
(c) Extempore   (d) Soliloquy

5 Easily duped or fooled
(a) Bigot   (b) Gullible
(c) Ridicule   (d) Venerable

6 Atonement for one's sins
(a) Elite   (b) Ignoramus
(c) Incendiary   (d) Repentance

7 Killing of one's own child
(a) Foeticide   (b) Filicide
(c) Infanticide   (d) Lupicide

8 A lover of work
(a) Oenophile   (b) Technophile
(c) Romanophile   (d) Ergophile

9 To give up a throne voluntarily
(a) Archer   (b) Bigot
(c) Abdicate   (d) Delegate

10 Words written on the tomb of a person
(a) Epigram   (b) Epitome
(c) Epicure   (d) Epitaph

PRACTICE SET 12 (OWS)

1 The quality of being particularly noticeable
(a) Salience   (b) Frivolous
(c) Immaterial   (d) Trivial

2 Of a disease or poison extremely severe or harmful in its effects
(a) Innocuous   (b) Virulent

(c) Naive   (d) Inoffensive

3 A person or thing that is likely to cause harm

(a) Menace   (b) Cordial
(c) Festal   (d) Blithe

4 Having or involving an extreme or irrational fear of or aversion to something
(a) Valiant   (b) Stout
(c) Phobic   (d) Foolhardy

5 Killer of prophet
(a) Mariticide   (b) Vaticide
(c) Patricide   (d) Sororicide

6 A person who preserves skin of animals
(a) Biloquist   (b) Philologist
(c) Taxidermist   (d) Oculist

7 A government by the military class
(a) Kratocracy   (b) Pantisocracy
(c) Stratocracy   (d) Mobocracy

8 Obsession for wine
(a) Ethnomania   (b) Oenomania
(c) Egomania   (d) Idolomania

9 A person's last performance
(a) Prognosis   (b) Elegy
(c) Memoir   (d) Swan song

10 Eating mud
(a) Equivorous   (b) Limivorous
(c) Calcivorous   (d) Fructivorous

Keys: 1-c, 2-b, 3-c, 4-c, 5-b, 6-d, 7-b, 8-d, 9-c, 10-d

Keys: 1-a, 2-b, 3-a, 4-c, 5-b, 6-c, 7-c, 8-b, 9-d, 10-b

PRACTICE SET 13 (OWS)

1 Giving undue favours to one's own kith and kin
 (a) Ableism (b) Iconoclast
 (c) Maiden (d) Nepotism

2 One who does not care for literature or art
 (a) Dictator (b) Hypocrite
 (c) Philistine (d) Primitive

3 Mania for travel
 (a) Dromomania (b) Hypomania
 (c) Megalomania (d) Nymphomania

4 One who has suddenly gained new wealth, power or prestige
 (a) Egotist (b) Imposter
 (c) Parvenu (d) Scullery

5 An associate in crime
 (a) Accomplice (b) Callous
 (c) Itinerant (d) Philistine

6 Man behaving more like a woman than as a man
 (a) Biped (b) Effeminate
 (c) Gregarious (d) Inalienable

7 Speaking with a stammer or lisp
 (a) Melliloquent (b) Dentiloquent
 (c) Fatiloquent (d) Stuttering

8 Excessive desire to work

 (a) Ergomania (b) Idolomania
 (c) Islomania (d) Ethnomania

9 That which is away from centre
 (a) Eccentric (b) Eclectic
 (c) Ellipsis (d) Equine

10 One who values practicality
 (a) Apotheosis (b) Pliable
 (c) Pragmatist (d) Realist

PRACTICE SET 14 (OWS)

1 Killing of birds
 (a) Herbicide (b) Avicide
 (c) Vulpicide (d) Matricide

2 Love for dogs
 (a) Paedophilia (b) Sinophile
 (c) Canophilia (d) Zoophilia

3 Lack of civic-mindedness or of patriotism
 (a) Iconomachy (b) Incivism
 (c) Shag (d) Clergy

4 Study of snakes
 (a) Philology (b) Phrenology
 (c) Ophilogy (d) Urology

5 Preferring or attracted to sunlight
 (a) Lithophilous (b) Heliophilous
 (c) Topophilia (d) Homophile

6 Mutual discourse
 (a) Soliloquy (b) Obloquy
 (c) Colloquy (d) Eloquence

7 Misappropriation of money
 (a) Abridgement (b) Condiment
 (c) Embezzlement (d) Bereavement

8 One who has the art of speaking in such a way that the sound seems to come from another person/place
 (a) Absolutist (b) Biblicist
 (c) Ventriloquist (d) Clavierist

9 One who changes sides
 (a) Ascetic (b) Turncoat
 (c) Virtuoso (d) Connoisseur

10 One who damages public property
 (a) Cynosure (b) Demagogue
 (c) Epicure (d) Vandal

Keys: 1-d, 2-c, 3-a, 4-c, 5-a, 6-b, 7-d, 8-a, 9-a, 10-c

Keys: 1-b, 2-c, 3-b, 4-c, 5-b, 6-c, 7-c, 8-c, 9-b, 10-d

PRACTICE SET 15 (OWS)	PRACTICE SET 16 (OWS)

1 One who loads and uploads ships
(a) Stevedore   (b) Transgressor
(c) Lapidist   (d) Reticent

2 Belief or opinion contrary to what is generally accepted
(a) Invocation   (b) Incognito
(c) Heresy   (d) Mercenary

3 Distorted representation of something
(a) Travesty   (b) Solemnity
(c) Seriousness   (d) Gravity

4 A feeling of intense longing for something
(a) Yearning   (b) Apathy
(c) Satiety   (d) Gratification

5 In exactly the same words as were used originally
(a) Verbatim   (b) Offbeat
(c) Divergent   (d) Contrary

6 Member of a band of robbers
(a) Cannibal   (b) Brigand
(c) Chauvinist   (d) Coquette

7 Showing strong feeling
(a) Meek   (b) Vehement
(c) Apathetic   (d) Impotent

8 A sheath for the blade of a sword
(a) Scabbard   (b) Denude
(c) Divulge   (d) Expose

9 One who has no money
(a) Polyglot   (b) Pauper
(c) Lunatic   (d) Recluse

10 The use of irony to mock or convey contempt
(a) Sanction   (b) Flatter
(c) Compliment   (d) Sarcasm

---

1 One who dies without a will
(a) Intestate   (b) Effeminate
(c) Fugitive   (d) Heretic

2 The upward force that a fluid exerts on a body floating in it
(a) Upthrust   (b) Plunge
(c) Submerge   (d) Capsize

3 To free somebody from all blame
(a) Highbrow   (b) Exonerate
(c) Escapism   (d) Henpeck

4 One who speaks less
(a) Bohemian   (b) Reticent
(c) Apostate   (d) Arbitrator

5 A person inclined to question or doubt accepted opinions
(a) Adherent   (b) Sceptic
(c) Zealot   (d) Disciple

6 A shady place under trees
(a) Debonair   (b) Bower
(c) Gourmand   (d) Fugitive

7 Small room for worship
(a) Bale   (b) Chapel
(c) Cache   (d) Brood

8 A person without home, job or property
(a) Narcissist   (b) Derelict
(c) Iconoclast   (d) Impregnable

9 A warning of impending danger
(a) Naive   (b) Monition
(c) Obtuse   (d) Daft

10 Concerned with beauty or the appreciation of beauty
(a) Foul   (b) Aesthetic
(c) Hideous   (d) Gross

Keys: 1-a, 2-c, 3-a, 4-a, 5-a, 6-b, 7-b, 8-a, 9-b, 10-d

Keys: 1-a, 2-a, 3-b, 4-b, 5-b, 6-b, 7-b, 8-b, 9-b, 10-b

PRACTICE SET 17 (OWS)

1. The crime of betraying one's country
   - (a) Treason
   - (b) Frankness
   - (c) Fidelity
   - (d) Allegiance

2. Fanatical and uncompromising pursuit of ideals
   - (a) Nonpartisan
   - (b) Zealotry
   - (c) Neutral
   - (d) Aloof

3. Seeking to harm someone in return for a perceived injury
   - (a) Affable
   - (b) Cordial
   - (c) Vengeful
   - (d) Benign

4. A military or political group that rules a country after taking power by force
   - (a) Junta
   - (b) Suffrage
   - (c) Emancipation
   - (d) Egalitarianism

5. Protection of or authority over someone
   - (a) Autonomous
   - (b) Tutelage
   - (c) Nonaligned
   - (d) Unaided

6. Optimistic in an apparently difficult situation
   - (a) Sanguine
   - (b) Pallid
   - (c) Pessimistic
   - (d) Sallow

7. Conformity to facts
   - (a) Veracity
   - (b) Deceit
   - (c) Hypothesis
   - (d) Theory

8. Search for and collect anything usable from discarded waste
   - (a) Scavenge
   - (b) Disperse
   - (c) Dissipate
   - (d) Scatter

9. Excessively lengthy speech
   - (a) Concision
   - (b) Verbiage
   - (c) Curt
   - (d) Succinct

10. An ornamented staff carried by rulers on ceremonial occasions as a symbol of sovereignty
    - (a) Spectacle
    - (b) Receptacle
    - (c) Sceptre
    - (d) Zephyr

Keys: 1-a, 2-b, 3-c, 4-a, 5-b, 6-a, 7-a, 8-a, 9-b, 10-c

PRACTICE SET 18 (OWS)

1. The state of being in short supply
   - (a) Plethora
   - (b) Myriad
   - (c) Scarcity
   - (d) Profusion

2. A person who lives outside his native country
   - (a) Indigenous
   - (b) Natal
   - (c) Expatriate
   - (d) Intrinsic

3. Have saliva dripping copiously from the mouth
   - (a) Cascade
   - (b) Inundate
   - (c) Sluice
   - (d) Slobber

4. Angry or bitter disagreement over fundamental issues
   - (a) Accord
   - (b) Strife
   - (c) Amity
   - (d) Affinity

5. An opinion or conclusion formed on the basis of incomplete information
   - (a) Proof
   - (b) Conjecture
   - (c) Clincher
   - (d) Averment

6. Protection or exemption from something, especially an obligation or penalty
   - (a) Castigation
   - (b) Immunity
   - (c) Penance
   - (d) Ostracism

7. The ability to make good judgements and take quick decisions
   - (a) Puerility
   - (b) Acumen
   - (c) Stupor
   - (d) Sanity

8. A high degree of skill
   - (a) Proficiency
   - (b) Maladroit
   - (c) Amateur
   - (d) Gawkiness

9. An urgent need or demand
   - (a) Vindication
   - (b) Satiety
   - (c) Redress
   - (d) Exigency

10. Believe in and follow the practices of
    - (a) Atheist
    - (b) Pagan
    - (c) Agnostic
    - (d) Adhere

Keys: 1-c, 2-c, 3-d, 4-b, 5-b, 6-b, 7-b, 8-a, 9-d, 10-d

PRACTICE SET 19 (OWS)

1 To move back and forth or sideways
   (a) Sojourn   (b) Tarriance
   (c) Traverse   (d) Breather

2 The remains of something that has been badly damaged
   (a) Pristine   (b) Immaculate
   (c) Wreckage   (d) Sterile

3 Deliberately destroy something for military advantage
   (a) Devotion   (b) Fidelity
   (c) Sabotage   (d) Ardour

4 The area near or surrounding a particular place
   (a) Horizon   (b) Vicinity
   (c) Distant   (d) Removed

5 Full of twists and turns
   (a) Tortuous   (b) Smooth
   (c) Cinch   (d) Facile

6 The practice of magic
   (a) Palpable   (b) Witchery
   (c) Substantial   (d) Corporal

7 Irritating inconvenience

   (a) Tranquillity   (b) Hassle
   (c) Harmony   (d) Rectitude

8 A punishment imposed for breaking a law, rule, or contract
   (a) Penalty   (b) Reprieve
   (c) Grace   (d) Amnesty

9 Complete with regard to every details

   (a) Thorough   (b) Lackadaisical
   (c) Lax   (d) Cursory

10 The faculty or power of using one's will
   (a) Antagonism   (b) Aversion
   (c) Rejection   (d) Volition

Keys: 1-c, 2-c, 3-c, 4-b, 5-a, 6-b, 7-b, 8-a, 9-a, 10-d

PRACTICE SET 20 (OWS)

1 Gratify an immoral or distasteful desire
   (a) Depress   (b) Frustrate
   (c) Offend   (d) Pander

2 Break up into small parts as the result of impact or decay
   (a) Disintegrate   (b) Juxtapose
   (c) Conjugate   (d) Entwine

3 Critical explanation or interpretation of a text, especially of scripture
   (a) Oblivion   (b) Nascence
   (c) Exegesis   (d) Naivete

4 Destruction or slaughter on a mass scale
   (a) Enshrine   (b) Cenotaph
   (c) Opulent   (d) Holocaust

5 Making a loud and confused noise
   (a) Reticent   (b) Clamorous
   (c) Laconic   (d) Bashful

6 Transfix or pierce with a sharp instrument
   (a) Impale   (b) Rampart
   (c) Aegis   (d) Bulwark

7 The action of discouraging an action or event through instilling doubt or fear of the consequences
   (a) Buoy   (b) Spur
   (c) Deterrence   (d) Exhilarate

8 Make someone less angry or hostile
   (a) Sullen   (b) Offend
   (c) Chafe   (d) Placate

9 Instruct or improve someone morally or intellectually
   (a) Hoodwink   (b) Allude
   (c) Beguile   (d) Edify

10 Characterized by bitterness or resentment
   (a) Piety   (b) Amity
   (c) Rancorous   (d) Fidelity

Keys: 1-d, 2-a, 3-c, 4-d, 5-b, 6-a, 7-c, 8-d, 9-d, 10-c

PRACTICE SET 21 (OWS)

1. Reduce or decrease in speed or intensity
   - (a) Expedite
   - (b) Slacken
   - (c) Impel
   - (d) Spur

2. A shake or tremble in a person's voice
   - (a) Permeate
   - (b) Rapacious
   - (c) Quaver
   - (d) Grove

3. Easily broken
   - (a) Fragile
   - (b) Pliable
   - (c) Malleable
   - (d) Ductile

4. Criticize in an abusive or angrily insulting manner
   - (a) Obeisance
   - (b) Veneration
   - (c) Approbation
   - (d) Revile

5. A remarkable concurrence of events or circumstances without apparent causal connection
   - (a) Jangle
   - (b) Coincidence
   - (c) Clamour
   - (d) Clinker

6. Comfort someone at a time of grief or disappointment
   - (a) Arouse
   - (b) Pique
   - (c) Fluster
   - (d) Console

7. Public disgrace arising from shameful conduct
   - (a) Opprobrium
   - (b) Kudos
   - (c) Plaudit
   - (d) Ovation

8. The action of driving or pushing forwards
   - (a) Propulsion
   - (b) Astern
   - (c) Abaft
   - (d) Propitiate

9. A state of disorder due to absence or non-recognition of authority or other controlling systems
   - (a) Anarchy
   - (b) Bridle
   - (c) Ascendancy
   - (d) Dominion

10. A liquid with healing, magical, or poisonous properties
    - (a) Viscous
    - (b) Potion
    - (c) Dulcet
    - (d) Luscious

Keys: 1-b, 2-c, 3-a, 4-d, 5-b, 6-d, 7-a, 8-a, 9-a, 10-b

PRACTICE SET 22 (OWS)

1. Rude in a mean-spirited and surly way
   - (a) Affable
   - (b) Churlish
   - (c) Cordial
   - (d) Genteel

2. Carry out a task clumsily or incompetently
   - (a) Bungle
   - (b) Adept
   - (c) Apt
   - (d) Adroit

3. Relating to or involved in crime
   - (a) Chaste
   - (b) Impeccant
   - (c) Licit
   - (d) Felonious

4. A person or thing that is a perfect example of a particular quality or type
   - (a) Epitome
   - (b) Abase
   - (c) Libertine
   - (d) Profligate

5. A person who moves stealthily about or loiters near a place with a view to committing a crime
   - (a) Scrupulous
   - (b) Prowler
   - (c) Veracious
   - (d) Unfeigned

6. A characteristic of one thing that is suggestive of another
   - (a) Antithetic
   - (b) Disparate
   - (c) Conjecture
   - (d) Reminiscence

7. A stately or impressive building housing a tomb or group of tombs
   - (a) Mausoleum
   - (b) Shanty
   - (c) Hovel
   - (d) Tepee

8. Respect and admiration
   - (a) Peccant
   - (b) Culpable
   - (c) Vicious
   - (d) Esteem

9. Exposed to the possibility of being attacked or harmed, either physically or emotionally
   - (a) Robust
   - (b) Tenacious
   - (c) Vulnerable
   - (d) Stout

10. Involving many carefully arranged parts or details; detailed and complicated in design and planni
    - (a) labyrinthine
    - (b) facile
    - (c) elaborate
    - (d) prodigious

Keys: 1-b, 2-a, 3-d, 4-a, 5-b, 6-d, 7-a, 8-d, 9-c, 10-b

PRACTICE SET 23 (OWS)

1 Working-class people regarded collectively

(a) Opulent   (b) Proletariat
(c) Gilded   (d) Affluent

2 A long, angry speech of criticism or accusation

(a) Obeisance   (b) Panegyric
(c) Homage   (d) Tirade

3 Portray in words

(a) Ensconce   (b) Depict
(c) Veil   (d) Obscure

4 The forming of a theory or conjecture without firm evidence

(a) Verification   (b) Substantiation
(c) Speculation   (d) Attestation

5 Regard something as being due to a cause

(a) Adventitious   (b) Superfluous
(c) Incidental   (d) Ascribe

6 Lasting for a very short time
(a) Ephemeral   (b) Immortal
(c) Incessant   (d) Perennial

7 Place or insert between one thing and another

(a) Oust   (b) Efface
(c) Purge   (d) Interpose

8 Making or spreading scandalous claims about someone with the intention of damaging their reputation

(a) Exemplary   (b) Laudable
(c) Scurrilous   (d) Stellar

9 Rub a part of the body to restore warmth or sensation

(a) Asunder   (b) Chafe
(c) Gelid   (d) Nippy

10 Showing a skilful use of underhand tactics to achieve goals

(a) Scrupulous   (b) Veracious
(c) Authentic   (d) Devious

Keys: 1-b, 2-d, 3-b, 4-c, 5-d, 6-a, 7-d, 8-c, 9-b, 10-d

PRACTICE SET 24 (OWS)

1 A deep cut or tear in skin or flesh

(a) Laceration   (b) Termination
(c) Cessation   (d) Desistance

2 Barely sufficient or adequate

(a) Scant   (b) Deluge
(c) Plethora   (d) Surfeit

3 Extreme self-confidence or audacity

(a) Petrified   (b) Abashed
(c) Skittish   (d) Chutzpah

4 The clandestine copying and distribution of literature banned by the state

(a) Wanton   (b) Brazen
(c) Flagrant   (d) Samizdat

5 Showing a lack of respect for people or things that are generally taken seriously

(a) Solemn   (b) Pious
(c) Devout   (d) Irreverent

6 Showing poor taste and quality
(a) Savour   (b) Pike
(c) Tacky   (d) Exquisite

7 The state or quality of being holy, sacred, or saintly

(a) Base   (b) Sanctity
(c) Vile   (d) Heinous

8 Relating to the study of the nature of god and religious belief

(a) Sceptic ism   (b) Atheism
(c) Impiety   (d) Theological

9 An artistic work, especially one on a large scale

(a) Ballad   (b) Sonnet
(c) Opus   (d) Limerick

10 Formally put an end to a system, practice, or institution

(a) Embark   (b) Commence
(c) Initiate   (d) Abolish

Keys: 1-a, 2-a, 3-d, 4-d, 5-d, 6-c, 7-b, 8-d, 9-c, 10-d

PRACTICE SET 25 (OWS)	PRACTICE SET 26 (OWS)

1 A plant, leaf, or flower becoming limp

(a) Bolster   (b) Invigorate
(c) Wilt   (d) Fortify

2 Reduce something in size, amount, or extent by a gradual series of steps

(a) Concoct   (b) Whittle
(c) Beget   (d) Exigency

3 One who speaks two languages fluently

(a) Bilingual   (b) Lexicologist
(c) Linguist   (d) Monolingual

4 The right to vote in political elections

(a) Suffrage   (b) Fetter
(c) Tether   (d) Coerce

5 Concern for one's own area or region at the expense of national or supranational unity

(a) Eschew   (b) Immolation
(c) Cede   (d) Provincialism

6 Lacking foresight or intellectual insight

(a) Sagacity   (b) Myopic
(c) Acumen   (d) Discern

7 Acutely distressing

(a) Palatable   (b) Harrowing
(c) Gratifying   (d) Suave

8 Revel in and make the most of something pleasing

(a) Abhor   (b) Bask
(c) Fret   (d) Edgy

9 Taste good food or drink and enjoy it to the full

(a) Acrid   (b) Savouring
(c) Acerb   (d) Caustic

10 A small piece of burning or glowing coal or wood in a dying fire

(a) Lumber   (b) Copse
(c) Grove   (d) Ember

---

1 Introductory part or lines to a discourse or play

(a) Prologue   (b) Blurb
(c) Monologue   (d) Epilogue

2 Someone not fit to be chosen

(a) Non-Eligible   (b) Ineligible
(c) Uneligible   (d) Imeligible

3 One who compiles a dictionary

(a) Lexicon   (b) Lexical
(c) Lexicography   (d) Lexicographer

4 A person who steals the writing of others

(a) Plagiarism   (b) Popular
(c) Plagiarist   (d) Nepotism

5 Animals living in water

(a) Mammals   (b) Aquatic
(c) Amphibian   (d) Gregarious

6 To destroy completely

(a) Bluster   (b) Chide
(c) Dawdle   (d) Annihilate

7 No longer in existence or use

(a) Invincible   (b) Delete
(c) Obsolete   (d) Inefficient

8 A cinema show held in the afternoon

(a) Entertainment   (b) Play
(c) Premiere   (d) Matinee

9 A handsome man

(a) Adonis   (b) Tycoon
(c) Debonair   (d) Cavalier

10 Intentional damage to arrest production

(a) Nemesis   (b) Sangfroid
(c) Sabotage   (d) Modus Operandi

Keys: 1-c, 2-b, 3-a, 4-a, 5-d, 6-b, 7-b, 8-b, 9-b, 10-d

Keys: 1-a, 2-b, 3-d, 4-c, 5-b, 6-d, 7-c, 8-d, 9-a, 10-c

PRACTICE SET 27 (OWS)

1. Causing annoyance or resentment

    (a) Congenial   (b) Galling
    (c) Amiable   (d) Mellow

2. Recklessly extravagant or wasteful in the use of resources

    (a) Profligate   (b) Churlish
    (c) Harpy   (d) Hoarder

3. Wrap or cover for warmth

    (a) Encourage   (b) Muffle
    (c) Divulge   (d) Expose

4. Keen interest or enthusiasm

    (a) Lassitude   (b) Lethargy
    (c) Avidity   (d) Soporific

5. Criticize unfairly

    (a) Accolade   (b) Obeisance
    (c) Denigrate   (d) Complimentary

6. The occurrence and development of events by chance in a happy or beneficial way

    (a) Debacle   (b) Affliction
    (c) Infelicity   (d) Serendipity

7. A system of religious belief; a faith
    (a) Nihilism   (b) Heresy
    (c) Impiety   (d) Creed

8. A formal speech, especially one given on a ceremonial occasion
    (a) Oration   (b) Reticent
    (c) Bashful   (d) Taciturn

9. Regard with great respect
    (a) Insolence   (b) Venerate
    (c) Flippancy   (d) Coarseness

10. Kill someone by covering their nose and mouth so that they suffocate
    (a) Bulwark   (b) Foster
    (c) Sentinel   (d) Smother

Keys: 1-b, 2-a, 3-b, 4-c, 5-c, 6-d, 7-d, 8-a, 9-b, 10-d

PRACTICE SET 28 (OWS)

1. A person who helps another to commit a crime

    (a) Colleague   (b) Accomplice
    (c) Assistant   (d) Supporter

2. One who walks in sleep

    (a) Omnipotent   (b) Somnambulist
    (c) Philanthropist   (d) Pedestrian

3. The act of killing one's own brother or sister

    (a) Homicide   (b) Suicide
    (c) Patricide   (d) Fratricide

4. Rules governing socially acceptable behaviour

    (a) Politeness   (b) Formality
    (c) Behaviour   (d) Etiquette

5. A person who is easily deceived or tricked

    (a) Tangible   (b) Trouble
    (c) Trickster   (d) Gullible

6. A place where birds are kept

    (a) Aquarium   (b) Aviary
    (c) Sanctuary   (d) Apiary

7. A gathering at a religious place
    (a) Congregation   (b) Spectators
    (c) Mob   (d) Audience

8. Art of working with metals

    (a) Meteorite   (b) Metaphysics
    (c) Metallurgy   (d) Metalloid

9. One who compiles a dictionary
    (a) Lexicographer   (b) Cartographer
    (c) Bibliographer   (d) Lapidist

10. A person who worships only one God

    (a) Polytheist   (b) Monotheist
    (c) Philogymist   (d) Theist

Keys: 1-b, 2-b, 3-d, 4-d, 5-d, 6-b, 7-a, 8-c, 9-a, 10-b

PRACTICE SET 29 (OWS)

1 That which cannot be heard
   (a) Invisible   (b) Inaudible
   (c) Hidden   (d) Slight

2 Incapable of being corrected
   (a) Inviolable   (b) Incredible
   (c) Incorrigible   (d) Impossible

3 One who does not tire easily
   (a) Indelible   (b) Indefatigable
   (c) Inflatable   (d) Indestructible

4 Incapable of being read
   (a) Vague   (b) Eligible
   (c) Unseen   (d) Illegible

5 Too unimportant to consider
   (a) Dimunitive   (b) Trivial
   (c) Nothing   (d) Noticeable

6 That which can be drawn into a thin wire
   (a) Brittle   (b) Ductile
   (c) Flexible   (d) Smooth

7 Impossible to satisfy
   (a) Contented   (b) Satisfiable
   (c) Satisfactory   (d) Insatiable

8 Liable to break easily
   (a) Bent   (b) Brittle
   (c) Thin   (d) Soft

9 An instrument for measuring the atmospheric pressure
   (a) Thermometer   (b) Altometer
   (c) Barometer   (d) Ammeter

10 The part of a country's government responsible for its legal system
   (a) Judiciary   (b) Legislature
   (c) Police   (d) Executive

Keys: 1-b, 2-c, 3-b, 4-d, 5-b, 6-b, 7-d, 8-b, 9-c, 10-a

PRACTICE SET 30 (OWS)

1 Strange in appearance
   (a) Bizarre   (b) Rustic
   (c) Geriatric   (d) Decrepit

2 The study of election.
   (a) Arachnology   (b) Philately
   (c) Philanthropy   (d) Psephology

3 Enigmatic person
   (a) Unique   (b) Unstable
   (c) Stable   (d) Unknowable

4 A group of islands
   (a) Islet   (b) Archipelago
   (c) Reef   (d) Atoll

5 Sudden involuntary muscular contraction.
   (a) Sprain   (b) Spasm
   (c) Spam   (d) Span

6 To renounce one's throne
   (a) Abdicate   (b) Arrogate
   (c) Abstain   (d) Abrogate

7 Make something less severe.
   (a) Aggravation   (b) Mediation
   (c) Palliation   (d) Reduction

8 Lively or high-spirited
   (a) Depression   (b) Grave
   (c) Vivacious   (d) Discouraged

9 One who does or studies without seriousness.
   (a) Dilettante   (b) Diligent
   (c) Deliberate   (d) Distracted

10 Not clear
   (a) Stupidity   (b) Obscure
   (c) Clarity   (d) Intensity

Keys: 1-a, 2-d, 3-d, 4-b, 5-b, 6-a, 7-c, 8-c, 9-a, 10-b

PART - B

(IDIOMS / PHRASES)

Idioms and Phrases are collection of words that aren't meant to be taken literally and usually have a cultural meaning behind them.

All the **"Idioms / Phrases"** provided in this chapter have been asked in SSC exams and compiled here for faster revision. *You should understand that sometimes options are not an exact match and students have to choose from the best available options out of the given 4 options in the question.*

SN	Idioms / Phrases (#R)	Meaning (as per SSC Papers)	Hindi
1	A bad hair day	A day on which everything seems to go wrong.	मनहूस दिन
2	A bad patch	A period of difficulty	कठिनाई का दौर
3	A bed of roses	An easy and happy situation	आरामदायक स्थिति
4	A bee hive	A busy place	व्यस्त जगह
5	A big draw	Huge attraction	बहुत बड़ा आकर्षण
6	A bird in hand is worth two in the bush	Having something for certain is better than the possibility of getting something better.	नौ नक़द न तेरह उधार (कुछ निश्चित रूप से होना, कुछ बेहतर पाने की उम्मीद से अच्छा है // नकद का काम उधार से काफी अच्छा होता है)
7	**A bird's eye view (4)**	A general view from above // good and comprehensive idea	ऊंचाई से विस्तृत दृश्य
8	**A Blessing in disguise (8)**	An apparent misfortune that eventually has good results. // a hidden favour // Something that seems bad turns out to be good	दुःख के भेष में सुख
9	**A blue-eyed boy (2)**	One who is favourite	आंखों का तारा (बहुत प्यारा)
10	**A bolt from the blue (10)**	Something unexpected and unpleasant // a complete surprise // a sudden calamity // an unexpected disaster	आकस्मिक घटना
11	**A bone of contention (6)**	Cause of dispute / cause for quarrel	झगड़े की जड़
12	**A bull in a China shop (3)**	An extremely awkward, clumsy person // A clumsy person in a delicate situation	शीशमहल में बंदर (अनाड़ी व्यक्ति)
13	A burning question	An important question	महत्वपूर्ण प्रश्न
14	**A cakewalk (5)**	Something very easy // an easy achievement // Extremely easy	अत्यंत सरल
15	A can of worms	A complicated situation or problem	जटिल परिस्थिति
16	**A carrot and stick approach (3)**	Rewards and punishments that influence someone's behavior	साम दाम दंड भेद
17	**A change of heart (3)**	A change in one's opinion // Different opinion about someone or something	विचार में बदलाव
18	**A child's play (2)**	Something that is very easy	बच्चों का खेल (आसान काम)
19	**A chip off the old block (7)**	Reminds them of one's father // someone similar in character to one's father // Resembling parents	जैसा बाप वैसा बेटा
20	**A close shave (6)**	Narrow escape from danger	बाल-बाल बचना
21	A closed book	A mystery	रहस्य

SN	Idioms / Phrases (#R)	Meaning (as per SSC Papers)	Hindi
22	**A close-fisted person (4)**	A miser	कंजूस आदमी
23	A cog in the machine	Very small part of a big organisation.	मामूली व्यक्ति
24	**A cold fish (2)**	Someone who seems unfriendly and who does not share his feelings.	भावनाओं को साझा नहीं करने वाला आदमी
25	A cuckoo in the nest	An unwelcome intruder	अवांछनीय घुसपैठिए
26	**A cut above something (2)**	Superior to	बेहतर
27	**A damp squib (2)**	A disappointing result // a situation or event which is much less impressive than expected	ऊंची दुकान फीका पकवान (निराशाजनक परिणाम)
28	A damsel in distress	A helpless woman	अबला नारी
29	**A dark horse (8)**	An unexpected winner // someone who unexpectedly succeeds // an unknown entry // a competitor of unknown capabilities	अप्रत्याशित विजेता
30	A dead loss	Completely useless	बेकार व्यक्ति
31	A diamond in the rough	Someone or something with potential or talent but lacking training or polish:	कोरा हीरा (छिपे गुणों वाला व्यक्ति)
32	**A dime a dozen (5)**	Very common and of no particular value.	कौड़ी के भाव (बेहद सस्ते)
33	A dog's breakfast	A total mess.	अव्यवस्था
34	**A dog's life (2)**	A miserable existence	दयनीय अस्तित्व
35	**A drop in a bucket (4)**	A very small part of something big or whole // Something small and unimportant, especially when compared with something else	ऊँट के मुंह में जीरा (बहुत कम)
36	**A drop in the ocean (2)**	A very small amount compared with what is needed or expected.	ऊँट के मुंह में जीरा (बहुत कम)
37	**A dry run (2)**	Rehearsal of an event	पूर्वाभ्यास
38	A fine state of affairs	An unpleasant situation	अप्रिय स्थिति
39	A fire in someone's belly	one who is energetic and enthusiastic about something	जोश से भरा हुआ
40	**A fish out of water (9)**	An uncomfortable position // in unfamiliar circumstances	असहज परिस्थिति
41	A fly on the wall	An unperceived observer	चोरी छिपे देखने वाला व्यक्ति
42	**A flying visit (2)**	A very short visit	संक्षिप्त-भेंट
43	**A fool's paradise (6)**	Being happy for foolish reasons // a state of happiness based on a person's not knowing about potential trouble.	हवाई महल (संभावित परेशानी नहीं जानने पर खुशी की स्थिति)
44	A gentleman at large	A man without a job	बेरोजगार आदमी
45	**A golden mean (2)**	Middle course between two extremes // neither too much nor too little	बीच का रास्ता

SN	Idioms / Phrases (#R)	Meaning (as per SSC Papers)	Hindi
46	A Good Samaritan	A helpful person	मददगार व्यक्ति
47	**A green horn (4)**	An inexperienced man	अनुभवहीन व्यक्ति
48	A grey area	An unclear situation	अस्पष्ट परिस्थिति
49	A hair in the butter	A challenging situation	चुनौतीपूर्ण स्थिति
50	A hair's breadth	Telling about the smallest possible amount or degree of something	बहुत बारीकी के साथ विवरण देना
51	**A hairbreadth escape (2)**	A narrow escape // narrow margin	बाल बाल बचना
52	**A hard nut to crack (12)**	Difficult task // a difficult problem to solve // A tough challenge // A difficult person // An inflexible person who is hard to convince	लोहे के चने चबाना (मुश्किल काम)
53	**A hornet's nest (3)**	An unpleasant situation // a troublesome situation // Raising controversy	अप्रिय स्थिति
54	**A hot potato (2)**	A controversial issue	विवादास्पद मुद्दा
55	**A house of cards (2)**	An insecure scheme	ताश का घर (असुरक्षित योजना)
56	**A kick in the teeth (2)**	A grave setback // Great disappointment	बड़ी असफलता
57	**A lame excuse (2)**	Unsatisfactory explanation // Weak excuse	असंतोषजनक बहाना
58	**A laughing stock (3)**	An object of laughter //an object of ridicule	हंसी का पात्र
59	A lean patch	A period of poor performance	असफलताओं का समय
60	**A left handed compliment (2)**	An ambiguous compliment // insulting remark appearing as praise	प्रशंसा के रूप में अपमानजनक टिप्पणी
61	**A leopard can't change its spots (2)**	It is impossible for one to change one's character	कोयला होय न ऊजला, नौ मन साबुन खाय (किसी के चरित्र को बदलना असंभव है)
62	A little bird told me	Used to indicate that the speaker knows something but chooses to keep the identity of their informant secret.	अपने मुखबिर की पहचान गुप्त रखने का तरीका
63	A little gush of gratitude	Friendly feeling	अनुकूल भावना
64	**A live wire (3)**	Lively and active	जिन्दादिल व्यक्ति
65	A long shot	Little chance of success	सफलता की कम संभावना
66	**A lot on your plate (3)**	To have a large number of problems to deal with // having many responsibilities	बहुत सारी जिम्मेदारियां
67	**A man of letters (4)**	Proficient in literary art // Scholar	विद्वान
68	A man of spirit is	A very courageous man	साहसी आदमी
69	**A man of straw (4)**	A man of no substance // A weak person	कमजोर व्यक्ति
70	**A mare's nest (4)**	A difficult/complicated situation	जटिल या भ्रामक स्थिति

SN	Idioms / Phrases (#R)	Meaning (as per SSC Papers)	Hindi
71	A month of Sundays	A long time	लम्बा समय
72	A moot point	Disputed	विवादित विषय
73	**A needle in a haystack (4)**	Something that is very difficult to locate // Attempting something impossible	घास के ढेर में सुई (ऐसी चीज जिसे ढूंढने में परेशानी हो)
74	A nig-nog	A fool	अक्ल का अंधा (मूर्ख व्यक्ति)
75	**A pain in the neck (2)**	Someone or something that is annoying / irritating or a nuisance	असहनीय आदमी
76	A Penelope's web	Endless	अनंत
77	**A penny for your thoughts (2)**	A way of asking what someone is thinking	कोई क्या सोच रहा है यह पूछने का तरीका
78	**A picture paints a thousand words (2)**	An image of a subject conveys its meaning more effectively than a description does.	एक चित्र में एक हजार शब्द होते है
79	**A piece of cake (8)**	A very easy task	बच्चों का खेल (आसान काम)
80	A piece of the pie	A share in money or business	पैसे में हिस्सेदारी
81	A rainy day	Time of difficulty	मुश्किल घड़ी (कठिनाई का समय)
82	A ray of hope	Something that provides a small amount of optimism in a difficult situation.	आशा की किरण
83	**A red letter day (12)**	An important day // a day that is pleasantly noteworthy or memorable // happy and significant day // a very special day	महत्वपूर्ण दिन
84	A red rag to a bull	An object, utterance, or act which is certain to provoke someone.	सांड को लाल कपड़ा दिखाना (मुसीबत को न्योता देना)
85	A rolling stone gathers no moss	A person who does not settle in one place for a long time, does not gain wealth, name or fame	अस्थिरता से कभी सफलता नहीं मिलती
86	A rotten apple	A single bad person or thing in a group	बुरी संगत
87	A sacred cow	A person never to be criticised	अनिन्दनीय व्यक्ति
88	**A safe pair of hands (2)**	A reliable person // A person who can be trusted to do something efficiently	विश्वसनीय व्यक्ति
89	**A sea change (3)**	A profound or notable transformation. // Complete transformation	पूर्ण परिवर्तन
90	**A shot in the arm (2)**	An encouraging stimulus. // something that gives encouragement	उत्साहवर्धक प्रोत्साहन
91	A sight for sore eyes	A person or thing that one is extremely pleased or relieved to see.	आँख की ठंडक

SN	Idioms / Phrases (#R)	Meaning (as per SSC Papers)	Hindi
92	A skeleton in the cupboard	An embarrassing fact to be kept secret	शर्मनाक गुप्त भेद
93	A slap on the wrist	A very mild punishment	बहुत हल्की सज़ा // चेतावनी
94	**A snake in the grass (10)**	A treacherous person // an unreliable and deceitful person // A secret enemy	आस्तीन का साँप (गुप्त शत्रु)
95	A sore point with	Something which hurts	दुखी करने वाली बात
96	**A square deal (2)**	A fair agreement // A fair and honest deal	उचित समझौता
97	A stiff-necked person	An obstinate person	अड़ियल व्यक्ति
98	A stitch in time saves nine	It is better to solve a problem straight away and not let it become bigger.	किसी समस्या का समाधान, उसके जादा बढ़ने से पहले कर देना अच्छा है
99	**A stone's throw away (9)**	At a short distance	थोड़ी दूरी पर
100	**A storm in a teacup (5)**	Big fuss over a small matter // A lot of anger and worry about trivial things	बात का बतंगड़
101	A stuffed shirt	Pompous person	आडंबरपूर्ण
102	A stumbling block	An obstacle to progress	सफलता मे बाधा
103	A thorn in the flesh	A source of continual annoyance or trouble.	जी का जंजाल
104	**A turning point (2)**	Anything that brings about changes // The time at which an important change starts	नया मोड़
105	A vexed question	Controversial	विवादास्पद प्रश्न
106	A walk of life	A person's occupation or position within society.	किसी व्यक्ति का पेशा या रुतबा
107	**A wet blanket (4)**	A person who discourages enjoyment or enthusiasm // someone who prevents other people from having fun	कबाब में हड्डी (मजा किरकिरा करने वाला)
108	**A white elephant (5)**	Costly and troublesome possession useless to its owner	महंगा और परेशानी का स्रोत
109	**A wild goose chase (11)**	Futile search // unprofitable adventure // A worthless hunt or chase	निर्थक खोज
110	**A wolf in sheep's clothing (2)**	Hypocrite // a dangerous person pretending to be harmless	भेड़ की खाल में भेड़िया
111	ABC of something	Essential fact	बुनियादी या सबसे महत्वपूर्ण तथ्य
112	**Above board (3)**	Honest and frank // without any secret	ईमानदार
113	**Above/Over one's head (2)**	Beyond one's understanding // beyond one's capability to understand something	समझ से परे
114	**Achilles' heel (4)**	A weakness or vulnerable point.	कमजोरी

SN	Idioms / Phrases (#R)	Meaning (as per SSC Papers)	Hindi
115	**Acid test (2)**	Definitive proof of truth or falsehood // A fact, event or situation that proves something	अग्नि परीक्षा (निश्चित प्रमाण)
116	**Actions speak louder than words (3)**	What you do is more important than what you say // What you do reveals the real you // Intentions can be judged by people's actions	कथनी से अधिक करनी बोलती है
117	Adam's ale	Water	पानी
118	**Add insult to injury (6)**	To further a loss with mockery to worsen an unfavourable situation. // Make a bad situation even worse	जले पर नमक छिड़कना (दुख: बढ़ाना)
119	After one's own heart	Sharing or having one's tastes or views.	मन कि बात
120	Aid and abet	To help someone to commit a crime	अपराध के लिए उकसाना या मदद करना
121	Aladdin's cave	a place that contains many interesting objects	अत्यधिक धन या रोचक वस्तुओं का स्थान
122	Alarums and excursions	Confused activity and uproar	भ्रमित गतिविधि
123	**Alive and kicking (3)**	In good health	अच्छे स्वास्थ्य में
124	All agog	Amazed	हैरान
125	**All and sundry (3)**	Everybody without distinction // All included	हर कोई बिना भेद के
126	All eyes	Watching eagerly	उत्सुकतापूर्वक देखना
127	All eyes and ears	To be attentive	आँख-कान खुले रखना (सतर्क रहना)
128	All hands on deck	Everyone available to help with a problem	समस्या के मदद के लिए सभी का उपलब्ध होना
129	All hat and no cattle	One who is full of big talk but lacks substance and action	डींगें हाँकने वाला
130	All in	Exhausted	पूरी तरह थका हुआ
131	All in a day's work	Part of a person's typical work	रोज़मर्रा का काम
132	All in all	having all authority	सभी अधिकार होना
133	**All moonshine (4)**	Far from reality // concocted // nonsense	दिखावटी
134	**All our might and main (2)**	Full force	एड़ी चोटी का जोर लगाना (पूरी ताकत से)
135	All over hell's half acre	Everywhere	सभी जगह
136	**All thumbs (2)**	Clumsy // physically awkward	अनाड़ी
137	Alma mater	Institution where I got education	जहाँ शिक्षा पाई वह संस्था
138	**Alpha and omega (2)**	Beginning and end	शुरुआत और अंत
139	**Alphabet soup (2)**	A metaphor for an abundance of abbreviations or acronyms	शब्दों के लघुरूप का जरूरत से ज्यादा प्रयोग

SN	Idioms / Phrases (#R)	Meaning (as per SSC Papers)	Hindi
140	Always a bridesmaid never a bride	Someone who is never the most important person in a particular situation	सबसे महत्वपूर्ण पद के बाद वाला स्थान
141	An about turn	Complete change of opinion	विचार का पूरा परिवर्तन
142	An account which is in the red	That which is overdrawn	ऐसा खाता जिसमें निकली गई राशि जमा की गई राशि से अधिक हो
143	An arm-chair critic	Someone who gives advice based on theory not practice	केवल सिद्धांत के आधार पर सलाह देने वाला व्यक्ति जो की व्यावहारिक रूप में काम नहीं आता
144	An arrow in the quiver	Strategies that can be followed	उपलब्ध विकल्पों में से एक विकल्प
145	An article of faith	A firmly held belief	दृढ़ विश्वास
146	An eagle eye	A careful or close watch	तेज निगाह
147	An eye opener	A shocking revelation	चौंकाने वाला खुलासा
148	**An iron hand (2)**	strict and harsh control	सख्त और कठोर नियंत्रण
149	**An iron will (3)**	A firm opinion // strong determination	मजबूत दृढ़ संकल्प
150	An olive branch	gesture of peace	शांति का प्रस्ताव
151	**An open book (3)**	One that held no secrets // one about whom it is easy to know everything	खुली किताब (बिना किसी रहस्य का)
152	An uphill task	Difficult task	मुश्किल कार्य
153	Apple of her mother's eye	A person of whom her mother is extremely fond and proud	आँख का तारा (अतिप्रिय होना)
154	**Apple of one's eye (6)**	Someone very precious or dear	आंखों का तारा (बहुत प्यारा)
155	Apple-cart	Spoil careful plans	काम बिगड़ जाना
156	**Apples and oranges (3)**	Two unlike things or people // Unequal comparisons	दो अलग चीजे
157	**Argus eyed (2)**	Observant // Vigilant	तेज़नजर
158	Around the clock	Day and night	दिन रात
159	As a matter of fact	Actually as it happens	असल में
160	As bald as a cue ball	Completely bald	पूरी तरह से गंजा
161	As clear as a bell	Readily understood	बहुत ही स्पष्ट
162	As clear as mud	Impossible to understand	समझना असंभव है
163	**As daft as a brush (2)**	Extremely silly	बेहद मूर्खतापूर्ण
164	**As fit as a fiddle (5)**	Strong and healthy // In a perfectly healthy condition	बहुत अच्छे स्वास्थ्य में
165	As good as gold	A person who is obedient and well-behaved	शिष्ट व्यक्ति
166	**As hard as a nail (3)**	Emotionless // unrelenting // to have no feelings	भावनाहीन
167	As high as a kite	Intoxicated with alcohol	नशे में धुत

SN	Idioms / Phrases (#R)	Meaning (as per SSC Papers)	Hindi
168	As the crow flies	The shortest route	नाक की सीध में (सबसे छोटा रास्ता)
169	As thick as two short planks	Extremely stupid	महामूर्ख
170	Ask for trouble	Act in a way that is likely to incur problems or difficulties.	आ बैल मुझे मार (मुसीबत मोल लेना)
171	Asleep at the wheel	Not attentive to one's duties	काम के प्रति चौकस नहीं रहना
172	Assume airs	Pretend superiority	श्रेष्ठता का बखान
173	At a loss	Unable to decide	निर्णय लेने में असमर्थ
174	**At a stretch (3)**	Continuously	लगातार
175	At any cost	Under any circumstances	किसी भी परिस्थितियों में
176	**At beck and call (3)**	At his disposal // to be dominated by someone	इशारे पर नाचने वाला (दूसरों के संकेत पर चलना)
177	**At daggers drawn (3)**	Enemies // hostile	दुश्मनी
178	At each other's throats	Arguing angrily	गुस्से में बहस करना
179	**At large (2)**	A criminal escaped or not yet captured.	भागा हुआ अपराधी
180	**At loggerheads (4)**	In conflict with someone // To disagree strongly	असहमति के कारण हिंसक विवाद
181	**At loose ends (2)**	In an uncertain situation	अनिश्चित स्थिति में
182	At one's elbow	Next to someone	किसी के समीप
183	**At one's wit's end (7)**	To be puzzled // not knowing what to do // Quite perplexed // Be overwhelmed with problems	समस्याओं से इतना चिंतित होना कि पता नहीं आगे क्या करना है
184	At random	In a random manner	अनियमित तरीके से
185	**At sea (4)**	At a loss // perplexed // confused	परेशान
186	At short notice	With little warning or time for preparation	कम समय में
187	**At sixes and sevens (2)**	In disorder or confusion	अव्यवस्था या भ्रम में
188	**At snail's pace (6)**	Do something very slowly	बहुत धीरे-धीरे
189	At somebody's expense	Paid for by someone	किसी और के लिए भुगतान करना
190	At stake	In danger	खतरे में, दांव पर
191	**At the drop of a hat/dime (9)**	Without any hesitation // instantly // without having planned beforehand	बहुत तेजी से बिना किसी हिचकिचाहट के तुरन्त घटित होना
192	**At the eleventh hour (10)**	At the very last moment // Just before the deadline	आखिरी मौके पर
193	At the top of your lungs	Extremely loudly.	पूरे जोर से चिल्लाना
194	At variance with	In opposite	विपक्ष में या अलग होना

SN	Idioms / Phrases (#R)	Meaning (as per SSC Papers)	Hindi
195	Average out	To produce a result that is even and balanced when looked at over a period of time	संतुलित होना
196	Babe in the woods	A young defenceless person	अबला नारी
197	Back in saddle	Resume duty	काम में वापस लौटना
198	Back me	Support	समर्थन करना
199	Back on one's feet	Well or successful again	फिर से अपने पैरों पर खड़ा होना (सुधार होना)
200	**Back out of (3)**	Withdraw from a commitment	मुकरना
201	**Back seat driver (3)**	Interfering in affairs without having knowledge	बिना ज्ञान के मामलों में दखल देना
202	**Back to square one (2)**	To return to the starting point	जहाँ के तहाँ (प्रारंभिक बिंदु पर लौटना)
203	**Back to the drawing board (6)**	Used to indicate that an idea has been unsuccessful and that a new one must be devised // plan it all over again	नये सिरे से बनाना
204	**Back up (2)**	Defend or support	सहारा देना
205	**Bad blood (6)**	Angry feeling // enmity // ill feeling	आपसी दुश्मनी
206	Bad hats	People of bad character	बुरे चरित्र के लोग
207	**Bag and baggage (2)**	With all one's belongings	बोरियां बिस्तर (सारा सामान)
208	**Ball is in your court (4)**	It is up to you to make the next decision or step // To be responsible for further action	जिम्मेदार होना
209	Banana oil	Nonsensical talk	निर्थक बात
210	Bang for the buck	More value for money	उचित मूल्य
211	Bark is worse than his bite	Threat is worse than the action taken	गरजने वाले बादल बरसते नहीं
212	**Barking up the wrong tree (7)**	Trying to do something in a way that will not work // Pursue a course of action that will most likely be futile	निर्थक प्रयास
213	Batten down the hatches	Prepare for a difficult situation	कठिन परिस्थिति के लिए तैयार होना
214	Be a dab hand at something	Skilled in a particular area	किसी विशेष क्षेत्र में कुशलता
215	Be a dead meat	To be in serious trouble	गंभीर संकट में पड़ना
216	**Be all ears (9)**	Listening intently // very attentive // To be ready and eager to listen	गौर से सुनना
217	Be all one to	Make no difference	कोई फर्क नहीं पड़ना
218	Be an old hat	Be outdated	अप्रचलित होना
219	Be at a loss for words	Not know what to say	निरुत्तर
220	Be behind the times	Be old fashioned	पुराने जमाने का

SN	Idioms / Phrases (#R)	Meaning (as per SSC Papers)	Hindi
221	**Be born with a silver spoon in the mouth (2)**	Be born in a rich family	अमीर परिवार में पैदा होना
222	Be down with	Suffering from	पीड़ित होना
223	**Be glad to see the back of (4)**	Be happy when a person leaves	व्यक्ति के जाने से खुश होना
224	**Be going places (2)**	Talented and successful	सफल होना
225	Be hard hit	Severely affected by something unpleasant	बहुत सताया हुआ
226	Be hard up	Have very little money	तंगहाल में
227	Be in force	In great strength or numbers.	ताकतवर
228	Be in someone's shoes	face the same situation as another person	किसी अन्य व्यक्ति के समान स्थिति का सामना करना
229	**Be in the air (3)**	When an emotion or idea is on everyone's mind. // under consideration // still to be settled	विचाराधीन
230	**Be in the red (2)**	To be in a loss or debt.	हानि में होना
231	**Be in two minds (3)**	Unable to decide // to be undecided // holding conflicting opinions	दुविधा में होना
232	Be left stranded	Unable to leave somewhere because of a problem.	फँसा हुआ रह जाना
233	Be like chalk and cheese	Be absolutely different	ज़मीन आसमान का अंतर (बिलकुल अलग)
234	Be Off	To go away	भाग जाना
235	Be on a high alert	Be watchful and ready to take action	चौकन्ना रहना
236	Be on the air	Broadcast over the radio or on tv.	रेडियो पर या टीवी पर आना
237	Be on the breadline	Be very poor	अत्यन्त ग़रीबी में
238	Be on the square	To act and speak honestly	ईमानदारी से काम करना
239	**Be out of order (2)**	A device not working properly or at all.	उपकरण का काम नहीं करना
240	**Be over the moon (2)**	Very pleased about something // Extremely happy	अति प्रसन्न
241	Be under no illusions	Be fully aware of the true state of affairs.	किसी भ्रम में न रहना, मामलों से पूरी तरह अवगत रहना
242	**Be under somebody's thumb (2)**	Be controlled by someone completely // under control of	किसी के मुट्ठी में होना
243	**Be wet behind the ears (5)**	Young and inexperienced	अनुभवहीन
244	Be worlds apart	Be very different.	बहुत अलग होना
245	Bear down	To move quickly towards someone in a determined and threatening way	गुस्से से किसी की ओर तेजी से बढ़ना
246	**Bear fruit (2)**	Produce positive results	मीठा फल
247	Bear garden	A place of noise and disturbance	शोर और अशांति का स्थान

SN	Idioms / Phrases (#R)	Meaning (as per SSC Papers)	Hindi
248	Bear in mind	Remember	ध्यान रखना
249	**Bear the brunt of (2)**	Suffer the worst of something // bear the maximum fury	सबसे ज़्यादा तकलीफ झेलने वाला
250	**Bear the palm (4)**	To win	जीतना
251	**Bear up with (2)**	Endure // to be strong enough to continue at a difficult time	सहना
252	Bear with	Have patience with	धैर्य रखना
253	**Beat around the bush (12)**	Avoiding the main topic // Speak in a round-about manner	घुमा–फिराकर बात करना
254	Beat one's brains out	To put forth one's maximum effort	भरसक प्रयास करना
255	Beauty is only skin deep	Physical appearance is no guide to a person's character	बाहरी सुन्दरता से बढ़ कर भीतरी गुण होते हैं
256	**Bed of roses (3)**	A pleasant situation // An enjoyable state	सुखद स्थिति
257	Beggar description	Cannot be described	जो वर्णित नहीं किया जा सकता
258	Behind closed doors	Do something secretly	चुपके से
259	Behind one's back	In one's absence	पीठ पीछे (अनुपस्थिति में)
260	Behind the scenes	Unknown to everyone	गुप्त रूप से
261	Bell the cat	Do the impossible task	बिल्ली के गले में घंटी बाँधना (असंभव कार्य करना)
262	Belly laugh	A loud and unrestrained laugh	ठहाका लगाकर हंसना
263	Below the belt	Cruel and unfair	अनीतिपूर्ण
264	**Bend over backwards (3)**	Make every effort to achieve something, especially to be fair or helpful. // To exert a lot of effort towards some end // Try to accommodate and please someone	हर संभव प्रयास करना
265	Beside oneself	Almost out of one's senses	आपे से बाहर
266	**Beside the mark (2)**	Irrelevant	असंगत होना
267	**Best of both worlds (7)**	A situation wherein someone has the privilege of enjoying two different opportunities // all the advantages // An ideal situation	दोनों हाथों में लड्डू (हर प्रकार से लाभ होना)
268	Best thing since sliced bread	Most useful innovation in a long time	बहुत ज्यादा अच्छा या उपयोगी
269	**Better late than never (2)**	Better to arrive late than not to come at all	देर आए दुरुस्त आए (दिर से आना अच्छा है कभी ना आने से)
270	**Between Scylla and Charybdis (3)**	Choice between two unpleasant alternatives	आगे कुआं पीछे खाई (दोनों विकल्प का खराब होना)
271	Between the devil and the deep sea	Between two great difficulties	आगे कुआं पीछे खाई (दो बड़ी मुश्किलों के बीच)

SN	Idioms / Phrases (#R)	Meaning (as per SSC Papers)	Hindi
272	**Between the horns of a dilemma (2)**	A difficult situation / choice	आगे कुआँ पीछे खाई (दो बड़ी मुश्किलों के बीच)
273	**Beyond the pale (2)**	Unreasonable or unacceptable	अस्वीकार्य
274	Beyond the shadow of a doubt	With certainty; for sure	संदेह की छाया से परे (निश्चित रूप से)
275	Bid fair	To seem likely	संभावना लगना
276	Big bucks	A lot of money	मोटी रकम
277	**Birds of the same feather (2)**	Persons of same character	एक ही थैली के चट्टे-बट्टे (सामान चरित्र के लोग)
278	**Bite off more than one can chew (9)**	To take more than one can deal with // to take on a task too big for oneself // To have tried to do something which is too difficult	अपनी क्षमता से अधिक काम लेना
279	**Bite someone's head off (2)**	Speak angrily without any reason // Respond to someone with anger that is often sudden or unprovoked	बेवजह गुस्सा करना
280	**Bite the bullet (4)**	To force yourself to do something unpleasant // To get something over with because it is inevitable	मजबूरी में स्वीकार करना
281	**Bite the dust (3)**	Suffer a defeat // to die	धूल चाटना (हार जाना)
282	Bite your tongue	Stop yourself from saying something	कुछ कहने से खुद को रोकना
283	Black out	Lost consciousness	बेहोश होना
284	Black ox	Misfortune	दुर्भाग्य
285	**Black sheep (4)**	one who is not accepted as part of a family or group because of one's bad conduct // Person with bad reputation // Disgrace for the family	कुल-कलंक (बुरी प्रतिष्ठा वाला व्यक्ति)
286	Blind alley	A situation in which no further progress can be made	आगे का रास्ता न मिलना
287	Blow a fuse	To react very angrily	आग बबूला होना
288	Blow his top	Be very angry	बहुत गुस्सा होना
289	**Blow one's own trumpet (10)**	Praise oneself // to boast about their achievements	अपने मुंह मियाँ मिट्ठू बनना (खुद की तारीफ खुद करना)
290	Blow over	Pass off	बीतना, गुज़रना
291	Blow up	To destroy by an explosion	विस्फोट करना
292	**Blue-blooded (3)**	Of noble birth	कुलीन
293	Bob's your uncle!	It becomes easily and quickly achievable	काम आसानी से हो जाना
294	Body and soul	With all your energy	जी जान से (पूरी ताकत के साथ)
295	boils down	sums up to	संक्षिप्त करना

SN	Idioms / Phrases (#R)	Meaning (as per SSC Papers)	Hindi
296	Bone to pick	Cause of quarrel	फसाद की जड़ (झगड़ा का कारण)
297	Bosom Friend	Close friend	करीबी दोस्त
298	Bottom line	The most important fact	सबसे महत्वपूर्ण तथ्य
299	Bread and butter	Means of livelihood	जीविकोपार्जन (मूलभूत जरूरत)
300	**Break in (2)**	Force entry // Enter a building illegally	बलपूर्वक प्रवेश करना
301	**Break new/fresh ground (4)**	Do or discover something new // To innovate or pioneer	नई खोज करना
302	**Break the ice (10)**	Initiate something // to start a conversation // To make someone comfortable	चुप्पी तोड़ना (बातचीत शुरू करना)
303	Breath of fresh air	someone or something new and refreshing	नया और स्फूर्तिदायक
304	Breathing down his neck	Watching all his actions closely	सिर पर सवार रहना (सभी कार्यों पर ध्यान देना)
305	Breathing the air	Useless tasks	बेकार के काम
306	Bring about	Cause to happen	पूरा करना
307	Bring home the bacon	To be successful	सफल होना, पैसे कमाना
308	**Bring the house down (2)**	Made the audience applaud enthusiastically	दर्शकों द्वारा तालियों से उत्साह बढ़ाना
309	Bring to one's knees	To force to submit	घुटनों पर लाना (हार मनवा लेना)
310	Broke a lance with	To argue against	विरुद्ध बहस करना
311	**Broke down (2)**	Wept bitterly // cried	टूट जाना
312	Broke off	Suddenly stopped	अचानक रुक जाना
313	Broke Priscian's head	To use bad grammar	खराब व्याकरण का उपयोग
314	Broke up	Disbanded itself	संबंध तोड़ना
315	Broken reed	Support that failed	विफल समर्थन
316	Brought about	Caused	कार्य-संपादन करना
317	brought to book	held accountable	स्पष्टीकरण माँगना
318	Brought up	Introduced for discussion	चर्चा के लिए पेश करना
319	Brown study	A mood of deep absorption or thoughtfulness (Reverie)	ध्यान में डूब जाना
320	Bugs me	Irritates me	परेशान करना
321	**Build castles in the air (5)**	Daydream // Have unrealistic ideas // to create impossible dreams or hopes	हवाई किले बनाना (कोरी कल्पना करना)
322	Bull's-eye	Something that is the centre of a target	तोते की आँख (लक्ष्य का केंद्र)
323	**Burn your boats (2)**	Do something that makes it impossible to return to the previous situation	पीछे लौटने के सभी रास्ते बंद कर देना

SN	Idioms / Phrases (#R)	Meaning (as per SSC Papers)	Hindi
324	**Bury the hatchet (11)**	To make peace // forget past quarrels // To settle disputes	झगड़ा ख़त्म करना
325	Butt in	Interrupt	दखल देना
326	Butter fingers	To be clumsy	अनाड़ी व्यक्ति
327	**Butterflies in the stomach (4)**	To be anxious and nervous	घबड़ाना
328	Button her lip	Stop talking	ज़बान पर ताला लगना (बात-चीत बंद करना)
329	By a whisker	By a small margin	बहुत कम अन्तर से
330	**By and By (2)**	Gradually	धीरे – धीरे
331	**By and large (2)**	In general // On the whole	सामान्यतः
332	By courtesy of	Given or allowed by	सौजन्य से
333	**By fair means or foul (2)**	In any way honest or dishonest	किसी भी तरह से (ईमानदार या बेईमान)
334	**By fits and starts (9)**	Unsteady // irregularly	अनियमित रूप से
335	**By hook or by crook (4)**	By any means, good or bad // Using whatever methods are necessary	कैसे भी करके
336	**By leaps and bounds (12)**	Very quickly // rapidly // Swiftly	दिन दुगनी रात चौगुनी (बहुत तेजी से)
337	By the same token	In the same way	एक समान तरीके से
338	**By the skin of one's teeth (5)**	By the narrowest margin // Having a narrow escape	बहुत कम अंतर से
339	Call down	To scold	डांटना
340	Call in question	Challenge	चुनौती देना
341	**Call it a day (7)**	Decide or agree to stop doing something // to give up work and go back to home	संन्यास लेना
342	Call off	Cancel something	रद्द करना
343	**Call on (2)**	Pay a visit	मिलने आना
344	Call upon	To order	काम के लिए बुलाना
345	Called for	Asked	किसी काम के लिए बुलाना
346	**Calls the shots (3)**	To be in control // to be the person in charge	निर्णय लेने का अधिकार होना
347	Came out of his shell	Became more sociable	अधिक मिलनसार बनना
348	Came up	was raised	उठाना या बढ़ाना
349	Can't cut the mustard	To be unable to do a job	नौकरी करने में असमर्थ होना
350	**Can't judge a book by its cover (2)**	We should not judge something primarily on its appearance	केवल बाहरी दिखावे से पूर्वानुमान नहीं लगाना चाहिए
351	Cap in hand	In a respectful manner	सम्मानजनक तरीके से
352	Capital punishment	Death sentence	मृत्यु दंड
353	Carry on	Continue doing something	जारी रखना

SN	Idioms / Phrases (#R)	Meaning (as per SSC Papers)	Hindi
354	**Carry out (2)**	Complete something // execute	पूरा करना
355	Carry the ball	Be in charge	जिम्मेदारी संभालना
356	Carry the can	To take the responsibility of some misdemeanour	गलती की जिम्मेदारी लेना
357	**Carry the day (5)**	win a victory	जीत हासिल करना
358	Carry weight	Be important	महत्वपूर्ण होना
359	Carve out a niche	Developed a specific position for himself	अपने लिए एक विशिष्ट स्थान बनाना
360	Cash-strapped	Impoverished	पैसे की तंगी
361	cast a slur upon	damaged	बदनामी कराना
362	Cast aside	To reject	बेकार समझ कर छोड़ देना
363	Casting pearls before swine	Offering good things to undeserving people	भैंस के आगे बीन बजाना
364	**Cat nap (2)**	To have disturbed sleep // brief sleep	संक्षिप्त नींद
365	Cat's paw	A person used as a tool by another	एक व्यक्ति का दूसरे द्वारा उपयोग किया जाना
366	**Catch 22 (2)**	A particular situation in which one cannot do any thing // A difficult situation in which the solution to a problem is impossible	ऐसी स्थिति जिसमें कुछ नहीं किया जा सकता
367	Catch a tartar	To deal with a person who is more than one's match	अपने से बलवान से जा भिड़ना
368	**Catch red handed (6)**	To catch someone doing something illegal // Caught in the act of committing the crime	रंगे हाथ (अपराध करते हुए) पकड़ना
369	Catch time by the forelock	Seize opportunity	अवसर का लाभ उठाना
370	Cat's whiskers	To be highly impressive	अत्यधिक प्रभावशाली
371	Change for the better	An improvement in the situation	पहले से बेहतर
372	Change hands	Pass from one person to another	एक व्यक्ति से दूसरे व्यक्ति के पास जाना
373	Changed colours	Turned pale	पीला पड़ जाना
374	Chapter and verse	Provided minute details	पूर्ण सटीक जानकारी
375	**Charley horse (2)**	Cramp	हाथ या पैर में ऐंठन या जकड़न
376	Chase rainbows	To pursue unrealistic goals	अवास्तविक लक्ष्यों का पीछा करना
377	**Cheek by jowl (2)**	Very close together	आस पास
378	Chew something over	Discuss or consider something at length	किसी बात पर विचार करना
379	Chew the fat	Gossip and make small talk	गप्पें मारना

SN	Idioms / Phrases (#R)	Meaning (as per SSC Papers)	Hindi
380	Chew the scenery	To act overly emotional	जरूरत से ज्यादा भावुक होकर काम करना
381	Chicken feed	Very little money	बहुत कम पैसा
382	**Chicken hearted (6)**	Timid // Cowardly	डरपोक
383	**Chicken out (2)**	To decide not to do something because you are too frightened // withdrew	डर जाना
384	**Child's play (3)**	Something that is very easy to do	बच्चों का खेल (आसान काम)
385	Children should be seen and not heard	Children should not speak in the presence of adults	बच्चों को वयस्कों की उपस्थिति में नहीं बोलना चाहिए
386	**Chill out (2)**	To calm down	शांत होना
387	Chinks in the armour	A weakness that can be taken advantage of	कमजोरी
388	Clam up	to become silent	मुँह बंद कर लेना
389	Clean hands	Innocent	मासूम
390	Clear the air	To deal openly with misunderstandings to get rid of them	संदेह दूर करना
391	**Cloak and dagger (2)**	An activity that involves mystery and secrecy	ऐसी गतिविधि जिसमें रहस्य और गोपनीयता शामिल हो
392	Close to one's heart	Dear and important to oneself	अत्यधिक प्रिय
393	Closed the book on	Stopped working on	काम करना बंद करना
394	Cloven hoof	The evil intention	बुरी नीयत
395	**Cock and bull story (9)**	An implausible story used as an explanation or excuse // absurd story // Improbable story // Wildly exaggerated or falsified story	बे-सिरपैर की या ऊट-पटांग बात
396	**Cold comfort (2)**	Slight satisfaction	झूठी तसल्ली
397	Comb through	To carefully look through	बारीकी से ध्यान देना
398	Come about	To happen	घटित होना
399	**Come hell or high water (2)**	No matter what // In spite of any obstacles	कठिनाइयों के बावजूद
400	**Come in handy (2)**	Turn out to be useful.	उपयोगी होना
401	Come of age	Reach maturity	वयस्क हो जाना
402	Come off	Be separated	अलग-थलग हो जाना
403	**Come rain or shine (3)**	Under any circumstances // whatever happens	किसी भी परिस्थिति में
404	**Come to blows (2)**	Get into a fight physically	हाथापाई होना
405	Come to grief	Have an accident // meet with disaster	दुर्घटना या असफल होना
406	**Come to light (3)**	Been revealed // To be known publicly	प्रकाश में आना (पता चलना)
407	Come to terms with something	To gradually accept a sad situation	हालात से समझौता कर लेना

SN	Idioms / Phrases (#R)	Meaning (as per SSC Papers)	Hindi
408	Come to the point	To speak plainly about the real issue	मुद्दे की बात करना
409	Come true	To happen in the way you had hoped	सपने सच होना
410	Come what may	No matter what happens.	चाहे जो हो जाए
411	Cook the books	To falsify financial records	हिसाब मे झोलझाल करना
412	Cool about working	Ready to work	काम करने के लिए तैयार
413	**Cool as a cucumber (5)**	Not nervous or emotional // to be calm and composed // cool as ice	धैर्यवान
414	Cool it	To relax	शांत होना
415	**Cool your heels (2)**	To be kept waiting // Unwillingly wait for something or someone	इंतजार करना
416	Cope with	Handle	सामना करना
417	Copycat	One who imitates another closely	नकलची बंदर
418	Cordoned off	Isolated	घेरा डालना
419	Cost (someone) dearly	To bring one suffering	महंगा पड़ना (घाटे का सौदा)
420	**Cost an arm and a leg (10)**	Very expensive // A large amount of money	बहुत महंगा पड़ना
421	**Couch potato (4)**	A lazy person // a person who watches too much television	आलसी व्यक्ति
422	Count one's blessings	Be grateful for what one has	जो मिला है उसमें खुश रहना
423	Cover up	Hide or conceal	छुपना
424	Crack up	Laugh out loud	जोर से हँसना
425	Crash and burn	To fail completely	पूरी तरह से विफल होना
426	Creature comforts	Luxuries	भौतिक - सुख
427	Cross out	Eliminate	काट देना
428	Cross that bridge	Solve the problem	समस्या का समाधान
429	**Cross that bridge when you come to it (3)**	Deal with something only when necessary // deal with a problem when and if it arises.	समस्या उत्पन्न होने पर ही उसे निपटाना
430	Cross your fingers	To hope that things will happen in the way that you want them to.	आशा करना कि चीजें उस तरह से होंगी जैसे आप चाहते हैं
431	Crossed swords	Disagreed	असहमत होना
432	Crunch time	A critical moment near the end of a game when decisive action is needed.	निर्णायक (महत्वपूर्ण) क्षण
433	Cry down	To depreciate	पद या प्रतिष्ठा में कमी होना
434	**Cry in the wilderness (2)**	An unrealistic demand // unpopular opinion // an unheeded warning	अलोकप्रिय राय
435	**Cry over spilt milk (8)**	To complain about a loss from the past // to regret about that which cannot be rectified // Feeling sorry over a mistake that cannot be changed	अब पछताए होत क्या जब चिड़िया चुग गई खेत

SN	Idioms / Phrases (#R)	Meaning (as per SSC Papers)	Hindi
436	**Cry wolf (2)**	To ask for help when you don't need it // To raise a false alarm	झूठमूठ का शोर मचाना
437	Crying for the moon	To make an impractical or unreasonable request	अव्यवहारिक या अनुचित अनुरोध करना
438	**Cup of tea (2)**	One's chosen or preferred thing // Something that pleases one	ऐसा काम जिसमें आप कुशल है
439	**Currying favour with (2)**	Ingratiate oneself with someone through obsequious behaviour	चापलूसी करना
440	Cut a poor figure	To put a bad impression	बुरा धारणा डालना
441	**Cut a sorry figure (2)**	Created a wrong impression	गलत छाप छोड़ना
442	**Cut and dried (2)**	Ready made // Already decided	बना बनाया
443	**Cut corners (5)**	Not do a thing well in order to save money or effort // Do something perfunctorily so as to save time or money // saving money	सबसे आसान, सस्ता या तेज़ (ग़लत) तरीके से करना
444	Cut down on	reduce	कम करना
445	Cut him off, without a shilling	Disinherited him	जमीन जायदाद से बेदखल करना
446	Cut in	Interrupt someone while they are speaking	बीच में टोकना
447	**Cut no ice with me (2)**	Had no influence on me	कोई प्रभाव नहीं पड़ना
448	Cut one short	To interrupt someone	बात-काटना
449	Cut short	Make shorter as if by cutting off	काट कर छोटा करना
450	**Cut the Gordian knot (2)**	Removed the difficulty // to perform a difficult task	अत्यन्त कठिन समस्या का समाधान करना
451	**Cut the mustard (2)**	To perform well // To succeed	अच्छा प्रदर्शन करना
452	**Cut to the chase (4)**	To start talking about the important aspects of something // come to the point	मुद्दे पर आना
453	Cut to the quick	Hurt intensely	भावनाओं को ठेस पहुँचाना
454	Dance to someone's tune	Do what others want you to do	उँगली पर नाचना (दूसरों के संकेत पर चलना)
455	Dead heat	Close contest that ends in a tie	बराबरी का मुकाबला
456	Dead in the water	No chance of succeeding or making any progress	सफल होने का कोई आशा नहीं
457	Dead set against	Disapproved	पूरी तरह से विरोध
458	Deep pockets	A lot of money	बहुत सारा पैसा
459	Die hard	Unwilling to change	दृढ़ या न झुकनेवाला
460	**Died in harness (3)**	Died while working // to die while in service	सेवा में रहते हुए मर जाना
461	Dig up dirt on someone	Discover damaging information about someone	किसी के भेद पता करना
462	**Do a good turn (3)**	To help someone // Render a service	किसी की सहायता करना

SN	Idioms / Phrases (#R)	Meaning (as per SSC Papers)	Hindi
463	Do a roaring trade	Highly successful	अत्यधिक सफल होना
464	Do away with	To abolish	खत्म करना
465	Do or die	To make a final effort	करो या मरो
466	Dog eat dog	Ruthlessly competitive	कड़ी प्रतिस्पर्धी
467	Dog in a manger	Selfish	स्वार्थी
468	Done for	Ruined	तबाह करना
469	**Donkey's years (5)**	A long time	बहुत लंबा समय
470	**Don't count your chickens before they hatch (2)**	Do not count on a good thing that has not yet happened	सफलता मिलने से पहले जश्न न मानना
471	**Don't put all your eggs in one basket (3)**	Don't put all your resources in one place	सब कुछ दाँव पर न लगाना
472	Dot one's i's and cross one's t's	Be detailed and exact	विस्तृत और सटीक होना
473	Down and out	Without money	दीन-हीन व्यक्ति
474	**Down in the dumps (2)**	Sad and depressed	हताश
475	Down in the mouth	To be depressed	उदास होना
476	Down the drain	Wasted or lost	बरबाद होना
477	Down the tubes	Failing completely	पूरी तरह से बर्बाद होना
478	**Down to earth (2)**	To be realistic // Practical and direct	आडंबर रहित (सरल और सच्चा)
479	Draconian law	Extremely severe law	बेहद कठोर कानून
480	**Drag one's feet (4)**	Be reluctant to act // Do something deliberately at a slow pace	टाल मटोल करना
481	**Draw a blank (5)**	To be unsuccessful // find no favour	खाली हाथ लौटना (असफल होना)
482	**Draw a line (4)**	To fix a limit // Accept something up to a particular point	सीमा निर्धारित करना
483	Draw first blood	Be the first to gain an advantage or score against an opponent	पहले फायदा उठाना
484	Dressed to kill	Dressed to attract attention	आकर्षक कपडे पहनना
485	Dressing-down	Give a scolding	फटकारना
486	Drew on his fancy	Used his imagination	कल्पना का इस्तेमाल करना
487	**Drive home (2)**	Emphasise // to emphasize an important point	महत्वपूर्ण बिंदु पर ज़ोर देना
488	**Drive someone up the wall (2)**	Make someone very irritated or angry.	किसी को बहुत चिढ़ या गुस्सा दिलाना
489	Drop in	Pay a casual visit	बिन बताए आना
490	**Drop names (2)**	Name famous people to impress others // Hinting at high connections	प्रसिद्ध लोगों का उल्लेख
491	Dropping like flies	Collapsing in large numbers	बड़ी संख्या में गिरना या मरना

SN	Idioms / Phrases (#R)	Meaning (as per SSC Papers)	Hindi
492	Dust and ashes	Something that is very disappointing	अत्यंत निराशाजनक
493	Eager beaver	A keen and enthusiastic person	कड़ी मेहनत करनेवाला अति उत्साही व्यक्ति
494	Eagle eye	An eye with sharp visual powers	तेज नजर
495	Ease somebody's mind	Alleviate someone's anxiety	किसी की चिंता को कम करना
496	Easier said than done	Be more easily talked about than put into practice.	कहना आसान है करना मुश्किल
497	Easy money	Make money without much effort, maybe illegally	हराम का पैसा // आसानी से पैसा बनाना
498	**Eat anyone's salt (2)**	To be one's guest	किसी का मेहमान होना
499	**Eats like a horse (4)**	Eats a lot of food	बहुत सारा खाना खाने वाला
500	Egg on	encourage	उकसाना
501	Egged you on	Urged	आग्रह करना
502	**Elbow grease (2)**	A lot of physical effort	बहुत ज्यादा मेहनत
503	**Elbow room (2)**	freedom to do what one wants	पर्याप्त जगह होना
504	**Ended in a fiasco (2)**	A complete failure	पूर्ण विफलता
505	Enough rope	Enough freedom for action	कार्रवाई के लिए पर्याप्त स्वतंत्रता
506	Evening of life	Old age	बुढ़ापा
507	**Every dark cloud has a silver lining (4)**	Every unpleasant situation has a positive side // difficult times will lead to better days // Something promising is there in any difficult situation	निराशा में भी आशा की झलक होती है
508	**Every dog has his day (2)**	Everyone has good luck or success at a point of time in their lives.	हर कुत्ते का दिन आता है
509	Every inch a gentleman	Completely gentleman	पूर्णतया सज्जन व्यक्ति
510	Evil twin	An imaginary double humorously invoked to explain or excuse uncharacteristic or reprehensible behaviour.	ऐसा डुप्लिकेट जो विपरीत गुण का हो
511	Excuse my French	Used to apologize for swearing.	गाली गलोज के लिए क्षमा याचना करना
512	**Eye wash (5)**	A deception // A pretence	आँखों में धूल झोंकना (धोखा देना)
513	Eyebrow raising	Something which surprises, shocks, or offends people.	आश्चर्य, आघात या संदेह की अभिव्यक्ति
514	**Face the music (12)**	Get reprimanded // be punished // to bear the consequences // Accept the blame	किये का परिणाम भुगतना
515	Face up to	To accept a difficult situation	कठिन परिस्थिति का सामना करना

SN	Idioms / Phrases (#R)	Meaning (as per SSC Papers)	Hindi
516	Faint hearted	Timid	डरपोक
517	**Fair weather friends (9)**	Friends in good times // supports only when easy and convenient // a friend who deserts you in difficulties // an unreliable friend // A selfish friend	स्वार्थी मित्र
518	Fair's fair	Just treatment	सबके साथ एक ही न्याय
519	**Fall back on (2)**	Resort to something // to seek support out of necessity	आश्रय लेना
520	**Fall flat (4)**	To fail to produce intended effect // to have no effect	असफल होना
521	Fall for	To be tricked or fooled by	बहकावे में आना
522	Fall short	To not reach a particular level // Had no effect	अपर्याप्त होना
523	Falling head over heels	Falling deeply in love with someone	प्यार में डूब जाना
524	**Fallout (2)**	To quarrel // Stop being friendly after an argument	झगडना
525	**Far cry from (2)**	To be very different from	एकदम अलग
526	Feast one's eyes on	Gaze at something with pleasure	किसी चीज को मजे से देखना
527	**Feather in one's cap (4)**	A new and additional distinction // an achievement // an accomplishment to be proud of	चार चाँद लगाना
528	**Feather one's own nest (7)**	Make money in an improper way // to profit in a dishonest way // promote their own interest	बेईमानी करके धनी होना
529	**Fed up (2)**	Annoyed	ऊब जाना
530	**Feel at sea (2)**	Feel lost or confused	भ्रमित महसूस करना
531	Feel blue	Gloomy	उदास होना
532	Feel his pulse	Find his views	किसी के विचार समझना
533	**Feel the pinch (3)**	Face financial difficulties	पैसे की तंगी होना
534	Fell back	Turned back	पीछे पलटना
535	Fell foul of	Got into trouble with	मुश्किल में पड़ना
536	Fell through	Failed	अनुत्तीर्ण होना
537	Few and far between	Rare or seldom-seen	दुर्लभ
538	**Fifth wheel (2)**	An unneeded person	अनावश्यक व्यक्ति
539	**Fight shy of me (4)**	To avoid encountering	मुठभेड़ से बचना
540	Fight your own battles	To try to overcome challenges without help from anyone else	अपनी लड़ाई खुद लड़ना
541	Find yourself in troubled waters	In a difficult situation or time	कठिन परिस्थिति
542	Finding their feet	Beginning to understand the work and feeling confident	काम को समझना और आत्मविश्वास महसूस करना

SN	Idioms / Phrases (#R)	Meaning (as per SSC Papers)	Hindi
543	Finish with something	Be through	समाप्त करना
544	Fire the imagination	To make someone feel very interested in something and excited about it	दिलचस्पी जगाना
545	First and foremost	Most important aspect	सबसे महत्वपूर्ण
546	Fit like a glove	To fit snugly	बहुत अच्छी तरह से फिट होना
547	Flash in the pan	Someone or something whose success or popularity is short-lived	क्षणिक सफलता
548	Flea market	A place where antiques and second-hand goods are sold	कबाड़ी बाज़ार
549	Flex one's muscles	give or make a show of one's strength	शक्ति प्रदर्शन करना
550	Floor	Puzzled	अचंभित
551	**Fly into a rage/passion (2)**	To become extremely angry	आग बबूला होना (अति क्रोधित होना)
552	**Fly off at a tangent (2)**	Starts discussing something irrelevant // Change the subject immediately	मुद्दे से भटकना
553	Fly the nest	Children leaving their parents' home to live on their own	अपने पैरों पर खड़ा होना
554	Flying off the handle	Suddenly becoming enraged	आग बबूला होना
555	Follow his nose	To go straight ahead	नाक की सीध में चलना
556	**Follow suit (2)**	To do as others have done	अनुकरण करना
557	**Foot the bill (3)**	To pay for something // pay for everything	हिसाब चुकाना
558	For better or worse	Under any circumstances	हर परिस्थिति में
559	**For good (5)**	Permanently // forever	सदा के लिए
560	For keeps	Forever	सदैव
561	**Forty winks (2)**	A short nap during the day	झपकी
562	Fought to the bitter end	Carried on a contest regardless of the consequences	परिणाम की परवाह किए बिना अंत तक लड़ना
563	Foul play	Unfair or dishonest behaviour	नियम विरुद्ध खेलना
564	Four corners of the earth	From all parts of the world	दुनिया के सभी हिस्सों से
565	From far and wide	From all directions	सभी दिशाओं से
566	**From rags to riches (2)**	Used to describe a person's rise from a state of extreme poverty to one of great wealth.	रंक से राजा (दरिद्र से धनवान होना)
567	From stem to stern	All the way from the front of a ship to the back.	पूरी तरह से
568	From the bottom of my heart	Sincerely	सच्चे दिल से
569	**Full of beans (8)**	Lively and energetic // Full of energy	जोश से भरा हुआ
570	**Full of hot air (3)**	Full of nonsense	बकवास से भरा हुआ

SN	Idioms / Phrases (#R)	Meaning (as per SSC Papers)	Hindi
571	Full of sound and fury	Merely loud and angry words but ineffective	कोलाहल
572	Full steam ahead	Move onward with determination	पूरा जोर लगाना
573	Gall and wormwood	Hateful	घृणास्पद
574	Game is up	Deception is at an end	भेद खुलना
575	Gate crasher	Uninvited guest	बिन बुलाए मेहमान
576	Gave away	Distributed	वितरित
577	**Gave the game away (2)**	Gave out the secret	पर्दाफाश करना
578	**Gave vent to something (3)**	Expressed forcefully	किसी पर भड़ास निकालना (गुस्सा व्यक्त करना)
579	Gear up for	Get ready for	तैयार होना
580	Gerrymander	In a manipulative and unfair way	जालसाज़ी करना
581	Get a foot in the door	To have a chance to do something	अवसर मिलना
582	Get a gold star	To earn a merit point for doing well	इनाम अर्जित करना
583	Get a second wind	To have renewed energy	नया जोश
584	**Get a taste of your own medicine (2)**	To be given the same treatment that you have given to others	जैसे को तैसा
585	Get away	To leave	छोड़ जाना
586	Get cracking	To start doing something	शुरुआत करना
587	**Get down to brass tacks (2)**	Start taking up the most important facts of a situation	मुद्दे की बात करना
588	Get into a soup	To make things difficult	मुसीबत मोल लेना
589	**Get on like a house on fire (2)**	To become friends quickly	जल्दी मित्र बनना
590	**Get on somebody's nerves (4)**	To be an irritant // annoys me	किसी का दिमाग खराब करना
591	Get one's dander up	Lose one's temper	आग बबूला होना
592	Get One's Ducks in a Row	have everything properly organized	जबरदस्त व्यवस्था
593	**Get out of hand (9)**	To become uncontrollable // get out of control	हाथ से निकलना (बेकाबू होना)
594	Get someone's goat	To irritate someone	अत्यधिक चिढ़ाना
595	**Get something off one's chest (3)**	Express something that has been worrying you, and you want to say	छाती का बोझ हल्का होना
596	Get the axe	Lose the job	नौकरी खो देना
597	**Get the ball rolling (2)**	To start doing something	शुरुआत करना
598	Get the hang of	Learn how to use	समझना
599	Get the message	Understand what is implied by a remark or action	भाव समझना
600	**Get the sack (2)**	Be dismissed	बर्खास्त होना

SN	Idioms / Phrases (#R)	Meaning (as per SSC Papers)	Hindi
601	Get the upper hand	To get an advantage	फायदा पाना
602	Get up on the wrong side of the bed	Start the day in a bad mood, which continues all day long	दिन की खराब शुरुआत
603	**Get wind of something (3)**	Hear about something // Come to know // To learn something secret	हवा लगना (खबर लगना)
604	Get your act together	organise your work in a better way	काम को बेहतर तरीके से करना
605	Get your money's worth	to pay and get something of good value	पैसा वसूल
606	Get your own way	Persuade other people to let you do what you want	अपनी बात मनवाना
607	**Getting a new lease of life (2)**	A chance to continue living or to become successful or popular again // Became energetic again	नया जीवन मिलना
608	Getting in everyone's hair	Annoying them	झुंझला देना
609	**Gift of the gab (12)**	Ability to speak eloquently // Talks well and persuasively	जिव्हा पर सरस्वती का वास (वाक्पटुता की क्षमता)
610	**Give a free hand (2)**	To exercise complete control over something // Complete liberty	खुली छूट देना
611	**Give a piece of one's mind (6)**	To rebuke someone strongly // speaking sharply // scolding // To reprimand	डाँटना
612	Give a wide berth to	To stay away from	दूर रहना
613	**Give and take (3)**	Adjustment // Obliging each other mutually	आपसी समझौता
614	**Give in (2)**	Yield	हार मानना
615	Give it a shot	Try something	कोशिश करना
616	Give it a whirl	To try out something	कोशिश करना
617	**Give me a hand with (2)**	Help me with // assist	मदद करना
618	**Give oneself airs (2)**	Pretend to be good	खुद को अच्छा दिखने की कोशिश करना
619	Give somebody a ring	Call someone on the telephone	टेलीफोन करना
620	**Give someone the cold shoulder (6)**	Deliberately ignore someone	जान बुझ कर नज़रअंदाज़ करना
621	Give up	stop doing it	हार मानना
622	**Give up the ghost (3)**	To die // To stop working	मरना / बंद पड़ना
623	Give way	Collapsed	ढह जाना, रास्ता देना
624	Giving a false alarm	A situation when people wrongly think that something bad is going to happen	झूठी चेतावनी
625	Gnash your teeth	Express rage	दाँत पीसना (गुस्सा होना)

SN	Idioms / Phrases (#R)	Meaning (as per SSC Papers)	Hindi
626	**Go against the grain (3)**	Something in conflict with one's value system // Doing things differently from what you usually do	स्वाभाविक रवैये के विपरीत होना
627	Go at equal speed	Keep up with	साथ चलना
628	Go belly up	Go bankrupt	दिवाला निकलना
629	Go bonkers	Become crazy	पागल होना
630	Go down in flames	fail completely	पूरी तरह से विफल होना
631	Go Dutch	Divide the costs	लागत को विभाजित करना
632	Go easy on something	Use only a small amount of	ज्यादा परेशान नहीं करना
633	Go for a song	To be sold cheaply	सस्ते में बेचा जाना
634	Go for the jugular	Attack all out	सब तरफ से हमला
635	Go getter	A real achiever	तेज़ी से तरक्की करने वाला
636	Go haywire	Became out of control	नियंत्रण से बाहर होना
637	Go off	Stop working	बंद
638	Go over	Review	समीक्षा करना
639	**Go the extra mile (2)**	Going above and beyond whatever is required for the task at hand // To make an extra effort	अतिरिक्त प्रयास करना
640	Go through a rough patch	to experience problems	समस्याओं का अनुभव करना
641	**Go through fire and water (3)**	Undergo any risk // to experience many dangers in order to achieve something	कोई भी खतरा मोल लेना
642	Go through the roof	Rise very high	बहुत ऊँचा
643	**Go to rack and ruin (2)**	Get into a bad condition // destroyed	मिट्टी में मिलाना (बर्बाद कर देना)
644	**Go to the dogs (5)**	To be ruined // Deteriorate shockingly	बरबाद हो जाना
645	Go to the wall	To fail	असफल होना
646	Go with the flow	Do what others are doing	धारा के साथ बहना
647	God's acre	A cemetery beside a church	चर्च के पास का कब्रिस्तान
648	**God's ape (2)**	A born fool	पैदाइशी मूर्ख
649	Goes about	Goes around	चारों ओर घूमना
650	Going over one's head	Beyond one's capacity to understand	समझ से बाहर
651	Got down to business	Began to work seriously	गंभीरता से काम करना
652	Got on well	Had a friendly relationship	दोस्ताना रिश्ता
653	Got the green light	Got permission to go ahead with something	हरी झंडी (अनुमति मिलना)
654	**Grease the palm (7)**	Bribe	मुट्ठी गरम करना (रिश्वत देना)
655	Great minds think alike	Said when two people have the same opinion or make the same choice	जब दो लोगों की राय एक जैसी हो

SN	Idioms / Phrases (#R)	Meaning (as per SSC Papers)	Hindi
656	**Green thumb (2)**	To have a natural interest in gardening // to have talent in gardening	बागवानी में रुचि
657	Green-eyed	Jealous	ईर्ष्यालु
658	**Grin/Beam from ear to ear (2)**	to smile a lot because of happiness	ठहाका लगाना
659	Had better	Should	चाहिए
660	Had gone down the drain	Was lost forever	हमेशा के लिए खो जाना
661	Hadn't a leg to stand on	Did not have much hope of getting it	ज्यादा उम्मीद नहीं होना
662	**Hale and hearty (2)**	Strong and healthy	चुस्त और तंदुरुस्त
663	Hand and glove	Very intimate terms	घनिष्ठ सम्बन्ध
664	**Hand in glove (5)**	In close association // in partnership for something dishonest	घनिष्ठ सम्बन्ध
665	Hand in hand	Together	साथ साथ
666	Hand over fist	Quickly and continuously	बहुत तेजी से
667	Handle with kid gloves	to treat someone with extreme care	बहुत सावधानी से
668	Hands down	Easily and without doubt	निसन्देह
669	**Hang in there (3)**	Don't give up // To persist in a difficult situation	हार नहीं मानना
670	Hang on every word	Listen very carefully	ध्यान से सुनना
671	Hang one's head	To be ashamed	सिर झुकाना (शर्मिंदा महसूस करना)
672	**Hang up one's boots (3)**	To take retirement from a sport	संन्यास लेना
673	**Hanging by a thread/a hair (2)**	Be in a dangerous situation	खतरनाक स्थिति में होना
674	**Hard and fast (4)**	That cannot be altered // strict // Fixed	अपरिवर्तनीय
675	Hard cash	Notes and coins as opposed to cheques and ATM cards	नक़द रूपया
676	**Hard of hearing (2)**	To be deaf // partially deaf	बहरा होना
677	Has a bee in her bonnet	Is an obsessed person	भूत सवार होना (जुनूनी व्यक्ति)
678	Has a face like thunder	is very angry	अत्यंत क्रोधित दिखाई देना
679	Haul over the coals	To scold	ख़बर लेना (डांटना)
680	Have a bone to pick with somebody	Disagree or be annoyed with someone	मुद्दा, जिस पर चर्चा की आवश्यकता हो
681	**Have a chip on one's shoulder (2)**	Entertaining a grudge over a past event // nurse a grudge	पुरानी घटना पर अभी तक ग़ुस्सा रहना
682	**Have a finger in every pie (3)**	To be meddlesome // to be involved in a large and varied number of activities or enterprises	एक से अधिक काम में फंसा होना

SN	Idioms / Phrases (#R)	Meaning (as per SSC Papers)	Hindi
683	Have a foot in the grave	Be close to death	कब्र में एक पैर होना (मृत्यु के करीब होना)
684	Have a long face	Look unhappy or disappointed	उदास चेहरा
685	Have a whale of a time	Have an exceptionally fun or exciting experience	मज़ेदार या रोमांचक अनुभव लेना
686	**Have an axe to grind (8)**	A private interest to serve // have a selfish interest // To have an ulterior motive	अपना उल्लू सीधा करना (निजी स्वार्थ)
687	Have green fingers	To be good at gardening	बाग़वानी में निपुणता
688	**Have one's hands full (2)**	To be very busy	बहुत व्यस्त होना
689	Have other fish to fry	Some important work to attend to	अन्य महत्वपूर्ण काम होना
690	Have the ball at your feet	To be in the best position to do something	कुछ करने की स्थिति में होना
691	Have the last laugh	To be victorious at the end of an argument	अंततः विजयी होना
692	Have your back to/against the wall	To be in a desperate situation with very few options	कठिन परिस्थिति में
693	Have your heart set on something	To want something very much	दिल से चाहना
694	**Having a soft spot for (2)**	To like someone a lot // Being fond of	प्यार होना
695	He who laughs last laughs loudest	He who focuses on winning in the long term is successful	लंबी रेस का घोडा
696	**Head in the clouds (2)**	To daydream // Cut off from reality	दिन में सपने देखना
697	Head over heels	Madly in love	प्यार में पागल
698	**Heads will roll (2)**	Dismissed or forced to resign	कड़ी सजा देना (नौकरी से निकाल कर)
699	**Heart and soul (2)**	Completely // With all the effort you can put	पूरी तरह से
700	Heart in the right place	Someone is good even if they sometimes behave in a wrong manner	दिल का अच्छा होना भले कभी गलती हो गयी हो
701	**Heart to heart talk (2)**	Frank talk // candid talk	दिल की बात
702	Hearts go out to	To feel sympathy for someone when they are distressed	किसी के प्रति सहानुभूति महसूस करना
703	Held up	Delayed	रुका हुआ
704	Helter-skelter	In disorderly haste	अस्त व्यस्त
705	**Herculean task (5)**	Very difficult task	मुश्किल काम
706	**High and dry (2)**	Neglected	नजरअंदाज किया हुआ
707	High and low	Everywhere	हर जगह
708	High and mighty	Arrogant	घमंडी
709	High handed	Overbearing	रोबदार

SN	Idioms / Phrases (#R)	Meaning (as per SSC Papers)	Hindi
710	High on the hog	To live in a luxurious or costly way	महंगे तरीके से रहना
711	High time	past the appropriate time	सही समय / सही समय के बाद का समय
712	Himalayan blunder	grave error	बहुत गंभीर गलती
713	His blood ran cold	He was frightened	हाथ-पैर ठंडे पड़ना (भयभीत होना)
714	Hit a bad patch	Experienced difficulty	कठिनाई का अनुभव
715	**Hit a brick wall (2)**	Not able to make any progress // Encounter an obstacle	किसी बाधा के कारण प्रगति नहीं कर पाना
716	Hit a dead end	reach a situation that leads to nothing further	आखिरी सिरा
717	Hit the books	To study very hard	बहुत मेहनत से पढ़ाई करना
718	**Hit the ceiling/roof (2)**	Explode in anger	आग बबूला होना
719	**Hit the nail on the head (7)**	Say or do something exactly right // to find exactly the right answer	सटीक जवाब देना
720	**Hobson's choice (4)**	No real choice at all // An apparently free choice where there is no real alternative	कोई विकल्प नहीं
721	Hocus pocus	Meaningless talk or activity, typically designed to trick someone	धोखा देने के लिए कि गयी व्यर्थ कि बात
722	Hold on	To wait for a short time	रुकना
723	**Hold one's tongue (3)**	Be silent // To keep quiet	ज़बान पर लगाम लगाना
724	Hold out	To endure a difficult situation	(कठिन स्थिति में) डटे रहना
725	Hold out an olive branch	do something to show that you want to end a disagreement with them	शान्ति का प्रस्ताव
726	Hold the fort	To take responsibility for a situation temporarily	देखभाल करना
727	Hold the key	To have control of something	किसी चीज पर नियंत्रण रखना
728	Hold up one's head	Be proud	गर्व होना
729	**Hold water (4)**	Seem acceptable // Appear to be valid or reasonable	स्वीकार्य
730	**Hold your horses (7)**	Be patient // To tell someone to stop and consider carefully // slow down	धैर्य रखना
731	**Hope against hope (2)**	Nurture an impossible hope	असंभव आशा
732	Horse around	To behave in a silly and noisy way	हुड़दंग मचाना
733	Horse sense	Basic common sense	मूलभूत व्यावहारिक बुद्धि
734	Horses for courses	Different people are suited for different jobs	अलग काम के लिए अलग विशेषज्ञ
735	How time flies!	Time seems to move quickly	समय तेजी से निकलता है
736	**Hue and cry (2)**	A noisy expression of anger	कोलाहल
737	Husband our resources	Save	व्यर्थ नहीं करना

SN	Idioms / Phrases (#R)	Meaning (as per SSC Papers)	Hindi
738	I can't think straight	Cannot think rationally due to being overwhelmed with emotion.	तर्कसंगत रूप से नहीं सोच पाना
739	Icing on the cake	Something that makes a good situation even better	सोने पे सुहागा (अतिरिक्त लाभ)
740	If it's not one thing, it's another	When one thing goes wrong, then another, and another	एक के बाद एक सब चीज़ गलत होने लगना
741	Ignorance is bliss	To remain ignorant of things that may cause stress	अज्ञानता परमानंद है // कुछ पता नहीं होना कभी कभी अच्छा होता है
742	**Ill at ease (3)**	to feel uncomfortable or worried in a situation	असहज होना
743	In a flutter	In a nervous state	हड़बड़ाहट में
744	In a fog	Confused and dazed	भ्रम में रहना
745	In a jiffy	Something that is done very quickly	पलक झपकाते
746	**In a nutshell (8)**	Briefly and concisely // express very briefly	संक्षेप में
747	**In a pickle (3)**	Experiencing a difficult situation // in trouble	कठिन परिस्थिति में
748	**In a tight corner (3)**	In a difficult situation	कठिन परिस्थिति में
749	**In apple pie order (2)**	In perfect order	सही क्रम में
750	In bad taste	Not suitable or offensive	अपमानजनक
751	**In black and white (7)**	In writing	लिखित रूप में
752	In cahoots with	In an alliance or partnership with.	साझेदारी में
753	**In cold blood (3)**	Angrily // cruelly, without any emotions // deliberately	निर्दयतापूर्वक
754	**In deep water (2)**	In great difficulty	बड़ी मुश्किल में
755	In dire straits	In a very bad or difficult situation	बहुत बुरी या कठिन परिस्थिति में
756	In Dutch	In trouble	मुसीबत में
757	**in full swing (2)**	very active // at the height of activity	पूरे जोरों शोरों से
758	In harmony with	In agreement with	समझौता में
759	In harness	In office	कार्यालय में
760	**In high spirits (7)**	Full of hope and enthusiasm // Joyful // Cheerful	उत्साह से भरपूर
761	In lieu of	In place of	बदले में
762	In line with	In agreement	सहमति में
763	In queer street	In debt	तंग हालत में
764	In raptures	extremely delighted	अत्यधिक उत्साह
765	In seventh heaven	Extremely happy	बेहद खुश
766	In the ascendant	Rising in power or influence	शक्ति में वृद्धि
767	In the blink of an eye	Within a very short period of time	पलक झपकते ही (तुरंत)

SN	Idioms / Phrases (#R)	Meaning (as per SSC Papers)	Hindi
768	In the blues	Cheerless and depressed	उदास
769	**In the dark (2)**	In ignorance // to not know something others are aware of	अज्ञानता में
770	**In the driver's seat (2)**	In charge or in control of a situation	स्थिति का नियंत्रण में होना
771	In the egg	In an early stage	प्रारंभिक चरण में
772	**In the eye of a storm (3)**	Deeply involved in a difficult or controversial situation which affects or interests a lot of people // Be in the middle of a difficult situation	मुसीबतों के बीच होना
773	**In the good books (3)**	In favour with	पक्ष में होना
774	In the heat of the moment	Saying or doing something without thinking due to anger	क्रोध के कारण बिना सोचे-समझे कुछ कह देना या करना
775	In the limelight	The centre of attraction	सुर्खियों में
776	**In the long run (5)**	Eventually/Ultimately	आखिरकार
777	In the loop	Informed regularly	नियमित रूप से सूचित करना
778	**In the nick of time (4)**	Just in time // At the last possible moment	सही समय पर
779	In the offing	Appear so on	शीघ्र होनेवाला
780	In the pink	In good health	अच्छा स्वास्थ्य में
781	In the red	In danger	खतरे में
782	In the running	Contesting the seat	प्रतियोगिता में भाग लेना
783	**In the same boat (9)**	To be in the same difficult situation as someone else	उसी कठिन परिस्थिति में होना
784	In the same breath	Say two contradictory things at the same time	एक ही समय में दो परस्पर विरोधी बातें
785	**In the soup (2)**	To be in trouble	मुसीबत में होना
786	In the swim	Well–informed and up–to–date	अच्छी तरह से सूचित होना
787	**In the teeth of (3)**	Inspite of something // directly against // in direct opposition to	प्रत्यक्ष विरोध में होना
788	**In vogue (2)**	Popular // in fashion	प्रचलन में
789	In your birthday suit	Not wearing any clothes	बिना कपड़े पहने
790	**Ins and outs (6)**	Detailed description // Full details	पूरा विवरण
791	Iron fist	Strictly	सख्ती से
792	It goes without saying	Something which is implied to be obvious	ज़ाहिर बात
793	**It's Greek to me (4)**	Incomprehensible // I cannot understand anything	समझ से बाहर
794	It's not rocket science	Used to say that you do not think that something is very difficult to do or to understand.	साधारण काम
795	Ivory towers	Detachment and seclusion	एकांत

SN	Idioms / Phrases (#R)	Meaning (as per SSC Papers)	Hindi
796	Jaundiced eye	A prejudiced view	पक्षपाती नज़र
797	Jog someone's memory	To cause someone to remember something	यादें ताज़ा करना
798	**Jump the gun (3)**	Start something too soon or act hastily	जल्दबाज़ी करना
799	Jumping down my throat	Scolding	फटकारना
800	Keep a civil tongue	Speak with great politeness	विनम्रता से बोलना
801	Keep a low profile	To avoid attracting attention to yourself	छिपकर रहना
802	Keep abreast of	Keep oneself updated	अवगत होना
803	Keep in check	To control something	नियंत्रण मे रखना
804	**Keep in touch (2)**	To maintain contact with another person	संपर्क बनाये रखना
805	**Keep one's head (3)**	Remain calm	शांत रहना
806	Keep someone in the loop	Give them all the information	जानकारी साझा करना
807	Keep under one's hat	To keep something a secret	गुप्त रखना
808	**Keep up appearances (2)**	To pretend to be happier or richer so as to conceal the real situation // maintained an expression of well being	दिखावा करना
809	Keep your chin up	Remain cheerful in difficult circumstances.	कठिन परिस्थितियों में भी प्रसन्न रहना
810	Keep your shirt on	To remain cool	क्रोध पर नियंत्रण रखना
811	Keep your wig on	To calm down	शांत होना
812	**Keep/hold something at bay (3)**	To control something and prevent it from causing you problems // Prevent someone from moving closer	दूर रखना
813	Keeps an open house	Welcomes all members	सभी का स्वागत करना
814	Kept a level head	Was sensible	समझदार होना
815	Kept a stiff upper lip	Remained expressionless	अपना दुःख दर्द जाहिर नहीं होने देना
816	Kick someone when they are down	To cause further trouble to someone already in a difficult situation	विपत्ती में फंसे व्यक्ति को और अधिक परेशानी में डालना
817	**Kick the bucket (4)**	To die	चल बसना (निधन होना)
818	**Kicked up a row (3)**	Made a great fuss // created a fuss // cause a disturbance	आसमान सिर पर उठाना (हंगामा करना)
819	Kicking his heels	Wasting time	समय की बरबादी करना
820	**Kill two birds with one stone (5)**	To serve two purposes at one time // To achieve two results with a single effort	एक तीर से दो शिकार करना
821	**Kith and kin (2)**	Relatives	रिश्तेदार
822	Kitty-corner	Things located diagonally opposite each other	तिरछा स्थित होना

SN	Idioms / Phrases (#R)	Meaning (as per SSC Papers)	Hindi
823	Knock down	To demolish	नष्ट करना
824	Know like the back of one's hand	to have detailed knowledge of something	रग रग से वाकिफ (गहराई से जानना)
825	**Know something inside out (2)**	To know everything about something // To know something thoroughly	गहराई से जानना
826	Knows how many beans make five	Well informed and intelligent	समझदार और बुद्धिमान होना
827	Laid down their arms	Surrendered	अपने शस्त्र डाल देना (आत्मसमर्पण करना)
828	Lap up	Accept eagerly	उत्सुकता पूर्वक स्वीकार करना
829	Large-hearted	Generous	दिलदार
830	Last but not least	Last in order of mention or occurrence but not last in importance.	अंतिम पर किसी से कम नहीं
831	Latched on to something	To become firmly attached	संलग्न होना
832	Late in the day	Too delayed to be of any use	बहुत ज्यादा देर कर देना
833	Latin and Greek	Incomprehensible	समझ से बाहर
834	laughs like a drain	Laugh loudly	जोर से हंसना
835	Laurels	To earn great prestige	पुरस्कार, ख्याति
836	**Lay out (2)**	Spend	व्यय करना
837	Laying it on thick	An exaggeration	बढ़ा-चढ़ा कर कहना
838	Laying off	Dismissal from jobs of	नौकरी से बरखास्त करना
839	**Lead someone by the nose (3)**	To dominate someone // To completely control someone	नकेल हाथ में रखना (पूर्ण नियंत्रण)
840	Lean and mean	Ready and efficient	सक्षम
841	Learn by heart	To memorize something	कंठस्थ करना
842	**Learn/Know the ropes (3)**	Learn to do particular jobs	काम के तरीके समझना
843	**Leave no stone unturned (10)**	Try every possible course of action in order to achieve something // to make all possible efforts	खून पसीना एक करना (हर मुमकिन प्रयास करना)
844	**Leaves you in the lurch (5)**	Leave someone in a helpless condition // desert someone in his difficulties	बिच मझधार में छोड़ देना
845	Left out in cold	to be ignored	नज़र-अंदाज करना
846	Left, right and centre	Happening in a lot of places or to a lot of people	सब जगह या सबके साथ घटित होना
847	**Lend me your ear (4)**	To politely ask for someone's full attention // to pay attention to	कान लगाकर सुनना (ध्यान से सुनना)
848	Lend someone a hand	To help or assist, especially voluntarily	सहायता करना
849	**Let bygones be bygones (2)**	Forget past offences or causes of conflict and be reconciled. // To forgive and forget	जो बीत गई सो बात गई (पुरानी बातों को भूल जाना)

SN	Idioms / Phrases (#R)	Meaning (as per SSC Papers)	Hindi
850	Let down	To fail	निराश करना
851	Let off steam	To work or play off excess energy	गुस्सा उतारना (शांत होना)
852	**Let sleeping dogs lie (4)**	Do not bring up an old controversial issue	सोते शेर को मत छेड़ो
853	Let something slip through one's fingers	To waste an opportunity to achieve something	अवसर खोना
854	**Let the cat out of the bag (5)**	Reveal a secret carelessly or by mistake	भेद खोलना
855	Let the chips fall where they may	Let something happen without bothering about the consequences	राम भरोसे छोड़ना (जो हो रहा है होने देना)
856	**Let the grass grow under one's feet (3)**	To remain idle	निष्क्रिय रहना
857	**Let your hair down (2)**	Behave uninhibitedly // To take it easy and relax	आराम से निश्चिंत रहना
858	Level playing field	A situation in which everyone has a fair and equal chance of succeeding	एक समान अवसर
859	Lie low	Try not to be noticed	छिपकर रहना
860	Like a dying duck in a thunderstorm	Dejected	घबराया हुआ
861	Like a phoenix	With a new life	नए जीवन के साथ
862	Like a shag on a rock	Completely alone	पूरी तरह से अकेला
863	Like pulling teeth	Extremely difficult	बेहद मुश्किल
864	Like talking to a brick wall	Inattentive	ध्यान ना देना
865	**Like two peas in a pod (2)**	Look very similar in appearance or character	एक जैसे
866	Lion's mouth	A dangerous situation	खतरनाक स्थिति
867	Little by little	gradually	धीरे-धीरे
868	**Live from hand to mouth (5)**	To have enough money to live on and nothing extra // miserably // consuming daily what little is earned	जैसे तैसे गुजर बसर करना
869	Loaded words	Words that carry more significance than their literal meaning	शाब्दिक अर्थ से अधिक महत्व होना
870	Lock horns	Fight with someone	लड़ना-झगड़ना
871	Lock, stock and barrel	Completely	पूरी तरह से
872	Long in the tooth	Too old to do something	बहुत ही बूढ़ा या पुराना
873	**Look after (2)**	Take care of	देखभाल करना
874	Look before you leap	Think carefully of the consequences	सोच समझकर कदम उठाना
875	**Look down upon (2)**	Regard with contempt // To consider someone inferior	तुच्छ समझना
876	Look into	To investigate	जांच करना
877	Look out	be careful	सावधान रहना

SN	Idioms / Phrases (#R)	Meaning (as per SSC Papers)	Hindi
878	Look sharp	Pay attention	ध्यान देना
879	Looking for greener pastures	Exploring new opportunities	नए अवसर तलाशना
880	Looking forward to	Expecting with pleasure	खुशी के साथ उम्मीद करना
881	**Loosen the purse strings (2)**	To increase the money available for expenditure	ज्यादा पैसे देना
882	Lose count of	forget the accurate total	गिनती भूलना
883	Lose face	Become embarrassed	पानी पानी होना (शर्मिंदा होना)
884	**Lose one's head (3)**	To lose self control // Panic	आपा खोना (गुस्सा होना)
885	Lose your marbles	To go insane	पागल हो जाना
886	Lose your touch	Not being as successful as previously	काम काज में पहले जैसी बात नहीं रहना
887	Loudmouth	One who talks boastfully	शेखी बघारना
888	Mad as a hatter	Eccentric	सिरफिरा
889	**Made a clean breast of (3)**	Confessed without reserve // confessed his crime	अपराध स्वीकार करना
890	Made light of	Treated it lightly	हल्के में लेना
891	Made off	ran away with	भाग जाना
892	Made out of whole cloth	Entirely false and fabricated	पूरी तरह से गलत और मनगढ़ंत
893	**Maiden speech (5)**	First speech	पहला भाषण
894	**Make a beeline for (5)**	Go straight to	बिलकुल सीधा जाना
895	Make a dent in	to reduce an amount of something, esp. money or work	कटौती करना
896	Make a fool of oneself	To be stupid	बेवकूफी करना
897	Make a fortune	To become rich	किस्मत चमकना (अमीर बनना)
898	Make a living	To earn enough money for things you need	जीवन यापन के लिए पैसे कमाना
899	Make a mockery of	There was no serious outcome	मज़ाक बनाना
900	Make a scene	Make a public disturbance or excited emotional display	तमाशा बनाना
901	Make an ass out of	Cause someone or oneself to look foolish or stupid	मूर्खतापूर्ण व्यवहार
902	Make away with	To remove or steal	चोरी कर लेना
903	Make believe that	Pretence	स्वांग रचना (ढोंग करना)
904	Make big time	Attain fame and success	सफलता प्राप्त करना
905	**Make head or tail of (3)**	understand // To figure out something	समझना
906	**Make no bones about (3)**	Did not have any hesitation in // To state something clearly	ज़रा भी नहीं हिचकिचाना

SN	Idioms / Phrases (#R)	Meaning (as per SSC Papers)	Hindi
907	Make no headway	Unable to progress ahead	प्रगति न कर पाना
908	Make off with	To run away	भागना (चुरा कर)
909	**Make one's flesh crawl/creep (3)**	To make someone feel disgusted, afraid, frightened // horrifying	डराना
910	**Make one's mark (2)**	Distinguish oneself // attain recognition	छाप छोड़ना (पहचान बनाना)
911	Make out	Understand someone or something with difficulty	मुश्किल से समझना
912	Make room	Make space	जगह बनाना
913	Make short work of something	Dispose of quickly	जल्दी समाप्त करना
914	Make up for	to replace something that is lost or damaged	क्षतिपूर्ति करना
915	**Make up with (someone) (2)**	Close or ignore the differences with (someone) // to settle their differences	मतभेद खत्म करना
916	Making hay while the sun shines	Taking advantage of a favourable opportunity	मौके पर चौका मारना (अनुकूल अवसर का लाभ उठाना)
917	Many a slip between the cup and the lip	Bad things may happen before the task is finished	काम शुरू होने से पहले नुकसान होना
918	Mark up	Increase the price	दाम बढ़ाना
919	**Mealy mouthed (2)**	Unwilling to state something // afraid to speak frankly	बात को टालने वाला
920	Measure up	Reach the level	स्तर पर पहुँचना
921	Mend your ways	Improve one's behaviour	व्यवहार में सुधार करना
922	Method to one's madness	Seeming disorderly yet having a structure	अपरंपरागत तरीके से करना
923	Milk and water	Weak ideas	कमजोर विचार
924	Mince matters	To confuse issues	भ्रमित होना
925	Mind your language	Tell someone to speak politely.	जबान संभाल के
926	Money does not grow on trees	Money is hard earned and limited	पैसे पेड़ पर नहीं उगते, मेहनत से कमाए जाते है
927	Monkey business	Behaviour that is not acceptable or is dishonest	धोखेबाजी
928	Months on end	Several months in a row	लगातार कई महीने
929	More or less	approximately	लगभग
930	**Mouth-watering (2)**	Stimulates appetite // Very tasty and appetising	मुँह में पानी लानेवाला
931	**Move heaven and earth (3)**	Make every effort to achieve something	ज़मीन आसमान एक करना (घोर प्रयत्न करना)

SN	Idioms / Phrases (#R)	Meaning (as per SSC Papers)	Hindi
932	Move the goalposts	Unfairly alter the conditions or rules of a procedure during its course	खेल के दौरान खेल की शर्तों या नियमों में अनुचित रूप से परिवर्तन करना
933	Much ado about nothing	Making a big fuss over a small thing	छोटी बात का बतंगड़ बनाना
934	Murdered in cold blood	A murder done without feeling	निर्दयतापूर्वक हत्या
935	Nail your colours to their mast	To make it obvious what your opinions or plans are	डंके की चोट पर कहना (ज़ाहिर करना)
936	Nail-biting	Suspenseful	दुविधापूर्ण
937	Neck and crop	Totally and completely	पूरी तरह से
938	Neither fish nor fowl	Something which can neither be categorized easily nor be accepted befittingly	अस्पष्ट / संशयपूर्ण
939	Never-never land	An imaginary utopian place or situation.	काल्पनिक आदर्शवादी जगह
940	New kid on the block	Newcomer to a particular place or sphere of activity.	क्षेत्र में एकदम नया
941	**Nine days' wonder (2)**	A dazzling short-lived spectacle of no real value // a short-lived sensation	चार दिन की चांदनी फिर अँधेरी रात (जो केवल थोड़े समय के लिए हो)
942	Nine times out of ten	In most cases	अधिकतर परिस्थितियों में
943	**Nip in the bud (4)**	To stop something at the start // Dropped at an early stage // To stop something before it has an opportunity to develop	शुरुआती समय में ही कुचल देना या नष्ट कर देना
944	No dice	Used to refuse a request or indicate that there is no chance of success.	साफ़ मना करना
945	No ifs and buts	No doubts	कोई शक नहीं
946	**No love lost between (4)**	Not on good terms // intense dislike // Persons who do not like each other at all	बहुत नफ़रत
947	No spring chicken	A person who is no longer young	जवानी खत्म होना
948	No strings attached	Without conditions or restrictions	बिना किसी शर्त
949	Not breathe a word	To remain silent about some secret	राज को राज रहने देना
950	**Not fit to hold a candle (2)**	Inferior // Cannot be compared to	पाँव की धूल होना (तुच्छ)
951	**Not hold water (2)**	Does not seem to be reasonable // Cannot be believed	अतार्किक तथ्य
952	Not make head or tail	not able to understand anything	समझ से बहार
953	**Not mince words (2)**	To speak in a direct way	मुँह पर कहना
954	**Not one's cup of tea (3)**	Not one's choice or preference	बस की बात न होना
955	Not playing with the full deck	either mentally, psychologically or intellectually deficient	मानसिक, मनोवैज्ञानिक या बौद्धिक रूप से कमी

SN	Idioms / Phrases (#R)	Meaning (as per SSC Papers)	Hindi
956	Not see eye to eye with somebody	To have different opinion	अलग विचार होना
957	Not to look a gift horse in the mouth	Not to find fault with the gifts received	उपहारों में कमियां नहीं निकालते
958	Not to mince matters	To speak out politely	विनम्रता से बात करना
959	Nothing doing	Not a chance	कोई मौका नहीं
960	Nothing ventured, nothing gained	One has to make every effort in order to achieve something	बिना जोखिम के सफलता असम्भव है
961	Now and again	Occasionally	कभी-कभी
962	**Null and void (2)**	Invalid // not binding	अमान्य
963	Odd man out	Person who doesn't fit into a group	असंगत
964	Of no avail	Useless	व्यर्थ
965	**Of the first water (2)**	Of the best quality	उत्तम गुणवत्ता का
966	Of the old school	Old fashioned in thought	पुराने जमाने की सोच वाला
967	**Off and on // On and Off (5)**	Occasionally // Periodically	कभी-कभी
968	Off the cuff	Without preparation	बिना सोचे समझे
969	**Off the hook (3)**	No longer in difficulty or trouble // Allowed to escape from blame	परेशानी से बाहर
970	Off the record	Not recorded for official publication; informally; in confidence	अनाधिकारिक
971	Off-colour	Feeling slightly ill	थोड़ा बीमार
972	Oily tongue	Flattery	चापलूसी
973	Old hand	Experienced	अनुभवि व्यक्ति
974	Old head on young shoulders	To be wise beyond his years	उम्र से अधिक बुद्धिमान
975	On a wing and a prayer	With only the slightest chance of success.	सफलता की थोड़ी सी संभावना
976	On account of	Because of	के कारण
977	On all hands	Everywhere	चारों ओर
978	**On cloud nine (9)**	Extremely happy and excited	सातवें आसमान पर (अत्यंत प्रसन्न होना)
979	On edge	Nervous and unable to relax	बेचैन
980	On good terms	Was friendly	मित्रता में
981	On one's guard	To be careful	सावधान रहना
982	On one's last legs	Near to death	अन्तिम घड़ी (मृत्यु के निकट)
983	**On purpose (2)**	deliberately // Intentionally	जानबूझकर
984	On shank's mare	On foot	पैदल
985	**On tenterhooks (5)**	In suspense and anxiety // anxious	चिंता में
986	On the back burner	To temporarily not deal with some matter because it is not urgent	ज्यादा जरूरी नहीं होने के वजह से बाद के लिए टालना

SN	Idioms / Phrases (#R)	Meaning (as per SSC Papers)	Hindi
987	On the ball	To be alert	चौकन्ना होना
988	**On the brink of (2)**	At the point of	कगार पर
989	On the brink of disaster	Very close to failure	आपदा के कगार पर
990	On the cards	Likely to happen	संभावित
991	On the cuff	On credit	उधार पर
992	On the double	at a fast pace	तेजी से
993	On the face of it	What appears on the surface	पहली नज़र में
994	On the horizon	An event that is likely to happen soon	जल्द ही होने की संभावना
995	On the level	Honest	ईमानदार
996	**On the same page (2)**	To understand and agree	समझकर सहमत होना
997	**On the spur of the moment (2)**	To act at once // acting impulsively without thinking	अचानक से
998	On the tip of my tongue	Readily available in my memory	जबान की नोक पर (स्मृति में उपलब्ध)
999	On the verge of	On the brink of	के कगार पर
1000	**On the wane (2)**	On the decline	क्षीण होना
1001	On the wrong side of sixty	To be older than sixty	साठ से अधिक उम्र का
1002	**On thin ice (3)**	In a precarious or risky situation	जोखिम भरी स्थिति में
1003	**Once and for all (5)**	Bring to an end // finally // conclusively	हमेशा के लिये
1004	**Once bitten, twice shy (2)**	An unpleasant experience induces caution // a bitter experience making one cautious for future	दूध का जला छाछ भी फूँक-फूँक कर पीता है (सोच समझ के काम करना)
1005	**Once in a blue moon (13)**	Rarely and infrequently	कभी कभार
1006	One track mind	always thinking of only one thing	सिर्फ एक चीज़ में केंद्रित
1007	Open-ended	Having no planned ending	पूर्व निर्धारित सीमा नहीं होना
1008	Out and out	Totally	पूरी तरह से
1009	Out at the elbows	Poor	गरीब
1010	Out for the count	In a deep, insensible sleep	घोड़े बेचकर सोना (गहरी नींद में)
1011	Out of bounds	Forbidden	वर्जित
1012	**Out of date (2)**	Something old fashioned	पुराने ज़माने का
1013	Out of my wits	Greatly confused	बहुत उलझन में
1014	Out of print	A book no longer available from the publisher	छपाई नहीं होना
1015	**Out of sorts (2)**	To be unwell	अस्वस्थ होना
1016	Out of spirits	Gloomy or sad	उत्साहहीन
1017	**Out of the blue (5)**	Completely unexpectedly	बिल्कुल अचानक

SN	Idioms / Phrases (#R)	Meaning (as per SSC Papers)	Hindi
1018	**Out of the question (3)**	Impossible	असंभव
1019	Out of the woods	No longer in trouble // out of danger	खतरे से बाहर
1020	Out of thin air	Appear suddenly	अचानक दिखाई देना
1021	Out of this world	Extraordinary	असाधारण
1022	Over and over again	Do something repeatedly	बार-बार करना
1023	Over egg the pudding	To spoil something by trying too hard to improve it	कुछ अच्छा करने की कोशिश में और बुरा हो जाना
1024	**Over head and ears (3)**	Completely	पूरी तरह
1025	**Over my dead body (2)**	Used to emphasize that one completely opposes something. // Opposing something fiercely	मेरी लाश से होकर
1026	Pale into insignificance	Seemed less important	कम महत्वपूर्ण लगना
1027	Palm off	To dispose off with the intent to deceive	धोखा देना
1028	Pandora's Box	A prolific source of trouble	मुसीबतों का पहाड़
1029	Paper over the cracks	To hide problems	समस्याओं को छिपाना
1030	**Part and parcel (3)**	Essential element // important part	अनिवार्य अंग
1031	Parthian shot	Parting hit	आख़ीरी दाँव
1032	Pass the baton	shift responsibility to others	जिम्मेदारी दूसरों पर टालना
1033	**Pass the buck (3)**	Refuse to accept responsibility // Blame someone for what you did wrong	पल्ला झाड़ना
1034	Pass the hat	To collect money	धन इकट्ठा करना
1035	Pat on the back	Praise or approval for doing something good	पीठ थपथपाना (शाबाशी देना)
1036	Pay heed to	Listen carefully with attention	ध्यान से सुनना
1037	**Pay lip service (4)**	Pretend to regard // To be insincere // Saying they agree although they do not support it	दिखावटी प्रेम या समर्थन
1038	Pay on the nail	Pay promptly	शीघ्र भुगतान करना
1039	Peas in a pod	Very similar	समान आकृति का
1040	Pedal to the metal	To drive very fast	बहुत तेज गाड़ी चलाना
1041	Pick a quarrel	to start a disagreement or argument	झगड़ा मोल लेना
1042	Pick and choose	Select only the best from choices	सर्वश्रेष्ठ का चयन करना
1043	Pick to pieces	Analyse critically	गंभीर रूप से विश्लेषण करना
1044	Picking holes in	Finding fault with	गलती ढूँढना
1045	Picks on someone	Treats badly	बुरा व्यवहार करना
1046	Pie in the sky	Something not possible	खयाली पुलाव (असंभव योजना)
1047	Pillar to post	One place to another	मारा-मारा फिरना

SN	Idioms / Phrases (#R)	Meaning (as per SSC Papers)	Hindi
1048	**Pin-money (2)**	Allowance made to a lady for her expenses // a small amount of money	जेब खर्च
1049	**Pipe dream (2)**	A dream or idea that is unlikely to happen // An illusory plan	असंभव सपना
1050	Plain as day	Very obvious and easy to understand	समझने में आसान
1051	Plain sailing	Was very easy	बहुत आसान
1052	**Play devil's advocate (2)**	To argue the opposite, just for the sake of argument	विपरीत तर्क करना
1053	Play for time	To make excuses or do things to gain time	बहाने बनाना
1054	Play it by ear	To do something without special preparation	बिना किसी विशेष तैयारी के कुछ करना
1055	Play one's ace	To use one's best weapon or resource	ब्रह्मास्त्र (सबसे बेहतर हथियार का उपयोग)
1056	Play safe	Avoid risks and take precautions	जोखिम से बचना
1057	Play truant	Stay away from duty	काम से अनुपस्थित रहना
1058	**Play with fire (2)**	To do something dangerous/risky	आग से खेलना (जोखिम भरा काम करना)
1059	**Played ducks and drakes (3)**	Spent lavishly // squandered // to use recklessly	आवश्यकता से अधिक खर्च करना
1060	Played havoc	Caused destruction	कहर बरपाना (नुकसान पहुंचाना)
1061	Playing to the gallery	Appeasing the masses	जनता को खुश करना
1062	**Playing with fire (3)**	To act in a dangerous and risky way	आग से खेलना (गंभीर जोखिम उठाना)
1063	**Pocket an insult (2)**	bear an insult quietly // Tolerate insult without protest	अपमान सहना
1064	**Point-blank (2)**	Directly // Close enough to hit the centre of the target	बहुत करीब से
1065	**Poke one's nose (2)**	To take interest in others' affairs // Interfere or meddle	टांग अड़ाना
1066	Pore over	Go through	ध्यान देना
1067	Pot-luck dinner	Dinner where everybody brings something to eat	रात का खाना जहाँ हर कोई कुछ न कुछ खाने के लिए लाता है
1068	Poured cats & dogs	Rained heavily	मूसलाधार बारिश
1069	Pouring cold water on	To discourage doing something	हतोत्साहित करना
1070	Provide a blueprint	Give a detailed plan or scheme	विस्तृत योजना
1071	**Pull a fast one (2)**	Play a trick // Trick someone	चाल चलना (धोखा देना)
1072	**Pull a long face (4)**	Look dejected // look sad	मुंह लटकाना (दुःखी होना)
1073	Pull a rabbit out of a hat	To do something unexpected	कुछ अजूबा करना

SN	Idioms / Phrases (#R)	Meaning (as per SSC Papers)	Hindi
1074	**Pull someone up (2)**	Criticise someone // Reprimand	आलोचना करना
1075	**Pull someone's leg (9)**	To make fool of // playing a joke with someone // To tease someone	किसी की टांग खींचना (मज़ाक उड़ाना)
1076	Pull something off	Make something happen	कुछ कर दिखाना (सफल होना)
1077	**Pull strings (2)**	Use personal influence	व्यक्तिगत प्रभाव का प्रयोग करना
1078	**Pull the plug (2)**	Prevent something from happening or continuing.	राह में रोड़े अटकाना (होने से रोकना)
1079	Pull the wool over someone's eyes	Deceive someone by telling lies.	आँखों में धूल झोंकना (धोखा देना)
1080	Pull together	Work harmoniously	मिलजुलकर काम करना
1081	**Pull up your socks (2)**	To put in extra effort	अधिक प्रयास करना
1082	**Pull yourself together (6)**	To calm oneself down and begin to think or act appropriately // To keep working constantly with attention // Regain composure	शांत होना, भावनाओं पर नियंत्रण रखकर काम करना
1083	Pulled all the stops	To do something with maximum effort or ability	आसमान-पाताल एक कर देना (पूरी कोशिश करना)
1084	Pulled the chestnuts out of fire.	Accomplishing a difficult job for someone else	किसी और के लिए खतरे में पड़ना
1085	Pulls no punches	Speaks frankly	खुलकर बोलना
1086	Put across	Effectively conveyed	प्रभावी ढंग से सूचित करना
1087	Put into action	To execute	पालन करना
1088	Put off	To delay	विलंब करना
1089	**Put one's foot down (6)**	Take a firm stand // asserted his authority // not to yield // refuse very firmly to do something	दृढ़तापूर्वक विरोध करना, अपने अधिकार का दावा करना
1090	Put one's cards on the table	To be honest	ईमानदार रहना
1091	**Put our heads together (2)**	Consult and work together // work in consultation	मिलकर काम करना
1092	Put someone's back up	To irritate someone	किसी को चिढ़ाना
1093	Put something by	Saves	बचत करना
1094	**Put two and two together (3)**	Reason logically // To deduce from given fact	ज्ञात तथ्यों से निष्कर्ष निकलना
1095	Put up the shutters	Went out of business	व्यापार बंद करना
1096	Put your best foot forward	Try as hard as one can	पुरजोर प्रयास करना
1097	**Putting the cart before the horse (3)**	Doing a thing in the wrong way	गलत तरीके से काम करना

SN	Idioms / Phrases (#R)	Meaning (as per SSC Papers)	Hindi
1098	Quicken the pulse	made some people excited or interested	धड़कन तेज़ करना
1099	Rained on the new bride's parade	To spoil a moment	अच्छे पल खराब करना
1100	**Raining cats and dogs (7)**	Raining extremely heavily	मूसलाधार बारिश होना
1101	Raise an alarm	warn of a dangerous situation	चेतावनी देना
1102	Raise the bar	To set higher goals	लक्ष्य ऊँचा करना
1103	Ran in the same groove	Moved in harmony	अच्छी सामंजस्ता
1104	Ran into	Met accidentally	अचानक मिलना
1105	Ran riot	Acted without restraint	अनियंत्रित व्यवहार
1106	**Rank and file (2)**	Ordinary workers in a company	साधारण कर्मचारी
1107	Rare bird	An exceptional person or thing; a rarity	दुर्लभ
1108	**Rat race (2)**	Fierce competition for power	कड़ी प्रतिस्पर्धा
1109	Reap the whirlwind	Suffer negative consequences as a result of one's actions	अपना बोया काटना (किये का परिणाम भुगतना)
1110	Red herrings	Clues intended to distract or mislead	छलावा
1111	**Red-tape (2)**	Official procedures causing delay // Official rules and bureaucracy that make it difficult to do something	दफ्तरशाही (अनावश्यक रूप से समय लेने वाली प्रक्रिया)
1112	Reinventing the wheel	Wasting one's time for things that have already been satisfactorily done	व्यर्थ के काम करना
1113	**Rest on one's laurels (2)**	To be satisfied with your achievements and not to make an effort to do anything else // To retire from active life	पुरानी ख्याति पर संतोष किए बैठे रहना
1114	Rides the high horse	Superior	खुद को श्रेष्ठ समझना
1115	Ring a bell	To sound familiar	जाना पहचाना लगना
1116	Ring fencing	Guarantee that funds allocated for a particular purpose will not be spent on anything else.	घेराबंदी
1117	Rip up old sores	To revive forgotten quarrel	पुराने घावों को कुरेदना (पुनः झगडा करना)
1118	**Rise like a phoenix (2)**	To become successful again // To emerge with a new life	फिर से सफल बनना
1119	Rise to the occasion	show you can deal with a situation successfully	खुद को योग्य साबित करना
1120	Rises with the lark	Very early	बहुत जल्दी उठना
1121	Roll back	To reduce, limit, decrease, or devalue	पीछे खदेड़ना
1122	Roll up your sleeves	Get ready to do something difficult	कमर कसना
1123	Root and branch	completely // wholly	पूरी तरह से
1124	Rose-coloured glasses	a positive outlook on life	सकारात्मक दृष्टिकोण

SN	Idioms / Phrases (#R)	Meaning (as per SSC Papers)	Hindi
1125	**Rub somebody the wrong way (2)**	Irked or irritated him // Annoy someone	गुस्सा दिलाना
1126	Ruffle somebody's feather	Annoy somebody	तंग करना
1127	**Rule the roost (4)**	To dominate // To make all the decisions // in complete control	हावी होना
1128	Run down	Criticise	आलोचना करना
1129	Run into	Incurred	दौर से गुजरना
1130	Run into rough weather	Experienced difficulties	काले बादल छाना (मुश्किल समय आना)
1131	**Run out of steam (3)**	To lose impetus or enthusiasm and stop doing something	उत्साह खत्म होना
1132	Sail close to the wind	Do something that is dangerous or even illegal	खतरनाक या अवैध काम करना
1133	Salad days	Adolescence	किशोरावस्था
1134	**Salt of the earth (4)**	A good , reliable, honest person	विश्वसनीय और ईमानदार व्यक्ति
1135	Saved by the bell	Saved at the last moment	अंतिम क्षण में बचाया गया
1136	**Saw through (2)**	Detected	पता चला
1137	**Scapegoats (2)**	Punished for others misdeeds	बलि का बकरा (दूसरों के गलती के लिए दोषी माना जाना)
1138	Second to none	As good as or better than all others	किसी से कम नहीं
1139	**See eye to eye (8)**	Be in full agreement // Agree with each other	पूर्णतः सहमत होना
1140	**See the light of day (2)**	Become publicly known	लोगों की नजर मे आना
1141	**Selling like hot cakes (3)**	To have a very good sale // To sell quickly	बहुत अच्छी बिक्री होना
1142	Send him packing	Terminate his services	नौकरी से निकालना
1143	Separate the wheat from the chaff	To separate the valuable from the worthless	अच्छे-बुरे की पहचान करना
1144	Set at liberty	To release	मुक्त कर देना
1145	Set forth	explained	व्याख्या करना
1146	Set the record straight	Give a correct account	सही विवरण देना
1147	Set the wheels in motion	To initiate a chain of events	काम शुरू करना
1148	Set their face against	Opposed strongly	दृढ़ता से विरोध करना
1149	**Shake off (3)**	Forget // to get rid of	भूल जाना
1150	Sharp as a tack	Mentally active	बहुत ही बुद्धिमान
1151	Sharp practices	Dishonest means	बेईमान तरीके

SN	Idioms / Phrases (#R)	Meaning (as per SSC Papers)	Hindi
1152	Shed light on	To explain a situation	किसी स्थिति को समझाना
1153	Shook in their shoes	Trembled with fear	डर से थर-थर काँपना
1154	Shoot through	Leave, typically to escape from or avoid someone or something.	खिसक जाना (छिप कर निकल जाना)
1155	shooting fish in a barrel	Exceptionally easy to do	बेहद आसान
1156	**Shot in the dark (2)**	An attempt that is not expected to succeed or very little chance of working // an attempt to guess something	अँधेरे में तीर चलाना (तुक्का मारना)
1157	Show white flag	Surrendered	आत्मसमर्पण करना
1158	Silver bullet	A simple and seemingly magical solution to a complicated problem	एक जटिल समस्या का एक सरल समाधान
1159	Sit in judgement	To criticize someone, especially when you have no right to do so	बिना अधिकार आलोचना करना
1160	**Sit on the fence (9)**	Not to take sides in a dispute // halting between two opinions // Remain undecided and unsure	दुविधा में होना
1161	Sit tight	Wait patiently	जमकर बैठे रहना
1162	Sitting on a gold mine	to own something potentially valuable	बेशुमार दौलत होना
1163	Sleep on it	To wait before making a decision	निर्णय लेने में समय लेना
1164	Slip off	Leave quietly	चुपचाप निकल जाना
1165	Slow and steady	Make consistent progress for success	निरंतर काम से सफलता मिलती है
1166	Smooth ruffled feathers	Make people feel less offended	लोगों को बुरा न लगने देना
1167	Smooth sailing	Easy progress	आसान
1168	Snowed under	Busy	व्यस्त होना
1169	So far so good	Things are going well so far	चीजें अब तक तो अच्छी चल रही हैं
1170	**Soft option (3)**	Easy and agreeable option // Do the thing that is easiest or least likely to cause trouble in a particular situation	आसान विकल्प
1171	Sought after	In great demand	काफी मांग में
1172	**Sow wild oats (2)**	To waste time by doing foolish things especially by having a lot of sexual relationships	अय्याशी करना
1173	Speak of the devil	The person we were just talking about showed up	शैतान का नाम लिया, शैतान हाजिर (जिसके बारे में बोला जा रहा हो उसका सामने आना)
1174	Speaks volumes	Gives enough proof // conveys a great deal	ठोस सबूत देना

SN	Idioms / Phrases (#R)	Meaning (as per SSC Papers)	Hindi
1175	**Spick and span (7)**	Clean and tidy	साफ़ – सुथरा
1176	**Spill the beans (12)**	To leak the secret // reveal a secret // Give away a secret	अनजाने में भेद खोल देना
1177	**Spin one's wheels (2)**	Expel much effort for little or no gain	बहुत कम लाभ के लिए बहुत ज्यादा प्रयास करना
1178	**Spread like wild fire (2)**	Spread rapidly	जंगल की आग की तरह फैलना
1179	**Square peg in a round hole (2)**	A misfit in the environment	बेमेल
1180	**Stab someone in the back (2)**	Betray someone.	पीठ में छुरा भोंकना (कपटपूर्ण व्यवहार)
1181	**Stand by (2)**	Support	समर्थन
1182	Stand for	Represent	पक्ष में
1183	Stand in one's own light	To act against one's own interest	अपने हित के विरुद्ध कार्य करना
1184	Stand-offish	Indifferent	तटस्थ रहना
1185	Standstill	Complete halt	ठहराव
1186	Start from scratch	Start entirely from the beginning	पूरी तरह से शुरू से शुरू करना
1187	Status quo	Unchanged position	वर्तमान स्थिति
1188	**Steal someone's thunder (2)**	Take credit for something someone else did // Get praise for doing something before someone	दूसरे का श्रेय छीनना
1189	**Stick to his guns (3)**	Maintain his own opinion	बात पर अड़े रहना
1190	Sticky fingers	An inclination to steal	चोरी करने की प्रवृत्ति
1191	**Stir up a hornet's nest (3)**	Caused anger in many people // Provoke trouble // To raise controversy	भीड़ को गुस्सा दिलाना
1192	Stole the show	Won everybody's praise	दर्शकों का दिल जीत लेना
1193	**Straight from the horse mouth (2)**	Hear something from someone who has direct, personal knowledge	विश्वसनीय सूत्रों से
1194	**Strain every nerve (5)**	Work very hard // to make utmost efforts	खून पसीना एक करना (कठिन परिश्रम करना)
1195	Straw in the wind	An indication of what might happen	संभावनाओं का सूक्ष्म संकेत
1196	Strike a bargain	To negotiate a deal	सौदा तय कर लेना
1197	**Strike while the iron is hot (2)**	To act at the right time // grab a favourable opportunity promptly	गरम लोहे पर हथौड़ा मारना (मौके का लाभ उठाना)
1198	Struck a chill to the heart	Aroused fear	दिल में डर पैदा करना
1199	Struck several bad patches	Had many professional difficulties	व्यवसाय-संबंधी मुश्किलें होना
1200	Suit you to a T	Look very good on your face	बहुत अच्छा जंचना
1201	Sum and substance	Essence	सारांश

SN	Idioms / Phrases (#R)	Meaning (as per SSC Papers)	Hindi
1202	Swan song	Last performance	अंतिम प्रदर्शन, अभिनय
1203	Sweeping statement	Generalised statement	व्यापक बयान
1204	Swept under the carpet	Kept hidden	छिपाकर रखा हुआ
1205	Swim with the tide	Agree with the popular opinion	प्रचलित तौर तरीके के अनुसार चलना
1206	**Swollen-headed (2)**	Pride	अभिमानी
1207	**Sword of Damocles (3)**	Imminent danger // a constant threat // an impending threat	सिर पर लटकती तलवार (होनेवाला खतरा)
1208	**Take a cue from someone (2)**	Learnt acting // be strongly influenced by someone	किसी से प्रभावित होकर सीखना
1209	Take a dim view of	disapprove of	घास नहीं डालना (अस्वीकार करना)
1210	Take away your breath	Astonishing	आश्चर्यचकित रह जाना
1211	**Take exception to (3)**	To object strongly	दृढ़ता से एतराज़ करना
1212	**Take heart (3)**	To take courage // to gain confidence	हिम्मत न हारना
1213	Take in their stride	Handle calmly	मुश्किल काम को आसानी से कर लेना
1214	Take something at face value	Accept something as it looks without thinking about whether it might, in fact, not be quite what it appears	बिना अधिक सोचे-विचारे स्वीकार कर लेना
1215	**Take the bull by the horns (3)**	To face a difficulty courageously // to face danger boldly	साहसपूर्वक मुसीबतों का सामना करना
1216	Take the heat	Receive criticism	आलोचना मिलना
1217	Take thee at thy word	Truly believe you	पूरी तरह विश्वास होना
1218	Take up room	Occupy space	कब्जा करना
1219	Take up the hatchet	Prepare for or go to war	युद्ध के लिए तैयार होना
1220	**Take with a pinch/grain of salt (5)**	Not believe completely something that you are told // To listen to something with considerable doubt // To believe with some scepticism	आँख मूँदकर विश्वास न करना (सन्देह होना)
1221	Taken fancy	Developed liking for	लट्टू होना (आकर्षित होना)
1222	**Takes after (5)**	To resemble // To be similar in appearance	एक जैसा होना
1223	**Taking a toll on (2)**	To harm or damage someone or something, especially in a gradual way	धीरे-धीरे नुकसान पहुँचाना
1224	Talked over	Discussed	विचार विमर्श करना
1225	**Talking through her hat (2)**	Talking nonsense	बकवास करना
1226	Tall tales	Boasting	डींग हांकना
1227	**Teething problems (2)**	Problems at the start of a new project	प्रारम्भिक कठिनाइयाँ

SN	Idioms / Phrases (#R)	Meaning (as per SSC Papers)	Hindi
1228	Tell upon	To affect adversely	प्रतिकूल प्रभाव डालना
1229	That ship has sailed	Too late to do something	कुछ करने के लिए बहुत देर हो जाना
1230	**The apple of discord (3)**	Reason for quarrel // Cause of animosity // something that causes friction	फसाद की जड़ (झगड़े का कारण)
1231	The ayes have it	The affirmative votes are in the majority	पक्ष में अधिक समर्थन
1232	**The bad egg (2)**	A dishonest or ill-behaved person	अविश्वसनीय व्यक्ति
1233	The bee's knees	Extraordinary	सर्वोत्कृष्ट
1234	The big fish	Main leaders	बड़ी हस्ती
1235	The calm before the storm	a period of quiet that comes before a time of activity, excitement, violence, etc.	आंधी के पहले की खामोशी
1236	The crux of the matter	The most important/critical point	सबसे महत्वपूर्ण पहलू
1237	The devil is beating his wife	The sun is shining while it rains	धूप के दौरान बारिश होना
1238	The die is cast	The decision has been taken	तीर कमान से निकल जाना (फैसला हो जाना)
1239	**The elephant in the room (3)**	A big problem everyone is ignoring or afraid to talk about // An obvious issue left unaddressed due to its sensitivity	बड़ी समस्या को नजरंदाज करना
1240	The gnomes of Zurich	Big international bankers	बड़े अंतर्राष्ट्रीय बैंकर या फाइनेंसर
1241	The grass is greener on the other side	Things appear better for others	दूर के ढोल सुहावने लगना (दूर की वस्तु अच्छी लगना)
1242	The graveyard shift	To work shift during the night, often from midnight to 8 A.M.	रात के शिफ्ट में काम
1243	The green-eyed monster	Jealousy	ईर्ष्यालु
1244	The jury is out	No decision has been reached	अनिर्णित
1245	**The last straw (5)**	Final problem in the series // A minor difficulty but coming on top of a series of difficulties, that makes a situation unbearable	स्थिति को असहनीय बनाने वाली आखिरी परेशानी
1246	**The Lion's share (6)**	The biggest and best part of a whole // The greatest and most desirable portion of something	सबसे बड़ा और बेहतर हिस्सा
1247	**The man in the street (3)**	Simple man // the ordinary man	आम आदमी
1248	The movers and shakers	People who have a lot of power and influence	प्रभावशाली व्यक्ति
1249	The nitty-gritty	The most important aspects or practical details of a subject or situation.	महत्वपूर्ण पहलू

SN	Idioms / Phrases (#R)	Meaning (as per SSC Papers)	Hindi
1250	**The pros and cons (3)**	For and against // advantages and disadvantages // consider all facts	नफा-नुकसान
1251	**The seamy side (2)**	The unpleasant aspects	अप्रिय पहलु
1252	The straw that broke the camel's back	To be the last in a series of events leading one to feel that it is intolerable	घटनाओं की श्रृंखला का अंतिम घटना जो असहनीय प्रतीत हो
1253	The tail is wagging the dog	The less important or subsidiary factor, person, or thing dominates a situation.	कम महत्वपूर्ण द्वारा नियंत्रित होना
1254	The thin end of the wedge	Start of harmful development	मामूली परेशानी जो बड़े परेशानी को जन्म देगा
1255	The tip of an iceberg	Something which is a small part of something much bigger	बड़ी समस्या की छोटी सी झलक
1256	The wheels have come off	Things start to fail or go wrong, especially after a period of success.	सफलता के बाद विफल होना
1257	Thick as thieves	Having a close friendship	घनिष्ट मित्रता
1258	Think on your feet	Adjust quickly to changes and make fast decisions	चुटकियों मे सही निर्णय लेना
1259	Threw a spanner	To do something that prevents a plan or activity from succeeding // Sabotage	कुछ ऐसा करना जो योजना को असफल करें
1260	Threw down the glove	Gave a challenge	चुनौती देना
1261	Through and through	completely	पूरी तरह से
1262	**Through thick and thin (11)**	Support under all circumstances // in times of good and bad fortune	हर हाल में
1263	**Throw caution to the winds (4)**	To do something without worrying about the risk // To behave recklessly	जोखिम भरा काम करना
1264	**Throw cold water (2)**	To discourage by showing indifference	पानी फेर देना (हतोत्साहित करना)
1265	**Throw in the towel (4)**	Acknowledge defeat // To admit defeat or failure	हार मान लेना
1266	Throw over	To refuse to accept // Reject	त्याग देना
1267	Throw up cards	Gave up my plan	मैदान-छोड़ देना (हार मानना)
1268	Throw up the sponge	To surrender	घुटने टेकना (पराजय स्वीकार करना)
1269	Tick all the boxes	To fulfil the required norms	आवश्यक मानदंडों को पूरा करना
1270	Tickled pink	Very pleased	बहुत खुश
1271	Tide over	to overcome	क़ाबू पा जाना
1272	Tide someone over	Give temporary help, usually financial	वित्तीय मदद करना
1273	Tie the knot	Get married	शादी के बंधन में बंधना
1274	Tighten one's belt	To cut one's expenditure	खर्च में कटौती करना

SN	Idioms / Phrases (#R)	Meaning (as per SSC Papers)	Hindi
1275	Till the cows come home	For a long, long time	अनिश्चित काल के लिए
1276	Time and again	Often	बार बार
1277	**Tit for tat (2)**	To do harm as done to you // Counter attack	जैसे को तैसा (जैसा कर्म वैसा फल)
1278	**To accept the gauntlet (2)**	To accept challenge	चुनौती स्वीकार करना
1279	**To add fuel to the fire (7)**	Make things worse // worsened the difficult situation	आग में घी डालना (किसी के गुस्से को ओर अधिक भडकाना)
1280	To aim for the stars	To set high goals	ऊँचा लक्ष्य निर्धारित करना
1281	**To air / to wash dirty linen in public (2)**	To discuss private affairs in public	निजी बातों को सबके सामने बोलना
1282	To and fro	Forward and backward	आगे और पिछे
1283	To angle	To fish	जाल बिछाना
1284	**To be all at sea (5)**	Puzzled // state of confusion // lost and confused	असमंजस की स्थिति
1285	To be at home	To be at ease	आराम से होना
1286	**To be devil's advocate (2)**	To present a counter argument just for the sake of it	खोट निकालने वाला
1287	**To be fair and square (4)**	To be honest // According to the rules	ईमानदार
1288	**To be in a fix (3)**	In a difficult situation // in puzzling state	उलझन में होना
1289	To be in a quandary	To be in a confusing situation	दुविधा में होना
1290	To be light years away	To be too distant for human beings to reach	बहुत ज्यादा दूर जहां पहुचना मुमकिन नहीं
1291	To be moved to tears	To be overwhelmed with emotion	भावना से आत्मविभोर होना
1292	To be off your food	To have no appetite	भूख न लगना
1293	To be on a roll	To be experiencing a successful period	सफलता अनुभव करना
1294	To be on pins and needles	To be in an agitated state of suspense	बेचैन होना
1295	**To be taken aback (4)**	To be surprised // shocked	हक्का-बक्का होना (चकित होना)
1296	To be thrown in at the deep end	Learn to do the difficult things too soon	नौसिखिये को मुशिकल काम देना
1297	To be tight-lipped	To keep quiet	मुंह सिलना (चुप रहना)
1298	**To be under the weather (14)**	To not feel well // To feel sick or unhealthy // To be in low spirits	बीमार होना
1299	**To beat a dead horse (2)**	To uselessly dwell on a subject far beyond its point of resolution. // a futile effort	निरर्थक प्रयास करना

SN	Idioms / Phrases (#R)	Meaning (as per SSC Papers)	Hindi
1300	**To beat a retreat (3)**	To run away in fear	दुम दबाकर भागना (घबरा कर भागना)
1301	To beat the air	To make efforts that are useless	व्यर्थ प्रयत्न करना
1302	To beat the clock	To perform a task within the time limit	समय पर काम कारना
1303	To beat the rap	To be acquitted of a crime	बरी होना
1304	To bid defiance	To disregard recklessly	आज्ञा का उल्लंघन करना
1305	**To blaze a trail (4)**	To lead the way as a pioneer // to initiate something new // To start a movement	नई राह दिखाना
1306	**To blow hot and cold (2)**	To be friendly and unfriendly at the same time // Vacillating	पल में तोला पल में माशा (कभी हाँ कभी ना करना)
1307	To blow one's own horn	To praise oneself	स्वयं की प्रशंसा करना
1308	**To break a leg (3)**	To wish good luck	भाग्य साथ होना
1309	To break into tears	To cry suddenly	रोना
1310	To break loose	To escape	नौ – दो ग्यारह होना (भाग जाना)
1311	To breathe one's last	To die	मरना
1312	**To bring to light (5)**	To reveal clearly	उजागर करना
1313	**To burn all bridges (2)**	To destroy all relations // doing something that makes it impossible to return to the previous situation later	पीछे लौटने के सभी रास्ते बंद करना
1314	**To burn one's fingers (3)**	To suffer financial losses // To get into trouble	अपने ही पैरो पर कुल्हाड़ी मरना (खुद को हानि पहुंचाना)
1315	To burn the candle at both ends	Work hard	अत्यधिक श्रम करना
1316	**To burn the midnight oil (4)**	To work till very late in the night	रात-दिन एक करना (देर रात्रि तक काम करना)
1317	**To call a spade a spade (4)**	To be frank // to speak in a straight forward manner // Say the truth about something, even if it is not pleasant	स्पष्ट रूप से कहना
1318	To catch someone's fancy	To appeal to someone	किसी को पसंद आना
1319	To catch up with	To come to their level	बराबरी करना
1320	To clear the decks	To remove obstructions	बाधाओं को हटाना
1321	**To clip one's wings (2)**	To restrict someone's freedom	पर काट देना (स्वतंत्रता को रोकना)
1322	To come clean	To make a honest disclosure	पूरी सच्चाई बता देना
1323	To come round	To become conscious again	होश में आना
1324	To cross one's mind	To think of something	विचार आना
1325	**To cudgel one's brains (2)**	To think hard	अक्ल के घोडे दौड़ना (दिमाग पर जोर डालना)

SN	Idioms / Phrases (#R)	Meaning (as per SSC Papers)	Hindi
1326	**To cut a long story short (2)**	To tell something briefly	संक्षेप में कहना
1327	To cut both ends	To argue in support of both side	दोनों पक्षों के समर्थन में तर्क देना
1328	To cut my teeth on	To gain experience	अनुभव हासिल करना
1329	To cut one short	To interrupt one	बीच में टोकना
1330	**To cut one's coat according to one's cloth (2)**	Live within one's means	जितनी चादर हो उतना ही पैर फैलाना चाहिये (अपनी आय के अनुसार व्यय करना)
1331	To cut the crackle	To stop talking and start working	बात बंद करके काम शुरू करना
1332	To die in harness	to continue occupation till death	काम करते हुए मरना
1333	To do the dishes	To wash and dry dishes	बर्तन धोना
1334	**To doctor the accounts (2)**	To manipulate the accounts	खाते में हेरफेर करना
1335	To draw the longbow	To exaggerate	बढ़ा-चढ़ाकर कहना
1336	**To eat a humble pie (8)**	To accept defeat // suffer humiliation // had to yield under pressure // Admit that you are wrong // To apologise humbly	नाक रगड़ना (हार मानना)
1337	**To eat one's own words (2)**	Forced to retract one's own statement // retract what one has said	अपने शब्द वापस लेना
1338	**To end in smoke (7)**	To come to nothing // end without any practical result // yielded no result	धुवें में उड़ना (कोई परिणाम न निकलना)
1339	To explore every avenue	To try every opportunity	हर संभव अवसर ढूँढना
1340	To fan the flames	To make a bad situation worse	स्थिति बदतर करना
1341	To feel at home	To feel comfortable	अपने घर की तरह अनुभव करना
1342	**To fight tooth and nail (6)**	To make every possible effort // with strength and fury // Fight very fiercely	जी जान से लड़ना
1343	**To fish in troubled waters (2)**	To make a profit out of disturbance	पराई आग में हाथ सेंकना (किसी की परेशानियों से अपनी स्वार्थ पूर्ति करना)
1344	**To flog a dead horse (9)**	To attempt to do the impossible // waste energy on an unalterable situation	मुर्दें में जान डालने की कोशिश करना (असंभव काम करना)
1345	**To foam at one's mouth (3)**	To get very angry // To be enraged and show it	आग बबूला होना (अति क्रोधित होना)
1346	To gain ground	To make progress	प्रगति करना
1347	To gather roses only	To seek all enjoyments of life	जीवन के सभी सुख की कामना
1348	**To get away with (2)**	To escape from something	बच निकलना

SN	Idioms / Phrases (#R)	Meaning (as per SSC Papers)	Hindi
1349	**To get cold feet (7)**	To experience nervousness or anxiety before one attempts to do something // Fear // Lose confidence	घबराहट होना
1350	**To get into hot water (8)**	To get into trouble // To be in a difficult situation in which you can be criticised	मुसीबत में पड़ना
1351	To get more kicks than half pence	Harsh treatment than rewards	अत्याचार करना
1352	To get one's own back	To get one's revenge	बदला लेना
1353	**To gird up the loins (2)**	To prepare for hard work // To prepare oneself for a difficult situation	कमर कस लेना (कड़ी मेहनत के लिए तैयार रहना)
1354	**To give the devil his due (2)**	To give encouragement even to the enemy // to give credit to even a notorious person	बुरे की भी प्रशंसा करना
1355	To give the slip	To escape	चंगुल से भाग निकलना
1356	**To go bananas (2)**	To become very excited or angry // Become irrational	बहुत क्रोधित होना
1357	To go nuts	To become crazy	पागल हो जाना
1358	To go off the air	To stop broadcasting a radio or tv programme	प्रसारण बंद करना
1359	To go red in the face	To feel embarrassed	शर्मिंदा महसूस करना
1360	**To go scot-free (2)**	To escape without punishment // unpunished	दण्ड से छुटकारा पाना
1361	To go the whole hog	To do it completely	पूरी तरह से करना
1362	To go to somebody's head	To damage or weaken your judgment // To make someone dizzy or slightly drunk	सर चढ़ना
1363	**To go/run around in circles (4)**	To waste one's time and energy doing trivial things // To keep doing something without achieving much // Make no progress in an argument or discussion	फालतू काम मे समय बर्बाद करना
1364	**To hail from (2)**	To come from	उत्पन्न होना
1365	**To hammer out (2)**	To arrive at an agreement	निर्णय या समझौते पर पहुंचना
1366	To hang together	To be connected with each other	एक दूसरे के साथ जुड़े रहना और मदद करना
1367	To have a blast	To have a good time	मस्ती करना
1368	**To have a gut feeling (3)**	Strong instinct // To feel an instinct or intuition	स्वाभाविक भावना
1369	To have a jaundiced eye	To be prejudiced	पक्षपातपूर्ण दृष्टिकोण
1370	To have a yen for	To have a very strong and continuous desire or craving for something	प्रबल लालसा होना
1371	To have at one's fingertips	Recall of factual information at one's command	जुबाँ पर होना (अच्छी तरह याद होना)

SN	Idioms / Phrases (#R)	Meaning (as per SSC Papers)	Hindi
1372	To have eggs on one's face	To be embarrassed because of one's action	अपनी हरकत से शर्मिंदा होना
1373	**To have second thoughts (2)**	To reconsider	पुनर्विचार करना
1374	To have something on the brain	To be obsessed with something	दिमाग में किसी चीज का जुनून होना
1375	**To have something up one's sleeve (3)**	To have a secret plan // have an alternative plan	गुप्त योजना
1376	**To heave a sigh of relief (2)**	To suddenly feel very happy because something unpleasant has not happened or has ended	राहत की सांस लेना
1377	To his heart's content	As much as he wanted to	जी भर के
1378	**To hit below the belt (3)**	To attack in an unfair manner	गलत तरीके से प्रहार करना
1379	**To hit the jackpot (2)**	To make money quickly // to find exactly what was sought	किस्मत का तारा चमकना (अचानक धन प्राप्त करना या जीतना)
1380	To hit the road	Begin one's journey	यात्रा शुरू करना
1381	**To hit the sack (6)**	To prepare for sleep // Went to bed	सोने की तैयारी करना
1382	To hold a brief for	To support someone's cause	किसी का समर्थन करना
1383	To hold good	To remain valid	लागु होना / मान्य होना
1384	**To judge a book by its cover (3)**	To evaluate people's worth by their outward appearance	बहरी दिखावे पर भरोसा करना
1385	**To jump on the bandwagon (5)**	To follow popular trends // Get involved in an activity because it is likely to succeed	बहती गंगा में हाथ धोना (लोकप्रिय प्रवृत्तियों को अपनाना)
1386	To keep a good table	To offer sumptuous food to one's guests	शानदार भोजन परोसना
1387	**To keep an eye on (2)**	To be cautions // To watch over attentively	नजर रखना (ध्यान रखना)
1388	**To keep body and soul together (3)**	To manage to live // to have just enough to sustain	गुजारा करना
1389	To keep in abeyance	In a state of suspension	ठंडे बस्ते में रखना (टालना)
1390	**To keep someone at arm's length (6)**	To be at a distance with someone // Avoid being friendly with someone // avoiding too much closeness	दूर से सलाम करना (दूरी बनाना)
1391	To keep the ball rolling	To maintain progress	जारी रखना
1392	**To keep the wolf away from the door (6)**	To keep off starvation // avoid starvation	भुखमरी से बचना
1393	**To keep under wraps (2)**	Secret	गुप्त रखना
1394	To keep up	To keep in touch	संपर्क बनाये रखना
1395	To know what's what	To know the facts of a situation	स्थिति के तथ्यों को जानना

SN	Idioms / Phrases (#R)	Meaning (as per SSC Papers)	Hindi
1396	To lag behind	To fail to maintain the pace or progress	पीछे छूट जाना
1397	To land a job	To be hired	नौकरी लगना
1398	To lead astray	To misguide	गुमराह करना
1399	**To let someone off (2)**	To release someone from blame // To punish someone lightly	गलती के लिए क्षमा करना
1400	To look blue	To be disheartened	धैर्यहीन दिखना
1401	To look down one's nose	To regard with contempt	किसी को तुच्छ समझना
1402	**To lose ground (3)**	Becoming less acceptable	पिछड़ना
1403	To lose one's temper	To become angry	आपा खोना (गुस्सा होना)
1404	To make a fuss about	An excessive display of attention or activity	उपद्रव करना
1405	**To make a mountain of a molehill (2)**	To give great importance to little things // exaggerate a minor problem	राई का पहाड़ बनाना (छोटी सी बात को बड़ा बनाना)
1406	To make a pile	To make a lot of money	बहुत पैसा कमाना
1407	**To make amends (3)**	To compensate // to correct a mistake	प्रायश्चित करना (भूल सुधारना)
1408	**To make both ends meet (5)**	To live within one's income // live within means // Manage expenses with just enough funds	किसी तरह से गुज़ारा करना
1409	To make do	Manage	काम चलाना
1410	To make matters worse	Make the situation worse	स्थिति को और खराब करना
1411	**To make one's blood boil (3)**	To make somebody furious // To be very angry	खून खौलाना (बहुत गुस्सा आना)
1412	**To make up one's mind (4)**	To decide what to do // Decide firmly	निश्चय करना
1413	To measure swords	to engage in competition	युद्ध, प्रतियोगिता में शामिल होना
1414	To meet one's Waterloo	To experience defeat	हार का अनुभव करना
1415	To mind one's p's and q's	To be careful about one's speech and behaviour	शिष्टाचार का पूरा ध्यान रखना
1416	**To miss the boat/bus (6)**	To miss an opportunity // lose an opportunity	मौक़ा गँवा बैठना
1417	To not have a clue	To not know about something	सुराग न होना
1418	**To paddle once own canoe (2)**	Manage in dependently // Depend on oneself	अपने पैरो पर खड़ा होना (आत्मनिर्भर होना)
1419	To pass away	Die	चल बसना (निधन होना)
1420	To pay off old scores	To take revenge	बदला लेना
1421	**To pay through the nose (5)**	Pay an extremely high price	भारी कीमत देना
1422	**To pick holes (2)**	To criticise someone	दूसरे के अन्दर कमियां ढूँढना
1423	To pick up the threads	To restart from the previous closing point	फिर से सँभलना

SN	Idioms / Phrases (#R)	Meaning (as per SSC Papers)	Hindi
1424	To pigeon hole	To typecast someone	फालतू काम देना
1425	To play fast and loose	To act in an unreliable way	अनैतिक तरीके से व्यवहार करना
1426	**To play second fiddle (2)**	Position has lesser importance than anybody else's. // Take a subordinate role	दूसरे दर्जे पर होना, महत्वहीन होना
1427	To play to the gallery	To seek to win approval	भीड़ को खुश करने वाला काम करना
1428	To pour oil in troubled water	To calm a dispute	झगड़े की आग को बुझाने की कोशिश करना
1429	To pull a fast one on someone	To cheat someone	धोखा देना
1430	**To put a spoke in one's wheel (3)**	To put a difficulty in the way of progress // thwarted in the execution of the plan	टाँग अड़ाना (बाधा डालना)
1431	To put an end to	Stop	समास करना
1432	To put in a nut-shell	To state something very concisely	संक्षेप में रखना
1433	To put one out of countenance	To make one feel ashamed	लज्जित करना
1434	To put one's foot in one's mouth	To accidentally embarrass or upset someone	गलती से किसी को शर्मिंदा करना
1435	To put one's hand to plough	To take up a difficult task // get busy working	काम में व्यस्त हो जाना
1436	To put something on hold	To postpone something	स्थगित करना
1437	**To put up with (4)**	Tolerate	बर्दाश्त करना
1438	To quit on someone	To stop helping someone, especially when the support is needed.	किसी को छोड़ना
1439	To raise a dust	To cause disruption or confusion	अशांति या भ्रम पैदा करना
1440	To raise a few eyebrows	To cause surprise or shock	आश्चर्य या आघात पहुँचाना
1441	**To read between the lines (11)**	Understand the hidden meaning // find more meaning than the words appear to express //understand what is implied but not stated directly // Discern the hidden meaning in the text	छिपा हुआ अर्थ निकालना // अनकहे भाव को समझना
1442	To roll out the red carpet	To give a grand welcome	भव्य स्वागत करना
1443	To rub salt in someone's wound	To make a bad or painful situation worse	जले पर नमक छिड़कना (दुख: बढ़ाना)
1444	To run across	To meet by chance	संयोग से मिलना
1445	To run amok	To run about in a frenzy	सिर पर खून सवार होना (नियंत्रण से बाहर)

SN	Idioms / Phrases (#R)	Meaning (as per SSC Papers)	Hindi
1446	To run around like a headless chicken	To do many things in a disorganised manner	अव्यवस्थित तरीके से काम करना
1447	To run one down	To disparage someone	किसी को नीचा दिखाना
1448	To scale up	To increase the size, amount or importance of	बढ़ाना
1449	To set aside	To move sideways	अलग रखना
1450	To set the Thames on fire	Do a heroic deed // To do wonderful or exciting things	अद्भुत या रोमांचक चीजें करना
1451	**To shed crocodile tears (4)**	To pretend to be sympathetic // to pretend grief // False tears	मगरमच्छ के आँसू बहाना (सहानुभूति का नाटक करना)
1452	**To show a clean pair of heels (2)**	To escape // ran away	नौ दो ग्यारह हो जाना (भाग जाना)
1453	To shun	To avoid deliberately and especially habitually	जानबूझकर दूर रहना
1454	**To smell a rat (14)**	Suspect a trick or deceit // detected something wrong // Have a reason to suspect something	दाल में काला होना (संदेह होना)
1455	To sound red alert	To rise an alarm	खतरे की घंटी बजाना (चौकस करना)
1456	To sow the dragon's teeth	To do something that inadvertently leads to trouble	कुछ ऐसा करना जिससे अनजाने में परेशानी हो
1457	**To speak one's mind (2)**	To express one's thoughts // to voice one's thoughts plainly	मन की बात करना
1458	To stand on his feet	To be independent	अपने पैरो पर खड़ा होना (आत्मनिर्भर होना)
1459	**To stand one's ground (3)**	Refused to yield // refuse to change your opinion	हार मानने से इनकार करना
1460	To stave off	Postpone	टाल देना
1461	To steal a march	To outshine	आगे निकलना
1462	To steal her brother's thunder	get more recognition than her brother for their success	ज्यादा ख्याति मिलना
1463	**To steer clear of (2)**	Avoid someone or something because it is dangerous for you	दूर रहना, टालना
1464	**To take a back seat (2)**	To become less important or to give up control over things	कम महत्वपूर्ण बनना
1465	To take a chill pill	To calm down	शांत होना
1466	**To take a stock of (4)**	To assess and evaluate before taking a decision // To think carefully	मूल्यांकन करना
1467	**To take for granted (2)**	To accept or assume without question	महत्व नहीं समझना
1468	**To take French leave (3)**	Absenting oneself without permission // Leave without any intimation	बिना अनुमति के अनुपस्थित रहना

SN	Idioms / Phrases (#R)	Meaning (as per SSC Papers)	Hindi
1469	**To take into account (2)**	To consider	ध्यान में रखना
1470	**To take one's hat off (5)**	To admire someone // Congratulations to	किसी की प्रशंसा करना
1471	**To take pains (4)**	To make efforts // Try hard	प्रयास करना
1472	To take someone for a ride	To deceive someone	धोखा देना
1473	**To take the bull by the horns (3)**	To handle difficulties // To deal with a difficult situation directly	साहसपूर्वक मुसीबतों का सामना करना
1474	**To take to heart (4)**	To grieve over // to be greatly affected // to consider something very seriously	दिल पर लेना (बहुत प्रभावित होना)
1475	**To take to one's heels (5)**	To run away // ran away in fear // ran off	दुम दबाकर भागना (डर कर भाग जाना)
1476	**To take to task (6)**	Punished // to rebuke // to scold someone // get an official reprimand	बुरी तरह से फटकारना
1477	To talk him over	To discuss something thoroughly // Convince	विचार विमर्श करना
1478	To the letter	In every detail	अक्षरशः (हूबहू)
1479	To the nines	To perfection	बहुत बढ़िया तरीके से
1480	To throw a fit	Express extreme anger	आग बबूला होना
1481	**To throw dust in one's eyes (3)**	To deceive // to mislead or confuse	आँखों में धूल झोंकना (धोखा देना)
1482	**To toe the line (2)**	To follow the lead // Follow the rules	आदेश का पालन करना
1483	**To turn a deaf ear (9)**	Disregard // refused to obey // to be indifferent // to pay no heed // neglected	कान पर जूँ तक न रेंगना (सुनी-अनसुनी कर देना)
1484	**To turn over a new leaf (5)**	To change one's behaviour for better // To begin again	नया जीवन शुरू करना
1485	To turn the corner	To pass the critical stage	मुसीबत के दिन पार कर लेना
1486	To walk on air	To be very happy	फूला नहीं समाना (बहुत खुश होना)
1487	**To win laurels (2)**	To achieve honours and glory	सफल होना
1488	To work like a dog	To work very hard	बहुत मेहनत करना
1489	**To wrangle over an ass's shadow (2)**	To quarrel over trifles	तुच्छ बात पर झगड़ा करना
1490	Toffee-nosed	A person who thinks he is of a high social class and looks down on people of lower class	दंभी/अहंकारी
1491	Token strike	Short strike held as a warning	सांकेतिक हड़ताल
1492	Tongue in cheek	In an ironic or insincere way.	व्यंगपूर्वक, मज़ाक में
1493	Too close for comfort	So close to be a cause idiom worry because of being unwelcome	इतने करीब की असहज महसूस हो
1494	Too close to call	A very narrow margin	बाल-बाल बचना

SN	Idioms / Phrases (#R)	Meaning (as per SSC Papers)	Hindi
1495	Too fond of her own voice	Does not listen properly to anyone else	घमंडी होना
1496	Too many chiefs and not enough Indians	An inefficient situation	ज्यादा मालिक कम कर्मचारी (अकुशल स्थिति)
1497	**Too many irons in the fire (3)**	Is engaged in too many enterprises at the same time	बहुत सारे कामों में उलझा हुआ होना
1498	Took a leap in the dark	Took a risk	अंधेरे में छलांग लगाना (जोखिम लेना)
1499	**Took exception (2)**	Objected	आपत्ति करना
1500	**Took to their heels (2)**	Ran away	बहुत ही तेज भागना
1501	Tooth and nail	With all their might	एड़ी चोटी का जोर लगाना (पूरी ताकत से)
1502	Touch all bases	Include everything	सब कुछ शामिल करना
1503	Touch and go	Uncertain	अनिश्चित
1504	Tricks of the trade	Special skills or knowledge	विशेष कौशल या ज्ञान
1505	True colours	Real character	वास्तविक चरित्र
1506	Trump card	That gives someone an advantage	तुरुप का पत्ता (सर्वोत्तम साधन)
1507	**Turn a blind eye (4)**	To ignore a situation, facts or reality	अँधा बन जाना (अनदेखा करना)
1508	Turn an honest penny	Make a legitimate living	ईमानदारी से पैसे कमाना
1509	**Turn down (3)**	Reject	अस्वीकार कर देना
1510	Turn turtle	Over-turn // turn upside down	उलट जाना
1511	Turn up	Appear	प्रस्तुत होना
1512	Turned his head	Cause to become conceited // Cause to become infatuated	घमण्डी बना देना, मुग्ध होना
1513	**Turned up one's nose (2)**	Treat offer with contempt // despises	नाक चढ़ाना (तिरस्कार करना)
1514	Twiddling one's thumbs	Feeling bored	ऊबना
1515	**Twist someone's arm (3)**	To force someone to do something by making it hard for them to refuse // persuade someone to do something	जबरन राजी करना
1516	**Under a cloud (7)**	Under suspicion // in disgrace // untrustworthy	शक के दायरे में
1517	Under duress	Under pressure	दबाव में
1518	Under his nose	Right in front of him	ठीक उसके सामने
1519	Under the gun	To be under pressure	दबाव में
1520	Up a blind alley	Following a course of action that is certain to lead to an undesirable outcome	अवांछनीय परिणाम वाला काम

SN	Idioms / Phrases (#R)	Meaning (as per SSC Papers)	Hindi
1521	Up against the wall	In an inextricable situation	कठिन स्थिति में फँसा हुआ
1522	**Up in arms (4)**	to be angry // protesting vigorously about something // In rebellion	खीजा हुआ, कड़ा विरोध करना
1523	Up in the air	Something that is unknown entirely	अनिश्चित होना
1524	**Up to the mark (2)**	As good as the others // up to the required standard	अच्छी हालत में
1525	**Upset someone's applecart (2)**	To cause trouble, especially by spoiling someone's plans	खेल बिगाड़ देना
1526	**Vanish into thin air (4)**	Completely disappear	गायब होना
1527	Vis-a-vis	In relation to // face-to-face	आमने–सामने
1528	Vote with your feet	Show their disapproval	असहमति जताना
1529	Walk the talk	To do what one says	वचन निभाना
1530	**Walk the tight rope (2)**	Be very cautious	नाज़ुक परिस्थिति से गुज़रना
1531	Walking on thin ice	doing something risky	खतरे का काम करना
1532	Want to curl up and die	Feel terribly ashamed and sorry	शर्म से डूब मरना
1533	Wash one's hands off something	Refuse to be responsible for something	पल्ला झाड़ना (जिम्मेदारी लेने से इनकार करना)
1534	Watching grass grow	Very boring	बहुत उबाऊ (बोरिंग)
1535	**Water under the bridge (2)**	Something I cannot change // used to say that something happened in the past and is no longer important or worth arguing about	पुरानी बात का अब महत्वपूर्ण नहीं होना
1536	**Weal and woe (3)**	Good times and bad times // joys and sorrows // In prosperity and adversity	अच्छा और बुरा समय
1537	**Wear and tear (2)**	Damage	घिस-पिस कर टूट जाना
1538	Wear someone out	to exhaust someone	किसी को थका देना
1539	Wear the green willow	Suffer unrequited love	खोए या बिना मिले प्यार के लिए दुखी होना
1540	**Wears his heart on his sleeve (3)**	Expresses his feelings openly // To show your true emotions	दिल खोल कर रख देना (अपनी भावनाओं को खुल कर बता देना)
1541	Weather the storm	Survive a period of difficulty	तूफ़ान का सामना करना (कठिन दौर से निपटना)
1542	Wee hours of the day	Dawn	भोर
1543	Went a long way	Helped considerably	काफी हद तक मदद करना
1544	Went pear-shaped	Went terribly wrong	बहुत गलत होना
1545	**Went to the winds (2)**	Dissipated	हवा में मिल जाना (फ़ेल जाना)
1546	Wet his whistle	Have a drink	शराब पीना

SN	Idioms / Phrases (#R)	Meaning (as per SSC Papers)	Hindi
1547	Wheels within wheels	Complication	जटिल समस्या जिसमें कई अलग-अलग चीजें शामिल हैं
1548	When it rains, it pours	Problems seem to happen together	कंगाली में आटा गीला (तकलीफे जब आती है तो हर तरफ से आती हैं)
1549	**When pigs fly (2)**	A way of saying that something will never happen. // A time that will never come	ऐसा जो कभी नहीं हो सकता
1550	When the balloon goes up	The situation turns unpleasant or serious	जब कठिनाई शुरू होगी
1551	Whet your appetite	To want something more	भूख बढ़ाना
1552	Whistle in the dark	Pretend to be unafraid	बेखौफ होने का नाटक करना
1553	White lie	A harmless or trivial lie	सफ़ेद झूठ
1554	Whole bag of tricks	Make use of all the possibilities or techniques to achieve something	सभी तकनीकों का उपयोग करना
1555	**Whole nine yards (2)**	The entirety of something	किसी चीज की संपूर्णता
1556	Whoop it up	Enjoying in a noisy way, usually in a group	धमाचौकड़ी मचाना
1557	Wide off the mark	Irrelevant	त्रुटिपूर्ण होना
1558	Wild and woolly	Uncouth in appearance or behaviour	दिखने या व्यवहार में जंगली
1559	**Will-o-the wisp (2)**	Something that is impossible to get or achieve // unreal imagining	असंभव कार्य
1560	Wine and dine	When somebody is treated to an expensive meal.	भव्यता से खान पान करवाना
1561	Wipe the floor with someone	To defeat someone	धूल चाटना (बुरी तरह से हराना)
1562	Wiped the nose	Cheated	धोखा देना
1563	With a fine tooth comb	to examine in great detail	बारीकी से देखना
1564	With a vengeance	Used to emphasize the degree to which something occurs	हद से ज्यादा होना
1565	With bated breath	In anxiety	उत्सुकता से
1566	With one voice	Unanimously	एक मत होकर
1567	**With open arms (2)**	Cordially // Warmly	खुले दिल से
1568	without rhyme or reason.	without a reasonable explanation	बिना मतलब के
1569	Word of mouth	Through the verbal sharing of information	मौखिक रूप से
1570	**Work against the clock (3)**	Work very fast to complete something within a deadline // work in great hurry, as fast as possible	बहुत तेजी से काम करना
1571	Work like a charm	To work very well	बहुत अच्छे से काम करना
1572	Work out	Exercise or develop a plan	व्यायाम करना
1573	Worked like a dream	A plan succeeded perfectly	बिना रुकावट के काम पूरा होना

SN	Idioms / Phrases (#R)	Meaning (as per SSC Papers)	Hindi
1574	Worth its weight in gold	Very valuable	बहुत ही मूल्यवान
1575	Wrap my head around it	To comprehend something that one considers challenging, confusing or a foreign concept	गुत्थी सुलझाना
1576	Yellow bellies	Cowards	डरपोक
1577	**Yeoman Service (2)**	Excellent service // Useful help in need	बहुत अच्छा काम
1578	Your guess is as good as mine	To have no idea of the answer	उत्तर पता नहीं होना
1579	Your number is up	The time has come when someone is doomed to suffer a disaster.	बड़ी संकट या मरने का समय आना
1580	Zip your lip	Keep quiet about something.	मुंह पर ताला लगाना (बिलकुल चुप रहना)

*Total **1580** Idioms asked **3058** times*

SN	Idioms / Phrases	Meaning (as per SSC Papers)	Hindi
1	To be under the weather (14)	To not feel well // To feel sick or unhealthy // To be in low spirits	बीमार होना
2	To smell a rat (14)	Suspect a trick or deceit // detected something wrong // Have a reason to suspect something	दाल में काला होना (संदेह होना)
3	Once in a blue moon (13)	Rarely and infrequently	कभी कभार
4	A hard nut to crack (12)	Difficult task // a difficult problem to solve // A tough challenge // A difficult person // An inflexible person who is hard to convince	लोहे के चने चबाना (मुश्किल काम)
5	A red letter day (12)	An important day // a day that is pleasantly noteworthy or memorable // happy and significant day // a very special day	महत्वपूर्ण दिन
6	Beat around the bush (12)	Avoiding the main topic // Speak in a round-about manner	घुमा-फिराकर बात करना
7	By leaps and bounds (12)	Very quickly // rapidly // Swiftly	दिन दुगनी रात चौगुनी (बहुत तेजी से)
8	Face the music (12)	Get reprimanded // be punished // to bear the consequences // Accept the blame	किये का परिणाम भुगतना
9	Gift of the gab (12)	Ability to speak eloquently // Talks well and persuasively	जिव्हा पर सरस्वती का वास (वाक्पटुता की क्षमता)
10	Spill the beans (12)	To leak the secret // reveal a secret // Give away a secret	अनजाने में भेद खोल देना
11	A wild goose chase (11)	Futile search // unprofitable adventure // A worthless hunt or chase	निरर्थक खोज
12	Bury the hatchet (11)	To make peace // forget past quarrels // To settle disputes	झगड़ा ख़त्म करना
13	Through thick and thin (11)	Support under all circumstances // in times of good and bad fortune	हर हाल में
14	To read between the lines (11)	Understand the hidden meaning // find more meaning than the words appear to express //understand what is implied but not stated directly // Discern the hidden meaning in the text	छिपा हुआ अर्थ निकालना // अनकहे भाव को समझना
15	A bolt from the blue (10)	Something unexpected and unpleasant // a complete surprise // a sudden calamity // an unexpected disaster	आकस्मिक घटना
16	A snake in the grass (10)	A treacherous person // an unreliable and deceitful person // A secret enemy	आस्तीन का साँप (गुप्त शत्रु)
17	At the eleventh hour (10)	At the very last moment // Just before the deadline	आखिरी मौके पर
18	Blow one's own trumpet (10)	Praise oneself // to boast about their achievements	अपने मुंह मियाँ मिट्ठू बनना (खुद की तारीफ खुद करना)

19	Break the ice (10)	Initiate something // to start a conversation // To make someone comfortable	चुप्पी तोड़ना (बातचीत शुरू करना)
20	Cost an arm and a leg (10)	Very expensive // A large amount of money	बहुत महंगा पड़ना
21	Leave no stone unturned (10)	Try every possible course of action in order to achieve something // to make all possible efforts	खून पसीना एक करना (हर मुमकिन प्रयास करना)
22	A fish out of water (9)	An uncomfortable position // in unfamiliar circumstances	असहज परिस्थिति
23	A stone's throw away (9)	At a short distance	थोड़ी दूरी पर
24	At the drop of a hat/dime (9)	Without any hesitation // instantly // without having planned beforehand	बहुत तेजी से बिना किसी हिचकिचाहट के तुरन्त घटित होना
25	Be all ears (9)	Listening intently // very attentive // To be ready and eager to listen	गौर से सुनना
26	Bite off more than one can chew (9)	To take more than one can deal with // to take on a task too big for oneself // To have tried to do something which is too difficult	अपनी क्षमता से अधिक काम लेना
27	By fits and starts (9)	Unsteady // irregularly	अनियमित रूप से
28	Cock and bull story (9)	An implausible story used as an explanation or excuse // absurd story // Improbable story // Wildly exaggerated or falsified story	बे-सिरपैर की या ऊट-पटांग बात
29	Fair weather friends (9)	Friends in good times // supports only when easy and convenient // a friend who deserts you in difficulties // an unreliable friend // A selfish friend	स्वार्थी मित्र
30	Get out of hand (9)	To become uncontrollable // get out of control	हाथ से निकलना (बेकाबू होना)
31	In the same boat (9)	To be in the same difficult situation as someone else	उसी कठिन परिस्थिति में होना
32	On cloud nine (9)	Extremely happy and excited	सातवें आसमान पर (अत्यंत प्रसन्न होना)
33	Pull someone's leg (9)	To make fool of // playing a joke with someone // To tease someone	किसी की टांग खींचना (मज़ाक उड़ाना)
34	Sit on the fence (9)	Not to take sides in a dispute // halting between two opinions // Remain undecided and unsure	दुविधा में होना
35	To flog a dead horse (9)	To attempt to do the impossible // waste energy on an unalterable situation	मुर्दे में जान डालने की कोशिश करना (असंभव काम करना)
36	To turn a deaf ear (9)	Disregard // refused to obey // to be indifferent // to pay no heed // neglected	कान पर जूँ तक न रेंगना (सुनी-अनसुनी कर देना)

37	A Blessing in disguise (8)	An apparent misfortune that eventually has good results. // a hidden favour // Something that seems bad turns out to be good	दुःख के भेष में सुख
38	A dark horse (8)	An unexpected winner // someone who unexpectedly succeeds // an unknown entry // a competitor of unknown capabilities	अप्रत्याशित विजेता
39	A piece of cake (8)	A very easy task	बच्चों का खेल (आसान काम)
40	Cry over spilt milk (8)	To complain about a loss from the past // to regret about that which cannot be rectified // Feeling sorry over a mistake that cannot be changed	अब पछताए होत क्या जब चिड़िया चुग गई खेत
41	Full of beans (8)	Lively and energetic // Full of energy	जोश से भरा हुआ
42	Have an axe to grind (8)	A private interest to serve // have a selfish interest // To have an ulterior motive	अपना उल्लू सीधा करना (निजी स्वार्थ)
43	In a nutshell (8)	Briefly and concisely // express very briefly	संक्षेप में
44	See eye to eye (8)	Be in full agreement // Agree with each other	पूर्णतः सहमत होना
45	To eat a humble pie (8)	To accept defeat // suffer humiliation // had to yield under pressure // Admit that you are wrong // To apologise humbly	नाक रगड़ना (हार मानना)
46	To get into hot water (8)	To get into trouble // To be in a difficult situation in which you can be criticised	मुसीबत में पड़ना
47	A chip off the old block (7)	Reminds them of one's father // someone similar in character to one's father // Resembling parents	जैसा बाप वैसा बेटा
48	At one's wit's end (7)	To be puzzled // not knowing what to do // Quite perplexed // Be overwhelmed with problems	समस्याओं से इतना चिंतित होना कि पता नहीं आगे क्या करना है
49	Barking up the wrong tree (7)	Trying to do something in a way that will not work // Pursue a course of action that will most likely be futile	निरर्थक प्रयास
50	Best of both worlds (7)	A situation wherein someone has the privilege of enjoying two different opportunities // all the advantages // An ideal situation	दोनों हाथों में लड्डू (हर प्रकार से लाभ होना)
51	Call it a day (7)	Decide or agree to stop doing something // to give up work and go back to home	संन्यास लेना
52	Feather one's own nest (7)	Make money in an improper way // to profit in a dishonest way // promote their own interest	बेईमानी करके धनी होना
53	Grease the palm (7)	Bribe	मुट्ठी गरम करना (रिश्वत देना)

54	Hit the nail on the head (7)	Say or do something exactly right // to find exactly the right answer	सटीक जवाब देना
55	Hold your horses (7)	Be patient // To tell someone to stop and consider carefully // slow down	धैर्य रखना
56	In black and white (7)	In writing	लिखित रूप में
57	In high spirits (7)	Full of hope and enthusiasm // Joyful // Cheerful	उत्साह से भरपूर
58	Raining cats and dogs (7)	Raining extremely heavily	मूसलाधार बारिश होना
59	Spick and span (7)	Clean and tidy	साफ़ - सुथरा
60	To add fuel to the fire (7)	Make things worse // worsened the difficult situation	आग में घी डालना (किसी के गुस्से को ओर अधिक भडकाना)
61	To end in smoke (7)	To come to nothing // end without any practical result // yielded no result	धुर्वे में उड़ना (कोई परिणाम न निकलना)
62	To get cold feet (7)	To experience nervousness or anxiety before one attempts to do something // Fear // Lose confidence	घबराहट होना
63	Under a cloud (7)	Under suspicion // in disgrace // untrustworthy	शक के दायरे में
64	A bone of contention (6)	Cause of dispute / cause for quarrel	झगड़े की जड़
65	A close shave (6)	Narrow escape from danger	बाल-बाल बचना
66	A fool's paradise (6)	Being happy for foolish reasons // a state of happiness based on a person's not knowing about potential trouble.	हवाई महल (संभावित परेशानी नहीं जानने पर खुशी की स्थिति)
67	Add insult to injury (6)	To further a loss with mockery to worsen an unfavourable situation. // Make a bad situation even worse	जले पर नमक छिड़कना (दुख: बढ़ाना)
68	Apple of one's eye (6)	Someone very precious or dear	आंखों का तारा (बहुत प्यारा)
69	At snail's pace (6)	Do something very slowly	बहुत धीरि-धीरे
70	Back to the drawing board (6)	Used to indicate that an idea has been unsuccessful and that a new one must be devised // plan it all over again	नये सिरे से बनाना
71	Bad blood (6)	Angry feeling // enmity // ill feeling	आपसी दुश्मनी
72	Catch red handed (6)	To catch someone doing something illegal // Caught in the act of committing the crime	रंगे हाथ (अपराध करते हुए) पकड़ना
73	Chicken hearted (6)	Timid // Cowardly	डरपोक
74	Give a piece of one's mind (6)	To rebuke someone strongly // speaking sharply // scolding // To reprimand	डाँटना
75	Give someone the cold shoulder (6)	Deliberately ignore someone	जान बुझ कर नज़रअंदाज़ करना

76	Ins and outs (6)	Detailed description // Full details	पूरा विवरण
77	Pull yourself together (6)	To calm oneself down and begin to think or act appropriately // To keep working constantly with attention // Regain composure	शांत होना, भावनाओं पर नियंत्रण रखकर काम करना
78	Put one's foot down (6)	Take a firm stand // asserted his authority // not to yield // refuse very firmly to do something	दृढतापूर्वक विरोध करना, अपने अधिकार का दावा करना
79	The Lion's share (6)	The biggest and best part of a whole // The greatest and most desirable portion of something	सबसे बड़ा और बेहतर हिस्सा
80	To fight tooth and nail (6)	To make every possible effort // with strength and fury // Fight very fiercely	जी जान से लड़ना
81	To hit the sack (6)	To prepare for sleep // Went to bed	सोने की तैयारी करना
82	To keep someone at arm's length (6)	To be at a distance with someone // Avoid being friendly with someone // avoiding too much closeness	दूर से सलाम करना (दूरी बनाना)
83	To keep the wolf away from the door (6)	To keep off starvation // avoid starvation	भुखमरी से बचना
84	To miss the boat/bus (6)	To miss an opportunity // lose an opportunity	मौक़ा गँवा बैठना
85	To take to task (6)	Punished // to rebuke // to scold someone // get an official reprimand	बुरी तरह से फटकारना
86	A cakewalk (5)	Something very easy // an easy achievement // Extremely easy	अत्यंत सरल
87	A dime a dozen (5)	Very common and of no particular value.	कौड़ी के भाव (बेहद सस्ते)
88	A storm in a teacup (5)	Big fuss over a small matter // A lot of anger and worry about trivial things	बात का बतंगड़
89	A white elephant (5)	Costly and troublesome possession useless to its owner	महंगा और परेशानी का स्रोत
90	As fit as a fiddle (5)	Strong and healthy // In a perfectly healthy condition	बहुत अच्छे स्वास्थ्य में
91	Be wet behind the ears (5)	Young and inexperienced	अनुभवहीन
92	Build castles in the air (5)	Daydream // Have unrealistic ideas // to create impossible dreams or hopes	हवाई किले बनाना (कोरी कल्पना करना)
93	By the skin of one's teeth (5)	By the narrowest margin // Having a narrow escape	बहुत कम अंतर से
94	Carry the day (5)	win a victory	जीत हासिल करना
95	Cool as a cucumber (5)	Not nervous or emotional // to be calm and composed // cool as ice	धैर्यवान

96	Cut corners (5)	Not do a thing well in order to save money or effort // Do something perfunctorily so as to save time or money // saving money	सबसे आसान, सस्ता या तेज़ (ग़लत) तरीके से करना
97	Donkey's years (5)	A long time	बहुत लंबा समय
98	Draw a blank (5)	To be unsuccessful // find no favour	खाली हाथ लौटना (असफल होना)
99	Eye wash (5)	A deception // A pretence	आँखों में धूल झोंकना (धोखा देना)
100	For good (5)	Permanently // forever	सदा के लिए
101	Go to the dogs (5)	To be ruined // Deteriorate shockingly	बरबाद हो जाना
102	Hand in glove (5)	In close association // in partnership for something dishonest	घनिष्ठ सम्बन्ध
103	Herculean task (5)	Very difficult task	मुश्किल काम
104	In the long run (5)	Eventually/Ultimately	आखिरकार
105	Kill two birds with one stone (5)	To serve two purposes at one time // To achieve two results with a single effort	एक तीर से दो शिकार करना
106	Leaves you in the lurch (5)	Leave someone in a helpless condition // desert someone in his difficulties	बिच मझधार में छोड़ देना
107	Let the cat out of the bag (5)	Reveal a secret carelessly or by mistake	भेद खोलना
108	Live from hand to mouth (5)	To have enough money to live on and nothing extra // miserably // consuming daily what little is earned	जैसे तैसे गुजर बसर करना
109	Maiden speech (5)	First speech	पहला भाषण
110	Make a beeline for (5)	Go straight to	बिलकुल सीधा जाना
111	Off and on // On and Off (5)	Occasionally // Periodically	कभी-कभी
112	On tenterhooks (5)	In suspense and anxiety // anxious	चिंता में
113	Once and for all (5)	Bring to an end // finally // conclusively	हमेशा के लिये
114	Out of the blue (5)	Completely unexpectedly	बिल्कुल अचानक
115	Strain every nerve (5)	Work very hard // to make utmost efforts	खून पसीना एक करना (कठिन परिश्रम करना)
116	Take with a pinch/grain of salt (5)	Not believe completely something that you are told // To listen to something with considerable doubt // To believe with some scepticism	आँख मूँदकर विश्वास न करना (सन्देह होना)
117	Takes after (5)	To resemble // To be similar in appearance	एक जैसा होना
118	The last straw (5)	Final problem in the series // A minor difficulty but coming on top of a series of difficulties, that makes a situation unbearable	स्थिति को असहनीय बनाने वाली आखिरी परेशानी
119	To be all at sea (5)	Puzzled // state of confusion // lost and confused	असमंजस की स्थिति

120	To bring to light (5)	To reveal clearly	उजागर करना
121	To jump on the bandwagon (5)	To follow popular trends // Get involved in an activity because it is likely to succeed	बहती गंगा में हाथ धोना (लोकप्रिय प्रवृत्तियों को अपनाना)
122	To make both ends meet (5)	To live within one's income // live within means // Manage expenses with just enough funds	किसी तरह से गुज़ारा करना
123	To pay through the nose (5)	Pay an extremely high price	भारी कीमत देना
124	To take one's hat off (5)	To admire someone // Congratulations to	किसी की प्रशंसा करना
125	To take to one's heels (5)	To run away // ran away in fear // ran off	दुम दबाकर भागना (डर कर भाग जाना)
126	To turn over a new leaf (5)	To change one's behaviour for better // To begin again	नया जीवन शुरू करना
127	A bird's eye view (4)	A general view from above // good and comprehensive idea	ऊंचाई से विस्तृत दृश्य
128	A close-fisted person (4)	A miser	कंजूस आदमी
129	A drop in a bucket (4)	A very small part of something big or whole // Something small and unimportant, especially when compared with something else	ऊंट के मुंह में जीरा (बहुत कम)
130	A green horn (4)	An inexperienced man	अनुभवहीन व्यक्ति
131	A man of letters (4)	Proficient in literary art // Scholar	विद्वान
132	A man of straw (4)	A man of no substance // A weak person	कमजोर व्यक्ति
133	A mare's nest (4)	A difficult/complicated situation	जटिल या भ्रामक स्थिति
134	A needle in a haystack (4)	Something that is very difficult to locate // Attempting something impossible	घास के ढेर में सुई (ऐसी चीज जिसे ढूंढने में परेशानी हो)
135	A wet blanket (4)	A person who discourages enjoyment or enthusiasm // someone who prevents other people from having fun	कबाब में हड्डी (मजा किरकिरा करने वाला)
136	Achilles' heel (4)	A weakness or vulnerable point.	कमजोरी
137	All moonshine (4)	Far from reality // concocted // nonsense	दिखावटी
138	At loggerheads (4)	In conflict with someone // To disagree strongly	असहमति के कारण हिंसक विवाद
139	At sea (4)	At a loss // perplexed // confused	परेशान
140	Ball is in your court (4)	It is up to you to make the next decision or step // To be responsible for further action	जिम्मेदार होना
141	Be glad to see the back of (4)	Be happy when a person leaves	व्यक्ति के जाने से खुश होना

142	Bear the palm (4)	To win	जीतना
143	Bite the bullet (4)	To force yourself to do something unpleasant // To get something over with because it is inevitable	मजबूरी में स्वीकार करना
144	Black sheep (4)	one who is not accepted as part of a family or group because of one's bad conduct // Person with bad reputation // Disgrace for the family	कुल-कलंक (बुरी प्रतिष्ठा वाला व्यक्ति)
145	Break new/fresh ground (4)	Do or discover something new // To innovate or pioneer	नई खोज करना
146	Butterflies in the stomach (4)	To be anxious and nervous	घबड़ाना
147	By hook or by crook (4)	By any means, good or bad // Using whatever methods are necessary	कैसे भी करके
148	Couch potato (4)	A lazy person // a person who watches too much television	आलसी व्यक्ति
149	Cut to the chase (4)	To start talking about the important aspects of something // come to the point	मुद्दे पर आना
150	Drag one's feet (4)	Be reluctant to act // Do something deliberately at a slow pace	टाल मटोल करना
151	Draw a line (4)	To fix a limit // Accept something up to a particular point	सीमा निर्धारित करना
152	Eats like a horse (4)	Eats a lot of food	बहुत सारा खाना खाने वाला
153	Every dark cloud has a silver lining (4)	Every unpleasant situation has a positive side // difficult times will lead to better days // Something promising is there in any difficult situation	निराशा में भी आशा की झलक होती है
154	Fall flat (4)	To fail to produce intended effect // to have no effect	असफल होना
155	Feather in one's cap (4)	A new and additional distinction // an achievement // an accomplishment to be proud of	चार चाँद लगाना
156	Fight shy of me (4)	To avoid encountering	मुठभेड़ से बचना
157	Get on somebody's nerves (4)	To be an irritant // annoys me	किसी का दिमाग खराब करना
158	Hard and fast (4)	That cannot be altered // strict // Fixed	अपरिवर्तनीय
159	Hobson's choice (4)	No real choice at all // An apparently free choice where there is no real alternative	कोई विकल्प नहीं
160	Hold water (4)	Seem acceptable // Appear to be valid or reasonable	स्वीकार्य
161	In the nick of time (4)	Just in time // At the last possible moment	सही समय पर
162	It's Greek to me (4)	Incomprehensible // I cannot understand anything	समझ से बाहर

163	Kick the bucket (4)	To die	चल बसना (निधन होना)
164	Lend me your ear (4)	To politely ask for someone's full attention // to pay attention to	कान लगाकर सुनना (ध्यान से सुनना)
165	Let sleeping dogs lie (4)	Do not bring up an old controversial issue	सोते शेर को मत छेड़ो
166	Nip in the bud (4)	To stop something at the start // Dropped at an early stage // To stop something before it has an opportunity to develop	शुरुआती समय में ही कुचल देना या नष्ट कर देना
167	No love lost between (4)	Not on good terms // intense dislike // Persons who do not like each other at all	बहुत नफ़रत
168	Pay lip service (4)	Pretend to regard // To be insincere // Saying they agree although they do not support it	दिखावटी प्रेम या समर्थन
169	Pull a long face (4)	Look dejected // look sad	मुंह लटकाना (दुःखी होना)
170	Rule the roost (4)	To dominate // To make all the decisions // in complete control	हावी होना
171	Salt of the earth (4)	A good , reliable, honest person	विश्वसनीय और ईमानदार व्यक्ति
172	Throw caution to the winds (4)	To do something without worrying about the risk // To behave recklessly	जोखिम भरा काम करना
173	Throw in the towel (4)	Acknowledge defeat // To admit defeat or failure	हार मान लेना
174	To be fair and square (4)	To be honest // According to the rules	ईमानदार
175	To be taken aback (4)	To be surprised // shocked	हक्का-बक्का होना (चकित होना)
176	To blaze a trail (4)	To lead the way as a pioneer // to initiate something new // To start a movement	नई राह दिखाना
177	To burn the midnight oil (4)	To work till very late in the night	रात-दिन एक करना (दिर रात्रि तक काम करना)
178	To call a spade a spade (4)	To be frank // to speak in a straight forward manner // Say the truth about something, even if it is not pleasant	स्पष्ट रूप से कहना
179	To go/run around in circles (4)	To waste one's time and energy doing trivial things // To keep doing something without achieving much // Make no progress in an argument or discussion	फालतू काम मे समय बर्बाद करना
180	To make up one's mind (4)	To decide what to do // Decide firmly	निश्चय करना
181	To put up with (4)	Tolerate	बर्दाश्त करना
182	To shed crocodile tears (4)	To pretend to be sympathetic // to pretend grief // False tears	मगरमच्छ के आँसू बहाना (सहानुभूति का नाटक करना)

183	To take a stock of (4)	To assess and evaluate before taking a decision // To think carefully	मूल्यांकन करना
184	To take pains (4)	To make efforts // Try hard	प्रयास करना
185	To take to heart (4)	To grieve over // to be greatly affected // to consider something very seriously	दिल पर लेना (बहुत प्रभावित होना)
186	Turn a blind eye (4)	To ignore a situation, facts or reality	अँधा बन जाना (अनदेखा करना)
187	Up in arms (4)	to be angry // protesting vigorously about something // In rebellion	खीजा हुआ, कड़ा विरोध करना
188	Vanish into thin air (4)	Completely disappear	गायब होना
189	A bull in a China shop (3)	An extremely awkward, clumsy person // A clumsy person in a delicate situation	शीशमहल में बंदर (अनाड़ी व्यक्ति)
190	A carrot and stick approach (3)	Rewards and punishments that influence someone's behavior	साम दाम दंड भेद
191	A change of heart (3)	A change in one's opinion // Different opinion about someone or something	विचार में बदलाव
192	A hornet's nest (3)	An unpleasant situation // a troublesome situation // Raising controversy	अप्रिय स्थिति
193	A laughing stock (3)	An object of laughter //an object of ridicule	हंसी का पात्र
194	A live wire (3)	Lively and active	जिन्दादिल व्यक्ति
195	A lot on your plate (3)	To have a large number of problems to deal with // having many responsibilities	बहुत सारी जिम्मेदारियां
196	A sea change (3)	A profound or notable transformation. // Complete transformation	पूर्ण परिवर्तन
197	Above board (3)	Honest and frank // without any secret	ईमानदार
198	Actions speak louder than words (3)	What you do is more important than what you say // What you do reveals the real you // Intentions can be judged by people's actions	कथनी से अधिक करनी बोलती है
199	Alive and kicking (3)	In good health	अच्छे स्वास्थ्य में
200	All and sundry (3)	Everybody without distinction // All included	हर कोई बिना भेद के

*Top **200** Idioms asked **1194** times.*

SN	Idioms / Phrases	Meaning
	SSC CGL Tier 1 2022 [IDIOMS/ PHRASES]	
1	Like a cakewalk	Easy task
2	All eyes	Watching eagerly
3	In weal and woe	In prosperity and adversity
4	A green horn	Inexperienced person
5	Bag and baggage	With all of one's possessions
6	in cold blood	deliberately
7	A skeleton in the cupboard	An embarrassing fact to be kept secret
8	Fly into a passion	To become angry suddenly
9	Break the ice	Make people meeting first time feel more comfortable
10	Beat around the bush	Avoid the main point by talking in a roundabout way
11	To smell a rat	To have reason to suspect
12	Fair and square	Honestly
13	at an arm's length	At a distance
14	Cut a poor figure	To put a bad impression
15	Bear the palm	To be a winner
16	Bob's your uncle!	It becomes easily and quickly achievable
17	beating about the bush	Speaking in a confusing manner without giving a correct answer
18	hit me below the hand	hit me below the belt
19	Himalayan blunder	grave error
20	donkey's years	a very long time
21	In hot waters	To be in trouble
22	Quicken the pulse	made some people excited or interested
23	Latin and Greek	Incomprehensible
24	elbow room	very little freedom
25	On the ball	To be alert
26	yellow bellies	Cowards
27	A rolling stone gathers no moss	A person who does not settle in one place for a long time, does not gain wealth, name or fame
28	born with a silver spoon in his mouth	born to riches and luxury
29	an olive branch	gesture of peace
30	cock and bull story	Wildly exaggerated or falsified story
31	in full swing	very active
32	let the cat out of the bag	To allow a secret to be **known**, usually without intending to
33	Take something at face value	Accept something as it looks without thinking about whether it might, in fact, not be quite what it appears
34	Turn over a new leaf	To begin again
35	A fair-weather friend	A selfish friend

36	Cudgel one's brain	To think hard
37	come in handy	Be useful
38	Play it by ear	To do something without special preparation
39	On cloud nine	Very happy
40	Heart in the right place	Someone is good even if they sometimes behave in a wrong manner
41	Down the tubes	Failing completely
42	put his foot down	refused to yield
43	Fair-weather friends	A person whose friendship cannot be relied on in times
44	cold feet.	feel too frightened to do something
45	greenhorn	Inexperienced
46	face the music	To accept unpleasant consequences
47	Lose your marbles	To go insane
48	He's sitting on the fence	He can't take a decision
49	take with a grain of salt	Not take too seriously
50	to and fro	Forward and backward
51	Eat humble pie	To apologise humbly
52	by leaps and bounds	Swiftly
53	Red tape	Official rules and bureaucracy that make it difficult to do something
54	in black and white	in writing
55	Steer clear of	Avoid someone or something because it is dangerous for you
56	Hold water	Appear to be valid or reasonable
57	slow and steady	Make consistent progress for success
58	ins and outs	Detailed description
59	went pear-shaped	Went terribly wrong
60	Aladdin's cave	a place that contains many interesting objects

SSC CGL Tier 2 2021 [IDIOMS/ PHRASES]

SN	Idioms / Phrases	Meaning
1	fight shy of	to avoid
2	bad blood	ill feeling
3	bury the hatchet	forget past quarrels
4	clam up	to become silent
5	forty winks	a short nap
6	hold your horses	slow down
7	all in all	having all authority
8	lend an ear	pay attention to
9	cut a sorry figure	create a poor impression

SSC CHSL Tier 1 2021 [IDIOMS/ PHRASES]

SN	Idioms / Phrases	Meaning
1	Hit the books	To study very hard

2	A piece of cake	An easy task
3	Crocodile tears	Pretended show of sorrow
4	To hold good	To remain valid
5	It's all Greek to me	I cannot understand anything
6	Pull a long face	To look sad
7	Bed of roses	Pleasant condition of life
8	fish out of water	Being uncomfortable and restless
9	Hobson's choice	A choice forced upon someone
10	Face up to	To accept a difficult situation
11	running around in circles	To be very active but with few results
12	Hale and hearty	Strong and healthy
13	Strain every nerve	To try extremely hard to do something
14	Jump the gun	To do something too soon
15	Dark horse	An unexpected winner
16	Be like chalk and cheese	Be absolutely different
17	green-eyed	jealous
18	Charley horse	Cramp
19	Carry the day	winning
20	White elephant	Costly but useless possession
21	To put someone's back up	To irritate someone
22	chip off the old block	Similar to one's parents in behaviour
23	High spirits	cheerful
24	Gear up for	Get ready for
25	Call upon	To order
26	Lose your touch	Not being as successful as previously
27	At one's elbow	Next to someone
28	Blow up	To destroy by an explosion
29	A fly on the wall	An unperceived observer
30	In the same boat	To be in the same difficult situation as someone else
31	hair's breadth	narrow margin
32	Grease someone's palm	Bribe someone
33	A storm in a tea cup	A lot of anger and worry about trivial things
34	Tell upon	To affect adversely
35	A snake in the grass	A deceitful person
36	Tit for tat	Counter attack
37	Win laurels	To gain honour
38	By the skin of one's teeth	Barely managed to escape
39	Safe pair of hands	A person who can be trusted to do something efficiently
40	Let down	To fail
41	Hard and fast	Strict
42	catch 22	A difficult situation in which the solution to a problem is impossible
43	Knock down	To demolish

44	Eat like a horse	Eat a lot of food
45	Beat around the bush	To avoid talking about what is important
46	Red letter day	Memorable day
47	Read between the lines	Understand something that is not said outright
48	A kick in the teeth	Great disappointment
49	Donkey's years	Long time
50	Go to the wall	To fail
51	Under the weather	Feeling ill
52	By leaps and bounds	Very quickly
53	Have a long face	Look unhappy or disappointed
54	The best of both worlds	An advantageous situation from two different things at a time
55	Get away	To leave
56	Between Scylla and Charybdis	Between two dangers
57	Be at a loose end	To have nothing to do
58	Have a soft spot for someone	To like someone a lot
59	Pull the plug	End something
60	At loggerheads	Disagreeing with
61	Playing devil's advocate	One who argues against something just for the sake of arguing
62	Back out	To withdraw from
63	Comparing apples with oranges	Unequal comparisons
64	Lion's share	Largest share
65	Get the axe	Lose the job
66	Wipe the floor with someone	To defeat someone
67	To pay lip service	To express loyalty, respect, or support for something insincerely
68	Every dog has his day	Everyone has good luck or success at a point of time
69	Come about	To happen
70	Break a leg	Wish someone good luck
71	Miss the boat	Miss an opportunity
72	On cloud nine	Extremely happy
73	Sum and substance	Essence
74	Under duress	Under pressure
75	Apple of one's eye	Very dear
76	Up in arms	In rebellion
77	Cut straight to the chase	Avoid unnecessary introduction and go to the more important part
78	Make one's blood boil	to make someone very angry
79	hard of hearing	partially deaf
80	Elbow grease	Hard physical efforts
81	Donkey's years	A very long time
82	make someone's flesh crawl/creep	to make someone feel disgusted, afraid, frightened

83	Start from scratch	Start entirely from the beginning
84	Chip off the old block	Someone who resembles their parent
85	to bite the bullet	Force oneself to do something unpleasant
86	Costs an arm and a leg	too expensive for us to buy
87	To bite the bullet	To be brave in a difficult situation
88	Call a spade a spade	talking too frankly
89	To draw a blank	To be unsuccessful at eliciting a response
90	Man of letters	Scholar
91	Jump the gun	Start something too soon or act hastily
92	In your birthday suit	Not wearing any clothes
93	Twist someone's arm	To try to force someone to do something
94	Cast aside	To reject
95	Tick all the boxes	To fulfil the required norms
96	Once in a blue moon	Very rarely
97	Child's play	An easy task
98	apple-cart	Spoil careful plans
99	Pocket an insult	Tolerate insult without protest
100	Be under a cloud	To be untrustworthy
101	Hit the sack	Go to sleep
102	In queer street	In debt
103	Snail's pace	Very slow
104	The movers and shakers	People who have a lot of power and influence
105	Snake in the grass	Treacherous person
106	Get one's dander up	Lose one's temper

SSC MTS Tier 1 2021 [IDIOMS/ PHRASES]		
SN	**Idioms / Phrases**	**Meaning**
1	raining cats and dogs	To rain very heavily
2	Ignorance is bliss	To remain ignorant of things that may cause stress
3	stealing the thunder	Get praise for doing something before someone
4	To smell a rat	To suspect something
5	Spill the beans	Give away a secret
6	on thin ice	In a risky situation
7	an iron hand	strict and harsh control
8	Come rain or shine	Whatever happens
9	Chase rainbows	To pursue unrealistic goals
10	Hold someone or something at bay	Prevent someone or something from moving closer
11	Have a whale of a time	Have an exceptionally fun or exciting experience
12	Crocodile tears	False tears
13	To take with a grain of salt	To believe with some scepticism
14	Make a living	To earn enough money for things you need
15	ring a bell	To sound familiar
16	Kick someone when they are down	To cause further trouble to someone already in a difficult situation

17	foaming at the mouth	To be enraged and show it
18	Back on one's feet	Well or successful again
19	Out of the blue	Completely unexpectedly
20	An iron hand	Strict control
21	In the heat of the moment	Saying or doing something without thinking due to anger
22	let the cat out of the bag	To reveal a secret
23	To raise a dust	To cause disruption or confusion
24	have an axe to grind	To have an ulterior motive
25	Keep an eye on	To watch over attentively
26	No spring chicken	A person who is no longer young
27	Move the goalposts	Unfairly alter the conditions or rules of a procedure during its course
28	crying for the moon	To make an impractical or unreasonable request
29	That ship has sailed	Too late to do something
30	In raptures	extremely delighted
31	Once in a blue moon	Very rarely
32	Hit the nail on the head	To be exactly right about something
33	flogging a dead horse	To waste time on useless things
34	drop in the bucket	A very small part of something big or whole
35	Below the belt	Cruel and unfair
36	Keep body and soul together	Stay alive during hard times
37	A piece of cake	A very easy task
38	Drop in the bucket	Something small and unimportant, especially when compared with something else
39	A leopard cannot change its spots	It is impossible to change who you are
40	Heart and soul	Completely
41	A gut feeling	An instinct or intuition
42	Go the extra mile	Going above and beyond whatever is required for the task at hand
43	Give someone a taste of their own medicine	Mistreat someone in the same way they have treated others
44	on cloud nine	Very happy
45	Barking up the wrong tree	Pursue a course of action that will most likely be futile
46	Add fuel to the fire	Worsen an already bad situation
47	smell a rat	Suspect trickery or deception
48	Gone bananas	become irrational
49	Hold the fort	To take responsibility for a situation temporarily
50	costed me an arm and a leg	is very expensive
51	flogging a dead horse	To waste time on useless things
52	drop in the bucket	A very small part of something big or whole
53	All eyes and ears	To be attentive

54	Beyond the shadow of a doubt	With certainty; for sure
55	All Greek to me	incomprehensible
56	An arm and a leg	A large amount of money
57	Get cold feet	To feel nervous about doing something
58	To blaze the trail	To start a movement
59	Leave no stone unturned	Make all possible efforts
60	A pipe dream	An illusory plan
61	Kill two birds with one stone	To achieve two things by doing a single action
62	Bite someone's head off	Respond to someone with anger that is often sudden or unprovoked
63	gird up your loins	To prepare oneself for a difficult situation
64	An eye opener	A shocking revelation
65	a bull in a China shop	A clumsy person in a delicate situation
66	Bury the hatchet	To settle disputes
67	every cloud has a silver lining	Every difficult situation has a hopeful aspect to it
68	Pull someone's legs	To tease someone
69	By hook or by crook	By any means
70	Bolt from the blue	To receive unexpected news
71	Castle in the air	Unrealistic plan
72	The last straw	The final problem in a series of problems that makes the situation intolerable
73	the lion's share	the largest portion
74	Through thick and thin	In good and bad times
75	Tricks of the trade	Special skills or knowledge
76	In a nutshell	Very briefly
77	One's cup of tea	One's chosen or preferred thing
78	Chew the scenery	To act overly emotional
79	Change of heart	Different opinion about someone or something
80	An eye wash	A pretence
81	To lead one by the nose	To control someone completely
82	Play with fire	To do something risky
83	Out for the count	In a deep, insensible sleep
84	Draw the line	To set a limit on something
85	in black and white	in writing
86	Long in the tooth	Too old to do something
87	through thick and thin	under all circumstances
88	The lion's share	The biggest and best part of a whole
89	To foot the bill	To make payment
90	shooting fish in a barrel	Exceptionally easy to do
91	Water under the bridge	Anything from the past that is not significant or important anymore
92	feather in his cap	An achievement to be proud of
93	a stone's throw	A short distance
94	Set the wheels in motion	To initiate a chain of events
95	To walk the tight rope	Be very cautious

| 96 | at the drop of a hat | Without delay |

	SSC CPO Paper 1 2022 [IDIOMS/ PHRASES]	
SN	**Idioms / Phrases**	**Meaning**
1	Throw caution to the wind	take risk
2	Cutting corners	Doing something poorly in order to save time or money
3	Call it a day	Stop working on something
4	close shave	A narrow escape
5	Blue blood	A person belonging to a high family
6	To make matters worse	Make the situation worse
7	Heart and soul	With all the effort you can put
8	apple-pie order	Completely arranged
9	Be on the breadline	Be very poor
10	Crying wolf	To ask for help when you don't need it
11	Belly laugh	A loud and unrestrained laugh
12	chip off the old block	A person who is similar in behaviour or actions to his/her parents
13	A mare's nest	Complicated situation
14	Beside oneself	Almost out of one's senses
15	cool as a cucumber	cool as ice
16	To give someone the cold shoulder	To ignore someone
17	True colours	Real character
18	burnt his fingers	To get into trouble
19	Butterflies in his stomach	a nervous feeling
20	Salt of the earth	A very good and honest person
21	An eagle eye	a vision
22	rained on the new bride's parade	To spoil a moment
23	At the drop of a dime	Something that can happen very fast without hesitation
24	All ears	To listening attentively
25	To pull someone's leg	To joke with someone
26	Snowed under	Busy
27	hard nuts to crack	An inflexible person who is hard to convince
28	beaming from ear to ear	Smiling broadly
29	At sea	At a loss or perplexed
30	under the weather	not very well
31	bird's eye view	good and comprehensive idea
32	the elephant in the room	A big problem everyone is ignoring or afraid to talk about
33	To stand one's ground	To maintain one's position
34	A slap on the wrist	A very mild punishment
35	A lot on one's plate	A lot to do
36	To be on thin ice	To be in a risky situation

37	A lame excuse	Weak excuse
38	hearts go out to	To feel sympathy for someone when they are distressed
39	Toffee-nosed	A person who thinks he is of a high social class and looks down on people of lower class
40	is in high spirits	Cheerful
41	Bear up	to be strong enough to continue at a difficult time
42	a black sheep	Disgrace for the family
43	the calm before the storm	a period of quiet that comes before a time of activity, excitement, violence, etc.
44	Burning your bridges	doing something that makes it impossible to return to the previous situation later
45	Wild goose chase	Futile search
46	Have an Axe to Grind	To have one's own interests to serve
47	Up in the air	Something that is unknown entirely
48	By hook or by crook	Using whatever methods are necessary
49	Once in a blue moon	Rarely
50	Hand and glove	Very intimate terms
51	Point blank	close enough to hit the centre of the target
52	bear garden	A place of noise and disturbance
53	Get on like a house on fire	Get on extremely well with someone
54	Against the clock	In a great hurry, as fast as possible
55	Get a second wind	To have renewed energy
56	To smell a rat	to recognize that something is not as it appears to be
57	So far so good	Things are going well so far
58	Hang in there	To persist in a difficult situation
59	Left, right and centre	Happening in a lot of places or to a lot of people
60	Spill the beans	Reveal a secret
61	Nine times out of ten	In most cases
62	To beat a retreat	To leave a situation
63	fair-weather friends	A person not reliable in difficult time
64	To throw caution to the wind	To do something without worrying about the risk
65	Be hard hit	Severely affected by something unpleasant
66	A black sheep	disgrace to his family
67	sit on the fence	A person's lack of decisiveness, neutrality or hesitance to choose between two sides in an argument or a competition
68	In a nutshell	Briefly
69	Go round in circles	Make no progress in an argument or discussion
70	a flying visit	a very short visit
71	In seventh heaven	Extremely happy
72	As good as gold	A person who is obedient and well-behaved

73	To judge a book by its cover	To evaluate people's worth by their outward appearance
74	Hold your horses	To tell someone to stop and consider carefully
75	Wet blanket	One who spoils other people's fun
76	the carrot and stick	Mixture of rewards and punishments
77	At the eleventh hour	Just before the deadline
78	the devil is beating his wife	The sun is shining while it rains

SSC CPO Paper 2 2020 [IDIOMS/ PHRASES]

SN	Idioms/Phrases	Meaning
1	Fair-weather friend	A person whose friendship cannot be relied on in difficult times
2	Full of beans	Happy and energetic
3	To take pains	To make efforts
4	Fifth wheel	An unneeded person
5	Make head or tail of something	To figure out something
6	Fight tooth and nail	Fight very fiercely
7	Hue and cry	A noisy expression of anger
8	A hard nut to crack	A difficult person
9	Hold your horses	Be patient
10	Give and take	Obliging each other mutually

SSC GD Constable 2021 [IDIOMS/ PHRASES]

SN	Idioms/Pharases	Meaning
1	To know what's what	To know the facts of a situation
2	To rub salt in someone's wound	To make a bad or painful situation worse
3	Flea market	A place where antiques and second-hand goods are sold
4	through thick and thin	in both, good times and bad times
5	moved heaven and earth	did everything possible
6	Out of the blue	Unexpectedly
7	Full steam ahead	Move onward with determination
8	cut down on	reduce
9	Loaded words	Words that carry more significance than their literal meaning
10	Pain in the neck	Someone or something that is annoying or a nuisance
11	Crack up	Laugh out loud
12	the lion's share	the largest part
13	Think on your feet	Adjust quickly to changes and make fast decisions
14	Go through the roof	Rise very high
15	To beat the clock	To perform a task within the time limit
16	As thick as two short planks	Extremely stupid
17	Take up room	Occupy space

18	Draw first blood	Be the first to gain an advantage or score against an opponent
19	Get out of hand	Lose control
20	To get wind of	To learn something secret
21	Hit the sack	Go to bed
22	give up	stop doing it
23	To spill the beans	To give away a secret
24	To take up the gauntlet	To accept a challenge
25	A cold fish	An unemotional person
26	Vanish into thin air	Disappear completely
27	Maiden speech	First speech
28	A dime a dozen	Something very common or of little value
29	To be on the same page	To agree on something
30	Tickled pink	Very pleased
31	Cool as a cucumber	Calm
32	Come to blows	Get into a fight physically
33	Play for time	To make excuses or do things to gain time
34	To breathe one's last	To die
35	Drop names	Name famous people to impress others
36	To beat around the bush	To avoid the main issue
37	To break new ground	To innovate or pioneer
38	To break into tears	To cry suddenly
39	To get out of hand	To become uncontrollable
40	Down in the dumps	In a depressed state of mind
41	Blow a fuse	To react very angrily
42	The apple of one's eye	A person who is very dear
43	All and sundry	Everyone
44	Hold your horses	Be patient
45	To break loose	To escape
46	Big bucks	A lot of money
47	A can of worms	A complicated situation or problem
48	Over and over again	Do something repeatedly
49	Worked like a dream	A plan succeeded perfectly
50	Mark up	Increase the price
51	On cloud nine	Very happy
52	In the long run	Eventually
53	Chicken hearted	Easily scared
54	Wee hours of the day	Dawn
55	Not breathe a word	To remain silent about some secret
56	To give up the ghost	To stop working
57	To pull a fast one on someone	To cheat someone
58	To kick the bucket	To die
59	Pass the baton	shift responsibility to others
60	Keep in touch	Maintain contact
61	Wear and tear	Damage caused by use

62	To aim for the stars	To set high goals
63	To do the dishes	To wash and dry dishes
64	Spick and span	Very neat and clean
65	At a snail's pace	Very slowly
66	Hand in hand	Together
67	Toe the line	Follow the rules
68	Elephant in the room	An obvious issue left unaddressed due to its sensitivity
69	Hands down	Easily and without doubt
70	To take pains	To make efforts
71	Child's play	Something that is very easy
72	Gift of the gab	Ability to speak confidently and clearly
73	Blue blood	Noble birth
74	Having a soft spot for	Being fond of
75	To be on pins and needles	To be in an agitated state of suspense
76	At the eleventh hour	At the very last minute
77	To put something on hold	To postpone something
78	Monkey business	Behaviour that is not acceptable or is dishonest
79	In the long run	Ultimately
80	Feel at sea	To feel lost or confused
81	In the same boat	In a similar situation
82	Down in the mouth	To be depressed
83	To take the bull by the horns	To deal with difficult situations courageously
84	In a fix	In a difficult situation
85	Open-ended	Having no planned ending
86	Ins and outs	Complete facts
87	See the light of day	Become publicly known
88	From far and wide	From all directions
89	Alive and kicking	Healthy and doing well
90	a blessing in disguise	event that seemed bad at first but resulted in something good later
91	To lose one's head	To become upset or angry
92	To take stock of	To think carefully
93	To get out of hand	To get out of control
94	Bite someone's head off	Speak angrily without any reason
95	Once in a blue moon	Taking place very rarely
96	A dog's life	A miserable life
97	To catch someone's fancy	To appeal to someone
98	Storm in a teacup	Anger or fuss about something trivial
99	To let someone off	To punish someone lightly
100	To blow one's own horn	To praise oneself
101	To go round in circles	To waste one's time and energy doing trivial things
102	Raining cats and dogs	Raining heavily
103	Between Scylla and Charybdis	Choice between two unpleasant alternatives

104	A fine state of affairs	An unpleasant situation
105	For good	Forever
106	Having the gift of the gab	Talks well and persuasively
107	On the cards	Likely to happen
108	spick and span	neat and tidy
109	Come of age	Reach maturity
110	To be off the hook	To escape a difficult situation
111	Odd man out	Person who doesn't fit into a group
112	Out of the blue	Completely unexpectedly
113	Hang up one's boots	Retire from a sport
114	Drag one's feet	Do something deliberately at a slow pace
115	Game is up	Deception is at an end
116	Dig up dirt on someone	Discover damaging information about someone
117	To land a job	To be hired
118	Once and for all	Finally
119	Under the weather	Slightly ill
120	To have a yen for	To have a very strong and continuous desire or craving for something
121	Go with the flow	Do what others are doing
122	Out of question	Impossible
123	make head or tail of	understand
124	To bear fruit	To produce positive results
125	Eagle eye	An eye with sharp visual powers
126	To lag behind	To fail to maintain the pace or progress
127	Lap up	Accept eagerly

SSC Stenographer 2022 [IDIOMS/ PHRASES]

SN	Idioms / Phrases	Meaning
1	To be in the driving seat	To be in charge or control of a situation
2	Hit the sack	Go to sleep
3	to turn over a new leaf	To start behaving in a better way
4	Hit the nail on the head	Do something exactly right
5	Separate the wheat from the chaff	To separate the valuable from the worthless
6	burnt his fingers	got into trouble
7	To win laurels	To achieve honours and glory
8	Break a leg	Good luck
9	Stir up a hornet's nest	To raise controversy
10	argus-eyed	Vigilant
11	chew the fat	Gossip and make small talk
12	Two peas in a pod	Look very similar in appearance or character
13	Break the ice	To begin a conversation to relieve the tension in an uncomfortable situation
14	To keep a good table	To offer sumptuous food to one's guests

15	apple of her mother's eye	A person of whom her mother is extremely fond and proud
16	By the skin of your teeth	To just barely get by or make it
17	Bite the bullet	To get something over with because it is inevitable
18	Blow hot and cold	Vacillating
19	By leaps and bounds	Rapidly
20	At the eleventh hour	At the last moment
21	got into hot water	Landed in trouble
22	Take away your breath	Astonishing
23	bore the palm	Won
24	Break fresh/new ground	To do something that was not done before
25	charley horse	Cramp
26	Chicken hearted	Someone who lacks courage and is easily frightened
27	Go through fire and water	To pass through all types of hardships

SSC JHT Paper I 2022 [IDIOMS/ PHRASES]

SN	Idioms / Phrases	Meaning
1	Stand your ground	refuse to change your opinion
2	go through a rough patch	to experience problems
3	Pick a quarrel	to start a disagreement or argument
4	with a fine tooth comb	to examine in great detail
5	A bird in hand is worth two in the bush	Having something for certain is better than the possibility of getting something better.
6	wear someone out	to exhaust someone

SSC Selection Post 2022 - 10th Level [IDIOMS/ PHRASES]

SN	Idioms / Phrases	Meaning
1	Hang in there	Don't give up
2	Go the extra mile	To make an extra effort
3	Hard cash	Notes and coins as opposed to cheques and ATM cards
4	Out of spirits	Gloomy or sad
5	break new ground	To do something innovative
6	Sit tight	Wait patiently
7	Hit the sack	Go to sleep
8	Fish out of water	To be out of your comfort zone
9	Better late than never	It is better to reach late than never arrive
10	Gift of the gab	A talent of speaking well
11	Get your own way	Persuade other people to let you do what you want
12	Bid fair	To seem likely
13	A bone of contention	A dispute
14	Stand in one's own light	To act against one's own interest
15	Throw cold water	To discourage by showing indifference
16	A dead loss	Completely useless

| 17 | Pull yourself together | Calm down |
| 18 | Under the weather | Feeling sick |

SSC Selection Post 2022 – 12th Level [IDIOMS/ PHRASES]

1	of two minds	holding conflicting opinions
2	feeling a bit under the weather	To feel sick or unhealthy
3	taking a back seat	To become less important or to give up control over things
4	not playing with the full deck	either mentally, psychologically or intellectually deficient
5	letting sleeping dogs lie	Do not bring up an old controversial issue
6	set forth	explained
7	laughs like a drain	Laugh loudly
8	Clear the air	To deal openly with misunderstandings to get rid of them
9	came up	was raised
10	Nothing ventured, nothing gained	One has to make every effort in order to achieve something

SSC Selection Post 2022 – Grad. Level [IDIOMS/ PHRASES]

1	A blessing in disguise	A good thing that seemed bad at first
2	It's a piece of cake	It's easy
3	Speak of the devil	The person we were just talking about showed up
4	Loosen the purse strings	allow more money to be spent
5	Hit the roof	Explode in anger
6	Grease someone's palm	To bribe someone
7	Lend someone a hand	To help or assist, especially voluntarily
8	Went from rags to riches	started life very poor and then later in life became very rich
9	Felt the pinch	Face financial difficulties
10	Dragged his feet	Do something deliberately at a slow pace
11	Got it off his chest	Express something that has been worrying you, and you want to say
12	Pull someone's leg	To joke with someone

SSC Delhi Police Constable 2022 [IDIOMS/ PHRASES]

SN	Idioms / Phrases	Meaning
1	Backed up	Supported
2	Better late than never	Better to arrive late than not to come at all
3	Let sleeping dogs lie	Stop discussing an issue
4	Call it a day	Stop working on something
5	Has a face like thunder	is very angry
6	Hit the nail on the head	Get something exactly right
7	Add insult to injury	To make a bad situation worse
8	The elephant in the room	The problem people are avoiding
9	Gave up the ghost	finally stopped working.

10	A picture paints a thousand words	An image of a subject conveys its meaning more effectively than a description does.
11	Bread and butter	Means of livelihood
12	Back to the drawing board	plan it all over again
13	Hang in there	Don't give up
14	Spill the beans	To give away a secret
15	A blessing in disguise	A good thing that seemed bad at first
16	When it rains, it pours	Problems seem to happen together
17	Blaze the trail	To start a movement
18	Hold out an olive branch	do something to show that you want to end a disagreement with them
19	Play devil's advocate	To argue the opposite, just for the sake of argument
20	Facing the music	Facing the consequences
21	By and by	Gradually
22	Stabbed in the back	Betraying someone
23	Between Scylla and Charybdis	Choice between two unpleasant alternatives
24	Fool's paradise.	A state of imaginary happiness
25	Bite off more than you can chew	Take on a project that you cannot finish
26	Eat like a horse	Eats a lot of food
27	A cog in the machine	Very small part of a big organisation.
28	ABC of something	Essential fact
29	Neck and crop	Totally and completely
30	in dire straits	In a very bad or difficult situation
31	burn the midnight oil	To work till very late in the night
32	Bosom Friend	Close friend
33	A mare's nest	A false invention
34	Jump on the bandwagon	Do what everyone else is doing
35	In a fool's paradise	Being happy for foolish reasons
36	The best of both worlds	An ideal situation
37	Milk and water	Weak ideas
38	Hold up one's head	Be proud
39	Take a dim view of	disapprove of
40	Pull someone's leg	To joke with someone
41	Plays a second fiddle	Position has lesser importance than anybody else's.
42	God's ape	Born fool
43	Crying over spilt milk	Feeling sorry over a mistake that cannot be changed
44	Feel the pinch	Face financial difficulties
45	Beauty is only skin deep	Physical appearance is no guide to a person's character
46	Took to his heels	To run away
47	Hornet's nest	Raising controversy
48	Give someone the cold shoulder	Ignore someone

SN	Idioms / Phrases	Meaning
	SSC IMD SA 2022 [IDIOMS/ PHRASES]	
1	a brown study	A state of reverie
2	To let the cat out of the bag	To reveal a secret
3	In a quandary	Confused
4	Raise the bar	Being better than before
5	Down in the mouth	Unhappy
6	Throw caution to the wind	Take a risk
7	Have at one's finger tips	Easily or conveniently accessed
8	Done up	Exhausted
9	Turn tail	To run away from difficulty
10	Jump on the bandwagon	Follow a trend
11	The ball is in your court	To refer to the person who is responsible for the next move
12	Sitting shotgun	Riding in the front passenger seat of a car
13	Between the devil and the deep blue sea	Between two equally unacceptable choices
14	under a cloud	In disgrace
15	A wet blanket	Someone who ruins other people's fun
16	Mumbo jumbo	Nonsense or meaningless speech
17	Rub a person up the wrong way	Annoy or offend a person
18	Kick the bucket	To die

PRACTICE SET 01 (Idioms)

1 After one's own heart

(a) Sharing or having one's tastes or views.

(b) Infatuation with a person which is not reciprocated.

(c) Memorise something by heart.

(d) Don't have the courage to do something bad for a good person.

2 Pull the wool over someone's eyes

(a) To protect someone.

(b) To keep oneself warm.

(c) Deceive someone by telling lies.

(d) To pretend to be blind to the other person's bad behaviour.

3 At somebody's expense

(a) Paid for by someone.

(b) To blame a crime on someone else.

(c) The unlucky persons who lose a race.

(d) If one person benefits it is always at the loss of another.

4 Cock and bull story

(a) An implausible story used as an explanation or excuse.

(b) A fairy tale told down generations.

(c) A story of animals with hidden morals.

(d) The meek can defeat the bully by being clever.

5 At large

(a) A very big opportunity.

(b) A criminal escaped or not yet captured.

(c) To have a big heart.

(d) A big appetite.

6 Head over heels

(a) To do things exactly opposite of what is expected.

(b) Madly in love.

(c) To do stupid things.

(d) To unknowingly dive into an unpleasant situation.

7 A walk of life

(a) An easy comfortable life not necessarily prosperous.

(b) The most important day of your life.

(c) A person's occupation or position within society.

(d) Walking is the best form of exercise.

8 Cut to the chase

(a) Come to the point.

(b) To run after somebody.

(c) To cut out the important bits of information.

(d) To take a short cut.

9 Be in force

(a) To enjoy a short period of fame or power.

(b) In great strength or numbers.

(c) A hateful act done in a haste.

(d) Be the current winner.

10 Make a scene

(a) To perform beautifully in front of an audience.

(b) Make a public disturbance or excited emotional display.

(c) To narrate an elaborate false story.

(d) Describe a scene in so much detail that it comes vivid.

Keys: 1-a, 2-c, 3-a, 4-a, 5-b, 6-b, 7-c, 8-a, 9-b, 10-b

PRACTICE SET 02 (Idioms)

1 Ask for trouble
(a) Act in a way that is likely to incur problems or difficulties.
(b) Be the self-appointed guardian of your neighbourhood.
(c) A clumsy person who keeps making mistakes.
(d) A person who has no work is bound to create trouble for others.

2 Drive someone up the wall
(a) To help someone achieve success.
(b) To overcome an obstacle by going over it.
(c) To close someone's path of escape.
(d) Make someone very irritated or angry.

3 At the top of your lungs
(a) Be a habitual smoker.
(b) Be breathless after an exhausting physical task.
(c) Feel suffocated in a very crowded place.
(d) Extremely loudly.

4 The wheels have come off
(a) To use something so much that it wears out.
(b) Things start to fail or go wrong, especially after a period of success.
(c) To do a shoddy job which is destined to fail.
(d) Make an excuse to avoid doing a task.

5 Be left stranded
(a) Unable to leave somewhere because of a problem.
(b) Suffer a bad hair day.
(c) Having only a single thing to hold on to save yourself.
(d) To be the last person on whom the blame falls on eventually.

6 All thumbs
(a) Permission from the concerned people to go ahead.
(b) A crowd cheering their favourite team.
(c) Physically awkward, especially with respect to the hands.
(d) An illiterate person who cannot sign his name.

7 A wet blanket
(a) A safety net of precaution from fires.
(b) A person who discourages enjoyment or enthusiasm.
(c) An extremely uncomfortable place to sleep.
(d) A trick to shoo away unwelcome guests.

8 A thorn in the flesh
(a) To fight despite being injured.
(b) A minor discomfort which is easily ignored.
(c) A source of continual annoyance or trouble.
(d) A person within close family whom you secretly hate.

9 A ray of hope
(a) Even in a very bad situation one should try to see a good thing.
(b) Good days are sure to follow difficult ones.
(c) Be very happy even if the reason is very small.
(d) Something that provides a small amount of optimism in a difficult situation.

10 Mind your language
(a) To put a lot of efforts to understand what the other person is trying to say.
(b) To speak first and think later.
(c) Tell someone to speak politely.
(d) To speak grammatically incorrect language.

Keys: 1-a, 2-d, 3-d, 4-b, 5-a, 6-c, 7-b, 8-c, 9-d, 10-c

PRACTICE SET 03 (Idioms)

1 Be in two minds
(a) Behave smart at some time and stupid at other.
(b) Unable to decide.
(c) Having a split personality disorder.
(d) Trying to do two things at the same time.

2 Wet behind the ears
(a) To take a bath.
(b) Lacking experience or be immature.
(c) To speak bad behind other's back.
(d) Not able to eavesdrop despite trying hard.

3 A bone of contention
(a) The only part to which two arguing parties agree.
(b) An issue over which there is continuing disagreement.
(c) A very expensive inherited property.
(d) To be happy with only a few things.

4 Zip your lip
(a) Keep quiet about something.
(b) To talk fast.
(c) To not think before speaking.
(d) The silence before a storm.

5 At short notice
(a) With little warning or time for preparation.
(b) To ignore something important at your own peril.
(c) To notice a small leak which can sink a ship.
(d) Inform somebody that they are fired from a job.

6 Alphabet soup
(a) A beautiful poem.
(b) A text which nourishes your soul.
(c) A book that is close to your heart.
(d) A confusing or confused mixture of things.

7 Be on the air
(a) Broadcast over the radio or on TV.
(b) Float like a bird.
(c) To pass bodily gases.
(d) Be very arrogant.

8 A diamond in the rough
(a) Someone or something with potential or talent but lacking training or polish:
(b) A person who dresses shabbily
(c) A diamond will shine out even when it is not polished.
(d) A person of character will shine through even in tough times.

9 Be worlds apart
(a) Travel a very long distance.
(b) To go from heaven to hell.
(c) Be very different.
(d) To sustain affection despite living very far away.

10 Silver bullet
(a) A very expensive solution used only as the last measure.
(b) A simple and seemingly magical solution to a complicated problem.
(c) A solution which is worse than the problem.
(d) A thing of beauty but which is actually deadly.

Keys: 1-b, 2-b, 3-b, 4-a, 5-a, 6-d, 7-a, 8-a, 9-c, 10-b

PRACTICE SET 04 (Idioms)

1 Come true

(a) Pray hard for your wishes.

(b) To happen in the way you had hoped.

(c) Day dream about success.

(d) Be finally proved that you were right.

2 Catch red-handed

(a) Apprehend someone in the course of wrongdoing.

(b) Successfully accomplish a difficult physical task.

(c) Catch someone with colour on his hands.

(d) Be warned of imminent danger.

3 Great minds think alike

(a) When an evil plan is hatched criminals agree.

(b) Said to those people who don't like each other to make them agree.

(c) Said when two people have the same opinion or make the same choice.

(d) Intelligent people will think of plans to which everybody will say yes.

4 A sea change

(a) A profound or notable transformation.

(b) An upcoming storm.

(c) Someone who appears turbulent on the outside but is actually calm deep inside.

(d) As you go deeper into the situation you will see a very different picture.

5 By courtesy of

(a) Be very polite.

(b) Do a philanthropic act forcefully.

(c) Be brave and face risks for the team.

(d) Given or allowed by.

6 In the same boat

(a) When the option that you have is equally bad as the situation you are in.

(b) Life like the river throws the same challenges for all boats.

(c) Be in the same difficult circumstances as others.

(d) Big and small boats suffer the same fate in a storm.

7 Chew something over

(a) Discuss or consider something at length.

(b) Grab what belongs to someone else.

(c) Take a large bite, more than you can eat.

(d) Talk while eating.

8 On a wing and a prayer

(a) A prayer can move mountains.

(b) A prayer has the strength to make you achieve great heights just like wings do.

(c) The more one gets into prayer the closer one feels to God.

(d) With only the slightest chance of success.

9 A drop in the ocean

(a) Even a small gesture means a lot to a needy person.

(b) To lose someone in a huge crowd.

(c) A scolding which has no effect on a stubborn person.

(d) A very small amount compared with what is needed or expected.

10 Count one's blessings

(a) To be blessed with the best things in life.

(b) Be grateful for what one has.

(c) Keep a track of your wealth or else you may lose it.

(d) Something which you thought lucky turns out to be bad luck.

Keys: 1-b, 2-a, 3-c, 4-a, 5-d, 6-c, 7-a, 8-d, 9-d, 10-b

PRACTICE SET 05 (Idioms)

1 Be in the air

(a) Harmful gaseous effluents from a factory.

(b) To fly like a bird or a plane.

(c) When an emotion or idea is on everyone's mind.

(d) To be confused.

2 Children should be seen and not heard

(a) The voice of children is often drowned in company of adults.

(b) Some children will seek attention by crying.

(c) Children should not speak in the presence of adults.

(d) Those children are likable who dress neatly.

3 Ease somebody's mind

(a) Alleviate someone's anxiety.

(b) Listen to somebody's grievances.

(c) Have the capacity to understand the other person's thoughts.

(d) Keep thinking about some person.

4 An axe to grind

(a) One cannot cut wood with a blunt axe.

(b) To have important jobs to do.

(c) Have an ulterior motive.

(d) A weapon is useful only when it is sharp.

5 At the eleventh hour

(a) At the last moment

(b) Very late at night.

(c) At a very odd time.

(d) Luckily have sufficient time to wrap up things.

6 The nitty-gritty

(a) The low level dirty job which is left to the lowermost subordinates.

(b) Those with grit and determination will not be defeated.

(c) The most important aspects or practical details of a subject or situation.

(d) Some people are born tough.

7 To quit on someone

(a) To fire someone from a job.

(b) To cheat with someone.

(c) To give up on a difficult person.

(d) To stop helping someone, especially when the support is needed.

8 Excuse my French

(a) Used to apologize for swearing.

(b) Said when one cannot speak the language of the other person correctly.

(c) Used to make a flimsy excuse.

(d) Used when you give up easily.

9 Chicken out

(a) Quickly move from one position to another in a game of chess or war.

(b) Be a lover of non-vegetarian delicacies.

(c) Be easily confused over small issues.

(d) To decide not to do something because you are too frightened.

10 A bad hair day

(a) A day which has a bad start will eventually become better.

(b) A day on which everything seems to go wrong.

(c) Don't worry over hair loss or else you will lose more.

(d) A day when you forget to comb your hair.

Keys: 1-c, 2-c, 3-a, 4-c, 5-a, 6-c, 7-d, 8-a, 9-d, 10-b

PRACTICE SET 06 (Idioms)

1 A penny for your thoughts

(a) A way of asking what someone is thinking.

(b) Another way of saying pennywise pound foolish.

(c) An idea is less worth a penny unless it is executed successfully.

(d) Willing to share a secret only at a price.

2 All in a day's work

(a) Even In routine work one can find Instances of fun.

(b) Something unusual or difficult accepted as part of someone's normal routine.

(c) A lot of work which is done in just one day.

(d) Work all day on a job that you love.

3 Blessing in disguise

(a) Good fortune always follows bad; that is the way of fate.

(b) An apparent misfortune that eventually has good results.

(c) If a curse makes one stronger than it is a blessing.

(d) A life of hardship does wonders for a person's character.

4 A picture paints a thousand words

(a) An image of a subject conveys its meaning more effectively than a description does.

(b) No words can do justice to a masterpiece.

(c) A great poem or script recreates a complete imagery.

(d) Your mind will create fanciful images based on the information that it gets.

5 To bid defiance

(a) To disregard recklessly

(b) To apologize

(c) To act in a like manner

(d) To bribe

6 A fool's paradise

(a) An average person appears smart in company of fools.

(b) A state of happiness based on a person's not knowing about potential trouble.

(c) A paradise is ruined when fools enter it.

(d) Pretending that everything is going fine when actually all is being lost.

7 Get on somebody's nerves

(a) To calm an anxious person.

(b) To be an irritant.

(c) Be angry with yourself but take out the anger on somebody else.

(d) To crack jokes at somebody's expense.

8 Eyebrow raising

(a) Pretend to like something or someone even when you dislike.

(b) Look up in defiance as a show of rebellion.

(c) A person finally getting due punishment.

(d) Something which surprises, shocks, or offends people.

9 Be glad to see the back of

(a) Be always welcome whenever you go back.

(b) Talk bad about somebody you hate behind t heir back.

(c) Be happy when a person leaves.

(d) Feel happy that you backed off from a fruitless plan.

10 With bated breath

(a) In dispute

(b) In anxiety

(c) In full detail

(d) In happy mood

Keys: 1-a, 2-b, 3-b, 4-a, 5-a, 6-b, 7-b, 8-d, 9-c, 10-b

PRACTICE SET 07 (Idioms)

1 Add insult to injury

(a) To further a loss with mockery to worsen an unfavourable situation.

(b) A disgrace becomes worse when friends and family disown you.

(c) The world usually slanders a fallen person rather than help him.

(d) A suffering is compounded if you are hurt at the same place again.

2 Tie the knot

(a) Get into a fight.

(b) Get angry.

(c) Get more complicated.

(d) Get married.

3 Easier said than done

(a) A task which is expected to be difficult turns out to be easy.

(b) Intentionally tell some one that a difficult task is easy.

(c) Be more easily talked about than put into practice.

(d) Once a difficult task is done it feels easy.

4 A red rag to a bull

(a) A few inspirational words can do wonderful things.

(b) An object, utterance, or act which is certain to provoke someone.

(c) A signal or symbol used to warn a person.

(d) All prepared and waiting for the signal to s tart.

5 Be under no illusions

(a) Not be duped by a cheater.

(b) Get out of a magic spell.

(c) Don't have the habit of daydreaming.

(d) Be fully aware of the true state of affairs.

6 Level playing field

(a) A game played where the weaker side is given an advantage to make it a fair fight.

(b) A situation in which everyone has a fair and equal chance of succeeding.

(c) A game where you progress level by level.

(d) A game which appears unfair but is actually fair.

7 To gird up the loins

(a) To be unable to decide

(b) To one's liking

(c) To be at strife

(d) To prepare for hard work

8 Evil twin

(a) Getting punished for the deeds of another person who is just like you.

(b) An imaginary double humorously invoked to explain or excuse uncharacteristic or reprehensible behaviour.

(c) When two people are alike then one will be good and the other evil.

(d) To show behaviour which randomly switches between good and evil.

9 Be in the red

(a) Be the top performer.

(b) To be in a loss or debt.

(c) Be in the list of people who are never invited.

(d) Be in the bad books of a person.

10 In cahoots with

(a) A marriage made in heaven.

(b) A group of criminals.

(c) With lot of determination.

(d) In an alliance or partnership with.

Keys: 1-a, 2-d, 3-c, 4-b, 5-d, 6-b, 7-d, 8-b, 9-b, 10-d

PRACTICE SET 08 (Idioms)

1 Choose a soft option

(a) Choose a comfortable place to spend the night.

(b) Target the weaker players to win the match.

(c) Do the thing that is easiest or least likely to cause trouble in a particular situation.

(d) Always choose comfort over hardship.

2 Achilles' heel

(a) A weakness which turns out to be a strength.

(b) A weakness or vulnerable point.

(c) A strength which eventually becomes your weakness.

(d) The point where you have converted your weakness in to your strength.

3 Come what may

(a) Welcome all visitors with open arms.

(b) No matter what happens.

(c) Insure all your property from all kinds of losses.

(d) Willing to become whatever fate has in store for your future.

4 Back seat driver

(a) A passenger who gives unwanted and/or unneeded directions to the driver.

(b) A person who gives unwanted advice is sometimes right.

(c) When too many people are controlling a project it is bound to fail.

(d) A person who acts as a remote control taking orders from others.

5 A bad patch

(a) A potholed road.

(b) A medical bandage.

(c) A period of difficulty.

(d) Shoddy repair work.

6 A dime a dozen

(a) A very expensive proposition.

(b) Something which appears cheap but which will prove expensive in the long run.

(c) Something which appears attractive but has zero value.

(d) Very common and of no particular value.

7 Burn the midnight oil

(a) To live a life of hardship.

(b) To waste away resources that could have helped in difficult times.

(c) Procrastinate and then work at the last minute to finish the task.

(d) Read or work late into the night.

8 Throw the towel in

(a) To challenge someone.

(b) To offer a signal of peace.

(c) To quit in defeat.

(d) To stop a bad situation from getting worse.

9 Can't judge a book by its cover

(a) If you love something dearly then you have to protect it.

(b) You shouldn't prejudge the value of something, by its outward appearance alone.

(c) To make a false opinion without even seeing that person is prejudice.

(d) A bad book needs a good cover to make it saleable.

10 Draconian law

(a) Written law

(b) Extremely severe law

(c) Oral law

(d) Lenient law

Keys: 1-c, 2-b, 3-b, 4-a, 5-c, 6-d, 7-d, 8-c, 9-b, 10-b

PRACTICE SET 09 (Idioms)

1 No dice
(a) A great gamble.
(b) Used to refuse a request or indicate that there is no chance of success.
(c) Be confident of the outcome.
(d) Make false assurances.

2 Keep at bay
(a) Keep y our loved ones protected even when they are faced with problems.
(b) To control something and prevent it from causing you problems.
(c) Hide your precious stuff.
(d) Be alert at all times.

3 Ring fencing
(a) The place where the sport of fencing is played by two opponents.
(b) Doubly protecting your assets.
(c) Guarantee that funds allocated for a particular purpose will not be spent on anything else.
(d) Be ready to fight for what is your right.

4 Keep your chin up
(a) Behave arrogantly in front of elders.
(b) Keep your self respect at all times.
(c) Remain cheerful in difficult circumstances.
(d) Pretend to be good when you have an evil plan.

5 Don't put all your eggs in one basket
(a) It is wise to have many baskets before you start collecting eggs.
(b) The strength of the safe has to be in proportion to the value of goods it has to protect.
(c) Have a fool proof plan before venturing on a risky mission.
(d) Don't risk everything on the success of one venture.

6 Let your hair down
(a) Behave uninhibitedly.
(b) Accept your deeds.
(c) Remove the mask.
(d) Feel fresh and rejuvenated.

7 Argus eyed
(a) A pretence
(b) Flatterer
(c) Short tempered
(d) Observant

8 Off the hook
(a) Everything prepared and kept ready for you.
(b) Accept something without checking its veracity.
(c) Put a person who is helping you into a difficult situation.
(d) No longer in difficulty or trouble.

9 As fit as a fiddle
(a) Very aggressive
(b) Strong and healthy
(c) Selfish friend
(d) Uncomfortable

10 New kid on the block
(a) A person who is acting smart to impress others.
(b) Be inexperienced in company of veterans.
(c) To block the path of success of outsiders.
(d) Newcomer to a particular place or sphere of activity.

Keys: 1-b, 2-b, 3-c, 4-c, 5-d, 6-a, 7-d, 8-d, 9-b, 10-d

PRACTICE SET 10 (Idioms)

1 Come in handy
(a) Be that type of a person who loves to work with his hands.
(b) Turn out to be useful.
(c) Always be ready to help strangers in need.
(d) Be always prepared for any kind of hardship.

2 Let bygones be bygones
(a) Even b ad memories become memorable.
(b) The past will return to haunt you unless you completely forget.
(c) Forget past offences or causes of conflict and be reconciled.
(d) Your past deeds will never leave you.

3 Heave a sigh of relief
(a) To suddenly feel very happy because something unpleasant has not happened or has ended.
(b) Be exhausted after a gruelling physical task.
(c) Get trapped in a tricky situation which you could have escaped easily.
(d) Feel sad that the good times have ended.

4 A lot on your plate
(a) A greedy person will collect more food than he can eat.
(b) A hungry person will devour if presented with food.
(c) To have a large number of problems to deal with.
(d) To be an expert in multi-tasking.

5 Come to terms with something
(a) To become friends with your opponents.
(b) Accept that you are a loser even though you have potential.
(c) Become unnecessarily depressed.
(d) To gradually accept a sad situation.

6 Under the weather
(a) Become a bit unpredictable like the weather.
(b) Slightly unwell or in low spirits.
(c) Feel optimistic simply because the weather is good.
(d) Feel depressed because you expect bad weather.

7 Be out of order
(a) Some goods which are out of stock.
(b) Do something against the court's ruling.
(c) A device not working properly or at all.
(d) Things kept in an organized manner.

8 A sight for sore eyes
(a) An ugly sight unpleasant to the eyes.
(b) When one becomes tired of watching too much TV or reading.
(c) A person or thing that one is extremely pleased or relieved to see.
(d) A beautiful sight that you can visualise even with closed eyes.

9 A cold fish
(a) Someone who seems unfriendly and who does not share his feelings.
(b) Something valuable preserved for a long time.
(c) A fish which can survive in freezing water.
(d) A lost business opportunity.

10 Bend over backwards
(a) Use unfair means to succeed.
(b) Make every effort to achieve something, especially to be fair or helpful.
(c) Lose self respect to please others.
(d) To step back from an unpleasant situation.

Keys: 1-b, 2-c, 3-a, 4-c, 5-d, 6-b, 7-c, 8-c, 9-a, 10-b

PRACTICE SET 11 (Idioms)

1 to hit the sack

(a) to prepare for sleep

(b) to die

(c) to take one's anger out

(d) to hit where it hurts the most

2 Hocus pocus

(a) walking in a zig-zag manner, especially under the influence of alcohol

(b) meaningless talk or activity, typically designed to trick someone

(c) rich people but who are shallow and greedy

(d) doing a job haphazardly

3 Fire the imagination

(a) Do something unbelievable.

(b) To destroy a person's dream s or ambition by giving discouraging advice.

(c) To make someone feel very interested in something and excited about it.

(d) Advice someone to be more practical in an effort to tackle a problem.

4 Pulling your leg

(a) To create trouble for others.

(b) To succeed by making others fail.

(c) To beg for a favour.

(d) To trick or lie to someone in a playful way.

5 Cut corners

(a) Remove the sharp edges now if you don't want to get hurt later.

(b) One has to sacrifice to achieve one's goals.

(c) Even a coward when cornered musters strength to fight back.

(d) Do something perfunctorily so as to save time or money.

6 Never-never land

(a) An imaginary utopian place or situation.

(b) A place that is worse than hell.

(c) A place that you know that you will never be able to visit.

(d) A place about which you have heard such stories that you would not like to go.

7 Every dog has his day

(a) The weakest will become the strongest, that is the cycle of life.

(b) Everyone will have good luck at some point in their lives.

(c) Loyalty will not go unrewarded.

(d) Every person has a talent, and one will discover it one day.

8 I can't think straight

(a) Faced with a dilemma.

(b) Accept that the puzzle is too difficult for you.

(c) Cannot think rationally due to being overwhelmed with emotion.

(d) Ask for advice on a difficult problem.

9 Kitty-corner

(a) Favourite place of cats.

(b) A place where ladies meet to party.

(c) A very small place.

(d) Things located diagonally opposite each other.

10 The tail is wagging the dog

(a) A situation where a small good thing makes everyone happy.

(b) The less important or subsidiary factor, person, or thing dominates a situation.

(c) A person who is always happy to meet you.

(d) Even smaller tasks become important if the whole project is to succeed.

Keys: 1-a, 2-b, 3-c, 4-d, 5-d, 6-a, 7-b, 8-c, 9-d, 10-b

PRACTICE SET 12 (Idioms)

1 Stab someone in the back
   (a) Praise someone.
   (b) Like someone secretly.
   (c) Betray someone.
   (d) Meet someone after a long time.

2 Shoot through
   (a) Pass with flying colours.
   (b) Practice a difficult task so many times that you can do it easily.
   (c) Reach your target by breaking through an obstacle.
   (d) Leave, typically to escape from or avoid someone or something.

3 It's not rocket science
   (a) A task so difficult that it has a slim chance of success.
   (b) Speak in jargon that is not understandable by laymen.
   (c) Used to say that you do not think that something is very difficult to do or to understand.
   (d) Refuse something that someone wants on a false pretext.

4 Pass the buck
   (a) Pass a person by awarding a few grace marks.
   (b) Borrow small amounts of money from your friends.
   (c) Offer help even without the other person asking for it.
   (d) Shift the responsibility for something to someone else.

5 Pull the plug
   (a) Behave greedily and take the most of the shared things for oneself.
   (b) Do something to stop the losses.
   (c) Prevent something from happening.
   (d) Play loud irritating music.

6 As high as a kite
   (a) Intoxicated with alcohol.
   (b) Feel light after meditation.
   (c) Feel jubilant after victory.
   (d) Behave arrogantly.

7 Cross that bridge when you come to it
   (a) A bridge is a path to a different world.
   (b) Deal with a problem when and if it arises.
   (c) It is always better to plan for an eventuality rather face it when you are unprepared.
   (d) If you are brave then you can overcome all hurdles.

8 A little bird told me
   (a) A secret which is known by everybody.
   (b) Used to indicate that the speaker knows something but chooses to keep the identity of their inform ant secret.
   (c) Have a strong network of spies from where you get reliable information from which you can profit.
   (d) A person unknowingly letting out a sec ret.

9 Rags to riches
   (a) It takes a lot of hard work to earn wealth.
   (b) To con someone and become rich by taking away their wealth.
   (c) Used to describe a person's rise from a state of extreme poverty to one of great wealth.
   (d) Earn wealth or reputation by unfair means.

10 Over my dead body
   (a) Used to emphasize that one completely opposes something.
   (b) Be dead sure of something.
   (c) Feel afraid of something or someone.
   (d) Feel unhealthy and very weak.

Keys: 1-c, 2-d, 3-c, 4-d, 5-c, 6-a, 7-b, 8-b, 9-c, 10-a

PRACTICE SET 13 (Idioms)

1 Tongue in cheek
 (a) In an ironic or insincere way.
 (b) Being practical.
 (c) Stop yourself from saying something hurtful.
 (d) Be gutsy and speak the unpleasant truth.

2 Pedal to the metal
 (a) Build something big by yourself.
 (b) Add more protection to an already strong shield.
 (c) To drive very fast.
 (d) Push a person to perform to its extreme.

3 Lend me your ear
 (a) To politely ask for someone's full attention.
 (b) Begging someone to listen to your grievances.
 (c) When nobody is willing to hear your side of the story.
 (d) Call someone for severe scolding.

4 Run out of steam
 (a) Lose impetus or enthusiasm.
 (b) To keep going even after losing all energy.
 (c) Have no more funds to proceed any further.
 (d) Build interest as you go along.

5 Last but not least
 (a) The class failure usually surprises everybody with success in real life.
 (b) The youngest child is the most mischievous.
 (c) The last task is the most difficult of a big project.
 (d) Last in order of mention or occurrence but not last in importance.

6 Go belly up
 (a) Go bankrupt.
 (b) Sleep after being very tired.
 (c) Eat food and rest.
 (d) Die unexpectedly.

7 A shot in the arm
 (a) Get hit by something.
 (b) Lose physical strength.
 (c) Lose motivation to do a task.
 (d) An encouraging stimulus.

8 Your number is up
 (a) When you win by betting on your lucky number
 (b) The time has come when someone is doomed to suffer a disaster.
 (c) Win a lottery or a lucky draw.
 (d) Be the chosen one from a large group.

9 When pigs fly
 (a) Day dreaming about fanciful things.
 (b) Talk nonsense when intoxicated.
 (c) Another way of saying that every dog has his day.
 (d) A way of saying that something will never happen.

10 Cost an arm and a leg
 (a) Very expensive.
 (b) Something which you can easily afford.
 (c) Buy something which is very critical to you.
 (d) It takes two very different people to make a workable pair.

Keys: 1-a, 2-c, 3-a, 4-a, 5-d, 6-a, 7-d, 8-b, 9-d, 10-a

PRACTICE SET 14 (Idioms)

1 Wine and dine
(a) Get drunk before dinner.
(b) A place where both alcohol and food is served.
(c) Live a hedonistic life.
(d) When somebody is treated to an expensive meal.

2 Cross your fingers
(a) Do nothing and hope that everything will fall in its place automatically.
(b) To express disapproval or dissatisfaction.
(c) Tell others that you will approve only on certain conditions.
(d) To hope that things will happen in the way that you want them to.

3 dance to someone's tune
(a) argue with others on petty matters
(b) delay in making a decision
(c) do what others want you to do
(d) be engaged in an energetic activity

4 leave no stone unturned
(a) leave the path halfway
(b) not make enough efforts
(c) turn everything upside down
(d) try everything possible

5 to air dirty linen in public
(a) to discuss private affairs in public
(b) to stand up and fight
(c) to continue to complain
(d) to hang out clothes in the open

6 throw in the towel
(a) drop something
(b) face the situation
(c) think of a solution
(d) admit defeat

7 tit for tat
(a) to reward people for the good done
(b) to do harm as done to you
(c) to make someone angry
(d) to take advantage of someone

8 bite your tongue
(a) talk for a long time
(b) be impossible to be understood
(c) get bruises in the mouth
(d) stop yourself from saying something

9 As clear as mud
(a) impossible to understand
(b) extremely dirty
(c) honest and legal
(d) completely suitable for someone

10 Spill the beans
(a) frighten someone
(b) make an excuse
(c) reveal a secret
(d) create difficulty

Keys: 1-d, 2-d, 3-c, 4-d, 5-a, 6-d, 7-b, 8-d, 9-a, 10-c

PRACTICE SET 15 (Idioms)

1 The crux of the matter

(a) the critical point

(b) the interesting thing

(c) the unknown point

(d) the lesser issue

2 Four corners of the earth

(a) from beginning to end

(b) from the very beginning

(c) from morning till night

(d) from all parts of the world

3 Hanging by a thread

(a) in a sorry or humble state

(b) be extremely weak

(c) unable to act as desired

(d) be in a dangerous situation

4 To shake off

(a) to denounce

(b) to get rid of

(c) to recollect

(d) to pass off

5 Going over one's head

(a) unable to take a decision

(b) beyond one's capacity to understand

(c) unable to function as one used to

(d) something one didn't expect

6 Mad as a hatter

(a) superstitious

(b) very upset

(c) eccentric

(d) old fashioned

7 feather your own nest

(a) make money unfairly

(b) win a competition

(c) be in a comfortable position

(d) disturb others in their work

8 Be an old hat

(a) be superstitious

(b) be outdated

(c) be crazy

(d) be foolish

9 GREEN THUMB

(a) to have talent in gardening

(b) to have talent in painting

(c) to be angry

(d) to be envious

10 HEAD IN THE CLOUDS

(a) to be very tall

(b) to feel giddy

(c) to be very lazy

(d) to daydream

Keys: 1-a, 2-d, 3-d, 4-b, 5-b, 6-c, 7-a, 8-b, 9-a, 10-d

PRACTICE SET 16 (Idioms)

1 To grease the palm

   (a) to give support

   (b) to bribe someone

   (c) to cheat someone

   (d) to give a massage

2 To bark up the wrong tree

   (a) to be wrong about the reason for something

   (b) to bury money under a tree and forget the place

   (c) to be mistaken about the name of a tree

   (d) to eat an unpalatable fruit by mistake

3 To take the bull by the horns

   (a) to face danger boldly

   (b) to escape unhurt

   (c) to act foolishly

   (d) to enjoy risky sports

4 Gift of the gab

   (a) receive a precious gift

   (b) achieve sudden greatness

   (c) have the ability to adapt

   (d) have the talent to speak well

5 Turn a deaf ear

   (a) to make someone deaf

   (b) to pay attention

   (c) to pay no heed

   (d) to listen carefully

6 Take to task

   (a) to assign work

   (b) to give an award

   (c) to praise

   (d) to rebuke

7 Have one's hands full

   (a) to be very rich

   (b) to be very clumsy

   (c) to be very busy

   (d) to be very generous

8 Face the music

   (a) face the enemy

   (b) enjoy the harmony

   (c) get appreciation

   (d) face the criticism

9 Pass the hat

   (a) to sell something

   (b) to collect money

   (c) to play a game

   (d) to avoid work

10 As the crow flies

   (a) to be uncertain

   (b) a long winding path

   (c) the shortest route

   (d) to be directionless

Keys: 1-b, 2-a, 3-a, 4-d, 5-c, 6-d, 7-c, 8-d, 9-b, 10-c

PRACTICE SET 17 (Idioms)

1 In a pickle

(a) in great pain

(b) in jubilation

(c) in trouble

(d) in deep sorrow

2 Red letter day

(a) a very special day

(b) a very hot day

(c) a frightful day

(d) a very cold day

3 Through thick and thin

(a) to be scared of small dangers

(b) passing through a thick forest

(c) support under all circumstances

(d) to be hard-hearted in times of loss

4 Rule the roost

(a) to make all the decisions

(b) to be prosperous but generous

(c) to frequently pick a quarrel

(d) to blindly follow others

5 at arm's length

(a) checking the length of fabric

(b) as close as one can touch

(c) avoiding too much closeness

(d) using one's arm to measure length

6 acid test

(a) a malicious way of taking revenge

(b) a test that shows how to harm someone

(c) proof that an attack has been made

(d) definitive proof of truth or falsehood

7 hand in glove

(a) doing work in the garden

(b) working together in the same office

(c) wearing gloves while working

(d) in partnership for something dishonest

8 dark horse

(a) someone who has a wheatish complexion

(b) someone who breeds race horses

(c) someone who unexpectedly succeeds

(d) someone who is fond of horse racing

9 late in the day

(a) too old to work

(b) too ripe to eat

(c) too dark to see anything

(d) too delayed to be of any use

10 draw a blank

(a) be unsuccessful

(b) be happy about something

(c) be unable to sketch

(d) be lucky in a game

Keys: 1-c, 2-a, 3-c, 4-a, 5-c, 6-d, 7-d, 8-c, 9-d, 10-a

PRACTICE SET 18 (Idioms)

1 bolt from the blue

  (a) winning after losing a game many times

  (b) something sudden that happens unexpectedly

  (c) someone who runs fast and wins a race

  (d) locking the doors to keep the rain out

2 left-handed compliment

  (a) praise that is given directly

  (b) insulting someone in front of others

  (c) insulting remark appearing as praise

  (d) making fun of someone to tease them

3 put your best foot forward

  (a) take care to dress well

  (b) walk very cautiously

  (c) try as hard as one can

  (d) check every step

4 at snail's pace

  (a) do something very carefully

  (b) be very persistent

  (c) do something very slowly

  (d) keep your moves secret

5 beat around the bush

  (a) hide behind a bush

  (b) make excuses

  (c) accept defeat

  (d) avoid the topic

6 a pain in the neck.

  (a) irritating

  (b) curious

  (c) argumentative

  (d) short tempered

7 make no headway

  (a) check if the head can pass through

  (b) unable to progress ahead

  (c) unable to overtake anyone

  (d) forced to fix a new goal

8 make short work of something

  (a) reduce the size

  (b) dispose of quickly

  (c) edit carefully

  (d) shorten some dress

9 in a nutshell

  (a) add nuts into something

  (b) put everything in a shell

  (c) packed very tightly

  (d) express very briefly

10 be an open book

  (a) one about whom it is easy to know everything

  (b) one who advises others to be frank and unsecretive

  (c) one who is fond of reading even when travelling

  (d) one who has written an examination without preparation

Keys: 1-b, 2-c, 3-c, 4-c, 5-d, 6-a, 7-b, 8-b, 9-d, 10-a

PRACTICE SET 19 (Idioms)

1 Man in the Street

(a) Man of talent

(b) A foolish man

(c) Simple man

(d) A dutiful person

2 Now and again

(a) Occasionally

(b) Always

(c) To be continued

(d) At present time or future

3 Yeoman service

(a) Service for short period

(b) Very costly service

(c) Useful help in need

(d) Work without preparation

4 Once and for all

(a) Bring to an end

(b) Remain alive

(c) Forever

(d) Something good for people

5 In the soup

(a) Avoiding responsibility

(b) Making progress

(c) In a difficult situation

(d) Giving a chance

6 In the nick of time

(a) In search of something

(b) Just in time

(c) In a hurry

(d) After a long period of time

7 At any cost

(a) Personally

(b) In a miserable situation

(c) Secretly

(d) Under any circumstances

8 An iron-will

(a) A firm opinion

(b) No longer in use

(c) By all means

(d) To make sacrifice

9 At the eleventh hour.

(a) The initial moment

(b) At the last possible moment

(c) At its usual time

(d) At the earliest possible time

10 A red letter day.

(a) A day when one feels lazy

(b) A day that is pleasantly noteworthy or memorable

(c) A sorrowful day

(d) Most dangerous day of one's life

Keys: 1-c, 2-a, 3-c, 4-a, 5-c, 6-b, 7-d, 8-a, 9-b, 10-b

PRACTICE SET 20 (Idioms)

1 A hair's breadth

(a) Telling about the smallest possible amount or degree of something

(b) Irresponsible pleasure sealing in an old age

(c) Praising someone's abilities and achievements

(d) Looking for something which is not clearly visible

2 In a flutter

(a) Effective

(b) Almost nothing

(c) In a nervous state

(d) Certain

3 Hornet's nest

(a) A troublesome situation

(b) To try utmost

(c) To ascertain

(d) To make peace

4 In the teeth of

(a) In fashion

(b) Inspite of something

(c) In brief

(d) Fail to keep position

5 come hell or high water

(a) No matter what

(b) Feeling ill

(c) Possible obstacles in one's path

(d) Something good and useful

6 All Greek to me

(a) Out of danger

(b) Incomprehensible

(c) Very dear

(d) Consulting seriously

7 Mealy mouthed

(a) Foolishly ideal

(b) Speaking harshly

(c) Unwilling to state something

(d) To speak something straightforwardly

8 No love lost

(a) Complimentary

(b) A seer's last creation

(c) Self satisfied

(d) Intense dislike

9 Out of sorts

(a) To be equal to

(b) To be unwell

(c) To make peace

(d) To ignore

10 Pay lip service

(a) Candidly

(b) Pretend to regard

(c) Encouraging

(d) To defend

Keys: 1-a, 2-c, 3-a, 4-b, 5-a, 6-b, 7-c, 8-d, 9-b, 10-b

PART - C
(SYNONYMS / ANTONYMS)

Synonyms means words that have similar meaning and **Antonyms** are words that have opposite meaning.

C1 is a list of words that have been asked in Synonyms as well as Antonyms sections of SSC exams, they are very important and are clubbed together.

C2 and C6 contains all words that have been asked for Synonyms and Antonyms respectively. Common words that have been asked in Synonyms and Antonyms have been removed from this part and added into C1 part.

All the **"Synonyms and Antonyms"** provided in this chapter have been asked in SSC exams and compiled here for faster revision. *You should understand that sometimes options are not an exact match and students have to choose from the best available options out of the given 4 options in the question.*

SN	WORD (Hindi Meaning)	Synonym	Antonym (Hindi Meaning)	#R
1	Abundant (प्रचुर)	Plentiful	Meagre, Scarce, Insufficient (अल्प, दुर्लभ)	13
2	Candid (निष्कपट, स्पष्ट)	Frank, Honest, Forthright	Devious, Cunning, Artful, Deceitful, Blunt, Biased (कुटिल, चालाक, धूर्त, धोखेबाज)	11
3	Abandon (छोड़ देना)	Forsake, Desert	Retain, Support (बनाये रखना)	10
4	Barren (बांझ)	Unproductive, Infertile, Desolate	Fertile (उपजाऊ)	10
5	Diligent (परिश्रमी)	Industrious, Hardworking, Assiduous, Untiring	Lazy (आलसी)	10
6	Lucid (स्पष्ट अर्थ का)	Clear	Vague, Confusing (अस्पष्ट)	10
7	Meagre (अल्प)	Inadequate	Plentiful, Sufficient (प्रचुर, पर्याप्त)	10
8	Obscene (अश्लील)	Indecent	Decent, Clear, Distinct (सभ्य, स्पष्ट, विशिष्ट)	10
9	Perilous (संकटपूर्ण)	Hazardous, Dangerous	Safe (सुरक्षित)	10
10	Prudent (विवेकी)	Cautious, Wise, Frugal	Unwise, Careless, Indiscreet, Wasteful (अविवेकी)	10
11	Cordial (दोस्ताना)	Friendly, Amicable, Warm	Hostile (शत्रुतापूर्ण)	9
12	Erudite (विद्वान)	Scholarly, Learned	Unscholarly, Ignorant (अज्ञानी)	9
13	Genuine (वास्तविक)	Original, Authentic, Real	Fake, Spurious, Dubious (नकली, झूठा)	9
14	Insolent (असभ्य)	Disrespectful, Rude, Bold	Humble, Submissive, Mannerly, Courteous (विनम्र, सभ्य)	9
15	Mitigate (कम करना)	Lessen, Reduce	Enhance, Intensify, Increase (बढ़ाना, तीव्र करना)	9
16	Persuade (राज़ी करना)	Coax, Convince	Dissuade, Prevent, Halt (रोक लगाना)	9
17	Transparent (पारदर्शक)	Lucid, Clear	Opaque (अपारदर्शी)	9
18	Turbulent (अशांत)	Violent, Agitation	Placid, Calm, Peaceful (शांत, शांतिपूर्ण)	9
19	Awkward (बेढंगा)	Clumsy	Convenient, Graceful (सुविधाजनक, गरिमापूर्ण)	8
20	Dubious (संदिग्ध)	Doubtful, Fishy	Likely, Certain (निश्चित)	8
21	Eccentric (सनकी)	Queer, Peculiar, Bizarre	Customary, Normal (प्रथागत/साधारण)	8
22	Humble (विनम्र)	Meek	Arrogant (घमंडी)	8
23	Impeccable (त्रुटिहीन)	Perfect, Flawless, Faultless	Inexact, Imperfect, Flawed (अशुद्ध, त्रुटिपूर्ण, दोषपूर्ण)	8

SN	WORD (Hindi Meaning)	Synonym	Antonym (Hindi Meaning)	#R
24	Morose (उदास)	Gloomy, Sullen	Cheerful (हंसमुख)	8
25	Obstinate (जिद्दी)	Stubborn	Flexible, Docile (विनम्र)	8
26	Opulent (धनी)	Rich, Luxurious, Sumptuous	Poor (गरीब)	8
27	Tranquil (शांत)	Peaceful, Calm, Sober	Stormy, Disturbed, Violent (अशांत, हिंसक)	8
28	Vigilant (सतर्क)	Watchful	Rash, Numb, Careless, Inattentive (गूंगा, लापरवाह)	8
29	Affluent (धनी)	Prosperous, Wealthy	Poor (गरीब)	7
30	Apparent (स्पष्ट)	Obvious, Manifest	Ambiguous, Hidden (अस्पष्ट)	7
31	Coarse (खुरदुरा, अशोधित)	Rough, Crude	Smooth, Gentle, Refined (कोमल)	7
32	Colossal (विशाल)	Enormous, Gigantic	Small, Minimal, Tiny, Teeny (छोटा)	7
33	Commence (आरंभ करना)	Start, Launch, Initiate	Conclude, Close, Terminate (समाप्त करना)	7
34	Demolish (ध्वस्त करना)	Dismantle	Build, Establish, Construct (बनाना)	7
35	Emerge (प्रकट होना)	Appear	Vanish, Disappear (गायब)	7
36	Futile (व्यर्थ)	Useless	Worthy, Productive, Fruitful, Useful (योग्य, उपयोगी)	7
37	Gloomy (उदास)	Murky, Dull	Bright, Radiant (दीप्तिमान)	7
38	Harmony (तालमेल)	Consensus, Peace	Strife, Conflict (विवाद)	7
39	Illicit (अवैध)	Illegal, Unlawful	Lawful, Legal (वैध, कानूनी)	7
40	Judicious (विवेकपूर्ण)	Wise, Cautious, Prudent	Rash (अविवेकी)	7
41	Liberty (स्वतंत्रता)	Freedom	Dependence, Slavery, Bondage (गुलामी, बंधन)	7
42	Peculiar (अजीब)	Strange	Usual, Normal (सामान्य)	7
43	Rectify (सुधारना)	Correct, Amend	Falsify (असत्य बनाना)	7
44	Sacred (धार्मिक)	Holy	Profane (अपवित्र)	7
45	Timid (डरपोक)	Coward, Shy, Humble	Brave, Bold (बहादुर)	7
46	Absurd (बेतुका)	Ridiculous	Sensible, Reasonable (समझदार)	6
47	Adversity (विपत्ति)	Misfortune, Misery	Prosperity (समृद्धि)	6
48	Amateur (नौसिखिया)	Beginner	Professional (पेशेवर)	6
49	Amiable (मैत्रीपूर्ण)	Friendly	Hostile (शत्रुतापूर्ण)	6
50	Benign (अनुकूल)	Favourable	Malignant (घातक)	6
51	Boisterous (कोलाहलपूर्ण)	Noisy, Clamorous	Calm, Peaceful, Restrained (शांत, संयमित)	6
52	Cease (रोकना)	Stop	Initiate, Continue, Start (जारी रखना)	6

SN	WORD (Hindi Meaning)	Synonym	Antonym (Hindi Meaning)	#R
53	Defile (अशुद्ध करना)	Corrupt	Purify, Honour, Elevate (शुद्ध करना, सम्मान करना)	6
54	Despair (निराशा)	Misery, Sad	Hope (आशा)	6
55	Eager (उत्सुक)	Keen	Disinterested, Indifferent (उदासीन)	6
56	Enigmatic (रहस्यपूर्ण)	Puzzling, Mysterious	Plain, Straightforward (सादा, सीधा)	6
57	Exaggerate (अतिशयोक्ति करना)	Magnify	Understate, Compress (परदा डालना, संक्षिप्त करना)	6
58	Fastidious (तुनक मिज़ाज)	Careful	Easy going, Adjustable (समझने वाला)	6
59	Lethal (घातक)	Malignant, Fatal	Harmless (हानिरहित)	6
60	Mundane (साधारण)	Ordinary, Everyday, Commonplace	Extraordinary (असाधारण)	6
61	Obstruct (रोक लगाना)	Block, Curb	Assist, Allow, Clear (सहायता/पास करना)	6
62	Pernicious (हानिकारक)	Injurious, Dangerous, Spiteful	Beneficial, Kind (लाभकारी, दयालु)	6
63	Precedence (प्रधानता)	Priority	Disruption (व्यवधान)	6
64	Redundant (अनावश्यक)	Unnecessary	Required, Concise (आवश्यक, संक्षिप्त)	6
65	Relevant (उपयुक्त)	Applicable	Inapplicable (अनुपयुक्त)	6
66	Reprimand (फटकार)	Rebuke, Reproach	Reward, Forgiveness, Compliment (क्षमा, प्रशंसा)	6
67	Sordid (घटिया)	Unpleasant, Dirty	Reputable (सम्मानित)	6
68	Spurious (अप्रामाणिक)	Fake	Authentic, Genuine (प्रामाणिक)	6
69	Stern (कठोर)	Strict	Lenient, Light (नरम, हलका)	6
70	Triumph (सफलता)	Victory	Defeat, Sorrow, Failure (हार, दुःख)	6
71	Abstain (संयम रखना)	Refrain	Indulge, Pursue (लिप्त होना)	5
72	Acute (धारदार)	Sharp	Blunt (भोथरा)	5
73	Affluence (संपन्नता)	Wealth, Richness	Poverty (दरिद्रता)	5
74	Agile (फुर्तीला)	Active, Quick, Nimble	Lethargic (सुस्त)	5
75	Benevolent (परोपकारी)	Kind, Generous	Malevolent, Merciless, Stingy (द्वेषी, निर्दयी, कंजूस)	5
76	Callous (कठोर)	Brutal	Caring, Sensitive, Sympathetic, Concerned (संवेदनशील, सहानुभूति, चिंतित)	5
77	Cogent (निश्चयात्मक)	Effective, Convincing, Rational	Impotent, Unconvincing (अविश्वसनीय)	5
78	Concise (संक्षिप्त)	Brief	Lengthy (लंबा)	5
79	Congenial (अनुकूल)	Favourable, Cordial, Compatible	Unpleasant (अप्रिय)	5
80	Curtail (घटाना)	Downsize	Resume, Enlarge, Lengthen (फिर से शुरू, बढ़ाना, लंबा करना)	5

SN	WORD (Hindi Meaning)	Synonym	Antonym (Hindi Meaning)	#R
81	Deliberate (जानबूझकर)	Intentional, Intended, Planned	Spontaneous (स्वाभाविक)	5
82	Dismal (निराशाजनक)	Gloomy	Cheerful (प्रफुल्लित)	5
83	Eminent (प्रतिष्ठित)	Famous, Prominent, Renowned	Ordinary, Inconspicuous (साधारण, अविशिष्ट)	5
84	Eradicate (मिटा देना)	Abolish, Uproot	Preserve (बचाना)	5
85	Eternal (निरन्तर)	Perpetual, Forever, Ageless, Everlasting	Temporary (अस्थायी)	5
86	Exceptional (असाधारण)	Extraordinary	Common, Unremarkable, Ordinary (साधारण)	5
87	Fatigue (थकान)	Tiredness, Weariness	Strength (ताकत)	5
88	Feeble (कमज़ोर)	Weak	Strong, Effective (प्रभावी)	5
89	Fragile (नाज़ुक, भंगुर)	Brittle	Tough, Strong (मजबूत)	5
90	Frail (दुर्बल)	Feeble, Fragile	Robust (सुदृढ़)	5
91	Industrious (मेहनती)	Diligent	Lethargic, Indolent (सुस्त, निष्क्रिय)	5
92	Insipid (बेस्वाद)	Bland	Tasty (स्वादिष्ट)	5
93	Intrepid (निडर)	Fearless, Gallant	Meek, Cowardly (डरपोक)	5
94	Invincible (अजय)	Unassailable, Unbeatable	Vulnerable, Powerless (कमजोर, शक्तिहीन)	5
95	Jubilant (उल्लसित)	Ecstatic, Rejoicing, Happy	Sorrowful, Depressed (उदास)	5
96	Lament (विलाप)	Mourn	Celebrate, Rejoice (आनंद)	5
97	Latent (छुपा हुआ)	Hidden	Obvious, Evident (स्पष्ट, प्रत्यक्ष)	5
98	Loathe (घृणा करना)	Abhor	Like, Love, Admire (पसंद, प्यार)	5
99	Malice (दुर्भावना)	Bitterness	Goodwill, Kindness (सद्भावना)	5
100	Modest (विनम्र)	Humble	Vain (अहंकारी)	5
101	Monotonous (नीरस, एकसमान)	Dull, Boring	Interesting, Varied (दिलचस्प, विभिन्न)	5
102	Morbid (रोगग्रस्त)	Depressed, Ghastly, Nasty	Cheerful (आनंदित)	5
103	Obscure (अस्पष्ट)	Confusing, Unknown	Clear (स्पष्ट)	5
104	Ominous (अशुभ)	Threatening	Auspicious (शुभ)	5
105	Pious (पवित्र)	Religious	Sinful (पापी)	5
106	Precarious (खतरनाक)	Perilous, Dangerous, Insecure	Safe (सुरक्षित)	5
107	Profuse (अत्यधिक)	Aplenty, Abundant	Sparse, Meager, Scant (अल्प)	5
108	Quiescent (निष्क्रिय)	Dull	Active, Animated (सक्रिय)	5
109	Remorse (अफसोस)	Regret	Indifference (उदासीनता)	5
110	Resolute (दृढ़)	Determined	Agreeable (स्वीकार्य)	5
111	Robust (मजबूत)	Healthy	Feeble (कमज़ोर)	5

SN	WORD (Hindi Meaning)	Synonym	Antonym (Hindi Meaning)	#R
112	Salient (मुख्य)	Prominent, Noticeable	Insignificant, Negligible (तुच्छ, नगण्य)	5
113	Taciturn (अल्पभाषी)	Silent, Reticent	Talkative (बातूनी)	5
114	Thrive (उन्नति करना)	Flourish, Prosper	Fail, Shrink (असफल होना, सिकुड़ना)	5
115	Thwart (बिगाड़ना)	Impede, Curb	Assist (सहायता करना)	5
116	Transient (क्षणिक)	Transitory, Fleeting, Temporary	Permanent (स्थायी)	5
117	Vanish (गायब)	Disappear	Emerge (उभरना)	5
118	Abrupt (एकाएक)	Sudden	Gradual, Smooth (धीरे-धीरे)	4
119	Absolve (दोषमुक्त करना)	Acquit, Pardon	Blame (दोष लगाना)	4
120	Accede (मान लेना)	Consent, Comply	Deny (मना करना)	4
121	Adept (निपुण)	Skilled	Inept (अयोग्य)	4
122	Admire (प्रशंसा)	Appreciate	Ridicule, Dislike (उपहास / नापसंद)	4
123	Admonish (डाँटना)	Chide	Praise, Applaud (प्रशंसा करना)	4
124	Advance (आगे बढ़ना)	Progress, Move Forward	Retreat (पीछे हटना)	4
125	Aggravate (भड़काना)	Irritate, Intensify	Alleviate (शान्त करना)	4
126	Allure (आकर्षित करना)	Tempt, Attract	Repulse (खदेड़ना)	4
127	Ample (प्रचुर)	Sufficient	Scarce, Meagre (अपर्याप्त)	4
128	Annoy (झुंझला देना)	Offend, Irritate	Satisfy, Comfort (संतुष्ट / आराम)	4
129	Arraign (दोष लगाना)	Prosecute	Free (मुक्त होना)	4
130	Assault (हमला)	Attack	Defend, Retreat (बचाव, पीछे हटना)	4
131	Assist (मदद करना)	Help, Facilitate, Aid	Obstruct (बाधा डालना)	4
132	Audacious (साहसी)	Bold	Cowardly (कायर)	4
133	Audacity (धृष्टता)	Boldness	Cowardice, Timidity (कायरता)	4
134	Authentic (विश्वसनीय)	Certain, Genuine	False (असत्य)	4
135	Baffled (चकित)	Confused	Composed (शांतचित्त)	4
136	Barbarous (असभ्य)	Crude	Civilized (सभ्य)	4
137	Bleak (उदास)	Depressing, Grim	Bright (उज्ज्वल)	4
138	Blunt (भौंथरा)	Dull	Sharp (नुकीला)	4
139	Brutal (क्रूर)	Savage, Cruel	Humane (दयालु)	4
140	Camouflage (छुप जाना)	Disguise	Reveal (दिखाना)	4
141	Censure (निंदा)	Criticise	Praise, Applause (प्रशंसा)	4
142	Chaste (पवित्र)	Pure	Corrupt (भ्रष्ट)	4
143	Clandestine (गुप्त)	Secret	Open, Honest (खुला, निष्कपट)	4
144	Comic (हास्य)	Funny	Tragic (दुखद)	4
145	Complacent (आत्मसंतुष्ट)	Satisfied, Smug	Concerned (चिंतित)	4
146	Conceited (अभिमानी)	Proud, Smug, Arrogant	Modest (विनम्र)	4

SN	WORD (Hindi Meaning)	Synonym	Antonym (Hindi Meaning)	#R
147	Consensus (आम सहमति)	Unanimity	Disagreement, Discord (असहमति, कलह)	4
148	Culpable (दोषी)	Guilty	Innocent, Blameless (निर्दोष)	4
149	Despise (घृणा)	Undervalue, Abhor	Admire (प्रशंसा)	4
150	Devout (धार्मिक)	Pious	Treacherous (अधर्मी)	4
151	Diffident (संकोची)	Timid	Confident, Aggressive (आत्मविश्वासी, आक्रामक)	4
152	Diminish (घटाना)	Reduce	Increase (बढ़ना)	4
153	Dispute (झगड़ा)	Quarrel	Concede, Agreement (हार मानना, समझौता करना)	4
154	Docile (आज्ञाकारी)	Submissive	Opposing, Unwilling (विरोधी, असम्मत)	4
155	Fasten (बान्धना)	Affix	Release (रिहाई)	4
156	Ferocious (उग्र)	Fierce	Mild, Gentle (विनम्र)	4
157	Fickle (अस्थिर)	Unstable	Constant, Stable, Firm (स्थिर)	4
158	Fictitious (काल्पनिक)	False	Real, Factual (असली)	4
159	Flimsy (कमज़ोर)	Weak, Feeble	Sturdy, Strong (तगड़ा)	4
160	Former (भूतपूर्व)	Previous	After, Latter (बाद)	4
161	Frugal (अल्पव्ययी, किफ़ायती)	Economical	Extravagant (खर्चीला)	4
162	Garrulous (बातूनी)	Talkative, Voluble, Talkative	Taciturn (अल्पभाषी)	4
163	Glee (आनंद)	Happiness	Woe (शोक)	4
164	Guile (छल कपट)	Cunning, Deceit	Honesty (ईमानदारी)	4
165	Haste (जल्दी)	Hurry	Delay (देरी)	4
166	Humane (दयालु)	Sympathetic	Cruel, Unkind (निर्दयी)	4
167	Impede (बाधा डालना)	Hinder	Expedite, Advance, Facilitate (प्रगति करना)	4
168	Incite (उत्तेजित करना)	Inflame	Prohibit, Discourage, Restrain (हतोत्साहित करना)	4
169	Incredible (अतुल्य, अविश्वसनीय)	Unbelievable	Possible, Believable (संभव, विश्वसनीय)	4
170	Indolent (आलसी, निष्क्रिय)	Lazy	Diligent, Lively (मेहनती, जीवंत)	4
171	Inept (अयोग्य)	Clumsy	Skillful, Talented, Competent (योग्य)	4
172	Innocuous (अहानिकर)	Harmless, Inoffensive	Pernicious, Harmful (हानिकारक)	4
173	Integration (एकीकरण)	Unity, Unification	Fragmentation (विखंडन)	4
174	Keen (इच्छुक)	Enthusiastic	Blunt, Dull (मंदबुद्धि)	4
175	Lavish (प्रचुर)	Expensive, Bountiful	Scarce, Frugal (दुर्लभ, अल्पव्ययी)	4
176	Lethargic (सुस्त)	Inactive, Lazy	Lively (जीवंत)	4
177	Lofty (ऊँचा)	Noble	Below (नीचे)	4

SN	WORD (Hindi Meaning)	Synonym	Antonym (Hindi Meaning)	#R
178	Magnificent (शानदार)	Splendid, Grand	Modest (विनम्र)	4
179	Marvellous (अद्भुत)	Wonderful	Terrible (ख़राब)	4
180	Meticulous (सतर्क)	Careful, Methodical, Perfectionist	Careless (लापरवाह)	4
181	Modern (आधुनिक)	New	Ancient (प्राचीन)	4
182	Nefarious (दुष्कर्मी)	Wicked, Iniquitous	Pleasing (सुखदायी)	4
183	Notorious (कुख्यात)	Disreputable	Popular, Reputed, Famous (प्रतिष्ठित, प्रसिद्ध)	4
184	Novel (अद्भुत, नया)	Unique	Banal, Old (तुच्छ, पुराना)	4
185	Pacify (शांत करना)	Calm Down, Soothe	Enrage (क्रोधित करना)	4
186	Paucity (कमी)	Shortage	Plethora, Surplus (बहुतायत, अतिरिक्त)	4
187	Penniless (कंगाल)	Broke	Rich (धनी)	4
188	Perceive (जानना समझना)	Notice, Recognise	Neglect (उपेक्षा)	4
189	Persist (अड़े रहना)	Insist, Continue	Cease, Discontinue (बन्द करना)	4
190	Plausible (संभाव्य)	Credible	Inconceivable, Implausible, Unlikely (अविश्वसनीय, असम्भव)	4
191	Praise (प्रशंसा करना)	Compliment	Accuse (आरोप लगाना)	4
192	Precise (सटीक)	Accurate	Vague (अस्पष्ट)	4
193	Predilection (पसंद)	Preference	Dislike, Aversion, Enmity (नापसंद, घृणा, शत्रुता)	4
194	Procrastinate (विलम्ब करना)	Delay	Expedite, Do (शीघ्र, करना)	4
195	Recede (कम होना)	Wane	Advance, Extend (उन्नति, विस्तार)	4
196	Reckless (लापरवाह)	Careless	Cautious (सतर्क)	4
197	Reluctant (अनिच्छुक)	Hesitant, Unwilling	Eager, Willing (तैयार, इच्छुक)	4
198	Revive (पुनर्जीवित करना)	Restore, Recover	Ruin, Damage (बर्बाद करना)	4
199	Savage (बर्बर)	Brutal	Civilized, Cultured (सभ्य)	4
200	Scanty (अल्प)	Limited, Meagre	Profuse (अधिक)	4
201	Serene (शांत, निर्मल)	Calm	Ruffled, Stressed (रूखा / अत्यधिक थका हुआ)	4
202	Slender (पतला)	Slim	Stout (मोटा)	4
203	Stable (स्थिर)	Anchored	Shaky (अस्थिर)	4
204	Stringent (सख्त)	Tough, Strict, Rigorous	Lenient (नरम)	4
205	Sufficient (पर्याप्त)	Enough	Inadequate (अपर्याप्त)	4
206	Trivial (मामूली)	Superficial	Profound (पारंगत)	4
207	Vacillate (निश्चय न कर पाना)	Waver, Irresolute	Decide (निश्चय करना)	4
208	Vice (बुराई)	Immorality	Virtue (गुण)	4
209	Wily (धूर्त)	Cunning, Artful, Crafty	Honest (ईमानदार)	4
210	Abeyance (ठहराव)	Inactivity, Suspension	Continuation (जारी रहना)	3

SN	WORD (Hindi Meaning)	Synonym	Antonym (Hindi Meaning)	#R
211	Abridge (संक्षेप करना)	Shorten	Stretch (फैलाना)	3
212	Absolute (पूर्ण)	Complete	Limited (सीमित)	3
213	Accomplish (सफल होना)	Achieve	Fail (असफल होना)	3
214	Adulation (चापलूसी)	Flattery, Adoration	Abuse (दुर्व्यवहार)	3
215	Affinity (लगाव, सहानुभूति)	Empathy	Aversion (घृणा)	3
216	Alleviate (कम करना)	Mitigate, Relieve	Aggravate (बढ़ाना)	3
217	Altruistic (परोपकारी)	Philanthropic	Selfish (स्वार्थी)	3
218	Ameliorate (सुधारना)	Improve	Worsen (बदतर करना)	3
219	Amicable (मैत्रीपूर्ण)	Friendly	Hostile (शत्रुतापूर्ण)	3
220	Anxiety (व्याकुलता)	Worry	Certainty (निश्चय)	3
221	Apex (शिखर)	Pinnacle	Base (नींव)	3
222	Apposite (उपयुक्त)	Appropriate	Inappropriate (अनुपयुक्त)	3
223	Arcane (गुप्त)	Mysterious, Hidden	Public (सार्वजनिक)	3
224	Articulate (सुस्पष्ट)	Distinct	Unclear (अस्पष्ट)	3
225	Ascend (ऊपर उठना)	Climb	Descend (नीचे उतरना)	3
226	Ascertain (सुनिश्चित करना)	Discover	Overlook, Disprove (अनदेखी करना, खंडन करना)	3
227	Attract (आकर्षित करना)	Fascinate, Entice	Repel (घृणा उत्पन्न करना)	3
228	Barbaric (असभ्य)	Uncivilized	Civilised (सभ्य)	3
229	Bare (नंगा)	Basic	Covered (ढका हुआ)	3
230	Barrier (अवरोध)	Bound	Opening (खुली जगह)	3
231	Beseech (याचना करना)	Beg	Command (हुक्म देना)	3
232	Brittle (नाज़ुक, भंगुर)	Fragile	Strong (मजबूत)	3
233	Cajole (फुसलाना)	Flatter, Entice	Repulse (प्रतिरोध करना)	3
234	Capable (सक्षम)	Competent	Inept (अयोग्य)	3
235	Capricious (मनमौजी)	Whimsical	Firm, Reasonable (दृढ़, तर्कसंगत)	3
236	Chastise (सज़ा देना)	Upbraid	Praise (प्रशंसा करना)	3
237	Cherish (पोषण करना)	Nurture	Abandon (छोड़ देना)	3
238	Chivalrous (शौर्यवान)	Heroic	Cowardly, Defiant (कायर)	3
239	Comely (मनोरम)	Pretty	Grotesque (विकृत)	3
240	Command (आदेश)	Instruct	Opposition, Permission (विपक्ष, अनुमति)	3
241	Conceit (अहंकार)	Vanity	Modesty, Humility (विनम्रता)	3
242	Confine (सीमित)	Restrict	Liberate (मुक्त करना)	3
243	Contaminate (दूषित करना)	Pollute	Cleanse (शुद्धी करना)	3
244	Contrary (विरोध)	Opposite	Agreeable (सहमत)	3
245	Copious (प्रचुर)	Plentiful	Scarce (दुर्लभ)	3
246	Courage (साहस)	Valour	Cowardice (कायरता)	3
247	Courteous (विनम्र)	Polite	Rude (अशिष्ट)	3

SN	WORD (Hindi Meaning)	Synonym	Antonym (Hindi Meaning)	#R
248	Culmination (समापन)	Climax	Beginning, Commencement (शुरुआत)	3
249	Cumbersome (भारी भरकम)	Heavy	Convenient (आसान)	3
250	Defy (विरोध करना)	Repel, Disobey	Yield (स्वीकार करना)	3
251	Delusion (भ्रम)	Illusion	Reality (हकीकत)	3
252	Demure (शर्मीला)	Sober	Strong, Bold (दृढ़, साहसिक)	3
253	Deny (इनकार करना)	Refuse	Agree, Accept (सहमत होना)	3
254	Derogatory (अपमानजनक)	Disparaging, Sarcastic	Complimentary (प्रशंसात्मक)	3
255	Deter (रोक लगाना)	Hinder	Incite, Encourage (प्रोत्साहित करना)	3
256	Detrimental (हानिकारक)	Harmful	Harmless, Benign (हानिरहित)	3
257	Devoid (खाली)	Empty	Full (भरा हुआ)	3
258	Dilate (फैलाना)	Widen	Contract, Compress (संकुचित करना)	3
259	Dilemma (दुविधा)	Predicament, Quandary	Solution (समाधान)	3
260	Disaster (आपदा)	Misfortune	Success (सफलता)	3
261	Dishevelled (अस्त व्यस्त)	Untidy	Tidy (साफ)	3
262	Distant (दूर)	Faraway	Close, Near (पास)	3
263	Dwindle (घटना)	Decrease	Increase (बढ़ना)	3
264	Efficacious (प्रभावी)	Effective	Ineffective, Useless (प्रभावहीन)	3
265	Efficient (कुशल)	Capable, Competent	Idle (बेकार)	3
266	Elated (उत्तेजित)	Exalted	Disheartened, Depressed (निराश)	3
267	Encountered (सामना करना)	Faced	Avoided (टालना)	3
268	Encourage (प्रोत्साहित करना)	Stimulate	Dishearten (निराश)	3
269	Enthusiasm (उत्साह)	Zeal	Lethargy (सुस्ती)	3
270	Evade (बच निकालना)	Avoid, Bypass	Confront (सामना करना)	3
271	Evasive (कपटपूर्ण)	Devious	Categorical, Frank (स्पष्ट, साफ़)	3
272	Exorbitant (अत्यधिक)	Excessive, High	Modest (मामूली)	3
273	Extinct (विलुप्त)	Abolished	Alive, Living (जीवित)	3
274	Exultation (उल्लास)	Jubilation	Agony (व्यथा)	3
275	Fake (नकली)	False	Real, Genuine (असली)	3
276	Fatuous (मूर्ख)	Silly, Irrational	Sensible (समझदार)	3
277	Felicity (परम सुख)	Bliss	Sorrow (शोक)	3
278	Fleeting (अस्थायी, क्षणभंगुर)	Momentary, Brief	Lasting (टिकाऊ)	3
279	Flourish (समृद्ध होना)	Thrive	Degenerate, Hinder (बिगड़ना, बाधा डालना)	3
280	Forsake (त्यागना)	Abandon, Desert	Revert (लौट आना)	3
281	Forthright (मुँहफट)	Outspoken	Devious (कुटिल)	3
282	Fortify (मजबूत करना)	Strengthen, Secure	Undermine (दुर्बल बना देना)	3
283	Frivolous (तुच्छ)	Puerile	Wise (विद्वान)	3
284	Gallant (वीर, शौर्य)	Courageous, Brave	Cowardly (कायरतापूर्ण)	3

SN	WORD (Hindi Meaning)	Synonym	Antonym (Hindi Meaning)	#R
285	Gather (एकत्र करना)	Congregate	Divide, Disperse (फैल जाना, छितराना)	3
286	Genial (मिलनसार)	Cordial	Boorish, Hostile (अशिष्ट, शत्रुतापूर्ण)	3
287	Graceful (गरिमापूर्ण)	Elegant	Awkward (बेढंगा)	3
288	Gregarious (सुसामाजिक)	Sociable	Unsociable, Introvert (एकांतप्रिय, अंतर्मुखी)	3
289	Grieve (शोक)	Mourn	Rejoice (आनंद)	3
290	Gullible (भोला-भाला)	Innocent	Wise (समझदार)	3
291	Haggard (थका मंदा)	Exhausted	Fresh (ताज़ा)	3
292	Handy (आसान)	Convenient	Heavy (भारी)	3
293	Harass (परेशान करना)	Bother, Molest	Relieve (दुःख दूर करना)	3
294	Hasty (जल्दबाज, अविचारी)	Quick	Cautious (सतर्क)	3
295	Haughty (घमंडी)	Conceited, Arrogant	Humble (नम्र)	3
296	Honest (ईमानदार)	Upright	Corrupt (भ्रष्ट)	3
297	Hospitable (सौहार्दपूर्ण)	Congenial	Rude (अशिष्ट)	3
298	Identical (समान)	Same, Similar	Different (अलग)	3
299	Immense (विशाल)	Massive	Tiny (बहुत छोटा)	3
300	Impetuous (जल्दबाजी में)	Hasty	Cautious (सावधानी से)	3
301	Impoverished (गरीब)	Penniless	Affluent, Rich (धनी)	3
302	Inception (आरंभ)	Beginning	Conclusion, Termination (समाप्ति)	3
303	Inclement (निर्दयी)	Unfavourable, Dignified	Mild (विनम्र)	3
304	Indelible (स्थायी)	Inerasable	Temporary (अस्थायी)	3
305	Indomitable (अदम्य, अजेय)	Unconquerable, Invincible	Cowardly (कायर)	3
306	Infirm (कमजोर)	Weak	Strong (बलवान)	3
307	Initiate (आरंभ करना)	Start	Finish, Conclude (खतम करना)	3
308	Inscrutable (रहस्यमय)	Inexplicable	Comprehensible (समझने योग्य)	3
309	Instant (तुरंत)	Immediate	Delayed, Gradual (विलंबित)	3
310	Integrate (जोड़ना)	Unite, Assimilate	Separate (अलग करना)	3
311	Jettison (बाहर फेंक देना)	Hurl, Eject	Accept (स्वीकार करना)	3
312	Just (न्याय संगत)	Fair	Corrupt (भ्रष्ट)	3
313	Knack (कुशलता)	Dexterity	Dullness, Inability (नीरसता, अक्षमता)	3
314	Lackadaisical (आलसी, भावुक)	Careless	Enthusiastic (उत्साही)	3
315	Laconic (संक्षिप्त)	Concise, Crisp, Brief	Verbose (शब्दाडंबरपूर्ण)	3
316	Loquacious (बातूनी)	Talkative	Taciturn (अल्पभाषी)	3
317	Mammoth (विशाल)	Gigantic, Enormous	Infinitesimal (अति सूक्ष्म)	3
318	Meander (दिशाहीन घूमना)	Curve, Wander	Determine (निर्धारित करना)	3
319	Mellow (मधुर)	Genial	Hard (कठिन)	3
320	Miniature (लघु)	Diminutive	Large (विशाल)	3
321	Naive (भोला)	Ingenuous	Artful, Experienced (धूर्त, अनुभवी)	3

SN	WORD (Hindi Meaning)	Synonym	Antonym (Hindi Meaning)	#R
322	Nascent (आरम्भ होना)	Budding	Withering (नष्ट होना)	3
323	Obedient (आज्ञाकारी)	Devoted	Disobedient (अवज्ञाकारी)	3
324	Obsequious (चापलूस)	Servile	Domineering (घमंडी)	3
325	Orthodox (परंपरागत)	Traditional	Heretical, Unconventional (विधर्मी, अपरंपरागत)	3
326	Ostracize (निष्कासित करना)	Expel, Banish	Patronize (संरक्षण देना)	3
327	Perennial (चिरस्थायी)	Lasting	Temporary (अस्थायी)	3
328	Peril (संकट)	Danger	Safety (सुरक्षा)	3
329	Perish (मर जाना)	Die, Decease	Thrive (फलना-फूलना)	3
330	Perseverance (दृढ़ता)	Endurance, Steadfastness	Indifference, Instability (उदासीनता/अस्थिरता)	3
331	Philanthropist (परोपकारी)	Benefactor, Humanitarian	Miser (लोभी)	3
332	Pinnacle (शिखर)	Summit, Culmination	Base (आधार)	3
333	Piquant (चटपटा)	Spicy, Appealing	Bland (बेस्वाद)	3
334	Predicament (कठिन परिस्थिति)	Plight, Dilemma	Solution (समाधान)	3
335	Prejudice (पक्षपात करना)	Bias	Fairness (निष्पक्षता)	3
336	Prevent (रोकना)	Avert, Block	Induce (प्रेरित करना)	3
337	Primitive (प्राचीन)	Basic, Ancient	Sophisticated (आधुनिकतम)	3
338	Proficient (कुशल)	Adept	Clumsy (अनाड़ी)	3
339	Progress (प्रगति)	Development	Decline, Retreat (पीछे हटना)	3
340	Prompt (शीघ्र)	Immediate, Quick	Sluggish (सुस्त)	3
341	Propitious (शुभ)	Hopeful, Auspicious	Inauspicious (अशुभ)	3
342	Prosperity (समृद्धि)	Wealth	Adversity (विपत्ति)	3
343	Provoke (भड़काना)	Arouse	Soothe, Appease (शांत करना)	3
344	Quash (रद्द करना, अस्वीकार करना)	Reject, Crush	Support (समर्थन करना)	3
345	Querulous (शिकायती)	Grouchy, Complaining	Uncomplaining (शिकायत न करने वाला)	3
346	Rampart (किले की दीवार)	Parapet	Ditch (खाई)	3
347	Rational (तर्कसंगत)	Logical	Illogical (विसंगत)	3
348	Rejuvenate (नया करना)	Update, Refresh	Suppress (दमन करना)	3
349	Relinquish (त्यागना)	Discard	Retain, Continue (बनाये रखना)	3
350	Reticent (अल्पभाषी)	Silent	Communicative, Talkative (मिलनसार)	3
351	Retreat (पीछे हटना)	Withdrawl	Advance (आगे बढ़ाना)	3
352	Reveal (प्रकट करना)	Disclose	Hide, Conceal (छिपाना)	3
353	Revoke (वापस लेना)	Repeal	Implement, Proclaim (लागू करना)	3
354	Rough (खुरदरा)	Coarse	Smooth (चिकना)	3
355	Sagacious (समझदार)	Judicious	Dull, Ignorant (अनभिज्ञ)	3
356	Sane (समझदार)	Sensible	Crazy (पागल)	3
357	Scarce (दुर्लभ)	Limited	Ample (प्रचुर)	3

SN	WORD (Hindi Meaning)	Synonym	Antonym (Hindi Meaning)	#R
358	Strange (अपरिचित)	Abnormal	Familiar (परिचित)	3
359	Strenuous (कठिन प्रयास)	Difficult, Formidable	Effortless (सहज)	3
360	Stupendous (आश्चर्यजनक)	Stunning	Terrible, Awful (भद्दा)	3
361	Stupor (अचम्भा)	Slumber	Consciousness (चेतना)	3
362	Sturdy (हट्टा कट्टा)	Tough	Feeble, Delicate (नाजुक)	3
363	Subsequent (आगामी)	Consecutive	Prior, Preceding (पहले, पूर्ववर्ती)	3
364	Subtle (कोमल)	Understated	Harsh (कठोर)	3
365	Superficial (सतही)	Shallow	Genuine (सच्चा)	3
366	Superfluous (अनावश्यक, अतिरिक्त)	Extra	Necessary (आवश्यक)	3
367	Surreptitious (गुप्त)	Secret, Secretive	Open (स्पष्ट)	3
368	Tedious (गैरदिलचस्प)	Dull	Interesting (दिलचस्प)	3
369	Terse (संक्षिप्त)	Brief	Polite, Verbose (शब्दाडंबरपूर्ण)	3
370	Treacherous (विश्वासघाती)	Unfaithful	Faithful (ईमानदार)	3
371	Uncanny (अलौकिक)	Mysterious, Spooky	Ordinary (साधारण)	3
372	Unruly (अनियंत्रित)	Lawless, Disobedient	Orderly (व्यवस्थित)	3
373	Urge (तीव्र इच्छा)	Impulse	Deter (रोक रखना)	3
374	Vacant (रिक्त)	Bare, Uninhabited	Occupied (व्यस्त)	3
375	Vanity (घमंड)	Conceit	Modesty, Humility (शील, नम्रता)	3
376	Vanquish (पराजित करना)	Defeat	Surrender (हार मानना)	3
377	Veracity (सच्चाई)	Truth	Deceit, Myth (धोखा / मिथक)	3
378	Vicious (अनैतिक, निर्दयी)	Cruel	Virtuous (नैतिक)	3
379	Vital (महत्वपूर्ण, अत्यावश्यक)	Essential, Crucial	Trivial (मामूली)	3
380	Vivid (चमकीला)	Lucid, Evocative	Murky (फीका)	3
381	Wary (होशियार)	Alert	Rash, Careless (जल्दबाज, लापरवाह)	3
382	Weary (थका मंदा)	Exhausted, Tired	Refreshed (तरोताजा)	3
383	Weird (अजीब)	Strange	Usual, Normal (सामान्य)	3
384	Zenith (शीर्ष बिंदु)	Summit	Nadir (सबसे निम्न बिंदु)	3
385	Aberration (असामान्यता, विचलन)	Deviation	Normality (सामान्यता)	2
386	Abjure (त्यागना)	Renounce	Acquire (प्राप्त करना)	2
387	Abolish (हटाना)	Eliminate	Continue (ज़ारी रखना)	2
388	Accord (सहमति)	Confer	Disagreement (असहमति)	2
389	Accustomed (अभ्यस्त)	Habituated	Unusual (असामान्य)	2
390	Acquire (प्राप्त)	Procure	Disperse (बिखेरना)	2
391	Adorn (सजाना)	Beautify	Disfigure (बिगाड़ना)	2
392	Alacrity (तत्परता)	Willingness	Indifference (उदासीनता)	2
393	Alert (सतर्क)	Watchful	Careless (लापरवाह)	2
394	Amass (एकत्र करना)	Gather	Distribute (वितरित करना)	2
395	Anxious (चिंतित)	Nervous	Calm (शांत)	2

SN	WORD (Hindi Meaning)	Synonym	Antonym (Hindi Meaning)	#R
396	Apparition (भूत-प्रेत)	Spirit	Realness (वास्तविकता)	2
397	Applause (वाहवाही)	Approval	Criticism (आलोचना)	2
398	Apprise (सूचित करना)	Inform	Hide (छिपा देना)	2
399	Ardent (उत्साही)	Passionate	Apathetic (उदासीन)	2
400	Arid (बंजर)	Dry	Wet, Fertile (उपजाऊ)	2
401	Assert (दृढ़ता से कहना)	Emphasize	Abandon (छोडना)	2
402	Astound (चकित करना)	To Bewilder	Clarify (स्पष्ट करना)	2
403	Attenuate (कमज़ोर होना)	Weaken	Strong (शक्तिशाली)	2
404	Avoid (टालना)	Evade	Meet (मिलना)	2
405	Bane (श्राप)	Curse	Boon (वरदान)	2
406	Banter (मज़ाक)	Repartee	Praise (प्रशंसा)	2
407	Beautiful (सुंदर)	Handsome	Ugly (कुरूप)	2
408	Beneficial (लाभदायक)	Advantageous	Harmful (हानिकारक)	2
409	Bliss (परमानंद)	Happiness	Sorrow (शोक)	2
410	Bountiful (प्रचुर)	Generous	Meager (अल्प)	2
411	Calamity (आपदा)	Catastrophe, Disaster	Happiness (खुशी)	2
412	Casual (अनौपचारिक)	Occasional	Formal (औपचारिक)	2
413	Caustic (कटु)	Acidic	Kind (दयालु)	2
414	Cavalier (घमंडी)	Gentleman	Humble (सादगीपूर्ण)	2
415	Chagrin (शर्मिंदगी, नाराजगी)	Embarrassment	Pleasure (खुशी)	2
416	Chronic (दीर्घकालीन, स्थायी)	Persistent	Infrequent (कभी-कभी)	2
417	Circuitous (घुमावदार)	Roundabout	Direct (सीधा)	2
418	Clamour (कोलाहल)	Uproar	Quiet (शांत)	2
419	Clumsy (अनाड़ी)	Unskilful	Graceful (गरिमापूर्ण)	2
420	Colloquial (बोल-चाल का)	Familiar	Formal (औपचारिक)	2
421	Compassion (दया)	Pity	Meanness (नीचता)	2
422	Compassionate (सहानुभूति)	Sympathetic	Heartless (बेरहम)	2
423	Conceal (छिपाना)	Hide	Reveal (प्रकट करना)	2
424	Concealed (गुप्त)	Disguised	Revealed (उजागर)	2
425	Confront (सामना करना)	Challenge	Avoid (टालना)	2
426	Conjecture (अनुमान)	Guess	Certainty (निश्चय)	2
427	Courageous (साहसी)	Valiant	Diffident (संकोची)	2
428	Crafty (चालाक)	Cunning	Unskilled (अनाड़ी)	2
429	Current (वर्तमानकालिक)	Present	Past (अतीत)	2
430	Damage (टूट-फूट)	Afflict	Mend (मरम्मत)	2
431	Debacle (पराजय)	Downfall	Success (सफलता)	2
432	Debonair (आकर्षक)	Elegant	Cheerless (निराश)	2
433	Decamp (भाग जाना)	Flee	Remain (ठहरना)	2
434	Decay (क्षय)	Decompose	Growth (वृद्धि)	2

SN	WORD (Hindi Meaning)	Synonym	Antonym (Hindi Meaning)	#R
435	Deliberately (जान - बूझकर)	Intentionally	Unintentionally (अनजाने में)	2
436	Delicate (नाज़ुक)	Fragile	Firm (दृढ़)	2
437	Delight (आनंद)	Joy	Sorrow (शोक)	2
438	Demented (पागल)	Idiotic	Sensible (समझदार)	2
439	Dense (घना)	Thick	Sparse (विरल)	2
440	Deplete (कम करना)	Reduce	Restore (पुनर्स्थापित करना)	2
441	Dexterity (निपुणता)	Adroitness	Ignorance (अज्ञानता)	2
442	Discontent (असंतोष)	Dissatisfaction	Satisfaction (संतोष)	2
443	Discreet (सावधान)	Careful	Tactless (अव्यावहारिक)	2
444	Disperse (छितराना)	Eject	Gather (एकत्र करना)	2
445	Dissuade (रोकना)	Discourage	Persuade (राजी करना)	2
446	Divulgence (पर्दाफाश)	Revelation	Repudiation (इनकार)	2
447	Doleful (दुख भरा)	Mournful	Cheerful (आनंदित)	2
448	Ebb (कम होना)	Sink	Flow (प्रवाहित होना)	2
449	Ebullient (जोशीला)	Enthusiastic	Dejected (उदास)	2
450	Elaborate (विस्तृत)	Detailed	Minimal (कम से कम)	2
451	Elegant (शिष्ट)	Graceful	Crude (अशिष्ट)	2
452	Eliminate (निकालना)	Remove, Exclude	Add (जोड़ना)	2
453	Eloquent (सुवक्ता)	Fluent	Inarticulate (व्यक्त करने में असमर्थ)	2
454	Emulate (अनुकरण करना)	Imitate	Neglect (उपेक्षा)	2
455	Encumbrance (ऋणभार)	Obstacle	Asset (संपत्ति)	2
456	Endeavour (प्रयत्न करना)	Attempt	Laziness (कामचोरी)	2
457	Enraged (खफ़ा)	Furious	Pleased (प्रसन्न)	2
458	Ensconce (छिपना)	Conceal	Unveil (दिखाना)	2
459	Epidemic (व्यापक (रोग))	Widespread	Limited (सीमित)	2
460	Epitome (प्रतीक, सारांश)	Type	Enlargement (विस्तारण)	2
461	Equanimity (संतुलन)	Calm	Agitation (उत्तेजना)	2
462	Erode (नष्ट करना)	Disintegrate	Fix (ठीक कर)	2
463	Esoteric (गुप्त, जटिल)	Abstruse	Familiar (परिचित)	2
464	Eternity (अनंत काल)	Forever	Bounds (सीमा)	2
465	Eventual (अंतिम)	Ultimate	Initial (प्रारंभिक)	2
466	Everlasting (चिरस्थायी)	Eternal	Transient (अस्थायी)	2
467	Evident (प्रत्यक्ष)	Clear	Indistinct, Hidden (अस्पष्ट)	2
468	Evince (व्यक्त करना)	Show	Conceal (छिपाना)	2
469	Exasperating (तंग करनेवाला)	Frustrating	Soothing (प्रसन्न करनेवाला)	2
470	Excruciating (कष्टदायी)	Piercing	Mild (मामूली)	2
471	Exotic (असाधारण)	Strange	Ordinary (साधारण)	2
472	Expensive (मूल्यवान)	Dear	Cheap (सस्ता)	2
473	Fallacy (भ्रम)	Bias	Truth (सच्चाई)	2

SN	WORD (Hindi Meaning)	Synonym	Antonym (Hindi Meaning)	#R
474	Fanatic (कट्टर)	Enthusiast	Tolerant (सहिष्णु)	2
475	Fascinating (आकर्षक)	Appealing	Repulsive (अरुचिकर)	2
476	Fidelity (वफ़ादारी)	Loyalty	Treachery (दगाबाजी)	2
477	Fiendish (क्रूर)	Cruel	Friendly (मित्रतापूर्ण)	2
478	Filthy (गंदा)	Dirty	Clean (स्वच्छ)	2
479	Flagitious (धोर अपराधी)	Criminal	Virtuous (धार्मिक)	2
480	Flaw (खोट)	Defect	Perfection (निपुणता)	2
481	Fragrance (सुगंध)	Aroma	Stench (दुर्गंध)	2
482	Frigid (बहुत ठंड़ा)	Freezing	Warm (गरम)	2
483	Genius (प्रतिभावान)	A Person With Uncommon Intellect	Dumb (बेवकूफ़)	2
484	Gradual (क्रमश:)	Continuous	Abrupt (एकाएक)	2
485	Gruesome (कुरूप)	Hideous	Gracious (सुन्दर)	2
486	Gumption (बुद्धिमानी)	Acumen	Stupidity (मूर्खता)	2
487	Guzzle (बहुत खाना पीना)	Imbibe	Starve (भूखा मरना)	2
488	Hesitate (हिचकिचाना)	Pause	Advance (अग्रसर होना)	2
489	Hostility (दुश्मनी)	Enmity	Friendship (मित्रता)	2
490	Ignoble (नीच)	Unworthy	Dignified (सम्मानित)	2
491	Ignominy (कलंक)	Disgrace, Dishonour	Glory (यश)	2
492	Illuminate (उजाला करना)	Brighten	Darken (अंधेरा करना)	2
493	Impertinent (उद्दंडतापूर्ण)	Impolite	Respectful (सम्मान पूर्ण)	2
494	Impolite (रूखा)	Rude	Courteous (विनम्र)	2
495	Incapacitate (असमर्थ बनाना)	Cripple	Facilitate (सुविधा देना)	2
496	Incessant (निरंतर)	Persistent	Intermittent (रुक-रुक कर)	2
497	Incorrigible (असंशोधनीय)	Unalterable	Reformable (संशोधनीय)	2
498	Indict (अभियोग लगाना)	Charge	Exonerate (दोषमुक्त करना)	2
499	Inevitable (अपरिहार्य, अटल)	Unavoidable	Avoidable (परिहार्य)	2
500	Inherent (अंतर्निहित)	Inborn	Extraneous (बाहरी)	2
501	Innate (जन्मजात)	Inherent	Acquired (अर्जित)	2
502	Invade (आक्रमण)	Ravage	Surrender (आत्मसमर्पण)	2
503	Irascible (चिड़चिड़ा)	Irritable	Amiable (सुशील)	2
504	Irresolute (अनिश्चित)	Undecided	Decisive (निश्चित)	2
505	Isolation (अलगाव, एकांत)	Separation	Association (संघ)	2
506	Jaded (थका हुआ)	Tired	Refreshed (ताज़ा)	2
507	Jeopardy (ख़तरा)	Risk, Peril	Safety (सुरक्षा)	2
508	Knowledge (ज्ञान)	Wisdom	Ignorance (अज्ञान)	2
509	Laborious (कठिन)	Assiduous	Facile (सरल)	2
510	Lassitude (थकान)	Sluggishness	Enthusiasm (उत्साह)	2
511	Levity (छिछोरापन)	Funniness	Gravity (गंभीरता)	2

SN	WORD (Hindi Meaning)	Synonym	Antonym (Hindi Meaning)	#R
512	Logical (तर्कसंगत)	Rational	Contradictory (असंगत)	2
513	Loyal (वफ़ादार)	Devoted	Fickle (चंचल)	2
514	Maestro (माहिर)	Genius	Amateur (शौक़ीन व्यक्ति)	2
515	Maintain (देखभाल करना)	Care	Abandon (छोड़ना)	2
516	Malevolent (बुरा चाहने वाला)	Despiteful	Kind (दयालु)	2
517	Manifest (स्पष्ट)	Obvious	Disguise (छिपाना)	2
518	Meek (विनम्र, आज्ञाकारी)	Submissive	Assertive (हठ धर्मी)	2
519	Melancholy (उदासी)	Sorrowful	Cheerful (हंसमुख)	2
520	Melodious (मधुर)	Tuneful	Tuneless (बेसुरा)	2
521	Muddle (अव्यवस्था)	Difficulty	Order (क्रम)	2
522	Nebulous (धुंधला)	Vague	Clear (स्पष्ट)	2
523	Notion (ख्याल)	Belief	Need (जरूरत)	2
524	Novice (नौसिखिया)	Beginner	Expert (विशेषज्ञ)	2
525	Nugatory (निरर्थक)	Futile	Productive (उत्पादक)	2
526	Obdurate (ज़िद्दी)	Stubborn	Amenable, Compassionate (विनम्र/दयालु)	2
527	Obsolete (अप्रचलित)	Outdated	Recent (नवीनतम)	2
528	Obvious (स्पष्ट)	Evident	Hidden (छिपा हुआ)	2
529	Old (पुराना)	Aged	New (नया)	2
530	Optimist (आशावादी)	Idealist	Pessimist (निराशावादी)	2
531	Opulence (संपन्नता)	Prosperity	Poverty (दरिद्रता)	2
532	Ostentation (आडम्बर)	Pomp	Modesty (विनम्रता)	2
533	Outrageous (शर्मनाक)	Shocking	Jolly (विनोदपूर्ण)	2
534	Pandemonium (कोलाहल)	Chaos	Harmony (सामंजस्य)	2
535	Paradox (विरोधाभास)	Puzzle	Evidence (प्रमाण)	2
536	Penitence (अफसोस करना)	Repentance	Brazenness (बेशर्मी)	2
537	Pensive (चिंताग्रस्त)	Reflective	Unreflective (असावधान)	2
538	Penury (गरीबी)	Poverty	Wealth (धन)	2
539	Permit (अनुमति)	Grant	Forbid (रोकना)	2
540	Pompous (आडंबरपूर्ण)	Boastful	Humble (विनम्र)	2
541	Porous (छिद्रयुक्त)	Permeable	Impermeable (अभेद्य)	2
542	Pragmatic (व्यावहारिक)	Realistic	Impractical (अव्यावहारिक)	2
543	Preposterous (ऊटपटांग)	Outrageous	Reasonable (वाजिब)	2
544	Proclaim (घोषित करना)	Declare	Conceal (छिपाना)	2
545	Protect (रक्षा करना)	Guard	Harm (हानि पहुंचाना)	2
546	Quaint (विचित्र)	Queer	Common (सामान्य)	2
547	Radiance (चमक)	Sparkle	Dullness (धुँधलापन)	2
548	Random (क्रमरहित)	Chance	Specific (विशिष्ट)	2
549	Ravish (मोह लेना)	Enthral	Repel (पीछे हटाना)	2

SN	WORD (Hindi Meaning)	Synonym	Antonym (Hindi Meaning)	#R
550	Receive (प्राप्त करना)	Get	Give (देना)	2
551	Regret (अफसोस)	Repent	Contentment (सन्तुष्टता)	2
552	Release (रिहाई)	Free	Confine (बन्द करना)	2
553	Rely (निर्भर होना)	Depend	Distrust (संदेह करना)	2
554	Remember (याद रखना)	Recall	Forget (भूलना)	2
555	Repulsive (घिनौना)	Disgusting	Pleasant (सुखद)	2
556	Rescind (रद्द कर देना)	Revoke	Reinstate (बहाल करना)	2
557	Retain (बनाये रखना)	Maintain	Release (मुक्त करना)	2
558	Revel (आनंद लेना)	Make Merry	Mourn (शोक मनाना)	2
559	Rigid (कठोर)	Inflexible	Flexible (लचीला)	2
560	Sanguine (आशावादी)	Buoyant	Hopeless (निराशाजनक)	2
561	Savoury (नमकीन/चटपटा)	Salty	Sweet (मीठा)	2
562	Scatter (तितर-बितर)	Disperse	Gather (संग्रह)	2
563	Scold (डपटना)	Chide	Praise (प्रशंसा)	2
564	Segregate (पृथक करना)	Isolate	Integrate (एकीकृत करना)	2
565	Seize (पकड़ना)	Catch	Loosen (ढीला करना)	2
566	Shrink (कम होना)	Diminish	Expand (फैलाना)	2
567	Sneer (उपहास)	Mock	Praise (प्रशंसा)	2
568	Solicit (विनती करना)	Request	Prohibit (मना करना)	2
569	Sombre (निराशाजनक)	Gloomy	Cheerful (हँसमुख)	2
570	Split (विभाजन)	Divide	Join (जुड़ना)	2
571	Startle (चौंकना)	Surprise	Soothe (शांत करना)	2
572	Stationary (स्थिर)	Fixed	Moving (गतिमान)	2
573	Steady (नियमित)	Abiding, Stable	Shaky (अस्थिर)	2
574	Sterile (बाँझ)	Barren	Fertile (उपजाऊ)	2
575	Stretch (विस्तार)	Extend	Compress (संक्षेप करना)	2
576	Sustenance (जीविका)	Aid	Starvation (भुखमरी)	2
577	Swift (तेज़)	Quick	Slow (धीरे)	2
578	Synthetic (कृत्रिम)	Fake	Natural (प्राकृतिक)	2
579	Tenacious (अटल)	Persistent	Yielding (समर्पण)	2
580	Threaten (धमकाना)	Intimidate	Commend (सराहना करना)	2
581	Toxic (विषैला)	Poisonous	Healthy (स्वास्थ्यवर्धक)	2
582	Traitor (गद्दार)	Deceiver	Patriot (देश-भक्त)	2
583	Trepidation (घबराहट)	Nervousness	Calm (शांत)	2
584	Truculent (उग्र, लड़ाकू)	Ferocious	Amiable (मिलनसार)	2
585	Tumult (हंगामा)	Uproar	Calmness (सन्नाटा)	2
586	Tyranny (अत्याचार)	Autocracy	Autonomy (स्वराज्य)	2
587	Vagrant (आवारा)	Drifter	Settled (स्थायी)	2
588	Vague (अस्पष्ट)	Unclear	Clear (स्पष्ट)	2

SN	WORD (Hindi Meaning)	Synonym	Antonym (Hindi Meaning)	#R
589	Valiant (बहादुर)	Courageous	Cowardly (कायरतापूर्ण)	2
590	Venial (क्षमा योग्य)	Pardonable	Unpardonable (अक्षम्य)	2
591	Vintage (प्राचीन)	Classic	Modern (आधुनिक)	2
592	Violent (हिंसक, उग्र)	Aggressive	Gentle (सुशील)	2
593	Virulent (घातक)	Deadly	Amicable (मैत्रीपूर्ण)	2
594	Vituperate (गाली देना)	Abuse	Praise (प्रशंसा)	2
595	Volition (इच्छा)	Choice	Compulsion (विवशता)	2
596	Vulgar (अश्लील)	Abusive	Refined (सभ्य)	2
597	Vulnerable (असुरक्षित)	Exposed	Secure (सुरक्षित)	2
598	Wavering (अस्थिर)	Fluctuating	Unchanging (स्थिर)	2
599	Wholesome (स्वास्थ्य के लिए अच्छा)	Sound	Impure (अशुद्ध)	2
600	Winsome (मनोहर)	Charming	Repelling (घिनौना)	2
601	Yell (चिल्लाना)	Shout	Whisper (धीरे-धीरे बोलना)	2
602	Yield (हार मानना)	Produce	Resist (विरोध करना)	2
603	Yoke (दासता)	Harness	Liberty (स्वतंत्रता)	2
604	Zest (उत्साह)	Enthusiasm	Monotonousness (नीरसता)	2

*Total **604** Combo (Syno+Anto) asked **2093** times*

SN	WORD	Hindi Meaning	Synonyms	#R
1	Abbreviate	संक्षिप्त करना	Shorten	
2	Abdicate	त्यागना	Abandon	
3	Abettor	अपराध में सहयोगी	Accomplice	
4	Ability	योग्यता	Capacity	
5	Ablaze	जलता हुआ, उत्तेजित	Furious	
6	Ablution	स्नान	Washing	
7	**Abnegation**	अस्वीकार	Denial, Renouncement	2
8	Abnormal	असामान्य	Unnatural	
9	Abode	घर	Dwelling	
10	Abolition	उन्मूलन	Cancellation	
11	Abort	बंद कर देना	End	
12	Abortive	निष्फल	Unsuccessful	
13	**Abrogate**	रद्द करना	Repeal, Abolish	3
14	Abruptly	एकाएक	Suddenly	
15	Absolutely	बिल्कुल	Definitely	
16	Absorbing	दिलचस्प	Engrossing	
17	**Abuse**	गाली	Scorn, Harm	2
18	Abysmal	बहुत खराब, बेबुनियाद	Bottomless	
19	Accessories	सहायक सामग्री	Attachments	
20	Acclaim	प्रशंसा करना	Praise	
21	Accountable	जवाबदेह	Answerable	
22	Accoutrements	उपकरण	Equipment	
23	Accredit	प्रमाणित करना	Certify	
24	**Accrue**	इकट्ठा करना	Accumulate, Collect, Gather	3
25	**Accurate**	शुद्ध	Precise, Correct, Exact	6
26	Accurately	शुद्धता से	Correctly	
27	Accused	अभियुक्त	Indicted	
28	**Achieve**	पाना	Accomplish, Succeed	4
29	Acknowledgement	अभिस्वीकृति	Confirmation	
30	**Acquaint**	परिचय कराना	Introduce, Familiarise	2
31	Acquiescent	बात मानने वाला	Tractable	
32	Active	कार्यरत	Busy	
33	Actuate	उकसाना	Move	
34	**Adapt**	अनुकूल बनाना	Adjust	2
35	Addicted	वशीभूत	Inclined	
36	**Adequate**	पर्याप्त	Sufficient, Enough	2
37	Adhere	पालन करना	Comply	
38	Adjust	अनुकूल बनाना	Adapt	
39	Adjustment	सामंजस्य	Balancing	

SN	WORD	Hindi Meaning	Synonyms	#R
40	Admonish	फटकार लगाना	To Reprimand	
41	Admonition	चेतावनी	Warning	
42	Adore	बहुत ही पसंद करना	Admire	
43	Adulterated	मिलावटी	Contaminated	
44	Advantageous	लाभदायक	Favourable	
45	Advent	आगमन	Arrival	
46	**Adversary**	विरोधी	Rival, Opponent	2
47	Adverse	विपरीत	Unfavourable	
48	Advocate	समर्थक	Support	
49	Affectionate	स्नेही	Sympathetic	
50	Afflict	सताना	Annoy	
51	Affront	अपमान	Insult	
52	Afraid	भयभीत	Scared	
53	Aggregate	कुल	Total	
54	Agitated	व्यथित, परेशान	Upset	
55	Agony	कष्ट	Pain	
56	Aim	उद्देश्य	Purpose	
57	Aisle	गलियारा	Passage	
58	Alarm	खतरे का संकेत	Panic	
59	**Allay**	शांत करना	Relieve	2
60	Allege	आरोप लगाना	Charge	
61	Allow	अनुमति देना	Permit	
62	Alluring	आकर्षक	Attractive	
63	Aloof	अलग-थलग	Detached	
64	Alter	बदलना	Transform	
65	Alteration	फेरबदल	Modification	
66	Altruist	परोपकारी	Philanthropist	
67	Amalgam	मिश्रण	Mixture	
68	Amaze	चकित करना	Astonish	
69	Amble	टहलना	Wander	
70	**Amend**	संशोधन	Alter, Rectify	2
71	Amorous	कामुक	Erotic	
72	**Amplify**	बढ़ाना	Magnify, Boost	2
73	Amusement	आनंद	Pleasure	
74	Amusing	मनोरंजक	Laughable	
75	Ancestor	पूर्वज	Forefather	
76	**Anger**	गुस्सा	Displeasure, Fury	2
77	Angry	गुस्सा	Enraged	
78	**Anguish**	दुख, पीड़ा	Agony, Ache, Sorrow	3
79	**Annihilate**	विनाश करना	Destroy	2

SN	WORD	Hindi Meaning	Synonyms	#R
80	Announce	घोषणा	Advertise	
81	Annoying	खीझ दिलाने वाला	Disturbing	
82	Annul	रद्द करना	Invalidate	
83	Anodyne	पीड़ानाशक	Benign	
84	Anomalous	असंगत, अजीब	Peculiar	
85	Answer	जवाब	Reply	
86	Antagonist	विरोधी	Opponent	
87	Anthology	संग्रह	Collection	
88	**Anticipate**	पूर्वानुमान	Expect	2
89	Anticipated	अपेक्षित	Predicted	
90	**Antipathy**	घृणा	Dislike	2
91	Antique	प्राचीन	Ancient	
92	Apathetic	उदासीन	Indifferent	
93	**Apathy**	उदासीनता	Indifference, Disinterest	2
94	Apex	शिखर	Top	
95	Aplomb	आत्मविश्वास	Self-Assurance	
96	Appalling	भयावह	Shocking	
97	Apparently	स्पष्ट रूप से	Seemingly	
98	Appeal	आकर्षण	Charm	
99	Appear	प्रतीत होना	Seem	
100	Appease	शान्त करना	Pacify	
101	Appeased	संतुष्ट	Pacified	
102	Application	इस्तेमाल	Implementation	
103	**Appraise**	आंकना	Judge, Assess	2
104	Apprehend	गिरफ्तार	Arrest	
105	Arbitrary	मनमाना	Random	
106	**Arduous**	कठिन	Difficult, Strenuous	2
107	**Aroma**	सुगन्ध	Scent	2
108	**Artful**	धूर्त	Cunning, Crafty	3
109	Ascription	आरोपण	Attribution	
110	Assemble	एकत्रित होना	Amass	
111	Assertion	दावा	Declaration	
112	Assertive	निश्चयात्मक	Domineering	
113	Assess	आकलन	Measure	
114	Astonish	चकित करना	Surprise	
115	Astonishment	आश्चर्य	Wonder	
116	Astute	धूर्त / चतुर	Shrewd	
117	**Atrocity**	अत्याचार	Violence, Barbarity	2
118	Attain	प्राप्त	Achieve	
119	**Attribute**	गुण	Characteristic, Quality	2

SN	WORD	Hindi Meaning	Synonyms	#R
120	**August**	गरिमापूर्ण, भव्य	Majestic, Dignified, Eminent	3
121	Aura	प्रभामंडल	Halo	
122	Auspicious	शुभ	Favourable	
123	**Austere**	सादा, सख्त	Strict, unadorned, Stern	3
124	Autocratic	निरंकुश	Dictatorial	
125	Avarice	लोभ	Greed	
126	Avenge	बदला लेना	Punish	
127	Aversion	घृणा	Dislike	
128	Avert	बचा लेना	Prevent	
129	Awe	श्रद्धा	Admiration	
130	Awry	विकृत	Crookedly	
131	**Baffle**	चकरा देना	Puzzle, Confuse, Perplex	6
132	Bafflement	उलझन	Confusion	
133	Ban	निषेध	Prohibit	
134	Banal	तुच्छ	Commonplace	
135	Bang	ज़ोर से मारना	Beat	
136	**Banish**	निर्वासित करना	Expel, Exile	3
137	Banner	पताका	Poster	
138	Bargain	मोल भाव करना	Deal	
139	**Bashful**	संकोची	Shy, Introverted	3
140	Batter	पीटना	Beat	
141	Battle	लड़ाई / युध्द	Combat	
142	Beckon	इशारे से बुलाना	Call	
143	**Beguile**	मोहना, ठगना	Deceive	2
144	Behaviour	व्यवहार	Conduct	
145	Behoove	योग्य होना	Necessary	
146	Belief	भरोसा	Faith	
147	**Belligerent**	लड़ाकू	Hostile, Antagonistic	2
148	Beneficiaries	लाभार्थी	Recipients	
149	**Benevolence**	भलाई	Kindness, Compassion	2
150	Bereft	वंचित	Deprived	
151	Bestial	गंवार / असभ्य	Brutish	
152	Bewilderment	घबराहट	Confusion	
153	Bewitched	मोहित	Captivated	
154	Bibliophile	पुस्तक प्रेमी	Booklover	
155	Bifurcated	दो शाखाओं में बांटना	Divided Into Two	
156	Bifurcation	द्विभाजन	Division	
157	**Bind**	बांधना	Unite, Fasten	2
158	Blabber	गप्पी, बक-बक करना	Nonsense	

SN	WORD	Hindi Meaning	Synonyms	#R
159	Blend	मिलना	Merge	
160	Blink	झिलमिलाना	Flicker	
161	**Blister**	छाला	Wound, Bubble	2
162	Bloom	फूल खिलना	Flower	
163	Blunder	बड़ी भूल	Mistake	
164	Board	खानपान	Food	
165	Boast	झूठा गर्व	Pride	
166	Bogus	जाली	Fake	
167	Boldness	निर्भिकता	Bravery	
168	Bolster	सहारा देना	Strengthen	
169	Bonanza	अप्रत्याशित लाभ	Bonus	
170	**Bonhomie**	मिलनसारिता	Companionship, Friendship	2
171	Brace	तैयार करना	Fortify	
172	Brat	बिगड़ैल बच्चा	Spoilt Child	
173	Breach	उल्लंघन	Violation	
174	Breakthrough	महत्वपूर्ण खोज	Discovery	
175	Breezy	हवादार	Airy	
176	Brevity	संक्षेप	Crispness	
177	**Brisk**	तेज	Quick	2
178	Brutalize	निर्दयी व्यवहार	Ill-Treat	
179	Bulky	भारी भरकम	Massive	
180	Bull-Headed	हठीला	Headstrong	
181	Bumptious	अहंकारी, घमण्डी	Conceited	
182	**Bustle**	हलचल	Haste, Rush	2
183	Cadence	लय ताल	Rhythm	
184	Calculation	हिसाब	Counting	
185	Caliber	क्षमता	Capacity	
186	**Calm**	शान्त	Peaceful, Relaxed, Quiet	3
187	Cancel	रद्द करना	Abolish	
188	Canny	चालाक	Clever	
189	**Cantankerous**	झगड़ालू	Quarrelsome	3
190	Capitulate	हथियार डालना	Surrender	
191	Caricature	व्यंग्य-चित्र	Grotesque	
192	Carnage	मार काट	Slaughter	
193	**Carouse**	खान पान कर आनंद मनाना	Frolic, Quaff	2
194	Catalyst	उत्प्रेरक	Activator	
195	**Catastrophe**	तबाही, आपदा	Calamity, Tragedy, Disaster	4
196	Cavort	कूदना	Jump	

SN	WORD	Hindi Meaning	Synonyms	#R
197	Celebrate	मनाना	Honour	
198	Ceremonial	शिष्टाचार-युक्त	Formal	
199	**Certain**	निश्चित	Sure	2
200	Chafe	झुँझलाना, क्रोध करना	Irritate	
201	Challenge	आपत्ति उठाना	Objection	
202	Change	परिवर्तन	Alter	
203	**Chaos**	अराजकता	Disorder, Mix-Up, Confusion, Turmoil, Disharmony, Disarray	6
204	Character	चरित्र	Trait	
205	Charisma	प्रतिभा	Charm	
206	Chary	सावधान	Cautious	
207	Chastised	दंड देना	Reprimanded	
208	Chauvinism	कट्टरता	Zealotry	
209	**Chide**	डाँटना	Rebuke, Scold	2
210	Choke	जाम होना	Block	
211	**Choosy**	चयनात्मक	Selective, Picky	2
212	Chorus	सहगान	Singing Group	
213	Citadel	गढ़	Fortress	
214	Clairvoyant	भविष्यसूचक	Prophetic	
215	Clasp	पकड़	Catch	
216	Clean	साफ	Honest	
217	Clement	दयालु	Mild	
218	Climax	चरम बिन्दु	Culmination	
219	Clinched	पक्का करना	Finalized	
220	Cloistered	तनहा	Isolated	
221	Cluster	समूह	Assemblage	
222	Coddle	लाड़ प्यार करना	Satisfy	
223	Coerce	मजबूर करना	Pressurize	
224	Coincidence	इत्तफ़ाक	Chance	
225	Collaborate	मिलकर काम करना	Collude	
226	Collate	एकत्र करना	Assemble	
227	Combustible	ज्वलनशील	Inflammable	
228	Commemorate	मनाना	Celebrate	
229	Commendable	सराहनीय	Praiseworthy	
230	Common	सामान्य	Usual	
231	**Commotion**	हल्ला गुल्ला	Disturbance, Fuss	2
232	Commute	परिवर्तित करना	Convert	
233	Compensate	कमी पूर्ति	Make Up For	
234	**Competent**	सक्षम	Capable	3

SN	WORD	Hindi Meaning	Synonyms	#R
235	Compliant	आज्ञाकारी	Submissive	
236	**Complicated**	जटिल	Complex	2
237	Comply	पालन करना	Obey	
238	Compose	संग्रह करना	Collect	
239	Comprehend	समझना	Understand	
240	**Compunction**	आत्मग्लानि	Scruples, Remorse	2
241	Concealed	गुप्त	Hidden	
242	Concede	मान जाना	Permit	
243	Concession	रिआयत	Allowance	
244	Conclude	समाप्त होना	End	
245	Concocted	मनगढ़ंत	Dubious	
246	Concurrence	सहमति	Agreement	
247	**Condemn**	निंदा करना	Criticize, Punish, Denounce	4
248	Condescending	प्रोत्साहक ढंग से	Patronising	
249	Condescension	नम्रता	Disdain	
250	**Condone**	ध्यान न देना	Overlook, Forgive	3
251	Confederate	संधि करना	Combined	
252	Confess	कबूल / स्वीकार करना	Admit, Acknowledge	
253	Confidential	गोपनीय	Secret	
254	Confiscated	ज़ब्त	Seized	
255	Conflagration	आग	Fire	
256	**Conflict**	टकराव	Clash, Battle	2
257	Confront	सामना करना	To Accost	
258	**Confusion**	अव्यवस्था	Muddle, Commotion	2
259	**Congregation**	मण्डली	Assembly, Meeting	2
260	Congruent	सर्वांगसम	Identical	
261	Congruous	उपयुक्त	Balanced	
262	Conjure	मंत्रमुग्ध करना	Appeal	
263	Conjurer	जादूगर	Magician	
264	Connoisseur	विशेषज्ञ	Discerning Judge	
265	Connote	भाव बतलाना	Convey	
266	Conscientious	ईमानदार	Honest	
267	**Consciousness**	चेतना	Awareness	2
268	Conscript	भरती होने वाला	Draftee	
269	Consequence	परिणाम	Outcome	
270	Consequent	फलस्वरूप	Ensuing	
271	Conservation	संरक्षण	Preservation	
272	Considerate	विचारशील	Thoughtful	
273	Consignee	पाने वाला	Nominee	

SN	WORD	Hindi Meaning	Synonyms	#R
274	Consort	सहचारी	Partner	
275	Conspicuous	प्रत्यक्ष	Evident	
276	**Consternation**	घबराहट	Dismay	2
277	Constrain	विवश करना	Restrict	
278	Constraint	प्रतिबंध	Control	
279	Consult	राय लेना	Discuss	
280	**Contemplation**	चिंतन	Meditation, Design	2
281	Contempt	घृणा	Hatred	
282	Contemptible	घृणित	Abhorrent	
283	Contingent	आकस्मिक	Accidental	
284	Contraband	वर्जित	Smuggled	
285	**Contradict**	खंडन	Confront, Refute	2
286	Contravene	अवहेलना करना	Breach	
287	**Contrite**	पछतावा	Regretful	2
288	Control	नियंत्रण करना	Regulate	
289	Controvert	प्रतिवाद करना	Contradict	
290	Convalesce	अच्छा हो जाना	Recover	
291	Converse	बातचीत	Talk	
292	Convert	परिवर्तित करना	Transform	
293	**Convict**	अपराधी	Criminal, Culprit	3
294	Cornucopia	जादा मात्रा में	Treasure Trove	
295	Corridor	बरामदा	Passage	
296	Corroborated	पुष्टि किया हुआ	Confirmed	
297	Counterfeit	नकली	Fake	
298	Cove	छोटी खाडी	Bay	
299	**Covenant**	प्रतिज्ञापत्र	Contract, Bond	2
300	Coveted	आकांक्षित	Desired	
301	Credible	विश्वसनीय	Believable	
302	Credulous	भोला	Gullible	
303	Creep	छुपकर सरक जाना	Tiptoe	
304	Crescendo	चढ़ाई, उत्कर्ष	Escalation	
305	Critically	गंभीर रूप से	Severely	
306	Criticised	आलोचना	Censured	
307	Crucial	अत्यंत महत्वपूर्ण	Vital	
308	Cruddy	मैला	Dirty	
309	Crude	कच्चा	Unrefined	
310	Cruel	क्रूर	Brutal	
311	Crumble	अधीन करना	Submissive	
312	Crusade	धर्मयुद्ध	Campaign	
313	Crust	उपरी तह	Shell	

SN	WORD	Hindi Meaning	Synonyms	#R
314	**Cunning**	धूर्त	Shrewd, Slick	2
315	Cupidity	लोभ	Greed	
316	Curative	उपचारात्मक	Healing	
317	Curious	जिज्ञासु	Inquisitive	
318	Cute	आकर्षक	Charming	
319	Cynicism	कुटिलता	Bitterness	
320	Dame	महिला	Lady	
321	Damp	नम	Wet	
322	Damsel	अविवाहित युवती	Maiden	
323	Dangerous	खतरनाक	Hazardous	
324	Dapper	ठाट बाटवाला	Stylish	
325	Daring	साहसी	Courageous	
326	Dauntless	निडर	Brave	
327	**Dearth**	अकाल	Scarcity, Shortage	3
328	Debilitate	दुर्बल करना	Weaken	
329	Deception	धूर्त	Cunning	
330	Deceptive	कपटी	Cheat	
331	**Decimated**	नाश करना	Destroyed	2
332	Decipher	अर्थ निकालना	Interpret	
333	Declension	पतन	Decay	
334	Decrease	घटना	Decline	
335	Decree	अदालती हुक्म	Verdict	
336	Decrepit	निर्बल	Feeble	
337	Decrepitude	निर्बलता	Feebleness	
338	Dedicate	समर्पित करना	Devote	
339	Dedicated	समर्पित	Committed	
340	Dedication	निष्ठा	Commitment	
341	Deepen	गहरा करना	Intensify	
342	Defect	दोष	Flaw	
343	**Defer**	टालना	Postpone, Delay	5
344	**Deference**	सम्मान	Respect, Obeisance, Compliance	3
345	Defiance	अवज्ञा, चुनौती	Resistance	
346	Defiant	अवज्ञाकारी	Rebellious	
347	**Deficiency**	कमी	Inadequacy, Shortage	2
348	**Deficient**	अपूर्ण	Lacking, Incomplete	2
349	**Definite**	निश्चित	Complete, Precise	2
350	Dejected	उदास	Depressed	
351	Delectable	स्वादिष्ट	Luscious	
352	**Delegate**	नियुक्त करना	Nominate, Representative	2

SN	WORD	Hindi Meaning	Synonyms	#R
353	Delicate	कोमल	Frail	
354	Delighted	आनंदपूर्ण	Joyful	
355	**Delineate**	वर्णन करना	Explain, Depict	2
356	Delinquent	अपराधी	Offending	
357	**Deluge**	बाढ़	Flood, Overflow	2
358	Demise	मृत्यु	Death	
359	Demonstrate	प्रदर्शित करना	Show	
360	Denial	इंकार	Dismissal	
361	Denouement	उपसंहार	Climax	
362	Depict	वर्णन करना	Characterize	
363	Deplore	विलाप करना	Regret	
364	Deposition	महाभियोग	Impeachment	
365	Deride	मज़ाक उड़ाना	Mock	
366	Derision	उपहास	Ridicule	
367	Derive	प्राप्त	Obtain	
368	Desert	परित्याग करना	Abandon	
369	Desiccated	शुष्क	Dry	
370	Desolate	उजड़ा हुआ	Bleak	
371	Desolate	सुनसान / अकेला	Lonely	
372	Desperation	निराशा	Hopelessness	
373	**Despicable**	धिनौना	Hateful, Contemptible	2
374	**Despondent**	हताश	Dejected, Depressed	2
375	Destitute	बदहाली	Indigent	
376	**Destroy**	नष्ट करना	Ruin, Demolish	2
377	Desultory	अनियमित	Frugal	
378	Detain	रोकना	Delay	
379	Detect	खोजना	Discover	
380	Deteriorate	ख़राब होना	Worsen	
381	**Determined**	निर्धारित	Resolved, Resolute	2
382	Detractors	आलोचक	Critics	
383	Devastate	नष्ट करना	Destroy	
384	Deviate	पथभ्रष्ट	Veer	
385	Dicey	अविश्वसनीय	Uncertain	
386	Dictator	तानाशाह	Tyrant	
387	Diffidence	संकोच	Meekness	
388	Dilettante	शौकीन	Amateur	
389	Diminutive	छोटा सा	Petite	
390	Disastrous	अनर्थकारी	Calamitous	
391	**Discern**	पहचानना	Discriminate, Perceive	2
392	**Discover**	खोजना	Find	2

SN	WORD	Hindi Meaning	Synonyms	#R
393	Discriminate	भेदभाव	Distinguish	
394	Disease	रोग	Illness	
395	Disgrace	कलंक	Dishonour	
396	Disgust	घृणा	Dislike	
397	Disheartened	निराश	Depressed	
398	Dishevel	बिखेरना	Clutter	
399	Disparity	असमानता	Difference	
400	Disproportionately	अनुपातहीन	Unreasonably	
401	**Disrupt**	भंग करना	Break, Disturb, Breach	3
402	**Disseminate**	फैलाना	Disperse, Circulate	2
403	Dissipated	छितराया हुआ / मिटा हुआ	Disappeared	
404	Dissolve	घोलना	Fade	
405	Distaste	अरुचि, घृणा	Loathing	
406	Distasteful	अरुचिकर	Unpleasant	
407	**Distinguished**	असाधारण	Acclaimed, Honoured	2
408	Distribute	वितरण करना	Circulate	
409	Divisive	बांटने वाला	Conflicting	
410	Divulge	भेद खोलना	Reveal	
411	Dodge	चकमा देना	Avoid	
412	Dour	रूखा	Morose	
413	**Drag**	खींचना	Pull	3
414	Dreaded	भयानक	Feared	
415	Drivel	बकवास	Blather	
416	Drizzle	बूंदा बांदी	Sprinkle	
417	Drowsy	निद्रालु	Sleepy	
418	Duct	नलिका	Canal	
419	Dulcet	मीठा	Sweet	
420	**Duo**	जोड़ी	Pair	2
421	Duplication	प्रतिलिपि	Copying	
422	Earn	कमाना	Achieve	
423	Echelon	उपाधि	Rank	
424	Eclectic	चयनशील	Diverse	
425	Economical	किफ़ायती	Thrifty	
426	**Ecstasy**	परमानंद	Joy, Happiness, Bliss	3
427	Efface	ख़त्म करना	Abolish	
428	Effect	नतीजा	Result	
429	Efficiency	दक्षता	Capability	
430	Effigy	पुतला	Dummy	
431	Elapsed	गुजर चुके	Ceased	
432	**Elastic**	लोचदार	Flexible	2

SN	WORD	Hindi Meaning	Synonyms	#R
433	Elegant	सुंदर	Graceful	
434	Elope	भागना	Abscond	
435	Elude	बच निकालना	Escape	
436	**Elusive**	मायावी	Intangible, Baffling	2
437	**Emancipate**	स्वतंत्र करना	Liberate	3
438	Embargo	पाबंदी	Barrier	
439	Embed	गाड़ना	Bury	
440	Embellish	सवाँरना	Decorate	
441	Embezzle	गबन करना	Misappropriate	
442	Emblem	प्रतीक	Symbol	
443	Embrace	स्वीकार करना	Accept	
444	Embroil	उलझाना	Confuse	
445	Emit	उत्सर्जित करना	Discharge	
446	**Emphasize**	ज़ोर देना	Stress, Significance	2
447	**Emphatic**	जोरदार	Firm, Vigorous	2
448	Empirical	प्रयोगात्मक	Practical	
449	Empty	रिक्त	Vacant	
450	Encroach	अतिक्रमण	Intrude	
451	Enforced	लागू किया	Imposed	
452	Engage	व्यस्त रखना	Occupy	
453	Engross	तल्लीन	Absorb	
454	**Engulf**	निगल जाना	Envelop, Inundate	2
455	Enhance	बेहतर करना	Improve	
456	**Enigma**	पहेली	Puzzle, Riddle	2
457	Enjoyable	आनंदमय	Delightful	
458	Enliven	सजीव करना	Cheer	
459	Ennui	नीरसता	Boredom	
460	**Enormous**	विशाल	Immense, Huge, Massive	4
461	Enrage	क्रोधित करना	Infuriate	
462	Entangle	फंसाना	Implicate	
463	**Enthrall**	मंत्रमुग्ध करना	Mesmerize, Enchant, Captivate	3
464	**Entice**	लुभाना	Lure, Entrap	2
465	Enumerate	सूची बनाना	List	
466	Enunciate	स्पष्ट उच्चारण करना	Articulate	
467	Envisage	परिकल्पना करना	Imagine	
468	**Equivocal**	अनेकार्थी	Ambiguous	2
469	Erect	उठाना	Raise	
470	Errand	कार्य	Assignment	
471	Erring	गलती से	Blundering	

SN	WORD	Hindi Meaning	Synonyms	#R
472	**Erroneous**	ग़लत	False, Invalid, Wrong, Inaccurate	5
473	Erstwhile	भूतपूर्व	Former	
474	**Espionage**	जासूसी	Spying	2
475	Essential	आवश्यक	Vital	
476	Esteem	आदर	Regard	
477	**Estimate**	अनुमान	Assess	2
478	Estranged	अलग-थलग	Separated	
479	Ethical	नैतिक	Equitable	
480	Eulogy	गुणगान	Praise	
481	**Eventually**	आखिरकार	Finally, Ultimately	2
482	Evidence	सबूत	Indication	
483	Evinced	दिखाई पड़ना	Showed	
484	Exaggerated	बढ़ा-चढ़ा कर कहना	Magnified	
485	Exaggeration	विस्तार	Amplification	
486	Exalt	प्रशंसा करना	Praise	
487	Exaltation	परमानंद	Ecstasy	
488	**Exasperate**	भड़काना	Infuriate	2
489	Exceed	ज़्यादा होना	Surpass	
490	Excerpt	अंश	Extract	
491	Excogitate	ईजाद करना	Invent	
492	Execrate	कोसना	Curse	
493	**Execute**	पालन करना	Implement	2
494	**Exempt**	मुक्त, छूट	Immune, Exclude	3
495	Exhaustible	समाप्त हो जानेवाला	Temporary	
496	Exhibited	प्रदर्शन किया	Displayed	
497	Exhort	उकसाना	Pressure	
498	Exorcise	भगाना	Expel	
499	Expandable	लचीला	Flexible	
500	**Expended**	लगभग समाप्त	Exhausted	2
501	**Explicit**	स्पष्ट	Clear, Lucid	2
502	Expose	बेनकाब	Reveal	
503	Expository	वर्णनात्मक	Illustrative	
504	Extract	निकालना	Withdraw	
505	Extravagantly	खर्चीले ढंग से	Expensively	
506	**Extricate**	मुक्त करना	Free, Remove	2
507	Extrovert	बहिर्मुखी	Talkative	
508	Exuberant	उत्सुक	Eager	
509	Exude	रिसना, टपकना	Ooze	
510	Fabulous	शानदार	Marvellous	

SN	WORD	Hindi Meaning	Synonyms	#R
511	Façade	मुखौटा	Frontage	
512	**Facile**	सहज	Oversimplified, Shallow	2
513	Facility	कौशल	Skill	
514	Facsimile	नकल	Replica	
515	Fare	प्रगति करना	Progress	
516	Fascinate	मंत्र मुग्ध करना	Captivate	
517	Fascination	आकर्षण	Appeal	
518	**Fatal**	जानलेवा	Deadly, Deadly	2
519	Favoured	पसंदीदा	Preferred	
520	**Feign**	बहाना करना	Pretend	3
521	Felicitated	सम्मानित	Congratulated	
522	Festivity	उत्सव का समय	Celebration	
523	Fetch	लाना	Bring	
524	Fiction	कल्पना	Fantasy	
525	Fillip	प्रोत्साहन	Boost	
526	Final	आख़िरी	Concluding	
527	Fissure	दरार	Cleavage	
528	**Flabbergasted**	स्तंभित	Dumbfounded, Astonished	2
529	Flagrant	घोर	Atrocious	
530	Flair	विशिष्ट योग्यता	Talent	
531	Flaunt	दिखावा	Exhibit	
532	Fleck	धब्बा	Spot	
533	Fledgling	अनुभवहीन मनुष्य	Apprentice	
534	Float	बहना, तैरना	Slide	
535	Flout	उपहास करना	Mock	
536	Fluke	अकस्मात सफलता	Chance	
537	Flung	छितराना, फेंकना	Threw	
538	Fluorescent	चमक	Glowing	
539	Flutter	स्पंदन	Flicker	
540	Foliage	वनस्पति	Greenery	
541	Foment	भड़काना	Incite	
542	**Forbid**	रोकना	Ban, Preclude, Prohibit	3
543	Foreboding	पूर्वाभास	Alarm	
544	**Forego**	त्यागना	Leave, Give Up	2
545	Forgive	माफ करना	Pardon	
546	Forsaken	छोड़ा हुआ	Abandoned	
547	Forswear	शपथपूर्वक त्यागना	Forsake	
548	Fortitude	साहस	Bravery	
549	Fossilize	मिलकर पत्थर बन जाना	Amalgamate	
550	Foundation	आधार	Base	

SN	WORD	Hindi Meaning	Synonyms	#R
551	Fowl	पक्षी	Bird	
552	Foyer	प्रवेश कक्ष	Lobby	
553	Frantic	उत्तेजित	Violent	
554	Fraternise	सहयोगी	Associate	
555	Fraudulent	कपटपूर्ण	Deceitful	
556	Freelance	आत्मनिर्भर,स्वच्छंद	Self-Employed	
557	**Fright**	भय	Dread	2
558	Frontier	सीमा	Boundary	
559	Fruitful	फलदायक	Productive	
560	Fundamental	आधारभूत	Basic	
561	Furbish	चमक लाना	Shine	
562	Furtive	गुप्त	Secretive	
563	**Fury**	रोष	Anger	3
564	Fuse	मिलना, जोड़ना	Combine	
565	Fustian	अभिमानी	Arrogant	
566	Futility	निर्थकता	Uselessness	
567	Gaff	गुप्त तरीका	Trick	
568	Gambol	उछल कूद करना	Frisk	
569	Garble	तोड़ना-मरोड़ना	Confuse	
570	**Garnish**	सजाना	Adorn, Embellish	3
571	Gasp	हांफना	Fight for Breath	
572	Gaudy	भड़कीला	Flashy	
573	**Generic**	सामान्य	Universal, General	2
574	Genre	शैली, प्रकार	Category	
575	Glare	चमक	Dazzle	
576	**Gleam**	चमक	Sheen, Shine	2
577	Glib	चालाक	Artful	
578	Glorious	शानदार	Splendid	
579	Glum	उदास	Dismal	
580	Gnome	बौना	Dwarf	
581	Gospel	धर्म शिक्षा	Faith	
582	**Gourmet**	पेटू	Gastronome, Epicure	2
583	**Grab**	लपकना	Catch, Seize	2
584	Grandeur	शानदार	Magnificence	
585	Grasp	पकड़ना	Clinch	
586	**Gratification**	संतुष्टि	Satisfaction, Contentedness	2
587	Gratuitous	अकारण	Spontaneous	
588	Grave	गंभीर	Serious	
589	Gravity	गंभीरता	Depth	

SN	WORD	Hindi Meaning	Synonyms	#R
590	Greed	लोभ	Cupidity	
591	Greet	नमस्कार	Welcome	
592	Grim	निर्दय	Stern	
593	Grisly	भयानक	Gruesome	
594	Groan	कराहना	Grumble	
595	Grudging	ईर्ष्यालु	Envious	
596	Gruff	कर्कश	Rough	
597	**Grumble**	बड़बड़ाना	Complain, Murmur, Groan	3
598	Guilt	अपराध बोध	Remorse	
599	Gullibility	भोलापन	Simplicity	
600	Hackneyed	घिसा-पिटा	Tired	
601	Hallucination	मतिभ्रम	Delusion	
602	**Hamper**	बाधा ड़ालना	Hinder, Restrict, Block	3
603	Hapless	अभागा	Unlucky	
604	Happiness	ख़ुशी	Bliss	
605	Hard	कठिन	Difficult	
606	Hardly	मुश्किल से	Barely	
607	**Hardship**	कष्ट	Misery, Tribulation	2
608	Hate	नफरत करना	Detest	
609	Hated	घृणित	Loathed	
610	**Hazardous**	खतरनाक	Dangerous, Risky	2
611	Hearsay	अफ़वाह	Buzz	
612	Hegemonic	आधिपत्य	Supremacy	
613	**Herald**	संदेशवाहक, घोषणा	Messenger, Announce	3
614	Herculean	बलशाली	Strong	
615	Heretic	विधर्मी	Cynic	
616	Hesitant	अनिच्छुक	Reluctant	
617	Hind	पिछला	Rear	
618	Hoax	झाँसा	Trick	
619	Holistic	सम्पूर्ण रूप से	Comprehensive	
620	Honour	सम्मान	Respect	
621	**Hoodwink**	आंख में धूल झोंकना	Deceive, Cheat, Defraud	3
622	Hoodwinked	छल करना	Deceived	
623	Horrid	भयंकर	Offensive	
624	Hound	शिकारी कुत्ता	Beagle	
625	Howl	चिल्लाना	Wail	
626	Huge	विशाल	Big	
627	**Humdrum**	नीरस	Monotonous,Boring	2
628	Humiliation	निरादर	Dishonour	
629	Humorous	हास्यपूर्ण	Witty	

SN	WORD	Hindi Meaning	Synonyms	#R
630	**Hurdle**	बाधा	Obstacle, Impediment	5
631	Hybrid	मिश्र प्रजाति	Composite	
632	Hyperbole	अतिशयोक्ति	Overstatement	
633	Hysteria	पागलपन	Madness	
634	Hysterical	मज़ेदार	Funny	
635	Iconic	आदर्श	Exemplary	
636	Ideology	विचारधारा	Belief	
637	**Idleness**	आलस्य	Lethargy	2
638	Ignominious	शर्मिंदा करने वाला	Disgraceful	
639	Ill-Bred	असभ्य	Uncouth	
640	Illness	बीमारी	Sickness	
641	Illogical	बेतुका	Absurd	
642	Imaginary	काल्पनिक	Fictitious	
643	**Imbecile**	मूर्ख	Idiot, Foolish, Dunce	3
644	**Imbue**	भर देना / मन में बिठा देना	Instil, Filled	2
645	**Imitate**	नकल	Copy, Ape, Mimic	4
646	Imitation	नकली	Artificial, Fake	
647	**Immerse**	डुबो देना	Submerge	2
648	**Imminent**	निकटस्थ	Forthcoming, Impending	2
649	Impair	कमजोर करना	Weakness	
650	Imparts	प्रसारित करना	Transmits	
651	Impasse	बन्द रास्ता	Deadlock	
652	Impediment	बाधा	Obstruction	
653	Imperial	साम्राज्य संबंधी	Sovereign	
654	Impervious	अभेद्य	Impenetrable	
655	**Impetus**	प्रेरणा	Encouragement, Incitement	2
656	**Impious**	अधर्मी	Irreverent, Irreligious	2
657	Implacable	टस से मस न होने वाला	Relentless	
658	**Implicit**	अंतर्निहित	Tacit, Unspoken	2
659	**Implore**	विनती करना	Plead	2
660	Importune	जिद करना	Appeal	
661	Impost	चुंगी	Tax	
662	Imprisonment	कारावास	Incarceration	
663	Imprudent	बेपरवाह	Careless	
664	Imputes	दोष लगाना	Attributes	
665	**Inadvertent**	बेपरवाह	Unintentional	2
666	Inanition	भोजन के कमी की वजह से सुस्ती	Lethargy	
667	Inarticulate	अस्पष्ट	Incoherent	
668	Incensed	क्रोधित	Exasperated	

SN	WORD	Hindi Meaning	Synonyms	#R
669	**Incessantly**	निरंतर	Continuously, Steadily	2
670	Incident	घटना	Event	
671	Inclination	रुझान	Aptitude	
672	Incognito	गुप्त रूप से	Anonymous	
673	**Incumbent**	आवश्यक	Required, Occupant	2
674	Index	सूची	Guide	
675	Indictment	अभियोग	Accusation	
676	**Indignation**	रोष	Anger, Offense	2
677	Indiscreet	असावधानीपूर्ण	Careless	
678	Indissoluble	स्थायी	Permanent	
679	Indistinguishable	समरूप	Equivalent	
680	Indulgence	अनुग्रह	Leniency	
681	Ineffable	अवर्णनीय	Inexpressible	
682	Ineluctable	अनिवार्य	Irremovable	
683	Inevitably	निश्चित रूप से	Certainly	
684	Inexpensive	सस्ता	Cheap	
685	Infamy	बदनामी	Notoriety	
686	Infatuation	मुग्धता	Passion	
687	Inference	निष्कर्ष	Conclusion	
688	Infructuous	निष्फल	Fruitless	
689	Infuriate	क्रोधित करना	Enrage	
690	Infuse	उड़ेलना	Fill	
691	**Ingenuous**	निष्कपट	Innocent, Candid	2
692	Inhibitor	अवरोध करनेवाला	Determent	
693	**Inimical**	विरोधी	Harmful, Hostile	3
694	Innuendo	इशारा	Implication	
695	**Insane**	पागल	Crazy, Mad	2
696	Insensitive	असंवेदनशील	Callous	
697	Insidious	घातक	Crafty	
698	Insignia	प्रतीक चिह्न	Symbol	
699	Inspire	प्रेरित करना	Animate	
700	Inspired	प्रेरित	Motivated	
701	Instigate	भड़काना	Kindle	
702	Instilled	मन में बिठाना	Inculcate	
703	Insult	अपमान	Offend	
704	Insuperable	अजेय	Insurmountable	
705	Integrant	अविभाज्य	Item	
706	Intensify	सशक्त करना	Strengthen	
707	Interdiction	निषेध आज्ञा	Decree	
708	**Interfere**	बाधा डालना	Obstruct, Restrict	2

SN	WORD	Hindi Meaning	Synonyms	#R
709	**Interference**	दखल अंदाजी	Obstruction, Barring	2
710	Interrogate	पूछताछ	Investigate	
711	Interspersed	छितराया हुआ	Scattered	
712	Intervene	हस्तक्षेप करना	Arbitrate	
713	**Intricate**	जटिल	Complex, Complicated	3
714	Intriguing	लुभावना	Gripping	
715	Inundated	भरमार कर देना, अभिभूत	Overwhelmed	
716	Invariable	स्थिर	Constant	
717	Invective	अपशब्द	Abusive	
718	Inventory	सामान सूची	Catalogue	
719	**Investigate**	जांच करना	Search, Examine	2
720	Invidious	अपमानजनक	Hateful	
721	Invigorating	स्फूर्तिदायक	Refreshing	
722	Invoice	चालान	Statement	
723	Iota	कण	Bit	
724	Irregular	अनियमित	Uneven	
725	Irreproachable	त्रुटिहीन	Faultless	
726	Irreverence	अपमान	Disrespect	
727	**Irrevocable**	अटल	Unalterable, Irreversible	2
728	**Isolate**	अलग	Detach, Secluded	2
729	Jabber	गपशप	Chatter	
730	Jangle	झगड़ा	Disagree	
731	**Jealous**	ईर्ष्या	Envied, Envious	2
732	Jostle	धक्का देना / ठेलना	Shove	
733	Jovial	आनन्दित	Joyous	
734	Jubilation	आनंदोत्सव	Rejoicing	
735	Junk	कचरा	Waste	
736	Juvenile	लड़कपन	Childish	
737	Keen	उत्सुक	Eager	
738	Kinship	रिश्तेदारी	Relationship	
739	Kiosk	गुमटी, छोटी दूकान	Store	
740	Kit	साज-सामान	Equipment	
741	**Knave**	धूर्त	Scoundrel, Rogue	2
742	Knavish	कपटी, बेईमान	Unscrupulous	
743	**Labyrinth**	भूलभुलैया	Meandering, Maze	2
744	Lacuna	अंतराल	Hiatus	
745	Laden	लदा हुआ, भरा हुआ	Full	
746	Laud	प्रशंसा	Acknowledge	
747	Launching	शुभारंभ	Introducing	
748	Lax	लापरवाह	Negligent	

SN	WORD	Hindi Meaning	Synonyms	#R
749	Layout	नक्शा	Arrangement	
750	Lean	दुबला	Thin	
751	Leisurely	आराम से	Relaxed	
752	**Lethargy**	सुस्ती	Drowsy, Hebetude	2
753	Level	समान स्तरीय	Flat	
754	Leverage	प्रभाव	Influence	
755	Liability	देनदारी	Debt	
756	Lighting Up	प्रकाश करना	Illuminating	
757	**Limpid**	पारदर्शक	Clear, Lucid	2
758	Lint	रोआँ	Fur	
759	Lithe	लचीला	Flexible	
760	Litter	कूड़ा–कर्कट	Trash	
761	Little	थोड़ा	Trivial	
762	**Livid**	आगबबूला	Furious	2
763	Lofty	ऊंचा	Towering	
764	Longevity	दीर्घायु	Durability	
765	Longing	लालसा	Yearning	
766	**Lousy**	घटिया	Awful, Terrible	2
767	Loyalty	वफादारी	Faithfulness	
768	Lucidity	स्पष्टता	Clarity	
769	Lucky	भाग्यशाली / शुभ	Auspicious	
770	Lucrative	लाभप्रद	Worthwhile	
771	Ludicrous	हास्यास्पद / ऊटपटांग	Crazy	
772	Lull	शान्त	Calm	
773	**Lure**	लुभाना	Attract	3
774	**Lurid**	सनसनीखेज़	Over-Bright, Shocking	2
775	**Lurk**	घात में रहना	Sneak, Prowl	2
776	**Luxuriant**	विलासी	Abundant, Lush, Flourishing	3
777	Lyrical	गीतात्मक	Musical	
778	Madness	पागलपन	Insanity	
779	Maestro	माहिर	Genius	
780	**Magnanimous**	उदार चरित्र	Charitable, Chivalrous	2
781	**Magnify**	बढ़ा देना	Enlarge, Expand	2
782	Malady	बीमारी	Illness	
783	Malign	बदनाम करना	Besmirch	
784	**Malignant**	घातक	Harmful, Vicious	2
785	**Mandate**	आदेशपत्र	Official Order, Command	2
786	**Mandatory**	अनिवार्य	Compulsory, Essential, Imperative	4

SN	WORD	Hindi Meaning	Synonyms	#R
787	Mandible	जबड़ा	Jaw	
788	**Mania**	उन्माद	Madness	2
789	Manual	नियम पुस्तिका	Handbook	
790	Masqueraded	स्वाँग रचना	Acted	
791	**Massive**	बड़ा	Huge	3
792	Mastery	प्रभुत्व	Authority	
793	Masticate	चबाना	Chew	
794	Mayhem	अफ़रा तफ़री	Chaos	
795	Meddle	हस्तक्षेप करना	Interfere	
796	Mediation	बीच बचाव	Intervention	
797	Mellifluous	मधुर	Dulcet	
798	Memoir	संस्मरण, वृत्तान्त	Diary	
799	**Menace**	खतरा	Threat, Nuisance	2
800	Mentor	गुरु	Guide	
801	Mercurial	अस्थिर	Volatile	
802	**Mercy**	दया	Sympathy, Clemency	2
803	Merge	मिलना	Blend	
804	Merry	खुश	Happy	
805	**Mimic**	अनुकरण करने वाला	Copy, Imitator	3
806	Mince	छोटे-छोटे टुकड़े करना	Crumble	
807	Mirage	दृष्टि भ्रम	Illusion	
808	Mirth	आनन्द	Delight	
809	Miscellaneous	अनेक प्रकार के	Various	
810	Misfortune	आपदा	Calamity	
811	Missive	राजनीतिक संदेश	Letter	
812	Mistake	गलती	Error	
813	Mock	उपहास करना	Taunt	
814	Mollify	शांत करना	Pacify	
815	Momentous	सबसे महत्वपूर्ण	Important	
816	Monolithic	विशालकाय	Huge	
817	Moral	नैतिक	Ethical	
818	Morale	हौसला	Self-Confidence	
819	**Mordant**	व्यंग्य मिश्रित	Bitter, Sarcastic	2
820	**Moribund**	मरता हुआ	Dying	2
821	Mortal	मरणशील	Deadly	
822	Motif	रूपरेखा	Design	
823	**Motive**	मकसद	Intention, Reason	2
824	Muddy	गंदा	Filthy	
825	Multitude	भीड़	Mass	
826	Munch	चबाना	Chew	

SN	WORD	Hindi Meaning	Synonyms	#R
827	Munificent	उदार	Generous	
828	Mutant	विकृत / अलग प्रकार का	Deviant	
829	Mutate	परिवर्तन	Change	
830	Naïve	भोला-भाला	Gullible	
831	Nap	झपकी	Siesta	
832	Naughty	शरारती	Impish	
833	Nauseous	घिनौना	Loathsome	
834	Neglected	उपेक्षित	Ignored	
835	Negotiation	मोल भाव	Bargaining	
836	Nexus	बंधन	Link	
837	Niggard	कंजूस	Miser	
838	Nimble	फुर्तीला	Agile	
839	**Nincompoop**	मूर्ख	Foolish, Fool	2
840	Noble	प्रतिष्ठित	Dignified	
841	**Nomadic**	घुमंतू	Roving, Wandering	2
842	Nonplussed	भौचक	Puzzled	
843	Noxious	हानिकारक	Harmful	
844	Nudge	हलके धक्के से ध्यान आकर्षित करना	Poke	
845	Numerous	बहुत	Several	
846	Nurture	पालन-पोषण करना	Grow	
847	Oasis	मरु उद्यान	Spring	
848	**Obligation**	दायित्व	Commitment, Duty	2
849	**Obligatory**	अनिवार्य	Necessary, Mandatory, Compulsory	3
850	**Obliterate**	पूर्ण विनाश	Annihilate, Abolish	2
851	Oblivious	अनजान	Ignorant	
852	Obnoxious	घृणित	Disgusting	
853	Observe	देखना	Watch	
854	Obsession	जुनून	Pre-Occupation	
855	Obstacle	बाधा	Barrier	
856	**Obstreperous**	कोलाहलमय	Noisy, Unruly	2
857	Obstruction	बाधा	Hindrance	
858	Obtain	हासिल करना	Achieve	
859	Obtrusive	बाधक	Prominent	
860	Occlude	अवरुद्ध करना	Obstruct	
861	Occult	अलौकिक	Supernatural	
862	**Occupies**	भर जाना	Fills	
863	Occur	घटित होना	Happen	
864	Odious	अप्रिय	Hateful	
865	Offend	परेशान करना	Annoy	

SN	WORD	Hindi Meaning	Synonyms	#R
866	Omission	छोड़ देना	Deletion	
867	Omniscient	अंतर्यामी	All-Knowing	
868	Onerous	कठिन	Arduous	
869	**Onus**	दायित्व	Responsibility, Burden	2
870	**Opinion**	विचार	View, Idea	2
871	Opportune	समय पर	Timely	
872	Optimal	सब से अच्छा	Best	
873	Oracular	रहस्यमय	Cryptic	
874	Ordained	घोषणा करना	Proclaimed	
875	Organising	आयोजन	Coordinating	
876	Ossify	हड्डी बन जाना	Make or become like a bone	
877	**Ostentatious**	भड़कीला, आडंबरपूर्ण	Flashy, Showy	2
878	Outraged	बेहद नाराज	Angry	
879	Ovation	अभिनंदन	Applause	
880	Over	समाप्त	Bygone	
881	Oversee	निरीक्षण करना	Supervise	
882	Overture	प्रस्तावना	Preamble	
883	**Overwhelmed**	व्याकुल, अभिभूत	Surprised, Awesome	2
884	Pace	रफ़्तार	Speed	
885	Pacific	शांत	Peaceful	
886	Pail	बाल्टी	Bucket	
887	Pale	फीका	Colourless	
888	Palliate	कम करना	Relieve	
889	Pallid	पीला पड़ना	Pale	
890	**Panacea**	रामबाण इलाज	Cure-All	2
891	Panic	उन्माद	Frenzy	
892	Panorama	चारों ओर का दृश्य	Scene	
893	**Paranoid**	शंकास्पद	Suspicious, Distrustful	2
894	Parity	समानता	Closeness	
895	**Parsimony**	कंजूसी	Miserliness, Frugality	2
896	Partisan	पक्षपाती	Biased	
897	Passion	जुनून	Desire	
898	**Pathetic**	दयनीय	Pitiful	2
899	Pathos	करुणा	Sorrow	
900	Patrol	पहरा देना	Inspect	
901	Patron	प्रायोजक	Sponsor	
902	Pawn	गिरवी रखना	Pledge	
903	Pedigree	वंशावली	Lineage	
904	Peevish	चिड़चिड़ा	Bad Tempered	

SN	WORD	Hindi Meaning	Synonyms	#R
905	Pejorative	अपमानजनक	Derogatory	
906	Penalise	दण्डित करना	Punish	
907	**Penchant**	विशेष रुचि	Liking, Fondness	3
908	Perceptive	ज्ञानविषयक / चतुर	Astute	
909	Perdurable	चिरस्थायी	Long-Lasting	
910	Perfidious	बेवफ़ा	Disloyal	
911	Perforate	छिद्र करना	Pierce	
912	Perils	ख़तरा	Hazards	
913	Periodic	नियमित	Regular	
914	Perjury	झूठी गवाही	Falsehood	
915	Perky	प्रफुल्लित	Cheerful	
916	Permeate	फैल जाना	Diffuse	
917	Perpetuate	स्थायी बनाना	Preserve	
918	Perplex	हैरान करना	Bewilder	
919	Perquisite	विशेषाधिकार	Privilege	
920	Persecution	अत्याचार	Oppression	
921	Persevere	दृढ़ रहना	Persist	
922	Perspicacious	चतुर	Shrewd	
923	Perspicuous	सुगम	Precise	
924	Pert	आकर्षक	Lively	
925	Pertinent	उपयुक्त	Relevant	
926	**Peruse**	ध्यान से पढ़ना	Examine, Read	2
927	Perverse	विकृत	Nefarious	
928	Pessimistic	निराशावादी	Cynical	
929	**Pester**	परेशान करना	Annoy	2
930	Petition	याचिका	Appeal	
931	Petrify	पत्थर बनाना	Harden	
932	Phonetic	ध्वनि-संबंधी	Spoken	
933	Pillage	डाका डालना	Desecrate	
934	Pioneer	पथप्रदर्शक	Primary	
935	Piquancy	चटपटापन	Flavouring	
936	Pitfall	ख़तरा	Hazard	
937	Pithy	संक्षिप्त	Brief	
938	Pity	दया	Mercy	
939	Plaudit	प्रशंसा	Praise	
940	Plea	दलील	Appeal	
941	Plead	निवेदन	Request	
942	**Pleasant**	सुखदायक	Amusing, Refreshing, Delightful	3
943	Pleasing	सुखदायी	Gratifying	

SN	WORD	Hindi Meaning	Synonyms	#R
944	Pleasure	आनंद	Happiness	
945	**Plebiscite**	जनमत संग्रह	Referendum	2
946	Pledged	प्रतिज्ञा करना	Promised	
947	Plentiful	प्रचुर	Ample	
948	Plight	दुर्दशा	Difficulty	
949	Plod	थके क़दमों से चलना	Drag	
950	Plump	मोटा	Fat	
951	Poach	अवैध शिकार करना	Hunt	
952	Podium	मंच	Dais	
953	**Poignant**	मार्मिक	Emotional, Sad, Touching	3
954	Polished	सभ्य	Cultured	
955	Pollute	दूषित	Contaminate	
956	Pollution	प्रदूषण	Contamination	
957	**Ponder**	विचार करना	Meditate, Contemplate	2
958	Populace	जनता	People	
959	Popular	लोकप्रिय	Favourite	
960	Populous	घनी आबादी वाला	Crowded	
961	Portray	वर्णन करना	Depict	
962	Posterior	पीठ-संबंधी	Dorsal	
963	Potent	शक्तिशाली	Powerful	
964	Practical	व्यावहारिक	Sensible	
965	Preamble	प्रस्तावना	Introduction	
966	Precision	सटीक	Accuracy	
967	Preferred	पसंदीदा	Favoured	
968	Premonition	पूर्व-सूचना	Forewarning	
969	Preponderance	प्रभुत्व	Dominance	
970	Prerogative	विशेषाधिकार	Privilege	
971	Presumptuous	अभिमानी	Arrogant	
972	Pretend	बहाना करना	Feign	
973	Prevalent	प्रचलित	Common	
974	Preventive	निवारक	Protective	
975	Principle	सिद्धांत	Axiom	
976	**Priority**	प्राथमिकता	Precedence, Preference	3
977	Proactive	अग्रसक्रिय	Enthusiastic	
978	**Probe**	जाँच	Investigate, Search	2
979	Procure	प्राप्त करना	Obtain	
980	**Prodigal**	फुजूलखर्ची	Wasteful, Lavish, Extravagant	5
981	Prodigious	अति विशाल	Immense	
982	Prodigy	प्रतिभाशाली	Genius	

SN	WORD	Hindi Meaning	Synonyms	#R
983	Profane	असभ्य	Coarse	
984	**Profess**	दावा करना	Admit, Declare	2
985	Profit	फ़ायदा	Benefit	
986	**Profligate**	अपव्ययी	Wasteful, Immoral	2
987	Prognosis	पूर्वानुमान	Forecast	
988	Prohibit	रोक लगाना	Ban	
989	Prohibition	निषेध	Exclusion	
990	Proliferate	पैदा करना	Reproduce	
991	Prolific	फलदायक	Productive	
992	Promiscuous	अविवेकी	Indiscriminate	
993	Promising	आशाजनक	Bright	
994	Promote	बढ़ावा देना	Boost	
995	Promotion	तरक्की	Elevation	
996	Prophylactic	रोगनिरोधी	Preventive	
997	Propinquity	निकटता	Nearness	
998	Propitiate	संतुष्ट करना	Appease	
999	Proposition	प्रस्ताव	Proposal	
1000	Proscribe	बहिष्कार करना	Ban	
1001	**Protest**	विरोध	Oppose, Object, Resist	3
1002	Protrude	उभरा होना	Bulge	
1003	Provoke	उत्तेजित करना	Enrage	
1004	Proximity	निकटता	Closeness	
1005	Pugnacious	लड़ाकू	Truculent	
1006	Pupils	छात्र	Students	
1007	Purge	शुद्ध करना	Evacuate	
1008	Puzzled	उलझा हुआ	Confused	
1009	Quack	ठग	Fake	
1010	Quake	काँपना	Tremble	
1011	Quandary	दुविधा	Dilemma	
1012	Quarantine	अलग करना	Isolation	
1013	Quarrelsome	झगड़ालु	Querulous	
1014	Quarry	शिकार	Victim	
1015	**Quest**	तलाश	Search	2
1016	Quicken	शीघ्र करना	Accelerate	
1017	Quintessential	सर्वोत्कृष्ट / आदर्श रूप	Typical	
1018	**Quiver**	काँपना	Tremble, Shake	2
1019	Rabid	कट्टर	Extreme	
1020	Radiant	कांतिमय	Glowing	
1021	**Radical**	पूर्ण	Absolute, Profound	2
1022	Ragged	फटा पुराना	Torn	

SN	WORD	Hindi Meaning	Synonyms	#R
1023	Rambling	दूर तक फैला हुआ	Long-Winded	
1024	Ramification	जटिल अनपेक्षित परिणाम	Consequence	
1025	Rampant	अनियंत्रित	Excessive	
1026	Random	अनियमित	Arbitrary	
1027	Rapid	तेज़	Quick	
1028	Rapturous	आनन्दित	Delighted	
1029	Rare	दुर्लभ	Scarce	
1030	**Ravage**	बरबाद कर देना	Demolish, Damage	2
1031	**Ravenous**	भूखा	Esurient, Starved	2
1032	Ravine	दर्रा	Abyss	
1033	**Realm**	क्षेत्र	Field, Dimension	2
1034	Rebellious	बेलगाम, अनियंत्रित	Unruly	
1035	Recapitulate	संक्षेप में दुहराना	Summarize	
1036	**Recapitulation**	संक्षिप्त	Recall, Summary	2
1037	Recently	हाल में	Lately	
1038	Receptacle	पात्र	Container	
1039	Recipients	प्राप्तकर्ता	Receivers	
1040	**Reckless**	लापरवाह	Thoughtless, Rash	2
1041	Recollect	याद करना	Remember	
1042	Recommend	सिफारिश	Approve	
1043	Reconcile	समझौता कराना	Resolve	
1044	Reconnoitre	खोज करना	Inspect	
1045	Recover	पुनः प्राप्त करना	Regain	
1046	Redeem	मुक्त करना	Save	
1047	Redundancy	फालतूपन	Excess	
1048	Refuge	शरण	Shelter	
1049	Regard	सम्मान	Respect	
1050	**Regime**	शासन	Authority, Rule	2
1051	Regress	पीछे हटना	Backslide	
1052	Regular	नियमित	Usual	
1053	Reiterate	दोहराना	Repeat	
1054	Rejoice	आनन्दित होना	Exult	
1055	Release	रिहाई	Acquit	
1056	**Reliable**	भरोसेमंद	Trusted, Dependable, Stable	4
1057	Relief	राहत	Aid	
1058	**Relish**	आनंद	Enjoy, Adore	3
1059	Remedial	उपचारात्मक	Corrective	
1060	Remedy	उपचार	Cure	
1061	Reminisce	याद दिलाना	Remember	

SN	WORD	Hindi Meaning	Synonyms	#R
1062	**Rendezvous**	पूर्वनिश्चित समय और स्थान पर मिलना	Pre-Arranged Meeting	2
1063	**Renounce**	त्यागना	Forsake, Abjure	2
1064	Renown	प्रसिद्ध	Fame	
1065	Repartee	हाजिर जवाबी	Response	
1066	Repeal	रद्द करना	Cancellation	
1067	Repeated	दोहराया गया	Reiterated	
1068	**Repel**	पीछे हटाना	Drive away, Resist	2
1069	Repercussion	प्रतिक्रिया	Reaction	
1070	Replace	जगह लेना	Substitute	
1071	Replaced	बदला गया	Substituted	
1072	Replenish	फिर से भरना	Restore	
1073	Replete	परिपूर्ण	Full	
1074	Repose	आराम करना	Rest	
1075	**Reproach**	धिक्कारना / फटकारना	Berate, Admonish	3
1076	Reproof	फटकार लगाना	Rebuke	
1077	Reprove	फटकार लगाना	Scold	
1078	Repudiate	त्याग करना	Renounce	
1079	Repugnance	घृणा	Aversion	
1080	Reputation	प्रतिष्ठा	Prestige	
1081	**Request**	निवेदन	Ask, Plea	2
1082	**Requisite**	आवश्यक	Obligatory, Precondition	2
1083	Resilient	लचीला	Supple	
1084	Resistant	अवरोध	Opposing	
1085	**Resolution**	संकल्प	Decision	2
1086	Respite	विराम	Hiatus	
1087	**Resplendent**	चमकीला	Dazzling, Magnificent	2
1088	Restive	अशांत	Restless	
1089	**Restrain**	नियंत्रित करना	Control, Constrain	2
1090	Restrict	रोकना	Prohibit	
1091	Result	परिणाम	Outcome	
1092	Resurgence	नवीनीकरण	Renewal	
1093	**Retaliate**	बदला लेना	Avenge, React	3
1094	Retaliated	जवाबी कार्रवाई	Reciprocated	
1095	Reticence	शांत रहना	Reserve	
1096	Retort	प्रत्युत्तर	Reply	
1097	Retrieve	वापस पा लेना	Recover	
1098	Revamp	मरम्मत करना	Restructure	
1099	Revelation	रहस्योद्घाटन	Break	
1100	Revenue	राजस्व	Income	
1101	**Revere**	आदर करना	Respect	2

SN	WORD	Hindi Meaning	Synonyms	#R
1102	Reverie	विचारों में खोना	Day-Dream	
1103	**Revile**	गाली देना	Abuse	3
1104	Revolt	विद्रोह	Riot	
1105	Rhythm	ताल	Tempo	
1106	Riddle	पहेली	Puzzle	
1107	Rift	टूटना	Break	
1108	Right	सही	Correct	
1109	Rind	छिलका	Peel	
1110	Rip	फाड़ना	Tear	
1111	Ripeness	परिपक्वता	Maturity	
1112	Rivalled	प्रतिद्वंद्री होना	Competed	
1113	Rivet	स्थिर रखना	Engage	
1114	Robbed	लूट	Plundered	
1115	Rotund	गोल-मटोल	Round	
1116	Rout	घोर पराजय	Defeat	
1117	Rowdy	फसादी	Boisterous	
1118	Royal	राजकीय	Kingly	
1119	Ruck	जनसाधारण	Mass	
1120	Ruin	बर्बाद करना	Despoil	
1121	Rumour	अफवाह	Hearsay	
1122	Ruse	चाल	Trick	
1123	Rushed	जल्दबाज़ी करना	Pressed	
1124	Saga	गाथा	Narrative	
1125	Salacious	कामातुर	Lustful	
1126	Salubrious	स्वास्थ्यवर्धक / लाभकारी	Beneficial	
1127	Salvage	बचाना	Save	
1128	**Sanction**	मंज़ूरी	Approval, Permit	2
1129	Sanguinity	आशावादिता	Optimism	
1130	**Sarcastic**	व्यंग्यात्मक	Arrogant, Caustic	2
1131	**Satiate**	संतृप्त करना	Satisfy	2
1132	Satisfaction	तसल्ली	Contentment	
1133	Satisfy	आनंद	Delight	
1134	Sauciness	ढिठाई	Impudence	
1135	Saucy	ज़िंदादिल	Cheeky	
1136	Savour	स्वाद	Taste	
1137	Scandalized	स्तंभित करना	Shocked	
1138	Scared	डर	Afraid	
1139	**Scintillating**	चमकता हुआ	Glittering	2
1140	Scion	वंशज	Heir	

SN	WORD	Hindi Meaning	Synonyms	#R
1141	**Scorn**	घृणा करना	Condemn, Despise, Mockery	3
1142	Scour	घिसना	Scrub	
1143	Scowl	भौंह चढ़ाना	Frown	
1144	Scrap	अस्वीकार करना	Reject	
1145	Scrawny	दुबला पतला	Skinny	
1146	Scream	चीखना	Cry	
1147	**Scrumptious**	स्वादिष्ट	Tasty, Delicious	2
1148	Scurrility	अति-दुष्ट व्यवहार	Atrocity	
1149	Scuttle	जल्दी-बाज़ी में चलना	Scamper	
1150	Secure	सुरक्षित	Protect	
1151	Seeking	पीछे लगे रहना	Pursuing	
1152	Seizure	ज़ब्ती	Capture	
1153	Selection	चयन	Preference	
1154	Sentiment	भावना	Feeling	
1155	Sequestered	एकांत	Secluded	
1156	Serendipity	आकस्मिक लाभ	Godsend	
1157	Serious	गंभीर	Earnest	
1158	Severity	कठिनाई	Seriousness	
1159	Sham	बनावटी	Fake	
1160	Sheath	आवरण	Coat	
1161	Shimmer	चमकना	Shine	
1162	Shine	चमक	Glitter	
1163	Shove	ठेलना	Poke	
1164	Shrewd	धूर्त / चतुर	Judicious	
1165	Shriek	चिल्लाकर बोलना	Yell	
1166	Shudder	कांपना	Shiver	
1167	Shuffle	हेर फेर	Stagger	
1168	Shy	शर्मीला / डरपोक	Timid	
1169	Silt	अवसाद	Residue	
1170	Similar	समरूप	Alike	
1171	Sinister	अशुभ	Evil	
1172	Sinuous	टेढ़ा मेढ़ा	Serpentine	
1173	**Slack**	ढीला	Feeble, Careless, Inactive	3
1174	Slim	पतला	Skinny	
1175	Slither	सरकते हुए जाना	Slide	
1176	Smear	धब्बा	Discolour	
1177	Smooth	समतल	Flat	
1178	**Smudge**	धब्बा	Stain	2
1179	Snaky	टेढ़ा मेढ़ा	Sinuous	

SN	WORD	Hindi Meaning	Synonyms	#R
1180	Snooze	झपकी लेना	Sleep	
1181	Sole	एकमात्र	Only	
1182	**Solemn**	गंभीर	Pensive, Serious, Dignified	3
1183	Solid	दृढ़	Firm	
1184	**Solitary**	अकेला	Lonely, Singular	4
1185	Somnolent	निद्रजनक	Drowsy	
1186	Soothe	शांत करना	Mollify	
1187	Sparkling	चमकता हुआ	Gleaming	
1188	Spectrum	विस्तृत श्रेणी	Range	
1189	Speculate	अनुमान लगाना	Guess	
1190	Spell Bound	सम्मोहित	Enthralled	
1191	Spill	गिरना	Drop	
1192	Spine	रीढ़ की हड्डी	Vertebrae	
1193	**Spirited**	साहसी	Ardent, Enthusiastic	2
1194	**Spontaneous**	स्वाभाविक	Impulsive	2
1195	**Sporadic**	छिट पुट	Scattered, Occasional, Infrequent	4
1196	**Spruce**	सजाना	Smart, Natty	2
1197	Spume	झाग	Foams	
1198	Spunky	साहसी	Enthusiastic	
1199	Spurn	तिरस्कार करना	Despise	
1200	Squalor	गन्दगी	Filthiness	
1201	Squawk	चीखना	Scream	
1202	Stagnant	गतिहीन	Motionless	
1203	Stamped	मुद्रांकित	Imprinted	
1204	Startled	आश्चर्यचकित	Amazed	
1205	Stentorian	बुलन्द	Extremely Loud	
1206	Stimulation	उत्तेजना	Provocation	
1207	Stoical	उदासीन	Apathetic	
1208	**Stray**	भटक जाना, बेघर	Wander, Homeless	2
1209	Stroll	चहलक़दमी	Walk	
1210	**Stubborn**	ज़िद्दी	Adamant, Obstinate	2
1211	Stun	चकित होना	Shock	
1212	Stupid	मूर्ख	Dull	
1213	**Stymie**	रोक लगाना	Impede, Hinder	2
1214	Subjugate	पराजित करना	Conquer	
1215	Submerge	डुबोना	Drown	
1216	Submission	आज्ञापालन	Compliance	
1217	Submissive	आज्ञाकारी	Obedient	
1218	Subside	कम होना	Descend	

SN	WORD	Hindi Meaning	Synonyms	#R
1219	Substitute	जगह लेना	Replace	
1220	Substitution	प्रतिस्थापन	Exchange	
1221	Successive	क्रमिक	Consecutive	
1222	**Succulent**	रसीला	Sucking, Juicy	2
1223	Suffix	अंत में जोड़ना	Addition	
1224	**Suitable**	उपयुक्त	Appropriate	2
1225	Sullen	रूठा हुआ	Grim	
1226	Sumptuous	आलीशान	Opulent	
1227	Superannuated	सेवा-निवृत्त	Retired	
1228	Supercilious	घमंडी	Arrogant	
1229	Supernatural	अलौकिक	Mystical	
1230	Supersede	निकाल फेंकना	Set Aside	
1231	Superstitious	अंध विश्वासी	Irrational	
1232	Supporting	सहायक	Agreeing	
1233	**Supreme**	सर्वोच्च	Head, Matchless	2
1234	**Surge**	तेज़ी से चढ़ना	Rush, Rise	2
1235	Surly	कर्कश और अमित्रतापूर्ण	Unfriendly	
1236	**Surmount**	काबू पाना	Overcome	2
1237	Survey	सर्वेक्षण	Examine	
1238	**Sustain**	बनाए रखना	Continue, Support	3
1239	Swap	अदला बदली	Exchange	
1240	Sybarite	ऐयाश	Debauchee	
1241	**Sycophant**	चापलूस	Flatterer	2
1242	Symptomatic	लक्षणात्मक	Characteristic	
1243	Systematically	व्यवस्थित ढंग से	Methodically	
1244	Taboo	निषेध	Unacceptable	
1245	Tackle	निपटना	Deal	
1246	Tag	उपनाम	Label	
1247	Tame	पालतू	Domesticated	
1248	Tangled	उलझा हुआ	Knotted	
1249	Tarnish	कलंकित करना	Damage	
1250	**Temerity**	ढिठाई	Audacity, Boldness	2
1251	Temperate	संतुलित	Moderate	
1252	**Tempest**	तूफ़ान	Storm	2
1253	Tenacity	दृढता	Firmness	
1254	Tend	देखभाल करना	Care For	
1255	Tenderness	दयालुता	Kindness	
1256	Tenet	धारणा	Belief	
1257	Tensile	तन्य	Stretchable	
1258	Tension	तनाव	Strain	

SN	WORD	Hindi Meaning	Synonyms	#R
1259	Tenuous	सूक्ष्म	Thin	
1260	Tepid	गुनगुना	Warm	
1261	Termination	समाप्ति	Conclusion	
1262	**Testify**	गवाही देना	Announce, Affirm	2
1263	Threat	ख़तरा	Risk	
1264	Threshold	दहलीज	Doorway	
1265	**Thrifty**	किफ़ायती	Economical, Frugal	2
1266	Tidy	साफ़ सुथरा	Orderly	
1267	Tilt	झुकाव	Slant	
1268	Timetable	समय सारणी	Schedule	
1269	**Tinsel**	सजाना	Decoration, Garnish	2
1270	Tirade	कड़ी निंदा	Rant	
1271	**Toil**	कठिन परिश्रम	Work Hard, Sweat	2
1272	Toilsome	कष्टमय	Tiresome	
1273	Tolerance	सहनशक्ति	Endurance	
1274	Torpid	निष्क्रिय	Inactive	
1275	Tousled	अस्त व्यस्त	Disarranged	
1276	Trail	रास्ता	Path	
1277	Tramp	घुमक्कड़	Wanderer	
1278	Transcend	हावी होना	Eclipse	
1279	Transition	परिवर्तन	Change	
1280	Transmission	परिवहन	Conveyance	
1281	Transmit	प्रसारित करना	Convey	
1282	Trauma	मानसिक आघात	Emotional Shock	
1283	Travail	पीड़ा	Agony	
1284	Tread	चलना	Walk	
1285	**Tremendous**	अद्भुत	Remarkable, Huge	2
1286	Trendy	प्रचलन में	Popular	
1287	Tribulation	पीड़ा	Suffering	
1288	Trimming	कतरन	Cutting	
1289	Trite	साधारण	Commonplace	
1290	Triumphant	विजयी	Victorious	
1291	Trust	भरोसा	Belief	
1292	Tryst	भेंट	Meeting	
1293	Umpteen	अनेक	Countless	
1294	Unanimous	एकमत	Undisputed	
1295	Unique	विशिष्ट	Exclusive	
1296	Utmost	अधिकतम	Greatest	
1297	Vagabond	आवारा	Tramp	
1298	Valedictory	बिदाई का	Terminal	

SN	WORD	Hindi Meaning	Synonyms	#R
1299	Valuable	मूल्यवान	Precious	
1300	Velocity	वेग	Speed	
1301	Venal	भ्रष्टाचारी	Corrupt	
1302	Venerable	माननीय	Esteemed	
1303	**Venerate**	सम्मानित करना	Revere, Respect	2
1304	**Venture**	जोखिम उठाना	Attempt, Undertaking	2
1305	Veracious	एकदम सही	Accurate	
1306	Verbatim	शब्द प्रति शब्द	Exactly	
1307	Verisimilitude	सत्य का आभास	Authenticity	
1308	Versatile	बहुमुखी	Flexible	
1309	Vertical	लम्बवत	Upright	
1310	Viable	करने योग्य	Workable	
1311	Vie	स्पर्धा करना	Compete	
1312	**Vindicate**	साबित करना	Justify, Exonerate	2
1313	**Vindictive**	प्रतिशोधी	Spiteful, Revengeful	3
1314	Violation	उल्लंघन	Breach	
1315	Virtuoso	गुणी कलाकार	Ace	
1316	Visceral	शारीरिक (आंत का)	Bodily	
1317	Visible	दृश्य	Apparent	
1318	**Vivacious**	जोशपूर्ण	Lively, Energetic, Sparky	4
1319	**Vocation**	पेशा	Occupation	2
1320	Void	रिक्त	Gap	
1321	**Voracious**	लालची	Greedy	2
1322	**Wander**	घूमना	Roam, Deviate	4
1323	Wane	घटना	Decline	
1324	Wastrel	खर्चीला	Spendthrift	
1325	Welter	उथल-पुथल	Turmoil	
1326	Whine	कराहना	Gripe	
1327	Whinny	ऊँचे स्वर में	Loud	
1328	Whirl	घूमना	Spin	
1329	Wistful	उदास	Sorrowful	
1330	Wobble	डगमगाना	Vibrate	
1331	Worth	क़ीमत	Value	
1332	Wrathful	क्रोधपूर्वक	Furious	
1333	Wreak	करना	Cause	
1334	Wrench	झटके से खींचना	Wrest	
1335	Wry	कुटिल	Crooked	
1336	Yardstick	मापदंड	Standard	
1337	**Yearn**	लालसा करना	Strong Desire, To Crave	2
1338	Yield	पैदावार	Harvest	
1339	Yield	राजी होना	Submit	

*Total **1339** Synonyms asked **1701** times.*

SN	WORD	Hindi Meaning	Synonyms	#R
1	Accurate	शुद्ध	Precise, Correct, Exact	6
2	Baffle	चकरा देना	Puzzle, Confuse, Perplex	6
3	Chaos	अराजकता	Disorder, Mix-Up, Confusion, Turmoil, Disharmony, Disarray	6
4	Defer	टालना	Postpone, Delay	5
5	Erroneous	ग़लत	False, Invalid, Wrong, Inaccurate	5
6	Hurdle	बाधा	Obstacle, Impediment	5
7	Prodigal	फुजूलखर्ची	Wasteful, Lavish, Extravagant	5
8	Achieve	पाना	Accomplish, Succeed	4
9	Catastrophe	तबाही, आपदा	Calamity, Tragedy, Disaster	4
10	Condemn	निंदा करना	Criticize, Punish, Denounce	4
11	Enormous	विशाल	Immense, Huge, Massive	4
12	Imitate	नकल	Copy, Ape, Mimic	4
13	Mandatory	अनिवार्य	Compulsory, Essential, Imperative	4
14	Reliable	भरोसेमंद	Trusted, Dependable,Stable	4
15	Solitary	अकेला	Lonely, Singular	4
16	Sporadic	छिट पुट	Scattered, Occasional, Infrequent	4
17	Vivacious	जोशपूर्ण	Lively, Energetic, Sparky	4
18	Wander	घूमना	Roam, Deviate	4
19	Abrogate	रद्द करना	Repeal, Abolish	3
20	Accrue	इकट्ठा करना	Accumulate, Collect, Gather	3
21	Anguish	दुख, पीड़ा	Agony, Ache, Sorrow	3
22	Artful	धूर्त	Cunning, Crafty	3
23	August	गरिमापूर्ण, भव्य	Majestic, Dignified, Eminent	3
24	Austere	सादा, सख्त	Strict, unadorned, Stern	3
25	Banish	निर्वासित करना	Expel, Exile	3
26	Bashful	संकोची	Shy, Introverted	3
27	Calm	शान्त	Peaceful, Relaxed, Quiet	3
28	Cantankerous	झगड़ालू	Quarrelsome	3
29	Competent	सक्षम	Capable	3
30	Condone	ध्यान न देना	Overlook, Forgive	3
31	Convict	अपराधी	Criminal, Culprit	3
32	Dearth	अकाल	Scarcity, Shortage	3
33	Deference	सम्मान	Respect, Obeisance, Compliance	3
34	Disrupt	भंग करना	Break, Disturb, Breach	3
35	Drag	खींचना	Pull	3
36	Ecstasy	परमानंद	Joy, Happiness, Bliss	3
37	Emancipate	स्वतंत्र करना	Liberate	3
38	Enthrall	मंत्रमुग्ध करना	Mesmerize, Enchant, Captivate	3
39	Exempt	मुक्त, छूट	Immune, Exclude	3

SN	WORD	Hindi Meaning	Synonyms	#R
40	Feign	बहाना करना	Pretend	3
41	Forbid	रोकना	Ban, Preclude, Prohibit	3
42	Fury	रोष	Anger	3
43	Garnish	सजाना	Adorn, Embellish	3
44	Grumble	बड़बड़ाना	Complain, Murmur, Groan	3
45	Hamper	बाधा डालना	Hinder, Restrict, Block	3
46	Herald	संदेशवाहक, घोषणा	Messenger, Announce	3
47	Hoodwink	आंख में धूल झोंकना	Deceive, Cheat, Defraud	3
48	Imbecile	मूर्ख	Idiot, Foolish, Dunce	3
49	Inimical	विरोधी	Harmful, Hostile	3
50	Intricate	जटिल	Complex, Complicated	3
51	Lure	लुभाना	Attract	3
52	Luxuriant	विलासी	Abundant, Lush, Flourishing	3
53	Massive	बड़ा	Huge	3
54	Mimic	अनुकरण करने वाला	Copy, Imitator	3
55	Obligatory	अनिवार्य	Necessary, Mandatory, Compulsory	3
56	Penchant	विशेष रुचि	Liking, Fondness	3
57	Pleasant	सुखदायक	Amusing, Refreshing, Delightful	3
58	Poignant	मार्मिक	Emotional, Sad, Touching	3
59	Priority	प्राथमिकता	Precedence, Preference	3
60	Protest	विरोध	Oppose, Object, Resist	3
61	Relish	आनंद	Enjoy, Adore	3
62	Reproach	धिक्कारना / फटकारना	Berate, Admonish	3
63	Retaliate	बदला लेना	Avenge, React	3
64	Revile	गाली देना	Abuse	3
65	Scorn	घृणा करना	Condemn, Despise, Mockery	3
66	Slack	ढीला	Feeble, Careless, Inactive	3
67	Solemn	गंभीर	Pensive, Serious, Dignified	3
68	Sustain	बनाए रखना	Continue, Support	3
69	Vindictive	प्रतिशोधी	Spiteful, Revengeful	3
70	Abnegation	अस्वीकार	Denial, Renouncement	2
71	Abuse	गाली	Scorn, Harm	2
72	Acquaint	परिचय कराना	Introduce, Familiarise	2
73	Adapt	अनुकूल बनाना	Adjust	2
74	Adequate	पर्याप्त	Sufficient, Enough	2
75	Adversary	विरोधी	Rival, Opponent	2
76	Allay	शांत करना	Relieve	2
77	Amend	संशोधन	Alter, Rectify	2
78	Amplify	बढ़ाना	Magnify, Boost	2
79	Anger	गुस्सा	Displeasure, Fury	2

SN	WORD	Hindi Meaning	Synonyms	#R
80	Annihilate	विनाश करना	Destroy	2
81	Anticipate	पूर्वानुमान	Expect	2
82	Antipathy	घृणा	Dislike	2
83	Apathy	उदासीनता	Indifference, Disinterest	2
84	Appraise	आंकना	Judge, Assess	2
85	Arduous	कठिन	Difficult, Strenuous	2
86	Aroma	सुगन्ध	Scent	2
87	Atrocity	अत्याचार	Violence, Barbarity	2
88	Attribute	गुण	Characteristic, Quality	2
89	Beguile	मोहना, ठगना	Deceive	2
90	Belligerent	लड़ाकू	Hostile, Antagonistic	2
91	Benevolence	भलाई	Kindness, Compassion	2
92	Bind	बांधना	Unite, Fasten	2
93	Blister	छाला	Wound, Bubble	2
94	Bonhomie	मिलनसारिता	Companionship, Friendship	2
95	Brisk	तेज	Quick	2
96	Bustle	हलचल	Haste, Rush	2
97	Carouse	खान पान कर आनंद मनाना	Frolic, Quaff	2
98	Certain	निश्चित	Sure	2
99	Chide	डाँटना	Rebuke, Scold	2
100	Choosy	चयनात्मक	Selective, Picky	2

*Total **100** Synonyms asked **296** times.*

SSC CGL Tier 1 2022 [SYNONYMS]

SN	Word - Synonym
1	Inundated - Overwhelmed
2	Keen - Enthusiastic
3	Perseverance - Steadfastness
4	Amend - Rectify
5	Impede - Hinder
6	Vivacious - Energetic
7	Mercy - Clemency
8	Tyranny - Autocracy
9	Wrathful - Furious
10	Old - Aged
11	Consensus - Agreement
12	Baffle - Puzzle
13	Fatigue - Tiredness
14	Belief - Faith
15	Inherent - Inborn
16	Anticipated - Predicted
17	Imparts - Transmits
18	Lighting Up - Illuminating
19	Flout - Mock
20	Obscene - Dirty
21	Antonym - Opposite
22	Ponder - Contemplate
23	Retaliated - Reciprocated
24	Erroneous - Inaccurate
25	Instilled - Inculcate
26	Empty - Vacant
27	Wavering - Fluctuating
28	Eager - Exhilarated
29	Abundant - Ample
30	Concealed - Disguised
31	Frugal - Economical
32	Calamity - Catastrophe
33	Demolish - Ruin
34	Chary - Cautious
35	Encountered - Experiencing
36	Anger - Fury
37	Apex - Pinnacle
38	Hoodwinked - Deceived
39	Permeate - Diffuse
40	Answer - Reply
41	Irrevocable - Irreversible
42	Ignoble - Unworthy
43	Request - Plea
44	Guile - Deceit
45	Muddy - Filthy
46	Vivid - Evocative
47	Futile - Fruitless
48	Morose - Gloomy
49	Distant - Faraway
50	Eccentric - Peculiar
51	Knowledge - Wisdom
52	Chide - Scold
53	Confusion - Commotion
54	Competent - Capable
55	Announce - Advertise
56	Sporadic - Occasional
57	Transient - Temporary
58	Modern - New
59	Moral - Ethical
60	Exaltation - Ecstasy
61	Illness - Sickness
62	Nexus - Link
63	Mutate - Change
64	Satisfaction - Contentment
65	Deliberate - Planned
66	Magnify - Expand
67	Remorse - Repentance
68	Stagnant - Motionless
69	Void - Gap
70	Perils - Hazards
71	Obligatory - Compulsory
72	Hysterical - Funny

SSC CGL Tier 2 2021 [SYNONYMS]

SN	Word - Synonym
1	Abandon - Leave
2	Incumbent - Occupant
3	Fictitious - Imaginary

SSC CHSL Tier 1 2021 [SYNONYMS]

SN	Word - Synonym
1	Devastate - Destroy
2	Vanity - Conceit
3	Profess - Declare
4	Allay - Relieve
5	Quaint - Queer
6	Rampart - Bulwark
7	Pugnacious - Truculent
8	Eccentric - Queer
9	Ludicrous - Crazy
10	Affront - Insult
11	Ravenous - Esurient
12	Destitute - Indigent
13	Salubrious - Beneficial
14	Boldness - Bravery
15	Banter - Repartee
16	Austere - Stern
17	Cunning - Slick
18	Abundant - Plentiful
19	Bafflement - Confusion
20	Confront - Challenge
21	Amble - Wander

SN	Word - Synonym
22	Benevolence - Compassion
23	Renounce - Forsake
24	Equivocal - Ambiguous
25	Hated - Loathed
26	Perilous - Treacherous
27	Loathe - Abhor
28	Perilous - Dangerous
29	Serendipity - Godsend
30	Sanguinity - Optimism
31	Expended - Exhausted
32	Expended - Exhausted
33	Scared - Afraid
34	Pace - Speed
35	Vacant - Uninhabited
36	Disseminate - Circulate
37	Ecstasy - Bliss
38	Startle - Surprise
39	Pleasing - Gratifying
40	Stymie - Hinder
41	Illogical - Absurd
42	Reconnoitre - Inspect
43	Rescind - Revoke
44	Opulence - Prosperity
45	Decipher - Interpret
46	Startle - Surprise
47	Overture - Preamble
48	Tranquil - Calm
49	Arraign - Prosecute
50	Admire - Appreciate
51	Incite - Inflame
52	Fleck - Spot
53	Excruciating - Piercing
54	Abrogate - Repeal
55	Greed - Cupidity
56	Laconic - Concise
57	Resplendent - Magnificent
58	Robbed - Plundered
59	Resolute - Strong
60	Quintessential - Typical
61	Slender - Frail
62	Chastise - Discipline
63	Bestial - Brutish
64	Deception - Cunning
65	Benign - Benevolent
66	Satiate - Satisfy
67	Savoury - Salty
68	Stupendous - Stunning
69	Imprisonment - Incarceration
70	Exorcise - Expel
71	Damage - Afflict
72	Renounce - Abjure

SSC MTS Tier 1 2021 [SYNONYMS]	
SN	Word - Synonym
1	Innate - Inherent
2	Luxuriant - Flourishing
3	Dissolve - Fade
4	Banish - Exile
5	Enforced - Imposed
6	Provoke - Arouse
7	Exaggerated - Magnified
8	Hurdle - Impediment
9	Laborious - Assiduous
10	Grieve - Mourn
11	Alleviate - Relieve
12	Intricate - Complicated
13	Extravagantly - Expensively
14	Pleasant - Delightful
15	Vivacious - Sparky
16	Imbecile - Dunce
17	Fatal - Deadly
18	Blunt - Dull
19	Probe - Search
20	Clandestine - Undercover
21	Garnish - Embellish
22	Uncanny - Spooky
23	August - Eminent
24	Mandate - Command
25	Bulky - Massive
26	Maestro - Genius
27	Definite - Precise
28	Proficient - Accomplished
29	Artful - Crafty
30	Tenderness - Kindness
31	Erring - Blundering
32	Penniless - Broke
33	Propitious - Auspicious
34	Sarcastic - Caustic
35	Revile - Abuse
36	Fright - Dread
37	Acute - Dire
38	Ardent - Passionate
39	Bloom - Flower
40	Vivid - Lucid
41	Confiscated - Seized
42	Satiate - Satisfy
43	Collaborate - Collude
44	Polished - Cultured
45	Slim - Skinny
46	Sporadic - Infrequent
47	Unique - Exclusive
48	Enthrall - Captivate
49	Enraged - Furious
50	Flagrant - Atrocious

51	Culpable - Guilty
52	Appeased - Pacified
53	Revile - Abuse
54	Fright - Dread
55	Interfere - Restrict
56	Dapper - Stylish
57	Scold - Chide
58	Voracious - Greedy
59	Impetus - Incitement
60	Reveal - Disclose
61	Eternity - Forever
62	Perceptive - Astute
63	Bustle - Rush
64	Reliable - Dependable
65	Encourage - Stimulate
66	Emphatic - Vigorous
67	Hesitant - Reluctant
68	Vanquish - Defeat
69	Expository - Illustrative
70	Sparkling - Gleaming
71	Delighted - Joyful
72	Imitate - Copy
73	Astute - Shrewd
74	Tidy - Orderly
75	Humble - Modest
76	Lethargic - Inactive
77	Occlude - Obstruct
78	Malign - Besmirch
79	Hasty - Expeditious
80	Demolish - Raze
81	Segregate - Isolate
82	Obtrusive - Prominent
83	Obstruct - Curb
84	Eccentric - Bizarre
85	Random - Chance
86	Modest - Humble
87	Gloomy - Depressing
88	Critically - Severely
89	Advent - Arrival
90	Merry - Happy
91	Sacred - Consecrated
92	Plausible - Credible
93	Intervene - Arbitrate
94	Sinister - Evil
95	Concede - Permit
96	Protest - Resist
97	Deficient - Incomplete
98	Callous - Brutal
99	Caustic - Acidic
100	Generic - General

SSC CPO Paper 1 2022 [SYNONYMS]

SN	Word - Synonym
1	Ruin - Despoil
2	Colossal - Gigantic
3	Radiant - Glowing
4	Delicate - Fragile
5	Glee - Mirth
6	Prodigal - Extravagant
7	Populous - Crowded
8	Lethargy - Hebetude
9	Reluctant - Hesitant
10	Peril - Danger
11	Erudite - Scholarly
12	Impasse - Deadlock
13	Prohibit - Ban
14	Restrain - Constrain
15	Guilt - Remorse
16	Progress - Development
17	Lethal - Deadly
18	Application - Implementation
19	Imputes - Attributes
20	Consciousness - Awareness
21	Addicted - Inclined
22	Hoax - Trick
23	Penchant - Liking
24	Peculiar - Unusual
25	Contrary - Opposite
26	Portray - Depict
27	Cogent - Rational
28	Pester - Annoy
29	Abridge - Shorten
30	Mirage - Illusion
31	Optimal - Best
32	Obsequious - Law-Abiding
33	Permit - Grant
34	Revoke - Repeal
35	Meagre - Scanty
36	Preposterous - Outrageous
37	Promote - Boost
38	Accredit - Certify
39	Conjure - Appeal
40	Profit - Benefit
41	Quandary - Dilemma
42	Rebellious - Unruly
43	Reputation - Prestige
44	Indignation - Offense
45	Bonhomie - Friendship
46	Partisan - Biased
47	Gourmet - Epicure
48	Stamped - Imprinted
49	Cornucopia - Treasure Trove
50	Obliterate - Abolish
51	Chaos - Disarray

SSC CPO Paper 2 2020 [SYNONYMS]

SN	Word - Synonym
1	Dilemma - Quandary
2	Enormous - Massive
3	Resolution - Decision

SSC GD Constable 2021 [SYNONYMS]

SN	Word - Synonyms
1	Jubilation - Rejoicing
2	Excerpt - Extract
3	Weary - Tired
4	Rambling - Long-Winded
5	Reckless - Rash
6	Aroma - Fragrance
7	Wily - Crafty
8	Enormous - Massive
9	Worth - Value
10	Seize - Catch
11	Sanction - Permit
12	Eternal - Everlasting
13	Adversary - Opponent
14	Baffle - Confuse
15	Steady - Stable
16	Sturdy - Tough
17	Sufficient - Enough
18	Lethal - Fatal
19	Alter - Transform
20	Adversity - Misfortune
21	Reliable - Dependable
22	Cute - Charming
23	Sustain (V) - Support
24	Sullen - Grim
25	Coarse - Crude
26	Disrupt - Disturb
27	Recover - Regain
28	Remedial - Corrective
29	Submissive - Obedient
30	Ample - Sufficient
31	Recommend - Approve
32	Substitution - Exchange
33	Threat - Risk
34	Visible - Apparent
35	Stun - Shock
36	Defy - Disobey
37	Plead - Request
38	Cruel - Brutal
39	Monotonous - Boring
40	Imperial - Sovereign
41	Competent - Capable
42	Radical - Profound
43	Lure - Attraction
44	Supreme - Matchless
45	Enjoyable - Delightful
46	Defer - Postpone
47	Eliminate - Exclude
48	Execute - Implement
49	Scour - Scrub
50	Dense - Thick
51	Aggregate - Total
52	Erect - Raise
53	Destroy - Demolish
54	Appeal - Charm
55	Choke - Block
56	Marvellous - Wonderful
57	Similar - Alike
58	Convert - Transform
59	Spurn - Despise
60	Humble - Meek
61	Assist - Aid
62	Secure (Verb - Protect
63	Noble - Dignified
64	Precarious - Insecure
65	Amusing - Laughable
66	Hurdle - Obstacle
67	Reliable - Trusted
68	Stray - Homeless
69	Estimate - Assess
70	Perceive - Recognise
71	Immerse - Submerge
72	Amiable - Friendly
73	Coincidence - Chance
74	Mirth - Delight
75	Restrain - Control
76	Vital - Crucial
77	Lure - Attract
78	Desert - Abandon
79	Facility - Skill
80	Kinship - Relationship
81	Accurate - Exact
82	Refuge - Shelter
83	Crust - Shell
84	Disgust - Dislike
85	Layout - Arrangement
86	Chaos - Turmoil
87	Turbulent - Violent
88	Absolutely - Definitely
89	Brutal - Cruel
90	Perforate - Pierce
91	Maintain - Care
92	Compose - Collect
93	Rift - Break
94	Grim - Stern
95	Hamper - Hinder

96	Bonanza - Bonus
97	Irregular - Uneven
98	Promotion - Elevation
99	Cunning - Shrewd
100	Shuffle - Stagger
101	Toil - Sweat
102	Keen - Eager
103	Venture - Attempt
104	Opinion - Idea
105	Regret - Repent
106	Gleam (V) - Shine
107	Level (Adj) - Flat
108	Adapt - Adjust
109	Amalgam - Mixture
110	Concise - Short
111	Obvious - Clear
112	Investigate - Examine
113	Achieve - Accomplish
114	Retrieve - Recover
115	Choosy - Picky
116	Treacherous - Unfaithful
117	Confine - Restrict
118	Mayhem - Chaos
119	Repel - Resist
120	Baffle - Confuse
121	Common - Usual
122	Bargain - Deal
123	Attract - Entice
124	Deliberate - Planned
125	Rapid - Quick
126	Fare - Progress

SSC Stenographer 2022 [SYNONYMS]

SN	Word - Synonym
1	Cumbersome - Clumsy
2	Vice - Immorality
3	Fortitude - Bravery
4	Camouflage - Disguise
5	Knave - Rogue
6	Lucky - Auspicious
7	Erudite - Scholarly
8	Bewilderment - Confusion
9	Aplomb - Self-Assurance
10	Courage - Valour
11	Audacious - Brave
12	Bibliophile - Booklover
13	Fastidious - Careful
14	Facile - Oversimplified
15	Rendezvous - Pre-Arranged Meeting
16	Flagitious - Criminal
17	Flaw - Defect

18	Utmost - Greatest
19	Dissipated - Disappeared
20	Magnanimous - Chivalrous
21	Sycophant - Flatterer
22	Yield - Produce
23	Organising - Coordinating
24	Gregarious - Sociable
25	Abandon - Relinquish
26	Hegemonic - Supremacy
27	Imbued - Filled
28	Capable - Suitable
29	Obligation - Duty
30	Ignominy - Dishonour
31	Omission - Deletion
32	Exaggeration - Amplification
33	Seizure - Capture
34	Confess - Acknowledge
35	Nimble - Agile
36	Observe - Watch
37	Clairvoyant - Prophetic
38	Miscellaneous - Various
39	Delegate - Representative
40	Naughty - Impish
41	Lucid - Comprehensible
42	Gullible - Naive
43	Compunction - Remorse
44	Catalyst - Activator

SSC JHT Paper I 2022 [SYNONYMS]

SN	Word - Synonym
1	Incident - Event
2	Squalor - Filthiness
3	Cordial - Gracious
4	Rushed - Pressed
5	Prerogative - Privilege
6	Threaten - Intimidate

SSC Selection Post 2022 - 10th Level [SYNONYMS]

SN	Word - Synonym
1	Gratification - Contentedness
2	Abridge - Shorten
3	Distribute - Circulate
4	Amaze - Astonish
5	Naïve - Gullible
6	Satisfy - Delight
7	Haughty - Arrogant
8	Turbulent - Disordered
9	Cordial - Amicable
10	Meagre - Scanty
11	Stupid - Dull
12	Emancipate - Liberate

SN	Word - Synonym
13	Shy - Timid
14	Submission - Compliance
15	Desolate - Lonely
16	Bashful - Introverted

SSC Selection Post 2022 - 12th Level [SYNONYMS]

SN	Word - Synonym
1	Sybarite - Debauchee
2	Evinced - Showed
3	Vindicate - Exonerate
4	Corroborated - Confirmed
5	Tenacious - Persistent

SSC Selection Post 2022- Grad. Level [SYNONYMS]

SN	Word - Synonym
1	Blink - Flicker
2	Dismal - Gloomy
3	Alacrity - Willingness
4	Abnegation - Renouncement
5	Embellish - Decorate
6	Compunction - Scruples

SSC Delhi Police Constable 2022 [SYNONYMS]

SN	Word - Synonym
1	Diligent - Industrious
2	Inspired - Motivated
3	Accrue - Gather
4	Vagrant - Drifter
5	Cordial - Friendly
6	Barrier - Obstacle
7	Baffled - Confused
8	Slack - Inactive
9	Notion - Belief
10	Awkward - Uncomfortable
11	Battle - Combat
12	Ordained - Proclaimed
13	Pessimistic - Cynical
14	Chastised - Reprimanded
15	Dicey - Uncertain
16	Exhibited - Displayed
17	Procrastinate - Postpone
18	Nascent - Budding
19	Vulgar - Abusive
20	Pupils - Students
21	Apathy - Disinterest
22	Peevish - Bad Tempered
23	Comely - Pretty
24	Courageous - Valiant
25	Criticised - Censured
26	Annoying - Disturbing
27	Venture - Undertaking
28	Facile - Shallow
29	Impetuous - Impulsive
30	Equivocal - Ambiguous
31	Timetable - Schedule
32	Adore - Admire
33	Zenith - Summit
34	Populace - People
35	Protect - Guard
36	Delineate - Depict
37	Rigid - Inflexible
38	Incognito - Anonymous
39	Opulent - Lavish
40	Seeking - Pursuing
41	Rendezvous - Meeting
42	Ripeness - Maturity
43	Venerate - Respect
44	Afraid - Scared
45	Calamity - Disaster
46	Decree - Verdict
47	Impertinent - Impolite
48	Dilettante - Amateur
49	Manifest - Obvious
50	Occupies - Fills
51	Obsolete - Outdated
52	Obstinate - Stubborn
53	Bifurcation - Division
54	Acute - Severe
55	Achieve - Accomplish

SSC IMD SA 2022 [SYNONYMS]

SN	Word - Synonym
1	Risky - Hazardous
2	Repentance - Regret
3	Basement - Cellar
4	Sublime - Astonish
5	Prohibit - Prevent
6	Insightful - Prudent
7	Hamper - Curb
8	Silent - Mute
9	Agreeable - Acceptable
10	Resurrect - Recharge
11	Gobble - Gulp
12	Ambiguous - Doubtful
13	Passion - Devotion
14	Clean - Tidy
15	Abrupt - Blunt
16	Perplex - Confuse
17	Predict - Foretell
18	Grim - Ghastly
19	Rival - Contender
20	Effective - Functional
21	Mesmerising - Spellbinding

PRACTICE SET 01 (SYNONYMS)

1 Mordant
- (a) Kind
- (b) Complimentary
- (c) Bitter
- (d) Peaceable

2 Implicit
- (a) Unspoken
- (b) Supply
- (c) Specific
- (d) Driven

3 Judicious
- (a) Hasty
- (b) Reckless
- (c) Irrational
- (d) Wise

4 Behoove
- (a) Behind
- (b) Bet
- (c) Necessary
- (d) Optional

5 Sustenance
- (a) Extras
- (b) Injury
- (c) Aid
- (d) Blockage

6 Conscientious
- (a) Concentrated
- (b) Honest
- (c) Scientific
- (d) False

7 Curtail
- (a) Downsize
- (b) Prolong
- (c) Lengthen
- (d) Extend

8 Inference
- (a) Beginning
- (b) Conclusion
- (c) Preparation
- (d) Discovery

9 Condemn
- (a) Commend
- (b) Complement
- (c) Denounce
- (d) Approve

10 Erroneous
- (a) Proper
- (b) Regretful
- (c) Dull
- (d) Invalid

PRACTICE SET 02 (SYNONYMS)

1 Expose
- (a) Hide
- (b) Bury
- (c) Reveal
- (d) Protect

2 Adversary
- (a) Helper
- (b) Assistant
- (c) Rival
- (d) Supporter

3 Hind
- (a) Front
- (b) First
- (c) Near
- (d) Rear

4 Fortify
- (a) Harm
- (b) Secure
- (c) Neglect
- (d) Loosen

5 Current
- (a) Antiquated
- (b) Uncommon
- (c) Old
- (d) Present

6 Adhere
- (a) Comply
- (b) Ignore
- (c) Release
- (d) Detach

7 Combustible
- (a) Unbreakable
- (b) Nonexplosive
- (c) Fragile
- (d) Inflammable

8 Embed
- (a) Pull
- (b) Bury
- (c) Dig Up
- (d) Rise

9 Enthrall
- (a) Free
- (b) Disgust
- (c) Mesmerize
- (d) Repel

10 Innuendo
- (a) Proof
- (b) Verification
- (c) Evidence
- (d) Implication

Keys: 1-C, 2-A, 3-D, 4-C, 5-C, 6-B, 7-A, 8-B, 9-C, 10-D

Keys: 1-C, 2-C, 3-D, 4-B, 5-D, 6-A, 7-D, 8-B, 9-C, 10-D

PRACTICE SET 03 (SYNONYMS)

1 Unruly
   (a) Cooperative   (c) Compliant
   (b) Disobedient   (d) Yielding

2 Ennui
   (a) Continuation   (c) Anger
   (b) Strange   (d) Boredom

3 Clandestine
   (a) Truthful   (c) Frank
   (b) Secret   (d) Upright

4 Cloistered
   (a) Isolated   (c) Improvement
   (b) Mendable   (d) Crowded

5 Laconic
   (a) Brief   (c) Lengthy
   (b) Verbose   (d) Unabridged

6 Propitious
   (a) Luxurious   (c) Sad
   (b) Pitiful   (d) Hopeful

7 Hyperbole
   (a) Spoliation   (c) Simplification
   (b) Overstatement (d) Injury

8 Lucid
   (a) Murky   (c) Dim
   (b) Clear   (d) Dumb

9 Incessantly
   (a) Ceasing   (c) Steadily
   (b) Irregularly   (d) Unevenly

10 Ruse
   (a) Rules   (c) Trick
   (b) Fuel   (d) Exchange

PRACTICE SET 04 (SYNONYMS)

1 Erode
   (a) Fix   (c) Preserve
   (b) Disintegrate   (d) Build

2 Entangle
   (a) Exclude   (c) Implicate
   (b) Clarify   (d) Release

3 Thwart
   (a) Impede   (c) Support
   (b) Aid   (d) Face

4 Handy
   (a) Hard   (c) Useless
   (b) Convenient   (d) Clumsy

5 Avenge
   (a) Punish   (c) Encourage
   (b) Cheer   (d) Comfort

6 Scrap
   (a) Hoard   (c) Store
   (b) Save   (d) Reject

7 Candid
   (a) Cruel   (c) Arrogant
   (b) Frank   (d) Sweet

8 Sane
   (a) Sensible   (c) Sensitive
   (b) Crazy   (d) Foolish

9 Opportune
   (a) Rarely   (c) Timely
   (b) Likely   (d) Barely

10 Pathetic
   (a) Powerful   (c) Purposeful
   (b) Plentiful   (d) Pitiful

Keys: 1-B, 2-D, 3-B, 4-A, 5-A, 6-D, 7-B, 8-B, 9-C, 10-C

Keys: 1-B, 2-C, 3-A, 4-B, 5-A, 6-D, 7-B, 8-A, 9-C, 10-D

PRACTICE SET 05 (SYNONYMS)		PRACTICE SET 06 (SYNONYMS)	
1 Whinny		**1 Thrifty**	
(a) Lazy	(c) Calm	(a) Grand	(c) Frugal
(b) Stop	(d) Loud	(b) Rigid	(d) Discreet
2 Perennial		**2 Stern**	
(a) Dangerous	(c) Dry	(a) Mellow	(c) Shrewd
(b) Lasting	(d) Perishable	(b) Proud	(d) Strict
3 Eminent		**3 Temperate**	
(a) Famous	(c) Bland	(a) Moderate	(c) Tentative
(b) Insignificant	(d) Typical	(b) Temporary	(d) Extreme
4 Conceited		**4 Defiance**	
(a) Factual	(c) Circular	(a) Deference	(c) Resistance
(b) Shy	(d) Proud	(b) Assistance	(d) Pretence
5 Winsome		**5 Reprimand**	
(a) Repulsive	(c) Ugly	(a) Reproach	(c) Eradicate
(b) Charming	(d) Repellent	(b) Reward	(d) Applaud
6 Amorous		**6 Resolute**	
(a) Detest	(c) Erotic	(a) Unsure	(c) Uncertain
(b) Correct	(d) Appreciate	(b) Determined	(d) Hesitant
7 Niggard		**7 Intrepid**	
(a) Kind	(c) Miser	(a) Gallant	(c) Insecure
(b) Unselfish	(d) Generous	(b) Cowardly	(d) Invisible
8 Echelon		**8 Pitfall**	
(a) Era	(c) Echo	(a) Haven	(c) Refuge
(b) Year	(d) Rank	(b) Retreat	(d) Hazard
9 Obligatory		**9 Vital**	
(a) Necessary	(c) Voluntary	(a) Trivial	(c) Insignificant
(b) Optional	(d) Liberalized	(b) Essential	(d) Needless
10 Conflagration		**10 Discover**	
(a) Fire	(c) Harmony	(a) Neglect	(c) Hide
(b) Conversation	(d) Shooting	(b) Find	(d) Ignore

Keys: 1-D, 2-B, 3-A, 4-D, 5-B, 6-C, 7-C, 8-D, 9-A, 10-A

Keys: 1-C, 2-D, 3-A, 4-C, 5-A, 6-B, 7-A, 8-D, 9-B, 10-B

PRACTICE SET 07 (SYNONYMS)

1 Abeyance
   (a) Revival   (c) Operation
   (b) Inactivity   (d) Continuation

2 Excogitate
   (a) Communication (c) Invent
   (b) Die   (d) Ignore

3 Virtuoso
   (a) Amateur   (c) Unskilled
   (b) Rookie   (d) Ace

4 Nascent
   (a) Nasal   (c) Budding
   (b) Mature   (d) Permanent

5 Attenuate
   (a) Weaken   (c) Strengthen
   (b) Expand   (d) Intensity

6 Omniscient
   (a) Illiterate   (c) All-Knowing
   (b) Arrogant   (d) Local

7 Jettison
   (a) Keep   (c) Embrace
   (b) Eject   (d) Retain

8 Prolific
   (a) Dead   (c) Famous
   (b) Productive   (d) Evidence

9 Enigmatic
   (a) Obvious   (c) Plain
   (b) Known   (d) Mysterious

10 Declension
   (a) Decay   (c) Improvement
   (b) Decision   (d) Increase

PRACTICE SET 08 (SYNONYMS)

1 Ignominious
   (a) Wonderful   (c) Innocuous
   (b) Disgraceful   (d) Generous

2 Orthodox
   (a) Civilized   (c) Traditional
   (b) Habitual   (d) Deliberate

3 Quest
   (a) Search   (c) Destination
   (b) Path   (d) Route

4 Ideology
   (a) Recognition   (c) Belief
   (b) Mark   (d) Contract

5 Meddle
   (a) Repair   (c) Elaborate
   (b) Manage   (d) Interfere

6 Anomalous
   (a) Indirect   (c) Unhealthy
   (b) Common   (d) Peculiar

7 Fleeting
   (a) Complete   (c) Ready
   (b) Momentary   (d) Lasting

8 Identical
   (a) Similar   (c) Detailed
   (b) Legible   (d) Perfect

9 Ostentatious
   (a) Distinct   (c) Flashy
   (b) Complete   (d) Trusted

10 Radiance
   (a) Depth   (c) Sparkle
   (b) Dryness   (d) Redness

Keys: 1-B, 2-C, 3-D, 4-C, 5-A, 6-C, 7-B, 8-B, 9-D, 10-A

Keys: 1-B, 2-C, 3-A, 4-C, 5-D, 6-D, 7-B, 8-A, 9-C, 10-C

PRACTICE SET 09 (SYNONYMS)

1. Debonair
   - (a) Elegant
   - (b) Awkward
   - (c) Clumsy
   - (d) Difficult

2. Rivet
   - (a) Heavy
   - (b) Joyous
   - (c) Engage
   - (d) Revolve

3. Glib
   - (a) Quiet
   - (b) Artful
   - (c) Dull
   - (d) Hard

4. Indissoluble
   - (a) Permanent
   - (b) Fundamental
   - (c) Detachment
   - (d) Inactive

5. Heretic
   - (a) Faithful
   - (b) Cynic
   - (c) Loyalist
   - (d) Righteous

6. Covenant
   - (a) Difference
   - (b) Conversation
   - (c) Bond
   - (d) Devotion

7. Obstreperous
   - (a) Noisy
   - (b) Quiet
   - (c) Restrained
   - (d) Silent

8. Deluge
   - (a) Famine
   - (b) Overflow
   - (c) Drip
   - (d) Filter

9. Defile
   - (a) Corrupt
   - (b) Hallow
   - (c) Sanctify
   - (d) Honour

10. Cruddy
    - (a) Creamy
    - (b) Dirty
    - (c) Spotless
    - (d) Greedy

PRACTICE SET 10 (SYNONYMS)

1. Recapitulation
   - (a) Summary
   - (b) Movement
   - (c) Prominence
   - (d) Readiness

2. Wary
   - (a) Rash
   - (b) Alert
   - (c) Lax
   - (d) Inattentive

3. Recede
   - (a) Intensify
   - (b) Wane
   - (c) Waver
   - (d) Increase

4. Accurate
   - (a) Real
   - (b) Sincere
   - (c) Precise
   - (d) Genuine

5. Dedication
   - (a) Contentment
   - (b) Trepidation
   - (c) Determination
   - (d) Commitment

6. Miniature
   - (a) Diminutive
   - (b) Mammoth
   - (c) Colossal
   - (d) Gigantic

7. Camouflage
   - (a) Exhibit
   - (b) Disguise
   - (c) Divulge
   - (d) Expose

8. Climax
   - (a) Preface
   - (b) Epilogue
   - (c) Culmination
   - (d) Prologue

9. Manual
   - (a) Thesaurus
   - (b) Handbook
   - (c) Directory
   - (d) Dictionary

10. Sordid
    - (a) Dirty
    - (b) Solid
    - (c) Clean
    - (d) Pure

Keys: 1-A, 2-C, 3-B, 4-A, 5-B, 6-C, 7-A, 8-B, 9-A, 10-B

Keys: 1-A, 2-B, 3-B, 4-C, 5-D, 6-A, 7-B, 8-C, 9-B, 10-A

PRACTICE SET 11 (SYNONYMS)

1 Replenish
   (a) Deplete   (c) Waste
   (b) Restore   (d) Drain

2 Veracious
   (a) Brave   (c) Accurate
   (b) Incorrect   (d) Arrogant

3 Hackneyed
   (a) Tired   (c) Uncommon
   (b) Fresh   (d) New

4 Accede
   (a) Admit   (c) Grown
   (b) Submit   (d) Consent

5 Terse
   (a) Brief   (c) Lengthy
   (b) Prolix   (d) Wordy

6 Poignant
   (a) Emotional   (c) Cold
   (b) Soothing   (d) Luxurious

7 Insuperable
   (a) Weak   (c) Beatable
   (b) Insurmountable   (d) Unstable

8 Volition
   (a) Dependence   (c) Villainy
   (b) Violence   (d) Choice

9 Barbarous
   (a) Refined   (c) Crude
   (b) Polite   (d) Civilized

10 Pejorative
   (a) Right   (c) Derogatory
   (b) Discussion   (d) Complimentary

PRACTICE SET 12 (SYNONYMS)

1 Adept
   (a) Alone   (c) Unknown
   (b) Skilled   (d) Kind-Hearted

2 Assist
   (a) Help   (c) Change
   (b) Mend   (d) Create

3 Attribute
   (a) Respect   (c) Praise
   (b) Speech   (d) Quality

4 Austere
   (a) Careless   (c) Generous
   (b) Strict   (d) Unwilling

5 Chronic
   (a) Persistent   (c) Ordinary
   (b) Common   (d) Temporary

6 Coerce
   (a) Pressurize   (c) Leave
   (b) Cajole   (d) Enchant

7 Concise
   (a) Lengthy   (c) Brief
   (b) Detailed   (d) Complex

8 Converse
   (a) Talk   (c) Oppose
   (b) Display   (d) Agree

9 Defer
   (a) Delay   (c) Dictate
   (b) Despair   (d) Dread

10 Devout
   (a) Revered   (c) Pious
   (b) Loyal   (d) Respectable

Keys: 1-B, 2-C, 3-A, 4-D, 5-A, 6-A, 7-B, 8-D, 9-C, 10-C

Keys: 1-B, 2-A, 3-D, 4-B, 5-A, 6-A, 7-C, 8-A, 9-A, 10-C

PRACTICE SET 13 (SYNONYMS)

1 Lackadaisical
 (a) Active   (c) Careless
 (b) Energetic   (d) Enthusiastic

2 Eclectic
 (a) Particular   (c) Selective
 (b) Electric   (d) Diverse

3 Meticulous
 (a) Perfectionist   (c) Inaccurate
 (b) Sloppy   (d) Faulty

4 Impetus
 (a) Implication   (c) Evidence
 (b) Encouragement   (d) Hindrance

5 Beguile
 (a) Deceive   (c) Deter
 (b) Warn   (d) Repel

6 Farcical
 (a) Serious   (c) Analytical
 (b) Absurd   (d) Lame

7 Carouse
 (a) Quaff   (c) Overlook
 (b) Grieve   (d) Ignore

8 Clement
 (a) Irritate   (c) Clingy
 (b) Cold   (d) Mild

9 Mollify
 (a) Pacify   (c) Provoke
 (b) Agitate   (d) Worry

10 Importune
 (a) Appeal   (c) Imply
 (b) Important   (d) Purchase

PRACTICE SET 14 (SYNONYMS)

1 Drag
 (a) Rest   (c) Push
 (b) Rush   (d) Pull

2 Dubious
 (a) Fishy   (c) Steady
 (b) Loyal   (d) Certain

3 Endeavour
 (a) Attempt   (c) Result
 (b) Achievement   (d) Success

4 Engulf
 (a) Enshrine   (c) Envelop
 (b) Entangle   (d) Encroach

5 Entice
 (a) Ensue   (c) Enrage
 (b) Entrap   (d) Entail

6 Exalt
 (a) Challenge   (c) Praise
 (b) Condemn   (d) Extract

7 Exempt
 (a) Prevent   (c) Hinder
 (b) Reduce   (d) Exclude

8 Garrulous
 (a) Talkative   (c) Throaty
 (b) Concise   (d) Guttural

9 Fuse
 (a) Correct   (c) Break
 (b) Unused   (d) Combine

10 Fury
 (a) Sorrow   (c) Fright
 (b) Cruelty   (d) Anger

Keys: 1-C, 2-D, 3-A, 4-B, 5-A, 6-B, 7-A, 8-D, 9-A, 10-A

Keys: 1-D, 2-A, 3-A, 4-C, 5-B, 6-C, 7-D, 8-A, 9-D, 10-D

PRACTICE SET 15 (SYNONYMS)

1 Perspicacious
   (a) Foolish   (c) Shrewd
   (b) Obscure   (d) Indistinct

2 Snaky
   (a) Clever   (c) Sinuous
   (b) Mild   (d) Wild

3 Divisive
   (a) Agreeing   (c) Cooperating
   (b) Conflicting   (d) Unifying

4 Gaff
   (a) Comp Lain   (c) Gesture
   (b) Trick   (d) Laugh

5 Supercilious
   (a) Modest   (c) Arrogant
   (b) Sociable   (d) Rational

6 Insolent
   (a) Shy   (c) Happy
   (b) Sorrowful   (d) Rude

7 Consternation
   (a) Dismay   (c) Composure
   (b) Happiness   (d) Assurance

8 Levity
   (a) Gravity   (c) Beloved
   (b) Funniness   (d) Baleful

9 Reprove
   (a) Praise   (c) Scold
   (b) Laud   (d) Commend

10 Jubilant
   (a) Happy   (c) Ancient
   (b) Aggressive   (d) Defeat

PRACTICE SET 16 (SYNONYMS)

1 Hostility
   (a) Sympathy   (c) Goodwill
   (b) Friendship   (d) Enmity

2 Inarticulate
   (a) Eloquent   (c) Inevitable
   (b) Incoherent   (d) Fluent

3 Indelible
   (a) Illegible   (c) Ineffective
   (b) Inerasable   (d) Illegal

4 Inept
   (a) Clumsy   (c) Strong
   (b) Fit   (d) Capable

5 Initiate
   (a) Show   (c) Sign
   (b) Start   (d) Slow

6 Insult
   (a) Apply   (c) Offer
   (b) Offend   (d) Remove

7 Intricate
   (a) Connected   (c) Complex
   (b) Complete   (d) Colourful

8 Lament
   (a) Afflict   (c) Torment
   (b) Mourn   (d) Distress

9 Lethal
   (a) Harmless   (c) Healthy
   (b) Fatal   (d) Strong

10 Mammoth
   (a) Magnificent   (c) Perilous
   (b) Miniscule   (d) Gigantic

Keys: 1-C, 2-C, 3-B, 4-B, 5-C, 6-D, 7-A, 8-B, 9-C, 10-A

Keys: 1-D, 2-B, 3-B, 4-A, 5-B, 6-B, 7-C, 8-B, 9-B, 10-D

PRACTICE SET 17 (SYNONYMS)		PRACTICE SET 18 (SYNONYMS)	

PRACTICE SET 17 (SYNONYMS)

1 Banal
   (a) Origin Al   (c) Distinctive
   (b) Commonplace   (d) Sharp

2 Contrite
   (a) Determined   (c) Devise
   (b) Specific   (d) Regretful

3 Devoid
   (a) Empty   (c) Sufficient
   (b) Complete   (d) Happy

4 Monolithic
   (a) Huge   (c) Minute
   (b) Written   (d) Cramped

5 Divulgence
   (a) Testimony   (c) Assent
   (b) Repudiation   (d) Revelation

6 To Admonish
   (a) To Reprimand   (c) To Panegyrize
   (b) To Rave   (d) To Eulogise

7 Blabber
   (a) Wary   (c) Sophic
   (b) Nonsense   (d) Sapient

8 Cogent
   (a) Invalid   (c) Inconclusive
   (b) Effective   (d) Unlikely

9 Precedence
   (a) Upraise   (c) Present
   (b) Insignificance   (d) Priority

10 Empirical
   (a) Practical   (c) Hypothetical
   (b) Unproved   (d) Theoretical

PRACTICE SET 18 (SYNONYMS)

1 Obstacle
   (a) Benefit   (c) Accessory
   (b) Clearance   (d) Barrier

2 Pensive
   (a) Reflective   (c) Spiteful
   (b) Spontaneous   (d) Tragic

3 Perplex
   (a) Deceive   (c) Complex
   (b) Bewilder   (d) Surprise

4 Precarious
   (a) Dangerous   (c) Valuable
   (b) Abundant   (d) Premature

5 Prevalent
   (a) Common   (c) Different
   (b) Unusual   (d) Rare

6 Rampant
   (a) Excessive   (c) Gentle
   (b) Rare   (d) Limited

7 Renown
   (a) Obscurity   (c) Wisdom
   (b) Fame   (d) Conceit

8 Repudiate
   (a) Enforce   (c) Regret
   (b) Sanction   (d) Renounce

9 Reticent
   (a) Silent   (b) Garrulous
   (c) Confident   (d) Extrovert

10 Sterile
   (a) Productive   (c) Sordid
   (b) Barren   (d) Pure

Keys: 1-B, 2-D, 3-A, 4-A, 5-D, 6-A, 7-B, 8-B, 9-D, 10-A

Keys: 1-D, 2-A, 3-B, 4-A, 5-A, 6-A, 7-B, 8-D, 9-A, 10-B

PRACTICE SET 19 (SYNONYMS)

1 Munificent
   (a) Stingy   (c) Careful
   (b) Generous   (d) Sparse

2 Fledgling
   (a) Wild   (c) Fugitive
   (b) Apprentice   (d) Ancient

3 Repugnance
   (a) Esteem   (c) Aversion
   (b) Respect   (d) Sympathy

4 Reminisce
   (a) Remember   (c) Forget
   (b) Discover   (d) Hang

5 Plaudit
   (a) Criticism   (c) Praise
   (b) Jeering   (d) Silence

6 Piquant
   (a) Flat   (c) Spicy
   (b) Pride   (d) Grumpy

7 Equanimity
   (a) Anxiety   (c) Arousal
   (b) Calm   (d) Upset

8 Despicable
   (a) Hateful   (c) Creditable
   (b) Disappointing   (d) Nonchalance

9 Pithy
   (a) Verbose   (c) Lengthy
   (b) Brief   (d) Unabridged

10 Mundane
   (a) Bounteous   (c) Exciting
   (b) Heavenly   (d) Everyday

PRACTICE SET 20 (SYNONYMS)

1 Taciturn
   (a) Reticent   (c) Phlegmatic
   (b) Talkative   (d) Placid

2 Tilt
   (a) Support   (c) Straighten
   (b) Cross   (d) Slant

3 Triumph
   (a) Victory   (c) Attack
   (b) Fight   (d) Peace

4 Vindictive
   (a) Forceful   (c) Helpful
   (b) Revengeful   (d) Watchful

5 Hybrid
   (a) Homogeneous   (c) Pure
   (b) Composite   (d) Love

6 Discreet
   (a) Described   (c) Rash
   (b) Careful   (d) Mundane

7 Invective
   (a) Invent   (c) Abusive
   (b) Expressive   (d) Invitation

8 Grave
   (a) Dead   (c) Serious
   (b) Still   (d) Sad

9 Felicity
   (a) Bliss   (c) Grief
   (b) Misery   (d) Trouble

10 Chafe
   (a) Chain   (c) Irritate
   (b) Safe   (d) Joy

Keys: 1-B, 2-B, 3-C, 4-A, 5-C, 6-C, 7-B, 8-A, 9-B, 10-D

Keys: 1-A, 2-D, 3-A, 4-B, 5-B, 6-B, 7-C, 8-C, 9-A, 10-C

SN	WORD	Antonyms	#R
1	Abate (समाप्त करना / कम करना)	Aggravate (और बढ़ा देना)	
2	Abbreviate (संक्षिप्त करना)	Expand (विस्तार करना)	
3	Abide (मान लेना / पालन करना)	Reject (अस्वीकार करना)	
4	Abolish (समाप्त करना)	Build (निर्माण करना)	
5	**Abominable (घटिया)**	Delightful, Admirable (आनंदप्रद)	2
6	Aboriginal (मूल निवासी)	Immigrant (अप्रवासी)	
7	Above (ऊपर)	Below (नीचे)	
8	Abscond (फ़रार होना)	Remain (टिकना)	
9	**Absorb (सोख लेना)**	Eject, Emit (निकालना)	2
10	**Abstract (निराकार, अमूर्त)**	Concrete (ठोस)	2
11	**Abundance (प्रचुरता)**	Scarcity (कमी)	3
12	Abusive (अपमानजनक)	Laudatory (प्रशंसात्मक)	
13	Abutting (सटा हुआ)	Far (दूर)	
14	Accelerate (गति बढ़ाना)	Delay (देरी करना)	
15	Accentuate (जोर देना)	Disparage (उपेक्षा करना)	
16	**Accept (स्वीकार)**	Reject, Deny (अस्वीकार)	4
17	Accessible (पहुंचने योग्य)	Restricted (वर्जित)	
18	Accolade (सम्मान)	Blame (दोष लगाना)	
19	**Accumulate (जमा करना)**	Disperse, Squandered (बिखेरना, गंवाना)	2
20	**Accusation (आरोप लगाना)**	Exculpation, Defend (सफ़ाई देना, बचाना)	2
21	Acerbic (कड़वा)	Bland (बेस्वाद)	
22	**Acknowledge (स्वीकार करना)**	Deny, Decline (मना करना)	2
23	Acquisition (अधिग्रहण)	Loss (नुकसान)	
24	**Acquit (दोषमुक्त करना)**	Condemn, Convict, Blame (दोष लगाना)	5
25	Acumen (कुशाग्र बुद्धि)	Stupidity (मूर्खता)	
26	**Adamant (अटल)**	Yielding, Gullible, Flexible (नर्म, लचीला)	5
27	Add (जोड़ना)	Remove (हटाना)	
28	Adipose (वसा)	Stringy (रेशेदार)	
29	Adjacent (सटा हुआ)	Distant (अलग)	
30	**Admirable (प्रशंसनीय)**	Unworthy, Blameworthy (अयोग्य, दोषयुक्त)	2
31	Admiration (प्रशंसा)	Contempt (निंदा)	
32	Admire (प्रशंसा करना)	Ridicule (उपहास)	
33	Adulteration (मिलावट)	Purification (शुद्धिकरण)	
34	Adultery (व्यभिचार)	Purity (पवित्रता)	
35	**Advanced (उन्नत)**	Retarded, Rudimentary (मंद)	2
36	Advocacy (समर्थन)	Discouragement (हतोत्साह)	
37	Affable (मिलनसार)	Surly (बदमिजाज़)	
38	Affiliation (संबंध)	Detachment (वियोग)	
39	**Affirm (स्वीकार करना)**	Refuse, Disagree, Denial (मना करना, असहमत होना)	4
40	**Affliction (यातना)**	Pleasure (आनंद)	2

SN	WORD	Antonyms	#R
41	Aggrandize (शक्ति बढ़ाना)	Belittle (महत्व घटाना)	
42	**Aggressive (आक्रामक)**	Peaceful, Calm (शांतिपूर्ण)	2
43	**Agitate (उत्तेजित करना)**	Pacify, Calm, Soothe (शांत करना)	3
44	**Agony (कष्ट)**	Pleasure, Ecstasy, Delight, Comfort (आनंद, उत्साह, आराम)	5
45	Agree (सहमत)	Oppose (विरोध)	
46	Agreement (समझौता)	Discord (अनबन)	
47	**Airy (हवादार)**	Stuffy (घुटन-भरा)	2
48	**Alien (विदेशी)**	Native (देशी)	2
49	Alight (उतरना)	Embark (चढ़ना)	
50	Alike (एक जैसे)	Different (अलग-अलग)	
51	Alive (ज़िन्दा)	Dead (मृत)	
52	Allergic (ऐलर्जी संबंधी)	Immune (प्रतिरक्षित)	
53	Alliance (संधि)	Separation (पृथक्करण)	
54	Alluring (मोहक)	Repulsive (अरुचिकर)	
55	Ally (मित्र)	Enemy (दुश्मन)	
56	**Altercation (तकरार)**	Compromise, Agreement (समझौता)	2
57	Altruism (परोपकारिता)	Spite (द्वेष करना)	
58	Always (हमेशा)	Never (कभी नहीं)	
59	**Ambiguous (अस्पष्ट)**	Precise, Clear, Certain (स्पष्ट)	5
60	Ambition (महत्वाकांक्षा)	Laziness (आलस्य)	
61	Ambitious (महत्वाकांक्षी)	Lazy (आलसी)	
62	Amorphous (अनाकार)	Definite (निश्चित)	
63	**Ample (प्रचुर)**	Meagre (अल्प)	3
64	Amuse (मन बहलाना)	Bore (उबा देना)	
65	Analogous (अनुरूप)	Disagreeing (भिन्न होना)	
66	Anarchic (अराजक)	Normal (साधारण)	
67	**Ancient (प्राचीन)**	Modern (आधुनिक)	2
68	Angst (आक्रोश)	Casualness (लापरवाही)	
69	Anile (बुढ़िया जैसा)	Young (युवा)	
70	**Animosity (बैर)**	Benevolence, Love (परोपकार, मोहब्बत)	2
71	**Antique (प्राचीन)**	Recent, Modern (हाल का, आधुनिक)	2
72	Antithesis (विपरीत)	Harmony (समानता)	
73	Antonym (विलोम शब्द)	Synonym (पर्याय शब्द)	
74	Anxieties (चिंता)	Placidity (शांतचित्तता)	
75	Apocryphal (मणगढ़ंत)	Authentic (विश्वसनीय)	
76	Appal (डराना)	Assure (आश्वासन)	
77	**Appalling (डरावना)**	Consoling, Appealing (सांत्वना, अपील)	2
78	**Applaud (सराहना)**	Denounce, Criticize, Censure (निंदा)	3
79	**Appoint (नियुक्त करना)**	Dismiss (खारिज)	3

SN	WORD	Antonyms	#R
80	Appreciation (प्रशंसा)	Antipathy (घृणा)	
81	Approach (पास आना)	Avoid (टाल जाना)	
82	**Approached (संपर्क किया)**	Retreated, Receded (पीछे हटा)	2
83	**Appropriate (उपयुक्त)**	Unsuitable, Irrelevant, Improper (अनुपयुक्त)	4
84	Approve (मंजूर)	Reject (अस्वीकार)	
85	Approximately (लगभग)	Exactly (बिल्कुल)	
86	Argue (तर्क करना)	Agree (सहमत होना)	
87	Arouse (उत्तेजित करना)	Cease (बंद करना)	
88	Arrogance (अहंकार)	Humility (विनम्रता)	
89	**Arrogant (अभिमानी)**	Modest, Humble, Humility (विनम्र)	6
90	Artifice (धोखा)	Truthfulness (सच्चाई)	
91	**Ascent (चढ़ाव)**	Descent (गिराव)	3
92	Asperity (रूखापन)	Civility (सभ्यता)	
93	Assaulted (हमला)	Guarded (पहरा)	
94	**Assemble (इकट्ठा करना)**	Disperse, Scatter (बिखेरना)	2
95	Assent (समर्थन)	Dissent (मतभेद)	
96	**Assiduous (परिश्रमी)**	Neglectful, Idle (बेपरवाह)	3
97	Assuage (शांत करना)	Provoke (उकसाना)	
98	Astonish (चकित करना)	Calm (शांत)	
99	Atheist (नास्तिक)	Believer (आस्तिक)	
100	Attachments (बंधन)	Opposition (विरोध)	
101	Attack (आक्रमण)	Defence (रक्षा)	
102	Attract (आकर्षित करना)	Deters (डराना)	
103	**Attract (आकर्षित)**	Repel (पीछे हटाना)	3
104	**Augment (बढ़ाना)**	Degrade, Decrease, Diminish (घटाना)	3
105	Auspicious (सौभाग्यशाली)	Unlucky (बदकिस्मत)	
106	Authenticated (प्रमाणीकृत)	Disprove (झूठा ठहराना)	
107	**Autonomy (स्वराज्य)**	Dependence (निर्भरता)	4
108	**Awake (जागना)**	Asleep, Hypnotized (सोना, सम्मोहित)	2
109	Aware (अवगत)	Ignorant (अनभिज्ञ)	
110	Babel (कोलाहल)	Quiet (शांत)	
111	Baffled (चकित)	Composed (शांत)	
112	Baffling (रहस्यमय)	Comprehensible (समझने लायक)	
113	Balmy (सुखदायी)	Hard (कठिन)	
114	Baneful (विनाशकारी)	Lucky (सौभाग्यशाली)	
115	Baroque (विचित्र)	Plain (सामान्य)	
116	Befuddle (मदहोश होना)	Explicate (समझना)	
117	Belittle (छोटा महसूस कराना)	Extol (प्रशंसा करना)	
118	**Beneath (नीचे)**	Above (ऊपर)	2
119	Benediction (आशीर्वाद)	Criticism (आलोचना)	

SN	WORD	Antonyms	#R
120	Benison (शुभकामना)	Execration (फटकार)	
121	Bequest (वसीयत, दान)	Withdraw (निकालना)	
122	**Betrayal (विश्वासघात)**	Loyalty, Stand By (स्वामिभक्ति)	2
123	**Better (बेहतर)**	Worse, Inferior (बदतर)	3
124	Betterment (सुधार होना)	Deterioration (बिगड़ना)	
125	Bewilder (उलझन में डालना)	Enlighten (स्पष्ट करना)	
126	Bias (पक्षपात)	Fairness (निष्पक्षता)	
127	Bifurcate (द्विशाखित)	Combine (जोड़ना)	
128	Bigot (कट्टर)	Liberal (उदार)	
129	**Bizarre (विचित्र)**	Usual, Ordinary (साधारण)	2
130	**Blame (आरोप)**	Praise, Compliment (प्रशंसा)	2
131	Bland (अरोचक)	Exciting (रोमांचक)	
132	Blasphemous (अपवित्रकारी)	Pious (पवित्र)	
133	Blemish (दोष)	Perfection (निपुणता)	
134	**Bless (आशीर्वाद)**	Curse (अभिशाप)	2
135	Blessed (भाग्यवान)	Cursed (अभिशप्त)	
136	Bliss (परमानंद)	Misery (कष्ट)	
137	Blissful (आनंदमय)	Miserable (दुखी)	
138	Blitz (तेज)	Obtuse (सुस्त)	
139	Bloated (फूला हुआ)	Deflated (पिचका हुआ)	
140	Block (रोक लगाना)	Clear (पास करना)	
141	**Bold (साहसिक)**	Timid (डरपोक)	3
142	Bondage (बंधन)	Liberty (स्वतंत्रता)	
143	Boring (अरुचिकर)	Exciting (रोमांचक)	
144	Bossy (धौंस देने वाला)	Polite (सभ्य)	
145	Boundaries (सीमा)	Cores (अन्तर्भाग)	
146	Boycott (बहिष्कार)	Welcome (स्वागत करना)	
147	Brashness (ढिठाई)	Timidity (कायरता)	
148	**Bravery (वीरता)**	Cowardice (कायरता)	2
149	**Brazen (बेशर्म)**	Modest (विनम्र)	2
150	Breadth (चौड़ाई)	Narrowness (संकीर्णता)	
151	Bridle (लगाम)	Release (रिहाई)	
152	**Brief (संक्षिप्त)**	Elaborate, Lengthy (विस्तृत)	2
153	Bright (चमकदार)	Bleak (बेरंग)	
154	Brindled (चितकबरा)	Unflecked (बेदाग)	
155	Broad (चौड़ा)	Narrow (संकीर्ण)	
156	**Brutality (निर्दयता)**	Humanity, Gentleness (मानवता)	2
157	Bucolic (ग्रामीण)	Urban (नगरीय)	
158	Bulk (थोक)	Handful (मुट्ठी भर)	
159	**Buoyant (तैरता हुआ)**	Weighted, Gloomy (भारी)	2

SN	WORD	Antonyms	#R
160	Burgeon (फलना फूलना)	Shrivel (सूखना)	
161	**Cacophony (कोलाहल)**	Harmony, Symphony (सामंजस्य)	3
162	Calculative (षड्यंत्रकारी)	Naive (भोला-भाला)	
163	**Callow (अनुभवहीन)**	Sophisticated (जटिल)	2
164	Calm (शान्त)	Excited (उत्तेजित)	
165	Camaraderie (सौहार्द)	Dislike (नापसंद, घृणा, शत्रुता)	
166	Canonical (धर्मवैधानिक)	Unorthodox (अपरंपरागत)	
167	Capacious (विशाल)	Cramped (तंग)	
168	Capitalise (लाभ उठाना)	Forfeit (ज़ब्ती)	
169	**Captivate (मंत्रमुग्ध होना)**	Distract, Disillusion (विचलित, मोह-भंग)	2
170	**Captivity (क़ैद)**	Liberty, Freedom (स्वतंत्रता)	3
171	Capture (कब्जा)	Release (रिहाई)	
172	Care (देखभाल)	Disregard (उपेक्षा)	
173	Carnal (शारीरिक)	Spiritual (आध्यात्मिक)	
174	Casual (आकस्मिक)	Planned (आयोजित)	
175	Casuistry (व्यर्थ उपदेश)	Certainty (निश्चितता)	
176	**Cautious (सतर्क)**	Negligent, Reckless (लापरवाह)	3
177	Celestial (स्वर्गीय)	Hellish (नारकीय)	
178	Centre (केंद्र)	Periphery (परिधि)	
179	Certainty (निश्चित)	Doubt (संदेह)	
180	Certify (प्रमाणित)	Disapprove (अस्वीकार करना)	
181	Cessation (समाप्ति)	Commencement (प्रारंभ)	
182	Chaotic (अस्तव्यस्त)	Organised (संगठित)	
183	Charity (दान पुण्य)	Stealing (चोरी)	
184	Charming (आकर्षक)	Repulsive (अरुचिकर)	
185	Cheerful (प्रसन्नतापूर्वक)	Gloomy (उदास)	
186	Chicken Hearted (डरपोक)	Courageous (निडर)	
187	Churlish (अभद्र)	Courteous (विनम्र)	
188	Cite (उल्लेख करना)	Forget (भूलना)	
189	Clammy (चिपचिपा)	Dry (सूखा)	
190	Clamorous (कोलाहलमय)	Suppression (अवरोध, रुकावट)	
191	Clash (टकराव)	Harmony (सामंजस्य)	
192	Classic (उत्कृष्ट)	Atypical (असामान्य)	
193	**Clear (स्पष्ट)**	Nebulous, Opaque, Murky, Dim (अस्पष्ट, अपारदर्शी, धुंधला)	3
194	Clench (जकड़ना)	Relax (ढीला करना)	
195	Cloudy (धुंधला)	Transparent (पारदर्शक)	
196	Coax (फुसलाना)	Dissuade (मना करना)	
197	**Coherent (सुसंगत)**	Disorganized, Illogical (अव्यवस्थित, अतार्किक)	2
198	Coincide (मेल खाना / एक जैसा होना)	Differ (अलग)	

SN	WORD	Antonyms	#R
199	Collaboration (सहभागिता)	Division (विभाजन)	
200	Collect (इकट्ठा करना)	Disperse (बिखेरना)	
201	**Combative (लड़ाकू)**	Peaceful (शांतिपूर्ण)	2
202	Comedy (हास्य)	Tragedy (शोकपूर्ण घटना)	
203	Comely (मनोहर)	Grotesque (विकृत)	
204	Comfort (सांत्वना)	Discontentment (असंतोष)	
205	Commiserate (हमदर्दी)	Indifferent (उदासीन)	
206	Committed (प्रतिबद्ध)	Uncertain (अनिश्चित)	
207	Compact (सघन)	Loose (ढीला)	
208	Compatriot (हमवतन)	Outsider (परदेशी)	
209	Compel (बल से कराना)	Dissuade (न करने के लिए समझाना)	
210	Compendium (सारांश)	Expansion (विस्तार)	
211	Competence (योग्यता)	Incompetence (अक्षमता)	
212	Complete (पूर्ण)	Partial (आंशिक)	
213	Complex (जटिल)	Simple (सरल)	
214	**Comply (आज्ञापालन करना)**	Oppose, Challenge (आपत्ति करना)	2
215	Comprehensive (विस्तृत)	Restricted (सीमित)	
216	Compress (दबाना/संक्षेप करना)	Enlarge (बड़ा करना)	
217	Compromise (समझौता)	Dissent (मतभेद)	
218	**Compulsory (अनिवार्य)**	Optional (ऐच्छिक)	3
219	Comrade (साथी)	Enemy (दुश्मन)	
220	Conceal (गुप्त रखना)	Reveal (प्रकट करना)	
221	**Conceit (अहंकार)**	Modesty, Humility (विनम्रता)	2
222	Conceive (विचार करना)	Misunderstand (गलत समझना)	
223	Concentrated (गाढ़ा)	Diluted (पतला)	
224	Conciliation (समझौता)	Confrontation (मुक़ाबला)	
225	Conclusive (निर्णयात्मक)	Ambiguous (अस्पष्ट)	
226	**Concur (सहमत होना)**	Disagree (असहमत)	3
227	Condense (संघनित करना)	Expand (फैलाना)	
228	Confident (आत्म विश्वासी)	Diffident (संकोची)	
229	**Confirm (निश्चित करना)**	Reject, Contradict (अस्वीकार करना)	2
230	**Conform (अनुरूप)**	Differ, Deviation (अलग, विचलन)	2
231	Confused (भ्रमित/अस्पष्ट)	Lucid (सुस्पष्ट)	
232	Congested (भरा हुआ)	Cleared (खाली)	
233	Connect (जुड़ना)	Detach (अलग होना)	
234	Conquer (जीतना)	Surrender (आत्मसमर्पण)	
235	Consanguinity (रक्तसंबंध)	Disunion (विच्छेद)	
236	**Consent (सहमति)**	Dissent, Interdiction (मतभेद)	3
237	Conserve (सुरक्षित रखना)	Destroy (नष्ट करना)	
238	Console (सांत्वना देना)	Agitate (आंदोलन करना)	

SN	WORD	Antonyms	#R
239	Consolidated (संयुक्त)	Weakened (कमजोर)	
240	Conspicuous (सुस्पष्ट)	Obscure (अस्पष्ट)	
241	**Constant (स्थिर)**	Varying, Fluctuating (परिवर्तनीय)	2
242	Constrict (सँकुचित करना)	Stretch (तानना)	
243	Construe (समझाना)	Obscure (अस्पष्ट)	
244	Consume (उपभोग करना)	Save (बचत करना)	
245	Consummate (उत्कृष्ट/संपूर्ण)	Inept (अयोग्य)	
246	Contemplate (विचार करना)	Ignore (अनसुनी करना)	
247	Contemplative (विचारशील)	Unreflective (असावधान)	
248	**Contented (संतुष्ट)**	Dissatisfied (असंतुष्ट)	2
249	Contentious (विवादास्पद)	Agreeable (सहमत)	
250	Contest (संघर्ष)	Stillness (स्थिरता)	
251	Contextual (संबंधित)	Unrelated (असंबंधित)	
252	Contiguous (मिला हुआ)	Separated (अलग-थलग)	
253	Continued (निरंतर)	Stopped (रोका हुआ)	
254	Contracts (सिकुड़ना)	Expand (फैलाना)	
255	Contradiction (परस्पर विरोध)	Agreement (समझौता)	
256	Contribute (योगदान करना)	Take (लेना)	
257	**Controlled (नियंत्रित)**	Excited, Agitated (उत्तेजित)	2
258	**Controversial (विवादास्पद)**	Undisputed, Indisputable, Agreement (निर्विवाद, समझौता)	3
259	Convene (आयोजित करना)	Disperse (भंग करना)	
260	Convenience (सहूलियत)	Hindrance (अड़चन)	
261	Convex (उत्तल)	Concave (अवतल)	
262	Convicted (दोषी ठहराया)	Acquitted (बरी कर दिया)	
263	Convincing (यक़ीनी)	Doubtable (संदेहास्पद)	
264	Convulsion (ऐंठन)	Restful (शांत)	
265	Cooperative (सहयोगी)	Unsupportive (असहयोगी)	
266	**Corroborate (समर्थन)**	Contradict, Oppose (खंडन करना)	2
267	Corrupt (भ्रष्ट)	Honest (ईमानदार)	
268	Countless (अनगिनत)	Limited (सीमित)	
269	Courageous (साहसी)	Diffident (संकोची)	
270	Courtesy (शिष्टाचार)	Rudeness (अशिष्टता)	
271	Courtly (सभ्य)	Rough (असभ्य)	
272	Covert (गुप्त)	Public (सार्वजनिक)	
273	Covetous (लालची)	Benevolent (भलाई करनेवाला)	
274	Cowardly (कायर)	Valiant (बहादुर)	
275	Cozen (धोखा देना)	Honest (ईमानदार)	
276	Create (सृजन करना)	Destroy (नष्ट करना)	
277	Credibility (विश्वसनीयता)	Improbability (असंभवता)	

SN	WORD	Antonyms	#R
278	Credit (जमा धन)	Debit (निकाला गया धन)	
279	Crestfallen (हताश, उदास)	Triumphant (विजयी)	
280	Crisp (करारा)	Tender (मुलायम)	
281	Critical (आलोचनात्मक)	Complimentary (प्रशंसात्मक)	
282	**Criticise (आलोचना करना)**	Commend, Approve, Praise (सराहना करना, मंजूर करना)	3
283	Crook (अपराधी)	Law (कानून)	
284	**Crooked (मुड़ा हुआ)**	Straight (सीधा)	3
285	**Crucial (महत्वपूर्ण)**	Trivial (तुच्छ)	2
286	Cruel (निर्दयी)	Kind (मेहरबान)	
287	Cryptic (गुप्त)	Definite (स्पष्ट)	
288	**Curb (नियंत्रण)**	Allow, Freedom (अनुमति, आजादी)	2
289	Curse (अभिशाप)	Boon (वरदान)	
290	Cursory (अधूरा)	Thorough (संपूर्ण)	
291	Curt (रूखा)	Polite (विनम्र)	
292	**Dainty (सजीला)**	Clumsy (बेढंगा)	2
293	Dank (नम)	Dry (सूखा)	
294	Darken (अंधेरा छाना)	Illuminated (प्रकाशित होना)	
295	Dashed (धराशायी)	Encouraged (प्रोत्साहित)	
296	Daunt (भयभीत करना)	Encourage (प्रोत्साहित करना)	
297	Dazzling (बहुत चमकीला)	Lackluster (फीका)	
298	Deathly (प्राणघातक)	Blooming (फलता-फूलता)	
299	Debauched (ऐयाश, पथभ्रष्ट)	Honourable (माननीय)	
300	Decay (क्षय)	Growth (वृद्धि)	
301	**Deceit (छल)**	Honesty, Plain (ईमानदारी, निष्कपट)	2
302	Deceive (धोखा देना)	Support (सहायता करना)	
303	Decimate (बरबाद करना)	Preserve (रक्षा करना)	
304	Decry (दोष देना)	Praise (प्रशंसा करना)	
305	Deep (गहरा)	Shallow (उथला)	
306	Defamatory (मानहानिकारक / अपमान सूचक)	Complimentary (प्रशंसासूचक)	
307	Defence (रक्षा)	Offence (अपराध)	
308	**Defend (बचाव)**	Surrender, Abandon (आत्मसमर्पण)	2
309	Deferential (आदरसूचक)	Arrogant (अभिमानी)	
310	Deficiency (कमी)	Excess (अति)	
311	**Deficit (अभाव)**	Abundance, Surplus (प्रचुरता)	2
312	Defuse (शांत करना)	Agitate (उत्तेजित करना)	
313	Dejected (उदास)	Cheerful (आनन्दित)	
314	**Delay (विलंभ / देरी)**	Advance, Haste (जल्दबाजी)	2
315	Delectation (आनंद)	Sorrow (शोक)	
316	**Delicious (स्वादिष्ट)**	Insipid, Distasteful (फीका, बेस्वाद)	2

SN	WORD	Antonyms	#R
317	Demand (मांग)	Supply (आपूर्ति)	
318	Demean (नीचा दिखाना)	Admire (प्रशंसा करना)	
319	Demote (पद घटाना)	Elevate (तरक्की)	
320	**Denounce (आरोप लगाना)**	Praise, Compliment (प्रशंसा करना)	3
321	Denounce (दोषी ठहराना)	Defended (बचाव करना)	
322	**Dense (सघन)**	Sparse (विरल)	3
323	Depict (शब्दों में वर्णन करना)	Hide (छिपा दना)	
324	Deplete (कम करना)	Expand (विस्तार करना)	
325	**Deport (निकाल देना)**	Permit (अनुमति देना)	2
326	Deposit (जमा)	Withdraw (निकालना)	
327	Depredation (विध्वंस)	Construction (निर्माण)	
328	Depth (गहराई)	Shallow (उथला)	
329	Derisive (व्यंग्यात्मक)	Respectful (सम्मान पूर्ण)	
330	**Descent (उतार)**	Ascent (चढ़ाव)	2
331	Desecrate (अपवित्र करना)	Sanctify (पवित्र करना)	
332	**Desecration (अपवित्रीकरण)**	Consecration, Veneration (पवित्रीकरण, मन्नत)	2
333	Deserter (भगोड़ा)	Loyalist (वफादार)	
334	Desiderate (कमी महसूस करना)	Disregard (उपेक्षा)	
335	Desire (इच्छा)	Apathy (उदासीनता)	
336	Desist (रोकना)	Continue (जारी रहना)	
337	Desperate (बेताब)	Content (संतुष्ट)	
338	Destination (मंज़िल)	Origin (प्रारंभ)	
339	Destroy (नष्ट करना)	Preserve (रक्षा करना)	
340	Destructive (विनाशकारी)	Constructive (रचनात्मक)	
341	Detachment (वैराग्य)	Subjectivity (आत्मीयता)	
342	**Detest (घृणा करना)**	Like, Adore (पसंद करना)	4
343	Developed (विकसित)	Backward (पिछड़ा)	
344	Deviate (भटकना)	Concentrate (ध्यान केन्द्रित करना)	
345	**Devious (चालाक)**	Straight, Sincere (सीधा)	3
346	Diabolical (शैतानी)	Moral (नैतिक)	
347	Dictatorship (तानाशाही)	Democracy (जनतंत्र)	
348	Differ (मतभेद होना)	Concur (सहमत होना)	
349	Difference (अंतर)	Similarity (समानता)	
350	Different (विभिन्न)	Similar (समान)	
351	Diffidence (संकोच)	Self-Assurance (आत्मविश्वास)	
352	Dignified (प्रतिष्ठित)	Ordinary (मामूली)	
353	Digress (पीछे हटना)	Stay (टिकना)	
354	Disable (अयोग्य बनाना // बंद करना)	Permit (मंजूरी देना)	
355	Disapprove (निंदा करना)	Commend (सराहना करना)	
356	Disarming (शांत करने वाला)	Detestable (घिनौना)	

SN	WORD	Antonyms	#R
357	Disavowal (इनकार)	Approval (स्वीकृति)	
358	**Discard (छोड़ना)**	Adopt, Accept (अपनाना)	2
359	Disclose (जाहिर करना)	Conceal (गुप्त रखना)	
360	Disconsolate (निराश)	Joyous (आनंदित)	
361	**Discord (कलह)**	Harmony (सामंजस्य)	2
362	Discordant (असहमत)	Agreeable (सहमत)	
363	Discreet (सावधान)	Heedless (असावधान)	
364	Discrimination (भेदभाव)	Equality (समानता)	
365	**Disdain (तिरस्कार)**	Admiration, Favour (प्रशंसा, एहसान)	2
366	Disgrace (अपमान)	Honour (सम्मान)	
367	Disgruntled (असंतुष्ट)	Pleased (प्रसन्न)	
368	Dishearten (हतोत्साह करना)	Encourage (उत्साहित करना)	
369	Disheveled (बिखेरा हुआ)	Ordered (सुव्यवस्थित)	
370	Disillusioned (निराशाग्रस्त)	Enthusiastic (उत्साहपूर्ण)	
371	Disjointed (संबंध तोड़ा हुआ)	Connected (जुड़ा हुआ)	
372	Dismal (निराशपुर्ण)	Cheerful (प्रसन्नतापूर्वक)	
373	Dismay (निराश करना)	Gladden (प्रसन्न करना)	
374	Disorderly (उल्टा पुल्टा)	Arranged (व्यवस्थित)	
375	Disparate (भिन्न)	Similar (समान)	
376	Dispatch (भेजना)	Acquire (प्राप्त करना)	
377	Dispensable (अनावश्यक)	Essential (आवश्यक)	
378	Dissension (कलह)	Harmony (सामंजस्य)	
379	Dissent (मतभेद)	Agreement (समझौता)	
380	Dissident (मतभेद करनेवाला)	Orthodox (परम्परावादी)	
381	Distinctive (विशेष)	Close (अभिन्न)	
382	Distract (विचलित करना)	Clarify (स्पष्टीकरण देना)	
383	Distraught (व्याकुल)	Serene (शांत)	
384	Distress (दु:ख)	Pleasure (आनंद)	
385	Distrustful (अविश्वासी)	Ingenuous (निष्कपट)	
386	Diurnal (दैनिक)	Nocturnal (रात्रिकालीन)	
387	**Diverge (अलग अलग होना)**	Collect, Converge (एकत्रित होना)	2
388	Divergence (विचलन)	Confluence (संगम)	
389	Diverse (भिन्न)	Identical (समान)	
390	Diversity (विविधता)	Uniformity (एकरूपता)	
391	Divest (वंचित करना)	Give (अदा करना)	
392	Divide (विभाजित करना)	Unite (जोड़ना)	
393	Dividing (विभाजक)	Connecting (संयोजक)	
394	Divine (दिव्य)	Lowly (नीच)	
395	**Divulge (भेद खोलना)**	Conceal, Hide (छिपाना)	3
396	Dogmatic (कट्टर)	Flexible (लचीला)	

SN	WORD	Antonyms	#R
397	Dominant (प्रभावशाली)	Submissive (विनम्र)	
398	Dominate (हावी)	Surrender (आत्मसमर्पण)	
399	**Dormant (निष्क्रिय)**	Active (सक्रिय)	4
400	Doubtful (अनिश्चित / संदिग्ध)	Decisive (निर्णायक)	
401	Downcast (निराश)	Cheerful (हंसमुख)	
402	Drab (फीका)	Bright (चमकदार)	
403	Drawn (तैयार)	Relaxed (आराम)	
404	**Dull (सुस्त)**	Keen, Exciting, Bright (उत्सुक, रोमांचक)	3
405	Dumb (गूंगा)	Vocal (वाणीमय)	
406	Dummy (दिखावटी)	Original (असली)	
407	Duplicate (नक़ल)	Original (मूल प्रति)	
408	Dwarf (बौना आदमी)	Giant (विशालकाय)	
409	Dwell (बस जाना)	Move On (आगे बढ़ना)	
410	Dye (रंग, रंजक)	Bleach (सफेद, विरंजक)	
411	**Dynamic (गतिशील)**	Static (स्थिर)	2
412	Earthly (पृथ्वी संबंधी)	Celestial (आकाशीय)	
413	Eccentric (विचित्र)	Customary (प्रचलित)	
414	Eccentricity (सनक)	Normalcy (सामान्य स्थिति)	
415	Effeminacy (कायरता)	Manliness (बहादुरपन)	
416	Effeminate (नारी जैसा)	Manly (मर्दाना)	
417	Effervescent (उत्तेजित)	Stale (पुराना)	
418	Egoist (अहंवादी)	Selfless (स्वार्थरहित)	
419	Egregious (अत्यंत)	Mild (सौम्य)	
420	Elasticity (लोच)	Rigidity (कठोरता)	
421	**Elegance (शिष्टता)**	Vulgarity, Gracelessness (असभ्यता, बेहयाई)	2
422	**Elementary (सामान्य)**	Complex (जटिल)	2
423	Elevation (ऊंचाई)	Depression (गिराव)	
424	**Emaciated (निर्बल)**	Fat, Healthy (स्वस्थ)	2
425	**Emancipation (मुक्ति)**	Bondage (गुलामी)	2
426	Embark (आरंभ करना)	Finish (खत्म करना)	
427	**Emerge (उभरना)**	Disappear (गायब होना)	2
428	Emigration (प्रवासी)	Immigration (आप्रवासन)	
429	Empathy (सहानुभूति)	Apathy (उदासीनता)	
430	Encourage (प्रोत्साहन)	Dishearten (उत्साह भंग करना)	
431	**Encouraged (प्रोत्साहित)**	Discouraged, Opposed (हतोत्साहित, विरोध)	2
432	Encroach (अतिक्रमण करना)	Keep Away (दूर रहना)	
433	End (समाप्त)	Start (शुरू)	
434	Endangered (संकटग्रस्त)	Protected (संरक्षित)	
435	**Endorse (समर्थन)**	Disapprove, Renounce (अस्वीकार करना)	2
436	Endow (प्रदान करना)	Deprive (वंचित)	

SN	WORD	Antonyms	#R
437	Endure (सहन करना)	Resist (प्रतिरोध करना)	
438	Enduring (स्थायी)	Transient (क्षणिक)	
439	Enigma (पहेली)	Clarity (स्पष्टता)	
440	Enlarge (विस्तार करना)	Condense (संक्षेप करना)	
441	Enlighten (प्रकाशित करना)	Befog (अंधेरा करना)	
442	Enlightened (ज्ञानसंपन्न)	Confounded (दंग/चकित)	
443	Enliven (सजीव करना)	Dishearten (उदास करना)	
444	Enmity (शत्रुता)	Amicability (मित्रतापूर्णता)	
445	Ennui (ग्लानि)	Excitement (उत्तेजना)	
446	**Enrich (बढ़ाना)**	Reduce, Deplete (कम करना)	3
447	Ensue (पीछे होना)	Precede (आगे होना)	
448	Enthusiasm (उत्साह)	Apathy (उदासीनता)	
449	Entice (लुभाना)	Repulse (खदेड़ना)	
450	Entire (संपूर्ण)	Partial (आंशिक)	
451	Entrance (प्रवेश)	Exit (निकास)	
452	Entrenched (जकड़ी हुई)	Transient (क्षणिक /अस्थायी)	
453	Ephemeral (अल्पकालिक)	Eternal (अनन्त)	
454	**Equilibrium (संतुलन)**	Imbalance (असंतुलन)	3
455	Equivalent (समतुल्य)	Dissimilar (भिन्न)	
456	Erase (मिटाना)	Create (बनाना)	
457	**Escalate (बढ़ाना)**	Reduce, Plunge (घटाना)	2
458	**Establish (स्थापित करना)**	Destroy, Displace (नष्ट करना)	2
459	Established (स्थापित)	Displaced (विस्थापित)	
460	Esteem (आदर)	Disregard (उपेक्षा)	
461	Estimate (आकलन)	Actual (वास्तविक)	
462	Eulogistic (प्रशंसात्मक)	Critical (आलोचनात्मक)	
463	Euphoria (उत्साह)	Lethargy (सुस्ती)	
464	Evanescent (क्षणभंगुर)	Permanent (स्थायी)	
465	**Evident (प्रत्यक्ष)**	Obscure, Doubtful (अस्पष्ट, संदिग्ध)	3
466	Evoke (आह्वान करना)	Stop (रोकना)	
467	Exasperation (रोष)	Enjoyment (आनन्द)	
468	Excelled (उत्कृष्ट प्रदर्शन)	Failed (असफल)	
469	Excitable (उत्तेजनीय)	Placid (शांत)	
470	Excited (उत्तेजित)	Bored (ऊबा हुआ)	
471	Exclusion (बहिष्करण)	Admittance (प्रवेश)	
472	Exclusive (छोड़ कर)	Inclusive (मिला कर)	
473	Excruciating (दुखदाई /कष्टदायी)	Mild (विनम्र)	
474	Exemplary (अनुकरणीय)	Unsatisfactory (असंतोषजनक)	
475	Exemptions (छूट)	Inclusions (सम्मिलन)	
476	Exhale (साँस छोड़ना)	Inhale (साँस लेना)	

SN	WORD	Antonyms	#R
477	**Exhaustive (संपूर्ण)**	Incomplete (अधूरा)	2
478	Exhausts (थका देना)	Invigorates (शक्ति देना)	
479	Exhume (खोद कर निकालना)	Hide (छिपाना)	
480	Exigent (अत्यावश्यक)	Usual (सामान्य)	
481	**Exodus (निर्गमन, प्रस्थान)**	Arrival, Influx (भीतर जाना)	2
482	**Exonerate (निर्दोषी ठहराना)**	Convict, Sentence, Engage (अपराधी घोषित करना, सज़ा देना)	4
483	**Expand (विस्तार)**	Contract, Shrink (सिकुड़न)	3
484	**Expansion (विस्तार)**	Contraction, Compression (संकुचन, संपीड़न)	2
485	Expedite (जल्दी करना)	Hinder (बाधा पहुंचाना)	
486	**Expel (निकाल देना)**	Absorb, Accept (सोख लेना)	2
487	Explicit (सुस्पष्ट)	Ambiguous (अस्पष्ट)	
488	**Expunge (निकालना)**	Insert, Add (डालना, जोड़ना)	3
489	Expurgate (बेकार चीज़ हटाना)	Permit (अनुमति देना)	
490	Exquisite (अति सुंदर)	Rough (असभ्य)	
491	**Extant (मौजूदा, प्रचलित)**	Extinct, Destroyed (विलुप्त, नष्ट)	2
492	Extensive (विस्तृत)	Intensive (गहन)	
493	Extenuate (शांत करना)	Strengthen (शक्तिशाली बनना)	
494	Extol (प्रशंसा करना)	Censure (निंदा करना)	
495	Extraneous (असंगत)	Relevant (संगत)	
496	Extravagance (फ़िज़ूलखर्ची)	Parsimony (कंजूसी)	
497	**Extravagant (फ़िज़ूल ख़र्च)**	Economical, Thrifty (किफायती)	3
498	Extreme (चरम)	Mild (सौम्य)	
499	Exultant (उल्लसित)	Depressed (उदास)	
500	Fabricate (निर्माण)	Break (टूटना)	
501	**Facilitate (सुविधा प्रदान करना)**	Hinder (बाधा पहुंचाना)	2
502	Faint (धुंधला)	Firm (दृढ़/मज़बूती से)	
503	Fair (निष्पक्ष)	Unjust (अन्यायपूर्ण)	
504	Fallible (पतनशील)	Unerring (अचूक)	
505	Fame (यश)	Disgrace (कलंक)	
506	Familiar (परिचित)	Strange (अपरिचित)	
507	Famished (भूखा)	Satiated (संतृप्त)	
508	**Famous (प्रसिद्ध)**	Obscure, Unknown (अज्ञात)	3
509	Fanatical (कट्टरता)	Liberal (उदारवादी)	
510	Far-Fetched (अवास्तविक)	Realistic (वास्तविक)	
511	Farsighted (दूरदर्शी)	Unwise (अज्ञानी)	
512	Fat (मोटा)	Lean (दुबला)	
513	**Fatigued (थका हुआ)**	Energised (जोश में)	2
514	**Feasible (संभव)**	Implausible, Impractical (असंभव)	2
515	**Fecund (उपजाऊ)**	Barren, Sterile, Sparse (बाँझ, विरल)	3

SN	WORD	Antonyms	#R
516	**Fertile (उपजाऊ)**	Barren (बंजर)	5
517	Fervent (उत्सुक)	Dispassionate (उदासीन)	
518	Fervour (जोश)	Apathy (उदासीनता)	
519	Festal (उत्सव-संबंधी)	Solemn (गंभीर)	
520	Fetter (बेड़ी डालना)	Liberate (स्वतंत्र करना)	
521	Feud (झगड़ा)	Harmony (सौहार्द)	
522	Finite (सीमित)	Endless (अनंत)	
523	Flabby (ढीला)	Firm (दृढ़)	
524	**Flamboyant (चमकीला)**	Understand, Modest (मामूली)	2
525	Flared (प्रदीप्त)	Darkened (अन्धेरा)	
526	Flaunt (दिखावा)	Cover (छिपाना)	
527	Flawless (निर्दोष)	Defective (दोषपूर्ण)	
528	Flee (भाग जाना)	Submit (समर्पण करना)	
529	**Flexible (लचीला)**	Rigid, Stiff, Defiant (कठोर)	7
530	Flicker (झिलमिलाहट)	Burn Steadily (नित्य जलनेवाला)	
531	**Flippant (गम्भीर न होना)**	Serious, Earnest (गंभीर, ईमानदार)	2
532	**Flood (बाढ़)**	Drought (सूखा)	2
533	**Florid (गहरे रंग का)**	Plain, Pale (सादा, फीका)	2
534	Fluctuate (उतार चढ़ाव)	Stabilize (स्थिर)	
535	Fluent (धाराप्रवाह)	Halting (लड़खड़ाता)	
536	Flummoxed (बेचैन करना)	Comfortable (आरामदायक)	
537	Focus (केन्द्रित करना)	Disperse (बिखेरना)	
538	Foe (शत्रु)	Companion (साथी)	
539	Foment (भड़काना)	Quell (शांत करना)	
540	Fondest (सबसे प्यारा)	Cold (भावना रहित)	
541	**Foreign (विदेश)**	Native (देशी)	2
542	Foreigner (विदेशी)	Native (मूल निवासी)	
543	Foremost (सबसे महत्वपूर्ण)	Unimportant (महत्वहीन)	
544	Foresight (दूरदर्शिता)	Indiscretion (मूर्खता)	
545	Forgo (त्यागना)	Conquer (जीतना)	
546	Forlorn (निराश)	Joyful, Elated (आनंदपूर्ण)	
547	**Formal (औपचारिक)**	Informal (अनौपचारिक)	2
548	Formidable (डरावना)	Trivial (तुच्छ)	
549	Foul (बेईमानी)	Fair (ईमानदारी)	
550	Frailty (निर्बलता)	Strength (मज़बूती)	
551	Frame (ढाँचा)	Disorganise (अव्यवस्थित)	
552	Freed (मुक्त किया गया)	Imprisoned (कैद किया हुआ)	
553	Freedom (आज़ादी)	Captivity (कारावास)	
554	Frenzy (बावलापन)	Calm (शान्त)	
555	Fret (झल्लाहट/चिंता करना)	Please (प्रसन्न करना)	

SN	WORD	Antonyms	#R
556	Friend (मित्र)	Foe (शत्रु)	
557	Friendly (मित्रतापूर्ण)	Hostile (शत्रुतापूर्ण)	
558	Friendship (मित्रता)	Enmity (शत्रुता)	
559	**Fritter (व्यर्थ नष्ट करना)**	Save, Hoard (बचाना, इकट्ठा करना)	2
560	**Frugality (कमखर्ची)**	Prodigality, Generosity (उदारता, दानशीलता)	2
561	Fruitless (निरर्थक)	Successful (सफल)	
562	Fugitive (भगोड़ा)	Captive (बंदी)	
563	Fulfil (पूरा करना)	Abandon (छोड़ देना)	
564	Furtive (गुपचुप)	Straight (स्पष्ट)	
565	Gaunt (दुबला-पतला)	Plump (मोटा)	
566	General (सामान्य)	Particular (विशिष्ट)	
567	**Generous (उदार)**	Stingy, Miserly, Inconsiderate (कंजूस, अविवेकी)	4
568	Genteel (सज्जन)	Uncivilized (असभ्य)	
569	Gentleman (सज्जन)	Boor (गंवार)	
570	Gigantic (विशाल)	Tiny (बहुत छोटा)	
571	Glad (हर्ष)	Gloomy (उदास)	
572	Glittering (शानदार)	Dull (फीका)	
573	Glossy (चमकदार)	Dull (फीका)	
574	Goodwill (ख्याति)	Hostility (शत्रुता)	
575	Gorgeous (मनमोहक)	Ordinary (साधारण)	
576	Graceful (गरिमापूर्ण)	Awkward (बेढंगा)	
577	**Gracious (दयालु)**	Miserable, Rude (दयनीय, दुखी)	2
578	**Gradual (धीरे-धीरे)**	Rapid (तीव्र)	2
579	Gradually (क्रमश:)	Abruptly (एकाएक)	
580	Grandiose (वैभवशाली)	Moderate (मध्यम)	
581	**Gratify (प्रसन्न करना)**	Disappoint, Annoy (निराश, झुंझला देना)	2
582	Grating (कर्कश)	Musical (मधुर)	
583	Grim (भयंकर)	Pleasant (सुहावना)	
584	**Grotesque (विकृत, कुरूप)**	Attractive, Natural, Plain (आकर्षक, सादा)	3
585	Group (समूह)	Individual (अकेला)	
586	Grudge (असन्तोष)	Goodwill (सद्भाव)	
587	Grumpy (तुनुकमिज़ाज)	Pleasant (हँसमुख)	
588	**Guilty (अपराधी)**	Innocent (मासूम)	4
589	Hail (ओला पड़ना)	Dribble (झीसी पड़नेवाला वर्षा)	
590	Halcyon (शान्तिपूर्ण)	Agitated (उत्तेजित)	
591	Harmonious (सुसंगत)	Discordant (असंगत)	
592	**Harmony (सामंजस्य)**	Hatred, Discord (नफरत, अनबन)	2
593	Harrowing (शोकजनक)	Pleasant (खुशनुमा)	
594	**Harsh (कठोर)**	Gentle, Lenient (कोमल, नरम)	4
595	Hassled (परेशान)	Relaxed (तनाव मुक्त)	

SN	WORD	Antonyms	#R
596	Haste (जल्दी)	Delay (विलंब)	
597	**Hazard (खतरा)**	Safety, Protection (सुरक्षा)	2
598	Hazardous (संकटपूर्ण)	Secure (सुरक्षित)	
599	Hazy (धुंधला)	Clear (स्पष्ट)	
600	Hearty (मिलनसार)	Aloof (अलग)	
601	Heed (सावधान रहना)	Neglect (असावधानी)	
602	Heedless (असावधान)	Observant (तेज़नज़र)	
603	Hefty (तगड़ा)	Slight (हलका)	
604	Hegemony (नेतृत्व)	Subordination (अधीनता)	
605	Heighten (बढ़ाना)	Decrease (कमी)	
606	**Heinous (घृणित)**	Agreeable, Delightful (सुखद)	2
607	Hereditary (अनुवांशिक)	Acquired (अर्जित)	
608	Hidden (छिपा हुआ)	Apparent (स्पष्ट)	
609	**Hideous (घिनौना)**	Beautiful, Charming, Attractive (सुंदर, आकर्षक)	3
610	Highlight (V.) (विशिष्टता दर्शाना)	Downplay (कम करके बताना)	
611	**Hilarious (उल्लसित)**	Sad, Humourless (दुखी)	2
612	**Hinder (बाधा पहुंचाना)**	Aid, Help (सहायता)	2
613	Hindrance (बाधा)	Advantage (सुविधा)	
614	Hoarse (कर्कश)	Smooth (कोमल)	
615	**Hollow (खोखला)**	Solid (ठोस)	2
616	**Hope (आशा)**	Doubt, Despair (संदेह, निराशा)	3
617	Hopeful (आशाजनक)	Pessimistic (निराशावादी)	
618	Horizontal (क्षैतिज)	Vertical (खड़ा)	
619	**Horrendous (भयानक)**	Pleasant (सुखदायक)	2
620	Hospitality (अतिथि सत्कार)	Coldness (उपेक्षा)	
621	**Hostile (शत्रुतापूर्ण)**	Amiable, Friendly, Sympathetic, Gentle, Favourable (दोस्ताना, सहानुभूति, कोमल)	10
622	Huddle (ढेर लगाना)	Sort (छाँटना)	
623	**Humility (विनम्रता)**	Pride, Arrogance, Vanity (अभिमान, अहंकार)	3
624	Hummock (टीला)	Ditch (खाई)	
625	Identical (समान)	Different (भिन्न)	
626	Identify (पहचान करना)	Overlook (अनदेखी करना)	
627	Idiosyncrasy (अनोखापन)	Generality (सामान्य)	
628	**Ignite (आग लगना)**	Extinguish (बुझाना)	2
629	**Ignorance (अज्ञान)**	Knowledge (ज्ञान)	3
630	Ignorant (अज्ञानी)	Learned (ज्ञानी)	
631	**Illusive (भ्रामक)**	Factual, Reality (वास्तविक)	2
632	Illustrious (शानदार)	Obscure (अस्पष्ट)	
633	Imbroglio (उलझन)	Composure (मानसिक संतुलन)	
634	**Immaculate (बेदाग)**	Filthy, Messy, Foul (गंदा, बेईमानी से)	3

SN	WORD	Antonyms	#R
635	Immoral (अनैतिक)	Decent (सभ्य)	
636	Immortal (अमर)	Temporary (अस्थायी)	
637	**Immune (प्रतिरक्षित)**	Vulnerable, Sensitive, Susceptible (असुरक्षित, नाज़ुक)	3
638	**Impartial (निष्पक्ष)**	Biased (पक्षपाती)	2
639	Impatient (उतावला)	Tolerant (सहनशील)	
640	Impel (उत्तेजित करना)	Repress (दबाना)	
641	Impressive (प्रभावशाली)	Ordinary (साधारण)	
642	**Impromptu (बिना पहले सोचे हुए)**	Premeditated, Prepared, Planned (पूर्व निर्धारित, तैयार)	3
643	Improvident (अपव्ययी)	Thrifty (किफ़ायती)	
644	**Impudent (बेशर्म)**	Polite, Modest, Respectful (सभ्य)	4
645	Impugnable (विवादास्पद)	Indubious (स्पष्ट)	
646	Impure (प्रदूषित)	Sterile (रोगाणुहीन)	
647	Impute (आरोप लगाना)	Defend (रक्षा करना)	
648	In Toto (पूर्णतया)	Partially (आंशिक रूप से)	
649	Inadvertently (अनजाने में)	Deliberately (जान - बूझकर)	
650	Incarcerate (क़ैद कर देना)	Release (रिहाई)	
651	Incentive (प्रोत्साहन)	Hindrance (बाधा)	
652	**Include (शामिल)**	Eliminate, Reject (हटाना, अस्वीकार करना)	2
653	**Incoherent (असंगत)**	Intelligible, Rational (सुगम)	2
654	Incongruous (असंगत)	Harmonious (सामंजस्यपूर्ण)	
655	Incorporate (शामिल करना)	Exclude (निकालना)	
656	Increase (बढ़ना)	Diminish (घटना)	
657	Indicted (दोषी ठहराया)	Released (मुक्त किया)	
658	Indifferent (उदासीन)	Attentive (सचेत)	
659	Indigenous (स्वदेशी)	Alien (विदेशी)	
660	Indignant (क्रोधित)	Pleased (प्रसन्न)	
661	Indispensable (अत्यावश्यक)	Superfluous (अनावश्यक)	
662	Induce (प्रेरित करना)	Prevent (रोकना)	
663	Inert (निष्क्रिय)	Active (सक्रिय)	
664	**Inertia (जड़ता)**	Vigour, Energy (शक्ति, ऊर्जा)	2
665	Inexpensive (सस्ता)	Dear (महंगा)	
666	**Infallible (अचूक)**	Imperfect, Faulty (त्रुटिपूर्ण)	2
667	Inferior (घटिया)	Superior (बेहतर)	
668	**Infinite (अनंत)**	Limited, Evanescent (सीमित)	2
669	Infirmity (दुर्बलता)	Strength (मज़बूती)	
670	Influenced (प्रभावित)	Bipartisan (द्विदलीय)	
671	Ingenious (प्रतिभावान)	Pedestrian (मामूली)	
672	Ingratiating (ख़ुशामद भरा)	Proud (अभिमानी)	
673	Inhale (साँस लेना)	Exhale (साँस छोड़ना)	
674	Inherent (अंतर्निहित)	Extraneous (बाहरी)	

SN	WORD	Antonyms	#R
675	**Inhibit (रोकना)**	Allow, Approve (स्वीकृति देना)	2
676	Iniquity (अधर्म)	Good (भलाई)	
677	Initiated (आरंभ करना)	Concluded (समापन करना)	
678	Innocent (मासूम)	Cunning (चालाक)	
679	Inoffensive (अहानिकर)	Rude (अशिष्ट, असभ्य)	
680	**Inordinate (अनियमित)**	Reasonable (उचित)	2
681	**Inquisitive (जिज्ञासु)**	Indifferent, Unconcerned, Ignore (उदासीन, बेपरवाह)	4
682	**Insatiable (लालची)**	Content, Fulfilled (संतुष्ट)	2
683	Inscrutable (रहस्यमय)	Comprehensible (समझने के योग्य)	
684	Insecure (असुरक्षित)	Confident (आत्मविश्वासी)	
685	Insert (डालना)	Extract (निकालना)	
686	Insidious (घातक)	Sincere (निष्कपट)	
687	Instinctive (स्वाभाविक)	Rational (तर्कसंगत)	
688	Insular (द्वीपीय, सीमित)	Cosmopolitan (सर्वदेशीय)	
689	Intangible (न छूने योग्य)	Concrete (ठोस)	
690	Intelligible (बोधगम्य)	Confused (परेशान)	
691	**Intense (बहुत ज़्यादा / अत्यधिक)**	Faint, Moderate (धुंधला, मध्यम)	2
692	**Intentional (जान-बूझकर)**	Accidental (आकस्मिक)	4
693	**Interim (अल्पकालीन)**	Permanent (स्थायी)	2
694	Interrogate (प्रश्न करना)	Reply (जवाब देना)	
695	**Intrinsic (आंतरिक)**	Extrinsic, Extraneous (बाहरी)	2
696	Inundate (बाढ लाना)	Underwhelm (उत्साहहीन करना)	
697	Inundation (सैलाब)	Drought (सूखा)	
698	Invaluable (अमूल्य)	Worthless (मूल्यहीन)	
699	Invert (पलटना)	Straighten (सीधा करना)	
700	Invigorate (स्फूर्ति से भर देना)	Tire (थका देना)	
701	Irk (गुस्सा दिलाना)	Please (आनंदित करना)	
702	Irrational (तर्कहीन)	Reasonable (तर्कसंगत)	
703	**Irrelevant (बेमतलब)**	Consequential, Meaningful (फल स्वरूप)	2
704	Irreversible (अपरिवर्तनीय)	Repairable (मरम्मत योग्य)	
705	Irritate (चिढ़ना)	Delight (आनंद)	
706	Jade (थका डालना)	Cheer (उत्साहित करना)	
707	Jeopardize (ख़तरे में डालना)	Protect (रक्षा करना)	
708	Jest (मज़ाक)	Gravity (गंभीरता)	
709	Jinx (बदकिस्मती)	Spell (जादू – टोना)	
710	Jolly (प्रसन्न)	Serious (गंभीर)	
711	**Jovial (उल्लासपूर्ण)**	Gloomy, Sorrowful (उदास)	2
712	Juicy (रसीला)	Dry (सूखा)	
713	**Kind (दयालु)**	Cruel, Meanness (निर्दयी, दरिद्रता)	2
714	Kindness (दयालुता)	Animosity (घृणा)	

SN	WORD	Antonyms	#R
715	Laborious (कठिन / श्रमसाध्य)	Facile (सहज)	
716	Lack-Lustre (बिना चमक का)	Radiant (चमकीला)	
717	Laid-Back (शांतचित्त)	Ambitious (महत्त्वाकांक्षी)	
718	Lambency (उज्ज्वलता)	Dullness (मंदता)	
719	**Languid (कमजोर)**	Energetic (शक्तिशाली)	2
720	Laudable (प्रशंसनीय)	Disrespected (अपमान)	
721	Launch (प्रारंभ करना)	Withdraw (वापस लेना)	
722	Lavish (खर्चीला)	Moderate (मध्य श्रेणी का)	
723	Lead (नेतृत्व करना)	Follow (अनुसरण करना)	
724	Learned (सीखा हुआ)	Instinctive (स्वाभाविक)	
725	Lechery (कामुकता)	Benevolence (परोपकार)	
726	Left (बचा हुआ)	Finished (समाप्त)	
727	Leisure (फुरसत)	Working (कार्यरत)	
728	**Lenient (उदार)**	Strict (कठोर)	3
729	Lessen (घटाना)	Increase (बढ़ाना)	
730	**Liberal (उदार)**	Intolerant, Stingy (असहिष्णु)	2
731	Liberation (आज़ादी)	Bondage (गुलामी)	
732	**Linger (देर तक ठहरना)**	Quicken, Leave (शीघ्र करना)	2
733	Lively (जीवंत)	Sluggish (सुस्त)	
734	**Loiter (टाल - मटोल करना)**	Hasten, Punctual (समयानुकूल)	2
735	Loosen (ढीला करना)	Fasten (जकड़ना)	
736	Loyalty (वफादारी)	Treason (विश्वासघात)	
737	Lugubrious (उदास)	Optimistic (आशावादी)	
738	Luminous (प्रकाशमान)	Dim (धुंधला)	
739	Lunacy (पागलपन)	Sanity (अक्लमंदी)	
740	Lustre (चमक)	Matte (चमकरहित)	
741	Luxury (विलासिता)	Poverty (दरिद्रता)	
742	Madden (क्रोधित करना)	Calm (शांत)	
743	Majority (बहुमत)	Minority (अल्पसंख्यक)	
744	Make (बनाना)	Break (तोड़ना)	
745	Malaise (अस्वस्थता)	Healthy (स्वस्थ)	
746	**Malicious (दुर्भावनापूर्ण)**	Benign, Decent (सौम्य)	2
747	Malignant (घातक)	Benign (अनुकूल)	
748	**Malleable (लचीला)**	Intractable, Stiff (हठीला)	2
749	Manage (सफल होना)	Fail (असफल होना)	
750	Manufacture (निर्माण)	Destroy (नष्ट करना)	
751	Marginal (किनारे का)	Core (भीतरी भाग)	
752	**Maverick (अपरंपरागत)**	Conventional, Conformist (परम्परागत)	3
753	Mean (घटिया)	Noble (प्रतिष्ठित)	
754	Meandering (घुमावदार)	Straight (सीधा)	

SN	WORD	Antonyms	#R
755	Meddle (दख़ल देना)	Ignore (अनदेखा करना)	
756	Mediocre (औसत दर्जे का)	Exceptional (असाधारण)	
757	Melodramatic (अतिनाटकीय)	Normal (सामान्य)	
758	Melody (राग)	Cacophony (कोलाहल)	
759	Menace (हानिकारक)	Comfort (आराम)	
760	Menacing (धमकाने वाला)	Helping (मदद करनेवाला)	
761	Mental (मानसिक)	Physical (शारीरिक)	
762	Meretricious (दिखावे का)	Natural (प्राकृतिक)	
763	Metropolitan (महानगर संबंधी)	Provincial (प्रान्तीय)	
764	Mettle (उत्साह)	Cowardice (कायरता)	
765	Migrate (स्थानांतरण करना)	Return (वापसी)	
766	**Minuscule (बहुत छोटा)**	Massive, Gigantic (विशाल)	2
767	Misanthropist (मानवद्वेषी)	Philanthropist (जन-हितैषी)	
768	**Miserable (दुखी)**	Happy, Cheerful, Joyful (खुश, खुशहाल)	4
769	**Misery (कष्ट)**	Bliss (परमानंद)	2
770	Mobile (चलता फिरता)	Standing (स्थायी)	
771	Moderate (मध्यम)	Extreme (अत्यधिक)	
772	Moil (कड़ी मेहनत करना)	Discourage (रोकने की कोशिश करना)	
773	Moist (नम)	Dry (सूखा)	
774	Monumental (अति महान)	Insignificant (तुच्छ)	
775	Moot (विवादास्पद)	Definite (निश्चित)	
776	Mortality (मरण)	Birth (जन्म)	
777	Mould (साँचे में ढालना)	Genuine (अकृत्रिम)	
778	**Mournful (शोकाकुल)**	Joyous (आनंदित)	2
779	Movement (गतिविधि)	Static (स्थिर)	
780	Multifaceted (बहुमुखी)	Simple (सरल)	
781	Multiple (बहुत)	Single (अकेला)	
782	Murky (अंधेरा)	Bright (दीप्तिमान)	
783	Muster (इकट्ठा करना)	Disperse (छितराना)	
784	Mutilate (विकृत करना)	Mend (मरम्मत करना)	
785	**Myopic (अदूरदर्शी)**	Farsighted (दूरदृष्टिता)	2
786	Myth (कल्पित)	Fact (तथ्य)	
787	Nab (पकड़ लेना)	Free (मुक्त करना)	
788	Nadir (पतन)	Zenith (सर्वोत्तम अवस्था)	
789	**Naive (सीधा-सादा)**	Experienced, Sophisticated (अनुभवी, जटिल)	2
790	Narrow (संकीर्ण)	Wide (चौड़ा)	
791	**Nasty (बुरा)**	Pleasant (सुखद)	2
792	**Native (मूल निवासी)**	Alien, Foreign, Exotic (विदेशी)	5
793	Neat (स्वच्छ)	Sloppy, Messy (मैला, अव्यवस्थित)	
794	Nebulous (अस्पष्ट)	Definite (निश्चित)	

SN	WORD	Antonyms	#R
795	**Neglect (लापरवाही)**	Care (देखभाल)	2
796	**Negligent (लापरवाह)**	Careful (सावधान)	3
797	Negotiate (मोल तोल)	Remain (टिकना)	
798	Nervous (घबराने वाला)	Composed (शांतचित्त)	
799	Never (कभी नहीं)	Always (हमेशा)	
800	**Niggardly (कंजूसी से)**	Lavishly, Generous (भव्य, उदार)	2
801	Noble (महान)	Servile (चापलूस)	
802	Noisily (ऊंचे स्वर से)	Quietly (चुपचाप)	
803	Nominate (मनोनीत)	Rejected (अस्वीकृत)	
804	Nonchalant (बेपरवाह)	Considerate (ध्यान रखने वाला)	
805	Nonconformist (संप्रदायवादी)	Conventional (परम्परागत)	
806	Nondescript (गुमनाम)	Distinguished (प्रसिद्ध)	
807	Normal (साधारण)	Strange (अजीब)	
808	Nourish (लालन-पालन)	Starve (भूखा)	
809	Nuisance (परेशानी)	Pleasure (आनंद)	
810	Numerous (प्रचुर)	Scarce (दुर्लभ)	
811	**Obese (मोटा)**	Thin, Slim, Skinny (पतला दुबला)	3
812	Obfuscate (उलझाना)	Clarify (स्पष्ट करना)	
813	Objective (निष्पक्ष)	Prejudiced (पक्षपातपूर्ण)	
814	Obligate (बाध्य करना)	Let Off (मुक्त करना)	
815	Obliging (उपकारी)	Unfriendly (अमित्रतापूर्ण)	
816	Oblivious (बेख़बर)	Conscious (सचेत)	
817	Obscure (अस्पष्ट)	Clear (स्पष्ट)	
818	Obsolescence (अप्रचलन)	Modernity (आधुनिकता)	
819	**Obstruct (बाधा)**	Assist, Allow (सहायता)	2
820	Obtuse (मंदबुद्धि)	Sharp-Witted (समझदार)	
821	Occupied (व्यस्त)	Free (मुक्त)	
822	Offbeat (असामान्य)	Conventional (परम्परागत)	
823	Officious (परेशान करनेवाला)	Timid (डरपोक)	
824	Offset (बराबर कर देना)	Disproportion (असमानता)	
825	Old (पुराना)	New (नया)	
826	Omit (छोड़ देना)	Include (शामिल)	
827	**Opaque (अपारदर्शक)**	Transparent, Clear (पारदर्शक, स्पष्ट)	4
828	Opponent (प्रतिद्वंद्री)	Supporter (समर्थक)	
829	**Oppose (विरोध)**	Favour, Encourage (समर्थन)	2
830	Opprobrium (अपमान)	Adulation (अतिप्रशंसा)	
831	Optimistic (आशावादी)	Pessimistic (निराशावादी)	
832	**Optional (ऐच्छिक)**	Compulsory (अनिवार्य)	2
833	Oral (मौखिक)	Written (लिखा हुआ)	
834	Orderly (व्यवस्थित)	Chaotic (अराजक)	

SN	WORD	Antonyms	#R
835	Originate (प्रारंभ करना)	Terminate (अंत करना)	
836	**Ostracise (बहिष्कृत करना)**	Welcome, Embrace (स्वागत करना)	2
837	Outlandish (विचित्र, बाहरी)	Ordinary (सामान्य)	
838	Outspoken (मुँहफट)	Secretive (रहस्यात्मक)	
839	**Outstanding (शानदार)**	Ordinary (सामान्य)	2
840	Overlook (अनदेखी करना)	Notice (ध्यान देना)	
841	Overrun (बढ़ जाना)	Surrender (त्यागना)	
842	**Overt (प्रत्यक्ष)**	Hidden, Concealed (छिपा हुआ)	3
843	Overweening (ज्यादा ही आत्मविश्वास)	Modest (आडंबरहीन)	
844	Pacifist (शांतिवादी)	Warmonger (युद्धोत्तेजक)	
845	Palatial (आलीशान)	Poor (गरीब)	
846	Pale (फीका)	Bright (तीव्र)	
847	Paltry (तुच्छ)	Substantial (पर्याप्त)	
848	Panegyric (प्रशंसात्मक)	Criticism (आलोचना)	
849	Panicky (घबराया हुआ)	Calm (शांत)	
850	Pardon (क्षमा)	Punish (सज़ा)	
851	Parochial (संकीर्ण)	Global (वैश्विक)	
852	**Parsimonious (किफ़ायती)**	Extravagant, Lavish (अतिशयोक्तिपूर्ण, भव्य)	2
853	Part (अंश / खंड)	Whole (पूरा)	
854	Particularly (विशेष रूप से)	Generally (आम तौर पर)	
855	Partner (साथी)	Opponent (प्रतिद्वंद्वी)	
856	Passive (निष्क्रिय)	Agitated (उत्तेजित)	
857	Passivity (निष्क्रियता)	Interest (दिलचस्पी)	
858	Peer (कुलीन)	Inferior (नीचा)	
859	Pellucid (पारदर्शक)	Murky (धुंधला)	
860	Penitent (पश्चात्तापी)	Unrepentant (अपश्चात्तापी)	
861	Penniless (कंगाल)	Rich (धनी)	
862	**Penurious (दरिद्र)**	Opulent, Munificent (धनी)	2
863	Penury (दरिद्रता)	Wealth (दौलत)	
864	Perfunctory (असावधान)	Careful (सावधान)	
865	Perish (मर जाना)	Grow (उत्पन्न होना)	
866	Permanent (स्थायी)	Temporary (अस्थायी)	
867	Permission (अनुमति)	Hindrance (बाधा)	
868	**Perpetrate (पाप करना)**	Prevent (प्रतिबंध करना)	2
869	**Perpetual (लगातार)**	Intermittent, Transitory (रुक-रुक कर, अस्थायी)	2
870	Perspicuity (स्पष्टता)	Vagueness (अस्पष्टता)	
871	Perturb (व्याकुल करना)	Soothe (शांत करना)	
872	Pessimist (निराशावादी)	Optimist (आशावादी)	
873	Pestering (तंग करना)	Pacifying (शांत करना)	
874	Petty (छोटा)	Big (बड़ा)	

SN	WORD	Antonyms	#R
875	Philanthropic (परोपकारी)	Self Centred (स्वकेन्द्रित)	
876	Phlegmatic (सुस्त)	Ardent (उत्साही)	
877	Pilferer (चोर)	Police (पुलिस)	
878	Placate (शांत करना)	Enrage (क्रोधित करना)	
879	Placid (शांत)	Stormy (तूफ़ानी)	
880	Plausible (संभाव्य)	Inconceivable (अकल्पनीय)	
881	**Pliable (लचीला)**	Rigid (कठोर)	2
882	Plunge (कूदना)	Rise (ऊपर उठना)	
883	**Polite (सभ्य)**	Rude (अशिष्ट)	2
884	**Pompous (गर्वित)**	Humble (विनीत)	2
885	Possess (दखल करना)	Release (छोड़ देना)	
886	Potent (प्रबल)	Weak (कमज़ोर)	
887	Potential (क्षमता)	Lacking (अभाव)	
888	**Precious (कीमती)**	Worthless, Cheap (बेकार, सस्ता)	3
889	Preclude (बंद करना)	Include (शामिल)	
890	Precocious (असामयिक)	Backward (पिछड़े)	
891	**Predecessor (पूर्वज)**	Successor (वारिस)	2
892	Premium (मूल्यवान)	Inferior (घटिया)	
893	Preserve (संरक्षित करना)	Neglect (ध्यान न देना)	
894	Prestige (प्रतिष्ठा)	Disregard (अनादर)	
895	Pretence (ढोंग)	Reality (असलियत)	
896	Prevail (जीत लेना)	Surrender (हार मानना)	
897	Previous (पिछला)	Current (वर्तमानकालिक)	
898	Prey (शिकार)	Predator (शिकारी)	
899	**Prim (नियमानुकूल)**	Informal, Dishevelled (अनौपचारिक)	2
900	Primary (प्राथमिक)	Secondary (माध्यमिक)	
901	Primed (दुरुस्त)	Unready (कच्चा)	
902	Primeval (अतिप्राचीन)	Recent (हाल का)	
903	Prior (पूर्व)	Subsequent (आगामी)	
904	Privilege (सुविधा)	Disadvantage (असुविधा)	
905	Probationer (परखाधीन)	Master (उस्ताद)	
906	Probity (ईमानदारी)	Deceit (छल)	
907	Proceed (आगे जाना)	Recede (दूर जाना)	
908	Proceeding (कार्यवाही)	Passiveness (निष्क्रियता)	
909	Produce (निर्माण करना)	Destroy (नष्ट करना)	
910	**Professional (पेशेवर)**	Amateur (शौक़ीन व्यक्ति)	2
911	**Profound (गहन)**	Superficial, Ignorant (सतही, अज्ञानी)	4
912	Profusion (प्रचुरता)	Scarcity (कमी)	
913	**Progressive (प्रगतिशील)**	Conservative (अपरिवर्तनवादी)	2
914	Prolific (फलदायक)	Unproductive (अनुत्पादक)	

SN	WORD	Antonyms	#R
915	Prolong (लंबा करना)	Shorten (छोटा करना)	
916	**Prominent (प्रसिद्ध)**	Obscure, Unknown, Inconspicuous (अस्पष्ट, अज्ञात, तुच्छ)	3
917	Proper (उचित)	Unsuitable (अनुचित)	
918	Prosper (उन्नति करना)	Decline (पतन)	
919	Protean (बहुरूपिया)	Unchanging (अपरिवर्तनीय)	
920	Protract (विलंब करना)	Advance (अग्रसर होना)	
921	Provide (प्रदान करना)	Deny (मना करना)	
922	Provident (दूरदर्शी)	Wasteful (अपव्ययी)	
923	Provincial (प्रांतीय)	Metropolitan (महानगर)	
924	**Provisional (अस्थायी)**	Permanent, Definite (स्थायी, निश्चित)	2
925	Pseudo (नक़ली)	Genuine (असली)	
926	Public (सार्वजनिक)	Private (निजी)	
927	Publicise (प्रचारित करना)	Withhold (रोक)	
928	Puissant (ओजस्वी)	Lazy (आलसी)	
929	Punctilious (बारीकियों पर ध्यान देने वाला)	Easy-Going (आरामपसंद)	
930	Pungent (तीखा)	Mild (सौम्य)	
931	Pure (पवित्र)	Indecent (अभद्र)	
932	Purloin (चुराना)	Compensate (कमी पूर्ति)	
933	Purportedly (कथित तौर पर)	Impossibly (असंभावना से)	
934	Putrefy (गलना, सड़ना)	Combine (जोड़ना)	
935	Quarrel (झगड़ा)	Harmony (सामंजस्य)	
936	Quell (शांत करना)	Agitate (उत्तेजित करना)	
937	Quiet (शांत)	Noisy (शोर)	
938	Rabble (निम्न वर्ग)	Elite (उच्च वर्ग)	
939	**Rambling (घुमावदार)**	Coherent, Direct (सुसंगत, सीधा)	2
940	Ramify (श्रेणी विभाजन होना)	Unite (सम्मिलित हो जाना)	
941	Rampage (हंगामा करना)	Harmony (सामंजस्य)	
942	**Rancid (बासी)**	Fresh (ताज़ा)	2
943	Ransack (लूटना)	Protect (रक्षा करना)	
944	**Rapid (तीव्र)**	Slow (धीरे)	4
945	Rapture (उत्साह)	Calmness (शांति)	
946	Rarely (कभी-कभार)	Frequently (बार-बार)	
947	Rash (जल्दबाजी)	Careful (सावधान)	
948	Ratification (पुष्टीकरण)	Disapproval (अस्वीकार)	
949	**Raucous (कर्कश)**	Subdued, Dulcet (सुरीला)	2
950	Ravaged (तबाह)	Restored (पुनः स्थापित किए गए)	
951	Raze (तोड़ना)	Build (बनाना)	
952	Rear (पिछला भाग)	Front (सामने का)	

SN	WORD	Antonyms	#R
953	Reason (विचार करना)	Charge (धावा बोलना)	
954	Reasonable (उचित)	Outrageous (बेहिसाब)	
955	Reassure (आश्वस्त)	Discourage (हतोत्साह करना)	
956	Rebate (छूट)	Increase (बढ़ना)	
957	**Rebellion (विद्रोह)**	Submission, Loyalty (अधीनता)	2
958	Rebuff (दुतकारना)	Praise (प्रशंसा)	
959	Rebuke (फटकार)	Flattery (चापलूसी)	
960	Recalled (स्मरण)	Forgotten (भुला दिया)	
961	Recluse (एकांतवासी)	Extrovert (बहिर्मुखी व्यक्ति)	
962	**Recondite (जटिल)**	Straightforward, Simple (सरल)	2
963	Recoup (दुबारा पाना)	Lose (खोना)	
964	Recovered (बरामद)	Lost (खोया)	
965	Rectitude (इंसाफ)	Infamy (बदनामी)	
966	**Refined (शुद्ध किया हुआ)**	Crude (कच्चा)	2
967	Refulgent (उज्ज्वल)	Dark (अंधेरा)	
968	Refute (खंडन करना)	Endorse (समर्थन)	
969	Reign (हुकूमत करना)	Yield (समर्पण करना)	
970	Reinforce (मजबूत करना)	Weaken (कमजोर)	
971	Relapse (पतन)	Improve (बेहतर बनाना)	
972	Relationship (संबंध)	Opposition (विरोध)	
973	Relaxed (तनाव मुक्त)	Tense (तनाव में)	
974	Relay (आगे भेजना)	Hold (रोक कर रखना)	
975	**Relentless (निष्ठुर)**	Yielding (बात मान लेनेवाला)	2
976	Remarkable (असाधारण)	Normal (साधारण)	
977	Remnant (अवशेष)	Whole (पूरा का पूरा)	
978	Remote (दूरस्थ)	Close (पास)	
979	Renaissance (नवजागरण)	Decadence (पतन)	
980	Renegade (स्वधर्मत्यागी)	Follower (अनुयायी)	
981	Renew (नवीनीकरण करना)	Exhaust (खत्म कर डालना)	
982	**Renowned (प्रसिद्ध)**	Unknown, Obscure (अनजान, अप्रसिद्ध)	2
983	**Repel (पीछे हटाना)**	Attract (आकर्षित करना)	2
984	Repress (दबाना)	Encourage (प्रोत्साहित करना)	
985	Reprieve (स्थगित करना)	Continuation (जारी रखना)	
986	Reprimanded (फटकारना)	Praised (सराहना की)	
987	Repugnant (प्रतिकूल)	Pleasant (सुहावना)	
988	Repulsion (घृणा)	Attraction (आकर्षण)	
989	**Repulsive (प्रतिकारक, अप्रिय)**	Attractive, Pleasing (आकर्षक, मनभावन)	4
990	**Reserved (संकोची)**	Communicative, Friendly (मिलनसार)	2
991	Resign (त्यागपत्र देना)	Join (नियुक्त होना)	
992	Resilience (लचीलापन)	Rigidity (कठोरता)	

SN	WORD	Antonyms	#R
993	**Resist (विरोध करना)**	Yield, Allow (स्वीकार करना)	2
994	**Resolve (संकल्प)**	Indecision, Refuse (असमंजस)	2
995	Resource (साधन)	Lack (अभाव)	
996	Responsible (ज़िम्मेदार)	Irresponsible (ग़ैर ज़िम्मेदार)	
997	Restore (सुधारना)	Damage (नष्ट करना)	
998	Restricted (सीमित)	Unbounded (अपार)	
999	Restrictive (प्रतिबंधक)	Liberal (उदारवादी)	
1000	**Resume (फिर आरम्भ करना)**	Finish, Cease (समाप्त)	2
1001	Retaliation (प्रतिशोध)	Reconciliation (सुलह)	
1002	Retard (धीमा करना)	Hurry (जल्दी करना)	
1003	Retrench (छटनी करना)	Recruit (नियुक्त करना)	
1004	Retrieve (सुधारना)	Damage (क्षति पहुँचाना)	
1005	Reveal (प्रकट करना)	Conceal (छिपाना)	
1006	Revered (आदरणीय)	Despised (तिरस्कृत)	
1007	Reverence (सम्मान)	Contempt (अपमान)	
1008	Reward (इनाम)	Punish (सज़ा देना)	
1009	Ribald (अशिष्ट)	Clean (स्वच्छ)	
1010	Ridiculous (बेतुका)	Reasonable (उचित)	
1011	Rife (परिपूर्ण)	Scarce (अपर्याप्त)	
1012	Rigorous (कठिन)	Lenient (नरम, हलका)	
1013	Rotund (गोल मटोल)	Slim (पतला)	
1014	Rough (खुरदुरा)	Smooth (कोमल)	
1015	Routine (सामान्य)	Different (विभिन्न)	
1016	Rueful (उदास)	Joyful (प्रफुल्लित)	
1017	**Ruefully (उदास)**	Cheerful, Defiant (प्रसन्नतापूर्वक, अवज्ञापूर्ण)	2
1018	Rugged (खुरदरा)	Smooth (कोमल)	
1019	Ruined (तबाह)	Mended (मरम्मत किया हुआ)	
1020	Rustic (देहाती)	Urban (शहरी)	
1021	**Ruthless (क्रूर)**	Kind, Compassionate (मेहरबान)	2
1022	Ruthlessly (बेरहमी से)	Leniently (उदारता से)	
1023	Sabotage (तोड़-फोड़)	Create (निर्माण करना)	
1024	Sacrifice (त्याग)	Acquire (प्राप्त)	
1025	Safe (सुरक्षित)	Insecure (असुरक्षित)	
1026	Sagacious (बुद्धिमान)	Dull (मंदबुद्धि)	
1027	Salve (ख़ुशामदी करना)	Blockage (रुकावट)	
1028	Sarcasm (ताना)	Flattery (खुशामद)	
1029	Savant (विद्वान)	Amateur (शौक़ीन)	
1030	Savoury (नमकीन/चटपटा)	Sweet (मीठा)	
1031	Scarcity (कमी)	Plenty (खूब)	
1032	Sceptic (संदेहवादी)	Believer (विश्वास करनेवाला)	

SN	WORD	Antonyms	#R
1033	Scholarly (विद्वत्तापूर्ण)	Ignorant (अनजान)	
1034	Scoff (हंसी उड़ाना)	Praise (प्रशंसा करना)	
1035	Scold (डांटना)	Praise (प्रशंसा करना)	
1036	Scorn (तिरस्कार)	Praise (प्रशंसा)	
1037	Scrimp (बचत करना)	Squander (गंवाना)	
1038	Scrutable (परीक्षा करने योग्य)	Occult (रहस्यमय)	
1039	Scurrilous (अपमानजनक)	Complimentary (प्रशंसात्मक)	
1040	Seamy (अनैतिक)	Pure (पवित्र)	
1041	Secede (किसी मंडली से हटना)	Unite (सम्मिलित होना)	
1042	Seclude (एकांत में रहना)	Socialize (घुलना मिलना)	
1043	Secure (सुरक्षित)	Endangered (संकटग्रस्त)	
1044	Sedate (शांत)	Exciting (उत्तेजित)	
1045	Seize (ज़ब्त करना)	Release (मुक्त करना)	
1046	Semblance (अनुरूपता)	Difference (अंतर)	
1047	Sentience (चेतना)	Disregard (उदासीनता)	
1048	Separable (अलग करने लायक)	Indivisible (अविभाज्य)	
1049	Servant (नौकर)	Master (स्वामी)	
1050	Servile (चापलूस)	Defiant (विद्रोही)	
1051	Sever (अलग करना)	Unite (सम्मिलित करना)	
1052	**Severe (कठोर)**	Mild, Gentle (सौम्य)	5
1053	Shabby (जर्जर)	Nice (सुहावना)	
1054	**Shallow (उथला)**	Deep (गहरा)	8
1055	Shimmering (झिलमिलाता)	Gloomy (उदास)	
1056	Shrewd (चालाक)	Naive (भोला)	
1057	Shun (दूर रहना / बचना)	Cherish (अच्छा लगना)	
1058	Siege (घेराबंदी)	Clearance (निकासी)	
1059	Simple (सरल)	Complex (जटिल)	
1060	Sinks (डूब जाना)	Floats (तैरना)	
1061	Skeptic (संदेहवादी)	Believer (विश्वास करनेवाला)	
1062	**Slacken (कम करना)**	Increase, Intensify (बढ़ना)	2
1063	Slander (बदनामी)	Admire (प्रशंसा करना)	
1064	Slave (दास)	Master (स्वामी)	
1065	Slavish (दास संबंधी)	Assertive (अड़ियल)	
1066	Sleek (आकर्षक)	Dull (फीका)	
1067	Slothful (आलसी)	Lively (जीवंत)	
1068	**Sluggish (सुस्त)**	Active, Alert (चौकन्ना)	2
1069	Slur (बदनामी)	Compliment (प्रशंसा)	
1070	Sly (धूर्त)	Honest (ईमानदार)	
1071	Smoulder (सुलगना)	Froze (जम जाना)	
1072	Smug (दंभी)	Modest (आडंबरहीन)	

SN	WORD	Antonyms	#R
1073	**Sober (शांत)**	Agitated, Drunk (उत्तेजित)	2
1074	Sobriety (संयम)	Drunkenness (मादकता)	
1075	Society (समाज)	Hate (नफ़रत)	
1076	**Soggy (गीला)**	Dry (सूखा)	2
1077	Solace (आश्वासन)	Disharmony (असामंजस्य)	
1078	Solitude (एकांत)	Company (साथ)	
1079	Somber (निराशाजनक)	Cheerful (हंसमुख)	
1080	Spacious (विशाल)	Cramped (तंग)	
1081	Span (फैलाव)	Concentrate (इकट्ठा)	
1082	Spare (अतिरिक्त)	Necessary (आवश्यक)	
1083	**Sparse (विरल)**	Abundant, Dense (सघन)	4
1084	Specific (विशिष्ट)	General (आम)	
1085	Spectacular (असाधारण)	Ordinary (साधारण)	
1086	Speculate (विचार करना)	Dismiss (खारिज करना)	
1087	Spellbound (मंत्रमुग्ध)	Disenchanted (मोहभंग)	
1088	**Spiritual (आध्यात्मिक)**	Physical, Material (भौतिक)	4
1089	Spry (फुर्तीला)	Lethargic (सुस्त)	
1090	**Squalid (मैला)**	Clean (साफ़)	3
1091	Squall (चिल्लाहट)	Peace (शांति)	
1092	**Squander (फिजूलखर्ची, धन लुटाना)**	Skimp, Hoard, Saving (कंजूसी, जमा करना, बचत)	3
1093	Stability (स्थिरता)	Inconsistency (असंगति)	
1094	**Stale (बासी)**	Fresh (ताज़ा)	2
1095	Stalwart (साहसी)	Cowardly (कायर)	
1096	Starve (भूखा मरना)	Stuff (परिपूर्ण करना)	
1097	**Stationary (स्थिर)**	Moving, Shifting, Unsteady (गतिशील, सरकाना, अस्थिर)	4
1098	Steep (ढालवांपन)	Flat (समतल)	
1099	Stiff (कठोर)	Tender (नरम)	
1100	Still (स्थिर)	Active (सक्रिय)	
1101	**Stingy (कंजूस)**	Generous, Extravagant (उदार, फ़िजूल ख़र्च)	5
1102	Stormy (अशांत, हिंसक)	Serene (शांत)	
1103	Stout (मोटा)	Thin (पतला)	
1104	Straighten (सीधा करना)	Crouching (झुकना)	
1105	Stratagem (कपट)	Frankness (सरलता)	
1106	Strident (कर्कश)	Noiseless (शांत)	
1107	Strife (कलह)	Peace (शांति)	
1108	Stunning (तेजस्वी)	Unattractive (बदसूरत)	
1109	Stupendous (शानदार / उम्दा)	Terrible (भयानक)	
1110	Suave (सौम्य)	Rude (अशिष्ट)	
1111	Suavity (मधुरता)	Misbehavior (दुराचार)	
1112	Subdued (नियंत्रित)	Excited (उत्साहित)	

SN	WORD	Antonyms	#R
1113	Subjective (जी या मन संबंधी)	Objective (पदार्थ संबंधी)	
1114	**Sublime (उत्कृष्ट)**	Ludicrous, Inferior (ऊटपटांग, हीन)	2
1115	Submissive (विनम्र)	Stubborn (ज़िद्दी)	
1116	**Substantial (पर्याप्त)**	Doubtful, Flimsy (अनिश्चित, छिछला)	2
1117	Subterfuge (छल)	Honesty (ईमानदारी)	
1118	Succeed (सफल होना)	Lose (हार जाना)	
1119	Successor (वारिस)	Predecessor (पूर्वज)	
1120	Succinct (संक्षिप्त)	Lengthy (लंबा)	
1121	Succinctly (संक्षेप)	Elaborately (विस्तार में)	
1122	Succumbed (हार मान लेना)	Overcame (जीतना)	
1123	Suffice (संतोष होना)	Dissatisfy (असंतोष)	
1124	Sullen (हठी)	Agreeable (सहमत)	
1125	Sultry (कामोत्तेजक)	Frigid (उदासीन)	
1126	Summit (शिखर)	Bottom (तल)	
1127	Summon (बुलवाना)	Dismiss (खारिज)	
1128	Sunder (अलग करना)	Combine (जोड़ना)	
1129	Supplant (कपट से हटाना)	Surrender (आत्मसमर्पण)	
1130	Supple (लचीला)	Brittle (भंगुर)	
1131	**Suppress (दबाना)**	Incite, Reveal, Release (उकसाना, प्रकट करना)	3
1132	Supreme (उच्चतम)	Inferior (नीचा)	
1133	Surveillance (निगरानी)	Neglect (लापरवाही)	
1134	Survival (उत्तरजीविता)	Extinction (विलुप्त होने)	
1135	**Susceptible (ग्रहणशील)**	Immune (प्रतिरक्षित)	2
1136	**Suspend (निलंबित करना)**	Continue, Persist (दृढ़ रहना)	2
1137	Suspicion (संदेह)	Trust (भरोसा)	
1138	Suspicious (संदेहजनक)	Trustworthy (भरोसेमंद)	
1139	Sweltering (तपना)	Freezing (जमना)	
1140	Swerve (मुड़ना)	Straighten (सीधा होना)	
1141	Swindle (धोखा देना)	Honesty (ईमानदारी)	
1142	Sympathy (सहानुभूति)	Cruelty (क्रूरता)	
1143	Synopsis (सार-संग्रह)	Amplification (विस्तारण)	
1144	Tacit (अल्पभाषी)	Explicit (सुस्पष्टवादी)	
1145	Tactful (शिष्ट)	Careless (लापरवाह)	
1146	Taint (कलंक)	Purify (शुद्ध)	
1147	Takes Off (उड़ना)	Lands (भूमि पर उतरना)	
1148	Talkative (बातूनी)	Withdrawn (गैर-मिलनसार)	
1149	Tame (शांत)	Upset (परेशान)	
1150	Tangible (वास्तविक / ठोस)	Abstract (काल्पनिक)	
1151	**Tardy (मंदा)**	Prompt, Quick, Early (शीघ्र)	3
1152	Tasty (स्वादिष्ट)	Insipid (फीका)	

SN	WORD	Antonyms	#R
1153	Taut (सख्त)	Slack (ढीला)	
1154	Tempestuous (तूफ़ानी)	Calm (शांत)	
1155	Temporal (सांसारिक)	Spiritual (आध्यात्मिक)	
1156	Temporary (अस्थायी)	Lasting (स्थायी)	
1157	Tempting (लुभाने वाला)	Repelling (घिनौना)	
1158	Tenacious (दृढ़)	Yielding (नर्म)	
1159	Tender (कोमल)	Rough (रूखा)	
1160	Tense (तना हुआ)	Relaxed (ढीला)	
1161	Tentative (संभावित)	Definite (निश्चित)	
1162	**Terminate (बर्खास्त)**	Begin, Commence (आरंभ करना)	2
1163	Terrible (भयानक)	Nice (सुहावना)	
1164	Testimony (गवाही)	Denial (इंकार)	
1165	Testimony (गवाही)	Disproof (खंडन)	
1166	Theoretical (सैद्धांतिक)	Practical (व्यावहारिक)	
1167	**Thorough (संपूर्ण)**	Cursory (सतही)	2
1168	Thoroughly (पूर्णता)	Superficially (अल्पज्ञता से)	
1169	Timorous (डरपोक)	Bold (साहसिक)	
1170	Tiresome (थकानेवाला)	Energising (स्फूर्तिदायक)	
1171	To Avert (टालना)	To Aid (मदद करना)	
1172	To Filch (चुराना)	To Philanthropy (परोपकार के लिए)	
1173	To Indict (अभियोग लगाना)	To Exonerate (दोषमुक्त करना)	
1174	To Maneuver (पैंतरेबाज़ी करना)	To Cease (समाप्त होना)	
1175	Tolerate (धैर्य धारण करना)	Disapprove (अस्वीकार करना)	
1176	**Traditional (परंपरागत)**	Unusual, Modern (असामान्य, आधुनिक)	4
1177	Tragedy (शोकपूर्ण घटना)	Fortune (सौभाग्य)	
1178	Tranquility (शांति)	Disturbance (अशांति)	
1179	Transience (क्षणिक होना)	Eternity (अनंत काल)	
1180	**Treacherous (नमक हराम)**	Faithful (वफादार)	3
1181	Treachery (धोखा)	Loyalty (ईमानदारी)	
1182	**Tremulous (डरपोक)**	Steady, Stable (स्थिर)	2
1183	Trenchant (प्रभावशाली)	Feeble (दुर्बल)	
1184	Trigger (शुरू करना)	Halt (रोक लगाना)	
1185	Tropical (उष्ण)	Cold (सर्द)	
1186	Turbid (मटमैला)	Clear (साफ़)	
1187	Turgid (आडम्बरी)	Humble (सादगीपूर्ण)	
1188	Tyrant (तानाशाह)	Benefactor (दान देनेवाला)	
1189	Tyro (नौसिखिए)	Professional (पेशेवर)	
1190	Ulterior (गुप्त)	Overt (प्रत्यक्ष)	
1191	Unanimity (सर्व-सम्मति)	Disagreement (मतभेद)	
1192	Unapproachable (पहुंच से बाहर का)	Accessible (पहुंचने योग्य)	

SN	WORD	Antonyms	#R
1193	Uncouth (अशिष्ट)	Refined (संस्कारयुक्त)	
1194	Underestimated (कम समझना)	Exaggerated (अतिशयोक्तिपूर्ण)	
1195	Undesirable (अनचाहा)	Advisable (उचित)	
1196	Unfair (अनुचित)	Just (न्याय संगत)	
1197	Unfeeling (निर्मम)	Affectionate (स्नेही)	
1198	Unfeigned (सच्चा)	Pretended (पाखंडी)	
1199	Unforeseen (आकस्मिक)	Expected (अपेक्षित होना)	
1200	Unfortunate (दुर्भाग्य)	Lucky (भाग्यशाली)	
1201	Unholy (अपवित्र)	Sacred (पवित्र)	
1202	Uniform (एकसमान)	Variable (परिवर्तनशील)	
1203	**Unitary (एकात्मक)**	Multiple, Incomplete (एकाधिक, अपूर्ण)	2
1204	United (संयुक्त)	Separated (विभाजित)	
1205	**Unprecedented (अभूतपूर्व)**	Known, Familiar (जानने वाला)	2
1206	**Unpredictable (अप्रत्याशित)**	Dependable, Reliable (भरोसेमंद, विश्वसनीय)	2
1207	Unscrupulous (अनैतिक)	Conscientious (ईमानदार)	
1208	Unusual (असामान्य)	Commonplace (सामान्य)	
1209	Unworthy (अयोग्य)	Deserving (योग्य)	
1210	Upgrade (उन्नति करना)	Demote (अवनति)	
1211	Uphold (समर्थन)	Oppose (विरोध)	
1212	**Urban (शहरी)**	Rural (ग्रामीण)	2
1213	Urbane (शिष्ट)	Crude (अशिष्ट)	
1214	**Usurp (हड़पना)**	Restore, Surrender, Release (पुनर्स्थापित, आत्मसमर्पण, त्यागना)	3
1215	Utilitarian (उपयोगी)	Unnecessary (अनावश्यक)	
1216	**Vacate (खाली करना)**	Occupy (दख़ल करना)	2
1217	Vacillation (चंचलता)	Steadfastness (दृढ़ता)	
1218	Vaguely (अस्पष्ट रूप से)	Distinctly (साफ़ तौर पर)	
1219	**Vain (अहंकारी)**	Modest (विनम्र)	2
1220	Valour (वीरता)	Cowardice (कायरता)	
1221	Vanguard (अग्र-दल)	Follower (अनुसरणकर्ता)	
1222	Variance (मतभेद)	Harmony (सौहार्द)	
1223	Variety (प्रकार)	Similarity (समानता)	
1224	Vast (व्यापक)	Small (छोटा)	
1225	**Veneration (आदर)**	Disrespect, Contempt (अनादर, अवमानना)	2
1226	Verbose (शब्दबहुल)	Brief (संक्षिप्त)	
1227	Verdant (हरा भरा)	Dying (मरता हुआ)	
1228	Verity (सचाई)	Falsehood (झूठ)	
1229	Versatile (अस्थायी)	Inflexible (अटल)	
1230	Veteran (अनुभवी)	Novice (नौसिखिए)	
1231	Vexatious (तंग करने वाला)	Soothing (संतुष्ट करनेवाला)	

SN	WORD	Antonyms	#R
1232	Vibrant (फुरतीला)	Listless (उदासीन)	
1233	Victor (विजेता)	Loser (परास्त)	
1234	Vigilance (जागरूकता)	Indifference (उदासीनता)	
1235	**Vigorous (जोरदार)**	Spiritless, Frail, Delicate (बेजान)	3
1236	Vile (नीच)	Decent (सभ्य)	
1237	Virtual (आभासी)	Authentic (विश्वसनीय)	
1238	**Virtue (गुण)**	Vice (बुराई)	4
1239	**Virtuous (धार्मिक)**	Vicious, Sinful (पापी)	2
1240	**Visionary (काल्पनिक)**	Pragmatist, Realist, Pragmatic (व्यावहारिक, यथार्थवादी)	3
1241	Vista (दृश्य)	Blindness (अंधापन)	
1242	Vitiate (नुकसान पहुंचाना)	Affirm (समर्थन करना)	
1243	Vivid (जीवंत)	Murky (उदास)	
1244	Vocal (स्वर)	Silent (मूक)	
1245	Vociferous (शोरगुलपूर्ण)	Silent (मौन)	
1246	Volatile (परिवर्तनशील)	Certain (निश्चित)	
1247	Voluble (बातूनी)	Reserved (संकोची)	
1248	Voluntary (स्वयंसेवी)	Mandatory (अनिवार्य)	
1249	Vulgar (अश्लील)	Refined (सुसंस्कृत)	
1250	Vulnerable (असुरक्षित)	Secure (सुरक्षित)	
1251	Waggish (मज़ाकिया)	Solemn (गंभीर)	
1252	Wane (कम होना)	Increase (बढ़ना)	
1253	Warm (गरम)	Cool (ठंडा)	
1254	Waver (डगमगाना)	Steady (स्थिर)	
1255	Wax (बढ़ना)	Wane (घटना)	
1256	Weakness (कमजोरी)	Strength (मज़बूती)	
1257	**Wicked (दुष्ट)**	Good, Righteous, Moral (अच्छा, धर्मी)	3
1258	**Widespread (बड़े पैमाने पर)**	Limited (सीमित)	2
1259	**Wisdom (बुद्धिमत्ता)**	Stupidity, Imbecility, Folly (मूर्खता)	3
1260	**Wither (मुरझाना)**	Bloom, Grow (फूल खिलना, उगाना)	2
1261	Woeful-Eyes (दुखी आंखें)	Cheerful (प्रसन्नतापूर्वक)	
1262	Worsen (बदतर)	Improve (बेहतर)	
1263	Wreck (विनाश)	Build (निर्माण)	
1264	**Zany (नासमझ)**	Sober, Serious (शांत, गंभीर)	2
1265	**Zeal (उत्साह)**	Apathy (उदासीनता)	2
1266	Zealous (उत्साही)	Indifferent (उदासीन)	
1267	Zenith (शीर्ष बिंदु)	Nadir (सबसे निम्न स्तर)	

*Total **1267** Anto asked **1693** times.*

SN	WORD	Antonyms	#R
1	Hostile (शत्रुतापूर्ण)	Amiable, Friendly, Sympathetic, Gentle, Favourable (दोस्ताना, सहानुभूति, कोमल)	10
2	Shallow (उथला)	Deep (गहरा)	8
3	Flexible (लचीला)	Rigid, Stiff, Defiant (कठोर)	7
4	Arrogant (अभिमानी)	Modest, Humble, Humility (विनम्र)	6
5	Acquit (दोषमुक्त करना)	Condemn, Convict, Blame (दोष लगाना)	5
6	Adamant (अटल)	Yielding, Gullible, Flexible (नर्म, लचीला)	5
7	Agony (कष्ट)	Pleasure, Ecstasy, Delight, Comfort (आनंद, उत्साह, आराम)	5
8	Ambiguous (अस्पष्ट)	Precise, Clear, Certain (स्पष्ट)	5
9	Fertile (उपजाऊ)	Barren (बंजर)	5
10	Native (मूल निवासी)	Alien, Foreign, Exotic (विदेशी)	5
11	Severe (कठोर)	Mild, Gentle (सौम्य)	5
12	Stingy (कंजूस)	Generous, Extravagant (उदार, फ़िज़ूल ख़र्च)	5
13	Accept (स्वीकार)	Reject, Deny (अस्वीकार)	4
14	Affirm (स्वीकार करना)	Refuse, Disagree, Denial (मना करना, असहमत होना)	4
15	Appropriate (उपयुक्त)	Unsuitable, Irrelevant, Improper (अनुपयुक्त)	4
16	Autonomy (स्वराज्य)	Dependence (निर्भरता)	4
17	Detest (घृणा करना)	Like, Adore (पसंद करना)	4
18	Dormant (निष्क्रिय)	Active (सक्रिय)	4
19	Exonerate (निर्दोषी ठहराना)	Convict, Sentence, Engage (अपराधी घोषित करना, सज़ा देना)	4
20	Generous (उदार)	Stingy, Miserly, Inconsiderate (कंजूस, अविवेकी)	4
21	Guilty (अपराधी)	Innocent (मासूम)	4
22	Harsh (कठोर)	Gentle, Lenient (कोमल, नरम)	4
23	Impudent (बेशर्म)	Polite, Modest, Respectful (सभ्य)	4
24	Inquisitive (जिज्ञासु)	Indifferent, Unconcerned, Ignore (उदासीन, बेपरवाह)	4
25	Intentional (जान-बूझकर)	Accidental (आकस्मिक)	4
26	Miserable (दुखी)	Happy, Cheerful, Joyful (खुश, खुशहाल)	4
27	Opaque (अपारदर्शक)	Transparent, Clear (पारदर्शक, स्पष्ट)	4
28	Profound (गहन)	Superficial, Ignorant (सतही, अज्ञानी)	4
29	Rapid (तीव्र)	Slow (धीरे)	4
30	Repulsive (प्रतिकारक, अप्रिय)	Attractive, Pleasing (आकर्षक, मनभावन)	4
31	Sparse (विरल)	Abundant, Dense (सघन)	4
32	Spiritual (आध्यात्मिक)	Physical, Material (भौतिक)	4
33	Stationary (स्थिर)	Moving, Shifting, Unsteady (गतिशील, सरकाना, अस्थिर)	4
34	Traditional (परंपरागत)	Unusual, Modern (असामान्य, आधुनिक)	4
35	Virtue (गुण)	Vice (बुराई)	4
36	Abundance (प्रचुरता)	Scarcity (कमी)	3
37	Agitate (उत्तेजित करना)	Pacify, Calm, Soothe (शांत करना)	3
38	Ample (प्रचुर)	Meagre (अल्प)	3
39	Applaud (सराहना)	Denounce, Criticize, Censure (निंदा)	3

SN	WORD	Antonyms	#R
40	Appoint (नियुक्त करना)	Dismiss (खारिज)	3
41	Ascent (चढ़ाव)	Descent (गिराव)	3
42	Assiduous (परिश्रमी)	Neglectful, Idle (बेपरवाह)	3
43	Attract (आकर्षित)	Repel (पीछे हटाना)	3
44	Augment (बढ़ाना)	Degrade, Decrease, Diminish (घटाना)	3
45	Better (बेहतर)	Worse, Inferior (बदतर)	3
46	Bold (साहसिक)	Timid (डरपोक)	3
47	Cacophony (कोलाहल)	Harmony, Symphony (सामंजस्य)	3
48	Captivity (क़ैद)	Liberty, Freedom (स्वतंत्रता)	3
49	Cautious (सतर्क)	Negligent, Reckless (लापरवाह)	3
50	Clear (स्पष्ट)	Nebulous, Opaque, Murky, Dim (अस्पष्ट, अपारदर्शी, धुंधला)	3
51	Compulsory (अनिवार्य)	Optional (ऐच्छिक)	3
52	Concur (सहमत होना)	Disagree (असहमत)	3
53	Consent (सहमति)	Dissent, Interdiction (मतभेद)	3
54	Controversial (विवादास्पद)	Undisputed, Indisputable, Agreement (निर्विवाद, समझौता)	3
55	Criticise (आलोचना करना)	Commend, Approve, Praise (सराहना करना, मंजूर करना)	3
56	Crooked (मुड़ा हुआ)	Straight (सीधा)	3
57	Denounce (आरोप लगाना)	Praise, Compliment (प्रशंसा करना)	3
58	Dense (सघन)	Sparse (विरल)	3
59	Devious (चालाक)	Straight, Sincere (सीधा)	3
60	Divulge (भेद खोलना)	Conceal, Hide (छिपाना)	3
61	Dull (सुस्त)	Keen, Exciting, Bright (उत्सुक, रोमांचक)	3
62	Enrich (बढ़ाना)	Reduce, Deplete (कम करना)	3
63	Equilibrium (संतुलन)	Imbalance (असंतुलन)	3
64	Evident (प्रत्यक्ष)	Obscure, Doubtful (अस्पष्ट, संदिग्ध)	3
65	Expand (विस्तार)	Contract, Shrink (सिकुड़न)	3
66	Expunge (निकालना)	Insert, Add (डालना, जोड़ना)	3
67	Extravagant (फ़िज़ूल ख़र्च)	Economical, Thrifty (किफायती)	3
68	Famous (प्रसिद्ध)	Obscure, Unknown (अज्ञात)	3
69	Fecund (उपजाऊ)	Barren, Sterile, Sparse (बाँझ, विरल)	3
70	Grotesque (विकृत, कुरूप)	Attractive, Natural, Plain (आकर्षक, सादा)	3
71	Hideous (घिनौना)	Beautiful, Charming, Attractive (सुंदर, आकर्षक)	3
72	Hope (आशा)	Doubt, Despair (संदेह, निराशा)	3
73	Humility (विनम्रता)	Pride, Arrogance, Vanity (अभिमान, अहंकार)	3
74	Ignorance (अज्ञान)	Knowledge (ज्ञान)	3
75	Immaculate (बेदाग)	Filthy, Messy, Foul (गंदा, बेईमानी से)	3
76	Immune (प्रतिरक्षित)	Vulnerable, Sensitive, Susceptible (असुरक्षित, नाजुक)	3
77	Impromptu (बिना पहले सोचे हुए)	Premeditated, Prepared, Planned (पूर्व निर्धारित, तैयार)	3
78	Lenient (उदार)	Strict (कठोर)	3
79	Maverick (अपरंपरागत)	Conventional, Conformist (परम्परागत)	3

SN	WORD	Antonyms	#R
80	Negligent (लापरवाह)	Careful (सावधान)	3
81	Obese (मोटा)	Thin, Slim, Skinny (पतला दुबला)	3
82	Overt (प्रत्यक्ष)	Hidden, Concealed (छिपा हुआ)	3
83	Precious (कीमती)	Worthless, Cheap (बेकार, सस्ता)	3
84	Prominent (प्रसिद्ध)	Obscure, Unknown, Inconspicuous (अस्पष्ट, अज्ञात, तुच्छ)	3
85	Squalid (मैला)	Clean (साफ़)	3
86	Squander (फिजूलखर्ची, धन लुटाना)	Skimp, Hoard, Saving (कंजूसी, जमा करना, बचत)	3
87	Suppress (दबाना)	Incite, Reveal, Release (उकसाना, प्रकट करना)	3
88	Tardy (मंदा)	Prompt, Quick, Early (शीघ्र)	3
89	Treacherous (नमक हराम)	Faithful (वफादार)	3
90	Usurp (हड़पना)	Restore, Surrender, Release (पुनर्स्थापित, आत्मसमर्पण, त्यागना)	3
91	Vigorous (जोरदार)	Spiritless, Frail, Delicate (बेजान)	3
92	Visionary (काल्पनिक)	Pragmatist, Realist, Pragmatic (व्यावहारिक, यथार्थवादी)	3
93	Wicked (दुष्ट)	Good, Righteous, Moral (अच्छा, धर्मी)	3
94	Wisdom (बुद्धिमत्ता)	Stupidity, Imbecility, Folly (मूर्खता)	3
95	Abominable (घटिया)	Delightful, Admirable (आनंदप्रद)	2
96	Absorb (सोख लेना)	Eject, Emit (निकालना)	2
97	Abstract (निराकार, अमूर्त)	Concrete (ठोस)	2
98	Accumulate (जमा करना)	Disperse, Squandered (बिखेरना, गंवाना)	2
99	Accusation (आरोप लगाना)	Exculpation, Defend (सफ़ाई देना, बचाना)	2
100	Acknowledge (स्वीकार करना)	Deny, Decline (मना करना)	2

*Total **100** Anto asked **351** times.*

SSC CGL Tier 1 2022 [ANTONYMS]	
SN	**Word - Antonym**
1	Sinks - Floats
2	Rebellion - Loyalty
3	Hospitality - Coldness
4	Trivial - Serious
5	Fertile - Barren
6	Casual - Formal
7	Conceit - Modesty
8	Blessed - Cursed
9	Mobile - Standing
10	Oppose - Encourage
11	Indispensable - Superfluous
12	Unprecedented - Familiar
13	Diversity - Uniformity
14	Precise - Rough
15	Left - Finished
16	Polite - Rude
17	Ambition - Laziness
18	Attracts - Deters
19	Severe - Gentle
20	Humble - Arrogant
21	Laborious - Facile
22	Dispatch - Acquire
23	Exemplary - Unsatisfactory
24	Polite - Rude
25	Native - Foreign
26	Ancient - Modern
27	Consent - Dissent
28	Valour - Cowardice
29	Guilty - Innocent
30	Ruthlessly - Leniently
31	Established - Displaced
32	Continued - Stopped
33	Immoral - Decent
34	Harmony - Hostility
35	Intrinsic - Extrinsic
36	Identify - Overlook
37	Persuade - Discourage
38	Leisure - Working
39	Cogent - Unconvincing
40	Undesirable - Advisable
41	Consent - Interdiction
42	Nonchalant - Considerate
43	Pacify - Aggravate
44	Penniless - Rich
45	Accept - Deny
46	Vivid - Murky
47	Immune - Susceptible
48	Antonym - Synonym
49	Bulk - Handful
50	Influenced - Bipartisan

51	Loyal - Fickle
52	Ravaged - Restored
53	Vigilant - Negligent
54	Advanced - Rudimentary
55	Anxiety - Relief
56	Hazard - Protection
57	Contracts - Expands
58	Part - Whole
59	Care - Disregard
60	Abundant - Minimal
61	Irresolute - Decisive
62	Everlasting - Transient
63	Acquisition - Loss
64	Cacophony - Symphony
65	Jeopardy - Safety
66	Strange - Mundane
67	Encourage - Dishearten
68	Appropriate - Improper
69	Feud - Harmony
70	Abominable - Admirable
71	Entrenched - Transient
72	Purportedly - Impossibly
73	Intense - Moderate
74	Cacophony - Harmony
75	Repulsive - Pleasant
76	Old - New
77	Incoherent - Rational
78	Dwindle - Complement
79	Inherent - Extraneous
80	Adversity - Fortune
81	Cease - Begin
82	Consolidated - Weakened

SSC CGL Tier 2 2021 [ANTONYMS]	
SN	**Word - Antonym**
1	Congenial - Mean
2	Impeccable - Blemished
3	Indolent - Energetic

SSC CHSL Tier 1 2021 [ANTONYMS]	
SN	**Word - Antonym**
1	Squalid - Clean
2	Maverick - Conformist
3	Ambiguous - Certain
4	Sacred - Profane
5	Treacherous - Faithful
6	Scarce - Abundant
7	Sturdy - Feeble
8	Tedious - Exciting
9	Siege - Clearance
10	Despair - Hope
11	Wax - Wane

12	Desiderate - Disregard
13	Famous - Obscure
14	Jaded - Refreshed
15	Praise - Condemn
16	Detrimental - Harmless
17	Dwarf - Giant
18	Primitive - Sophisticated
19	Succumbed - Overcame
20	Variance - Harmony
21	Former - Latter
22	Savage - Civilised
23	Pseudo - Genuine
24	Assiduous - Idle
25	Ebb - Flow
26	Sceptic - Believer
27	Flummoxed - Comfortable
28	Pure - Indecent
29	Marvellous - Terrible
30	Ardent - Apathetic
31	Attract - Repel
32	Clamour - Quiet
33	Suffice - Dissatisfy
34	Recondite - Simple
35	Vulgar - Refined
36	Impudent - Polite
37	Judicious - Foolish
38	Comely - Grotesque
39	Reinforce - Weaken
40	Dispensable - Essential
41	Exonerate - Convict
42	Pretence - Reality
43	Precocious - Backward
44	Terse - Verbose
45	Exaggerate - Understate
46	Delay - Haste
47	Annoy - Comfort
48	Vain - Modest
49	Absurd - Sensible
50	Cheerful - Gloomy
51	Meagre - Plentiful
52	Doubtful - Decisive
53	Ignominy - Glory
54	Frivolous - Serious
55	Fanatic - Tolerant
56	Comic - Tragic
57	Approached - Receded
58	Uniform - Variable
59	Perfunctory - Careful
60	Defile - Purify
61	Squalid - Clean
62	Susceptible - Immune

SSC MTS Tier 1 2021 [ANTONYMS]	
SN	Word - Antonym
1	Credibility - Improbability
2	Frail - Robust
3	Stormy - Serene
4	Impartial - Biased
5	Eradicate - Conserve
6	Mundane - Exceptional
7	Agitate - Soothe
8	Insatiable - Fulfilled
9	Alleviate - Aggravate
10	Moil - Discourage
11	Obedient - Resistant
12	Evident - Indistinct
13	Sturdy - Delicate
14	Miniature - Mammoth
15	Vicious - Gentle
16	Overrun - Surrender
17	Impure - Sterile
18	Insecure - Confident
19	Resolute - Wavering
20	Brashness - Timidity
21	Hideous - Attractive
22	Laudable - Disrespected
23	Unfeigned - Pretended
24	Irrelevant - Meaningful
25	Impressive - Ordinary
26	Flared - Darkened
27	Impolite - Courteous
28	Abundant - Scarce
29	Ambitious - Lazy
30	Fleeting - Lasting
31	Flexible - Defiant
32	Vanish - Emerge
33	Outstanding - Ordinary
34	Glad - Gloomy
35	Strenuous - Effortless
36	Relapse - Improve
37	Robust - Weak
38	Sprightly - Lethargic
39	Scold - Praise
40	Irrational - Reasonable
41	Divergence - Confluence
42	Baffled - Composed
43	Evident - Hidden
44	Inception - Termination
45	Benign - Violent
46	Exclusion - Admittance
47	Rigorous - Lenient
48	Ebullient - Dejected
49	Detrimental - Benign
50	Cryptic - Definite

51	Flexible - Defiant		4	Spurious - Genuine
52	Blissful - Miserable		5	Hostile - Favourable
53	Fatuous - Sensible		6	Scanty - Abundant
54	Malleable - Stiff		7	Asperity - Civility
55	Heinous - Delightful		8	Spry - Lethargic
56	Preserve - Neglect		9	Deplete - Restore
57	Invigorate - Tire		10	Concise - Lengthy
58	Serene - Agitated		11	Annoy - Satisfy
59	Rational - Illogical		12	Assiduous - Idle
60	Relentless - Yielding		13	Stupendous - Terrible
61	Simple - Complex		14	Obstruct - Assist
62	Pragmatic - Impractical		15	Consummate - Inept
63	Obscure - Obvious		16	Novice - Expert
64	Laconic - Verbose		17	Colloquial - Formal
65	Console - Agitate		18	Straighten - Crouching
66	Admirable - Blameworthy		19	Awkward - Adroit
67	Seclude - Socialize		20	Wily - Honest
68	Escalate - Plunge		21	Opulent - Destitute
69	Variety - Similarity		22	Discontent - Satisfaction
70	Demote - Elevate		23	Compress - Enlarge
71	Forthright - Devious		24	Novel - Traditional
72	Rejuvenate - Suppress		25	Rife - Scarce
73	Salient - Insignificant		26	Excelled - Failed
74	Pestering - Pacifying		27	Fascinating - Repulsive
75	Flabby - Firm		28	Vigorous - Frail
76	Upgrade - Demote		29	Intense - Faint
77	Improvident - Thrifty		30	Separable - Indivisible
78	Perilous - Safe		31	Indelible - Temporary
79	Enlightened - Confounded		32	Pensive - Unreflective
80	Harmony - Discord		33	Dilemma - Solution
81	Sagacious - Dull		34	Sane - Crazy
82	Courageous - Diffident		35	Vacant - Occupied
83	Tangible - Abstract		36	Assaulted - Guarded
84	Decay - Growth		37	Vociferous - Silent
85	Endure - Resist		38	Reprieve - Continuation
86	Zenith - Nadir		39	Sordid - Honourable
87	Refute - Endorse		40	Capitalise - Forfeit
88	Steady - Shaky		41	Coincide - Differ
89	Luminous - Dim		42	Utilitarian - Unnecessary
90	Hilarious - Humourless		43	Underestimated - Exaggerated
91	Abate - Aggravate		44	Tempting - Repelling
92	Obvious - Hidden		45	Uncanny - Ordinary
93	Brutality - Gentleness		46	Disgruntled - Pleased
94	Cowardly - Valiant		47	Subterfuge - Honesty
95	Lucid - Ambiguous		48	Controlled - Agitated
96	Wicked - Moral		49	Vituperate - Praise
			50	Penitent - Unrepentant

SSC CPO Paper 1 2022 [ANTONYMS]

SN	Word - Antonym			
1	Emulate - Neglect		51	Vigorous - Delicate
2	Resume - Cease		52	Approximately - Exactly
3	Dull - Bright		53	Amateur - Professional
			54	Barbaric - Civilised
			55	Detachment - Subjectivity

56	Integrate - Separate
57	Better - Inferior

SSC CPO Paper 2 2020 [ANTONYMS]	
SN	**Word - Antonym**
1	Perseverance - Indifference
2	Shallow - Deep
3	Relevant - Inapplicable

SSC GD Constable 2021 [ANTONYMS]	
SN	**Word - Antonyms**
1	Generous - Inconsiderate
2	Commence - Conclude
3	Stable - Shaky
4	Appoint - Dismiss
5	Impel - Repress
6	Retard - Hurry
7	Certainty - Doubt
8	Assuage - Provoke
9	Connect - Detach
10	Vaguely - Distinctly
11	Callous - Caring
12	Erase - Create
13	Innocent - Cunning
14	Cautious - Reckless
15	Betterment - Deterioration
16	Volatile - Certain
17	Dull - Keen
18	Possess - Release
19	Deny - Agree
20	Advance - Retreat
21	Candid - Biased
22	Benign - Malignant
23	Delicious - Distasteful
24	Just - Corrupt
25	Gallant - Cowardly
26	Hearty - Aloof
27	Dispute - Agreement
28	Invert - Straighten
29	Fictitious - Factual
30	Spellbound - Disenchanted
31	Prudent - Wasteful
32	Criticise - Approve
33	Vital - Trivial
34	Precarious - Safe
35	Vulnerable - Secure
36	Alert - Careless
37	Hesitate - Advance
38	Detest - Adore
39	Deny - Accept
40	Enthusiasm - Lethargy
41	Loathe - Admire
42	Beneath - Above
43	Ravish - Repel
44	Beseech - Command
45	Crisp - Tender
46	Reign - Yield
47	Bleak - Bright
48	Malice - Kindness
49	Arouse - Cease
50	Clumsy - Graceful
51	Violent - Gentle
52	Mettle - Cowardice
53	Maintain - Abandon
54	Remember - Forget
55	Petty - Big
56	Defend - Abandon
57	Ample - Scarce
58	Opponent - Supporter
59	Deposit - Withdraw
60	Sparse - Dense
61	Peculiar - Normal
62	Progress - Decline
63	Reverence - Contempt
64	Obscure - Clear
65	Diverge - Converge
66	Chaste - Corrupt
67	Monotonous - Varied
68	Persuade - Halt
69	Deceive - Support
70	Opaque - Clear
71	Aggressive - Calm
72	Frivolous - Wise
73	Ignorance - Knowledge
74	Damage - Mend
75	Collect - Disperse
76	Resource - Lack
77	Tropical - Cold
78	Monumental - Insignificant
79	Guilty - Innocent
80	Distinctive - Close
81	Ample - Meagre
82	Reticent - Talkative
83	Ally - Enemy
84	Overlook - Notice
85	Abstract - Concrete
86	Paltry - Substantial
87	Abundant - Insufficient
88	Dissuade - Persuade
89	United - Separated
90	Remorse - Indifference
91	Stout - Thin
92	Beneficial - Harmful
93	Naive - Experienced

94	Desperate - Content
95	Emerge - Disappear
96	Regret - Contentment
97	Humble - Arrogant
98	Oppose - Favour
99	Emerge - Disappear
100	Resist - Allow
101	Persist - Discontinue
102	Dummy - Original
103	Bold - Timid
104	Hindrance - Advantage
105	Vast - Small
106	Bliss - Sorrow
107	Immune - Sensitive
108	Lenient - Strict
109	Emerge - Disappear
110	Specific - General
111	Demolish - Construct
112	Assert - Abandon
113	Retreat - Advance
114	Never - Always
115	Allure - Repulsion
116	Obedient - Disobedient
117	Discreet - Tactless
118	Dull - Exciting
119	Peculiar - Familiar
120	Emerge - Vanish
121	Severe - Mild
122	Originate - Terminate
123	Awkward - Graceful
124	Captivity - Freedom
125	Contextual - Unrelated
126	Rash - Careful

SSC Stenographer 2022 [ANTONYMS]	
SN	**Word - Antonym**
1	Renegade - Follower
2	Malice - Goodwill
3	Adipose - Stringy
4	Perceive - Neglect
5	Dazzling - Lackluster
6	Rabble - Elite
7	Privilege - Disadvantage
8	Propitious - Inauspicious
9	Wisdom - Imbecility
10	Confused - Lucid
11	Extravagant - Economical
12	Acumen - Stupidity
13	Vain - Modest
14	Prudent - Imprudent
15	Enigmatic - Comprehensible
16	Distrustful - Ingenuous

17	Boundaries - Cores
18	Emigration - Immigration
19	Languid - Energetic
20	Permission - Hindrance
21	Diligent - Inactive
22	Admire - Ridicule
23	Callous - Sensitive
24	Precedence - Disruptions
25	Infinite - Evanescent
26	Gracious - Rude
27	Abide - Reject
28	Primeval - Recent
29	Solitude - Company
30	Blitz - Obtuse
31	Defile - Clean
32	Savoury - Sweet
33	Anxieties - Placidity
34	Fame - Disgrace
35	Woeful-Eyes - Cheerful
36	Terse - Polite
37	Native - Exotic
38	Intrinsic - Extraneous
39	Reluctant - Eager
40	Haughty - Humble
41	Denounced - Defended
42	Fanatical - Liberal

SSC JHT Paper I 2022 [ANTONYMS]	
SN	**Word - Antonym**
1	Mitigate - Agitate
2	Blame - Compliment
3	Faint - Firm
4	Cogent - Impotent

Selection Post 2022 - 10th Level [ANTONYMS]	
SN	**Word - Antonym**
1	Majority - Minority
2	Native - Foreign
3	Testimony - Denial
4	Unfortunate - Lucky
5	Prejudice - Fairness
6	Rarely - Frequently
7	Dense - Sparse
8	Bliss - Misery
9	Dictatorship - Democracy
10	Cease - Begin
11	Conceal - Reveal
12	Liberty - Dependence
13	Intentional - Accidental
14	Dainty - Clumsy
15	Identical - Different

16	Previous - Current
17	Better - Worse
18	Conquer - Surrender

Selection Post 2022 - 12th Level [ANTONYMS]

1	Zeal - Apathy
2	Rescind - Reinstate
3	Frail - Stout
4	Winsome - Repelling
5	Penurious - Munificent

Selection Post 2022 - Grad. Level [ANTONYMS]

1	Delusion - Reality
2	Eager - Reluctant
3	Fertile - Barren
4	Frame - Disorganise
5	Unholy - Sacred
6	Kindness - Animosity

SSC Delhi Police Constable 2022 [ANTONYMS]

SN	Word - Antonym
1	Expel - Accept
2	Proper - Unsuitable
3	Yoke - Liberty
4	Casuistry - Certainty
5	Foreigner - Native
6	Ancient - Modern
7	Spectacular - Ordinary
8	Fondest - Cold
9	Maverick - Conventional
10	Succinctly - Elaborately
11	General - Particular
12	Strident - Noiseless
13	Competence - Incompetence
14	Precious - Worthless
15	Humane - Barbaric
16	Plausible - Inconceivable
17	Precarious - Secure
18	Airy - Stuffy
19	Fulfil - Abandon
20	Excruciating - Mild
21	Veracity - Deceit
22	Zest - Monotonousness
23	Generous - Miserly
24	Reveal - Conceal
25	Appropriate - Irrelevant
26	Mean - Noble
27	Murky - Bright
28	Optimist - Pessimist
29	Extravagance - Parsimony
30	Cooperative - Unsupportive
31	Eccentric - Customary
32	Trivial - Important
33	Obdurate - Compassionate
34	Inception - Conclusion
35	Foe - Companion
36	Countless - Limited
37	Perish - Thrive
38	Expensive - Cheap
39	Recoup - Lose
40	Praise - Condemn
41	Enticed - Repulsed
42	Mystify - Bewilder
43	Exultation - Agony
44	Adulation - Abuse
45	Shallow - Deep
46	Wisdom - Folly
47	Veracity - Myth
48	Trenchant - Feeble
49	Dismal - Cheerful
50	Desire - Apathy
51	Encumbrance - Asset
52	Subjective - Objective
53	Stupor - Consciousness
54	Brief - Lengthy
55	Pious - Sinful

SSC IMD SA 2022 [ANTONYMS]

SN	Word - Synonym
1	Hostile - Friendly
2	Treachery - Loyalty
3	Juvenile - Adult
4	Victim - Hunter
5	Vital - Limited
6	Opacity - Transparency
7	Emancipate - Confined
8	Intentional - Accidental
9	Vagabond - Dweller
10	Flat - Bumpy
11	Proceeding - Halted
12	Plentiful - Scarce
13	Spiritual - Irreverent
14	Partial - Fair
15	Ally - Antagonist
16	Plight - Convenience
17	Expedited - Delayed
18	Brave - Weakness

PRACTICE SET 01 (Antonym)

1 Exhume
   (a) Dig   (b) Reveal
   (c) Hide   (d) Resurrect

2 Baneful
   (a) Harmful   (b) Cruel
   (c) Disastrous   (d) Lucky

3 Jubilant
   (a) Happy   (b) Excited
   (c) Sorrowful   (d) Celebrating

4 Predicament
   (a) Trouble   (b) Hardship
   (c) Condition   (d) Solution

5 Baroque
   (a) Decorative   (b) Bizarre
   (c) Plain   (d) Rich

6 Myopic
   (a) Farsighted   (b) Biased
   (c) Careless   (d) Blind

7 Preposterous
   (a) Ridiculous   (b) Excessive
   (c) Incredible   (d) Reasonable

8 Forgo
   (a) Forfeit   (b) Neglect
   (c) Conquer   (d) Pass

9 Anile
   (a) Senile   (b) Young
   (c) Foolish   (d) Soft

10 Usurp
   (a) Annex   (b) Surrender
   (c) Grab   (d) Displace

PRACTICE SET 02 (Antonym)

1 Virtual
   (a) Fundamental   (b) Implied
   (c) Indirect   (d) Authentic

2 Rustic
   (a) Homely   (b) Simple
   (c) Urban   (d) Plain

3 Barren
   (a) Fertile   (b) Depleted
   (c) Empty   (d) Waste

4 Flourish
   (a) Garnish   (b) Hinder
   (c) Amplify   (d) Develop

5 Triumph
   (a) Joy   (b) Jubilee
   (c) Pride   (d) Sorrow

6 Elementary
   (a) Easy   (b) Fundamental
   (c) Primary   (d) Complex

7 Proficient
   (a) Clumsy   (b) Capable
   (c) Effective   (d) Expert

8 Divine
   (a) Beautiful   (b) Lowly
   (c) Celestial   (d) Heavenly

9 Courtesy
   (a) Cordiality   (b) Rudeness
   (c) Culture   (d) Gentleness

10 Estimate
   (a) Assessment   (b) Conclude
   (c) Opinion   (d) Actual

Keys: 1-c, 2-d, 3-c, 4-d, 5-c, 6-a, 7-d, 8-c, 9-b, 10-b

Keys: 1-d, 2-c, 3-a, 4-b, 5-d, 6-d, 7-a, 8-b, 9-b, 10-d

PRACTICE SET 03 (Antonym)		PRACTICE SET 04 (Antonym)	

1 Perpetual
- (a) Continual
- (b) Ceaseless
- (c) Enduring
- (d) Transitory

2 Peer
- (a) Equal
- (b) Look
- (c) Match
- (d) Inferior

3 Evince
- (a) Manifest
- (b) Comply
- (c) Declare
- (d) Prove

4 Exquisite
- (a) Elaborate
- (b) Consummate
- (c) Sensitive
- (d) Rough

5 Grumpy
- (a) Cross
- (b) Bad Tempered
- (c) Irritable
- (d) Pleasant

6 Officious
- (a) Timid
- (b) Intrusive
- (c) Rude
- (d) Busy

7 Digress
- (a) Stray
- (b) Stay
- (c) Deviate
- (d) Drift

8 Arraign
- (a) Accuse
- (b) Charge
- (c) Indict
- (d) Free

9 Florid
- (a) Busy
- (b) Plain
- (c) Flowery
- (d) Pretentious

10 Incarcerate
- (a) Release
- (b) Confine
- (c) Detain
- (d) Commit

1 Conceive
- (a) Misunderstand
- (b) Accept
- (c) Expect
- (d) Assume

2 Suspend
- (a) Cease
- (b) Discontinue
- (c) Eliminate
- (d) Persist

3 Tranquil
- (a) Violent
- (b) Quiet
- (c) Calm
- (d) Easy

4 Shrewd
- (a) Clever
- (b) Naive
- (c) Brainy
- (d) Artful

5 Suspicious
- (a) Doubtful
- (b) Jealous
- (c) Wondering
- (d) Trustworthy

6 Superfluous
- (a) Excessive
- (b) Necessary
- (c) Lavish
- (d) Abundant

7 Humility
- (a) Meekness
- (b) Reserve
- (c) Arrogance
- (d) Shyness

8 Chicken hearted
- (a) Obedient
- (b) Courageous
- (c) Fearful
- (d) Doubtful

9 Nobel
- (a) Wellborn
- (b) Gentle
- (c) Servile
- (d) Kingly

10 Applause
- (a) Acclaim
- (b) Cheers
- (c) Criticism
- (d) Praise

Keys: 1-d, 2-d, 3-b, 4-d, 5-d, 6-a, 7-b, 8-d, 9-b, 10-a

Keys: 1-a, 2-d, 3-a, 4-b, 5-d, 6-b, 7-c, 8-b, 9-c, 10-c

PRACTICE SET 05 (Antonym)	PRACTICE SET 06 (Antonym)

1 Capacious
- (a) Cramped
- (b) Broad
- (c) Comfortable
- (d) Generous

2 Abutting
- (a) Touching
- (b) Far
- (c) Bordering
- (d) Joining

3 Punctilious
- (a) Careful
- (b) Formal
- (c) Exact
- (d) Easy-Going

4 Stratagem
- (a) Frankness
- (b) Ruse
- (c) Gimmick
- (d) Ploy

5 Antithesis
- (a) Opposite
- (b) Reverse
- (c) Harmony
- (d) Conflict

6 Lechery
- (a) Lust
- (b) Binge
- (c) Excess
- (d) Benevolence

7 Assiduous
- (a) Active
- (b) Neglectful
- (c) Diligent
- (d) Zealous

8 Voluble
- (a) Reserved
- (b) Talkative
- (c) Fluent
- (d) Gabby

9 Chaste
- (a) Proper
- (b) Neat
- (c) Corrupt
- (d) Controlled

10 Clamorous
- (a) Noisy
- (b) Confusion
- (c) Disturbance
- (d) Suppression

1 Miniscule
- (a) Dwarf
- (b) Small
- (c) Gigantic
- (d) Meagre

2 Perpetrate
- (a) Execute
- (b) Prevent
- (c) Perform
- (d) Commit

3 Succinct
- (a) Curt
- (b) Lengthy
- (c) Terse
- (d) Pithy

4 Exotic
- (a) Alien
- (b) Ordinary
- (c) Colourful
- (d) Curious

5 Inordinate
- (a) Undue
- (b) Extreme
- (c) Exorbitant
- (d) Reasonable

6 Jeopardize
- (a) Threaten
- (b) Imperil
- (c) Protect
- (d) Hazard

7 Corroborate
- (a) Confirm
- (b) Contradict
- (c) Approve
- (d) Verify

8 Morose
- (a) Sullen
- (b) Cheerful
- (c) Unsatisfied
- (d) Mournful

9 Denounce
- (a) Applaud
- (b) Criticise
- (c) Blame
- (d) Vilify

10 Opaque
- (a) Frosty
- (b) Dull
- (c) Hazy
- (d) Clear

Keys: 1-a, 2-b, 3-d, 4-a, 5-c, 6-d, 7-b, 8-a, 9-c, 10-d

Keys: 1-c, 2-b, 3-b, 4-b, 5-d, 6-c, 7-b, 8-b, 9-a, 10-d

PRACTICE SET 07 (Antonym)		PRACTICE SET 08 (Antonym)	

1 Efficacious

  (a) Powerful   (b) Useless

  (c) Successful   (d) Good

2 Deathly

  (a) Blooming   (b) Wasted

  (c) Horrible   (d) Sick

3 Rectitude

  (a) Goodness   (b) Infamy

  (c) Honesty   (d) Character

4 Rotund

  (a) Fat   (b) Broad

  (c) Dumpy   (d) Slim

5 Turbulence

  (a) Disorder   (b) Agitation

  (c) Peace   (d) Fight

6 Candid

  (a) Artful   (b) Free

  (c) Objective   (d) Plain

7 Decimate

  (a) Preserve   (b) Destroy

  (c) Execute   (d) Abate

8 Fritter

  (a) Blow   (b) Dwindle

  (c) Dissipate   (d) Save

9 Egregious

  (a) Noticeable   (b) Gross

  (c) Mild   (d) Obvious

10 Dainty

  (a) Clumsy   (b) Attractive

  (c) Light   (d) Rare

1 Dense

  (a) Sparse   (b) Jammed

  (c) Crammed   (d) Piled

2 Exaggerate

  (a) Heighten   (b) Amplify

  (c) Compress   (d) Overdo

3 Instant

  (a) Immediate   (b) Current

  (c) Quick   (d) Delayed

4 Reserved

  (a) Placid   (b) Communicative

  (c) Quiet   (d) Modest

5 Hasty

  (a) Sudden   (b) Cautious

  (c) Reckless   (d) Urgent

6 Accessible

  (a) Reachable   (b) Stressed

  (c) Attainable   (d) Restricted

7 Meagre

  (a) Minor   (b) Plentiful

  (c) Scarce   (d) Common

8 Urban

  (a) Rural   (b) Alien

  (c) Casual   (d) Modern

9 Sparse

  (a) Dense   (b) Strong

  (c) Thin   (d) Weak

10 Inferior

  (a) Ulterior   (b) Exterior

  (c) Interior   (d) Superior

Keys: 1-b, 2-a, 3-b, 4-d, 5-c, 6-a, 7-a, 8-d, 9-c, 10-a

Keys: 1-a, 2-c, 3-d, 4-b, 5-b, 6-d, 7-b, 8-a, 9-a, 10-d

PRACTICE SET 09 (Antonym)	PRACTICE SET 10 (Antonym)

1 Prim

(a) Particular	(b) Informal
(c) Straight	(d) Nice

2 Articulate

(a) Unclear	(b) Enunciate
(c) Eloquent	(d) Coherent

3 Cozen

(a) Cheat	(b) Catch
(c) Burn	(d) Honest

4 Consensus

(a) Accord	(b) Discord
(c) Consent	(d) Unity

5 Incorrigible

(a) Hopeless	(b) Incurable
(c) Reformable	(d) Loser

6 Purloin

(a) Steal	(b) Filch
(c) Lift	(d) Compensate

7 Deferential

(a) Civil	(b) Submissive
(c) Arrogant	(d) Polite

8 Temporal

(a) Material	(b) Fleshly
(c) Earthly	(d) Spiritual

9 Sordid

(a) Dirty	(b) Black
(c) Corrupt	(d) Reputable

10 Disarming

(a) Detestable	(b) Charming
(c) Silk	(d) Convincing

---

1 Manual

(a) Thesaurus	(b) Handbook
(c) Directory	(d) Dictionary

2 Sordid

(a) Dirty	(b) Solid
(c) Clean	(d) Pure

3 Absurd

(a) Sensitive	(b) Sentimental
(c) Selfish	(d) Sensible

4 Accept

(a) Reject	(b) Acquire
(c) Obtain	(d) Release

5 Acquit

(a) Evict	(b) Forgive
(c) Convict	(d) Clear

6 Affinity

(a) Empathy	(b) Attraction
(c) Preference	(d) Aversion

7 Agony

(a) Anxiety	(b) Distress
(c) Comfort	(d) Misery

8 Arrogance

(a) Superiority	(b) Sweetness
(c) Humility	(d) Vanity

9 Ascent

(a) Descent	(b) Depression
(c) Decent	(d) Distant

10 Brutal

(a) Fierce	(b) Sane
(c) Savage	(d) Humane

Keys: 1-b, 2-a, 3-d, 4-b, 5-c, 6-d, 7-c, 8-d, 9-d, 10-a

Keys: 1-b, 2-c, 3-d, 4-a, 5-c, 6-d, 7-c, 8-c, 9-a, 10-d

PRACTICE SET 11 (Antonym)	PRACTICE SET 12 (Antonym)

1 Gratify

(a) Satisfy (b) Enchant

(c) Disappoint (d) Pamper

2 Bigot

(a) Intolerant (b) Extremist

(c) Racist (d) Liberal

3 Obscene

(a) Indecent (b) Immoral

(c) Decent (d) Offensive

4 Flamboyant

(a) Glamorous (b) Modest

(c) Colourful (d) Sporty

5 Objective

(a) Prejudiced (b) Detached

(c) Straight (d) Fair

6 Illusive

(a) Delusive (b) Mystery

(c) Delusive (d) Factual

7 Procrastinate

(a) Delay (b) Defer

(c) Do (d) Drag

8 Inquisite

(a) Examine (b) Interrogate

(c) Dig (d) Ignore

9 Mould

(a) Genuine (b) Shape

(c) Slice (d) Sculpt

10 Guile

(a) Cleverness (b) Suspicious

(c) Dishonesty (d) Honesty

1 Comic

(a) Absurd (b) Amusing

(c) Tragic (d) Awkward

2 Covetous

(a) Mercenary (b) Avaricious

(c) Acquisitive (d) Benevolent

3 Crucial

(a) Imperative (b) Trivial

(c) Pivotal (d) Critical

4 Deficit

(a) Adhere (b) Credit

(c) Surplus (d) Remove

5 Dense

(a) Thick (b) Opaque

(c) Condensed (d) Sparse

6 Eminent

(a) Exalted (b) Impressive

(c) Inconspicuous (d) Distinguished

7 Escalate

(a) Raise (b) Enlarge

(c) Reduce (d) Heighten

8 Exceptional

(a) Uncommon (b) Unimaginable

(c) Unthinkable (d) Unremarkable

9 Expansion

(a) Extension (b) Inflation

(c) Compression (d) Augmentation

10 Extravagant

(a) Pauper (b) Generous

(c) Thrifty (d) Deficit

Keys: 1-c, 2-d, 3-c, 4-b, 5-a, 6-d, 7-c, 8-d, 9-a, 10-d

Keys: 1-c, 2-d, 3-b, 4-c, 5-d, 6-c, 7-c, 8-d, 9-c, 10-c

PRACTICE SET 13 (Antonym)	PRACTICE SET 14 (Antonym)

1 Loathe

| (a) Like | (b) Decline |
| (c) Hate | (d) Abhor |

2 Nascent

| (a) Developing | (b) Germinal |
| (c) Maturing | (d) Withering |

3 Absolve

| (a) Acquit | (b) Clear |
| (c) Excuse | (d) Blame |

4 Demure

| (a) Strong | (b) Shy |
| (c) Backward | (d) Afraid |

5 Artifice

| (a) Truthfulness | (b) Trick |
| (c) Skill | (d) Scheme |

6 Inept

| (a) Clumsy | (b) Artless |
| (c) Inadept | (d) Skilful |

7 Inhibit

| (a) Check | (b) Stop |
| (c) Frustrate | (d) Allow |

8 Angst

| (a) Casualness | (b) Anxiety |
| (c) Insecurity | (d) Disturbed |

9 Banter

| (a) Teasing | (b) Praise |
| (c) Fun | (d) Gossip |

10 Adjacent

| (a) Nearby | (b) Joining |
| (c) Remote | (d) Bordering |

---

1 Finite

| (a) Finished | (b) Endless |
| (c) Bound | (d) Limited |

2 Foreign

| (a) Rustic | (b) Rural |
| (c) Indian | (d) Native |

3 Gather

| (a) Disperse | (b) Distract |
| (c) Dispute | (d) Display |

4 Illuminate

| (a) Add | (b) Erase |
| (c) Light | (d) Darken |

5 Liberty

| (a) Slavery | (b) Autonomy |
| (c) Reservation | (d) Freedom |

6 Meagre

| (a) Inadequate | (b) Plentiful |
| (c) Scanty | (d) Premium |

7 Notorious

| (a) Vicious | (b) Infamous |
| (c) Famous | (d) Disgraceful |

8 Pardon

| (a) Mercy | (b) Punish |
| (c) Grace | (d) Kindness |

9 Progressive

| (a) Moving | (b) Conservative |
| (c) Repeated | (d) Aristocratic |

10 Prolong

| (a) Prevent | (b) Allow |
| (c) Increase | (d) Shorten |

Keys: 1-a, 2-d, 3-d, 4-a, 5-a, 6-d, 7-d, 8-a, 9-b, 10-c

Keys: 1-b, 2-d, 3-a, 4-d, 5-a, 6-b, 7-c, 8-b, 9-b, 10-d

PRACTICE SET 15 (Antonym)		PRACTICE SET 16 (Antonym)	

1 Resolute

(a) Agreeable   (b) Determined

(c) Constant   (d) Faithful

2 Defile

(a) Pollute   (b) Abuse

(c) Shame   (d) Honour

3 Hummock

(a) Ridge   (b) Hill

(c) Upland   (d) Ditch

4 Preclude

(a) Include   (b) Prevent

(c) Impede   (d) Stop

5 Progress

(a) Gain   (b) March

(c) Retreat   (d) Rise

6 Discordant

(a) Aggressive   (b) Agreeable

(c) Noisy   (d) Differ

7 Adjure

(a) Order   (b) Require

(c) Advise   (d) Disclaim

8 Allergic

(a) Affected   (b) Immune

(c) Sensitive   (d) Afraid

9 Captivate

(a) Disillusion   (b) Attract

(c) Grip   (d) Delight

10 Eventual

(a) Future   (b) Last

(c) Overall   (d) Initial

---

1 Transient

(a) Temporal   (b) Stationary

(c) Celestial   (d) Permanent

2 Tyrant

(a) Rival   (b) Benefactor

(c) Patron   (d) Champion

3 Vigilant

(a) Visible   (b) Elusive

(c) Careful   (d) Careless

4 Weakness

(a) Illness   (b) Strength

(c) Disability   (d) Bravery

5 Scanty

(a) Profuse   (b) Small

(c) Precise   (d) Concise

6 Scarce

(a) Seldom   (b) Scanty

(c) Few   (d) Plentiful

7 Severe

(a) Mediocre   (b) Meticulous

(c) Morose   (d) Mild

8 Sober

(a) Nervous   (b) Serious

(c) Agitated   (d) Calm

9 Stale

(a) Fresh   (b) Flat

(c) Dry   (d) Sour

10 Stationary

(a) Tired   (b) Still

(c) Shifting   (d) Motionless

Keys: 1-a, 2-d, 3-d, 4-a, 5-c, 6-b, 7-d, 8-b, 9-a, 10-d

Keys: 1-d, 2-b, 3-d, 4-b, 5-a, 6-d, 7-d, 8-c, 9-a, 10-c

PRACTICE SET 17 (Antonym)	PRACTICE SET 18 (Antonym)

1 Baffling
- (a) Puzzling (b) Comprehensible
- (c) Mystifying (d) Unclear

2 Brindled
- (a) Tabby (b) Spotted
- (c) Stippled (d) Unflecked

3 Extant
- (a) Extinct (b) Present
- (c) Immediate (d) Around

4 Analogous
- (a) Similar (b) Parallel
- (c) Related (d) Disagreeing

5 Haggard
- (a) Fresh (b) Weak
- (c) Pale (d) Tire

6 Scholarly
- (a) Learned (b) Ignorant
- (c) Cultured (d) Trained

7 Nefarious
- (a) Evil (b) Pleasing
- (c) Rotten (d) Infernal

8 Deserter
- (a) Criminal (b) Loyalist
- (c) Refugee (d) Runaway

9 Halcyon
- (a) Calm (b) Gentle
- (c) Palmy (d) Agitated

10 Drawn
- (a) Tense (b) Thin
- (c) Relaxed (d) Drained

1 Calamity
- (a) Happiness (b) Failure
- (c) Suffering (d) Tragedy

2 Wholesome
- (a) Impure (b) Healthy
- (c) Pure (d) Safe

3 Airy
- (a) Stuffy (b) Graceful
- (c) Indifferent (d) Light

4 Convulsion
- (a) Cramp (b) Shaking
- (c) Restful (d) Disaster

5 Squall
- (a) Wind (b) Scream
- (c) Cry (d) Peace

6 Gullible
- (a) Innocent (b) Silly
- (c) Wise (d) Naive

7 Celestial
- (a) Heavenly (b) Blessed
- (c) Hellish (d) Holy

8 Mellow
- (a) Ripe (b) Mature
- (c) Rich (d) Hard

9 Melancholy
- (a) Destroyed (b) Moody
- (c) Low (d) Cheerful

10 Dank
- (a) Dry (b) Close
- (c) Sticky (d) Moist

Keys: 1-b, 2-d, 3-a, 4-d, 5-a, 6-b, 7-b, 8-b, 9-d, 10-c

Keys: 1-a, 2-a, 3-a, 4-c, 5-d, 6-c, 7-c, 8-d, 9-d, 10-a

PRACTICE SET 19 (Antonym)	PRACTICE SET 20 (Antonym)

1 Reprimand

(a) Forgiveness   (b) Punishment

(c) Lecture   (d) Blame

2 Effervescent

(a) Bouncy   (b) Lively

(c) Stale   (d) Resilient

3 Verdant

(a) Grassy   (b) Lush

(c) Dying   (d) Fresh

4 Fecund

(a) Sparse   (b) Productive

(c) Rich   (d) Pregnant

5 Exorbitant

(a) Expensive   (b) High

(c) Cruel   (d) Modest

6 Unprecedented

(a) Exceptional   (b) Bizarre

(c) Known   (d) Fantastic

7 Secede

(a) Quit   (b) Resign

(c) Withdraw   (d) Unite

8 Vigilant

(a) Observant   (b) Aroused

(c) Numb   (d) Active

9 Docile

(a) Controllable   (b) Opposing

(c) Mild   (d) Subservient

10 Quaint

(a) Different   (b) Common

(c) Old-Fashioned   (d) Erratic

---

1 Fluent

(a) Degrading   (b) Inappropriate

(c) Halting   (d) Insensitive

2 Public

(a) Ready   (b) Private

(c) Common   (d) Restricted

3 Adept

(a) Ignorance   (b) Lacuna

(c) Inept   (d) Inexperience

4 Taint

(a) Construct   (b) Clear

(c) Purify   (d) Repair

5 Release

(a) Hide   (b) Bury

(c) Close   (d) Confine

6 Hostile

(a) Joyful   (b) Helpful

(c) Friendly   (d) Violent

7 Redundant

(a) Repentant   (b) Surplus

(c) Singular   (d) Required

8 Calculative

(a) Naïve   (b) Gentle

(c) Docile   (d) Careful

9 Retrench

(a) Revamp   (b) Belie

(c) Deviate   (d) Recruit

10 Amateur

(a) Novice   (b) Professional

(c) Lover   (d) Apprentices

Keys: 1-a, 2-c, 3-c, 4-a, 5-d, 6-c, 7-d, 8-c, 9-b, 10-b

Keys: 1-c, 2-b, 3-c, 4-c, 5-d, 6-c, 7-d, 8-a, 9-d, 10-b

PART - D
(SPELLING)

Spelling may be defined as the forming of words from letters according to accepted usage.

In **spelling** questions 4 options will be given and you will be asked to choose the correct / wrong spelling.

SN	Correct Spelling (#R)
1	**Abandon (4)**
2	Abase
3	**Abbreviate (2)**
4	Abbreviations
5	**Abdicate (2)**
6	Abductor
7	Aberrance
8	Aberrant
9	Aberration
10	**Abhorrent (2)**
11	**Ability (2)**
12	Abnegation
13	Abnormality
14	Abolish
15	Aborigines
16	Abridge
17	Abroad
18	Abscess
19	Abscission
20	**Absence (5)**
21	Absent
22	**Absolute (2)**
23	Absolutely
24	Absorb
25	Abstinence
26	Abstinent
27	Abstract
28	**Abstruse (2)**
29	**Abundance (3)**
30	Abundant
31	Abyssal
32	Academic
33	**Accede (2)**
34	**Accelerate (3)**
35	Acceleration
36	Accent
37	Accentuate
38	**Acceptable (3)**
39	**Acceptance (3)**
40	Access
41	Accessibility
42	**Accessible (2)**
43	**Accessory (3)**
44	**Accident (3)**
45	**Accidentally (3)**
46	**Acclaim (9)**
47	Acclimatise
48	**Accommodate (16)**
49	**Accommodation (6)**
50	**Accommodative (2)**
51	Accompaniment
52	**Accompany (3)**
53	**Accomplice (4)**
54	Accomplish
55	**Accomplishment (2)**
56	Accost
57	Accountancy
58	Accountant
59	**Accredited (3)**
60	**Accumulate (5)**
61	**Accurate (2)**
62	Accuse
63	**Accustomed (5)**
64	**Achieve (6)**
65	**Achievement (6)**
66	**Acknowledge (5)**
67	**Acknowledgement (2)**
68	**Acoustic (8)**
69	**Acquaint (2)**
70	**Acquaintance (5)**
71	**Acquiesce (2)**
72	Acquiescence
73	**Acquire (6)**
74	**Acquisition (3)**
75	Acquit
76	**Acquittal (2)**
77	Acquitted
78	**Acrimonious (2)**
79	Acrimony
80	Across
81	**Actually (4)**
82	Actuation
83	**Adamant (4)**
84	Adapt
85	Adaptation
86	Addiction
87	Addition
88	Additional
89	**Address (8)**
90	Addressee
91	Adept
92	Adequacy
93	**Adequate (3)**
94	Adherent
95	Adjacent
96	**Adjourn (3)**
97	Adjournment
98	Adjust
99	Administration
100	**Administrator (2)**
101	Admirable
102	Admiration
103	Admissible
104	**Admission (2)**
105	Admittance
106	Admitted
107	**Admonish (4)**
108	**Admonition (3)**
109	**Adolescence (2)**
110	**Adolescent (2)**
111	Adopt
112	**Adorn (2)**
113	Adrenaline
114	Adroit
115	Adroitness
116	Adulterant
117	**Adulteration (3)**
118	Advancements
119	Advantage
120	**Advantageous (2)**
121	**Adventure (5)**
122	Adventurous
123	**Adversary (2)**
124	**Adverse (2)**
125	**Advertise (4)**
126	**Advertisement (5)**
127	Advice
128	**Advisable (4)**
129	Advise
130	**Advisory (2)**
131	Advocate
132	Aerodynamic
133	Aeroplane
134	Aerosol
135	**Aesthetic (5)**
136	Aestivation
137	Affectionate
138	**Affidavit (2)**
139	**Affiliate (3)**
140	**Affiliation (2)**
141	Affirm
142	**Affliction (4)**
143	**Affluence (2)**
144	**Afforestation (2)**
145	**Aggravate (8)**
146	**Aggression (6)**
147	**Aggressive (4)**
148	Agitate
149	Agitation
150	Ago
151	Agrarian
152	**Agreement (4)**
153	Agriculture
154	Aircraft
155	Airdrome
156	Airliner
157	**Aisle (2)**
158	Alacritous
159	**Alert (2)**
160	**Algebra (2)**
161	Alien
162	**Alienate (2)**
163	**Alignment (2)**
164	Alimentary
165	**Alimony (2)**
166	Alive
167	Alkali
168	**Allegation (2)**
169	**Allegorical (2)**
170	**Allergic (3)**
171	**Allergy (2)**
172	Alleviate
173	**Alleviation (2)**
174	**Alliance (3)**
175	Alligator
176	Alliterate
177	**Alliteration (3)**
178	Allopathy
179	Allotment
180	Allotted
181	**Allowance (3)**
182	Almanac
183	**Almighty (3)**
184	Alphabet
185	Alpine
186	**Already (4)**
187	Altar
188	**Alternate (2)**
189	**Altitude (4)**
190	Aluminium
191	Alumni
192	Amass
193	**Amateur (5)**
194	**Ambassador (3)**
195	**Ambiguous (2)**
196	**Ambition (4)**
197	**Ambitious (3)**
198	Ambulance
199	Ambush

200 **Amenable (2)**	251 **Appeal (4)**	302 Ascertain	353 Automatic	
201 Amendment	252 Appealing	303 Ascetic	354 **Autonomy (2)**	
202 Amiable	253 **Appearance (4)**	304 Asleep	355 Autopsy	
203 **Amicable (3)**	254 **Appease (2)**	305 Assassin	356 **Autumn (3)**	
204 Ammunition	255 Appeasement	306 **Assassinate (3)**	357 **Auxiliary (4)**	
205 **Amnesia (2)**	256 Appended	307 **Assassination (4)**	358 Available	
206 Amorphous	257 Appetite		359 Avalanche	
207 Amount	258 Applause	308 **Assembly (3)**	360 Avarice	
208 Amplification	259 Appliances	309 Assert	361 Avaricious	
209 Amusement	260 **Application (3)**	310 **Assertion (2)**	362 **Aversion (2)**	
210 Analogues	261 **Appreciate (5)**	311 **Assessment (2)**	363 Aviary	
211 Analysable	262 **Appreciation (2)**	312 **Assiduous (3)**	364 **Aviation (2)**	
212 Analysis	263 Apprehensive	313 **Assignment (2)**	365 Awakening	
213 **Anarchy (4)**	264 Apprentice	314 **Assimilate (2)**	366 Awesome	
214 Ancestors	265 **Approach (6)**	315 **Assistance (2)**	367 **Awful (2)**	
215 Ancestral	266 Approachable	316 **Associate (3)**	368 Awfully	
216 Anchor	267 **Appropriate (4)**	317 Assuage	369 Bachelor	
217 Ancillary	268 Appropriation	318 Assurable	370 Baffling	
218 Aneurysm	269 **Approval (2)**	319 **Assurance (2)**	371 **Baggage (2)**	
219 Angel	270 Approve	320 Assure	372 Bail	
220 Angriest	271 Aptitude	321 **Assuredly (3)**	373 Bailout	
221 **Anguish (2)**	272 **Aquarium (5)**	322 Astonished	374 **Balloon (3)**	
222 Animated	273 Aquatic	323 Astound	375 Banality	
223 Annex	274 Aqueous	324 Atheist	376 Barbarian	
224 Annexations	275 Arachis	325 **Athlete (2)**	377 Barbaric	
225 **Annihilate (3)**	276 **Arbitrary (2)**	326 Atmosphere	378 Barrage	
226 **Anniversary (3)**	277 Arbitrates	327 **Atrocious (3)**	379 Barrel	
227 Annotate	278 Archaeology	328 Attach	380 **Barren (2)**	
228 **Announcement (2)**	279 Archery	329 **Attack (2)**	381 **Barricade (3)**	
	280 Architect	330 Attain	382 Barrier	
229 Annoyance	281 **Architecture (4)**	331 **Attempt (2)**	383 Batch	
230 Annunciation	282 **Argue (2)**	332 Attend	384 **Battalion (3)**	
231 **Anomaly (2)**	283 **Argument (6)**	333 **Attendance (4)**	385 Battery	
232 **Anonymous (4)**	284 Aristocracy	334 Attendant	386 Beaker	
233 Antarctic	285 Aristocrat	335 **Attention (6)**	387 Beast	
234 Antecedent	286 Armature	336 **Attitude (3)**	388 Beautician	
235 Antibodies	287 Aromatic	337 Attorney	389 Beautiful	
236 Antics	288 Arraign	338 **Attract (2)**	390 Beautifully	
237 Antidote	289 **Arrangement (4)**	339 Attractive	391 Becoming	
238 Antioxidant		340 Auction	392 Bedridden	
239 **Antiseptic (2)**	290 Array	341 **Audacious (3)**	393 **Beggar (5)**	
240 **Anxiety (3)**	291 **Arrival (2)**	342 Audacity	394 Beggarly	
241 **Anxious (3)**	292 **Arrogance (3)**	343 **Audible (3)**	395 Begin	
242 Apartheid	293 Arrogant	344 **Audience (5)**	396 Beginner	
243 Apartment	294 Article	345 Auditorium	397 **Beginning (12)**	
244 Apathy	295 **Articulate (2)**	346 Augustan	398 **Beguile (2)**	
245 **Apology (2)**	296 Artillery	347 **Auspicious (3)**	399 Beguiling	
246 Appalling	297 Artless	348 Austere	400 **Behave (3)**	
247 Apparatus	298 Ascendance	349 Authorities	401 Behold	
248 **Apparel (2)**	299 Ascendant	350 **Authority (2)**	402 Beige	
249 **Apparent (2)**	300 Ascension	351 **Autocracy (2)**	403 **Belief (2)**	
250 **Apparently (8)**	301 Ascent	352 Automated	404 **Believe (11)**	

405 Believing
406 Belittle
407 **Belligerent (4)**
408 Bellow
409 Bellowing
410 Belly
411 Bemoan
412 Bench
413 Benchmark
414 **Beneath (3)**
415 Benefactor
416 **Beneficial (4)**
417 **Beneficiary (4)**
418 **Benefit (5)**
419 Benevolence
420 **Benevolent (4)**
421 **Benign (5)**
422 Bereave
423 Bereavement
424 Bereaving
425 Bereft
426 Berry
427 **Besiege (4)**
428 Betray
429 Better
430 Beverage
431 Bewitched
432 Biannual
433 Bibliography
434 Bifurcated
435 Bilingual
436 **Billion (2)**
437 Binocular
438 Biopic
439 **Biscuit (2)**
440 Biscuits
441 Bitter
442 **Bizarre (3)**
443 Black
444 Blackboard
445 Blade
446 Blame
447 Blandishment
448 Blandness
449 Blare
450 Bleak
451 Blemish
452 Blessed
453 Blessing
454 Blight
455 Blind
456 Bliss

457 **Blister (2)**
458 **Blithesome (3)**
459 **Blizzard (2)**
460 Blockage
461 Blonde
462 Blossom
463 Board
464 Boast
465 Boasting
466 Boisterous
467 Bombastic
468 Bombshell
469 Bonafide
470 Bonfire
471 **Booty (2)**
472 Boredom
473 Borrow
474 Borrowing
475 Bottleneck
476 Bouncing
477 **Boundary (4)**
478 **Bouquet (8)**
479 **Boutique (2)**
480 Bovine
481 Bowlegged
482 Boxing
483 Bracelet
484 Brag
485 Brakes
486 Branding
487 Breath
488 Breathe
489 Brevity
490 Bridges
491 **Bridle (2)**
492 **Briefcase (2)**
493 Brighten
494 Brilliant
495 Brisk
496 **Bristle (2)**
497 Bristles
498 **Brittle (2)**
499 Broadcaster
500 Brochure
501 Brood
502 Brought
503 Brusque
504 **Brutal (2)**
505 Brutality
506 Budget
507 **Budgetary (2)**
508 Buffet

509 **Building (2)**
510 **Bulletin (3)**
511 Bullying
512 **Bungalow (2)**
513 Buoyant
514 **Bureaucracy (8)**
515 **Bureaucrat (6)**
516 Burglary
517 Burlesque
518 **Business (11)**
519 Businessman
520 Buying
521 Cabbage
522 Cacophony
523 **Cactus (4)**
524 Cadre
525 Calamitous
526 Calamity
527 **Calculate (3)**
528 **Calendar (5)**
529 **Callous (2)**
530 **Camaraderie (2)**
531 Camera
532 **Camouflage (4)**
533 Campaign
534 **Campaigns (4)**
535 Camphor
536 Cancel
537 Cancellation
538 Cannibal
539 Capabilities
540 **Capable (2)**
541 **Capacity (2)**
542 Capillary
543 **Capricious (3)**
544 Capture
545 **Caravan (2)**
546 Carbonated
547 **Career (3)**
548 Careful
549 Caribbean
550 **Carnivorous (2)**
551 **Carriage (3)**
552 **Carrier (3)**
553 **Carrying (2)**
554 Cashier
555 Cassette
556 Castigated
557 Casualty
558 **Catalogue (2)**
559 Catastrophe
560 **Catch (2)**

561 Category
562 Caterpillar
563 Caused
564 Causeway
565 **Cautious (4)**
566 Cautiously
567 Cavalier
568 Cease
569 **Ceiling (3)**
570 Celebrant
571 **Celebrate (2)**
572 **Celebration (4)**
573 Celebrity
574 **Celestial (2)**
575 Celibate
576 **Cemetery (4)**
577 Censure
578 **Centenarian (2)**
579 Central
580 Century
581 Cereal
582 Cerebral
583 **Ceremonial (3)**
584 **Ceremony (5)**
585 **Certain (2)**
586 Certainty
587 **Certificate (2)**
588 **Challenge (2)**
589 Challenging
590 **Chameleon (2)**
591 Champagne
592 **Champion (2)**
593 Chancellor
594 Chandelier
595 **Changeable (5)**
596 Changes
597 Channel
598 **Character (2)**
599 **Characteristic (3)**
600 Chargeable
601 **Charisma (2)**
602 Charitable
603 Charity
604 Chauffer
605 **Chauffeur (2)**
606 Chauvinist
607 Chemist
608 **Chemistry (2)**
609 **Chirpy (2)**
610 Chivalrous
611 **Chocolate (4)**

#	Word	#	Word	#	Word	#	Word
612	Choir	661	Commensurate	710	**Concise (2)**	759	**Consequence (2)**
613	Choose	662	**Commentary (4)**	711	Concomitant	760	Consequent
614	Christmas	663	Commercially	712	Concrete	761	Consequently
615	**Chronic (2)**	664	Commiserate	713	Concurrence	762	Conservative
616	**Chronology (2)**	665	Commissariat	714	Concurrently	763	Considerate
617	**Circuit (3)**	666	**Commission (3)**	715	Concussion	764	**Consignment (2)**
618	**Circuitous (2)**	667	**Commit (9)**	716	**Condemn (2)**		
619	Circumlocution	668	**Commitment (7)**	717	Condemnation	765	Consistency
620	Circumstances			718	Condensing	766	Consistent
621	Circumventing	669	**Committee (14)**	719	**Condition (2)**	767	**Consolation (2)**
622	Circus	670	**Commotion (2)**	720	Condom	768	Consolidation
623	Citizen	671	**Communication (2)**	721	Condone	769	Constituency
624	Clairvoyant			722	Conducive	770	Constitute
625	**Clandestine (3)**	672	**Community (2)**	723	Conduct	771	Constitution
626	Clarify	673	Compact	724	Conductor	772	Constraint
627	Classic	674	Company	725	**Conference (3)**	773	**Construction (2)**
628	Classical	675	Comparable	726	**Confession (3)**		
629	Classicist	676	**Comparison (2)**	727	**Confidence (2)**	774	**Consumerism (2)**
630	**Classification (3)**	677	**Compassionate (5)**	728	**Confident (2)**		
631	Clattering			729	Confidential	775	Consummate
632	Cleaver	678	Compatible	730	Confidents	776	Consummation
633	Clemency	679	Compel	731	Configuration	777	**Contagious (4)**
634	**Clever (2)**	680	Compelling	732	Confirmed	778	Contain
635	Client	681	Compere	733	Confiscate	779	Contemplate
636	Climate	682	**Competence (2)**	734	Confluence	780	**Contemporary (5)**
637	**Clock (2)**	683	Competency	735	Conform		
638	Cloistered	684	Competent	736	Conformist	781	Contemptible
639	Closure	685	**Competition (2)**	737	Confusion	782	**Contemptuous (2)**
640	Clothes	686	Competitive	738	Congenital		
641	Coadunation	687	**Competitor (2)**	739	**Conglomerate (2)**	783	**Content (3)**
642	Coalesce	688	Complacency			784	**Contentious (2)**
643	**Coalescence (2)**	689	**Complacent (3)**	740	Congratulations	785	**Contextual (2)**
644	**Coalition (3)**	690	**Complaint (3)**	741	Congregate	786	Contiguous
645	Coarse	691	Complaisance	742	Congregation	787	**Continent (2)**
646	Coercion	692	Complaisant	743	Coniferous	788	Contingency
647	**Collaborate (4)**	693	**Complement (2)**	744	Conjectural	789	Continual
648	**Colleague (5)**	694	**Completely (2)**	745	**Conjecture (4)**	790	**Continuance (3)**
649	Collection	695	Completion	746	Conjoined	791	**Continuation (2)**
650	College	696	Compliment	747	Conjugate		
651	**Collide (2)**	697	**Composition (3)**	748	Conjure	792	Continuity
652	Colonel	698	Composure	749	Connect	793	**Continuous (2)**
653	Colonize	699	Comprehension	750	**Connivance (2)**	794	**Continuously (2)**
654	Colossal	700	Comprehensive	751	**Connoisseur (9)**		
655	**Column (3)**	701	**Compromise (2)**	752	**Conquer (5)**	795	Contortion
656	**Combination (7)**	702	**Compulsory (2)**	753	**Conscience (6)**	796	Contraction
657	**Comedian (3)**	703	Conceal	754	**Conscientious (11)**	797	Contractor
658	**Commemorate (5)**	704	**Conceit (4)**			798	**Contradiction (4)**
		705	Conceivable	755	**Conscious (9)**		
659	**Commencement (2)**	706	**Conceive (6)**	756	**Consciousness (2)**	799	Contraption
		707	**Concentrate (2)**			800	Contrary
660	**Commendation (2)**	708	Conciliation	757	**Consensus (5)**	801	Contribution
		709	Conciliatory	758	**Consent (2)**		

802 Controversial	850 Craftmanship	902 Cylinder	954 Demeanour
803 **Controversy (2)**	851 Crater	903 Cynic	955 **Demolish (4)**
804 Contusion	852 Crayon	904 Daughter	956 Demonstrated
805 Convalescence	853 **Creativity (2)**	905 Dealer	957 Demonstrations
806 Convene	854 **Creator (2)**	906 Debates	958 Demoralize
807 **Convenience (5)**	855 Creature	907 **Debilitate (2)**	959 Denial
808 Convent	856 Credential	908 Debtor	960 Denounce
809 **Conversation (2)**	857 Credible	909 Decaffeinated	961 Dental
	858 Creditable	910 Decease	962 Deodorize
810 Converse	859 **Credulous (2)**	911 Deceit	963 Department
811 Conversion	860 Cremator	912 **Deceive (12)**	964 Dependence
812 **Convert (2)**	861 Crevice	913 Decency	965 **Dependent (2)**
813 **Conveyance (2)**	862 **Cricketer (2)**	914 Decennial	966 Deplorable
814 Convict	863 Criminal	915 Deception	967 Depressed
815 Conviction	864 Cringe	916 Decibel	968 Depression
816 **Convincing (2)**	865 Criteria	917 Decide	969 Deprived
817 Convoluted	866 Criterion	918 **Decision (2)**	970 **Descendant (2)**
818 Cooking	867 Criticism	919 **Decisive (2)**	971 **Descent (3)**
819 **Cooperate (4)**	868 Cropping	920 Declension	972 **Describe (3)**
820 **Cooperation (2)**	869 Croton	921 Declination	973 **Desecration (2)**
821 Copulate	870 Crouching	922 Decorative	974 Desert
822 Corollary	871 Cruel	923 Decrease	975 **Desiccate (3)**
823 Corporate	872 **Cruelly (2)**	924 Defamation	976 **Design (2)**
824 **Corporation (2)**	873 Crunchy	925 Defence	977 Designated
825 Correlative	874 Crushing	926 **Defer (2)**	978 Desire
826 Correspond	875 Crust	927 Deferred	979 Despatch
827 **Correspondence (2)**	876 Crystal	928 **Defiance (2)**	980 **Desperate (5)**
	877 Crystallisation	929 **Deficiency (2)**	981 Despise
828 **Correspondent (2)**	878 Cube	930 **Deficient (5)**	982 Despotic
	879 Cubicle	931 Define	983 Dessert
829 Corresponding	880 Cuddle	932 **Definite (4)**	984 Destabilised
830 Corrigendum	881 Cuisine	933 **Definitely (10)**	985 Destiny
831 Corrigible	882 Culminate	934 **Definition (7)**	986 Destress
832 Corroborate	883 Cultural	935 Deflate	987 Destruction
833 **Corrupt (3)**	884 **Cumbersome (2)**	936 Deforestation	988 **Detach (3)**
834 **Corruption (2)**	885 **Curiosity (3)**	937 Deform	989 Detail
835 Cortege	886 **Curious (4)**	938 Deities	990 Detainees
836 Cosmetic	887 Currently	939 **Delegate (4)**	991 Detect
837 Cosmopolitan	888 **Curriculum (2)**	940 Delegation	992 Detective
838 **Councillor (2)**	889 Curry	941 Delete	993 Deter
839 **Counsellor (2)**	890 Curse	942 Deliberate	994 **Detergent (2)**
840 **Countenance (7)**	891 Cursor	943 Deliberately	995 Deteriorate
	892 Cursory	944 **Delicate (2)**	996 Determination
841 **Counterfeit (2)**	893 Curtail	945 **Delicious (7)**	997 Determining
842 Countless	894 Curtsy	946 Delight	998 **Deterred (2)**
843 Countries	895 Curvaceous	947 Delightful	999 Deterrent
844 **Courageous (2)**	896 **Cushion (2)**	948 Deliquescence	1000 Detest
845 Courier	897 **Custard (2)**	949 Delirious	1001 Detrimental
846 **Courteous (5)**	898 **Custody (3)**	950 Deliver	1002 Devastation
847 Cousin	899 **Custom (2)**	951 Delivery	1003 **Develop (3)**
848 Couture	900 **Customary (2)**	952 Demagogue	1004 **Development (3)**
849 Cracker	901 Cyclist	953 Demarcation	

1005 Deviate
1006 **Deviation (2)**
1007 Device
1008 Devilish
1009 Devious
1010 **Devote (2)**
1011 Devotion
1012 Devout
1013 Dexterous
1014 Diabetes
1015 Diabolical
1016 Diagnose
1017 Diagnosis
1018 Diagonal
1019 **Dialogue (2)**
1020 **Diamond (2)**
1021 **Diaphragm (2)**
1022 **Diarrhoea (3)**
1023 Dictate
1024 **Dictionary (5)**
1025 **Diesel (2)**
1026 **Dietician (2)**
1027 **Difference (5)**
1028 **Different (2)**
1029 Differentiate
1030 Differently
1031 **Difficult (2)**
1032 Diffidence
1033 Diffuse
1034 Diffusion
1035 Dignitary
1036 **Dilapidated (2)**
1037 **Dilemma (8)**
1038 Diligence
1039 Diligent
1040 Dilution
1041 Dimension
1042 Diminish
1043 Diminution
1044 Dining
1045 **Dinosaur (2)**
1046 Director
1047 Directory
1048 Disallow
1049 **Disappear (4)**
1050 **Disappoint (3)**
1051 **Disappointment (3)**
1052 **Disapproval (2)**
1053 **Disapprove (2)**
1054 **Disaster (2)**
1055 **Disastrous (4)**

1056 **Discern (3)**
1057 Disciple
1058 Disciplinarian
1059 **Discipline (7)**
1060 **Discomfort (2)**
1061 Disconcerted
1062 Discourage
1063 Discovered
1064 **Discovery (2)**
1065 **Discrepancy (2)**
1066 Discretion
1067 **Discrimination (2)**
1068 Discriminatory
1069 **Discussion (3)**
1070 Disease
1071 Disenchantment
1072 Disenfranchised
1073 Disguise
1074 Disguising
1075 Dishevelled
1076 Disillusionment
1077 Disinterest
1078 Dislodge
1079 Dismay
1080 Disobedient
1081 Disorientation
1082 **Disparage (2)**
1083 Disparaging
1084 Disparate
1085 Disparity
1086 Disposable
1087 Disposal
1088 **Disrupt (2)**
1089 **Dissatisfied (3)**
1090 Disseminate
1091 Disseminating
1092 Dissimulation
1093 Dissuade
1094 **Distance (2)**
1095 Distillation
1096 Distract
1097 Distraction
1098 **Disturbance (3)**
1099 Dithering
1100 **Dive (2)**
1101 Diversified
1102 Divert
1103 **Divide (2)**
1104 **Divine (2)**
1105 Division
1106 Divulge

1107 Docile
1108 **Doctor (2)**
1109 **Domicile (3)**
1110 **Dominant (4)**
1111 Dominate
1112 Dominion
1113 Donations
1114 Dormitory
1115 Doubt
1116 Doubtful
1117 Doubtfully
1118 Downtrodden
1119 Drainage
1120 Drastic
1121 **Dreadful (3)**
1122 Dreamy
1123 Dreary
1124 Dribble
1125 **Drought (2)**
1126 Drunkenness
1127 **Dubious (2)**
1128 Duly
1129 Dumbbell
1130 Durable
1131 **Duration (2)**
1132 Dwarf
1133 **Dwelling (4)**
1134 Dwindle
1135 Dyeing
1136 Dysentery
1137 Dysfunction
1138 Eager
1139 Eagle
1140 Early
1141 Earn
1142 **Earnest (2)**
1143 Earring
1144 Earthiness
1145 Earthquake
1146 Easier
1147 **Eccentricity (2)**
1148 Ecclesiastical
1149 Echelon
1150 Echo
1151 **Eclipse (2)**
1152 Ecological
1153 Ecology
1154 **Economic (2)**
1155 **Economy (2)**
1156 **Ecstasy (4)**
1157 Ecumenical
1158 Eczema

1159 Edge
1160 **Edible (4)**
1161 Edition
1162 Educate
1163 Education
1164 Eerie
1165 Effect
1166 Effective
1167 Effectively
1168 Effervescent
1169 **Efficient (6)**
1170 Efficiently
1171 Effigy
1172 Efflorescence
1173 Effluents
1174 Effort
1175 Effusively
1176 **Eighth (4)**
1177 Eighty
1178 **Elaborate (3)**
1179 Elastic
1180 **Election (4)**
1181 **Electorate (2)**
1182 **Electric (3)**
1183 Electrolyte
1184 Electron
1185 Electronics
1186 Elegance
1187 **Elegant (2)**
1188 **Elementary (6)**
1189 Elephantine
1190 Eleven
1191 Eligibility
1192 **Eligible (3)**
1193 Eliminate
1194 Elite
1195 Elocution
1196 **Eloquent (6)**
1197 **Embankment (3)**
1198 **Embarrass (7)**
1199 **Embarrassing (2)**
1200 **Embarrassment (7)**
1201 Embattle
1202 Embellish
1203 **Embodiment (2)**
1204 Embody
1205 Embrace
1206 Embroidery
1207 **Emergency (3)**

1208 **Emigrate (3)**
1209 **Eminent (5)**
1210 Emission
1211 Emolument
1212 **Emphasis (2)**
1213 Emphasize
1214 Emphatic
1215 Employed
1216 Emporium
1217 Enables
1218 **Encourage (3)**
1219 **Encouragement (4)**
1220 **Encyclopaedia (2)**
1221 Encyclopedia
1222 Endeavor
1223 **Endeavour (2)**
1224 Endogenous
1225 Endurance
1226 Energy
1227 Enervating
1228 Enforcement
1229 Engage
1230 **Engineer (2)**
1231 Engineering
1232 Engraving
1233 Enigmatic
1234 Enjoin
1235 Enlighten
1236 Enlist
1237 **Enmity (5)**
1238 Enormous
1239 Ensue
1240 **Ensure (3)**
1241 **Enthusiasm (5)**
1242 Enthusiastic
1243 Entirely
1244 Entity
1245 Entrance
1246 Entrant
1247 Entreat
1248 **Entrepreneur (5)**
1249 Entrepreneur-ship
1250 Entrust
1251 **Envelope (2)**
1252 **Environment (6)**
1253 Environmental
1254 Envisage

1255 Envoy
1256 Episcopal
1257 **Equality (2)**
1258 Equanimity
1259 Equanimous
1260 Equation
1261 Equilateral
1262 **Equilibrium (3)**
1263 Equine
1264 **Equipment (4)**
1265 **Equipped (2)**
1266 Equitable
1267 **Equivalent (3)**
1268 **Equivocal (2)**
1269 **Equivocation (2)**
1270 **Eradication (6)**
1271 Eraser
1272 Erode
1273 Erosion
1274 Erratic
1275 **Erroneous (5)**
1276 Escalation
1277 Escalator
1278 **Escapade (2)**
1279 **Essence (2)**
1280 **Essential (3)**
1281 Essentially
1282 Establish
1283 **Esteem (5)**
1284 **Estimate (2)**
1285 Estimation
1286 Eternal
1287 Ethereal
1288 **Etiquette (4)**
1289 Euphemism
1290 Evacuate
1291 Evacuation
1292 Evaluation
1293 Evaporation
1294 Evasion
1295 Eventually
1296 **Evidence (4)**
1297 Evidently
1298 Evince
1299 **Evocation (3)**
1300 Evolution
1301 Evolve
1302 Exacerbate
1303 Exacerbating
1304 Exact
1305 **Exaggerate (3)**

1306 **Exaggeration (3)**
1307 Example
1308 Exasperated
1309 Exasperation
1310 Excavation
1311 **Exceed (4)**
1312 **Excellence (3)**
1313 Excellent
1314 **Except (2)**
1315 **Exception (2)**
1316 Exceptionable
1317 **Exceptional (2)**
1318 **Excess (2)**
1319 **Excessive (3)**
1320 **Exchange (2)**
1321 **Excite (2)**
1322 **Excitement (2)**
1323 **Exclaim (2)**
1324 **Exclamation (4)**
1325 Exclamatory
1326 Excretory
1327 **Excruciating (2)**
1328 Excursion
1329 Excuse
1330 Execution
1331 **Executive (5)**
1332 **Exemplary (2)**
1333 **Exemplify (2)**
1334 **Exempt (2)**
1335 Exercise
1336 **Exhale (2)**
1337 **Exhaust (6)**
1338 Exhaustive
1339 **Exhibit (4)**
1340 Exhibition
1341 Exhibitionist
1342 **Exhilarate (4)**
1343 Exhilaration
1344 **Existence (8)**
1345 Existential
1346 Exonerate
1347 Expanse
1348 Expansion
1349 Expansive
1350 **Expect (2)**
1351 **Expedient (2)**
1352 **Expedition (4)**
1353 **Expel (2)**
1354 Expenditure
1355 Expense
1356 **Experience (2)**

1357 **Experiment (7)**
1358 Experimental
1359 **Expertise (2)**
1360 Expire
1361 **Explain (3)**
1362 Explained
1363 **Explanation (6)**
1364 **Expletive (2)**
1365 **Explicit (2)**
1366 Explode
1367 **Exploit (2)**
1368 **Exploitation (2)**
1369 Exploration
1370 Exploring
1371 Explosion
1372 Exponent
1373 Express
1374 **Expression (2)**
1375 **Exquisite (2)**
1376 Extempore
1377 **Extension (3)**
1378 Extensive
1379 Exterminated
1380 External
1381 Extinct
1382 Extirpate
1383 Extortion
1384 **Extract (6)**
1385 **Extravagant (2)**
1386 Extravert
1387 Extrusion
1388 Exuberance
1389 **Exuberant (4)**
1390 Exuberantly
1391 Exultation
1392 Fable
1393 **Fabulous (3)**
1394 Facade
1395 Facilitation
1396 Facsimile
1397 Fahrenheit
1398 Failure
1399 Fair
1400 Faithful
1401 **Faithfully (2)**
1402 **Fallacious (4)**
1403 Fallible
1404 False
1405 Falsification
1406 Faltering
1407 **Familiar (2)**
1408 Family

1409 Famous
1410 Farther
1411 **Fascinate (5)**
1412 Fascinating
1413 **Fascination (3)**
1414 Fascism
1415 Fascist
1416 **Fashion (3)**
1417 Fasten
1418 **Fastidious (2)**
1419 Fasting
1420 Fatal
1421 Fatalist
1422 Fatality
1423 Fatally
1424 Fattening
1425 Favourite
1426 Feasible
1427 Feature
1428 **February (2)**
1429 Feeling
1430 Feign
1431 Felicitate
1432 **Femininity (2)**
1433 Fermentation
1434 **Ferocious (2)**
1435 Fertile
1436 Feudal
1437 Fictitious
1438 **Field (2)**
1439 Fiend
1440 **Fierce (3)**
1441 **Fiery (3)**
1442 Fifteenth
1443 **Fifty (2)**
1444 Fighting
1445 Figure
1446 Filial
1447 Filling
1448 Finally
1449 Finance
1450 Financial
1451 Financially
1452 Finery
1453 Fiscal
1454 Fission
1455 Fitter
1456 Fixation
1457 Flamboyant
1458 Flame
1459 Flapped
1460 Flare

1461 **Flashy (2)**
1462 **Flavour (2)**
1463 Flawless
1464 **Flexible (3)**
1465 Flippant
1466 Flock
1467 Flood
1468 Floor
1469 **Flounder (2)**
1470 Flour
1471 Flourish
1472 Flower
1473 Floweriest
1474 Fluorescence
1475 Fluorescent
1476 Fluttering
1477 Focal
1478 Foliage
1479 Fomentation
1480 Foot
1481 Forbearance
1482 Forbidding
1483 **Forcibly (3)**
1484 Forebear
1485 Forecast
1486 **Foreign (7)**
1487 **Foreigner (2)**
1488 **Foreseeable (4)**
1489 Foretell
1490 **Forfeit (4)**
1491 Forgo
1492 Forlorn
1493 Fortieth
1494 Fortify
1495 Forts
1496 **Fortuitous (2)**
1497 **Fortunate (4)**
1498 Forty
1499 **Forward (3)**
1500 Fossil
1501 Fourteenth
1502 Fourth
1503 Foyer
1504 **Fraction (2)**
1505 Fractional
1506 Fragmentation
1507 Fragrance
1508 Frailty
1509 Frantic
1510 Fraud
1511 Fraudster
1512 **Freedom (3)**

1513 **Freeze (2)**
1514 Frenetically
1515 Frenzied
1516 Frequency
1517 **Frequent (2)**
1518 Freshen
1519 Fridge
1520 **Friend (3)**
1521 Frieze
1522 **Fright (2)**
1523 Frigid
1524 Frigidity
1525 Frisk
1526 Frolicked
1527 Front
1528 Frost
1529 Frosty
1530 Froth
1531 Frothiest
1532 **Frown (3)**
1533 Frozen
1534 Fruitful
1535 Frustrated
1536 **Fugitive (2)**
1537 Fulcrum
1538 **Fulfil (4)**
1539 **Fulfilment (2)**
1540 Fundamental
1541 Funereal
1542 **Furious (2)**
1543 Furl
1544 Furnace
1545 Further
1546 Fuse
1547 **Futile (2)**
1548 **Future (2)**
1549 Gadget
1550 **Gaiety (4)**
1551 Gait
1552 Galaxy
1553 Gallant
1554 **Gallery (4)**
1555 Galley
1556 Gallop
1557 Gangster
1558 Garbage
1559 Gargantuan
1560 Garment
1561 **Garrison (2)**
1562 Gauche
1563 **Gauge (3)**
1564 Gauze

1565 Gazelle
1566 **Gazette (2)**
1567 **General (2)**
1568 Generate
1569 **Generation (2)**
1570 **Generosity (3)**
1571 **Generous (2)**
1572 Genius
1573 Gentry
1574 **Genuine (3)**
1575 Geography
1576 **Geometry (2)**
1577 Gesticulate
1578 Giant
1579 Giddyap
1580 Giggle
1581 **Gimmick (2)**
1582 **Ginger (2)**
1583 **Girdle (2)**
1584 Glacier
1585 Glade
1586 **Glamorous (2)**
1587 **Glamour (2)**
1588 Gleam
1589 Gleaming
1590 Glitch
1591 Glitter
1592 **Global (2)**
1593 **Gloomy (2)**
1594 **Glorious (2)**
1595 **Glory (2)**
1596 **Gloss (2)**
1597 Glossary
1598 Glove
1599 **Glutton (2)**
1600 **Gnaw (2)**
1601 Goals
1602 **Gobble (2)**
1603 Goddess
1604 Goggles
1605 **Gorgeous (3)**
1606 **Gorilla (2)**
1607 Gossip
1608 Gothic
1609 Gourd
1610 Gourmandize
1611 **Gourmet (2)**
1612 Governance
1613 **Government (4)**
1614 **Governor (2)**
1615 Graceful
1616 **Gracious (3)**

1617 Gradation
1618 Gradual
1619 Graduate
1620 **Grammar (11)**
1621 Grammatic
1622 Grammatical
1623 **Grandeur (5)**
1624 Grandly
1625 **Graphic (2)**
1626 **Grateful (3)**
1627 Gratification
1628 Gratifying
1629 Gratuitous
1630 Gravity
1631 Greenery
1632 **Gregarious (3)**
1633 **Grief (2)**
1634 **Grievance (3)**
1635 **Grieve (3)**
1636 **Grievous (2)**
1637 Grind
1638 Gritty
1639 Groan
1640 Groggy
1641 **Groom (2)**
1642 Groove
1643 **Groovy (3)**
1644 Grotesque
1645 **Ground (2)**
1646 Group
1647 Growl
1648 Grumble
1649 **Guarantee (9)**
1650 Guaranty
1651 **Guard (4)**
1652 **Guardian (4)**
1653 Guerrilla
1654 **Guidance (4)**
1655 Guide
1656 **Guilty (4)**
1657 Guise
1658 Gullet
1659 Gullible
1660 Gunner
1661 Gutter
1662 Guzzle
1663 Gymnastic
1664 Gynaecology
1665 Gypsy
1666 Habitation
1667 Habitual
1668 Haematite

1669 Haemoglobin
1670 Haemorrhage
1671 Halloween
1672 **Hallucinate (2)**
1673 **Hallucination (3)**
1674 Handful
1675 Handicapped
1676 **Handkerchief (4)**
1677 Handling
1678 Handsome
1679 Haphazard
1680 **Happened (2)**
1681 Happiness
1682 **Harass (3)**
1683 **Harassment (4)**
1684 Harbour
1685 Harmony
1686 Harness
1687 **Hasten (3)**
1688 **Hasty (2)**
1689 Haughtily
1690 Haughtiness
1691 Haunted
1692 Haunting
1693 **Hazard (2)**
1694 Hazardous
1695 Hazy
1696 **Headache (2)**
1697 Headmaster
1698 **Headmistress (2)**
1699 Healthiest
1700 Heartbeat
1701 Heavenly
1702 Heavily
1703 **Hegemony (2)**
1704 **Height (2)**
1705 Heighten
1706 **Heinous (3)**
1707 **Heiress (2)**
1708 Heist
1709 **Helicopter (2)**
1710 **Hereditary (3)**
1711 **Heresy (3)**
1712 Heretic
1713 Heritage
1714 **Hesitancy (2)**
1715 **Hesitate (2)**
1716 **Heterogeneous (4)**

1717 Hiatus
1718 Hibernate
1719 Hideous
1720 Hierarchical
1721 **Hierarchy (4)**
1722 **Highlight (2)**
1723 **Hilarious (2)**
1724 **Hindrance (3)**
1725 Hippopotamus
1726 Hitch
1727 **Hoarse (2)**
1728 Hoist
1729 Hold
1730 Holiday
1731 Hollered
1732 Homage
1733 Homely
1734 Homeopathy
1735 **Homoeopath (2)**
1736 Homonym
1737 **Honorarium (3)**
1738 **Honorary (3)**
1739 Hopelessness
1740 **Horizontal (2)**
1741 Horoscope
1742 Horrible
1743 Horrid
1744 Horrific
1745 **Horror (3)**
1746 Horticulture
1747 Hospitable
1748 Hospital
1749 **Hospitality (3)**
1750 Hostage
1751 **Hostel (2)**
1752 **Hostile (3)**
1753 Hostility
1754 Hotel
1755 Hover
1756 Huddle
1757 Humane
1758 **Humanitarian (3)**
1759 Humanitarian-ism
1760 Humbly
1761 **Humiliate (2)**
1762 Humiliation
1763 Humongous
1764 **Humorous (5)**
1765 Humour
1766 Hurdle

1767 **Hygiene (4)**
1768 **Hygienic (2)**
1769 **Hypnotist (2)**
1770 Hypochondria
1771 **Hypocrisy (2)**
1772 Hypothesis
1773 Hysterically
1774 Ideal
1775 Idealize
1776 **Identically (2)**
1777 Identifiable
1778 **Identification (2)**
1779 **Ideology (2)**
1780 **Idiosyncrasy (3)**
1781 **Idiotic (2)**
1782 Idleness
1783 Idyllic
1784 Ignition
1785 Ignominious
1786 **Ignorance (5)**
1787 Ignorant
1788 **Illegal (3)**
1789 **Illegible (6)**
1790 **Illegitimate (6)**
1791 **Illicit (2)**
1792 **Illicitly (2)**
1793 **Illiterate (7)**
1794 Illogical
1795 **Illumination (3)**
1796 Illusion
1797 Illustrious
1798 Ill-will
1799 Imagery
1800 **Imaginary (2)**
1801 Imagination
1802 Imitate
1803 Imitation
1804 **Immaculate (4)**
1805 Immature
1806 **Immediacy (2)**
1807 **Immediate (7)**
1808 **Immediately (4)**
1809 **Immense (2)**
1810 Immersive
1811 Immigrant
1812 **Immigration (2)**
1813 Imminent
1814 Immunize
1815 **Impact (2)**
1816 Impartial
1817 **Impeach (2)**
1818 **Impeccable (3)**

1819 Impediment	1869 Indication	1919 Injury	1971 **Interfere (3)**
1820 Impending	1870 Indigenous	1920 Inkling	1972 Interference
1821 Impenetrable	1871 Indispensable	1921 **Innocence (3)**	1973 Intermediate
1822 Imperative	1872 **Indisposition (2)**	1922 **Innocent (2)**	1974 Interminable
1823 Imperial	1873 Indistinguishable	1923 **Innocuous (2)**	1975 Intermittent
1824 Impersonators		1924 Innovate	1976 Intermittently
1825 Impervious	1874 **Individual (4)**	1925 Innovation	1977 Internet
1826 Impetuous	1875 Individualise	1926 Innumerable	1978 Interpretation
1827 Implant	1876 Individuals	1927 **Inoculate (3)**	1979 Interrogation
1828 Implement	1877 Indolence	1928 Inoculation	1980 **Interrupt (4)**
1829 Implements	1878 Indomitable	1929 Inquietude	1981 **Interruption (2)**
1830 **Implicate (3)**	1879 **Inedible (2)**	1930 Inquiry	1982 Intervention
1831 Implication	1880 Ineffectual	1931 **Inquisitive (3)**	1983 Interview
1832 Implore	1881 Inefficient	1932 Inscrutable	1984 Intimation
1833 **Impoverish (2)**	1882 Inept	1933 Insects	1985 Intrepid
1834 Impractical	1883 Inequality	1934 Insecurities	1986 **Intrigue (3)**
1835 **Impression (3)**	1884 Inertia	1935 Insidious	1987 Intriguing
1836 Impressionable	1885 **Inevitable (4)**	1936 Insignificant	1988 Introvert
1837 **Imprudence (2)**	1886 Inexplicable	1937 Insipid	1989 Intruder
1838 Impudence	1887 Inextinguishable	1938 **Insistence (2)**	1990 Intubate
1839 Impunity	1888 Infallible	1939 Insolence	1991 Inundate
1840 Inability	1889 Infatuation	1940 **Insoluble (2)**	1992 Invalid
1841 **Inadvertent (2)**	1890 Infection	1941 Insolvency	1993 Invasion
1842 Inapplicable	1891 Infectious	1942 Inspector	1994 Invent
1843 Incandescent	1892 Inferior	1943 Inspire	1995 Inventor
1844 Incautious	1893 Infertile	1944 **Install (2)**	1996 **Investigate (2)**
1845 Incident	1894 Infest	1945 Installation	1997 Investigating
1846 **Incidentally (3)**	1895 Infidel	1946 **Instalment (3)**	1998 Invisible
1847 Incision	1896 Infiltrate	1947 Instance	1999 **Invitation (2)**
1848 Incite	1897 Infinitely	1948 Instant	2000 **Invite (3)**
1849 **Inclusion (2)**	1898 Infinitive	1949 **Instantaneous (2)**	2001 **Inviting (2)**
1850 Incommunicable	1899 **Inflammable (2)**	1950 Instead	2002 Invoke
1851 Inconclusive	1900 Inflammatory	1951 Institute	2003 Involve
1852 Incongruous	1901 **Influence (5)**	1952 **Institutional (2)**	2004 Inward
1853 **Inconvenience (2)**	1902 Informal	1953 Institutionalized	2005 Iodine
1854 Incorporate	1903 Information	1954 Instructor	2006 Ironing
1855 Incorrect	1904 Informational	1955 Instrumental	2007 Irradiate
1856 **Incorrigible (2)**	1905 Infrastructure	1956 Insufficient	2008 **Irrational (2)**
1857 **Incredible (4)**	1906 **Ingenious (2)**	1957 Insult	2009 Irrefutable
1858 **Incredulous (2)**	1907 Ingenuity	1958 Insure	2010 Irregular
1859 **Increment (2)**	1908 Ingenuous	1959 Integral	2011 **Irrelevant (5)**
1860 Incremental	1909 Ingratitude	1960 **Integrate (2)**	2012 Irreligious
1861 Incriminating	1910 **Ingredient (2)**	1961 Integrity	2013 **Irreparable (2)**
1862 Incubate	1911 **Ingredients (2)**	1962 **Intelligence (4)**	2014 **Irresistible (5)**
1863 Indecisiveness	1912 Inherent	1963 **Intelligent (4)**	2015 **Irrespective (2)**
1864 **Indefatigable (2)**	1913 Inherit	1964 Intelligibility	2016 Irresponsible
1865 Indefinite	1914 Inheritance	1965 Intend	2017 **Irreverent (2)**
1866 **Independence (3)**	1915 Inimical	1966 Intensify	2018 Irreversible
1867 **Independent (3)**	1916 Initially	1967 Intention	2019 **Irrevocable (3)**
1868 Indicate	1917 Initiate	1968 Intentional	2020 **Irrigation (2)**
	1918 Injection	1969 Interest	2021 **Irritable (3)**
		1970 **Interesting (2)**	2022 Irritant

2023 **Irritate (2)**
2024 **Irritating (2)**
2025 Irritation
2026 Itch
2027 Itinerant
2028 **Itinerary (3)**
2029 Jailor
2030 Janitor
2031 January
2032 Jarring
2033 Jasmine
2034 Javelin
2035 **Jealous (9)**
2036 **Jealousy (3)**
2037 Jeopardy
2038 **Jewellery (3)**
2039 Jingoistic
2040 **Jocular (2)**
2041 Jocularly
2042 Jostle
2043 **Journey (4)**
2044 Journeys
2045 Jovial
2046 Joyous
2047 **Jubilant (2)**
2048 Judge
2049 Judgement
2050 Judicial
2051 Judiciary
2052 **Judicious (2)**
2053 Jumble
2054 **Junior (2)**
2055 Jurist
2056 Justice
2057 Justifiable
2058 **Juvenile (2)**
2059 Juxtapose
2060 Juxtaposition
2061 Kangaroo
2062 Keen
2063 Keep
2064 Kernel
2065 Ketchup
2066 **Kettle (2)**
2067 Kicked
2068 Kindergarten
2069 Kindle
2070 Kinetic
2071 Kingdom
2072 Kitchen
2073 **Kleptomaniac (2)**

2074 Knead
2075 **Knight (3)**
2076 Knives
2077 Knowing
2078 **Knowledge (6)**
2079 **Knowledgeable (2)**
2080 Labelling
2081 **Laboratory (5)**
2082 Laborious
2083 Labour
2084 Labourer
2085 Labyrinth
2086 Lacquer
2087 Lamentable
2088 Landscape
2089 **Language (2)**
2090 Languish
2091 **Lantern (2)**
2092 Laparoscopy
2093 **Lapped (2)**
2094 Lapse
2095 **Lascivious (2)**
2096 Lateral
2097 Latitude
2098 Latter
2099 Laudable
2100 Laughable
2101 Laughing
2102 **Laughter (2)**
2103 Launderette
2104 Laurel
2105 Lawyer
2106 Layer
2107 Leader
2108 Lease
2109 Leave
2110 **Lecture (2)**
2111 Legacy
2112 Legend
2113 **Legible (5)**
2114 **Legionnaire (6)**
2115 Legislator
2116 Legitimacy
2117 Legitimate
2118 **Leisure (10)**
2119 Lenient
2120 Leopard
2121 Lesson
2122 **Lethargy (4)**
2123 Leverage
2124 Liable

2125 **Liaison (4)**
2126 Libertarian
2127 **Library (4)**
2128 **License (4)**
2129 Lieutenant
2130 Lifelessness
2131 Limitless
2132 **Liquefier (2)**
2133 Listener
2134 Literal
2135 **Literary (2)**
2136 Literate
2137 **Literature (2)**
2138 Litigants
2139 Liveable
2140 **Livelihood (2)**
2141 Living
2142 Lizard
2143 Loafer
2144 Loathsome
2145 Local
2146 **Location (2)**
2147 Loiter
2148 **Lonely (3)**
2149 Longitude
2150 Longitudinal
2151 **Loopholes (2)**
2152 Loot
2153 Lopsided
2154 Loquacity
2155 Lose
2156 Loud
2157 Loving
2158 Lubricant
2159 Lucid
2160 Lucrative
2161 Ludicrous
2162 Luggage
2163 Lugubrious
2164 **Luminescent (2)**
2165 Luminous
2166 Lunacy
2167 **Luscious (2)**
2168 **Lustrous (2)**
2169 Luxuriant
2170 Luxuries
2171 **Luxurious (4)**
2172 Luxury
2173 Lyre
2174 **Machiavellian (5)**
2175 Machine

2176 Machinery
2177 Magazine
2178 Magisterial
2179 **Magnanimous (4)**
2180 **Magnificent (10)**
2181 **Maintain (4)**
2182 **Maintenance (10)**
2183 Majestic
2184 **Malicious (2)**
2185 **Malignant (2)**
2186 Maligned
2187 **Malleable (3)**
2188 Malnourished
2189 Mammal
2190 **Manageable (2)**
2191 **Management (3)**
2192 Manager
2193 **Mandatory (2)**
2194 Mangled
2195 Manhandle
2196 **Manifestation (2)**
2197 **Manipulate (3)**
2198 **Manipulates (3)**
2199 **Manipulation (3)**
2200 Mannered
2201 **Manners (2)**
2202 **Manoeuvre (5)**
2203 Mansion
2204 Mantle
2205 Manual
2206 **Manufacture (2)**
2207 Manufacturing
2208 Marathon
2209 Marinate
2210 **Marriage (3)**
2211 Married
2212 Marshal
2213 Martinet
2214 **Marzipan (2)**
2215 Mascot
2216 Masculine
2217 **Massacre (2)**
2218 Massage
2219 Massive
2220 Master
2221 Match
2222 Matchless
2223 **Material (2)**

2224 Maternal
2225 Maternity
2226 **Mathematician (3)**
2227 **Mathematics (4)**
2228 Matriarchy
2229 Matrix
2230 **Matter (2)**
2231 Mattress
2232 Mature
2233 Maturity
2234 **Maximum (2)**
2235 **Meadow (4)**
2236 Meagre
2237 Meaningful
2238 **Measure (3)**
2239 Mechanic
2240 Mechanical
2241 **Mechanism (2)**
2242 Medal
2243 **Medallion (2)**
2244 **Meddle (3)**
2245 **Mediate (2)**
2246 **Medieval (5)**
2247 **Mediocre (5)**
2248 Meditation
2249 Meditative
2250 **Megalomaniac (2)**
2251 Melancholy
2252 **Mellifluence (2)**
2253 Melodious
2254 Melodrama
2255 **Melody (2)**
2256 Membrane
2257 Memento
2258 Memoir
2259 Memorial
2260 Menace
2261 **Mendacious (2)**
2262 Mention
2263 **Mentor (2)**
2264 **Mercenary (4)**
2265 Meritocratic
2266 Meritorious
2267 Messenger
2268 Metabolic
2269 Metal
2270 Metallic
2271 Metallurgy
2272 Metaphor
2273 Metaphysics

2274 **Meticulous (2)**
2275 Midday
2276 Midget
2277 Migraine
2278 **Migrant (2)**
2279 **Mileage (2)**
2280 **Milieu (4)**
2281 Militant
2282 Military
2283 **Millennia (4)**
2284 **Millennium (9)**
2285 Milliner
2286 Million
2287 **Millionaire (3)**
2288 Millipede
2289 **Mimic (2)**
2290 Mimicry
2291 **Miniature (3)**
2292 Minimum
2293 **Mining (7)**
2294 Minister
2295 Ministry
2296 Minus
2297 **Minuscule (5)**
2298 Minute
2299 **Miraculous (2)**
2300 Mirage
2301 Misalliance
2302 **Misanthrope (2)**
2303 **Miscellaneous (9)**
2304 **Mischief (2)**
2305 **Mischievous (4)**
2306 Miscreant
2307 Misdemeanour
2308 Miserable
2309 Misled
2310 Mismatch
2311 **Misogynist (3)**
2312 Misogynous
2313 Misrepresent
2314 **Missing (2)**
2315 Mission
2316 Missionary
2317 **Misspell (2)**
2318 Mistaken
2319 **Modern (2)**
2320 Modification
2321 **Moisture (2)**
2322 Molestation
2323 Momentary
2324 Momentous

2325 Moments
2326 **Monarch (3)**
2327 Monarchy
2328 Monologue
2329 Monopoly
2330 Monotheistic
2331 **Monotonous (3)**
2332 Monumental
2333 Morose
2334 Mortal
2335 **Mortgage (2)**
2336 Mortified
2337 Motivate
2338 Mountaineer
2339 **Moustache (3)**
2340 Mousy
2341 **Movement (3)**
2342 Muddle
2343 Muesli
2344 Multifarious
2345 Multinational
2346 **Multiple (2)**
2347 Mumble
2348 **Mundane (2)**
2349 Municipality
2350 Murderous
2351 Murmur
2352 **Murmuring (2)**
2353 Muscle
2354 **Musician (2)**
2355 Musk
2356 **Mutineers (2)**
2357 Mutter
2358 **Mutual (2)**
2359 **Mysterious (3)**
2360 Mystery
2361 Mythical
2362 **Narcissism (2)**
2363 **Narrate (2)**
2364 Narrative
2365 Narrator
2366 Narrowest
2367 Nascent
2368 Nation
2369 Nationalise
2370 **Nationalist (2)**
2371 Natural
2372 Naturalistic
2373 **Nature (3)**
2374 Naturopathy
2375 Naughty
2376 **Nausea (2)**

2377 Nautical
2378 **Navigation (4)**
2379 Nebulous
2380 **Necessary (10)**
2381 Necessitate
2382 **Necessity (2)**
2383 Need
2384 **Nefarious (3)**
2385 Negation
2386 Negative
2387 **Negativity (2)**
2388 **Neglect (2)**
2389 **Negligence (3)**
2390 **Negligible (3)**
2391 **Negotiate (3)**
2392 **Negotiation (2)**
2393 Neighbour
2394 Neighbouring
2395 **Neither (3)**
2396 Nemesis
2397 Neolithic
2398 Neoplasm
2399 Nephew
2400 Nerve
2401 **Nervous (3)**
2402 Netiquette
2403 Neurological
2404 Neuron
2405 Neurosurgeon
2406 Neutral
2407 Neutralise
2408 Neutrality
2409 Neutron
2410 Never
2411 Nibble
2412 **Niece (4)**
2413 Nightingale
2414 **Nineteen (2)**
2415 **Nineteenth (2)**
2416 Ninth
2417 **Ninety (2)**
2418 Nirvana
2419 Nobility
2420 **Nocturnal (2)**
2421 Nomenclature
2422 Nonchalant
2423 **Non-commis-sioned (3)**
2424 Noncommittal
2425 **Normally (2)**
2426 Nostalgic
2427 Nosy

2428 **Noticeable (5)**
2429 Noticing
2430 Notification
2431 Notional
2432 **Notoriety (2)**
2433 **Notorious (3)**
2434 Noun
2435 Nourish
2436 **Nourishment (3)**
2437 November
2438 Novice
2439 Nuclear
2440 **Nuisance (4)**
2441 Numerous
2442 Nuptial
2443 Nursery
2444 **Nurture (2)**
2445 **Obedient (2)**
2446 Obeisance
2447 Objectionable
2448 Objective
2449 Oblique
2450 Obliterate
2451 Obnoxious
2452 Obscene
2453 **Obscure (2)**
2454 Obsequious
2455 Observatory
2456 Observer
2457 **Obsessive (2)**
2458 Obsolescing
2459 Obsolete
2460 Obstacle
2461 **Obvious (2)**
2462 **Occasion (10)**
2463 **Occasionally (3)**
2464 Occupancy
2465 Occupant
2466 Occupation
2467 **Occur (2)**
2468 Occurred
2469 **Occurrence (6)**
2470 Occurring
2471 October
2472 Ocular
2473 Odour
2474 **Offence (2)**
2475 Offered
2476 Offering
2477 Officiate
2478 Offshoot
2479 Offspring

2480 **Olfactory (5)**
2481 Oligopoly
2482 Omelette
2483 **Ominous (3)**
2484 **Omission (7)**
2485 **Omitted (2)**
2486 **Onerous (2)**
2487 Opaque
2488 Opening
2489 Operator
2490 Opinion
2491 Opponents
2492 Opportunities
2493 **Opportunity (5)**
2494 **Opposition (2)**
2495 Oppressed
2496 Oppression
2497 Optimal
2498 Optimist
2499 Option
2500 Opulence
2501 **Opulent (2)**
2502 Orchard
2503 **Orchestra (4)**
2504 **Ordinance (2)**
2505 Ordinarily
2506 Organic
2507 **Orientation (2)**
2508 **Original (3)**
2509 Ornamental
2510 Ornate
2511 Orthopaedic
2512 **Oscillate (3)**
2513 Ostentation
2514 Ostracise
2515 Outcome
2516 **Outrageous (2)**
2517 Overall
2518 Overreact
2519 Override
2520 Packet
2521 Paediatrician
2522 Paint
2523 Paired
2524 Palace
2525 Palanquins
2526 Palatable
2527 Palladium
2528 Palliative
2529 Palmistry
2530 Paltry
2531 Pamphlet

2532 Pancreas
2533 Panic
2534 Panicked
2535 Pantomime
2536 **Parachute (2)**
2537 Parakeets
2538 **Parallel (8)**
2539 Parallelogram
2540 Paramilitary
2541 **Parapet (2)**
2542 Paraphernalia
2543 Parentage
2544 Parity
2545 **Parliament (2)**
2546 Parody
2547 **Parsimonious (2)**
2548 Partial
2549 Participant
2550 Participation
2551 Particle
2552 **Particular (3)**
2553 Particularly
2554 Partisanship
2555 Partly
2556 **Partner (6)**
2557 Passage
2558 **Passenger (3)**
2559 Passion
2560 Passive
2561 Password
2562 Paste
2563 **Pastor (2)**
2564 Pasture
2565 **Pathetic (2)**
2566 **Patience (2)**
2567 Patient
2568 Patrimony
2569 **Patriotism (2)**
2570 **Patronage (2)**
2571 Patronise
2572 Pauper
2573 Peace
2574 **Peaceful (2)**
2575 Pearl
2576 Peasant
2577 Peculiar
2578 Peddle
2579 Pedestal
2580 **Pedestrian (3)**
2581 Penalty
2582 Pendant

2583 **Penetrate (4)**
2584 Peninsula
2585 Penitent
2586 Pensive
2587 People
2588 Perceivable
2589 **Perceive (5)**
2590 Percentage
2591 Percolation
2592 Percussion
2593 Percussive
2594 Perennially
2595 Perfect
2596 Perfection
2597 Perfectionist
2598 Perfidy
2599 Perforate
2600 **Performance (3)**
2601 Peripheral
2602 Periphery
2603 Perishable
2604 Perjury
2605 Permafrost
2606 **Permanent (6)**
2607 Permissible
2608 Permission
2609 **Permit (2)**
2610 Permitting
2611 **Pernicious (3)**
2612 Perpetuate
2613 Perpetuity
2614 Persecution
2615 **Perseverance (6)**
2616 Perseverant
2617 **Persistence (2)**
2618 **Persistent (2)**
2619 Personal
2620 **Personnel (5)**
2621 Perspicuous
2622 Perspiration
2623 **Persuade (2)**
2624 **Persuasion (3)**
2625 Pertinacious
2626 Perturb
2627 **Peruse (2)**
2628 Pervade
2629 Perverted
2630 Pessimism
2631 Pessimist
2632 Pester
2633 Petite

2634 **Pharaoh (2)**
2635 **Pharmaceutical (2)**
2636 Pharmacy
2637 **Phenomenon (2)**
2638 Philanthropist
2639 **Philosophy (2)**
2640 Phlegmatic
2641 Photograph
2642 Physician
2643 Physics
2644 Piano
2645 Picking
2646 Pickle
2647 **Picnic (2)**
2648 Picnicked
2649 **Picture (2)**
2650 Pictures
2651 Picturesque
2652 Pie
2653 **Piece (3)**
2654 **Pierce (4)**
2655 Piercing
2656 **Piety (2)**
2657 **Pigeon (2)**
2658 Pilgrim
2659 Pilgrimage
2660 Pillion
2661 Pioneer
2662 Pious
2663 Pitch
2664 Piteous
2665 Pitiful
2666 Plagiarist
2667 Plagiarize
2668 **Plaintiff (2)**
2669 Planning
2670 Plantain
2671 **Plaque (2)**
2672 **Plateau (3)**
2673 Platinum
2674 Platter
2675 Plausible
2676 Player
2677 **Playful (2)**
2678 **Playwright (2)**
2679 Plead
2680 **Pleasant (3)**
2681 Please
2682 Plebeian
2683 Pledge

2684 Plenary
2685 Plenty
2686 Plight
2687 Plough
2688 Plump
2689 Plunge
2690 Plural
2691 Pneumatic
2692 **Pneumonia (3)**
2693 **Poetry (2)**
2694 Poignant
2695 Policeman
2696 **Politician (2)**
2697 Pollen
2698 Pollutant
2699 Pollution
2700 Pomegranate
2701 **Pompous (3)**
2702 Pontifical
2703 Popular
2704 Popularly
2705 Portfolio
2706 Portion
2707 Portray
2708 **Portuguese (2)**
2709 **Possess (5)**
2710 Possesses
2711 **Possession (7)**
2712 Possessions
2713 **Possibility (3)**
2714 Possible
2715 Posthumous
2716 Posthumously
2717 Postulate
2718 **Posture (2)**
2719 Potassium
2720 Potatoes
2721 **Potential (2)**
2722 **Practical (2)**
2723 Practically
2724 **Practice (4)**
2725 Pragmatic
2726 Prankster
2727 **Preamble (2)**
2728 Precariously
2729 **Precaution (2)**
2730 Precede
2731 **Precedent (2)**
2732 Preceding
2733 **Precious (8)**
2734 Precipitate
2735 Precipitation

2736 **Precise (2)**
2737 **Precision (3)**
2738 Precursor
2739 Predict
2740 Predilection
2741 **Predominant (2)**
2742 Preface
2743 **Prefer (3)**
2744 **Preferable (3)**
2745 **Preference (3)**
2746 Preferential
2747 Preferred
2748 Prehistoric
2749 **Premier (3)**
2750 **Premium (2)**
2751 Preparation
2752 **Prepare (2)**
2753 Preposterous
2754 Prerequisite
2755 Prescience
2756 **Presence (2)**
2757 **Present (2)**
2758 Presentable
2759 Presentation
2760 Presenter
2761 **Preserve (2)**
2762 Presidential
2763 **Pressure (3)**
2764 Pressurised
2765 Prestige
2766 Prestigious
2767 **Presume (2)**
2768 **Presumptuous (2)**
2769 Pretence
2770 **Pretensions (4)**
2771 **Prevalent (5)**
2772 Prevaricate
2773 Prevent
2774 Preview
2775 Previous
2776 Prey
2777 Pried
2778 Priestly
2779 Primarily
2780 **Primary (2)**
2781 Primate
2782 Primitive
2783 Primitivism
2784 Princely
2785 Principal
2786 Principally

2787 Principle
2788 Printed
2789 **Priority (2)**
2790 Prisoner
2791 Private
2792 **Privilege (12)**
2793 Proactivity
2794 **Probable (2)**
2795 Probably
2796 Problem
2797 Problematic
2798 **Procedure (4)**
2799 **Proceed (2)**
2800 Proceedings
2801 Processing
2802 **Procession (2)**
2803 Proclaim
2804 **Procrastination (2)**
2805 **Procure (2)**
2806 Procurement
2807 Prodigy
2808 Production
2809 **Productive (2)**
2810 **Profession (3)**
2811 **Professional (4)**
2812 **Professor (5)**
2813 Proficient
2814 **Profuse (2)**
2815 **Progress (3)**
2816 **Progression (2)**
2817 Proliferate
2818 **Prolific (2)**
2819 Prologue
2820 Prolong
2821 Prominent
2822 Promiscuous
2823 Promise
2824 Promote
2825 Promotion
2826 Promulgate
2827 Pronounce
2828 **Pronunciation (3)**
2829 Propaganda
2830 Propel
2831 **Propeller (2)**
2832 **Propensity (2)**
2833 Property
2834 Prophesy
2835 Prophet
2836 Propitiate

2837 Proportion
2838 Proportionate
2839 **Propose (2)**
2840 Prosecutor
2841 **Prospect (2)**
2842 **Prosper (2)**
2843 Prosperity
2844 **Prosperous (2)**
2845 Protag
2846 Protect
2847 Protection
2848 **Protein (3)**
2849 Protest
2850 Protestors
2851 Protocol
2852 Protrude
2853 Protuberance
2854 Proverbial
2855 **Providence (2)**
2856 **Provision (4)**
2857 **Provoke (2)**
2858 Proximate
2859 Prudent
2860 Prudently
2861 **Pseudonym (4)**
2862 Pseudonymous
2863 Psychiatrist
2864 Psychiatry
2865 Psychological
2866 Psychologist
2867 **Psychology (3)**
2868 Psychometric
2869 Publication
2870 **Puddle (2)**
2871 **Punctuation (2)**
2872 **Pungent (3)**
2873 Punishment
2874 Pupil
2875 Puppeteer
2876 Puppies
2877 Purify
2878 **Puritanical (2)**
2879 Purity
2880 Purport
2881 Purposefully
2882 **Pursue (3)**
2883 **Pursuit (4)**
2884 Purvey
2885 Quadrangle
2886 **Quadrant (2)**
2887 Quadruple
2888 Qualification

2889 Quandary
2890 Quantify
2891 Quantitative
2892 Quantity
2893 **Quarantine (3)**
2894 **Quarrel (5)**
2895 **Quarrelled (3)**
2896 Quarrelsome
2897 Quasi
2898 Quaver
2899 **Queer (2)**
2900 Question
2901 Questionable
2902 **Questionnaire (3)**
2903 **Queue (3)**
2904 Quick
2905 **Quiet (2)**
2906 **Quieten (3)**
2907 Quietly
2908 Quinine
2909 Quintessence
2910 Quizzes
2911 Quotation
2912 Quote
2913 Quotient
2914 Radiant
2915 Radiator
2916 Radicalism
2917 Radius
2918 Raged
2919 Rambunctious
2920 Rampant
2921 Random
2922 Rankle
2923 Rapport
2924 Rascal
2925 Rational
2926 Rationale
2927 Rationing
2928 Raucous
2929 **Ravishing (2)**
2930 **Readable (2)**
2931 Realised
2932 **Reality (2)**
2933 **Realm (5)**
2934 Rebel
2935 **Rebellious (2)**
2936 Rebuttal
2937 Recalcitrant
2938 Recapitulate
2939 **Recede (7)**

2940 **Receipt (9)**
2941 **Receive (6)**
2942 **Recent (2)**
2943 **Receptacle (2)**
2944 Reception
2945 **Recession (3)**
2946 **Recipient (2)**
2947 Recluse
2948 Recognisable
2949 Recognition
2950 **Recommend (6)**
2951 Recommenda-
tion
2952 Reconciliation
2953 Recondite
2954 **Reconnaissance (2)**
2955 Recruit
2956 Recruitment
2957 Rectify
2958 Recuperate
2959 **Recurrent (2)**
2960 **Refer (3)**
2961 **Referee (4)**
2962 **Reference (5)**
2963 **Referred (4)**
2964 Reflection
2965 **Refrigerator (4)**
2966 **Refurbish (2)**
2967 Refusal
2968 Refute
2969 Regrettable
2970 **Regular (2)**
2971 **Regularization (2)**
2972 **Regulate (4)**
2973 **Rehabilitation (3)**
2974 **Rehearsal (3)**
2975 **Reign (2)**
2976 **Reimbursement (2)**
2977 Reinforcement
2978 Reinstate
2979 Reiterate
2980 **Rejuvenation (3)**
2981 **Release (2)**
2982 Relegate
2983 Relentless
2984 **Relevant (3)**
2985 **Reliable (2)**

2986 **Reliance (2)**
2987 **Reliant (2)**
2988 **Relieve (3)**
2989 Religiosity
2990 **Religious (3)**
2991 **Relish (2)**
2992 Reluctant
2993 **Remarkable (3)**
2994 **Remember (2)**
2995 **Remembrance (3)**
2996 Reminder
2997 **Reminiscence (3)**
2998 **Reminiscent (2)**
2999 **Remission (2)**
3000 **Remittance (3)**
3001 Remitted
3002 **Remnant (3)**
3003 Remonstrate
3004 **Remuneration (4)**
3005 **Remunerative (2)**
3006 **Renaissance (2)**
3007 Render
3008 Rendezvous
3009 Repel
3010 Repent
3011 Repentance
3012 Repentant
3013 **Repercussion (5)**
3014 Repertoire
3015 **Repetition (3)**
3016 Repetitive
3017 Replaceable
3018 Replaced
3019 Replacement
3020 Reply
3021 Repository
3022 **Representation (2)**
3023 **Representative (2)**
3024 Reprimanded
3025 Reproduce
3026 Repugnance
3027 Repulsive
3028 Reputed
3029 **Require (2)**
3030 Requirement

3031 Requisite
3032 Research
3033 **Resemblance (2)**
3034 **Resemble (2)**
3035 Resentment
3036 **Reservoir (2)**
3037 Resettlement
3038 Reside
3039 Residual
3040 Residue
3041 Resist
3042 **Resistance (4)**
3043 Resistivity
3044 Resolute
3045 **Resonate (2)**
3046 Resourceful
3047 Respectable
3048 Respectful
3049 Resplendence
3050 **Resplendent (9)**
3051 Response
3052 Responsibilities
3053 Responsibility
3054 **Restaurant (6)**
3055 Restore
3056 Resultant
3057 Resurrect
3058 Retaliate
3059 Retort
3060 **Retrieve (3)**
3061 **Retrospect (2)**
3062 Return
3063 Reveal
3064 Revellers
3065 Revenge
3066 **Revenue (2)**
3067 Reverberate
3068 Reverberation
3069 **Revere (2)**
3070 Reverence
3071 Reverent
3072 Reversal
3073 **Reverse (2)**
3074 Review
3075 Revise
3076 Revision
3077 Revolutionary
3078 Revolutionize
3079 Rhapsodic
3080 **Rhapsody (2)**
3081 Rhinoceros

3082 **Rhyme (2)**
3083 **Rhythm (3)**
3084 Ride
3085 Ridge
3086 **Ridiculous (3)**
3087 Rifle
3088 Right
3089 **Righteous (3)**
3090 **Rivalry (3)**
3091 **Roast (2)**
3092 Roaster
3093 **Robbery (2)**
3094 Robust
3095 Rockery
3096 Rocket
3097 **Rogue (3)**
3098 Rotate
3099 Rotten
3100 Round
3101 Routine
3102 **Rudimentary (2)**
3103 **Rumble (2)**
3104 Ruminate
3105 Running
3106 Rupee
3107 Rusk
3108 Rustle
3109 Ruthless
3110 Sabbatical
3111 Sabotage
3112 Saccharine
3113 Sacrament
3114 Sacred
3115 **Sacrifice (4)**
3116 **Sacrilege (3)**
3117 Sacrilegious
3118 Sacrosanct
3119 Sadly
3120 Salary
3121 Saleable
3122 Salient
3123 Sanctimonious
3124 **Sanctity (2)**
3125 **Sanctuaries (7)**
3126 Sandwich
3127 **Sanguine (2)**
3128 Sarcasm
3129 Sartorial
3130 **Satellite (2)**
3131 Satiate
3132 Satire

3133 Savage
3134 Savoury
3135 Scale
3136 Scanty
3137 **Scarce (2)**
3138 Scarcity
3139 Scavenge
3140 Scavenger
3141 **Scenery (4)**
3142 **Scenic (2)**
3143 **Schedule (6)**
3144 **Scheme (3)**
3145 Schizophrenia
3146 Scholar
3147 Science
3148 Scientific
3149 **Scientist (3)**
3150 Scimitars
3151 Scintillate
3152 **Scintillating (3)**
3153 **Scintillators (2)**
3154 **Scissors (2)**
3155 Scoreboard
3156 Scorn
3157 Scorpion
3158 Scramble
3159 **Scripture (2)**
3160 Scrupulous
3161 **Scrutinize (2)**
3162 Scrutiny
3163 Seasonal
3164 Secluded
3165 **Secondary (2)**
3166 **Secrecy (5)**
3167 Secretariat
3168 **Secretary (5)**
3169 Secrete
3170 Secretion
3171 Secure
3172 Securities
3173 Security
3174 Sediment
3175 Seeing
3176 Segments
3177 Segregate
3178 Segregation
3179 **Seize (3)**
3180 Seizing
3181 Seldom
3182 **Selection (2)**
3183 **Semblance (2)**
3184 Sensation

3185 Sense
3186 Sensible
3187 **Sentiment (3)**
3188 Sentimentalist
3189 Sentimentally
3190 Sentry
3191 Separable
3192 **Separate (13)**
3193 Separately
3194 **Separation (3)**
3195 Sequence
3196 **Serendipity (2)**
3197 Serene
3198 **Serenity (2)**
3199 **Sergeant (5)**
3200 Serial
3201 **Serious (2)**
3202 Sermonise
3203 **Serpent (2)**
3204 **Serrated (2)**
3205 Serum
3206 **Servant (2)**
3207 **Service (3)**
3208 **Session (2)**
3209 Settle
3210 Seventeenth
3211 Several
3212 Severity
3213 Shade
3214 Shadow
3215 Shameful
3216 Sheath
3217 Sheet
3218 **Shield (2)**
3219 **Shining (2)**
3220 Shoddy
3221 Shopaholic
3222 Shortfall
3223 Showpiece
3224 Shrewd
3225 Shrines
3226 Shrinkage
3227 Siege
3228 Sieve
3229 Signage
3230 Significance
3231 Silhouette
3232 Simulation
3233 **Simultaneous (3)**
3234 **Sincere (2)**
3235 Sincerely

3236 Sincerity	3288 **Stagnation (2)**	3340 **Substitution (2)**	3387 **Surveillance (2)**
3237 Sinhalese	3289 Stain	3341 **Subtle (2)**	3388 Survey
3238 Sinister	3290 Stampede	3342 **Subway (2)**	3389 Survival
3239 Sizable	3291 Starvation	3343 **Succeed (2)**	3390 Susceptible
3240 Size	3292 **Stationary (4)**	3344 **Success (3)**	3391 Suspense
3241 Skilful	3293 Statistician	3345 **Successful (4)**	3392 Suspension
3242 Slander	3294 Statutory	3346 **Succession (2)**	3393 **Suspicion (2)**
3243 Slaughter	3295 Stereotype	3347 Successive	3394 **Suspicious (3)**
3244 Sledge	3296 Stigmatic	3348 Succinct	3395 Sustain
3245 Sleek	3297 Stimulate	3349 Succulent	3396 Swallow
3246 Slip	3298 Stingy	3350 **Succumb (4)**	3397 **Sweater (2)**
3247 Sloth	3299 Stipulate	3351 Suddenly	3398 Swimming
3248 Smallish	3300 Stocked	3352 **Suffering (2)**	3399 Swindle
3249 Smelled	3301 Stoically	3353 **Sufficient (2)**	3400 **Swivelling (2)**
3250 Smelly	3302 Stooped	3354 Suggested	3401 Sycophant
3251 Snatch	3303 Storage	3355 **Suggestion (2)**	3402 Syllabi
3252 Socialite	3304 Straightest	3356 Sultry	3403 Symbolical
3253 Society	3305 Straightway	3357 **Summary (4)**	3404 Symmetry
3254 Solicitation	3306 Strain	3358 Summon	3405 Sympathize
3255 **Solitary (2)**	3307 Strangled	3359 **Sumptuous (3)**	3406 Sympathy
3256 **Soluble (2)**	3308 **Stratagem (2)**	3360 Sundry	3407 Symphony
3257 **Solution (3)**	3309 **Strategy (5)**	3361 **Supercilious (2)**	3408 Symptomatically
3258 **Solvent (2)**	3310 Streamlining	3362 Superficial	3409 Symptoms
3259 Somnambulist	3311 **Strength (2)**	3363 **Superfluous (2)**	3410 Synchronize
3260 Souvenir	3312 Strengthen	3364 **Superintendent (2)**	3411 Syndicate
3261 Sovereign	3313 Stressed		3412 Syndrome
3262 **Sovereignty (2)**	3314 Stretch	3365 **Superior (3)**	3413 Synergism
3263 **Spacious (4)**	3315 Stridency	3366 **Superiority (2)**	3414 Synthetic
3264 Sparkling	3316 Stringent	3367 Supernumerary	3415 Syringe
3265 Sparrow	3317 Strings	3368 **Supersede (4)**	3416 System
3266 **Special (2)**	3318 Stripe	3369 **Superstition (2)**	3417 Systematic
3267 **Specialist (2)**	3319 Strived	3370 **Superstitious (5)**	3418 **Systematically (2)**
3268 Speciality	3320 **Structural (2)**		
3269 Specific	3321 Structure	3371 **Supplement (2)**	3419 Tackle
3270 Specified	3322 **Struggle (2)**	3372 **Supplementary (3)**	3420 Tactful
3271 Specifying	3323 Stubble		3421 Tactfully
3272 Spectacles	3324 **Studious (2)**	3373 Support	3422 Tactics
3273 Spectacular	3325 Study	3374 Supporters	3423 Tactile
3274 Speculative	3326 Stupefaction	3375 Supporting	3424 Tailor
3275 **Speech (2)**	3327 Stupefy	3376 Suppose	3425 Talent
3276 Spelling	3328 Stylistics	3377 **Suppress (2)**	3426 Tamarind
3277 Spoilage	3329 **Submission (2)**	3378 **Suppression (2)**	3427 Tamper
3278 Sponsor	3330 **Submitted (2)**	3379 Suppressor	3428 **Tangible (2)**
3279 Spontaneity	3331 Subscribe	3380 **Supreme (2)**	3429 **Tapestry (2)**
3280 Spontaneous	3332 Subsequence	3381 **Surely (2)**	3430 Tariff
3281 Spoonful	3333 Subsequent	3382 Surprise	3431 Tattle
3282 **Spurious (2)**	3334 Subsequently	3383 **Surrender (2)**	3432 **Teacher (2)**
3283 Square	3335 Subservient	3384 **Surreptitious (2)**	3433 Technician
3284 Squawked	3336 Subsistence		3434 Technique
3285 Squirrel	3337 Substantial	3385 Surround	3435 Technological
3286 Staggered	3338 Substantially	3386 **Surroundings (3)**	3436 **Technology (2)**
3287 Stagnant	3339 **Substantive (5)**		3437 Tedious

3438 **Telepathy (3)**
3439 **Television (2)**
3440 Temperament
3441 **Temperate (2)**
3442 **Temperature (6)**
3443 **Tempest (2)**
3444 Temple
3445 **Temporary (4)**
3446 **Temptation (2)**
3447 **Tendency (4)**
3448 Tender
3449 Tenor
3450 Tentative
3451 Tenth
3452 Tenure
3453 Terabyte
3454 Terminal
3455 Terminology
3456 Termite
3457 Terrestrial
3458 **Terrible (4)**
3459 **Territory (4)**
3460 **Terrorism (2)**
3461 Terrorist
3462 Texture
3463 Thanksgiving
3464 Theoretical
3465 Theorise
3466 **Therapeutic (2)**
3467 **Thermometer (2)**
3468 **Thesaurus (2)**
3469 Thespian
3470 Thorough
3471 **Thoroughfare (2)**
3472 Thoroughly
3473 Thrashing
3474 Threatened
3475 **Threshold (4)**
3476 Thriller
3477 Thrilling
3478 Thrive
3479 Throttle
3480 Throttled
3481 Throughout
3482 Thrust
3483 Thunderous
3484 Thwart
3485 Thyroid
3486 Timely
3487 **Tinker (2)**

3488 Titillate
3489 Tobacco
3490 Toffee
3491 Together
3492 **Tolerance (3)**
3493 **Tolerant (2)**
3494 **Tolerate (2)**
3495 Tomatoes
3496 **Tomorrow (4)**
3497 **Tongue (4)**
3498 Tonsure
3499 Torches
3500 Tornado
3501 Torrent
3502 Tourist
3503 Traceable
3504 Tractor
3505 **Tradition (2)**
3506 Traditional
3507 **Traffic (3)**
3508 Trafficking
3509 Traipse
3510 **Tranquillity (4)**
3511 Tranquillize
3512 Transcend
3513 Transferred
3514 **Transition (3)**
3515 Translate
3516 Translucent
3517 Transmission
3518 **Transmit (2)**
3519 Transparent
3520 Transpire
3521 **Traumatic (2)**
3522 Traverse
3523 **Treacherous (2)**
3524 Treachery
3525 Treasure
3526 Treasury
3527 **Tremendous (3)**
3528 Trespasser
3529 Triangulation
3530 Tribe
3531 Trickery
3532 Trickster
3533 Triple
3534 **Triumph (2)**
3535 **Trivial (3)**
3536 **Tropical (6)**
3537 Trouble
3538 Trousers
3539 Trousseau

3540 Truism
3541 **Truly (4)**
3542 Trusted
3543 Trustworthy
3544 Truthful
3545 Tryst
3546 **Tuition (5)**
3547 Tumble
3548 **Tumultuous (2)**
3549 Tunnel
3550 Turbulence
3551 Turmeric
3552 Turmoil
3553 Turtle
3554 **Twelfth (4)**
3555 Twinkle
3556 Twisted
3557 Typical
3558 Tyrannical
3559 **Tyranny (6)**
3560 Tyrant
3561 Ubiquitous
3562 Ulterior
3563 Ultimate
3564 Umbilical
3565 Umbrella
3566 **Unanimous (2)**
3567 Unassailable
3568 Unassuming
3569 Unattractiveness
3570 Uncle
3571 Undergarment
3572 Understand
3573 Undoubtedly
3574 Undulate
3575 Unduly
3576 Unfathomable
3577 Unflappable
3578 Unforgettable
3579 **Unfortunately (2)**
3580 **Unique (3)**
3581 Unison
3582 **University (2)**
3583 Unlawful
3584 Unmanageable
3585 Unmindful
3586 **Unnecessary (2)**
3587 Unnerve
3588 Unnerving
3589 Unorganised
3590 Unparalleled

3591 Unprecedented
3592 **Unpretentious (3)**
3593 Unravel
3594 **Unruffled (2)**
3595 Unruly
3596 Unsurpassable
3597 Unsustainable
3598 Untie
3599 Until
3600 Upcoming
3601 Upheaval
3602 **Uproar (2)**
3603 Uprooted
3604 Urchins
3605 Usable
3606 Usual
3607 Usually
3608 Usurp
3609 Utterance
3610 **Vaccination (3)**
3611 Vaccine
3612 Vacillation
3613 **Vacuum (2)**
3614 Vacuum-Cleaner
3615 Vagabond
3616 **Vague (2)**
3617 **Valediction (4)**
3618 Valiant
3619 Valour
3620 **Valuable (3)**
3621 Value
3622 Variability
3623 Variety
3624 Vassal
3625 Vastness
3626 Vegetable
3627 **Vegetarian (3)**
3628 Vegetation
3629 Vehemence
3630 **Vehicle (3)**
3631 Vein
3632 Velocity
3633 Vendetta
3634 Venerable
3635 **Vengeance (2)**
3636 Venison
3637 Ventilation
3638 Verbal
3639 Verification
3640 **Verisimilitude (2)**

3641 Veritable	3693 Weary	3745 Yoghurt
3642 Vermilion	3694 **Weather (4)**	3746 Zealot
3643 Versatile	3695 Website	3747 **Zealous (2)**
3644 Versus	3696 **Wednesday (3)**	3748 Zenith
3645 Vessel	3697 **Weird (4)**	3749 Zoologist
3646 **Veterinary (3)**	3698 **Welfare (3)**	
3647 Vial	3699 Wench	
3648 **Vicarious (2)**	3700 Wherefore	*Total **3749** Spelling asked **6322** times.*
3649 Vicinity	3701 Whether	
3650 **Vicious (9)**	3702 Whimper	
3651 Vicissitude	3703 **Whimsical (2)**	
3652 Victims	3704 Whine	
3653 **Victorious (4)**	3705 Whip	
3654 Victory	3706 **Whisper (2)**	
3655 Video	3707 Whistle	
3656 Vigorously	3708 Whiten	
3657 **Village (3)**	3709 Whither	
3658 **Villain (3)**	3710 Wholesome	
3659 Violation	3711 Wholly	
3660 **Violence (4)**	3712 Whorl	
3661 Violent	3713 Wiggle	
3662 **Violin (3)**	3714 Wildernesses	
3663 Virtual	3715 Wilful	
3664 Virtually	3716 Willingness	
3665 **Virtuous (5)**	3717 Winch	
3666 Viscous	3718 Winning	
3667 Vise	3719 **Wisdom (2)**	
3668 Visibility	3720 Wish	
3669 Visible	3721 Wit	
3670 Visionary	3722 Witch	
3671 Visualise	3723 Withdrawal	
3672 **Vivacious (2)**	3724 Wither	
3673 Vividly	3725 Withhold	
3674 Vocal	3726 **Witness (3)**	
3675 Vociferous	3727 Woollen	
3676 **Vogue (2)**	3728 Worried	
3677 Volcano	3729 Worshipped	
3678 **Voluntary (6)**	3730 Worthwhile	
3679 Volunteer	3731 Wrap Up	
3680 Voracious	3732 Wreak	
3681 Voracity	3733 Wreathe	
3682 Voyage	3734 Wriggle	
3683 Waiter	3735 **Wrinkle (2)**	
3684 Waiting	3736 **Writing (2)**	
3685 Wakeful	3737 Written	
3686 Wantonly	3738 Xenophobia	
3687 Warden	3739 Xylophone	
3688 Wariness	3740 Yacht	
3689 Warrant	3741 Yearn	
3690 **Warrior (2)**	3742 Yesterday	
3691 Washing	3743 Yeti	
3692 Wealth	3744 **Yield (2)**	

SN	Correct Spelling (#R)
1	Accommodate (16)
2	Committee (14)
3	Separate (13)
4	Beginning (12)
5	Deceive (12)
6	Privilege (12)
7	Believe (11)
8	Business (11)
9	Conscientious (11)
10	Grammar (11)
11	Definitely (10)
12	Leisure (10)
13	Magnificent (10)
14	Maintenance (10)
15	Necessary (10)
16	Occasion (10)
17	Acclaim (9)
18	Commit (9)
19	Connoisseur (9)
20	Conscious (9)
21	Guarantee (9)
22	Jealous (9)
23	Millennium (9)
24	Miscellaneous (9)
25	Receipt (9)
26	Resplendent (9)
27	Vicious (9)
28	Acoustic (8)
29	Address (8)
30	Aggravate (8)
31	Apparently (8)
32	Bouquet (8)
33	Bureaucracy (8)
34	Dilemma (8)
35	Existence (8)
36	Parallel (8)
37	Precious (8)
38	Combination (7)
39	Commitment (7)
40	Countenance (7)
41	Definition (7)
42	Delicious (7)
43	Discipline (7)
44	Embarrass (7)
45	Embarrassment (7)
46	Experiment (7)
47	Foreign (7)
48	Illiterate (7)
49	Immediate (7)
50	Mining (7)
51	Omission (7)
52	Possession (7)
53	Recede (7)
54	Sanctuaries (7)
55	Accommodation (6)
56	Achieve (6)
57	Achievement (6)
58	Acquire (6)
59	Aggression (6)
60	Approach (6)
61	Argument (6)
62	Attention (6)
63	Bureaucrat (6)
64	Conceive (6)
65	Conscience (6)
66	Efficient (6)
67	Elementary (6)
68	Eloquent (6)
69	Environment (6)
70	Eradication (6)
71	Exhaust (6)
72	Explanation (6)
73	Extract (6)
74	Illegible (6)
75	Illegitimate (6)
76	Knowledge (6)
77	Legionnaire (6)
78	Occurrence (6)
79	Partner (6)
80	Permanent (6)
81	Perseverance (6)
82	Receive (6)
83	Recommend (6)
84	Restaurant (6)
85	Schedule (6)
86	Temperature (6)
87	Tropical (6)
88	Tyranny (6)
89	Voluntary (6)
90	Absence (5)
91	Accumulate (5)
92	Accustomed (5)
93	Acknowledge (5)
94	Acquaintance (5)
95	Adventure (5)
96	Advertisement (5)
97	Aesthetic (5)
98	Amateur (5)
99	Appreciate (5)
100	Aquarium (5)
101	Audience (5)
102	Beggar (5)
103	Benefit (5)
104	Benign (5)
105	Calendar (5)
106	Ceremony (5)
107	Changeable (5)
108	Colleague (5)
109	Commemorate (5)
110	Compassionate (5)
111	Conquer (5)
112	Consensus (5)
113	Contemporary (5)
114	Convenience (5)
115	Courteous (5)
116	Deficient (5)
117	Desperate (5)
118	Dictionary (5)
119	Difference (5)
120	Eminent (5)
121	Enmity (5)
122	Enthusiasm (5)
123	Entrepreneur (5)
124	Erroneous (5)
125	Esteem (5)
126	Executive (5)
127	Fascinate (5)
128	Grandeur (5)
129	Humorous (5)
130	Ignorance (5)
131	Influence (5)
132	Irrelevant (5)
133	Irresistible (5)
134	Laboratory (5)
135	Legible (5)
136	Machiavellian (5)
137	Manoeuvre (5)
138	Medieval (5)
139	Mediocre (5)
140	Minuscule (5)
141	Noticeable (5)
142	Olfactory (5)
143	Opportunity (5)
144	Perceive (5)
145	Personnel (5)
146	Possess (5)
147	Prevalent (5)
148	Professor (5)
149	Quarrel (5)
150	Realm (5)
151	Reference (5)
152	Repercussion (5)
153	Secrecy (5)
154	Secretary (5)
155	Sergeant (5)
156	Strategy (5)
157	Substantive (5)
158	Superstitious (5)
159	Tuition (5)
160	Virtuous (5)
161	Abandon (4)
162	Accomplice (4)
163	Actually (4)
164	Adamant (4)
165	Admonish (4)
166	Advertise (4)
167	Advisable (4)
168	Affliction (4)
169	Aggressive (4)
170	Agreement (4)
171	Already (4)
172	Altitude (4)
173	Ambition (4)
174	Anarchy (4)
175	Anonymous (4)
176	Appeal (4)
177	Appearance (4)
178	Appropriate (4)
179	Architecture (4)
180	Arrangement (4)
181	Assassination (4)
182	Attendance (4)
183	Auxiliary (4)
184	Belligerent (4)
185	Beneficial (4)
186	Beneficiary (4)
187	Benevolent (4)
188	Besiege (4)
189	Boundary (4)
190	Cactus (4)
191	Camouflage (4)
192	Campaigns (4)
193	Cautious (4)
194	Celebration (4)
195	Cemetery (4)
196	Chocolate (4)
197	Collaborate (4)
198	Commentary (4)
199	Conceit (4)
200	Conjecture (4)

*Top **200** Spelling asked **1206** times.*

SSC CGL Tier 1 2022			
SN	**Correct Spelling**		
1	Erroneous	49	Rhythm	99	Sergeant
2	Finery	50	Symbolical	100	Compact
3	Heist	51	Justice	101	Compel
4	Cringe	52	Judge	102	Currently
5	Defer	53	Attorney	103	Savage
6	Piercing	54	Lawyer	104	Assiduous
7	Sleek	55	Hysterically	105	Disapproval
8	Pie	56	Frisk	106	Devastation
9	Itch	57	Reply	107	Conjoined
10	Disenfranchised	58	Rusk	108	Equilibrium
11	Slaughter	59	Foliage	109	Athlete
12	Cropping	60	Irritating	110	Practically
13	Trafficking	61	Pedestrian	111	Benefitted
14	Tyrannical	62	Enervating	112	Antarctic
15	Gleaming	63	Beguiling	113	Thyroid
16	Cemetery	64	Adopt	114	Disaster
17	Accommodate	65	Access	115	System
18	Intruder	66	Abandon	116	Distance
19	Necessary	67	Abase	117	Armature
20	Aborigines	68	Delight	118	Apparently
21	Texture	69	Stripe	119	Committed
22	Sledge	70	Fright	120	Disciplined
23	Savoury	71	Knight	121	Accommodative
24	Tamper	72	Innocence	122	Magnanimous
25	Benign	73	Governance	123	Aggressive
26	Mortified	74	Enforcement	124	Benevolent
27	Insecurities	75	Insufficient	125	Architecture
28	Dismay	76	Colleague	126	Serrated
29	Besieged	77	Harassment	127	Nuisance
30	Besieged	78	Humorous	128	Convalescence
31	Adolescent	79	Perceivable	129	Languish
32	Belief	80	Warden	130	Altitude
33	Beneath	81	Policeman	131	Discussion
34	Belly	82	Engineer	132	Longitudinal
35	Bellow	83	Doctor	133	Publication
36	Clemency	84	Tranquillity	134	Password
37	Avaricious	85	Tyranny	135	Research
38	Hegemony	86	Serenity	136	Popular
39	Nostalgic	87	Harmony	137	Sabbatical
40	Associate	88	Movement	138	Confluence
41	Professional	89	Ketchup	139	Sinhalese
42	Dubious	90	Precise	140	Conform
43	Nefarious	91	Flashy	141	Mythical
44	Consummate	92	Demolish	142	Squawked
45	Raucous	93	Conduct	143	Questionnaire
46	Occurrence	94	Biopic	144	Committee
47	Rhyme	95	Handful	145	Intervention
48	Timely	96	Artillery	146	Outcome
		97	Efficient	147	Hippopotamus
		98	Craftmanship	148	Embarrassing

SN	Correct Spelling	SN	Correct Spelling	SN	Correct Spelling
149	Slip	199	Deforestation	1	Glamour
150	Moments	200	Substantial	2	Quarantine
151	Repetitive	201	Regrettable	3	Guarantee
152	Streamlining	202	Consequences	4	Queue
153	Construction	203	Couture	5	Philosophy
154	Barbaric	204	Benchmark	6	Geography
155	Evolution	205	Knight	7	Economics
156	Contradiction	206	Aggravate	8	Psychology
157	Abhorrent	207	Subsistence	9	Stingy
158	Condensing	208	Musk	10	Culminate
159	Hereditary	209	Decide	11	Pitch
160	Bouquet	210	External	12	Hasty
161	Hygiene	211	Angel	13	Nocturnal
162	Mortgage	212	Hierarchical	14	Irrespective
163	Champagne	213	Guarantee	15	Repulsive
164	Manoeuvre	214	Structural	16	Scoreboard
165	Noticeable	215	Downtrodden	17	Acquaintance
166	Technological	216	Diabetes	18	Treacherous
167	Advancements	217	Anguish	19	Serendipity
168	Millennium	218	Excruciating	20	Malicious
169	Thrilling	219	Exacerbating	21	Radicalism
170	Caribbean	220	Traumatic	22	Primitivism
171	Assassination	221	Strings	23	Raged
172	Ruthless	222	Ecological	24	Debates
173	Inquisitive	223	Assessment	25	Harass
174	Perseverant	224	Comprehensive	26	Kinetic
175	Conscientious	225	Inoculation	27	Inkling
176	Exploring	226	Continuous	28	Jocular
177	Laparoscopy	227	Success	29	Argument
178	Generate	228	Goals	30	Corporation
179	Intermittent	229	Achievement	31	Surreptitious
180	Guise	230	Protestors	32	Deception
181	Piece	231	Enmity	33	Interpretation
182	Amateur			34	Tremendous
183	Pollen			35	Persistent
184	Mousy	**SSC CGL Tier 2 2021**		36	Pronunciation
185	Quasi	SN	Correct Spelling	37	Committee
186	Quaver	1	Parallel	38	Develop
187	Flawless	2	Premium	39	Reference
188	Rudimentary	3	Penalty	40	Beginning
189	Primitive	4	Passage	41	Accessories
190	Impractical	5	Plantain	42	Dominant
191	Anonymous	6	Platinum	43	Pamphlet
192	Insidious	7	Plateau	44	Politician
193	Deceived	8	Plaque	45	Particular
194	Eczema	9	Inquiry	46	Queue
195	Convoluted	10	Nobility	47	Recommend
196	Foreseeable	11	Enmity	48	Opposition
197	Problematic	12	Incite	49	Humiliate
198	Exhilarate				

SSC CHSL Tier 1 2021

50	Ignorant	100	Decaffeinated	150	Colleague		
51	Intelligent	101	Supplementary	151	Equine		
52	Fascinate	102	Noticeable	152	Equilateral		
53	Persistence	103	Xylophone	153	Equilibrium		
54	Audience	104	Oligopoly	154	Equanimity		
55	Comprehension	105	Robust	155	Encouragement		
56	Competence	106	Zenith	156	Achievement		
57	Attendance	107	Nosy	157	Advertisement		
58	Kangaroo	108	Venison	158	Environment		
59	Vivacious	109	Yearn	159	Cavalier		
60	Ambiguous	110	Ruminate	160	Elegant		
61	Itinerary	111	Informational	161	Charisma		
62	Inscrutable	112	Personnel	162	Dominate		
63	Banality	113	Informal	163	Gothic		
64	Conscientious	114	Personal	164	Neutron		
65	Giddyap	115	Enthusiasm	165	Frosty		
66	Question	116	Accomplishment	166	Deceive		
67	Brusque	117	Convenience	167	Apology		
68	Boisterous	118	Auxiliary	168	Extravert		
69	Blizzard	119	Occurrence	169	Lugubrious		
70	Blonde	120	Accommodation	170	Collaborate		
71	Movement	121	Privilege	171	Reconciliation		
72	Career	122	Erroneous	172	Huddle		
73	Carrier	123	Consciousness	173	Hostile		
74	Freedom	124	Encyclopaedia	174	Horror		
75	Summary	125	Euphemism	175	Hospital		
76	Emigrate	126	Embarrassment	176	Mandatory		
77	Rivalry	127	Leverage	177	Amnesia		
78	Grandeur	128	Oscillate	178	Courteous		
79	Superstitious	129	Bonfire	179	Frigidity		
80	Superstitious	130	Ensue	180	Neutrality		
81	Superstitious	131	Ministry	181	Satire		
82	Superstitious	132	Attention	182	Augustan		
83	Efficient	133	Attitude	183	Partisanship		
84	Layer	134	Mimicry	184	Discipline		
85	Committee	135	Guide	185	Conscious		
86	Field	136	Guilty	186	Privilege		
87	Martinet	137	Guard	187	Believe		
88	Congenital	138	Global	188	Facilitation		
89	Phlegmatic	139	Beautician	189	Resplendent		
90	Ocular	140	Mathematician	190	Jingoistic		
91	Luxurious	141	Musician	191	Segregation		
92	Innocent	142	Technician	192	Crouching		
93	Zealous	143	Acquaint	193	Innocuous		
94	Judicial	144	Memorial	194	Demolish		
95	Argument	145	Guarantee	195	Shoddy		
96	Performance	146	Monotonous	196	Expelled		
97	Valuable	147	Opportunity	197	Sartorial		
98	Secretary	148	Warrant	198	Implicate		
99	Nuptial	149	Conversation	199	Sabotage		

200	Characteristic	250	Wish	300	Shrines
201	Appearance	251	Whip	301	Deities
202	Controversy	252	Wisdom	302	Mercenary
203	Definitely	253	Freedom	303	Narrowest
204	Curiosity	254	Boredom	304	Instantaneous
205	Maturity	255	Kingdom	305	Presumptuous
206	Creativity	256	Trustworthy	306	Illegitimate
207	Generosity	257	Bonafide	307	Lascivious
208	Imprudence	258	Solution	308	Vengeance
209	Conscience	259	Cultural	309	Management
210	Necessity	260	Queer	310	Enthusiasm
211	Reprimanded	261	Antibodies	311	Bibliography
212	Spacious	262	Brag	312	Intelligence
213	Lyre	263	Rascal	313	Succession
214	Irrespective	264	Tactile	314	Assassinate
215	Soluble	265	Concentrate	315	Complacent
216	Audacious	266	Domicile	316	Aquarium
217	Incredible	267	Customary	317	Occasion
218	Baffling	268	Unfortunately	318	Humorous
219	Prevalent	269	Sloth	319	Mysterious
220	Retrospect	270	Beast	320	Scissors
221	Gourmet	271	Wantonly	321	Copulate
222	Magnanimous	272	Repetition	322	Ignition
223	Clandestine	273	Portray	323	Portion
224	Commiserate	274	Procedure	324	Horticulture
225	Decennial	275	Separate	325	Alimony
226	Nausea	276	Admonish	326	Hallucinate
227	Curriculum	277	Avarice	327	Structural
228	Possession	278	Adverse	328	Halloween
229	Jealous	279	Beige	329	Certificate
230	Suspicious	280	Investigate	330	Channel
231	Luxurious	281	Invite	331	Champion
232	Correspondence	282	Invent	332	Challenge
233	Campaign	283	Involve	333	Tryst
234	Experiment	284	Sinister	334	Yoghurt
235	Accommodation	285	Adroitness	335	Serene
236	Protocol	286	Dexterous	336	Shopaholic
237	Medal	287	Gauche	337	Hilarious
238	Opponents	288	Hegemony	338	Demolish
239	Imitate	289	Nebulous	339	Magnificent
240	Absolute	290	Elephantine	340	Gargantuan
241	Absent	291	Committee	341	Hallucinate
242	Absorb	292	Inoculate	342	Hiatus
243	Abstract	293	Leisure	343	Sacrilege
244	Supersede	294	Medieval	344	Launderette
245	Indefatigable	295	Millennium	345	Effervescent
246	Autopsy	296	Demonstrated	346	Unorganised
247	Anonymous	297	Percussion	347	Efficient
248	Wit	298	Orchestra	348	Saleable
249	Witch	299	Brought	349	Loquacity

SN	Correct Spelling
350	Atheist
351	Intrepid
352	Affluence
353	Knowledge
354	Marinate
355	College
356	Jocular
357	Bowlegged
358	Palanquins
359	Urchins
360	Businessman
361	Appetite
362	Reliance
363	Success
364	Confidence
365	Meritorious
366	Traumatic
367	Stigmatic
368	Exhibitionist
369	Hereditary
370	Forts
371	Garrisoned
372	Military
373	Immigration
374	Administrator
375	Admission
376	Exploitation

SSC MTS Tier 1 2021

SN	Correct Spelling
1	Monotonous
2	Meticulous
3	Narrative
4	Exhilarate
5	Privilege
6	Indispensable
7	Perseverance
8	Inadvertent
9	Tender
10	Consent
11	Millennia
12	Monotheistic
13	Hypothesis
14	Prehistoric
15	Appease
16	Aberrant
17	Arbitrary
18	Insipid
19	Tendency
20	Imprudence
21	Mismatch
22	Securities
23	Essentially
24	Fiscal
25	Ventilation
26	Missing
27	Balloon
28	Inability
29	Barricade
30	Prosperity
31	Bouquet
32	Dissatisfied
33	Maintains
34	Freedom
35	Accede
36	Accost
37	Abstruse
38	Abnegation
39	Definitely
40	Envisage
41	Psychologist
42	Emergency
43	Transition
44	Distract
45	Shadow
46	Fraction
47	Chocolate
48	Separate
49	Encourage
50	Councillors
51	Rudimentary
52	Conscious
53	Coalesce
54	Reliant
55	Height
56	Believe
57	Fiery
58	Foreign
59	Strangled
60	Dominion
61	Solitary
62	Persecution
63	Library
64	Hopelessness
65	Feeling
66	Blessed
67	Television
68	Entirely
69	Unravel
70	Equilibrium
71	Compelling
72	Ecstasy
73	Adamant
74	Amorphous
75	Despotic
76	Contentious
77	Tolerate
78	Autocracy
79	Bureaucracy
80	Autonomy
81	Anarchy
82	Escapade
83	Resonate
84	Progression
85	Discovery
86	Suggested
87	Chauffeur
88	Specialist
89	Anchor
90	Compere
91	Precursor
92	Acknowledge
93	Religiosity
94	Ancestors
95	Continent
96	Indefatigable
97	Building
98	Experiences
99	Immersive
100	Institutionalized
101	Tremendous
102	Local
103	Vehicle
104	Focal
105	Vocal
106	Available
107	Website
108	Beneficial
109	Discern
110	Harass
111	Repercussions
112	Appealing
113	Disturbance
114	Implicate
115	Miniature
116	Patience
117	Foreign
118	Secondary
119	Evince
120	Portfolio

121	Equipment	171	Bombastic	221	Conducive
122	Strengthen	172	Arachis	222	Apparently
123	Instrumental	173	Benign	223	Bottleneck
124	Reversal	174	Artless	224	Endogenous
125	Sacrifice	175	Showpiece	225	Majestic
126	Upcoming	176	Simultaneous	226	Flexible
127	Competitive	177	Interview	227	Stringent
128	Autocracy	178	Executive	228	Faltering
129	Bureaucracy	179	Expression	229	Exploitation
130	Autonomy	180	Yesterday	230	Conversation
131	Anarchy	181	Meaningful	231	Revenue
132	Escapade	182	Content	232	Passion
133	Resonate	183	Laughing	233	Inoculate
134	Progression	184	Prominent	234	Legitimate
135	Discovery	185	Immigrant	235	Engage
136	Remember	186	Chauvinist	236	Credential
137	Contribution	187	Contemporary	237	Habitual
138	Bureaucrat	188	Cosmopolitan	238	Lopsided
139	Harness	189	Bizarre	239	Adventurous
140	Beguile	190	Infatuation	240	Admonish
141	Blandishment	191	Fortunate	241	Aggravate
142	Bereft	192	Perfection	242	Assertion
143	Assiduous	193	Surely	243	Accumulate
144	Wariness	194	Master	244	Prestigious
145	Monumental	195	Perturb	245	Breathe
146	Disenchantment	196	Perceive	246	Smelled
147	Awakening	197	Pigeon	247	Institute
148	Exceptionable	198	Passive		
149	Deceive	199	Custody		
150	Mortal	200	Fifty		

	SSC CPO Paper 1 2022	
	SN	**Correct Spelling**

151	Appearance	201	Swimming	1	Vociferous
152	Crater	202	Borrowing	2	Affliction
153	Mantle	203	Sovereign	3	Episcopal
154	Volcano	204	Preserve	4	Innocuous
155	Earthquake	205	Investigating	5	Manipulate
156	Contentious	206	Terrorist	6	Postulate
157	Prevaricate	207	Assembly	7	Stipulate
158	Refute	208	Picking	8	Calculate
159	Revere	209	Picture	9	Abscission
160	Secure	210	Fighting	10	Abstruse
161	Company	211	Influence	11	Incision
162	Lonely	212	Suddenly	12	Abyssal
163	Livelihood	213	Nascent	13	Ensure
164	Veritable	214	Malleable	14	Pharaoh
165	Purposefully	215	Disseminate	15	Strategy
166	Penetrate	216	Obsequious	16	Fulfilment
167	Propensity	217	Perfidy	17	Address
168	Constituency	218	Misanthrope	18	Discovered
169	Demolish	219	Relentless	19	Campaigns
170	Patronise	220	Ingenuous	20	Demonstrations

21	Auxiliary	71	Centenarian	121	Perseverance
22	Acclaim	72	Mercenary	122	Interminable
23	Believe	73	Extracted	123	Intubate
24	Absence	74	Expected	124	Incredible
25	Illicit	75	Extracted	125	Incredulous
26	Illegal	76	Acceptable	126	Assembly
27	Impunity	77	Irreversible	127	Discipline
28	Illegible	78	Spoilage	128	Group
29	Panic	79	Modification	129	Leader
30	Panicked	80	Inedible	130	Fluorescence
31	Picnicked	81	Alliterate	131	Forebear
32	Picnic	82	Elementary	132	Forgo
33	Inflammatory	83	Illiterate	133	Flounder
34	Neurological	84	Alimentary	134	Cushion
35	Numerous	85	Column	135	Scientist
36	Metabolic	86	Scale	136	Posthumously
37	Bail	87	Peace	137	Laboratory
38	Definitely	88	Square	138	Whorl
39	Destress	89	Conference	139	Winch
40	Realised	90	Circumstances	140	Weird
41	Perspicuous	91	Indefinite	141	Wench
42	Purvey	92	Inevitable	142	Conceive
43	Peruse	93	Knowing	143	Appropriate
44	Pervade	94	Cooking	144	Terminology
45	Wriggle	95	Living	145	Believe
46	Wreathe	96	Loving	146	Difficulty
47	Wiggle	97	Commitment	147	Thesaurus
48	Wreak	98	Development	148	Dictionary
49	Membrane	99	Management	149	Dinosaurs
50	Solvent	100	Deprived	150	Frieze
51	Highlight	101	Vial	151	Fortunate
52	Exuberant	102	Vassal	152	Funereal
53	Nefarious	103	Vise	153	Fortuitous
54	Sermonise	104	Voracity	154	Quarrelsome
55	Acquittal	105	Metaphysics	155	Ecclesiastical
56	Chivalrous	106	Study	156	Bovine
57	Pried	107	Nature	157	Calamitous
58	Prophet	108	Realty	158	Measure
59	Prodigy	109	Deficient	159	Subscribe
60	Protag	110	Washing	160	Rectify
61	Impoverish	111	Waiting	161	Branding
62	Ostracise	112	Dyeing	162	Medallion
63	Necessitate	113	Seeing	163	Elaborate
64	Grandeur	114	Serrated	164	Complemented
65	Connoisseur	115	Prey	165	Quadrant
66	Reputed	116	Seizing	166	Mirage
67	Entrepreneur	117	Crushing	167	Missing
68	Successful	118	Diarrhoea	168	Mistaken
69	Aquatic	119	Pseudonym	169	Mission
70	Notorious	120	Connoisseur	170	Investigated

SN	Correct spelling
171	Accident
172	Mangled
173	Victims

SSC CPO Paper 2 2020

SN	Correct spelling
1	Attempt
2	Attract
3	Attain
4	Attend
5	Virtuous
6	Glorious
7	Anxious
8	Precious
9	Carriage
10	Clock
11	Camera
12	Caravan

SSC GD Constable 2021

SN	Correct spelling
1	Glorious
2	Conscious
3	Vicious
4	Courteous
5	Synergism
6	Lifelessness
7	Incredulous
8	Recapitulate
9	Observatory
10	Adolescence
11	Metallurgy
12	Prologue
13	Orchard
14	Archery
15	Monarch
16	Anarchy
17	Eligible
18	Relevant
19	Illicit
20	Tactics
21	Charity
22	Overall
23	Hitch
24	Affirm
25	Palace
26	Peddle
27	Packet
28	Paint
29	Metallic
30	Vigorously
31	Crystallisation
32	Carrying
33	Misanthrope
34	Mascot
35	Socialite
36	Alumni
37	Translate
38	Transcend
39	Transpire
40	Transmit
41	Black
42	Blade
43	Blame
44	Blare
45	Absence
46	Conference
47	Expense
48	Entrance
49	People
50	Render
51	Together
52	Gnaw
53	Zealous
54	Joyous
55	Nervous
56	Furious
57	Occasion
58	Occurrence
59	Offering
60	Auction
61	Hotel
62	Strain
63	Mutter
64	Guard
65	Agreement
66	Aggression
67	Agitate
68	Aggravate
69	Innocence
70	Essence
71	Conveyance
72	Convenience
73	Abbreviations
74	Fluttering
75	Menace
76	Notoriety
77	Cuisine
78	Mundane
79	Beverage
80	Celestial
81	Pauper
82	Awesome
83	Buffett
84	Mischief
85	Player
86	Ideal
87	Aristocrat
88	Filling
89	Mathematics
90	Indecisiveness
91	Gullible
92	Dissimulation
93	Magnanimous
94	Discipline
95	Guidance
96	Guarantee
97	Appreciate
98	Glade
99	Gleam
100	Glitch
101	Glove
102	Fright
103	Friend
104	Freeze
105	Frigid
106	Curious
107	Assistance
108	Participant
109	Exchanged
110	Cereal
111	Tunnel
112	Whistle
113	Rustle
114	Paediatrician
115	Assassination
116	Bureaucracy
117	Philanthropist
118	Erode
119	Eraser
120	Erosion
121	Erratic
122	Commitment
123	Bouquet
124	Procedure
125	Quarantine
126	Voluntary
127	Stationary
128	Dictionary
129	Delivery

130	Response	180	Calamity	230	Sincere
131	Congratulations	181	Affliction	231	Laughter
132	Felicitate	182	Casualty	232	Disturbance
133	Anniversary	183	Experimental	233	Compulsory
134	Collection	184	Equipment	234	Audience
135	Consolidation	185	Electrolyte	235	Potential
136	Corresponding	186	Environmental	236	Committee
137	Complaint	187	Specialist	237	Harbour
138	Recession	188	Increment	238	Premier
139	Remission	189	Exploration	239	Orchestra
140	Precision	190	Ridiculous	240	Glossary
141	Omission	191	Incidentally	241	Hover
142	Rotate	192	Commercially	242	Monarch
143	Rotten	193	Purify	243	Adorn
144	Robbery	194	Possibility	244	Dreary
145	Round	195	Complaint	245	Capture
146	Procedure	196	Worried	246	Nurture
147	Labelling	197	Warrior	247	Structure
148	Precautions	198	Passenger	248	Lecture
149	Precipitation	199	Vein	249	Conscientious
150	Continuously	200	Quick	250	Fasten
151	Sensible	201	Certain	251	Business
152	Feasible	202	Contain	252	Plunge
153	Compatible	203	Sumptuous	253	Evolve
154	Accessible	204	Summary	254	Cushion
155	Dictate	205	Suffering	255	Custody
156	Decision	206	Sundry	256	Curtail
157	Difference	207	Specifying	257	Custard
158	Dictionary	208	Spoonful	258	Boutique
159	Future	209	Vegetable	259	Honorarium
160	Flavour	210	Opening	260	Aquarium
161	Leisure	211	Drainage	261	Bungalow
162	Figure	212	Prosperous	262	Negotiate
163	Substitution	213	Sumptuous	263	Referee
164	Habitation	214	Pompous	264	Miraculous
165	Estimation	215	Precious	265	Satellite
166	Presentation	216	Criteria	266	Accuse
167	Valuable	217	Solitary	267	Progress
168	Infectious	218	Legible	268	Acclaim
169	Precious	219	Individual	269	Vicious
170	Special	220	Hospitality	270	Proactivity
171	Bureaucracy	221	Hoist	271	Pronunciation
172	Scavenge	222	Hostel	272	Procrastination
173	Warier	223	Hold	273	Prolong
174	Inheritance	224	Overreact	274	Commitment
175	Miscellaneous	225	Disobedient	275	Persuasion
176	Misalliance	226	Disapprove	276	Gregarious
177	Miscreant	227	Proportionate	277	Magnificent
178	Misrepresent	228	Collide	278	Unflappable
179	Disaster	229	Jealous	279	Unassuming

280	Unruffled	330	Flame	380	Contingency
281	Unanimous	331	Flock	381	Volunteer
282	Terabyte	332	Flare	382	Laurel
283	Terrestrial	333	Flood	383	Religious
284	Terminal	334	Appliances	384	Mutual
285	Termite	335	Circuit	385	Whine
286	Pickle	336	Phenomenon	386	Injury
287	Picture	337	Associated	387	Thrust
288	Piano	338	Schemes	388	Shield
289	Picnic	339	Malnourished	389	Attach
290	Array	340	Integrated	390	Immaculate
291	Express	341	Recognisable	391	Impediment
292	Exclaim	342	Submission	392	Immense
293	Community	343	Omission	393	Immature
294	Nineteen	344	Commission	394	Fraudster
295	Neutralise	345	Remission	395	Gangster
296	Noun	346	Defiance	396	Prankster
297	Nationalise	347	Pretence	397	Trickster
298	Domicile	348	Reliance	398	Refusal
299	Peninsula	349	Alliance	399	Equipment
300	Cannibal	350	Illusion	400	Starvation
301	Pharmacy	351	Brilliant	401	Baggage
302	Maintenance	352	Scrutiny	402	Imperative
303	Referee	353	Abandon	403	Exceptional
304	Restaurant	354	Considerate	404	Integrated
305	Millennium	355	Separate	405	Intensify
306	Accommodate	356	Disparate	406	Influence
307	Intrigue	357	Desperate	407	Superior
308	Unique	358	Melody	408	Intermediate
309	Quarantine	359	Melodrama	409	Interfere
310	Absolutely	360	Melodious	410	Necessary
311	Adaptation	361	Malignant	411	Separate
312	Abandon	362	Futile	412	Ability
313	Accurate	363	Future	413	Definitely
314	Batch	364	Furnace	414	Schedule
315	Catch	365	Fertile	415	Sheath
316	Yacht	366	Procure	416	Shade
317	Snatch	367	Massacre	417	Sheet
318	Develop	368	Mediocre	418	Pitiful
319	Occur	369	Mediocre	419	Tactful
320	Regulate	370	Delicious	420	Guilty
321	Writing	371	Progress	421	Plead
322	Resist	372	Present	422	Conference
323	Betray	373	Approve	423	Presence
324	Reverse	374	Private	424	Reference
325	Specific	375	Privilege	425	Difference
326	Laboratory	376	Prevalent	426	Medallion
327	Government	377	Previous	427	Mechanical
328	Advertisement	378	Mercenary	428	Mediate
329	Tactfully	379	Versatile	429	Meddle

SN	Correct Spelling
430	Procrastination
431	Alliteration
432	Superintendent
433	Hallucination
434	Threatened
435	Thermometer
436	Thanksgiving
437	Throughout
438	Buying
439	Bouncing
440	Boxing
441	Beginning
442	Configuration
443	Capillary
444	Auxiliary
445	Corollary
446	Ancillary
447	Witness
448	Embarrass
449	Harassment
450	Suppress
451	Consensus
452	Existence
453	Guarantee
454	Believe
455	Arrogance
456	Effective
457	Imitation
458	Fascinating
459	Necessary
460	Adequate
461	Attendance
462	Occurrence
463	Arrogant
464	Appeal
465	Immediate
466	Attention
467	Submitted
468	Omitted
469	Committed
470	Remitted
471	Fatal
472	Tackle
473	Brutal
474	Metal
475	Mechanism
476	Excretory
477	Aluminium
478	Manufacturing
479	Resistivity
480	Successful
481	Strategy
482	Definition
483	Continuously

SSC Selection Post 2022 - 10th Level

SN	Correct Spelling
1	Twisted
2	Kicked
3	Printed
4	Handicapped
5	Ornate
6	Jewellery
7	Tonsure
8	Mundane
9	Conceived
10	Abdicate
11	Abbreviate
12	Juvenile
13	Dumbbell
14	Electorate
15	Promise
16	Custom
17	Strength
18	Pollution
19	Professor
20	Immediately
21	Trusted
22	Incident
23	Bullying
24	Faithful
25	Unlawful
26	Awful
27	Dreadful
28	Tenth
29	Ninth
30	Nineteenth
31	Eighth
32	Refer
33	Conceit
34	Deceive
35	Counterfeit
36	Protein
37	Camouflage
38	Business
39	Building
40	Camphor
41	Leisure
42	Threshold
43	Supersede
44	Filial
45	Horror
46	Advantage
47	Attitude
48	Receipt
49	Hierarchy
50	Heiress
51	Notorious
52	Ethereal
53	Acknowledgement
54	Agreement
55	Excitement
56	Disappointment
57	Beginning
58	Believing
59	Bellowing
60	Becoming
61	Consensus
62	Confession
63	Battalion
64	Battery
65	Gaiety
66	Adequacy
67	Curiosity
68	Frailty
69	Superstitions
70	Prevalent
71	Duly
72	Sadly
73	Wholly
74	Truly
75	Cosmetic
76	Turmeric
77	Detergent
78	Playful
79	Believe
80	Size
81	Receive
82	Relieve

SSC Selection Post 2022 - 12th Level

SN	Correct Spelling
1	Citizen
2	Jailor
3	Blackboard
4	Bailout
5	Abroad
6	Alive
7	Asleep
8	Adjust

9	Advocate	9	Aesthetic	59	Accessory
10	Capacity	10	Forfeit	60	Contemporary
11	Library	11	Hideous	61	Reservoir
12	Imagination	12	Acquit	62	Endeavour
13	Homonym	13	Percentage	63	Pseudonym
14	Exclamation	14	Storage	64	Patriotism
15	Optimal	15	Parentage	65	Combination
16	Versus	16	Shrinkage	66	Internet
17	Adverse	17	Fridge	67	Netiquette
18	Terrible	18	Educate	68	Etiquette
19	Visible	19	Install	69	Pungent
20	Management	20	Refrigerator	70	Smelly

SSC Selection Post 2022 - Grad. Level

1	Hollered	21	Solution	71	Carbonated
2	Need	22	Ambition	72	Aerosol
3	Manager	23	Impression	73	Humongous
4	Service	24	Dilution	74	Acrimonious
5	Present	25	Destabilised	75	Reservoir
6	Heritage	26	Stocked	76	Sacrilege
7	Understand	27	Atmosphere	77	Reliable
8	Appreciate	28	Permafrost	78	Impartial
9	Arguments	29	Crunchy	79	Misled
10	Fruitful	30	Elegance	80	Pragmatic
11	Aggressive	31	Definite	81	Department
12	Natured	32	Dilemma	82	Government
13	Drastic	33	Wholesome	83	Committee
14	Changes	34	Novice	84	Congregation
15	Climate	35	Tangible	85	Pester
16	Recent	36	Colum	86	Opulent
17	Garrison	37	Community	87	Plausible
18	Threshold	38	Particularly	88	Original
19	Pedestrian	39	Heinous	89	Acknowledge
20	Posthumous	40	Vicinity	90	Maintenance
21	Ignorance	41	Nation	91	Jewellery
22	Rebuttal	42	Ambition	92	Memento
23	Embarrassing	43	Depression	93	Retrieve
24	Incautious	44	Expression	94	Audience
		45	Mentor	95	Delicate

SSC Delhi Police Constable 2022

SN	Correct Spelling				
1	Supreme	46	Eloquent	96	Assert
2	Ultimate	47	Tornado	97	Assembly
3	Perfect	48	Parliament	98	Assuredly
4	Eternal	49	Hoarse	99	Diversified
5	Permitting	50	Roast	100	Segments
6	Enables	51	Cynic	101	Familiar
7	Wrap Up	52	Personnel	102	Environment
8	Efficiently	53	Trivial	103	Regulate
		54	Triumph	104	Temperature
		55	Trouble	105	Chameleon
		56	Tribe	106	Lucid
		57	Paramilitary	107	Lose
		58	Necessary	108	Loot

109	Loud		159	Countless		26	Discreet
110	Neuron		160	Manageable		27	Maintain
111	Enlist		161	Brevity		28	Concerned
112	Neither		162	Rumble		29	Comparable
113	Weather		163	Horrific		30	Calendar
114	Character		164	Withhold		31	Controversial
115	Inclusion		165	Economy		32	Arrangement
116	Criterion		166	Traverse		33	Allotment
117	Representation		167	Productive		34	Acceptable
118	Sentry		168	Privilege		35	Accommodation
119	Roast		169	Organic		36	Foreigner
120	Morose		170	Practice		37	Exceptionable
121	Tomatoes		171	Tenor		38	Commission
122	Aircraft		172	Speech		39	Fragrance
123	Aerodynamic		173	Handsome		40	Theory
124	Airliner		174	Crevice		41	Serene
125	Airdrome		175	Domicile		42	Dependable
126	Separated		176	Conscious		43	Indispensable
127	Animated		177	Entrant		44	Homophones
128	Narrated		178	Yeti		45	Synonyms
129	Designated		179	Antics		46	Antonyms
130	Handling		180	Tyranny		47	Homonyms
131	Chronic					48	Gamble

SSC IMD SA 2022

SN	Correct Spelling

132	Lunacy		1	Cylinder		49	Galloping
133	Vehicle		2	Colander		50	Grievance
134	Delegation		3	Consider		51	Geography
135	Executive		4	Calendar		52	Whimsical
136	Orchestra		5	Beginning		53	Surgical
137	Parliament		6	Colonel		54	Bicycle
138	Fair		7	Circumstance		55	Popsicle
139	Foot		8	Attendance		56	Luggage
140	Relished		9	Helpful		57	Instance
141	Enthusiastic		10	Outcome		58	Laborious
142	Witness		11	Specific		59	Kneeling
143	Ago		12	Separate		60	Apparatus
144	Astonished		13	Situations		61	Inconsiderate
145	Indistinguishable		14	Rational		62	Commence
146	Psychology		15	Resilient		63	Certain
147	Entrepreneur		16	Respond		64	Acknowledge
148	Heretic		17	Conspiracy		65	Courageous
149	Weird		18	Conspicuously		66	Manageable
150	Sanguine		19	Patriarchy		67	Foreseeable
151	Untie		20	Patriotic			
152	Camaraderie		21	Glamorous			
153	Presence		22	Guarantee			
154	Environment		23	Grammar			
155	Disrupt		24	Gradual			
156	Tumultuous		25	Spun			
157	Limitless						
158	Soluble						

PRACTICE SET 01 (Spelling)

1 Select the correctly spelt word.

  (a) arrogence   (b) attendence

  (c) apearance   (d) abundance

2 Select the correctly spelt word.

  (a) jewlry   (b) defnition

  (c) scramble   (d) acceptence

3 Select the correctly spelt word.

  (a) pious   (b) pios

  (c) pieos   (d) piuos

4 Select the correctly spelt word.

  (a) revarberation   (b) riverberation

  (c) revirberation   (d) reverberation

5 Select the correctly spelt word.

  (a) mischevious   (b) miscariage

  (c) misdemeanour   (d) misnomar

6 Select the correctly spelt word.

  (a) eccumenikal   (b) ecumenical

  (c) ecuemenicel   (d) ekumanical

7 Select the wrongly spelt word.

  (a) idyllic   (b) idiotic

  (c) prolific   (d) miopic

8 Select the correctly spelt word.

  (a) peece   (b) peice

  (c) piece   (d) peac

9 Select the correctly spelt word.

  (a) complacency   (b) complacensy

  (c) cumplacency   (d) complicency

10 Select the correctly spelt word.

  (a) hetrogenous   (b) heterogineous

  (c) heterogenious   (d) heterogeneous

Keys: 1-d, 2-c, 3-a, 4-d, 5-c, 6-b, 7-d, 8-c, 9-a, 10-d

PRACTICE SET 02 (Spelling)

1 Select the correctly spelt word.

  (a) luxery   (b) luxry

  (c) lugzury   (d) luxury

2 Select the wrongly spelt word.

  (a) whimsical   (b) contiguous

  (c) spectaculer   (d) adjacent

3 Select the correctly spelt word.

  (a) consistency   (b) consistancy

  (c) consistensy   (d) consistansy

4 Select the correctly spelt word.

  (a) terbulence   (b) turbulance

  (c) turbulence   (d) turbulense

5 Select the correctly spelt word.

  (a) mischievous   (b) mischievious

  (c) mischeivous   (d) mischeivious

6 Select the wrongly spelt word.

  (a) matter   (b) meadow

  (c) megre   (d) measure

7 Select the wrongly spelt word.

  (a) mendacious   (b) obnoxcious

  (c) pernicious   (d) ferocious

8 Select the correctly spelt word.

  (a) pharmaceautical   (b) pharmacutical

  (c) pharmaceutical   (d) farmaceutical

9 Select the wrongly spelt word.

  (a) quadruple   (b) quagmaire

  (c) quadrangle   (d) quadrant

10 Select the wrongly spelt word.

  (a) cease   (b) seize

  (c) besiege   (d) beseach

Keys: 1-d, 2-c, 3-a, 4-c, 5-a, 6-c, 7-b, 8-c, 9-b, 10-d

PRACTICE SET 03 (Spelling)	PRACTICE SET 04 (Spelling)

PRACTICE SET 03 (Spelling)

1 Select the wrongly spelt word.

  (a) renassaince   (b) remuneration

  (c) remonstrate   (d) rendezvous

2 Select the correctly spelt word.

  (a) perticular   (b) particuler

  (c) particular   (d) perticuler

3 Select the correctly spelt word.

  (a) sensasion   (b) sansassion

  (c) sansation   (d) sensation

4 Select the correctly spelt word.

  (a) puritannical   (b) puritanical

  (c) purritanical   (d) purritaniccal

5 Select the wrongly spelt word.

  (a) earn   (b) eerie

  (c) early   (d) eagel

6 Select the correctly spelt word.

  (a) acommodate   (b) accommodate

  (c) acomodate   (d) accomodate

7 Select the correctly spelt word.

  (a) reprimond   (b) resplendant

  (c) repositary   (d) requisite

8 Select the correctly spelt word.

  (a) achievement   (b) acknoledgement

  (c) accreditted   (d) accoustomed

9 Select the wrongly spelt word.

  (a) congregate   (b) conglomerate

  (c) cajoule   (d) confiscate

10 Select the correctly spelt word.

  (a) desperete   (b) disparat

  (c) desperate   (d) desparate

Keys: 1-a, 2-c, 3-d, 4-b, 5-d, 6-b, 7-d, 8-a, 9-c, 10-c

PRACTICE SET 04 (Spelling)

1 Select the wrongly spelt word.

  (a) poignant   (b) relevent

  (c) prevalent   (d) malignant

2 Select the wrongly spelt word.

  (a) transferred   (b) referred

  (c) sufferred   (d) deferred

3 Select the wrongly spelt word.

  (a) exchange   (b) exercise

  (c) exclaim   (d) exite

4 Select the wrongly spelt word.

  (a) settle   (b) satallite

  (c) satiate   (d) session

5 Select the correctly spelt word.

  (a) tantative   (b) substentive

  (c) remunerative   (d) speculetive

6 Select the wrongly spelt word.

  (a) emerjency   (b) delegate

  (c) mandatory   (d) appreciate

7 Select the wrongly spelt word.

  (a) nerve   (b) neglect

  (c) negative   (d) nerveous

8 Select the wrongly spelt word.

  (a) comparable   (b) committee

  (c) consceince   (d) commission

9 Select the correctly spelt word.

  (a) advertizment   (b) adversery

  (c) advantegious   (d) adventurous

10 Select the wrongly spelt word.

  (a) controversial   (b) conquer

  (c) contamporary   (d) cooperation

Keys: 1-b, 2-c, 3-d, 4-b, 5-c, 6-a, 7-d, 8-c, 9-d, 10-c

PRACTICE SET 05 (Spelling)

1 Select the correctly spelt word.

  (a) casset   (b) cassette

  (c) casete   (d) cassat

2 Select the correctly spelt word.

  (a) rhapsodic   (b) rapsodic

  (c) rapcodic   (d) rapsodich

3 Select the wrongly spelt word.

  (a) composition   (b) grammer

  (c) literature   (d) poetry

4 Select the wrongly spelt word.

  (a) profesional   (b) preferential

  (c) proverbial   (d) presidential

5 Select the correctly spelt word.

  (a) deliquancy   (b) friquency

  (c) discrepency   (d) hesitancy

6 Select the wrongly spelt word.

  (a) begining   (b) winning

  (c) mining   (d) running

7 Select the wrongly spelt word.

  (a) fomentation   (b) bureaucrecy

  (c) plateau   (d) horizontal

8 Select the correctly spelt word.

  (a) pedestrean   (b) pedestrian

  (c) padestrian   (d) pedistrian

9 Select the wrongly spelt word.

  (a) efficient   (b) sufficient

  (c) magnificient   (d) proficient

10 Select the correctly spelt word.

  (a) benevolence   (b) benevolene

  (c) benevolens   (d) benevelence

Keys: 1-b, 2-a, 3-b, 4-a, 5-d, 6-a, 7-b, 8-b, 9-c, 10-a

PRACTICE SET 06 (Spelling)

1 Select the wrongly spelt word.

  (a) telepathy   (b) antepathy

  (c) sympathy   (d) apathy

2 Select the correctly spelt word.

  (a) persue   (b) purseue

  (c) pursue   (d) persoue

3 Select the correctly spelt word.

  (a) persemonious   (b) persimonoius

  (c) parsemonious   (d) parsimonious

4 Select the correctly spelt word.

  (a) startegy   (b) stratagie

  (c) strategy   (d) stratagy

5 Select the wrongly spelt word.

  (a) complement   (b) compliment

  (c) supplement   (d) requirment

6 Select the correctly spelt word.

  (a) systamatically   (b) systematically

  (c) systematicaly   (d) systimatically

7 Select the correctly spelt word.

  (a) tuetion   (b) tuttion

  (c) tuition   (d) tution

8 Select the wrongly spelt word.

  (a) reproduce   (b) reverse

  (c) require   (d) resembel

9 Select the wrongly spelt word.

  (a) impetuous   (b) impetinent

  (c) imperial   (d) implication

10 Select the wrongly spelt word.

  (a) earnest   (b) infest

  (c) detest   (d) againest

Keys: 1-b, 2-c, 3-d, 4-c, 5-d, 6-b, 7-c, 8-d, 9-b, 10-d

PRACTICE SET 07 (Spelling)

1 Select the wrongly spelt word.

  (a) embankment   (b) deliberately

  (c) preceding   (d) proleferous

2 Select the wrongly spelt word.

  (a) literature   (b) literal

  (c) literecy   (d) literary

3 Select the correctly spelt word.

  (a) reeciet   (b) reciept

  (c) receipt   (d) reiceit

4 Select the wrongly spelt word.

  (a) assesment   (b) assignment

  (c) alignment   (d) inherent

5 Select the correctly spelt word.

  (a) chooze   (b) chooj

  (c) chuse   (d) choose

6 Select the wrongly spelt word.

  (a) accelarate   (b) accumulate

  (c) accomplice   (d) accommodate

7 Select the correctly spelt word.

  (a) gaiety   (b) gaity

  (c) gaeity   (d) gayety

8 Select the correctly spelt word.

  (a) stagnetion   (b) stagnasion

  (c) stagnation   (d) stegnation

9 Select the correctly spelt word.

  (a) genuine   (b) genaral

  (c) guillty   (d) generus

10 Select the wrongly spelt word.

  (a) mercenary   (b) machinery

  (c) missionery   (d) visionary

Keys: 1-d, 2-c, 3-c, 4-a, 5-d, 6-a, 7-a, 8-c, 9-a, 10-c

PRACTICE SET 08 (Spelling)

1 Select the wrongly spelt word.

  (a) variety   (b) anxiety

  (c) gaitey   (d) society

2 Select the correctly spelt word.

  (a) cemetery   (b) cemetry

  (c) symetry   (d) cemetary

3 Select the wrongly spelt word.

  (a) tailor   (b) sculpter

  (c) doctor   (d) fitter

4 Select the correctly spelt word.

  (a) allienate   (b) aliennate

  (c) alienatte   (d) alienate

5 Select the correctly spelt word.

  (a) deceit   (b) deceipt

  (c) decept   (d) deciept

6 Select the correctly spelt word.

  (a) contrapsion   (b) cunstruction

  (c) controdiction   (d) controversy

7 Select the wrongly spelt word.

  (a) acquire   (b) acquatic

  (c) acquittal   (d) acquiesce

8 Select the wrongly spelt word.

  (a) accomplice   (b) accompaniment

  (c) accomplishment   (d) accomodation

9 Select the correctly spelt word.

  (a) posess   (b) possess

  (c) posses   (d) possus

10 Select the wrongly spelt word.

  (a) prefer   (b) defer

  (c) difer   (d) refer

Keys: 1-c, 2-a, 3-b, 4-d, 5-a, 6-d, 7-b, 8-d, 9-b, 10-c

PRACTICE SET 09 (Spelling)	PRACTICE SET 10 (Spelling)

1 Select the wrongly spelt word.

(a) lapped (b) murmurred

(c) deterred (d) worshipped

2 Select the wrongly spelt word.

(a) celebrity (b) celebrate

(c) celeberation (d) celebrant

3 Select the wrongly spelt word.

(a) deflate (b) deform

(c) define (d) definate

4 Select the correctly spelt word.

(a) laibertarian (b) libertarian

(c) liebertarian (d) liberterian

5 Select the correctly spelt word.

(a) refridgerator (b) refregerator

(c) refreggerator (d) refrigerator

6 Select the correctly spelt word.

(a) rennassance (b) renaissance

(c) rennaiscence (d) rennaissance

7 Select the wrongly spelt word.

(a) noticable (b) negligible

(c) neighbouring (d) nuisance

8 Select the correctly spelt word.

(a) calandar (b) colendar

(c) calendar (d) calender

9 Select the wrongly spelt word.

(a) amelirate (b) zealot

(c) penetrate (d) stain

10 Select the wrongly spelt word.

(a) whether (b) weathere

(c) whither (d) wither

Keys: 1-b, 2-c, 3-d, 4-b, 5-d, 6-b, 7-a, 8-c, 9-a, 10-b

---

1 Select the correctly spelt word.

(a) happened (b) happenned

(c) hapened (d) hapenned

2 Select the wrongly spelt word.

(a) board (b) bliss

(c) behaive (d) better

3 Select the correctly spelt word.

(a) compitation (b) fascination

(c) assemilation (d) vindicasion

4 Select the correctly spelt word.

(a) anticeptic (b) anteceptic

(c) anticeptique (d) antiseptic

5 Select the wrongly spelt word.

(a) particle (b) discern

(c) consize (d) nurture

6 Select the wrongly spelt word.

(a) inexplicable (b) inevitable

(c) inextinguishable (d) inexpressable

7 Select the correctly spelt word.

(a) inergy (b) energy

(c) enerzy (d) enerzi

8 Select the correctly spelt word.

(a) compitition (b) distruction

(c) contruction (d) repetition

9 Select the correctly spelt word.

(a) judicious (b) juditious

(c) judiceous (d) judecious

10 Select the wrongly spelt word.

(a) earring (b) gourrmet

(c) torrent (d) carrying

Keys: 1-a, 2-c, 3-b, 4-d, 5-c, 6-d, 7-b, 8-d, 9-a, 10-b

PRACTICE SET 11 (Spelling)

1 Select the wrongly spelt word.

   (a) metaphor   (b) expletive

   (c) allegary   (d) parody

2 Select the correctly spelt word.

   (a) adolescence   (b) adolescance

   (c) adolescense   (d) adolesense

3 Select the correctly spelt word.

   (a) commemorete   (b) comemorate

   (c) commemmorate   (d) commemorate

4 Select the wrongly spelt word.

   (a) attendence   (b) preference

   (c) providence   (d) evidence

5 Select the correctly spelt word.

   (a) proffession   (b) profetion

   (c) profesion   (d) profession

6 Select the correctly spelt word.

   (a) revolutionize   (b) revoulutionize

   (c) revvolutionize   (d) revollutionize

7 Select the correctly spelt word.

   (a) janury   (b) novamber

   (c) february   (d) octuber

8 Select the correctly spelt word.

   (a) inumerable   (b) innumarable

   (c) innumereble   (d) innumerable

9 Select the correctly spelt word.

   (a) conscentious   (b) consenteous

   (c) conscientious   (d) concentious

10 Select the correctly spelt word.

   (a) consensus   (b) consenzas

   (c) concensus   (d) concensas

Keys: 1-c, 2-a, 3-d, 4-a, 5-d, 6-a, 7-c, 8-d, 9-c, 10-a

PRACTICE SET 12 (Spelling)

1 Select the wrongly spelt word.

   (a) comencement   (b) continuation

   (c) resentment   (d) triangulation

2 Select the wrongly spelt word.

   (a) trivial   (b) tution

   (c) tyranny   (d) typical

3 Select the correctly spelt word.

   (a) obidient   (b) obediemt

   (c) obedient   (d) obeydient

4 Select the wrongly spelt word.

   (a) admonish   (b) aborigin

   (c) aberration   (d) agrarian

5 Select the correctly spelt word.

   (a) acquaintence   (b) acquintance

   (c) acquiantance   (d) acquaintance

6 Select the wrongly spelt word.

   (a) postar   (b) pastor

   (c) posture   (d) pasture

7 Select the wrongly spelt word.

   (a) responsibility   (b) oppertunity

   (c) possibility   (d) generosity

8 Select the wrongly spelt word.

   (a) continuance   (b) continuity

   (c) continutie   (d) continual

9 Select the wrongly spelt word.

   (a) expire   (b) explain

   (c) expereince   (d) except

10 Select the wrongly spelt word.

   (a) mathametician   (b) statistician

   (c) dietician   (d) physician

Keys: 1-a, 2-b, 3-c, 4-b, 5-d, 6-a, 7-b, 8-c, 9-c, 10-a

PRACTICE SET 13 (Spelling)

1 Select the correctly spelt word.

(a) fourtyeth   (b) fourtieth

(c) fortieth   (d) fortyth

2 Select the wrongly spelt word.

(a) synonimous   (b) anonymous

(c) unanimous   (d) pseudonymous

3 Select the correctly spelt word.

(a) acommodation   (b) accommodation

(c) acomodation   (d) accomodation

4 Select the wrongly spelt word.

(a) peruse   (b) persuade

(c) persuit   (d) pursue

5 Select the correctly spelt word.

(a) voceferous   (b) tennacious

(c) piccaresque   (d) opulent

6 Select the wrongly spelt word.

(a) illiterate   (b) tolarate

(c) co-operate   (d) irritate

7 Select the correctly spelt word.

(a) acquasition   (b) acquision

(c) acquesition   (d) acquisition

8 Select the correctly spelt word.

(a) broadcaster   (b) broodcaster

(c) boardcaster   (d) brodcaster

9 Select the correctly spelt word.

(a) manipulate   (b) menipulate

(c) manepulate   (d) manipulete

10 Select the wrongly spelt word.

(a) sacrosanct   (b) sacrelege

(c) sacred   (d) sacrament

Keys: 1-c, 2-a, 3-b, 4-c, 5-d, 6-b, 7-d, 8-a, 9-a, 10-b

PRACTICE SET 14 (Spelling)

1 Select the correctly spelt word.

(a) haroscope   (b) harosecope

(c) horoscope   (d) haroescope

2 Select the wrongly spelt word.

(a) dining   (b) shining

(c) determining   (d) begining

3 Select the wrongly spelt word.

(a) allitration   (b) allowanace

(c) almighty   (d) almanc

4 Select the wrongly spelt word.

(a) indomitable   (b) furmidable

(c) amicable   (d) admirable

5 Select the correctly spelt word.

(a) scissors   (b) sweatter

(c) clettering   (d) teribble

6 Select the correctly spelt word.

(a) cartificate   (b) sertificate

(c) certificate   (d) sartifikate

7 Select the wrongly spelt word.

(a) emphasis   (b) emolument

(c) emporium   (d) emmision

8 Select the wrongly spelt word.

(a) barrier   (b) berrel

(c) berry   (d) barren

9 Select the wrongly spelt word.

(a) aggrassive   (b) agriculture

(c) agitation   (d) agreement

10 Select the wrongly spelt word.

(a) sergent   (b) silhouette

(c) session   (d) somnambulist

Keys: 1-c, 2-d, 3-a, 4-b, 5-a, 6-c, 7-d, 8-b, 9-a, 10-a

PRACTICE SET 15 (Spelling)

1 Select the wrongly spelt word.

   (a) histry   (b) chemistry

   (c) psychiatry   (d) palmistry

2 Select the wrongly spelt word.

   (a) beginning   (b) ordinery

   (c) disguising   (d) dignitary

3 Select the correctly spelt word.

   (a) turbulance   (b) obeisence

   (c) perservarance   (d) surveillance

4 Select the correctly spelt word.

   (a) roberry   (b) leisure

   (c) restaurent   (d) meazure

5 Select the wrongly spelt word.

   (a) extract   (b) eligible

   (c) extension   (d) explaination

6 Select the correctly spelt word.

   (a) shcolar   (b) scholar

   (c) scoler   (d) schollar

7 Select the correctly spelt word.

   (a) counterfiet   (b) countorfeit

   (c) counterfeit   (d) counterfate

8 Select the wrongly spelt word.

   (a) relieve   (b) protein

   (c) deceit   (d) frieght

9 Select the wrongly spelt word.

   (a) prioratise   (b) picturise

   (c) visualise   (d) individualise

10 Select the wrongly spelt word.

   (a) unnecessary   (b) unscruplous

   (c) unparalleled   (d) unprecedented

Keys: 1-a, 2-b, 3-d, 4-b, 5-d, 6-b, 7-c, 8-d, 9-a, 10-b

PRACTICE SET 16 (Spelling)

1 Select the correctly spelt word.

   (a) execption   (b) ecseption

   (c) ecxeption   (d) exception

2 Select the correctly spelt word.

   (a) ebulient   (b) jubilant

   (c) iminent   (d) tolerent

3 Select the wrongly spelt word.

   (a) anniversery   (b) bureaucracy

   (c) heresy   (d) secrecy

4 Select the wrongly spelt word.

   (a) receive   (b) conceive

   (c) perceive   (d) decieve

5 Select the wrongly spelt word.

   (a) competent   (b) repentent

   (c) penitent   (d) consistent

6 Select the correctly spelt word.

   (a) concious   (b) complascent

   (c) contemptible   (d) corigible

7 Select the correctly spelt word.

   (a) rejuvenation   (b) rejvenation

   (c) rejuenation   (d) rejevanation

8 Select the correctly spelt word.

   (a) entirty   (b) gratious

   (c) discern   (d) contestent

9 Select the wrongly spelt word.

   (a) assure   (b) assuredly

   (c) assurable   (d) assurence

10 Select the correctly spelt word.

   (a) asiduous   (b) nefarious

   (c) macaber   (d) loqacious

Keys: 1-d, 2-b, 3-a, 4-d, 5-b, 6-c, 7-a, 8-c, 9-d, 10-b

PRACTICE SET 17 (Spelling)

1 Select the wrongly spelt word.

(a) personel (b) personnel

(c) notional (d) nationalist

2 Select the wrongly spelt word.

(a) influence (b) inequality

(c) inefficent (d) independence

3 Select the correctly spelt word.

(a) perjary (b) perjury

(c) parjury (d) perjery

4 Select the correctly spelt word.

(a) superfluous (b) superflous

(c) superfluos (d) superflouss

5 Select the correctly spelt word.

(a) privilege (b) previlege

(c) prevelege (d) privelage

6 Select the wrongly spelt word.

(a) submitted (b) admitted

(c) comitted (d) omitted

7 Select the correctly spelt word.

(a) manegeable (b) managable

(c) manageble (d) manageable

8 Select the correctly spelt word.

(a) ommineous (b) omineous

(c) ominous (d) omenous

9 Select the correctly spelt word.

(a) accommodation (b) accomodation

(c) acommodation (d) accomodetion

10 Select the wrongly spelt word.

(a) hasitate (b) hasty

(c) hazard (d) hazy

Keys: 1-a, 2-c, 3-b, 4-a, 5-a, 6-c, 7-d, 8-c, 9-a, 10-a

PRACTICE SET 18 (Spelling)

1 Select the correctly spelt word.

(a) nesessary (b) necessary

(c) necessery (d) necassery

2 Select the wrongly spelt word.

(a) courageous (b) outrageous

(c) languoreous (d) spacious

3 Select the correctly spelt word.

(a) necter (b) necassary

(c) puntuation (d) pungent

4 Select the correctly spelt word.

(a) entrepreneurship (b) leadeship

(c) scholership (d) partnarship

5 Select the wrongly spelt word.

(a) repent (b) serpent

(c) flagrent (d) reverent

6 Select the correctly spelt word.

(a) supremecy (b) suppressor

(c) surfiet (d) surender

7 Select the wrongly spelt word.

(a) opulence (b) oppression

(c) oppurtunity (d) opposition

8 Select the correctly spelt word.

(a) succesively (b) acquaintance

(c) commissionner (d) exaggerrate

9 Select the correctly spelt word.

(a) mariage (b) marryiage

(c) marrage (d) marriage

10 Select the correctly spelt word.

(a) saccarine (b) sacarine

(c) sachharine (d) saccharine

Keys: 1-b, 2-c, 3-d, 4-a, 5-c, 6-b, 7-c, 8-b, 9-d, 10-d

PRACTICE SET 19 (Spelling)

1 Select the wrongly spelt word.

(a) rapport (b) support

(c) repport (d) purport

2 Select the wrongly spelt word.

(a) curious (b) curse

(c) curry (d) cursore

3 Select the correctly spelt word.

(a) occassion (b) occasion

(c) occation (d) ocassion

4 Select the correctly spelt word.

(a) semblence (b) samblance

(c) semblance (d) samblence

5 Select the correctly spelt word.

(a) peivailege (b) previledge

(c) previllage (d) privilege

6 Select the wrongly spelt word.

(a) callous (b) career

(c) calander (d) carriage

7 Select the correctly spelt word.

(a) mantion (b) mentoin

(c) mension (d) mention

8 Select the wrongly spelt word.

(a) comparison (b) communication

(c) compitition (d) comparable

9 Select the correctly spelt word.

(a) taelant (b) clevar

(c) centiment (d) serenity

10 Select the correctly spelt word.

(a) vagebond (b) vegabonde

(c) vegabond (d) vagabond

PRACTICE SET 20 (Spelling)

1 Select the wrongly spelt word.

(a) commit (b) comedian

(c) committee (d) comunication

2 Select the correctly spelt word.

(a) accomplish (b) hieghten

(c) repitition (d) aggrravate

3 Select the wrongly spelt word.

(a) fourtieth (b) seventeenth

(c) fifteenth (d) fourteenth

4 Select the wrongly spelt word.

(a) unnerve (b) unnerving

(c) unnecessary (d) unnecesserily

5 Select the correctly spelt word.

(a) campagnes (b) campaigns

(c) campaines (d) campaignes

6 Select the correctly spelt word.

(a) maintainence (b) maintenence

(c) maintenance (d) mentainance

7 Select the wrongly spelt word.

(a) examplify (b) example

(c) exhale (d) exempt

8 Select the wrongly spelt word.

(a) therapeutic (b) bureaucretic

(c) thermometer (d) barricade

9 Select the wrongly spelt word.

(a) representation (b) verification

(c) amplification (d) liberalisetion

10 Select the correctly spelt word.

(a) arguement (b) argument

(c) argeument (d) arguemant

Keys: 1-c, 2-d, 3-b, 4-c, 5-d, 6-c, 7-d, 8-c, 9-d, 10-d

Keys: 1-d, 2-a, 3-a, 4-d, 5-b, 6-c, 7-a, 8-b, 9-d, 10-b

SN	Vocabulary	Meaning (Synonyms)	Hindi
1	**Abet**	assist, aid, help, lend a hand, support	सहयोग देना
2	**Abetment**	to encourage, support, or countenance by aid or approval, usually in wrongdoing	दुरुत्साहन
3	**Abeyance**	a state of temporary disuse or suspension.	दुविधा
4	**Abhor**	regard with disgust and hatred.	घृणा करना
5	**Abjure**	renounce, relinquish, reject, dispense with, forgo, forswear, disavow, abandon	त्यागना
6	**Ablation**	the surgical removal of body tissue.	पृथक करना
7	**Abnegation**	renunciation, rejection, refusal, abandonment, abdication, surrender	अस्वीकार
8	**Abominable**	loathsome, detestable, hateful, odious, obnoxious, despicable	घिनौना
9	**Absconding**	run away, escape, bolt, clear out, flee, make off, take flight, take off, fly, decamp	फरार
10	**Absurd**	preposterous, ridiculous, ludicrous, farcical, laughable	बेतुका
11	**Accolades**	honour, recognition, privilege, award, gift, title; prize, laurels	सम्मान
12	**Accomplice**	abetter, accessory, partner in crime, associate, confederate	साथी
13	**Accrete**	grow by accumulation or coalescence.	साथ उगना
14	**Accretion**	accumulation, collecting, gathering	अभिवृद्धि
15	**Accrue**	result, arise, follow, ensue, emanate, stem, spring, flow	इकट्ठा करना
16	**Acquiescence**	permit, consent to, agree to, allow, assent to, give one's consent to, accept	रज़ामंदी
17	**Acrimonious**	bitter, rancorous, caustic, acerbic, scathing, sarcastic, acid, harsh	उग्र
18	**Acrimony**	bitterness, rancour, resentment, ill feeling, ill will, bad blood, animosity	कटुता
19	**Acumen**	astuteness, awareness, shrewdness, acuity, sharpness	कुशाग्रता
20	**Adroit**	skilful, adept, dexterous, deft, agile, nimble, nimble-fingered, handy; More	निपुण
21	**Advent**	arrival, appearance, emergence, materialization, surfacing	आगमन
22	**Adversary**	opponent, rival, enemy, foe, nemesis, antagonist	विरोधी
23	**Aegis**	patronage, sponsorship, backing, protection, shelter, umbrella, charge, keeping, care, supervision, guidance	संरक्षण
24	**Agglomeration**	collection, mass, cluster, lump, clump, pile, heap, bunch, stack, bundle, quantity	ढेर

SN	Vocabulary	Meaning (Synonyms)	Hindi
25	**Aghast**	horrified, appalled, astounded, amazed, dismayed, thunderstruck	भौचक्का
26	**Agnostic**	sceptical, doubting, questioning, unsure, cynical, unbelieving,	संशयवादी
27	**Agony**	extreme physical or mental suffering.	व्यथा, कष्ट
28	**Albeit**	though	यद्यपि
29	**Alibi**	cover for, give an alibi to, provide with an alibi, shield, protect	अन्यत्र उपस्थिति
30	**Allegory**	parable, analogy, metaphor, symbol, emblem	रूपक
31	**Alleviate**	reduce, ease, relieve, take the edge off, deaden, dull, diminish, lessen, weaken	कम करना
32	**Altercation**	a noisy argument or disagreement, especially in public	विवाद, तकरार
33	**Ambiguity**	ambivalence, equivocation	अस्पष्टता
34	**Ambit**	the scope, extent, or bounds of something.	सीमा
35	**Ambivalent**	equivocal, uncertain, unsure, doubtful, indecisive, inconclusive, irresolute, in two minds	उभयभावी
36	**Ambush**	surprise attack, trap, snare, pitfall, lure	घात लगाना
37	**Ameliorate**	make (something bad or unsatisfactory) better.	सुधारना
38	**Amicable**	friendly, good-natured, cordial, civil, courteous, polite, easy, easy-going, neighbourly, brotherly, fraternal, harmonious	मैत्रीपूर्ण
39	**Amicus**	an impartial adviser to a court of law in a particular case.	न्यायमित्र
40	**Amity**	friendly relations.	मेल – जोल
41	**Ample**	enough, sufficient, adequate	प्रचुर
42	**Anarchy**	lawlessness, absence of government, nihilism, mobocracy, revolution	अराजकता
43	**Angst**	anxiety, fear, dread, apprehension, worry, perturbation	चिंता
44	**Anguish**	agony, pain, torment, torture, suffering, distress, angst, misery, sorrow, grief, heartache, heartbreak	दुख, पीड़ा
45	**Animus**	motivation to do something	विरोधपूर्ण भावना
46	**Annihilation**	complete destruction or obliteration.	विनाश
47	**Anodyne**	painkilling drug or medicine.	पीड़ा–नाशक
48	**Anoint**	consecrate, sanctify, bless, ordain, hallow	तेल लगाना
49	**Antiquity**	ancient times, the ancient past, classical times, former times	प्राचीन काल
50	**Anxiety**	worry, concern, apprehension, apprehensiveness, consternation	चिंता

SN	Vocabulary	Meaning (Synonyms)	Hindi
51	**Apathy**	indifference, lack of interest, lack of enthusiasm, lack of concern, unconcern, uninterestedness	उदासीनता
52	**Apostate**	dissenter, heretic, nonconformist	स्वधर्मत्यागी
53	**Appeasement**	conciliation, placation, pacification, propitiation, palliation, allaying	मनौती
54	**Apprehended**	understand, comprehend, realize, recognize, appreciate, discern, perceive	गिरफ्तार, आशंका करना
55	**Apprehension**	anxiety, angst, alarm, worry, uneasiness, unease	डर
56	**Apprise**	inform, notify, tell, let know, advise, brief, intimate, make aware of	सूचित करना
57	**Aquifer**	a body of permeable rock which can contain or transmit groundwater.	जलभृत
58	**Archaic**	obsolete, obsolescent, out of date, anachronistic, old-fashioned	प्राचीन
59	**Archetype**	a very typical example of a certain person or thing.	मूलरूप आदर्श
60	**Ardent**	passionate, avid, impassioned, fervent, fervid, zealous, wholehearted, eager, vehement, intense, fierce, fiery	उत्साही
61	**Arduous**	onerous, taxing, difficult, hard, heavy, laborious, burdensome, strenuous	कठिन
62	**Arraign**	indict, prosecute, put on trial, bring to trial	दोष लगाना
63	**Articulate**	eloquent, fluent, communicative, effective, persuasive, coherent	स्पष्ट
64	**Ascension**	the action of rising to an important position or a higher level.	अधिरोहण
65	**Askance**	with an attitude or look of suspicion or disapproval.	तिरछी
66	**Aspersion**	vilification, disparagement, denigration, defamation	आक्षेप
67	**Assertion**	declaration, contention, statement, claim, submission, postulation, averment, opinion, proclamation	अभिकथन
68	**Assertive**	confident, forceful, self-confident, positive, bold, decisive, assured, self-assured	निश्चयात्मक
69	**Assiduous**	diligent, careful, meticulous, thorough, sedulous, attentive, industrious, laborious, hard-working, conscientious	परिश्रमी
70	**Assimilate**	absorb, take in, acquire, pick up, grasp, comprehend, understand	पचाना

SN	Vocabulary	Meaning (Synonyms)	Hindi
71	**Assuage**	relieve, ease, alleviate, soothe, mitigate, dampen	शांत करना
72	**Astounding**	amazing, astonishing, staggering, shocking, surprising, breathtaking	अद्भुत
73	**Astute**	shrewd, sharp, sharp-witted, razor-sharp, acute, quick, quick-witted	चतुर
74	**Atrocity**	act of barbarity, act of brutality, act of savagery, act of wickedness, cruelty, abomination, enormity, outrage	अत्याचार
75	**Attrition**	wearing down, wearing away, weakening, debilitation, enfeebling, sapping	संघर्षण
76	**Auspices**	a divine or prophetic token.	तत्त्वावधान
77	**Avenge**	take revenge for, take vengeance for, exact retribution for, requite	बदला लेना
78	**Aversion**	dislike of, distaste for, disinclination, abhorrence, hatred, hate	घृणा
79	**Avert**	turn away, prevent, stop, avoid.	टालना
80	**Awry**	amiss, wrong, not right	विकृत
81	**Babble**	prattle, rattle on, gabble, chatter, jabber, twitter, go on, run on, prate, ramble	प्रलाप
82	**Bamboozle**	cheat or fool.	धोखा देना
83	**Banal**	trite, hackneyed, clichéd, platitudinous, vapid, commonplace, ordinary	साधारण, तुच्छ
84	**Banish**	exile, expel, expatriate	निर्वासित करना
85	**Barrage**	bombardment, gunfire, cannonade, battery, blast, broadside	बाँध
86	**Bastion**	rampart, bulwark, parapet, fortification, buttress, outwork, projection	बुर्ज
87	**Bedlam**	uproar, pandemonium, commotion, mayhem, confusion, unrest	हंगामा
88	**Beeline**	a straight line between two places.	सीधा रास्ता
89	**Befuddle**	confused, muddled, addled, bewildered, disoriented	मदहोश होना
90	**Beget**	father, sire, engender, generate, spawn, create	उत्पन्न करना
91	**Behest**	instruction, bidding, request, requirement	आज्ञा
92	**Beleaguer**	besieged, under siege, blockaded, surrounded, encircled, hemmed in	घेरा डालना
93	**Belied**	contradict, be at odds with, call into question, give the lie to	झुठलाना
94	**Belittling**	disparage, denigrate, run down, deprecate, depreciate, downgrade, play down	छोटा करना

SN	Vocabulary	Meaning (Synonyms)	Hindi
95	**Belligerent**	hostile, aggressive, threatening, antagonistic, pugnacious, bellicose, truculent, confrontational	लड़ाकू
96	**Benevolent**	kind, kindly, kind-hearted, warm-hearted, tender-hearted, big-hearted, good-natured, good, gracious, tolerant, benign	भलाई करनेवाला
97	**Benign**	kindly, kind, warm-hearted, good-natured, friendly, warm, affectionate	दयालु
98	**Bereaved**	be deprived of a close relation or friend through their death.	वंचित
99	**Bereft**	deprived of or lacking (something).	कमी होना
100	**Bicker**	argue about petty and trivial matters.	कलह
101	**Bigot**	dogmatist, partisan, sectarian, prejudiced person	कट्टर
102	**Bigotry**	prejudice, bias, partiality, partisanship, sectarianism, discrimination	कट्टरता
103	**Billow**	puff up / out, balloon (out), swell, fill out, bulge out, belly out	तरंग
104	**Bizarre**	strange, peculiar, odd, funny, curious, offbeat, outlandish, eccentric	विचित्र
105	**Blasphemous**	sacrilegious, profane, irreligious, irreverent, impious	तिरस्कारी, अपवित्रकारी
106	**Blasphemy**	profanity, profaneness, sacrilege, irreligiousness, irreverence	ईश – निंदा
107	**Blatant**	flagrant, glaring, obvious, undisguised, unconcealed, overt, open	ज़बरदस्त
108	**Blaze**	fire, flames, conflagration, inferno, holocaust, firestorm	दहकना
109	**Bleak**	bare, exposed, desolate, stark, arid, desert, denuded, lunar, open, empty	बेरंग
110	**Blithely**	in a happy or carefree manner	सानंद
111	**Blitz**	bombardment, battery, bombing, onslaught, barrage, sally	बम बरसाना
112	**Blot**	spot, dot, mark, speck, fleck, blotch, smudge, patch	धब्बा
113	**Bluff**	try to deceive someone as to one's abilities or intentions.	धोखा
114	**Blurb**	a short description of a book, film, or other product written for promotional purposes.	विज्ञापन
115	**Bluster**	blow fiercely, blast, gust, storm, roar, rush	धमकी
116	**Bogus**	fake, faked, spurious, false, fraudulent, sham	जाली
117	**Bolster**	support or strengthen.	आधार

SN	Vocabulary	Meaning (Synonyms)	Hindi
118	**Bombast**	bluster, pomposity, ranting, rant, nonsense, empty talk, humbug, wind	आडंबर
119	**Boomerang**	backfire, recoil, reverse, rebound, come back, bounce back, spring back, return, ricochet	प्रतिगामी
120	**Botch**	bungle, do badly, do clumsily, make a mess of, mismanage	पैवंद लगाना
121	**Bottleneck**	traffic jam, jam, congestion, hold-up, gridlock, queue, tailback	रास्ते का संकीर्ण
122	**Bountiful**	abundant, plentiful, ample, bumper, superabundant	प्रचुर
123	**Bounty**	reward, prize, award, recompense, remuneration, commission	इनाम
124	**Bourgeois**	middle-class, property-owning, propertied, shopkeeping	पूंजीपति
125	**Bravura**	virtuoso, magnificent, outstanding, exceptional, exceptionally good, excellent	उनकी कुशलता
126	**Brazen**	bold, shameless, as bold as brass, brazen-faced, forward	बेशर्म
127	**Brink**	edge, verge, margin, rim, lip	कगार
128	**Briquettes**	a block of compressed coal dust or peat used as fuel.	कोयले की ईंट
129	**Buff**	a yellowish-beige colour.	बादामी रंग का
130	**Bulwark**	wall, rampart, fortification, parapet, stockade, palisade, barricade, embankment	बांध
131	**Bumbling**	acting in a confused or ineffectual way; incompetent.	अनाड़ी
132	**Bungle**	mishandle, mismanage, mess up, make a mess of, botch, spoil, mar	घपला
133	**Burgeoned**	grow rapidly, increase rapidly / exponentially, expand, spring up, shoot up, swell, explode, boom	तेजी से बढ़ते
134	**Buttress**	prop, support, abutment, shore, pier, reinforcement, stanchion, stay	समर्थन देना
135	**Cacophony**	din, racket, noise, discord, dissonance, discordance, caterwauling	कोलाहल
136	**Cadaver**	a corpse	शव
137	**Calibrate**	adjust (experimental results) to take external factors into account or to allow comparison with other data.	जांच करना
138	**Callous**	heartless, unfeeling, uncaring, cold, cold-hearted, hard	कठोर
139	**Capacious**	roomy, commodious, spacious, ample, big, large, sizeable, generous	विशाल

SN	Vocabulary	Meaning (Synonyms)	Hindi
140	**Capsized**	overturn, turn over, turn upside down, upset, upend, knock over, flip over, tip over, topple over, invert	नाव को उलटना
141	**Carcasses**	corpse, cadaver, dead body, body, remains, skeleton, relics	कंकाल
142	**Carnage**	slaughter, massacre, mass murder, mass destruction	नरसंहार
143	**Cascade**	waterfall, falls, water chute, cataract, rapids, torrent	झरना
144	**Cataclysmic**	disastrous, catastrophic, calamitous, tragic, devastating	दुर्घटना
145	**Catastrophe**	disaster, calamity, cataclysm, crisis, holocaust, ruin, ruination	तबाही, आपदा
146	**Catchment**	the action of collecting water, especially the collection of rainfall over a natural drainage area.	जलग्रह
147	**Cavalcade**	procession, parade, motorcade, carcade, cortège	घुड़सवार–दल
148	**Caveat**	warning, caution, admonition, monition, red flag, alarm bells	चेतावनी
149	**Celestial**	heavenly, astronomical, extraterrestrial, stellar, planetary	आकाशीय, स्वर्गीय
150	**Chasm**	gorge, abyss, canyon, ravine, gully, gulf, pass, defile	खाई
151	**Chicanery**	trickery, deception, deceit, deceitfulness, duplicity, dishonesty	वाक्छल
152	**Chide**	scold, chastise, upbraid, berate, castigate, lambaste, rebuke, reprimand, reproach, reprove, admonish	डाँटना
153	**Chirpy**	cheerful and lively.	ज़िंदादिल
154	**Chunk**	lump, hunk, wedge, block, slab, square, nugget	टुकड़ा
155	**Churn**	be turbulent, heave, boil, swirl, toss, seethe, foam, froth	मंथन
156	**Circumspect**	cautious, wary, careful, chary, guarded, on one's guard	चौकस
157	**Circumvent**	avoid, get round, find a way round, evade, get past, bypass, sidestep	दरकिनार
158	**Clamour**	din, racket, loud noise, uproar, tumult, babel, shouting, yelling	कोलाहल
159	**Clandestine**	secret, covert, furtive, surreptitious, stealthy, cloak-and-dagger, hole-and-corner, hole-in-the-corner, closet, behind-the-scenes, backstairs	गुप्त
160	**Clutter**	litter, make untidy, make a mess of, mess up, throw into disorder, disarrange, jumble	अव्यवस्था

SN	Vocabulary	Meaning (Synonyms)	Hindi
161	Coalescence	to grow together or into one body	संघीकरण
162	Coalition	alliance, union, partnership, affiliation, bloc, caucus	गठबंधन
163	Coax	persuade, wheedle, cajole, talk into something, get round, prevail on, beguile	फुसलाना
164	Codify	systematize, systemize, organize, arrange, order, marshal, set out, chart, structure	संहिताबद्ध करना
165	Coercion	force, compulsion, constraint, duress, oppression, enforcement, harassment, intimidation	बलप्रयोग
166	Coercive	relating to or using force or threats.	बलपूर्वक
167	Cogent	convincing, compelling, strong, forceful, powerful, potent	प्रभावशाली, निश्चयात्मक
168	Collegium	an advisory or administrative board	अधिशासी समिति
169	Colloquial	informal, conversational, everyday, casual, non-literary	बोल-चाल का
170	Combat	battle, fighting, action, hostilities, conflict, armed conflict, war, warfare	युद्ध
171	Commemorative	memorial, remembrance, celebratory, celebrative	स्मरणीय
172	Commendable	admirable, praiseworthy, laudable, estimable, meritorious, creditable	सराहनीय
173	Commensurable	measurable by the same standard.	अनुरूप
174	Commotion	disturbance, racket, uproar, tumult, ruckus, clamour, brouhaha, furore	हल्ला गुल्ला
175	Compel	force, coerce into, pressurize into, pressure, impel, drive, press, push	मजबूर
176	Compendious	succinct, pithy, short and to the point, short and sweet, potted, thumbnail, brief	संक्षिप्त
177	Complicit	involved with others in an activity that is unlawful or morally wrong.	सहापराधिता
178	Conceal	hide, keep out of sight, keep hidden, secrete	छिपाना
179	Conceded	admit or agree that something is true after first denying or resisting it.	स्वीकार किया
180	Concocted	make up, think up, dream up, fabricate, invent, contrive	मनगढ़ंत
181	Concomitant	attendant, accompanying, associated, collateral, related	सहगामी
182	Condone	deliberately ignore, not take into consideration, disregard, take no notice of	माफ करना, जाने देना
183	Conducive	good for, helpful to, instrumental in, calculated to produce, productive of	अनुकूल

SN	Vocabulary	Meaning (Synonyms)	Hindi
184	Conduit	channel, duct, pipe, tube, gutter, groove, furrow, trough	नलिका
185	Confiscate	impound, seize, commandeer, requisition, appropriate, expropriate, take possession of, sequester	जब्त कर लिया
186	Conglomerate	a thing consisting of a number of different and distinct parts or items that are grouped together.	समूह
187	Conjectur	guess, speculation, surmise, fancy, notion, belief, suspicion, presumption	अनुमान
188	Conjecture	guess, speculation, surmise, fancy, notion, belief, suspicion, presumption, assumption, theory	अनुमान
189	Connived	deliberately ignore, overlook, not take into consideration, disregard	बढ़ावा देना
190	Connotation	overtone, undertone, undercurrent, implication, hidden meaning	अर्थ
191	Consigned	assign, allocate, place, put, entrust, grant, remit, hand down, bequeath	भेजा हुआ
192	Consonance	agreement, concord, accord, accordance, harmony, unison	तालमेल
193	Consortium	an association, typically of several companies.	संघ
194	Consternation	dismay, perturbation, anxiety, distress, disquiet, disquietude, discomposure, angst	घबराहट
195	Contagion	contamination, infection, disease, illness, infirmity, pestilence	छूत
196	Contempt	scorn, disdain, disrespect, deprecation, disparagement	निन्दनीय, घृणा
197	Contention	disagreement, dispute, disputation, argument, variance	विवाद
198	Contentious	controversial, disputable, debatable, disputed, contended, open to question / debate, moot, vexed	विवादास्पद
199	Contextual	depending on or relating to the circumstances that form the setting for an event, statement, or idea.	प्रासंगिक
200	Contrived	forced, strained, studied, artificial, affected, put-on, pretended, false, feigned	काल्पनिक
201	Conundrum	difficulty, quandary, dilemma	पहेली
202	Coquettishly	flirtatious manner	नखरेबाज़
203	Cordon	prevent access to or from an area or building by surrounding it with police or other guards.	घेराबंदी कर दी

SN	Vocabulary	Meaning (Synonyms)	Hindi
204	**Cornucopia**	an ornamental container shaped like a goat's horn. // an abundant supply of good things of a specified kind.	जादा मात्रा में
205	**Corollary**	a proposition that follows from (and is often appended to) one already proved.	परिणाम
206	**Corroborate**	confirm, verify, endorse, ratify, authenticate	पुष्टि करना
207	**Coterminous**	having the same boundaries or extent in space, time, or meaning	सीमा
208	**Counterfeit**	fake, faked, copied, forged, feigned, simulated, sham, spurious	नक़ली
209	**Coup**	seizure of power, overthrow, takeover, ousting, deposition, regime change	तख़्तापलट
210	**Covets**	desire, be consumed with desire for, crave, have one's heart set on	लोभ
211	**Coyness**	archness, simpering, coquettishness, flirtatiousness, kittenishness	शर्मीलापन
212	**Credence**	acceptance, belief, faith, trust, confidence, reliance, traction	विश्वास
213	**Credible**	acceptable, trustworthy, reliable, dependable, sure, good,	विश्वसनीय
214	**Crude**	unrefined, unpurified, unprocessed, untreated	कच्चा
215	**Crumble**	disintegrate, fall down, fall to pieces, fall apart, collapse	चूर चूर होना, कमज़ोर पड़ना
216	**Crunch**	munch, chew noisily, chomp, champ, bite, gnaw, masticate	संकट
217	**Cull**	reduce the population of (a wild animal) by selective slaughter.	चुनना
218	**Culminate**	come to a climax, come to a crescendo, come to a head, reach a finale, peak, climax, reach a pinnacle; build up to	समापन
219	**Cumbersome**	unwieldy, unmanageable, awkward, clumsy, ungainly, inconvenient, incommodious	बोझिल
220	**Curb**	a check or restraint on something.	नियंत्रण
221	**Curt**	terse, brusque, abrupt, clipped, blunt, short, monosyllabic	रूखा
222	**Dabble**	splash, dip, paddle, wet, moisten, dampen, immerse, trail	भिगोना
223	**Dastard**	a dishonourable or despicable man.	बदमाश
224	**Daunting**	intimidating, formidable, disconcerting, unnerving, unsettling	कठिन
225	**Dearth**	lack, scarcity, scarceness, shortage, shortfall, want, deficiency	अकाल

SN	Vocabulary	Meaning (Synonyms)	Hindi
226	**Debacle**	fiasco, failure, catastrophe, disaster, disintegration, mess, wreck	पराजय, विध्वंस
227	**Debauch**	destroy or debase the moral purity of; corrupt.	भ्रष्टाचार
228	**Debilitate**	weakening, enfeebling, enervating, enervative, devitalizing, draining, sapping, wearing, exhausting, tiring	दुर्बल
229	**Decennial**	recurring every ten years.	दस वर्ष का
230	**Decrepit**	dilapidated, rickety, run down, broken-down, tumbledown, ramshackle	निर्बल
231	**Deferred**	postpone, put off, adjourn, delay, hold over / off, put back	स्थगित
232	**Deft**	skilful, adept, adroit, dexterous, agile, nimble, neat, nimble-fingered, handy	चतुर
233	**Defunct**	disused, no longer in use, unused, inoperative, non-functioning	मृत
234	**Deleterious**	harmful, damaging, detrimental, injurious, inimical, hurtful, bad, adverse, disadvantageous, unfavourable, unfortunate	हानिकारक
235	**Deliberate**	intentional, calculated, conscious, done on purpose, intended, planned	जानबूझकर
236	**Delineate**	describe, set forth, set out, present, outline, depict, portray	वर्णन करना
237	**Delinquency**	crime, wrongdoing, criminality, lawbreaking, lawlessness, misconduct	अपराध
238	**Deluge**	flood, flash flood, torrent.	बाढ़
239	**Demagogue**	rabble-rouser, political agitator, agitator, soapbox orator	प्रजानायक
240	**Demeanour**	manner, air, attitude, appearance, look, aspect, mien	आचरण
241	**Demonic**	devilish, diabolic, diabolical, fiendish, satanic, Mephistophelian	राक्षसी
242	**Demure**	modest, unassuming, meek, mild, reserved, retiring, quiet, shy, bashful	संकोची
243	**Denigrate**	disparage, belittle, diminish, deprecate, cast aspersions on, decry	बदनाम करना
244	**Denouement**	outcome, upshot, consequence, result, end result, end, ending, termination, culmination, climax	अंतिम परिणाम
245	**Denunciation**	public condemnation of someone or something.	निंदा
246	**Deplore**	abhor, be shocked by, be offended by, be scandalized by	विलाप करना

SN	Vocabulary	Meaning (Synonyms)	Hindi
247	**Deprecate**	disapprove of, deplore, abhor, find unacceptable, be against, frown on, take a dim view of	प्रतिकूल इच्छा प्रकट करना
248	**Deprivation**	poverty, impoverishment, penury, privation, hardship, destitution	हानि
249	**Dereliction**	dilapidation, disrepair, decrepitude, deterioration, ruin, rack and ruin	कर्तव्य का त्याग
250	**Derisive**	mocking, ridiculing, jeering, scoffing	व्यंग्यात्मक
251	**Derogatory**	disparaging, denigratory, belittling, diminishing, slighting, deprecatory	अपमानजनक
252	**Desist**	abstain, refrain, forbear, hold back, keep	रोकना
253	**Desolate**	barren, bleak, stark, bare, dismal, grim	उजाड़
254	**Destitute**	penniless, impoverished, poverty-stricken	निराश्रित
255	**Deterrence**	the action of discouraging an action or event through instilling doubt or fear of the consequences	निवारण
256	**Deterrent**	disincentive, discouragement, dissuasion, damper, brake, curb, check, restraint	हतोत्साह करनेवाला
257	**Detractor**	a person who disparages someone or something.	आलोचक
258	**Detrimental**	harmful, damaging, injurious, hurtful, inimical, deleterious, dangerous, destructive	हानिकारक
259	**Diabolism**	worship of the Devil.	जादू की विद्या, शैतानी
260	**Diaspora**	the dispersion of the Jews beyond Israel.	प्रवासी
261	**Dichotomy**	division, separation, divorce, split, gulf, chasm	विरोधाभास
262	**Dictum**	pronouncement, proclamation, direction, injunction, assertion	अभ्युक्ति
263	**Diktat**	an order or decree imposed by someone in power without popular consent.	अलोकप्रिय और कड़ा आदेश
264	**Dilapidate**	run down, tumbledown, ramshackle, broken-down, in disrepair, shabby	जीर्ण
265	**Dilemma**	quandary, predicament, difficulty, problem, puzzle, conundrum	दुविधा
266	**Diligent**	industrious, hard-working, assiduous	मेहनती
267	**Diminutive**	tiny, small, little, petite, minute, miniature, mini, minuscule, microscopic	छोटा सा
268	**Dioramas**	a scenic painting, viewed through a peephole, in which changes in colour and direction of illumination simulate changes in the weather, time of day, etc.	चित्रावली
269	**Dire**	terrible, dreadful, appalling, frightful, awful, horrible	सख्त जरूरत

SN	Vocabulary	Meaning (Synonyms)	Hindi
270	**Discontent**	dissatisfaction, disaffection, discontentment, discontentedness, disgruntlement	असंतोष
271	**Discordant**	inharmonious, unharmonious, unmelodic, unmusical, tuneless, off-key, dissonant	प्रतिकूल
272	**Discrete**	separate, distinct, individual, detached, unattached, disconnected	अलग
273	**Disdain**	contempt, scorn, scornfulness, contemptuousness, derision	तिरस्कार
274	**Disgruntle**	dissatisfied, discontented, aggrieved, resentful, fed up, displeased, unhappy	ख़फ़ा
275	**Dismal**	dingy, dim, dark, gloomy, sombre, dreary, drab, dull, desolate, bleak	निराशाजनक
276	**Dismantle**	take apart, take to pieces, take to bits, pull apart, pull to pieces, deconstruct	विघटित
277	**Disparity**	discrepancy, inconsistency, imbalance, inequality, incongruity, unevenness, disproportion	असमानता
278	**Dispel**	banish, eliminate, dismiss, chase away, drive away, drive off, get rid of,	दूर हो जाना
279	**Disruptive**	troublemaking, troublesome, unruly, rowdy, disorderly, undisciplined	हानिकारक
280	**Dissent**	disagreement, lack of agreement, difference of opinion, argument, dispute, demur;	मतभेद
281	**Dissenter**	dissident, dissentient, objector, protester, disputant, rejectionist	असंतुष्ट, भिन्न-मतावलंबी
282	**Dissuade**	discourage, deter, prevent, disincline, turn aside, divert, sidetrack	रोकना
283	**Distort**	warp, twist, contortion, bend, buckle, deformation, deformity	बिगाड़ना
284	**Distraught**	worried, upset, distressed, fraught, devastated, shattered	व्याकुल
285	**Dither**	hesitate, falter, waver, teeter, vacillate, oscillate, fluctuate	बेचैनी
286	**Doldrums**	depression, melancholy, gloom, gloominess, glumness, downheartedness, dejection, despondency, dispiritedness	उदासी
287	**Dole**	unemployment benefit, state benefit, government benefit, benefit, benefit payments, social security	खैरात
288	**Douse**	drench, soak, souse, saturate, drown, flood, inundate, deluge, wet, splash	भिगोना
289	**Downtrodden**	oppressed, subjugated, persecuted, subdued, repressed, tyrannized, ground down	रौंदा हुआ

SN	Vocabulary	Meaning (Synonyms)	Hindi
290	**Drab**	lacking brightness or interest; drearily dull.	नीरसता
291	**Draconian**	harsh, severe, strict, extreme, drastic, stringent, tough, swingeing, cruel, brutal	कठोर
292	**Drudgery**	hard work, menial work, donkey work, toil, toiling, labour	कठिन परिश्रम
293	**Drumbeat**	a stroke or pattern of strokes on a drum.	ढोल की आवाज
294	**Dubious**	doubtful, uncertain, unsure, in doubt, hesitant	संदिग्ध
295	**Duress**	coercion, compulsion, force, pressure, pressurization, intimidation, threats, constraint, enforcement, exaction	अवरोध
296	**Dwindle**	diminish, decrease, reduce, get smaller, become smaller, grow smaller	सूखना
297	**Dystopian**	relating to or denoting an imagined place or state in which everything is unpleasant or bad, typically a totalitarian or environmentally degraded one.	मनहूस
298	**Ebb**	receding, going out, flowing back, retreat, retreating	अवनति
299	**Eccentric**	unconventional, uncommon, abnormal, irregular, aberrant, anomalous	सनकी
300	**Echelons**	level, rank, grade, step, rung, tier, stratum, plane, position, order, division	कतारबंदी
301	**Ectomorphic**	characterized by a lean slender body build with slight muscular development.	कृशता सम्बन्धी
302	**Edifice**	building, structure, construction, erection, pile, complex, assembly	भवन
303	**Eerie**	uncanny, sinister, ghostly, spectral, unnatural, unearthly	भयानक
304	**Eerily**	in a strange and frightening manner.	डरते हुए
305	**Efficacy**	the ability to produce a desired or intended result.	प्रभावोत्पादकता
306	**Effigy**	statue, statuette, carving, sculpture, graven image, model, dummy, figure	पुतला
307	**Effusive**	gushing, gushy, unrestrained, unreserved, extravagant, fulsome, demonstrative, lavish	प्रवाहपूर्ण
308	**Egalitarian**	believing in or based on the principle that all people are equal and deserve equal rights and opportunities.	समानाधिकारवादी
309	**Eloquent**	persuasive, expressive, articulate, fluent	वाक्पटु
310	**Elucidate**	explain, make clear, make plain, illuminate	स्पष्ट करना
311	**Elusive**	difficult to find, catch, or achieve.	मायावी
312	**Emanate**	emerge, flow, pour, proceed, issue, ensue, come out, come forth	निर्गत होना

SN	Vocabulary	Meaning (Synonyms)	Hindi
313	Emanating	emerge, flow, pour, proceed, issue, ensue, come out, come forth, spread out, come	निकलती
314	Embark	go on board a ship or aircraft.	चढ़ना, शुरू करना
315	Embezzlement	misappropriation, theft, stealing, robbing, robbery, thieving, pilfering, pilferage, appropriation, abstraction	ग़बन
316	Embolden	give courage, make brave / braver, encourage, hearten, strengthen	उत्साह देना
317	Embroil	involve, entangle, ensnare, enmesh, catch up, mix up, bog down, mire	उलझाना
318	Eminent	illustrious, distinguished, renowned, esteemed, pre-eminent	प्रख्यात
319	Empathy	the ability to understand and share the feelings of another.	सहानुभूति
320	Enamour	in love with, infatuated with, besotted with, smitten with, love-struck by	मोहित
321	Encroachment	intrusion into, trespass on, invasion of, infiltration of, incursion into, obtrusion into	अतिक्रमण
322	Endemic	(of a disease or condition) regularly found among particular people or in a certain area.	स्थानीय
323	Enfeeble	weaken, make weak, make feeble, debilitate, incapacitate, indispose, prostrate	ढीला छोड़ना
324	Engrossing	preoccupy, absorb, engage	मनोरंजक
325	Enmeshed	entangle, ensnare, snare, trap, entrap, ensnarl, embroil	जाल में फंसना
326	Enormity	wickedness, evilness, vileness, baseness, blackness	दुष्टता
327	Enraged	very angry; furious	ख़फ़ा
328	Ensconced	settle, install, establish, park, shut, plant, lodge, position, seat, entrench	विराजमान
329	Ensemble	whole, whole thing, entity, unit, unity, body, piece, object, discrete item	समवेत
330	Entail	necessitate, make necessary, require, need, demand	आवश्यक
331	Enthral	captivate, charm, enchant, bewitch, fascinate, beguile	रोमांचित
332	Entrench	establish, settle, ensconce, lodge, set, root, install	मोर्चाबंदी बांधना
333	Envisage	foresee, predict, forecast, foretell, anticipate, expect.	परिकल्पना की गई
334	Ephemeral	transitory, transient, fleeting, passing, short-lived, momentary	अल्पकालिक

SN	Vocabulary	Meaning (Synonyms)	Hindi
335	**Epithet**	sobriquet, nickname, byname, title, name, label, tag; description, descriptive word / expression / phrase	विशेषण
336	**Eponymous**	(of a thing) named after a particular person or group.	नामस्रोत
337	**Equitable**	fair, just	न्यायसंगत
338	**Equivocation**	prevarication, vagueness, qualification, ambiguity, uncertainty, ambivalence	गोल-मोल बात
339	**Erode**	wear away / down, abrade, scrape away, grind down	खिसक
340	**Errant**	erring or straying from the accepted course or standards.	भटकनेवाला
341	**Erratic**	unpredictable, inconsistent, changeable, variable, inconstant	अनियमित
342	**Erred**	make a mistake, be wrong, be in error, be mistaken, mistake	गलती
343	**Erroneous**	wrong, incorrect, mistaken, in error, inaccurate, not accurate, inexact, not exact, imprecise, invalid	ग़लत
344	**Escalating**	increase rapidly, soar, rocket, shoot up, mount, surge, spiral, grow rapidly	तीव्र करना
345	**Eschew**	abstain from, refrain from, give up, forgo	त्याग करना
346	**Espionage**	spying, undercover work, cloak-and-dagger activities, surveillance	जासूसी
347	**Euphemism**	polite term, substitute, mild alternative, indirect term, understatement, underplaying	व्यंजना
348	**Euphoria**	elation, happiness, joy, joyousness, delight, glee, excitement	उत्साह
349	**Evict**	expel (someone) from a property, especially with the support of the law.	बेदख़ल करना
350	**Evocation**	the action of invoking a spirit or deity.	उदबोधन
351	**Evocative**	reminiscent, suggestive, redolent	विचारोत्तेजक
352	**Exacerbated**	aggravate, make worse, worsen, inflame, compound	ख़राब करना
353	**Exaggerate**	overstate, overemphasize, overstress, overestimate, overvalue	अतिशयोक्तिपूर्ण
354	**Exalted**	high, high-ranking, elevated, prominent, superior, lofty, grand	उत्साहपूर्ण
355	**Excavator**	a person who excavates an archaeological site.	उत्खनक
356	**Excruciating**	agonizing, extremely painful, severe, acute, intense, extreme, savage	कष्टदायी
357	**Execrable**	appalling, awful, dreadful, terrible, frightful, atrocious	घिनौना

SN	Vocabulary	Meaning (Synonyms)	Hindi
358	Exhort	urge, encourage, call on, enjoin, adjure, charge, try to persuade, press, pressure, put pressure on, use pressure on, pressurize	उकसाना
359	Exodus	mass departure, withdrawal, evacuation, leaving	निर्गमन, प्रस्थान
360	Exonerate	absolve, clear, acquit, declare innocent, find innocent, pronounce not guilty	निर्दोषी ठहराना
361	Exorbitant	extortionate, excessively high, extremely high, excessive, sky-high, prohibitive	अत्यधिक
362	Exotic	foreign, non-native, tropical	विदेशागत
363	Expatriate	emigrant, living abroad, working abroad, non-native	प्रवासी
364	Expedite	speed up, accelerate, hurry, hasten, step up, quicken, precipitate, rush	शीघ्र
365	Expedite	speed up, accelerate, hurry, hasten, step up, quicken, precipitate, rush	शीघ्र
366	Expedition	journey, voyage, tour, odyssey	अभियान
367	Expeditious	speedy, swift, quick, rapid, fast	शीघ्र
368	Explicit	clear, direct, plain, obvious, straightforward, clear-cut	स्पष्ट
369	Extravaganza	spectacular, display, spectacle, exhibition	ऊटपटाँग या असंगत बर्ताव
370	Facade	front, frontage, face, aspect, elevation, exterior, outside	मुखौटा
371	Facile	simplistic, superficial, oversimple, oversimplified	सरल-प्रकृति
372	Fag	chore, slog, grind, drudgery, exertion, trouble, bother, pain	थकान
373	Fallacy	misconception, mistaken belief, misbelief, delusion, false notion, mistaken impression	भ्रम
374	Fallible	error-prone, erring, errant, liable to err, prone to err, open to error	पतनशील
375	Fanatic	a person filled with excessive and single-minded zeal, especially for an extreme religious or political cause.	कट्टर
376	Fanciful	ornate, exotic, imaginative, creative, fancy	काल्पनिक
377	Farce	slapstick comedy, broad comedy, slapstick, burlesque	स्वांग
378	Farcical	ridiculous, preposterous, ludicrous, absurd, laughable, risible, nonsensical	विनोदपूर्ण
379	Fastidious	scrupulous, punctilious, painstaking, meticulous, assiduous	ढीठ, हठी

SN	Vocabulary	Meaning (Synonyms)	Hindi
380	**Fathom**	understand, comprehend, work out, fathom out, make sense of, grasp	थाह लेना
381	**Fearmongering**	the action of deliberately arousing public fear or alarm about a particular issue.	डर का व्यापार
382	**Feeble**	weak, weakly, weakened, puny, wasted, frail, infirm, delicate, sickly	कमज़ोर
383	**Felony**	a crime regarded in the US and many other judicial systems as more serious than a misdemeanour.	घोर अपराध
384	**Ferocious**	a ferocious beast"	क्रूर
385	**Fervour**	passion, ardour, intensity, zeal, vehemence, vehemency	जोश
386	**Festoons**	a chain or garland of flowers, leaves, or ribbons, hung in a curve as a decoration.	माला
387	**Fickle**	capricious, changeable, variable, volatile, mercurial, vacillating, fitful, irregular	अस्थिर
388	**Fiddle**	fraud, swindle, fix, wangle, confidence trick, ruse, wile	तुच्छ बातों में लगे रहना
389	**Fidelity**	loyalty, allegiance, obedience, constancy, fealty, homage	सत्य के प्रति निष्ठा
390	**Fidget**	move restlessly, wriggle, squirm, twitch, jiggle, writhe, twist, shuffle, be jittery	विकल होना
391	**Fiefdom**	a territory or sphere of operation controlled by a particular person or group.	जागीर
392	**Fierce**	ferocious, savage, vicious	उग्र
393	**Fig**	a soft pear-shaped fruit with sweet dark flesh and many small seeds, eaten fresh or dried.	साज़-सिंगार
394	**Figment**	invention, production, creation, concoction, fabrication	मनगढ़ंत
395	**Filibuster**	delaying tactics, stonewalling, procrastination, obstruction, delaying, blocking	जलडाकू
396	**Fillip**	something which acts as a stimulus or boost to an activity.	प्रोत्साहन
397	**Flagrant**	blatant, glaring, obvious, overt, evident	ज्वलंत
398	**Flair**	aptitude, talent, gift, knack, instinct, natural ability, ability, capability	विशिष्ट योग्यता
399	**Flak**	criticism, censure, disapproval, disapprobation, hostility, complaints	विमान भेदी गोलाबारी
400	**Flamboyant**	ostentatious, exuberant, confident, lively, buoyant, animated, energetic	आकर्षक
401	**Flank**	the right or left side of a body of people such as an army, a naval force, or a soccer team.	नज़दीक होना

SN	Vocabulary	Meaning (Synonyms)	Hindi
402	**Flounder**	struggle, thrash, thresh, flail, toss and turn, twist and turn, pitch	छटपटाना
403	**Flout**	defy, refuse to obey, go against, rebel against, scorn, disdain, show contempt for	अवज्ञा
404	**Flutter**	flit, flitter	लहराना, उड़ना, फड़फड़ाना
405	**Foibles**	weakness, weak point, weak spot, failing, shortcoming, flaw, imperfection,	दोष
406	**Foil**	thwart, frustrate, counter, oppose, baulk, disappoint	विफलता
407	**Foist**	impose, force, thrust, offload, unload, dump, palm off, fob off	थोपना
408	**Foray**	a sudden attack or incursion into enemy territory, especially to obtain something; a raid.	धावा
409	**Foregone**	past, former, earlier, previous, prior, bygone, old, of old, ancient, long-ago	त्याघना
410	**Foresee**	anticipate, predict, forecast, expect, envisage, envision	पूर्वानुमान
411	**Forgo**	go without (something desirable).	त्यागना
412	**Forlorn**	unhappy, sad, miserable, sorrowful, dejected, despondent	निराश
413	**Formidable**	intimidating, forbidding, redoubtable, daunting, alarming, frightening	भयावह
414	**Fracas**	disturbance, quarrel, scuffle, brawl, affray, tussle, melee	कोलाहल
415	**Fractious**	grumpy, grouchy, crotchety, in a (bad) mood, cantankerous	झगड़ालू, अनियंत्रित
416	**Fragile**	breakable, easily broken, brittle, frangible, smashable, splintery	नाज़ुक
417	**Fray**	unravel, wear, wear thin, wear out, wear away, wear through, become worn	दंगा
418	**Frenzy**	hysteria, madness, mania, insanity, derangement, dementedness, delirium	उन्माद
419	**Fretful**	feeling or expressing distress or irritation.	चिड़चिड़ा
420	**Frivolous**	flippant, glib, waggish, joking, jokey, light-hearted, facetious, fatuous, inane	तुच्छ
421	**Frugal**	thrifty, sparing, economical, saving	मितव्ययी
422	**Fudge**	compromise, cover-up, halfway house	ठगना
423	**Fugitive**	escapee, escaper, runaway, deserter, refugee, renegade	भगोड़ा
424	**Fulminate**	protest, rail, rage, rant, thunder, storm, declaim, inveigh, speak out, make / take a stand	फूटना

SN	Vocabulary	Meaning (Synonyms)	Hindi
425	**Furlough**	leave of absence, especially that granted to a member of the services or a missionary.	लम्बी छुट्टी
426	**Furore**	commotion, uproar, outcry, disturbance, hubbub, hurly-burly, fuss, upset, tumult	उत्तेजना
427	**Futile**	fruitless, vain, pointless	व्यर्थ
428	**Fuzzy**	downy, down-covered, frizzy, woolly, velvety, silky, silken, satiny	अस्पष्ट
429	**Gaffe**	blunder, mistake, error, slip	चूक
430	**Gallow**	hanging, being hanged, the noose, the rope, the gibbet, the scaffold	फांसी
431	**Galvanize**	shock or excite (someone) into taking action.	प्रेरित करना
432	**Gamut**	range, spectrum, span, sweep, compass, scope, area, breadth	विस्तार
433	**Gargantuan**	enormous, extremely big, extremely large, massive, huge, colossal, vast	विशाल
434	**Garner**	gather, collect, accumulate, amass, assemble	संचित करना
435	**Garnish**	decorate or embellish	सजाना
436	**Gastronomy**	the practice or art of choosing, cooking, and eating good food.	पाक
437	**Gauntlet**	a strong glove with a long, loose wrist.	लोहे का दस्ताना
438	**Genesis**	origin, source, root, beginning, commencement, start, outset	उत्पत्ति
439	**Gestation**	pregnancy, development, incubation, maturation	गर्भावस्था
440	**Ghastly**	causing great horror or fear.extremely unwell , very objectionable , unpleasant.	भयंकर
441	**Ghettos**	a part of a city, especially a slum area, occupied by a minority group or groups.	पृथक–बस्ती
442	**Giggle**	titter, snigger, snicker, tee-hee, give a half-suppressed laugh	डरते हुए हँसना
443	**Gimmick**	publicity device, stunt, contrivance, eye-catching novelty, scheme, trick, dodge, ploy, stratagem	नौटंकी
444	**Glean**	obtain, get, take, draw, derive, extract, cull, garner, gather	बीनना
445	**Glimmer**	gleam, shine, glint, flicker, shimmer, glisten, glow, twinkle, sparkle	झलमलाना
446	**Glimpse**	catch sight of, catch / get a glimpse of, see briefly, get a sight of, notice	झलक
447	**Glut**	surplus, excess, surfeit, superfluity, overabundance	भरमार
448	**Goad**	provoke, spur, prick, sting, prod, egg on, hound, badger	उसकाव

SN	Vocabulary	Meaning (Synonyms)	Hindi
449	**Grapple**	engage in a close fight or struggle without weapons; wrestle.	हाथापाई करना
450	**Gravitate**	move, head, be pulled, drift	केंद्र की ओर झुकना
451	**Grievous**	serious, severe, grave, bad, critical, dreadful, terrible, awful	क्षतिकर
452	**Grim**	bleak, dreary, dismal, dingy, wretched, miserable, disheartening, depressing, cheerless, comfortless	भयंकर, भयानक
453	**Grisly**	gruesome, ghastly, frightful, horrid, horrifying, fearful, hideous	भयानक
454	**Growl**	snarl, bark, yap, bay	गुर्राना
455	**Grub**	larva, maggot; caterpillar,dig, excavate, burrow	खोदना,कीड़ा
456	**Gruelling**	exhausting, tiring, fatiguing, wearying, enervating, taxing, draining, sapping	थकानेवाला
457	**Gruesome**	grisly, ghastly, frightful, horrid, horrifying, fearful, hideous, macabre, spine-chilling, horrible	भीषण
458	**Grumble**	complain, moan, groan, whine, mutter, grouse, bleat, carp, cavil	बड़बड़ाना
459	**Guise**	likeness, external appearance, appearance, semblance, form	भेष
460	**Gullible**	credulous, over-trusting, over-trustful, trustful, easily deceived / led, easily taken in, exploitable, dupable, deceivable	आसानी से धोखा खानेवाला
461	**Gusty**	blustery, breezy, windy, squally, gusting, blustering	वातमय
462	**Gutted**	bitterly disappointed or upset.	निराश
463	**Hamlet**	a small settlement, generally one smaller than a village, and strictly (in Britain) one without a church.	छोटा गांव
464	**Hapless**	unfortunate, unlucky, luckless, out of luck, ill-starred, ill-fated	बदकिस्मत
465	**Harangues**	a lengthy and aggressive speech.	उग्र भाषण देना
466	**Harbinger**	herald, sign, indicator, indication	सन्देशवाहक
467	**Harrowing**	acutely distressing.	शोकजनक
468	**Hassle**	inconvenience, bother, nuisance, problem, struggle, difficulty, annoyance	परेशानी
469	**Haulage**	a charge for the commercial transport of goods.	पार करना
470	**Haunting**	evocative, affecting, moving, touching, emotive, expressive, powerful	नित्य आनेवाला
471	**Haywire**	out of control, out of order, erratic, faulty, not functioning properly	व्याकुल

SN	Vocabulary	Meaning (Synonyms)	Hindi
472	**Hazardous**	dangerous, risky, unsafe, perilous, precarious, insecure, tricky, unpredictable, uncertain	संकटपूर्ण
473	**Hearken**	to listen or give respectful attention	ध्यान देना
474	**Hearsay**	information received from other people which cannot be substantiated; rumour.	अफ़वाह
475	**Heckle**	jeer, taunt, jibe at, shout down, shout at, boo, hiss, disrupt	सवालों से बात काटना
476	**Heckled**	interrupt (a public speaker) with derisive or aggressive comments or abuse.	सवालों से बात काटना
477	**Hegemony**	leadership or dominance, especially by one state or social group over others.	नेतृत्व
478	**Heinous**	odious, wicked, evil, atrocious, monstrous, disgraceful, abominable, detestable, contemptible	जघन्य
479	**Heist**	a robbery.	डकैती
480	**Hiatus**	pause, break, interval, interruption, suspension, intermission	ख़ाली जगह
481	**Hillock**	mound, small hill, prominence, eminence, elevation, rise	छोटी पहाड़ी
482	**Hindsight**	understanding of a situation or event only after it has happened or developed.	दीर्घदर्श
483	**Hinterlands**	the back of beyond, the middle of nowhere, the backwoods, the wilds, the bush, remote areas, a backwater	आंतरिक इलाके
484	**Hoax**	a humorous or malicious deception.	छल
485	**Holocaust**	cataclysm, disaster, catastrophe, destruction, devastation, demolition, annihilation	प्रलय
486	**Homage**	respect, recognition, admiration, esteem, adulation, acclaim	श्रद्धा
487	**Hone**	sharpen, make sharper, make sharp, whet, strop, grind, file, put an edge on	प्रखर करना
488	**Honorarium**	fee, payment, consideration, allowance	मानदेय
489	**Hooch**	alcoholic drink, especially inferior or illicit whisky.	अवैध शराब
490	**Horrendous**	extremely unpleasant, horrifying, or terrible.	खराब
491	**Hubris**	arrogance, conceit, conceitedness, haughtiness, pride, vanity, self-importance, self-conceit, pomposity	अभिमान
492	**Hurl**	throw, toss, fling, pitch, cast, lob, launch, flip, catapult, shy, dash, send	उछालना
493	**Ignominy**	shame, humiliation, embarrassment	कलंक, बदनामी
494	**Imminent**	impending, at hand, close, near, approaching, fast approaching, coming	निकटस्थ

SN	Vocabulary	Meaning (Synonyms)	Hindi
495	Impeccable	flawless, faultless, unblemished, spotless, stainless, untarnished	त्रुटिहीन
496	Impediment	hindrance, obstruction, obstacle, barrier, bar, handicap, block, check	बाधा
497	Impend	imminent, at hand, close, close at hand, near, nearing, approaching, coming, forthcoming, upcoming, to come, on the way, about to happen, upon us	आसन्न
498	Imperative	vitally important, of vital importance, all-important, vital, crucial	अनिवार्य
499	Impervious	impermeable, impenetrable, impregnable, waterproof, watertight, water-resistant, water-repellent	प्रबल
500	Impetus	momentum, propulsion, impulsion, impelling force, motive force, driving force	प्रेरणा
501	Impinge	affect, have an effect on, have a bearing on, touch, influence	टकराना
502	Implacably	unappeasable, unpacifiable, unplacatable, unmollifiable	संगदिल
503	Implead	prosecute or take proceedings against.	पक्षकार बनाना
504	Implosion	sudden failure or collapse of an organization or system	अन्तःस्फोट
505	Impoverished	weaken, sap, exhaust, drain, empty, diminish	गरीब
506	Impromptu	unrehearsed, unprepared, unscripted, extempore, extemporized	बिना पहले सोचे हुए
507	Impudent	impertinent, insolent, cheeky, audacious, brazen, shameless, immodest	बेशर्म
508	Impugned	call into question, challenge, question, dispute, query, take issue with, impeach	बहस करना
509	Impunity	exemption from punishment or freedom from the injurious consequences of an action.	दण्ड मुक्ति
510	Incapacitation	to deprive of ability, qualification, or strength; make incapable or unfit; disable	अशक्तता
511	Incarceration	imprisonment, internment, confinement, detention	कैद करना
512	Inception	establishment, institution, foundation, founding, formation, initiation	आरंभ
513	Incessant	ceaseless, unceasing, constant, continual, unabating, interminable	निरंतर
514	Inchoate	just begun and so not fully formed or developed; rudimentary.	अस्फुटित
515	Incoherence	the quality of being illogical, inconsistent, or unclear.	बेतरतीबी

SN	Vocabulary	Meaning (Synonyms)	Hindi
516	Inconclusive	not leading to a firm conclusion or result; not ending doubt or dispute.	दुविधा में पड़ा हुआ
517	Incongruous	not in harmony or keeping with the surroundings or other aspects of something.	बेमेल
518	Inconsolable	heartbroken, broken-hearted, unable to be comforted, unable to be consoled, grief-stricken, prostrate with grief	गमगीन
519	Incredulity	disbelief, incredulousness, lack of belief, unbelief, lack of credence, doubt	अविश्वास
520	Inculcate	instil, implant, fix, ingrain, infuse, impress, imprint, introduce	मन में बैठाना
521	Incumbent	binding, obligatory, mandatory, necessary, compulsory, required, requisite, essential, imperative	आवश्यक
522	Incur	suffer, sustain, experience, bring upon oneself	अपने ऊपर लेना
523	Incursion	an invasion or attack, especially a sudden or brief one.	चढ़ाई
524	Indictment	charge, accusation, arraignment, citation, summons	अभियोग
525	Indomitable	invincible, unconquerable, unbeatable, unassailable, impregnable	अदम्य
526	Inebriate	make (someone) drunk; intoxicate.	नशे में धुत
527	Ineluctable	unable to be resisted or avoided; inescapable.	अनिवार्य
528	Inept	incompetent, unskilful, unskilled, inexpert, amateurish, crude, rough	अयोग्य
529	Inescapable	unavoidable, inevitable, ineluctable, ineliminable, inexorable	अनिवार्य
530	Inexorable	intransigent, unbending, unyielding, inflexible, unswerving, unwavering,	निष्ठुर
531	Inexorably	in a way that is impossible to stop or prevent.	निष्ठुर
532	Inexplicable	unaccountable, unexplainable, incomprehensible, unfathomable, impenetrable, insoluble, unsolvable, baffling,	अकथनीय
533	Inextricably	in a way that is impossible to disentangle or separate.	अलंघनीय
534	Infallible	unerring, error-free, unfailing, faultless, flawless, impeccable	अचूक
535	Influx	inundation, inrush, rush, stream, flood, incursion, ingress	अंतःप्रवेश
536	Infusion	the introduction of a new element or quality into something.	आसव
537	Ingenious	inventive, creative, imaginative, original, innovative, resourceful, enterprising	प्रतिभावान

SN	Vocabulary	Meaning (Synonyms)	Hindi
538	**Ingratitude**	ungratefulness, thanklessness, unthankfulness, lack of gratitude	कृतघ्नता
539	**Inimical**	harmful, injurious, detrimental, deleterious, pernicious, damaging, hurtful	विरोधी
540	**Innate**	inborn, natural, inbred, congenital, inherent, intrinsic, instinctive, intuitive	जन्मजात
541	**Innocuous**	harmless, safe, non-dangerous, non-poisonous, non-toxic	अहानिकर
542	**Inquisitive**	unduly curious about the affairs of others; prying.	जिज्ञासु
543	**Inscribe**	carve, write, engrave, etch, cut, chisel	अंकित किया
544	**Inscrutable**	enigmatic, unreadable, impenetrable, mysterious, impossible to interpret, cryptic	रहस्यमय
545	**Insidious**	stealthy, subtle, surreptitious, sneaking, cunning, crafty, Machiavellian	कपटी, घातक
546	**Insinuation**	implication, inference, suggestion, hint, intimation	आक्षेप
547	**Insular**	ignorant of or uninterested in cultures, ideas, or peoples outside one's own experience.	द्वीपीय, सीमित
548	**Insularity**	narrow-mindedness, blinkered approach / attitude, parochialism	संकीर्णता
549	**Insurgent**	rebel, revolutionary, revolutionist, mutineer, agitator, subversive, guerrilla, anarchist, terrorist	विद्रोही
550	**Intangible**	impalpable, untouchable, imperceptible to the touch, non-physical	न छूने योग्य
551	**Interlocutor**	a person who takes part in a dialogue or conversation.	वार्ताकार
552	**Interlude**	interval, intermission, break, recess, pause, respite, rest, breathing space, halt	अन्तराल
553	**Internecine**	mutually distructive, deadly, bloody, violent, fierce, destructive, ruinous	परस्पर-विध्वंसी
554	**Intransigent**	unwilling or refusing to change one's views or to agree about something.	सैद्धांतिक
555	**Intricacy**	details, especially of an involved or perplexing subject.	गूढ़ता
556	**Intriguing**	arousing one's curiosity or interest; fascinating.	दिलचस्प
557	**Inundation**	flood, overflow, deluge, torrent, influx	सैलाब
558	**Invective**	abuse, insults, vituperation, expletives, swear words, swearing	अपशब्द

SN	Vocabulary	Meaning (Synonyms)	Hindi
559	Invigorate	revitalize, energize, refresh, revive, vivify, brace, rejuvenate, enliven, liven up, perk up, wake up, animate	स्फूर्तिदायक
560	Invoke	pray to, call on, appeal to, plead with, supplicate	आह्वान
561	Irrevocable	irreversible, unrectifiable, irremediable, irreparable, unrepairable	अटल
562	Jeopardise	threaten, endanger, imperil, menace, risk, put at risk, expose to risk	ख़तरे में डालना
563	Jester	joker, comedian, comic, humorist, wag, wit, funny man / woman, prankster	विदूषक
564	Jingoism	extreme patriotism, blind patriotism, chauvinism	अंधराष्ट्रीयता
565	Jostle	push, elbow, or bump against (someone) roughly, typically in a crowd.	मुठभेड़
566	Jubilant	overjoyed, exultant, triumphant, joyful, jumping for joy, rejoicing, cock-a-hoop	उल्लसित
567	Juggernaut	a huge, powerful, and overwhelming force.	विशालकाय वाहन
568	Jugglery	the art or practice of a juggler. ,manipulation or trickery especially to achieve a desired end.	बाजीगरी
569	Juncture	a particular point in events or time.	समय
570	Juxtaposition	the fact of two things being seen or placed close together with contrasting effect.	तुलना
571	Laborious	arduous, hard, heavy, difficult, strenuous, gruelling, murderous	व्यवसायी
572	Lacklustre	uninspired, uninspiring, unimaginative, dull, humdrum, colourless	मंद
573	Laggards	straggler, loiterer, lingerer, dawdler, sluggard, slug, snail, delayer	सुस्त
574	Lambast	criticize, castigate, chastise, censure, condemn, take to task, harangue, attack, rail at, rant at, revile	आलोचना की
575	Lament	wail, wailing, lamentation, moan, moaning, groan, weeping,	विलाप
576	Languish	weaken, grow weak, deteriorate, decline, go into a decline	दुर्बल
577	Laudable	praiseworthy, commendable, admirable, meritorious	प्रशंसनीय
578	Laxity	lack of strictness or care.	ढील
579	Leeway	freedom, scope, room to manoeuvre, latitude, elbow room, slack, space	गुंजाइश
580	Lethargic	sluggish and apathetic	आलसी
581	Levant	run away, typically leaving unpaid debts.	भाग जाना

SN	Vocabulary	Meaning (Synonyms)	Hindi
582	**Lexicon**	the vocabulary of a person, language, or branch of knowledge.	शब्दकोश
583	**Liaise**	cooperate, work together, collaborate	संबंध स्थापित करना
584	**Libtard**	a person with left-wing political views.	उदार पंथी
585	**Limbo**	oblivion, void, non-existence, neither heaven nor hell	जेल
586	**Liturgy**	ritual, worship, service, ceremony, rite, observance, celebration	मरणोत्तर गित
587	**Loggerhead**	a reddish-brown turtle with a very large head, occurring chiefly in warm seas	आपस में भिड़े
588	**Loiter**	linger, potter, wait, skulk	टाल – मटोल करना
589	**Lucrative**	producing a great deal of profit.	लाभप्रद
590	**Ludicrous**	absurd, ridiculous, farcical, laughable, risible, preposterous, foolish, idiotic, stupid	ऊटपटांग
591	**Lumpen**	lumpy and misshapen; ugly and ponderous.	जर्जर
592	**Lynch**	hang, hang by the neck	वध
593	**Lynched**	hang, hang by the neck	वध करना
594	**Mace**	staff, club, cudgel, stick, shillelagh, bludgeon, blackjack, truncheon	गदा
595	**Maelstrom**	turbulence, tumult, turmoil, uproar, commotion, disorder, jumble, disarray, chaos	भंवर
596	**Magnanimous**	generous, charitable, benevolent, beneficent, open-handed	उदार
597	**Makeshift**	acting as an interim and temporary measure.	अस्थायी
598	**Malaise**	unhappiness, restlessness, uneasiness, unease, melancholy	अस्वस्थता
599	**Malfeasance**	wrongdoing	दुराचार
600	**Malicious**	spiteful, malevolent, hostile, bitter, venomous, poisonous, evil-intentioned	दुर्भावनापूर्ण
601	**Malign**	harmful, evil, bad, baleful, hostile, inimical, destructive, malevolent	हानिकारक
602	**Manoeuvre**	operation, exercise, activity, move, movement, action	पैंतरेबाज़ी
603	**Massacre**	slaughter, butcher, murder, kill, annihilate, exterminate, execute, liquidate, eliminate, destroy, decimate	नरसंहार
604	**Maul**	to injure by a rough beating, shoving, or the like; bruise	क्षतविक्षत करना
605	**Maven**	an expert or connoisseur.	प्रवीण
606	**Mayhem**	chaos, disorder, confusion, havoc, bedlam, pandemonium, tumult	हाथापाई

SN	Vocabulary	Meaning (Synonyms)	Hindi
607	**Meagre**	inadequate, scanty, scant, paltry, limited, restricted, modest, insufficient, sparse, spare, deficient	अल्प
608	**Meddled**	interfere, butt in, intrude, intervene, interlope, pry, poke, nose	हस्तक्षेप करना
609	**Mediocre**	ordinary, common, commonplace, indifferent, average, middle-of-the-road	औसत दर्जे का
610	**Melancholy**	desolation, sadness, pensiveness, woe, sorrow, melancholia	उदासी
611	**Mete**	dispense, hand out, apportion, distribute, issue, deal out	बाँटना
612	**Microcosm**	a community, place, or situation regarded as encapsulating in miniature the characteristics of something much larger	मनुष्य का सूक्ष्म दर्शन
613	**Milieu**	environment, background, backdrop, setting, context, atmosphere	परिवेश
614	**Millennial**	denoting or relating to a period of a thousand years.	हज़ार साल का
615	**Minuscule**	tiny, minute, microscopic, nanoscopic, very small, little	बहुत छोटा
616	**Mirage**	optical illusion, hallucination, phantasmagoria, apparition	मृगतृष्णा
617	**Mire**	entangle, tangle up, embroil, enmesh, catch up, mix up, involve, bog down	दलदल
618	**Miscreant**	a person who has done something wrong or unlawful.	बदमाश
619	**Missive**	message, communication, letter, word, note, memorandum, line, report	राजनीतिक संदेश
620	**Mitigate**	alleviate, reduce, diminish, lessen, weaken, lighten, attenuate	कम करना
621	**Modicum**	little bit, small amount, particle, degree, speck, fragment, scrap, crumb, grain	अल्पांश
622	**Moiety**	each of two parts into which a thing is or can be divided.	आधा भाग
623	**Momentous**	important, significant, epoch-making, historic, apocalyptic, headline, fateful	सबसे महत्वपूर्ण
624	**Mongers**	a person who encourages a particular activity, especially one that causes trouble	सौदागर
625	**Mongrelised**	cause to become mixed in race, composition, or character.	संकर जाति का बनाना
626	**Monomaniacal**	an inordinate or obsessive zeal for or interest in a single thing, idea, subject, or the like	एकोन्मादी
627	**Moot**	debatable, open to debate, open to discussion	विवादास्पद

SN	Vocabulary	Meaning (Synonyms)	Hindi
628	**Moratorium**	embargo, ban, prohibition, suspension, postponement, stay, stoppage, halt	रोक
629	**Morbid**	ghoulish, macabre, unhealthy, gruesome, grisly, grotesque	रोगी, विकृत
630	**Moribund**	being in the state of dying :approaching death	मरता हुआ
631	**Morphed**	change smoothly from one image to another by small gradual steps using computer animation techniques.	बदलना
632	**Motif**	design, pattern, decoration, figure, shape, logo	मूल भाव
633	**Motley**	miscellaneous, disparate, diverse, assorted, sundry, varied	मिश्रित
634	**Muckraking**	the action of searching out and publicizing scandal about famous people.	कीचड़ उछालने वाले
635	**Mucky**	dirty, filthy, grimy, muddy, mud-caked, grubby, messy, soiled	मलिन
636	**Mulling**	ponder, consider, think over / about, reflect on, contemplate, deliberate	सोचना
637	**Mundane**	humdrum, dull, boring, tedious, monotonous, tiresome, wearisome	सांसारिक
638	**Murky**	dark, gloomy, grey, leaden, dull, dim, overcast, cloudy, clouded, sunless, foggy	धुंधला
639	**Muzzle**	snout, nose, mouth, jaws, maw	नालमुख
640	**Myriad**	multitude, a large / great number / quantity, a lot, scores, quantities, mass	असंख्य
641	**Mystic**	spiritual, religious, transcendental, transcendent, paranormal	रहस्यवादी
642	**Nascent**	(especially of a process or organization) just coming into existence and beginning to display signs of future potential.	नवजात
643	**Navigate**	plan and direct the course of a ship, aircraft, or other form of transport, especially by using instruments or maps.	मार्गनिर्देशन करना
644	**Nefarious**	(typically of an action or activity) wicked or criminal.	कुटिल
645	**Nexus**	a connection or series of connections linking two or more things.	बंधन
646	**Nimbleness**	agility, litheness, sprightliness, light-footedness, nimble-footedness	फुर्तीला
647	**Nonchalance**	(of a person or manner) feeling or appearing casually calm and relaxed; not displaying anxiety, interest, or enthusiasm.	बेपरवाह
648	**Notorious**	infamous, of ill repute, with a bad reputation / name, ill-famed, scandalous	कुख्यात

SN	Vocabulary	Meaning (Synonyms)	Hindi
649	**Noxious**	poisonous, toxic, deadly, virulent	हानिकारक
650	**Nuance**	fine distinction, subtle distinction / difference, shade	अति सूक्ष्म अंतर
651	**Nudge**	poke, elbow, dig, prod, jog, jab, butt	हलके धक्के से ध्यान आकर्षित करना
652	**Nuisance**	source of annoyance / irritation, annoyance, inconvenience, bore, bother	परेशानी
653	**Nutshell**	the hard woody covering around the kernel of a nut	संक्षेप
654	**Obeisance**	respect, homage, worship, adoration, reverence, veneration	श्रद्धा
655	**Obfuscate**	obscure, confuse, make obscure / unclear, blur, muddle, jumble, complicate, garble, muddy, cloud, befog	उलझाना
656	**Obligation**	duty, commitment, responsibility, moral imperative	दायित्व
657	**Obnoxious**	extremely unpleasant.	घृणित
658	**Obscurantism**	the practice of deliberately preventing the facts or full details of something from becoming known.	प्रगतिविरोध
659	**Obsequious**	obedient or attentive to an excessive or servile degree	चापलूस
660	**Obtrusive**	conspicuous, prominent, noticeable, obvious, pronounced, unmistakable	निकला हुआ
661	**Obviate**	preclude, prevent, remove, get rid of, do away with, get round, rule out, eliminate, make unnecessary	अनावश्यक बनाना
662	**Octogenarian**	a person who is between 80 and 89 years old.	अस्सी साल का बुढ़ा
663	**Ominous**	giving the worrying impression that something bad is going to happen; threateningly inauspicious	अमंगल
664	**Onerous**	burdensome, heavy, inconvenient, troublesome, awkward, crushing	कठिन
665	**Onslaught**	a fierce or destructive attack.	हमला
666	**Onus**	burden, responsibility, liability, obligation, duty, weight, load, charge, mantle, encumbrance	दायित्व
667	**Opportune**	auspicious, propitious, favourable, advantageous, heaven-sent, golden, good	समय पर
668	**Oppressive**	harsh, cruel, brutal, repressive, crushing, tyrannical,	दमनकारी

SN	Vocabulary	Meaning (Synonyms)	Hindi
669	**Opulent**	luxurious, sumptuous, palatial, lavishly appointed, lavish, deluxe, rich, lush, luxuriant, splendid, magnificent, grand	धनी
670	**Orator**	speaker, public speaker, speech-maker, lecturer, declaimer, rhetorician	वक्ता
671	**Ordeal**	painful / unpleasant experience, trial, tribulation, test	कठिन परीक्षा
672	**Ostensible**	apparent, seeming, outward, surface, superficial, professed, supposed, avowed, presumed,	ख़याली
673	**Ostentatious**	characterized by pretentious or showy display; designed to impress.	भड़कीला, आडंबरपूर्ण
674	**Ostracise**	exclude, shun, spurn, cold-shoulder, give someone the cold shoulder	बहिष्कृत करना
675	**Ousted**	drive out, expel, force out, throw out, remove, remove from office / power, eject	बेदख़ल
676	**Outcry**	shout, exclamation, cry, yell, howl, whoop, roar, scream, shriek	चिल्लाहट, हाहाकार
677	**Outlandish**	weird, queer, offbeat, far out, freakish, grotesque, quirky,	विचित्र, बाहरी
678	**Outmanoeuvre**	outflank, circumvent, bypass, shake / throw off, get around	मात कर देना
679	**Outrage**	shocking, disgraceful, scandalous, atrocious, appalling, abhorrent, monstrous	अपमानजनक
680	**Overhaul**	a thorough examination of machinery or a system, with repairs or changes made if necessary.	जीर्णोद्धार करना
681	**Overtures**	prelude, introduction, opening, introductory movement, voluntary	प्रस्ताव
682	**Pacifist**	peace-lover, conscientious objector, passive resister, peacemaker	शांतिवादी
683	**Paeans**	song of praise, hymn, psalm, anthem, shout of praise, alleluia	विजय का गीत
684	**Palanquin**	(in India and the East) a covered litter for one passenger, consisting of a large box carried on two horizontal poles by four or six bearers.	पालकी
685	**Palpable**	perceptible, perceivable, visible, noticeable	स्पर्शनीय
686	**Paltry**	small, meagre, trifling, insignificant, negligible, inadequate, insufficient, scant	तुच्छ
687	**Pander**	gratify or indulge (an immoral or distasteful desire or taste or a person with such a desire or taste).	बढ़ावा देना

SN	Vocabulary	Meaning (Synonyms)	Hindi
688	**Paradigm**	a typical example or pattern of something; a pattern or model.	मिसाल
689	**Paradox**	contradiction, contradiction in terms, self-contradiction	विरोधाभास
690	**Parity**	equality, equivalence, uniformity, sameness, consistency	समानता
691	**Parochial**	narrow-minded, small-minded, provincial, insular, narrow, small-town, inward-looking	संकीर्ण
692	**Parsimoniously**	thrifty, frugal, penurious, niggardly, penny-pinching, miserly, tight-fisted	किफ़ायती
693	**Partisan**	supporter, follower, adherent, devotee, champion, backer	पक्षपातपूर्ण
694	**Patronise**	treat condescendingly, treat with condescension, condescend to	सहायता देना
695	**Paucity**	the presence of something in only small or insufficient quantities or amounts.	कमी
696	**Pauperise**	make poor	गरीबी
697	**Pawn**	puppet, dupe, hostage, counter, cog	गिरवी रखना
698	**Peg**	spike, pin, nail, dowel, skewer, rivet, brad, screw, bolt, hook, stick, nog	खूंटी
699	**Penchant**	a strong or habitual liking for something or tendency to do something.	विशेष रुचि
700	**Perceptible**	able to be seen or noticed.	प्रत्यक्ष
701	**Percolate**	filter, drain, drip, ooze, seep, trickle, dribble, strain, leak, leach	प्रसारित हो जाना
702	**Percolation**	Percolation is the process of a liquid slowly passing through a filter	टपकन
703	**Peremptory**	brusque, imperious, high-handed, brisk, abrupt, summary, commanding	आज्ञासूचक, आदेशपूर्ण
704	**Perfunctory**	cursory, desultory; quick, brief, hasty, hurried, rapid, passing, fleeting, summary; token,	असावधान
705	**Perilous**	dangerous, fraught with danger, hazardous, risky, unsafe, treacherous	जोखिम
706	**Pernicious**	harmful, damaging, destructive, injurious, hurtful, detrimental, deleterious, dangerous	हानिकारक
707	**Perpetrator**	a person who carries out a harmful, illegal, or immoral act	अपराधी
708	**Perpetual**	everlasting, never-ending, eternal, permanent, unending, endless	लगातार
709	**Perpetuate**	keep alive, keep going, keep in existence, preserve, conserve, sustain	स्थायी बनाना

SN	Vocabulary	Meaning (Synonyms)	Hindi
710	**Perplex**	puzzle, baffle, mystify, bemuse, bewilder, confound, confuse, nonplus, disconcert, dumbfound, throw	हैरान करना
711	**Perquisite**	a benefit which one enjoys or is entitled to on account of one's job or position.	विशेषाधिकार
712	**Persuasive**	convincing, effective, cogent, compelling, potent, forceful, eloquent, impressive, weighty, influential, sound, valid	प्रेरक
713	**Pertinent**	relevant, to the point, apposite, appropriate, suitable, fitting	उचित
714	**Perturb**	worry, upset, unsettle, disturb, concern, trouble, make anxious	व्याकुल करना
715	**Pervasive**	prevalent, penetrating, pervading, permeating, extensive, ubiquitous	व्यापक
716	**Perversion**	distortion, misrepresentation, falsification, travesty	विकृति
717	**Pessimism**	defeatism, negative thinking, negativity, expecting the worst, doom and gloom	निराशावाद
718	**Petite**	small, dainty, diminutive, slight, little, tiny, elfin, delicate	छोटी कद-काठी की स्त्री
719	**Piece-Meal**	a little at a time, piece by piece, bit by bit, gradually, slowly, in stages	क्रम से
720	**Piliferage**	Inventory control: Reduction in inventory caused by shoplifting, Marine insurance: Theft of a few pieces or a small quantity of a relatively large shipment.	चोरी
721	**Pique**	stimulate, arouse, rouse, provoke, whet, awaken	मनमुटाव
722	**Pittance**	a very small amount, a tiny amount, an insufficient amount, next to nothing, very little	अल्प भाग
723	**Pivotal**	central, crucial, vital, critical, focal, essential, key	केंद्रीय
724	**Placard**	notice, poster, public notice, sign, bill, sticker, advertisement	घोषणापत्र
725	**Plagiarism**	the practice of taking someone else's work or ideas and passing them off as one's own.	साहित्यिक चोरी
726	**Plantain**	a low-growing plant which typically has a rosette of leaves and a slender green flower spike, occurring widely as a weed of lawns.	केला
727	**Platitude**	cliché, truism, commonplace	साधारण बात
728	**Plebiscite**	the direct vote of all the members of an electorate on an important public question such as a change in the constitution.	जनमत संग्रह

SN	Vocabulary	Meaning (Synonyms)	Hindi
729	**Plenitude**	an abundance	विपुलता
730	**Plentiful**	abundant, copious, ample, profuse, rich, lavish, liberal, generous	प्रचुर
731	**Plenum**	an assembly of all the members of a group or committee.	विस्तृत बैठक
732	**Plethora**	a large or excessive amount of something.	बहुतायत
733	**Plexus**	an intricate network or web-like formation.	जाल
734	**Plight**	a dangerous, difficult, or otherwise unfortunate situation.	दुर्दशा
735	**Plummeted**	plunge, fall headlong, hurtle, nosedive, dive, drop, crash	तेज़ी से गिरना
736	**Plunder**	pillage, loot, rob, raid, ransack, strip, fleece, ravage	लूट
737	**Plunge**	jump, dive, hurl oneself, throw oneself, fling oneself, launch oneself	डुबकी
738	**Poignant**	touching, moving, sad, saddening, affecting, pitiful, piteous, pitiable	मार्मिक
739	**Polemic**	diatribe, invective, denunciation, denouncement, rant, tirade, broadside, attack, harangue, verbal onslaught	विवादात्मक
740	**Ponder**	think about, give thought to, consider, review, reflect on, mull over	विचार करना
741	**Posterity**	future generations, succeeding generations, those who come after us	भावी पीढ़ी
742	**Pragmatic**	dealing with things sensibly and realistically in a way that is based on practical rather than theoretical considerations.	व्यावहारिक
743	**Precarious**	uncertain, insecure, unreliable, unsure	संकटपूर्ण, खतरनाक
744	**Precedent**	model, exemplar, example, pattern, previous case, prior case	मिसाल
745	**Precinct**	area, zone, sector, district, section, quarter, region	सीमा
746	**Precocious**	advanced, old beyond one's years, forward, ahead of one's peers, mature	असामयिक
747	**Predecessor**	former / previous holder of the post, forerunner, precursor, antecedent	पूर्वज
748	**Predicament**	difficult situation, awkward situation, mess, difficulty, problematic situation, issue, plight, quandary, trouble	स्थिति
749	**Preemptive**	relating to the purchase of goods or shares by one person or party before the opportunity is offered to others.	रिक्तिपूर्व

SN	Vocabulary	Meaning (Synonyms)	Hindi
750	Prelude	an action or event serving as an introduction to something more important.	प्रस्तावना
751	Premature	untimely, early, too soon, too early, before time	असामयिक
752	Preposterous	absurd, ridiculous, foolish, stupid, ludicrous, farcical, laughable, comical	ऊटपटांग
753	Prerogative	entitlement, right, privilege, advantage, due, birthright	विशेषाधिकार
754	Prevail	win, win out, win through, triumph, be victorious, be the victor, gain the victory, carry the day, carry all before one, finish first	जीतना
755	Prevalent	widespread, prevailing, frequent, usual, common, general, universal, pervasive	प्रचलित
756	Pristine	immaculate, in perfect condition, perfect, in mint condition, as new, unspoilt	प्राचीन
757	Proactive	disposed to take action or effectuate change	सक्रिय
758	Probity	integrity, honesty, uprightness, decency, morality, rectitude, goodness, virtue	ईमानदारी
759	Proclamation	decree, order, edict, command, rule, ruling, announcement, declaration	घोषणा
760	Proclivity	liking, inclination, tendency, leaning, disposition, propensity, bent, bias	झुकाव
761	Procurement	the action or occupation of acquiring military equipment and supplies	खरीद
762	Prodigy	child genius, genius, wonder child, mastermind, virtuoso	प्रतिभाशाली
763	Profligacy	reckless extravagance or wastefulness in the use of resources	आवारगी
764	Profligate	wasteful, extravagant, spendthrift, improvident, prodigal, immoderate	अपव्ययी
765	Progeny	a descendant or the descendants of a person, animal, or plant; offspring.	संतान
766	Proliferation	rapid increase, growth, multiplication, spread, escalation, expansion, build-up	प्रसार
767	Prolific	productive, creative, inventive, fertile	फलदायक
768	Promulgation	to make known by open declaration; publish; proclaim formally or put into operation (a law, decree of a court, etc.)	प्रचार
769	Proselytise	promote, present, spread, proclaim, peddle, propound, preach, back	धर्मांतरण
770	Protagonist	supporter, upholder, adherent, backer, proponent, advocate	नायक
771	Protract	prolong	विलंब करना

SN	Vocabulary	Meaning (Synonyms)	Hindi
772	**Proximity**	closeness, nearness, presence, juxtaposition, propinquity	निकटता
773	**Prudent**	acting with or showing care and thought for the future.	दूरदर्शी
774	**Psephological**	the scientific study of elections	चुनाव विश्लेषक
775	**Pseudonym**	pen name, assumed name, incognito	उपनाम
776	**Punitive**	harsh, severe, stiff, austere, cruel, savage, stringent, burdensome	दंडात्मक
777	**Purport**	gist, substance, drift, implication, intention, meaning	अर्थ लगाना
778	**Purview**	the scope of the influence or concerns of something.	परिधि
779	**Putative**	generally considered or reputed to be.	ख्यात
780	**Quagmire**	swamp, morass, bog, peat bog, marsh, mire, quag, marshland	दलदल
781	**Quandry**	dilemma, plight, predicament, state of uncertainty, state of perplexity	व्याकुलता, नाज़ुक हालत
782	**Quarantine**	a state, period, or place of isolation in which people or animals that have arrived from elsewhere or been exposed to infectious or contagious disease are placed.	अलग करना
783	**Quell**	put an end to, stamp out, put a stop to, end, finish, get rid of	शांत करना
784	**Queshed**	cancel, reverse, rescind, repeal, revoke, retract, countermand, withdraw, take back, rule against, disallow, overturn, override	मिटा देना
785	**Quibbling**	find fault with, raise trivial objections to, complain about, object to	वक्रोक्ति
786	**Quintessential**	typical, prototypical, stereotypical, archetypal, classic, model, essential, standard, stock, representative	सर्वोत्कृष्ट
787	**Quirky**	eccentric, idiosyncratic, unconventional, unorthodox, unusual, off-centre	विचित्र
788	**Ramification**	consequence, result, aftermath, outcome, effect, upshot, issue, sequel	उपशाखा
789	**Rampage**	rush wildly / madly, riot, run riot, go on the rampage, run amok	हंगामा करना
790	**Rampant**	(especially of something unwelcome) flourishing or spreading unchecked.	अनियंत्रित
791	**Rampart**	defensive wall, embankment, earthwork, parapet	किले की दीवार
792	**Ransack**	plunder, pillage, steal from, raid, rob, loot, rifle, sack	तोड़फोड़

SN	Vocabulary	Meaning (Synonyms)	Hindi
793	**Rapport**	affinity, close / special relationship, (mutual) understanding, bond, empathy	घनिष्ठता
794	**Rapprochement**	an establishment or resumption of harmonious relations	मेल-मिलाप
795	**Rapturous**	ecstatic, joyful, joyous, elated, euphoric,	मनमौजी
796	**Ratcheted**	a situation or process that is perceived to be changing in a series of irreversible steps.	शाफ्ट
797	**Raucous**	harsh, strident, screeching, squawky, squawking, sharp, grating, discordant	कर्कश
798	**Ravage**	lay waste, devastate, ruin, leave in ruins, destroy, wreak havoc on, leave desolate, level, raze, demolish, wipe out, wreck, damage	बरबाद कर देना
799	**Rebellion**	uprising, revolt, insurrection, mutiny, revolution	विद्रोह
800	**Rebound**	recover in value, amount, or strength after a decrease or decline.	प्रतिक्षेप
801	**Rebuff**	reject, turn down, spurn, refuse, decline, repudiate	प्रतिघात, झिड़क देना, अस्वीकार
802	**Rebuttal**	refutation, denial, disproving, counter-argument, countering, invalidation, negation	खंडन
803	**Recalcitrant**	having an obstinately uncooperative attitude towards authority or discipline.	आज्ञा न माननेवाला
804	**Reckon**	calculate, compute, work out, put a figure on, figure	अनुमान लगाना
805	**Reconnaissance**	preliminary survey, survey, exploration, observation	पूर्व-परीक्षण
806	**Recourse**	option, possibility, alternative, possible course of action, resort	सहारा
807	**Recuperate**	get better, recover, convalesce, get back to normal, get well	स्वस्थ हो जाना
808	**Recuse**	excuse oneself from a case because of a potential conflict of interest or lack of impartiality	जांच से हटना
809	**Redundant**	unnecessary, not required, inessential, unessential, needless, unneeded	निरर्थक
810	**Refurbish**	renovate, recondition, rehabilitate, revamp, make over, overhaul, restore	नवीनीकरण
811	**Reimpose**	impose (something, especially a law or regulation) again after a lapse.	पुनः लागू
812	**Reinstate**	restore, return to a former position, return to power, put back, replace	पुनः स्थापित करना
813	**Reinvigorate**	give new energy or strength to.	फिर ताजा करना

SN	Vocabulary	Meaning (Synonyms)	Hindi
814	**Reiterated**	say something again or a number of times, typically for emphasis or clarity.	दोहराया
815	**Rejig**	organize (something) differently; rearrange	बदलाव
816	**Rekindle**	revive (something lost or lapsed).	फिर से जलाना
817	**Relegate**	downgrade, lower, lower in rank / status, put down, move down	बाहर निकाल देना
818	**Relent**	change one's mind, do a U-turn, back-pedal, back down	तरस खाना
819	**Reliable**	dependable, good, well founded	विश्वसनीय
820	**Relinquish**	voluntarily cease to keep or claim; give up.	त्यागना
821	**Relish**	condiment, accompaniment, sauce, dressing, flavouring	आनंद
822	**Reluctant**	unwilling, disinclined, unenthusiastic, grudging, resistant, resisting	अनिच्छुक
823	**Reminiscent**	similar to, comparable with, inviting / bearing comparison with	याद ताजा
824	**Remission**	cancellation, setting aside, suspension, revocation, repeal	क्षमा
825	**Remittance**	payment, settlement, money, fee	प्रेषित धन
826	**Remunerative**	lucrative, well paid, financially rewarding, financially worthwhile, moneymaking	पारिश्रमिक–संबंधी
827	**Render**	give, provide, supply, furnish, make available	लौटाना
828	**Rendition**	performance, rendering, interpretation, presentation	प्रतिपादन
829	**Renege**	default on, fail to honour, go back on, break, back out of, pull out of	इनकार
830	**Renunciatory**	relinquishment, giving up, abandonment, resignation, abdication	त्याग
831	**Repartee**	banter, badinage, witty conversation, bantering, raillery, witticism, crosstalk	हाजिर जवाबी
832	**Repatriate**	send (someone) back to their own country.	अपने देश को लौट आना
833	**Repose**	rest, relaxation, inactivity, restfulness, stillness, idleness	आराम करना
834	**Reprehensible**	deplorable, disgraceful, discreditable, disreputable, despicable	निन्दा
835	**Repressive**	oppressive, authoritarian, despotic, tyrannical, tyrannous, dictatorial, fascist, autocratic, undemocratic, anti-democratic	दमन का
836	**Reprieve**	grant a stay of execution to, cancel / postpone / commute / remit someone's punishment	दण्डविराम
837	**Repudiate**	reject, renounce, abandon, forswear, give up, turn one's back on	त्याग करना

SN	Vocabulary	Meaning (Synonyms)	Hindi
838	**Requisite**	necessary, required, prerequisite, essential, indispensable, vital	आवश्यक
839	**Resentment**	bitterness, indignation, irritation, pique, displeasure, dissatisfaction	नाराज़गी
840	**Resilient**	flexible, pliable, pliant, supple, plastic, elastic, springy, rubbery	लचीलाता
841	**Resplendent**	attractive and impressive through being richly colourful or sumptuous.	देदीप्यमान
842	**Resurgent**	increasing or reviving after a period of little activity, popularity, or occurrence.	पुनरुत्थानशील
843	**Retaliate**	fight back, strike back, hit back, respond, react, reply, reciprocate	बदला लेना
844	**Reticence**	reserve, introversion, restraint, inhibition, diffidence, shyness	शांत रहना
845	**Retrieve**	get back, recover, regain (possession of), win back, recoup, reclaim	पुनः प्राप्त
846	**Retrograde**	backward, backwards, reverse, rearward, directed backwards	पतित
847	**Revel**	celebrate, make merry, have a party, party, feast, eat, drink	आनंद लेना
848	**Reverberate**	resound, echo, re-echo, repeat, resonate, pulsate	गूंजना
849	**Revile**	criticize, censure, condemn, attack, inveigh against, rail against, lambaste	गाली देना
850	**Rhetoric**	oratory, eloquence, power of speech, command of language	वक्रपटुता
851	**Ridicule**	mockery, derision, laughter, scorn, scoffing, contempt	उपहास
852	**Rife**	widespread, general, common, universal, extensive	व्याप्त
853	**Rift**	crack, fault, flaw, split, break, breach, fissure, fracture, cleft, crevice	दरार
854	**Rig**	equip, kit out, fit out / up, supply, outfit, furnish, accoutre, array	धांधली
855	**Rigour**	meticulousness, thoroughness, carefulness, attention to detail, diligence	कठोरता
856	**Riposte**	retort, counter, rejoinder, sally, return, retaliation, answer, reply	जवाबी हमल
857	**Ripple**	wavelet, wave, undulation, ripplet, ridge, crease, wrinkle, ruffle	लहर
858	**Riven**	torn apart, split, rent, ripped apart, ruptured, severed	विखंडित
859	**Rivulet**	a small stream of water or another liquid.	छोटी नदी

SN	Vocabulary	Meaning (Synonyms)	Hindi
860	**Robust**	strong, vigorous, sturdy, tough, powerful, powerfully built, solidly built	मजबूत
861	**Rubble**	debris, remains, ruins, wreckage	मलवा
862	**Ruckus**	a row or commotion.	हंगामा
863	**Rue**	bitterly regret (something one has done or allowed to happen) and wish it undone.	पछताना
864	**Rumbling**	an early indication or rumour of dissatisfaction or incipient change.	कुलबुलाना
865	**Ruminate**	think about, contemplate, consider, give thought to	चिंतन करना
866	**Ruthless**	merciless, pitiless, cruel, heartless, hard-hearted, hard, stony-hearted	क्रूर
867	**Sabotage**	wreck, deliberately damage, vandalize, destroy, obstruct, disrupt, cripple, impair	नुक़सान पहुंचाना
868	**Sacrilege**	desecration, profanity, profaneness, profanation, blasphemy	अपवित्रीकरण
869	**Sacrosanct**	sacred, hallowed, respected, inviolable, inviolate, unimpeachable	पुण्यमय
870	**Salience**	the political salience of religion has a considerable impact	प्रमुखता
871	**Sanctity**	holiness, godliness, sacredness, blessedness, saintliness, sanctitude	पवित्रता
872	**Sanguine**	optimistic, bullish, hopeful, buoyant, positive, disposed to look on the bright side	आशावादी
873	**Sarcophagus**	a stone coffin, typically adorned with a sculpture or inscription and associated with the ancient civilizations of Egypt, Rome, and Greece.	पत्थर की बनी हुई कब्र
874	**Satire**	mockery, ridicule, derision, scorn, caricature	व्यंग्य
875	**Scant**	little, little or no, minimal, hardly any, limited, negligible, barely sufficient	अल्प
876	**Scaremongers**	alarmist, prophet of doom, Cassandra, voice of doom	आतंक फैलाना
877	**Scathing**	devastating, withering, blistering, extremely critical, searing	हानि पहुंचाने वाला
878	**Schism**	division, split, rift, breach, rupture, break, separation, severance, estrangement, alienation, detachment	फूट
879	**Scion**	cutting, graft, slip	वंशज
880	**Scourge**	whip, horsewhip, lash, strap, birch, switch, flail	महान कष्ट
881	**Scribble**	write hurriedly, write untidily, write illegibly, scratch, scrawl, doodle	घसीटना

SN	Vocabulary	Meaning (Synonyms)	Hindi
882	**Scruples**	qualms, twinge of conscience, compunction, hesitation, reservations	संदेह
883	**Scuffle**	fight, struggle, tussle, brawl, fracas, rumpus, melee, free-for-all	हाथापाई
884	**Scurrilous**	abusive, vituperative, derogatory, disparaging, denigratory, pejorative	अपमानजनक
885	**Scuttle**	scamper, scurry, scramble, bustle, skip, trot, hurry, hasten, make haste, rush	जल्दी-बाज़ी में चलना
886	**Secession**	withdrawal, break, breakaway, separation, severance, schism, apostasy, leaving, quitting, split, splitting, disaffiliation	अपगमन
887	**Sedentary**	sitting, seated, desk-bound, desk, inactive, still	गतिहीन
888	**Sedition**	conduct or speech inciting people to rebel against the authority of a state or monarch.	राज – द्रोह
889	**Serendipity**	chance, happy chance, accident, happy accident, fluke	नसीब
890	**Shambles**	chaos, mess, muddle, confusion, disorder, disarray, disorganization	खंडहर
891	**Shanty**	a small, crudely built shack.	कुटिया
892	**Shoddy**	poor-quality, inferior, second-rate, third-rate, low-grade, cheap, cheapjack, tawdry	तुच्छ
893	**Shun**	avoid, evade, eschew, steer clear of, shy away from, fight shy of	सीधे खड़े हो
894	**Simulacrum**	an image or representation of someone or something	कपटरूप
895	**Sinister**	menacing, threatening, ominous, forbidding, baleful, frightening	भयावह
896	**Skew**	neither parallel nor at right angles to a specified or implied line; askew; crooked.	तिरछा
897	**Skirmish**	fight, battle, clash, conflict, encounter, confrontation, engagement	झड़प
898	**Skullduggery**	trickery, swindling, fraudulence, double-dealing, sharp practice	छल-कपट
899	**Slackness**	not using due diligence, care, or dispatch :negligent.	ढिलाई
900	**Slain**	kill, murder, put to death, do to death, put to the sword, butcher, cut down, cut to pieces	हत्या करना
901	**Sleuths**	private detective, detective, private investigator, investigator	गुप्तचर
902	**Slew**	turn or slide violently or uncontrollably.	मोड़
903	**Slippage**	the action or process of slipping or subsiding.	गिरावट
904	**Slither**	move smoothly over a surface with a twisting or oscillating motion.	सरकते हुए जाना

SN	Vocabulary	Meaning (Synonyms)	Hindi
905	**Sluggish**	inactive, quiet, slow, slow-moving, slack, flat, depressed, stagnant, static	सुस्त
906	**Slump**	sit heavily, flop, flump, collapse, sink, fall, subside; sag, slouch	मंदी
907	**Slush**	sentimentality, mawkishness, over-sentimentality, emotionalism, overemotionalism	कीचड़, नरम मिट्टी
908	**Smacked**	slap, hit, strike, spank, cuff, clout, thump, punch, rap, swat, thwack	मारना
909	**Smorgasbord**	a wide range of something; a variety.	एक संग्रह जिसमें कई तरह की चीजें होती हैं
910	**Snag**	obstacle, difficulty, complication, catch, hitch, stumbling block, pitfall	रोड़ा
911	**Snowballed**	increase rapidly in size, intensity, or importance.	तेज़ी से बढ़ जाना
912	**Snub**	insult, slight, affront, humiliate, treat disrespectfully	अपमान
913	**Solidarity**	unanimity, unity, like-mindedness, agreement, accord, harmony, consensus	एकजुटता
914	**Spate**	a large number of similar things coming in quick succession.	आवेश
915	**Spew**	emit, discharge, eject, expel, belch out, pour out, spout, disgorge	उबकाई
916	**Splurge**	an act of spending money freely or extravagantly.	शेख़ी
917	**Spree**	a spell or sustained period of unrestrained activity of a particular kind.	आनंद का उत्सव
918	**Spruce**	neat, well groomed, well turned out, well dressed, besuited, smart,	सजाना
919	**Spur**	stimulus, incentive, encouragement, stimulant, stimulation	प्रेरणा
920	**Spurious**	bogus, fake, not genuine, specious, false, factitious, counterfeit, fraudulent	जाली, कृत्रिम
921	**Spurn**	refuse, decline, say no to, reject, rebuff, scorn, turn down	अस्वीकार करना
922	**Spurt**	squirt, shoot, spray, fountain, jet, erupt	उछाल
923	**Squandered**	waste, misspend, misuse, throw away, dissipate, fritter away	गंवाना
924	**Squeamish**	scrupulous, principled, conscientious, fastidious, particular, punctilious, finicky, fussy, prissy, prudish	नकचढ़ा

SN	Vocabulary	Meaning (Synonyms)	Hindi
925	**Stagger**	lurch, walk unsteadily, reel, sway, teeter, totter, stumble	लड़खड़ाहट
926	**Stance**	posture, body position, pose, attitude	स्वरूप
927	**Standalone**	(of computer hardware or software) able to operate independently of other hardware or software.	अकेले कर सकना
928	**Stark**	sharply delineated, sharp, sharply defined, well focused, crisp, distinct, obvious, evident, clear, clear-cut	पुष्ट
929	**Starvation**	suffering or death caused by lack of food	भुखमरी
930	**Staunch**	stalwart, loyal, faithful, trusty, committed, devoted, dedicated, dependable, reliable, steady, constant	निष्ठावान
931	**Steadfast**	loyal, faithful, committed, devoted, dedicated, dependable, reliable, steady, true, constant, staunch	दृढ़
932	**Stealth**	furtiveness, secretiveness, secrecy, surreptitiousness, sneakiness	चुपके
933	**Straddle**	sit / stand astride, bestride, bestraddle	पैर फैलाकर बैठना
934	**Strenuous**	arduous, difficult, hard, tough, taxing, demanding	दृढ़
935	**Strewn**	scatter, spread, disperse, distribute, litter, toss, sprinkle, sow,	बिखरे
936	**Strident**	harsh, raucous, rough, grating, rasping, jarring, loud, stentorian	तेज़
937	**Strife**	conflict, friction, discord, disagreement, dissension, variance	विवाद
938	**Stringent**	strict, firm, rigid, rigorous, severe, harsh, tough, tight, exacting, demanding	कड़ी से कड़ी
939	**Stubble**	bristles, whiskers, designer stubble, hair, facial hair, beard	कड़ा बाल
940	**Stultify**	hamper, impede, obstruct, thwart, frustrate, foil, suppress	मूर्ख बनाना
941	**Stupendous**	amazing, astounding, astonishing, extraordinary, remarkable, wonderful, prodigious	विस्मयकारी, बृहत्
942	**Stutterer**	to speak with involuntary disruption or blocking of speech (as by repetition or prolongation of vocal sounds)	हकलाना
943	**Subdued**	sombre, low-spirited, downcast, sad, dejected, depressed, low, gloomy	नियंत्रित
944	**Subjugation**	the action of bringing someone or something under domination or control.	दमन

SN	Vocabulary	Meaning (Synonyms)	Hindi
945	**Submerged**	flood, inundate, deluge, engulf, swamp, immerse, drown	जलमग्न
946	**Subpoena**	require (a document or other evidence) to be submitted to a court of law.	शास्तिलेख
947	**Succour**	help, aid, bring aid to, give help to, give / render assistance to, assist,	सहायता
948	**Succumb**	yield, give in, give way, submit, surrender, capitulate, cave in	मर जाना
949	**Supplant**	replace, displace, supersede, take the place of, take over from, substitute for, undermine	उखाड़ना, हटाना
950	**Surfeit**	an excessive amount of something.	अतिरेक
951	**Surveillance**	observation, scrutiny, watch, view, inspection,	निगरानी
952	**Swathe**	a broad strip or area of something.	पट्टा
953	**Sycophant**	toady, creep, crawler, fawner, flatterer, flunkey, truckler, groveller, doormat, lickspittle	चापलूस
954	**Tactical**	calculated, planned, plotted, prudent, strategic	सामरिक
955	**Tame**	domesticate, break, train, master, subdue, subjugate	पालतू
956	**Tandem**	having two things arranged one in front of the other.	एक के पीछे एक
957	**Tantamount**	equivalent to, equal to, amounting to, as good as, more or less, synonymous with, virtually the same as,	समान
958	**Tantrum**	fit of temper, fit of rage, fit of pique, fit, outburst, flare-up, blow-up, pet, paroxysm	नखरे
959	**Tardy**	slow in action or response; sluggish	मंदा
960	**Tarnish**	become discoloured, discolour, stain, rust, oxidize, corrode, deteriorate	कलंकित करना
961	**Tatters**	rags, scraps, shreds, bits, pieces, bits and pieces, torn pieces, ragged pieces	फटे कपड़े
962	**Tawdry**	gaudy, flashy, showy, garish, loud	भड़कीला
963	**Teem**	be full of, be filled with, be alive with, be brimming with, be overflowing with	भरा हुआ
964	**Temptation**	desire, urge, itch, impulse, inclination	प्रलोभन
965	**Tenacity**	persistence, pertinacity, determination, perseverance, doggedness, tenaciousness, single-mindedness, strength of will	तप, सख्त पकड़
966	**Tenuous**	slight, insubstantial, flimsy, negligible, weak, fragile	सूक्ष्म
967	**Tepid**	unenthusiastic, apathetic, half-hearted, indifferent	गुनगुना
968	**Terse**	curt, brusque, abrupt, clipped, blunt, gruff, short, brief, concise	संक्षिप्त

SN	Vocabulary	Meaning (Synonyms)	Hindi
969	**Theocracy**	a system of government in which priests rule in the name of God or a god.	थेअक्रसी
970	**Thrash**	hit, beat, flog, whip, horsewhip, scourge, lash, flagellate, flail, strap, birch	पीटना
971	**Thrive**	flourish, prosper, grow vigorously, develop well, burgeon, bloom, blossom	फलना
972	**Thwart**	prevent (someone) from accomplishing something.	विफल
973	**Tilt**	a sloping position or movement	झुकाव
974	**Tinker**	try to mend / improve, work amateurishly on, fiddle with	ठठेरा
975	**Tirade**	diatribe, invective, polemic, denunciation, rant, broadside	कड़ी निंदा
976	**Titular**	nominal, in title / name only, formal, official, ceremonial	शीर्षक
977	**Tizzy**	a state of nervous excitement or agitation.	घबराहट
978	**Topple**	fall, tumble, overturn, overbalance, tip, keel, drop, pitch, plunge, capsize	गिर पड़ना
979	**Torpedo**	a cigar-shaped self-propelled underwater missile designed to be fired from a ship or submarine or dropped into the water from an aircraft and to explode on reaching a target.	जहाज तोड़ने का गोला
980	**Totalitarian**	authoritarian, autocratic, autarchic, dictatorial, tyrannical, oppressive	अधिनायकवादी
981	**Totalitarianism**	a system of government that is centralized and dictatorial and requires complete subservience to the state	सर्वसत्तावाद
982	**Traction**	grip, friction, adhesion, purchase, resistance	संकर्षण
983	**Trample**	tread on and crush.	रौंद
984	**Tranche**	a portion of something, especially money.	अंश
985	**Tranquillity**	peace, peacefulness, restfulness, repose, reposefulness, calm, calmness	शांति
986	**Transcend**	be or go beyond the range or limits of (a field of activity or conceptual sphere).	हावी होना
987	**Transient**	transitory, temporary, short-lived, short-term, ephemeral, impermanent, brief, short, momentary	क्षणिक
988	**Travails**	engage in painful or laborious effort.	गम
989	**Trawler**	a fishing boat used for trawling.	जालदार जहाज़
990	**Treacherous**	traitorous, disloyal, perfidious, faithless, unfaithful, duplicitous, false-hearted	नमक हराम
991	**Tremendous**	very great, huge, enormous, immense, colossal, massive	अद्भुत

SN	Vocabulary	Meaning (Synonyms)	Hindi
992	**Tremors**	trembling, shaking, shakiness, tremble, shake, quivering, quiver	झटके
993	**Trenchant**	incisive, cutting, pointed, piercing, penetrating, sharp, keen	कटु, तीव्र
994	**Trepidation**	a feeling of fear or anxiety about something that may happen	घबराहट
995	**Trifle**	unimportant thing / matter, trivial thing / matter, triviality, thing / matter of no consequence	तुच्छ वस्तु
996	**Triumvirate**	the office of triumvir in ancient Rome, a group of three people who are in control of an activity or organization:	तिकड़ी
997	**Trounced**	defeat utterly, beat hollow, win a resounding victory over	पीटना
998	**Trudge**	plod, tramp, drag oneself, walk heavily, walk slowly, plough, slog, footslog, toil, trek, clump, clomp, lumber	पैदल चलना
999	**Tryst**	a private romantic rendezvous between lovers.	गुप्त भेंट
1000	**Tug**	pull, pluck	खींचातानी
1001	**Tumultuous**	loud, deafening, thunderous, thundering, ear-shattering, ear-splitting	उतार-चढ़ाव भरे
1002	**Turf**	grass and the surface layer of earth held together by its roots.	मैदान
1003	**Turmoil**	confusion, upheaval(s), turbulence, tumult, disorder, commotion, disturbance	उथल-पुथल
1004	**Turpitude**	wickedness, immorality, depravity, corruption, corruptness, vice, degeneracy	अधमता
1005	**Tussle**	scuffle, fight, struggle, skirmish, brawl, scrimmage, scramble, scrum	संघर्ष
1006	**Tutelage**	protection of or authority over someone or something; guardianship.	संरक्षण
1007	**Tweak**	pull sharply, twist, tug, pinch, nip, twitch, squeeze, jerk	मरोड़ना
1008	**Ubiquitous**	omnipresent, ever-present, present everywhere, everywhere, all-over, all over the place	सर्वव्यापक
1009	**Unabated**	without any reduction in intensity or strength.	ताकत में बिना किसी कमी के
1010	**Unanimous**	united, in complete agreement, in complete accord, of one mind	एकमत
1011	**Unctuosity**	the quality of being excessively flattering or ingratiating.	चाटुकारिता

SN	Vocabulary	Meaning (Synonyms)	Hindi
1012	**Undaunted**	unafraid, undismayed, unalarmed, unflinching, unshrinking, unabashed	निडर
1013	**Unencumbered**	not having any burden or impediment.	अभारग्रस्त
1014	**Unfazed**	not disconcerted or perturbed.	बेफिक्र
1015	**Unfettered**	unrestrained, unrestricted, unconstrained, free, unbridled, untrammelled, unchecked, unconfined, unimpeded	निरंकुश
1016	**Unflappable**	having or showing calmness in a crisis.	स्थिर
1017	**Unfurl**	make or become spread out from a rolled or folded state, especially in order to be open to the wind.	फैलाना
1018	**Unhinged**	mentally unbalanced; deranged.	घबराना
1019	**Unprecedented**	unparalleled, unequalled, unmatched, unrivalled, without parallel	अभूतपूर्व
1020	**Unsavoury**	unpalatable, unappetizing, unpleasant, distasteful	बेस्वाद
1021	**Unscrupulous**	unprincipled, unethical, immoral, amoral, conscienceless, untrustworthy, shameless, reprobate, exploitative, corrupt	अनैतिक
1022	**Untenable**	indefensible, undefendable, unarguable, insupportable, refutable	असमर्थनीय
1023	**Upheaval**	disruption, upset, disturbance, trouble, turbulence	उथल-पुथल
1024	**Usurious**	relating to or characterized by usury; extortionate.	अति ब्याज लेने वाला
1025	**Utterance**	remark, comment, word, expression, statement, observation, declaration	कथन
1026	**Vague**	indistinct, indefinite, indeterminate, unclear; More	अस्पष्ट
1027	**Vainglorious**	excessively proud of oneself or one's achievements; overly vain.	गुमानी
1028	**Valedictory**	farewell, goodbye, leaving, parting	बिदाई का
1029	**Valiant**	brave, fearless, courageous, valorous, plucky, intrepid, heroic	बहादुर
1030	**Valorise**	raise or fix the price or value of (a commodity or currency) by artificial means, especially by government action.	मूल्यवर्धन
1031	**Vandal**	a person who deliberately destroys or damages property belonging to others.	उपद्रवादी
1032	**Vanguard**	forefront, van, advance guard, avant-garde, spearhead	अग्र-दल
1033	**Vantage**	point of view, viewpoint, standpoint, stance, stand, view, opinion, position	सहूलियत

SN	Vocabulary	Meaning (Synonyms)	Hindi
1034	Vehemently	in a forceful, passionate, or intense manner; with great feeling.	जोरदार
1035	Vendetta	feud, blood feud, quarrel, argument, falling-out, wrangle, clash, altercation, dispute	प्रतिशोध
1036	Veneer	a thin decorative covering of fine wood applied to a coarser wood or other material.	मुखावरण
1037	Venture	travel, journey, go, move, proceed, progress, set out, set forth	उद्यम
1038	Veracity	conformity to facts; accuracy.	सच्चाई
1039	Verbatim	word for word, letter for letter, line for line, to the letter, literally, exactly, precisely	शब्द प्रति शब्द
1040	Veritable	used for emphasis, often to qualify a metaphor.	यथार्थ
1041	Versatile	adaptable, flexible, all-round, multifaceted, multitalented	बहुमुखी
1042	Veteran	a person who has had long experience in a particular field.	अनुभवी
1043	Vetted	screen, assess, evaluate, appraise, weigh up, examine	निरीक्षण किया
1044	Vex	annoy, irritate, infuriate, anger, incense, inflame, enrage, irk	तंग करना
1045	Vexatious	annoying, vexing, irritating, irksome, displeasing, infuriating, maddening, exasperating, provoking, galling	तंग करने वाला
1047	Viable	workable, feasible, practicable, practical, applicable	करने योग्य
1048	Vibrant	spirited, lively, full of life, full of spirit, high-spirited, energetic, sprightly	फुरतीला
1049	Vicinity	surrounding district, surrounding area, neighbourhood, locality, locale	आस-पास
1050	Vicious	brutal, ferocious, savage, violent, dangerous, ruthless, remorseless, merciless	शातिर
1051	Vigilant	watchful, on the lookout, observant, sharp-eyed, keen-eyed, gimlet-eyed	जागरूक
1052	Vigorous	robust, healthy, in good health, hale and hearty, strong	जोरदार
1053	Vindicate	acquit, clear, absolve, free from blame, declare innocent, exonerate, exculpate,	साबित करना
1054	Virulent	poisonous, toxic, venomous, noxious, deadly, lethal, fatal, mortal	विषैला
1055	Vital	essential, indispensable, crucial, key, necessary	महत्वपूर्ण, अत्यावश्यक
1056	Vitiate	spoil or impair the quality or efficiency of.	भ्रष्ट करना

SN	Vocabulary	Meaning (Synonyms)	Hindi
1057	**Vitriolic**	acrimonious, rancorous, bitter, caustic, mordant, acerbic, astringent, acid, acrid	कटु
1058	**Vociferous**	expressing or characterized by vehement opinions; loud and forceful.	कोलाहलकारी
1059	**Void**	invalid, null and void, null, nullified, cancelled, revoked, rescinded,	निरर्थक
1060	**Volition**	the faculty or power of using one's will.	इच्छाशक्ति
1061	**Vulnerable**	in danger, in peril, in jeopardy, at risk, endangered, unsafe, unprotected	चपेट में
1062	**Wanton**	deliberate, wilful, malicious, malevolent, spiteful, vicious, wicked, evil, cruel	प्रचंड
1063	**Wean**	accustom (someone) to managing without something which they have become dependent on	अलग करना
1064	**Welter**	confusion, jumble, tangle, clutter, mess, hotchpotch	उथल-पुथल
1065	**Whiff**	faint smell, brief smell, trace, sniff, scent, odour, aroma	हल्की गन्ध
1066	**Whim**	impulse, urge, notion, fancy, whimsy, foible, idea, caprice	तरंग, झक
1067	**Whimsical**	fanciful, playful, mischievous, waggish, quaint, fantastic, unusual	सनकी
1068	**Whip**	flog, scourge, flagellate, lash, birch, switch, tan, strap	कोड़ा
1069	**Whittle**	pare, shave, peel, cut, hew, trim, carve, shape, model	छीलना
1070	**Winnowed**	blow a current of air through (grain) in order to remove the chaff.	फटकना
1071	**Wrath**	extreme anger.	कोप
1072	**Wrench**	tug, pull, jerk, jolt, wrest, heave, twist;	ऐंठन
1073	**Xenophobia**	dislike of or prejudice against people from other countries.	विदेशियों के प्रति विकर्षण या घृणा
1074	**Yearn**	long, pine, crave, desire, want, want badly, wish, have / feel a longing, covet	लालसा करना
1075	**Zeal**	passion, zealousness, committedness, ardour, love, fervour, fire, avidity	उत्साह
1076	**Zealot**	fanatic, enthusiast, extremist, radical, Young Turk, diehard, activist	कट्टरपंथी
1077	**Zeitgeist**	the defining spirit or mood of a particular period of history as shown by the ideas and beliefs of the time.	युगचेतना

SN	Word	Meaning
1	**accept**	to receive
	except	with the exclusion of
2	**advice**	recommendation (noun)
	advise	to recommend (verb)
3	**adverse**	unfavorable
	averse	opposed to
4	**affect**	to influence (verb); emotional response (noun)
	effect	result (noun); to cause (verb)
5	**aisle**	space between rows
	isle	island
6	**allude**	to make indirect reference to
	elude	to avoid
7	**allusion**	indirect reference
	illusion	false idea, misleading appearance
8	**already**	by this time
	all ready	fully prepared
9	**alright**	OK
	all right	everything is okay
10	**altar**	sacred platform or place
	alter	to change
11	**altogether**	thoroughly
	all together	everyone/everything in one place
12	**a lot**	a quantity; many of something
	allot	to divide or portion out
13	**angel**	supernatural being, good person
	angle	shape made by joining 2 straight lines
14	**are**	plural form of "to be"
	our	plural form of "my"
15	**accent**	pronunciation common to a region
	ascent	the act of rising or climbing
	assent	consent, agreement
16	**assistance**	help
	assistants	helpers
17	**bare**	nude, unadorned
	bear	to carry; an animal
18	**beside**	close to; next to
	besides	except for; in addition
19	**boar**	a wild male pig
	bore	to drill a hole through
20	**board**	piece of wood
	bored	uninterested
21	**born**	brought into life
	borne	past participle of "to bear" (carry)

SN	Word	Meaning
22	**breath**	air taken in (noun)
	breathe	to take in air (verb)
23	**brake**	device for stopping
	break	destroy; make into pieces
24	**buy**	to purchase
	by	next to; through the agency of
25	**canvas**	heavy cloth
	canvass	to take a survey; a survey
26	**capital**	major city
	capitol	government building
27	**choose**	to pick
	chose	past tense of "to choose"
28	**clothes**	garments
	cloths	pieces of fabric
29	**coarse**	rough
	course	path; series of lectures
30	**complement**	something that completes
	compliment	praise, flattery
31	**continuous**	without stopping
	continual	repeated with breaks in between
32	**conscience**	sense of morality
	conscious	awake, aware
33	**corps**	regulated group
	corpse	dead body
34	**council**	governing body
	counsel	advice; to give advice
35	**dairy**	place where milk products are processed
	diary	personal journal
36	**disinterested**	impartial or neutral
	uninterested	bored or lacking interest
37	**descent**	downward movement
	dissent	disagreement
38	**dessert**	final, sweet course in a meal
	desert	to abandon; dry, sandy area
39	**device**	a plan; a tool or utensil
	devise	to create
40	**discreet**	modest, prudent behavior
	discrete	a separate thing, distinct
41	**do**	a verb indicating performance or execution of a task
	dew	water droplets condensed from air
	due	as a result of
42	**dominant**	commanding, controlling
	dominate	to control

SN	Word	Meaning
43	**die**	to lose life; one of a pair of dice
	dye	to change or add color
44	**dyeing**	changing or adding color
	dying	losing life
45	**elicit**	to draw out
	illicit	illegal, forbidden
46	**eminent**	prominent
	imminent	about to happen
47	**emigrate**	to leave one country or region to settle in another
	immigrate	to enter another country and reside there
48	**envelop**	to surround (verb)
	envelope	container for a letter (noun)
49	**ensure**	to make sure by double checking
	assure	to guarantee
	insure	to provide insurance
50	**everyday**	routine, commonplace, ordinary (adj.)
	every day	each day, succession (adj. + noun)
51	**fair**	light skinned; just, honest; a carnival
	fare	money for transportation; food
52	**farther**	at a greater(measurable) distance
	further	in greater(non-measurable) depth
53	**few**	that can be counted
	less	that can't be counted
54	**formally**	conventionally, with ceremony
	formerly	previously
55	**forth**	forward
	fourth	number four in a list
56	**gorilla**	animal in ape family
	guerrilla	soldier specializing in surprise attacks
57	**good**	The word "good" is an adjective.
	well	The word "well" is an adverb.
58	**hear**	to sense sound by ear
	here	in this place
59	**heard**	past tense of "to hear"
	herd	group of animals
60	**hoard**	a hidden fund or supply, a cache
	horde	a large group or crowd, swarm
61	**hole**	opening
	whole	complete; an entire thing
62	**human**	relating to the species homo sapiens
	humane	compassionate
63	**its**	possessive form of "it"
	it's	contraction for "it is"

SN	Word	Meaning
64	knew	past tense of "know"
	new	fresh, not yet old
65	know	to comprehend
	no	negative
66	i	I is a subject prounoun and it's used for the subject of the sentence
	me	Me is an object pronoun
67	later	after a time
	latter	second one of two things
68	lead	heavy metal substance; to guide
	led	past tense of "to lead"
69	lessen	to decrease
	lesson	something learned and/or taught
70	lightning	storm-related electricity
	lightening	making lighter
71	loose	unbound, not tightly fastened
	lose	to misplace
72	maybe	perhaps (adv.)
	may be	might be (verb)
73	meat	animal flesh
	meet	to encounter
	mete	to measure; to distribute
74	metal	a hard organic substance
	medal	a flat disk stamped with a design
	mettle	courage, spirit, energy
75	miner	a worker in a mine
	minor	underage person (noun); less important (adj.)
76	moral	distinguishing right from wrong; lesson of a fable or story
	morale	attitude or outlook usually of a group
77	passed	past tense of "to pass"
	past	at a previous time
78	patience	putting up with annoyances
	patients	people under medical care
79	peace	absence of war
	piece	part of a whole; musical arrangement
80	peak	point, pinnacle, maximum
	peek	to peer through or look furtively
	pique	fit of resentment, feeling of wounded vanity
81	pedal	the foot lever of a bicycle or car
	petal	a flower segment
	peddle	to sell
82	personal	intimate; owned by a person
	personnel	employees

SN	Word	Meaning
83	**plain**	simple, unadorned
	plane	to shave wood; aircraft (noun)
84	**precede**	to come before
	proceed	to continue
85	**presence**	attendance; being at hand
	presents	gifts
86	**principal**	foremost (adj.); administrator of a school (noun)
	principle	moral conviction, basic truth
87	**quiet**	silent, calm
	quite	very
88	**rain**	water drops falling; to fall like rain
	reign	to rule
	rein	strap to control an animal (noun); to guide or control (verb)
89	**raise**	to lift up
	raze	to tear down
90	**rational**	having reason or understanding
	rationale	principles of opinion, beliefs
91	**respectfully**	with respect
	respectively	in that order
92	**reverend**	title given to clergy; deserving respect
	reverent	worshipful
93	**right**	correct; opposite of left
	rite	ritual or ceremony
	write	to put words on paper
94	**road**	path
	rode	past tense of "to ride"
95	**scene**	place of an action; segment of a play
	seen	viewed; past participle of "to see"
96	**sense**	perception, understanding
	since	measurement of past time; because
97	**sight**	scene, view, picture
	site	place, location
	cite	to document or quote (verb)
98	**stationary**	standing still
	stationery	writing paper
99	**straight**	unbending
	strait	narrow or confining; a waterway
100	**taught**	past tense of "to teach"
	taut	tight
101	**than**	used to introduce second element; compared to
	then	at that time; next
102	**their**	possessive form of "they"
	there	in that place

SN	Word	Meaning
	they're	contraction for "they are"
103	through	finished; into and out of
	threw	past tense of "to throw"
	thorough	complete
104	to	toward
	too	also; very (used to show emphasis)
	two	number following one
105	track	course, road
	tract	pamphlet; plot of ground
106	waist	midsection of the body
	waste	discarded material; to squander
107	waive	forgo, renounce
	wave	flutter, move back and forth
108	weak	not strong
	week	seven days
109	weather	climatic condition
	whether	if
	wether	a neutered male sheep
110	where	in which place
	were	past tense of "to be"
111	which	one of a group
	witch	female sorcerer
112	whose	possessive for "of who"
	who's	contraction for "who is"
113	your	possessive for "of you"
	you're	contraction for "you are"
	yore	time long past

SN	Select the most appropriate homonym to fill in the blank.	Answer
	Homonym Questions asked in Delhi Police Head Constable 2022	
1	He is not a _______ Don't misunderstand him. 1) cheat 2) chit 3) sheath 4) chid	**cheat**
2	The person who used to _______ the girl got arrested last week. 1) stalk 2) laugh at 3) like 4) adore	**stalk**
3	You need to _______ your car in the designated area. 1) park 2) took 3) put 4) stand	**park**
4	The room was _______ with fans. 1) cooled 2) coaled 3) cold 4) cowled	**cooled**
5	Leaving his friend, Ramu said, "Next time we meet, I will _______ you a drink". 1) bye 2) bi 3) by 4) buy	**buy**
6	The _______ of a cow is used as manure. 1) don 2) dun 3) dunk 4) dung	**dung**
7	The institute is known for _______ discipline. 1) marked 2) marshal 3) marginal 4) martial	**martial**
8	A huge _______will be erected outdoors for the birthday celebrations. 1) tenth 2) dent 3) tend 4) tent	**tent**
9	_______worship is a predominant part of some religions. 1) Idyl 2) Idle 3) Idol 4) Idyll	**Idol**
10	The old doors _______ whenever they are opened. 1) crick 2) cry 3) creak 4) creek	**creak**
11	Do any of the students still _______ letters to their families? 1) right 2) writ 3) write 4) rite	**write**
12	The _______ pierced through the skin. 1) teeth 2) stick 3) nail 4) stone	**nail**
13	In case of a snake _______, villagers in many places do not go to the hospital. They prefer witch doctors. 1) byte 2) bite 3) bight 4) bait	**bite**
14	Sometimes, when a speaker changes his pitch of voice, it conveys a different _______ to the listeners. 1) cense 2) sense 3) cents 4) scents	**sense**
15	She is not keeping _______ these days. 1) good 2) well 3) notes 4) better	**well**
16	He declared himself a _______ saying he can predict anything. 1) sear 2) seer 3) sere 4) cere	**seer**
17	The _______ of musicians are amazing. 1) bunch 2) band 3) choir 4) group	**band**

SN	Phrasal Verb	Meaning
1	**Abide by**	to respect or obey a decision, a law or a rule
2	**Account for**	to explain, give a reason
3	**Add up**	to make sense // to come to the expected total
4	**Advise against**	to recommend not doing something
5	**Agree with**	to have the same opinion as someone else
6	**Aim at**	to point a weapon at someone
7	**Allow for**	to take into consideration
8	**Appeal to**	to plead or make a request
9	**Apply for**	to make a formal request for something
10	**Ask around**	ask many people the same question
11	**Ask for**	to request something
12	**Ask out**	invite on a date
13	**Back away**	to move backwards, in fear or dislike
14	**Back down**	to withdraw, concede defeat
15	**Back off**	when you leave an emotional situation // to allow someone to handle something alone
16	**Back up**	to give support or encouragement
17	**Bank on**	to base your hopes on something / someone
18	**Beat up**	when someone punches, kicks, or hits someone repeatedly using fists or with an object
19	**Beef up**	to make changes or an improvement
20	**Believe in**	to feel confident about something or someone
21	**Bite off**	to use your teeth to bite a piece of something
22	**Black out**	to faint, lose consciousness
23	**Block off**	to separate using a barrier
24	**Blow away**	when the wind moves an object from where it was
25	**Blow off**	when the wind removes something from its place
26	**Blow out**	to extinguish or make a flame stop burning
27	**Blow up**	explode // add air
28	**Boil down to**	to have determined or analyzed the solution or reason for something
29	**Boot up**	to start a computer by loading an operating system
30	**Break away**	to separate from a crowd
31	**Break down**	to go out of order, cease to function // divide into smaller parts
32	**Break in**	force entry to a building
33	**Break into**	to enter by force
34	**Break off**	to remove a part of something with force
35	**Break out**	to start suddenly // to escape from a place
36	**Break through**	to make a way through a barrier or a surface
37	**Break up**	to come to an end (marriage, relationship)
38	**Bring back**	to return something you've borrowed
39	**Bring down**	make unhappy
40	**Bring over**	to bring someone from one place or area to another

SN	Phrasal Verb	Meaning
41	**Bring up**	to raise a child
42	**Brush off**	to remove something (dust particle, insect, etc)
43	**Brush up**	to improve, refresh one's knowledge of something
44	**Build in/into**	to add a fixture or component to a certain area or place through construction
45	**Bump into**	to meet by chance or unexpectedly
46	**Burn down**	when someone uses fire to destroy a structure
47	**Burn out**	stop working
48	**Burn up**	to destroy something with heat or fire
49	**Burst out**	to suddenly do or say something
50	**Butt in**	to interrupt a conversation or activity
51	**Call around**	phone many different places/people
52	**Call back**	to return a phone call
53	**Call in**	to request that someone come and help
54	**Call off**	to cancel
55	**Call on**	ask for an answer or opinion
56	**Call up**	to summon before an authority
57	**Calm down**	to become more relaxed, less angry or upset
58	**Care for**	to nurture or take care of someone
59	**Carry away**	to do something out of the ordinary due to strong emotions
60	**Carry on**	to continue
61	**Carry out**	to do something as specified
62	**Catch on**	to understand or realize something
63	**Catch up**	to move faster to reach someone that is ahead of you
64	**Cheat on**	when you are emotionally and/or sexually unfaithful to your girlfriend/boyfriend or spouse
65	**Check in**	arrive and register at a hotel or airport
66	**Check out**	to pay one's bill and leave // look at carefully
67	**Cheer up**	become happier
68	**Chicken out**	to refrain from doing something because of fear
69	**Chip in**	help
70	**Chop up**	to cut something into pieces with a knife
71	**Clam up**	to refuse to speak
72	**Clamp down on**	to act strictly to prevent something
73	**Clean out**	to clean or clear the inside of something thoroughly
74	**Clean up**	tidy, clean
75	**Clear out**	to remove things completely from an area or place
76	**Clear up**	to do something to solve a problem or a misunderstanding
77	**Clog up**	when something in a drain or valve prevents the flow of water or other liquids
78	**Close down**	when the activities or services of a business permanently end
79	**Close off**	to block an entrance or pathway
80	**Come about**	when something happens or occurs

SN	Phrasal Verb	Meaning
81	**Come across**	find unexpectedly
82	**Come apart**	separate
83	**Come back**	to return to a place
84	**Come down**	to move from a higher to a lower position or from north to south // become sick
85	**Come forward**	volunteer for a task or to give evidence
86	**Come from**	originate in
87	**Come in**	when someone enters a place, building, or room
88	**Come off**	when something is removed or breaks off from where it was originally attached to
89	**Come on**	to appear on television or be heard on the radio
90	**Come out**	to leave a place
91	**Come over**	to make a visit
92	**Come through**	when someone expected arrives
93	**Come up**	when something appears or happens, either expected or unexpected
94	**Come up with**	when you think of a solution, idea, plan, or excuse
95	**Con into**	to persuade someone to do something through lies and deception
96	**Con out of**	to persuade someone to give or do something through lies and deception
97	**Cool off**	to lose temperature
98	**Count on**	to rely or depend on
99	**Count up**	to count all of something or people in a group
100	**Cover up**	to use something to conceal something else
101	**Crack down**	to take more action than usual against wrongdoing
102	**Cross off**	to remove or delete someone from a list
103	**Cross out**	draw a line through
104	**Cut back**	consume less
105	**Cut down**	to reduce in number or size
106	**Cut in**	interrupt
107	**Cut off**	to completely remove or separate // stop providing
108	**Cut out**	to remove something using a knife or a pair of scissors
109	**Cut up**	when you use a knife or scissors to cut something into several pieces
110	**Deal with**	to handle, take care of (problem, situation)
111	**Die down**	to calm down, become less strong
112	**Do away with**	to dispose of something
113	**Do over**	to do something again in order to improve or correct mistakes
114	**Do up**	fasten, close prepare
115	**Do with**	to make a connection between two or more things
116	**Do without**	to manage without
117	**Doze off**	to go to sleep unintentionally

SN	Phrasal Verb	Meaning
118	**Drag on**	to last longer than expected
119	**Draw up**	to write (contract, agreement, document)
120	**Dress up**	wear nice clothing
121	**Drop back**	move back in a position/group
122	**Drop in/ by/ over**	come without an appointment
123	**Drop off**	to deliver someone
124	**Drop out**	to leave school without finishing
125	**Dry off**	to dry something or a surface quickly
126	**Dry out**	to remove water or other liquid from a container
127	**Dry up**	when all the liquid and/or moisture evaporates
128	**Ease off**	to reduce, become less severe or slow down (pain, traffic, work)
129	**Eat out**	eat at a restaurant
130	**Eat up**	when someone consumes all their food
131	**Empty out**	to remove everyone or everything from a space
132	**End in**	to finish in a certain way // result in
133	**End up**	to finally reach a state, place or action
134	**Fall apart**	break into pieces
135	**Fall behind**	to move slower than others
136	**Fall down**	to fall to the ground
137	**Fall for**	when you have an intense attraction to something or someone
138	**Fall off**	when something drops to a lower level
139	**Fall out**	to fall from or through something
140	**Fall over**	to go to sleep
141	**Fall through**	to fail // doesn't happen
142	**Feel up to**	when you have/don't have the energy to do something
143	**Fight back**	to make a new effort against an opponent
144	**Figure on**	to expect or plan for something
145	**Figure out**	to understand, find the answer
146	**Fill in / out**	to complete (a form/an application)
147	**Fill up**	to fill something completely
148	**Find out**	discover
149	**Fix up**	to set right
150	**Flip out**	to become very mad or lose control over your emotions
151	**Float around**	when an object or a person is near, but you cannot pinpoint the exact location
152	**Focus on**	to concentrate on something
153	**Follow up**	to find out more about something, or take further action in regards to it
154	**Fool around**	to waste time doing unimportant or silly things
155	**Freak out**	when someone becomes irrationally upset or angry, sometimes to the point of confusion

SN	Phrasal Verb	Meaning
156	Get ahead	to become successful in the professional environment or make consistent progress in life
157	Get along	to have good interactions with others
158	Get around	have mobility
159	Get around to	to do something that needed to get done at an earlier time
160	Get at	to imply
161	Get away	to escape // do without being noticed or punished
162	Get back at	retaliate, take revenge
163	Get back into	become interested in something again
164	Get behind	to learn, work, or progress more slowly than others
165	Get by	to manage to cope or to survive
166	Get down	to move to a lower place or level
167	Get in	to enter
168	Get into	to enter
169	Get off	to leave (bus, train, plane)
170	Get off on	to enjoy or be excited especially in a sexual way
171	Get on	to board (bus, train, plane)
172	Get out	to leave
173	Get out of	to avoid doing something
174	Get over	to recover from (illness, disappointment)
175	Get over with	to finish something that needs to get done
176	Get rid of	to eliminate
177	Get round	finally find time to do
178	Get across	communicate, make understandable
179	Get back	receive something you had before // return
180	Get through	when a message, meaning, or idea is understood or accepted
181	Get to	to arrive to or assist someone to a place
182	Get together	to meet
183	Get up	to rise, leave bed
184	Give away	to give something for free or without expecting anything in return
185	Give back	return a borrowed item
186	Give in	to surrender to something
187	Give out	to distribute something
188	Give up	stop trying
189	Go about	to take the necessary steps to get something done
190	Go after	follow // achive
191	Go against	compete, oppose
192	Go ahead	start, proceed
193	Go along with	to accept or agree with a decision, rule, opinion, etc
194	Go around	to follow a circular path
195	Go away	to move or travel from one place to another place
196	Go back	to return to a place, time, activity, or a person

SN	Phrasal Verb	Meaning
197	**Go back on**	when you fail to fulfill a promise you made to someone
198	**Go beyond**	to be more than or better than what is normal or expected
199	**Go by**	to pass someone quickly
200	**Go down**	to move to a lower position, place, price, level, etc
201	**Go for**	to try to obtain
202	**Go in for**	to enter a place or area for a specific reason
203	**Go in/into**	to enter a place, room, building, etc usually through a door
204	**Go off**	to leave unannounced
205	**Go on**	when something takes place
206	**Go out**	leave home to go on a social event
207	**Go over**	to review something
208	**Go through**	to continue firmly or obstinately to the end
209	**Go up**	to move or extend to a higher level or farther north
210	**Go with**	to accompany someone to a place
211	**Go without**	suffer lack or deprivation
212	**Goof around**	to waste time doing silly or unimportant things
213	**Gross out**	to be disgusted with someone
214	**Grow apart**	stop being friends over time
215	**Grow back**	regrow
216	**Grow into**	grow big enough to fit
217	**Grow out of**	to become too big or too tall for your clothes
218	**Grow up**	become an adult
219	**Hand back**	when you return something to the person who owns it after the person has given it to you
220	**Hand down**	give something used to somebody else
221	**Hand in**	to submit (report, homework)
222	**Hand out**	to distribute
223	**Hand over**	to give upon request or demand
224	**Hang around**	to spend time in a place or an area
225	**Hang in**	stay positive
226	**Hang on**	wait a short time
227	**Hang out**	to spend time relaxing with a group of friends
228	**Hang up**	end a phone call
229	**Have on**	to wear clothing, cosmetics, perfume, etc
230	**Head back**	to go to a place where you've been before or where you started from
231	**Head for**	when a situation becomes more likely
232	**Head toward**	to move in the direction where someone is
233	**Hear about**	when you learn details about something or someone
234	**Hear of**	when you learn about something or someone
235	**Heat up**	to make something warmer or cause a rise in temperature
236	**Help out**	to assist people with something

SN	Phrasal Verb	Meaning
237	**Hit on**	to suddenly have a solution to a problem or an interesting idea
238	**Hold against**	when you don't forgive or have little respect for someone because of something they did
239	**Hold off**	to delay something
240	**Hold on**	wait a short time
241	**Hold onto**	hold firmly using your hands or arms
242	**Hold out**	to extend your hand or an object in front of you
243	**Hold back**	prevent from doing/going // hide an emotion
244	**Hold up**	to hold someone up in the air // rob
245	**Hook up**	when you connect two electrical devices together
246	**Hurry up**	to do something quickly
247	**Iron out**	to resolve by discussion, eliminate differences
248	**Join in**	to participate
249	**Join up**	to engage in, become a member of
250	**Keep at**	to continue doing an activity even though it may be difficult
251	**Keep away**	to avoid getting close to someone
252	**Keep down**	to make sound, music and noise minimal
253	**Keep from**	to stop yourself or other people from doing something
254	**Keep off**	to avoid discussing a particular subject or topic
255	**Keep on**	to continue doing something
256	**Keep out**	stop from entering
257	**Keep to**	when you don't share information
258	**Keep up**	to stay at the same level as someone
259	**Kick back**	to illegally pay extra money to someone as part of the price
260	**Kick off**	to begin, start
261	**Kick out**	to force someone to leave an organization or place
262	**Knock off**	to use force to cause someone to fall from its place, whether intentionally or accidentally
263	**Knock out**	when someone is struck hard enough to cause them to lose consciousness
264	**Knock over**	to make contact with something or someone in such a way it or they fall
265	**Know about**	to have knowledge of or be familiar with something
266	**Lay down**	to place something on a surface or an object
267	**Lay off**	when a company or business ends a worker's employment
268	**Lead up to**	when a period of time or a series of events cause an event, situation or conversation to happen
269	**Leave behind**	when you don't take something or someone with you when you leave
270	**Leave off**	to accidentally or intentionally not include a person or thing on a list
271	**Leave out**	to omit, not mention

SN	Phrasal Verb	Meaning
272	**Leave over**	when you have a portion that still remains from something after you have used or eaten the rest of it
273	**Let off**	to allow someone to leave a car, bus, train etc
274	**Let on**	to tell something that is a secret or private
275	**Let out**	when you give permission for someone to leave or be released from a place
276	**Let down**	fail to support or help, disappoint
277	**Let in**	allow to enter
278	**Let up**	when someone becomes less intense or strong
279	**Lie around**	to be lazy or to not do anything
280	**Lift up**	to raise someone to a higher level
281	**Light up**	to illuminate something
282	**Lighten up**	when a conversation is changed or a person changes to become less serious
283	**Line up**	to form in a row one after another or side-by-side
284	**Live with**	to share the same residence
285	**Lock in**	to secure people or things behind a closed door
286	**Lock out**	when you don't have the key or passcode to enter a secured place
287	**Lock up**	when you shut the windows and doors of a place or building
288	**Log in (or on)**	sign in (to a website, database etc)
289	**Log out (or off)**	sign out (of a website, database etc)
290	**Look after**	to take care of
291	**Look around**	to turn your head to see what or who is around you
292	**Look at**	to divert your eyes to someone
293	**Look down on**	to consider as inferior
294	**Look for**	to try to find something
295	**Look forward to**	to await or anticipate with pleasure
296	**Look into**	to investigate
297	**Look on**	to be a spectator at an event
298	**Look out**	be careful, vigilant, and take notice
299	**Look over**	to examine or inspect something or someone
300	**Look up**	search and find information in a reference book or database
301	**Look up to**	to admire
302	**Luck out**	to have exceptionally good luck
303	**Make for**	to go in a certain direction, typically in a hurry
304	**Make fun of**	to laugh at/ make jokes about
305	**Make of**	to understand the meaning of something
306	**Make up**	invent, lie about something // apply cosmetics to // forgive each other in a relationship
307	**Mess up**	when something is dirty or unorganized
308	**Mix up**	to mistake one thing or person for another

SN	Phrasal Verb	Meaning
309	**Monkey around with**	to try to play with or repair a device that you have no true knowledge about
310	**Move in**	to arrive in a new home or office
311	**Move out**	to leave your home/office for another one
312	**Narrow down**	to reduce the number of options or possibilities
313	**Nod off**	to fall asleep
314	**Own up**	to admit or confess something
315	**Pass away**	to die
316	**Pass out**	to faint
317	**Pass up**	to let go by without accepting or taking advantage of // decline
318	**Pay back**	to reimburse
319	**Pay for**	to purchase merchandise // be punished for doing something bad
320	**Pay off**	to repay money that is owed to a person or entity
321	**Pay up**	to pay all the money that is owed or asked for
322	**Pick on**	to tease and/or criticize someone over a period of time
323	**Pick out**	choose
324	**Pick up**	to get someone from somewhere
325	**Pile up**	to put things in a pile or heap
326	**Piss off**	[informal] to be angry about something
327	**Plan ahead**	to prepare for a future event or situation
328	**Plan for**	to prepare for a big event or expectation in the future
329	**Plan on**	when you have the intention to do something
330	**Plug in**	to connect an electrical device to an electrical outlet
331	**Plug up**	to block a narrow passage such as a hole, drain, or pipe
332	**Point out/to**	indicate with your finger
333	**Print out**	to produce a hard copy of a computer document
334	**Pull off**	to succeed in doing something difficult or tricky
335	**Pull out**	when something or someone leaves a place
336	**Pull over**	to drive your vehicle to the side of the road to stop
337	**Pull through**	to recover from an injury or illness
338	**Punch in**	to enter data or record time on a device
339	**Punch out**	to record the time you leave the workplace using a special clock
340	**Put away**	to place something where it cannot be seen or isn't in the way of other things
341	**Put back**	when something is causing a project to slow down
342	**Put down**	to bring to an end
343	**Put in**	when you invest or make a deposit in this example, the amount almost always separates the verb
344	**Put off**	to postpone // to become offended by someone
345	**Put on**	put clothing/ accessories on your body
346	**Put out**	to extinguish

SN	Phrasal Verb	Meaning
347	**Put past**	to not be surprised by a person's actions [always used with the negative]
348	**Put to**	to cause someone to be in a certain state or to do something extra
349	**Put together**	to assemble or connect the parts of something
350	**Put up**	to move an object to a higher level
351	**Put up to**	to encourage or persuade someone to do something
352	**Put up with**	to tolerate or accept something that you'd rather not
353	**Rely on**	to count on, depend on, trust
354	**Ring up**	to call someone on the phone
355	**Rip off**	when someone asks for a price for something that is too high, when someone cheats or steals
356	**Rip up**	to tear something (ie paper, cloth, etc) into pieces
357	**Rule out**	to eliminate
358	**Run across**	to move or run from one side to the other
359	**Run around**	to go from one place to another in a hurry
360	**Run away**	leave unexpectedly, escape
361	**Run down**	to hit someone with a vehicle
362	**Run into**	meet unexpectedly
363	**Run out**	have none left
364	**Run over**	drive a vehicle over a person or thing
365	**Run up**	to run from a lower elevation or level to a higher elevation or level
366	**Screw on**	to ensure the top of a container/bottle is sealed
367	**Screw out of**	to cheat or deceive someone
368	**Screw up**	to make a mistake or do something really bad
369	**See about**	to seriously think about doing something
370	**Sell out**	when all the inventory of a particular product has been purchased
371	**Send back**	return
372	**Set off**	to start a journey
373	**Set up**	arrange, organize, trap
374	**Settle down**	to begin living a stable and routine life
375	**Settle for**	to accept something even though it's not what you want or need
376	**Shake up**	to mix something in a container by shaking it
377	**Shop around**	to compare prices
378	**Show off**	to brag or want to be admired
379	**Show up**	to appear/arrive
380	**Shut off**	to stop the operation of an electrical or mechanical device
381	**Shut up**	to stop talking
382	**Shut up (impolite)**	to be silent, stop talking
383	**Sign in**	to write your name on a list to indicate the day and time you arrived at a certain place

SN	Phrasal Verb	Meaning
384	**Sign out**	to write your name on a list to indicate the day and time of your departure
385	**Sit down**	to take a seat
386	**Sleep over**	stay somewhere for the night
387	**Slow down**	to do something slower
388	**Sneak in/into**	to enter a place quietly to avoid being seen or heard
389	**Sneak out**	to leave a place without being noticed
390	**Sort out**	organize, resolve a problem
391	**Space out**	when someone's attention is not in the present moment
392	**Stand around**	to stand in one place when you should be doing something
393	**Stand for**	to support or represent an idea, belief, etc
394	**Stand up**	to rise from a sitting position
395	**Start off**	the beginning of an event, activity or time period
396	**Start out**	to begin a trip or venture to some place
397	**Start up**	to start something
398	**Stay off**	to avoid discussing a certain subject or topic
399	**Stay out**	to spend time out of your own home
400	**Stay up**	to remain in a place that is higher than ground level
401	**Step on**	to place your foot on something or someone
402	**Stick around**	to stay in a place or with someone for any period of time
403	**Stick out**	to extend something outward
404	**Stick to**	continue doing something // limit yourself to particular thing
405	**Stick up**	to use a weapon, especially a gun, to rob someone
406	**Stick up for**	to defend
407	**Stick with**	to continue to use or do something
408	**Stop off**	to make a quick stop on your way to a destination
409	**Stop over**	to visit someone for a short period of time
410	**Straighten out**	to make something straight
411	**Stress out**	to feel very worried, nervous or anxious
412	**Switch off**	stop the energy flow, turn off
413	**Switch on**	start the energy flow, turn on
414	**Take after**	to resemble, in appearance or character
415	**Take apart**	purposely break into pieces
416	**Take back**	return an item
417	**Take care of**	to look after
418	**Take in**	to be successfully tricked or deceived by someone
419	**Take off**	start to fly
420	**Take on**	to hire or engage staff
421	**Take out**	to remove // extract
422	**Take out on**	to direct your anger towards someone
423	**Take up on**	when you accept an invitation or offer from someone
424	**Talk down to**	to talk to someone as if they are less intelligent than you by conveying a tone of voice or attitude that says so

SN	Phrasal Verb	Meaning
425	**Talk into**	to convince someone to do something
426	**Talk out of**	to convince someone not to do something
427	**Talk to**	to have a conversation with someone
428	**Tear down**	to deconstruct a building or home
429	**Tear off**	to remove with force
430	**Tear up**	rip into pieces
431	**Tell apart**	to be able to differentiate something or someone from something or someone else
432	**Tell off**	to reprimand/criticize severely
433	**Tell on**	to inform an authoritative figure about what someone else did
434	**Think about**	to consider something prior to making a final decision
435	**Think ahead**	to think and plan carefully for a future situation or event
436	**Think back**	remember
437	**Think over**	to consider
438	**Think up**	to use your imagination to create a plan, idea, or a solution
439	**Throw away**	dispose of
440	**Throw out**	when you get rid of something by putting it in a trash can, bin, etc
441	**Throw up**	to vomit or puke
442	**Track down**	to locate someone after a long search
443	**Trade in**	to exchange something old for something new
444	**Trick into**	to convince or persuade someone to believe something untrue or to do something for you
445	**Try on**	to wear something to see if it suits or fits
446	**Try out**	to compete / show that you are qualified to do something
447	**Turn around**	when someone moves until it faces the opposite direction
448	**Turn down**	to refuse
449	**Turn in**	to give someone to the police or someone of authority
450	**Turn into**	to transform
451	**Turn off**	to stop a device from functioning // something that causes loss of interest
452	**Turn on**	to excite sexually
453	**Turn out**	to attend an event, meeting, etc
454	**Turn over**	to move an object so that the part that is on top becomes the bottom and vice versa
455	**Turn up**	appear suddenly
456	**Use up**	to completely consume or use a product
457	**Wake up**	stop sleeping
458	**Warm up**	prepare body for exercise
459	**Wash off**	to remove dirt with soap and water
460	**Wash up**	to clean your face, hands, body, etc
461	**Watch out**	to be careful

SN	Phrasal Verb	Meaning
462	**Wear down**	to make the surface disappear due to friction
463	**Wear off**	fade away
464	**Wear out**	to become unusable due to aging
465	**Wind up**	to operate a mechanical device by turning its handle
466	**Wipe off**	to completely remove or clean something
467	**Wipe out**	to clean the inside of something
468	**Wipe up**	to remove liquid from a surface using a sponge, towel etc
469	**Work in**	to make time in a busy schedule for a person or an activity
470	**Work out**	exercise // make a calculation
471	**Work up**	to gradually improve at or make progress in something
472	**Wrap up**	to cover something with some kind of special paper
473	**Zip up**	to close an item that has a zipper

SN	Words	Definition
1	Acarophobia	Fear of mites
2	Acerophobia	Fear of sourness
3	Acousticophobia	Fear of sound
4	Acrophobia / Hypsophobia	Fear of high places
5	Aerophobia	Fear of air travel
6	Agoraphobia	Fear of open places
7	Ailurophobia	Fear of cats
8	Algophobia	Fear of pain
9	Americophobia	Fear of American people and things
10	Androphobia	Fear of men
11	Anemophobia	Fear of wind
12	Anginophobia	Fear of narrowness
13	Anglophobia	Fear of English people and things
14	Anthophobia	Fear of flowers
15	Anthropophobia	Fear of people
16	Antlophobia	Fear of floods
17	Apeirophobia	Fear of infinity
18	Apiphobia	Fear of bees
19	Arachnophobia	Fear of spiders
20	Asthenophobia	Fear of weakness
21	Astrapophobia	Fear of lightning
22	Atelophobia	Fear of imperfection
23	Atephobia	Fear of ruin
24	Autophobia / Ermitophobia	Fear of loneliness
25	Bacillophobia / Microbiophobia	Fear of microbes
26	Bacteriophobia	Fear of bacteria
27	Ballistophobia	Fear of bullets
28	Bathophobia	Fear of depth
29	Batophobia	Fear of high buildings
30	Batrachophobia	Fear of reptiles
31	Belonephobia	Fear of needles
32	Blennophobia	Fear of slime
33	Bromidrosiphobia	Fear of body odour
34	Brontophobia / Tonitrophobia / Keraunophobia	Fear of thunder
35	Carcinophobia	Fear of cancer
36	Cardiophobia	Fear of heart disease
37	Cheimaphobia	Fear of cold
38	Chionophobia	Fear of snow
39	Chrematophobia	Fear of money
40	Chromophobia	Fear of colour
41	Chronophobia	Fear of time
42	Chrysophobia / Aurophobia	Fear of gold
43	Cibophobia / Sitophobia	Fear of food

SN	Words	Definition
44	**Claustrophobia**	Fear of enclosed places
45	**Clinophobia**	Fear of bed
46	**Cnidophobia**	Fear of insect stings
47	**Coitophobia**	Fear of coitus
48	**Cometophobia**	Fear of comets
49	**Coprophobia**	Fear of faeces
50	**Coprostasophobia**	Fear of constipation
51	**Cremnophobia**	Fear of steep cliffs (precipices)
52	**Cryophobia**	Fear of ice
53	**Cyberphobia**	Fear of computers
54	**Cynophobia**	Fear of dogs
55	**Cyrnophobia**	Fear of waves
56	**Demophobia / Ochlophobia**	Fear of crowds
57	**Dermatosiophobia / Dermatopathophobia**	Fear of skin disease
58	**Dikephobia**	Fear of justice
59	**Doraphobia**	Fear of fur
60	**Ecclesiophobia**	Fear of church
61	**Eisoptrophobia**	Fear of mirrors
62	**Electrophobia**	Fear of electricity
63	**Eleutherophobia**	Fear of freedom
64	**Emetophobia**	Fear of vomiting
65	**Enetophobia**	Fear of pins
66	**Entomophobia**	Fear of insects
67	**Eosophobia**	Fear of dawn
68	**Epistolophobia**	Fear of correspondence
69	**Eremophobia**	Fear of solitude
70	**Ergophobia**	Fear of work
71	**Erotophobia**	Fear of sex
72	**Erythrophobia**	Fear of blushing
73	**Febriphobia**	Fear of fever
74	**Francophobia / Gallophobia**	Fear of French people and things
75	**Gamophobia**	Fear of marriage
76	**Gephyrophobia**	Fear of bridges
77	**Germanophobia / Teutophobia**	Fear of German people and things
78	**Geumatophobia**	Fear of taste
79	**Graphophobia**	Fear of writing
80	**Gymnophobia**	Fear of nudity
81	**Gynophobia**	Fear of women
82	**Hadephobia / Stygiophobia**	Fear of hell
83	**Haemophobia**	Fear of blood
84	**Hagiophobia**	Fear of saints
85	**Hamartophobia**	Fear of sin
86	**Haptophobia**	Fear of touch

SN	Words	Definition
87	**Harpaxophobia**	Fear of robbers
88	**Hedonophobia**	Fear of pleasure
89	**Heliophobia**	Fear of sun
90	**Helminthophobia**	Fear of worms
91	**Hierophobia**	Fear of priests
92	**Hippophobia**	Fear of horses
93	**Hodophobia**	Fear of travel
94	**Homichlophobia**	Fear of fog
95	**Homophobia**	Fear of homosexuals
96	**Hormephobia**	Fear of shock
97	**Hydrophobia**	Fear of water
98	**Hydrophobophobia**	Fear of rabies
99	**Hygrophobia**	Fear of dampness
100	**Hypegiaphobia**	Fear of responsibility
101	**Hypnophobia**	Fear of sleep
102	**Ichthyophobia**	Fear of fish
103	**Iconophobia**	Fear of religious works of art
104	**Ideophobia**	Fear of ideas
105	**Italophobia**	Fear of Italian people and things
106	**Kakorrhaphiaphobia**	Fear of failure
107	**Katagelophobia**	Fear of ridicule
108	**Kenophobia**	Fear of voids
109	**Kinetophobia**	Fear of motion
110	**Kleptophobia**	Fear of stealing
111	**Koniophobia**	Fear of dust
112	**Kopophobia**	Fear of fatigue
113	**Lalophobia / Laliophobia**	Fear of stuttering
114	**Lalophobia / Laliophobia / Glossophobia / Phonophobia**	Fear of speech
115	**Leprophobia**	Fear of leprosy
116	**Limnophobia**	Fear of lakes
117	**Linonophobia**	Fear of string
118	**Logophobia**	Fear of words
119	**Lyssophobia / Maniphobia**	Fear of insanity
120	**Mastigophobia**	Fear of beating
121	**Mechanophobia**	Fear of machinery
122	**Metallophobia**	Fear of metal
123	**Microphobia**	Fear of small things
124	**Musicophobia**	Fear of music
125	**Musophobia**	Fear of mice
126	**Mysophobia**	Fear of dirt
127	**Necrophobia**	Fear of corpses
128	**Nelophobia**	Fear of glass
129	**Neophobia**	Fear of new things

SN	Words	Definition
130	**Nephophobia**	Fear of clouds
131	**Nosophobia**	Fear of illness
132	**Nyctophobia**	Fear of night
133	**Ochlophobia**	Fear of mobs
134	**Ochophobia**	Fear of vehicles
135	**Odontophobia**	Fear of teeth
136	**Oikophobia**	Fear of home
137	**Olfactophobia / Osmophobia**	Fear of smell
138	**Ommetaphobia**	Fear of eyes
139	**Oneirophobia**	Fear of dreams
140	**Onomatophobia**	Fear of names
141	**Ophidiophobia**	Fear of snakes
142	**Ornithophobia**	Fear of birds
143	**Paedophobia**	Fear of children
144	**Panophobia / Pantophobia**	Fear of everything
145	**Papaphobia**	Fear of Pope
146	**Parasitophobia**	Fear of parasites
147	**Pathophobia / Nosophobia**	Fear of disease
148	**Patroiophobia**	Fear of heredity
149	**Pediculophobia**	Fear of lice
150	**Peniaphobia**	Fear of poverty
151	**Phagophobia**	Fear of swallowing
152	**Pharmacophobia**	Fear of drugs
153	**Phasmophobia**	Fear of ghosts
154	**Philosophobia**	Fear of philosophy
155	**Phobophobia**	Fear of fear
156	**Photophobia**	Fear of light
157	**Phronemophobia**	Fear of thinking
158	**Phthisiophobia**	Fear of tuberculosis
159	**Pinaciphobia / Katastichophobia**	Fear of lists
160	**Pnigerophobia**	Fear of smothering
161	**Pogonophobia**	Fear of beards
162	**Poinephobia**	Fear of punishment
163	**Politicophobia**	Fear of politics
164	**Potamophobia**	Fear of rivers
165	**Potophobia**	Fear of drink
166	**Pteronophobia**	Fear of feathers
167	**Pyrophobia**	Fear of fire
168	**Rhabdophobia**	Fear of magic
169	**Russophobia**	Fear of Russian people and things
170	**Satanophobia**	Fear of Satan
171	**Scabiophobia**	Fear of scabies
172	**Sciophobia**	Fear of shadows
173	**Scotophobia**	Fear of Scottish people and things

SN	Words	Definition
174	**Scotophobia**	Fear of darkness
175	**Selaphobia**	Fear of flesh
176	**Siderodromophobia**	Fear of rail travel
177	**Siderophobia**	Fear of stars
178	**Sinophobia**	Fear of Chinese people and things
179	**Stasophobia**	Fear of standing
180	**Symmetrophobia**	Fear of symmetry
181	**Syphilophobia**	Fear of venereal disease
182	**Tachophobia**	Fear of speed
183	**Taphephobia**	Fear of burial alive
184	**Technophobia**	Fear of technology
185	**Telephonophobia**	Fear of telephone
186	**Teratophobia**	Fear of giving birth to monsters
187	**Thalassophobia**	Fear of sea
188	**Thanatophobia**	Fear of death
189	**Thassophobia**	Fear of idleness
190	**Theophobia**	Fear of God
191	**Thermophobia**	Fear of heat
192	**Tocophobia**	Fear of childbirth
193	**Topophobia**	Fear of places
194	**Toxiphobia**	Fear of poison
195	**Traumatophobia**	Fear of injury
196	**Trichophobia**	Fear of hair
197	**Triskaidekaphobia**	Fear of thirteen
198	**Trypanophobia / Vaccinophobia**	Fear of inoculation
199	**Tyrannophobia**	Fear of tyrants
200	**Uranophobia**	Fear of heaven
201	**Xenophobia**	Fear of foreigners
202	**Zelotypophobia**	Fear of jealousy
203	**Zoophobia**	Fear of animals

SN	Words	Definition
1	**Ablutomania**	mania for washing oneself
2	**Aboulomania**	pathological indecisiveness
3	**Agromania**	intense desire to be in open spaces
4	**Andromania**	nymphomania
5	**Anglomania**	craze or obsession with England and the English
6	**Anthomania**	obsession with flowers
7	**Aphrodisiomania**	abnormal sexual interest
8	**Arithmomania**	obsessive preoccupation with numbers
9	**Balletomania**	abnormal fondness for ballet
10	**Bibliomania**	craze for books or reading
11	**Bruxomania**	compulsion for grinding teeth
12	**Cacodemomania**	pathological belief that one is inhabited by an evil spirit
13	**Catapedamania**	obsession with jumping from high places
14	**Chinamania**	obsession with collecting china
15	**Choreomania**	dancing mania or frenzy
16	**Clinomania**	excessive desire to stay in bed
17	**Copromania**	obsession with feces
18	**Cytheromania**	nymphomania
19	**Dacnomania**	obsession with killing
20	**Demonomania**	pathological belief that one is possessed by demons
21	**Dinomania**	mania for dancing
22	**Dipsomania**	abnormal craving for alcohol
23	**Discomania**	obsession for disco music
24	**Doramania**	obsession with owning furs
25	**Doromania**	obsession with giving gifts
26	**Drapetomania**	intense desire to run away from home
27	**Dromomania**	compulsive longing for travel
28	**Ecdemomania**	abnormal compulsion for wandering
29	**Egomania**	irrational self-centered attitude or self-worship
30	**Eleutheromania**	manic desire for freedom
31	**Empleomania**	mania for holding public office
32	**Enosimania**	pathological belief that one has sinned
33	**Entheomania**	abnormal belief that one is divinely inspired
34	**Epomania**	craze for writing epics
35	**Ergasiomania**	excessive desire to work; ergomania
36	**Ergomania**	excessive desire to work; workaholism
37	**Erotomania**	abnormally powerful sex drive
38	**Etheromania**	craving for ether
39	**Ethnomania**	obsessive devotion to one's own people
40	**Eulogomania**	obsessive craze for eulogies
41	**Flagellomania**	abnormal enthusiasm for flogging
42	**Florimania**	craze for flowers
43	**Francomania**	craze or obsession with France and the French
44	**Gallomania**	craze or obsession with France and the French

SN	Words	Definition
45	**Gamomania**	obsession with issuing odd marriage proposals
46	**Graecomania**	obsession with Greece and the Greeks
47	**Graphomania**	obsession with writing
48	**Gynaecomania**	abnormal sexual obsession with women
49	**Habromania**	insanity featuring cheerful delusions
50	**Hagiomania**	mania for sainthood
51	**Hellenomania**	obsession with Greece and the Greeks; Graecomania
52	**Hexametromania**	mania for writing in hexameter
53	**Hieromania**	pathological religious visions or delusions
54	**Hippomania**	obsession with horses
55	**Hydromania**	irrational craving for water
56	**Hylomania**	excessive tendency towards materialism
57	**Hypermania**	severe mania
58	**Hypomania**	minor mania
59	**Hysteromania**	nymphomania
60	**Iconomania**	obsession with icons or portraits
61	**Idolomania**	obsession or devotion to idols
62	**Infomania**	excessive devotion to accumulating facts
63	**Islomania**	craze or obsession for islands
64	**Italomania**	obsession with Italy or Italians
65	**Kleptomania**	irrational predilection for stealing
66	**Klopemania**	kleptomania
67	**Logomania**	pathological loquacity
68	**Lypemania**	extreme pathological mournfulness
69	**Macromania**	delusion that objects are larger than natural size
70	**Megalomania**	abnormal tendency towards grand or grandiose behaviour
71	**Melomania**	craze for music
72	**Methomania**	morbid craving for alcohol
73	**Metromania**	insatiable desire for writing verse
74	**Micromania**	pathological self-deprecation or belief that one is very small
75	**Monomania**	abnormal obsession with a single thought or idea
76	**Morphinomania**	habitual craving or desire for morphine
77	**Musomania**	obsession with music
78	**Mythomania**	lying or exaggerating to an abnormal extent
79	**Narcomania**	uncontrollable craving for narcotics
80	**Necromania**	sexual obsession with dead bodies; necrophilia
81	**Nosomania**	delusion of suffering from a disease
82	**Nostomania**	abnormal desire to go back to familiar places
83	**Nymphomania**	excessive or crazed sexual desire
84	**Oenomania**	obsession or craze for wine
85	**Oligomania**	obsession with a few thoughts or ideas
86	**Oniomania**	mania for making purchases
87	**Onomamania**	mania for names
88	**Onomatomania**	irresistible desire to repeat certain words

SN	Words	Definition
89	**Onychotillomania**	compulsive picking at the fingernails
90	**Opiomania**	craving for opium
91	**Opsomania**	abnormal love for one kind of food
92	**Orchidomania**	abnormal obsession with orchids
93	**Parousiamania**	obsession with the second coming of Christ
94	**Pathomania**	moral insanity
95	**Peotillomania**	abnormal compulsion for pulling on the penis
96	**Phagomania**	excessive desire for food or eating
97	**Phaneromania**	habit of biting one's nails
98	**Pharmacomania**	abnormal obsession with trying drugs
99	**Phonomania**	pathological tendency to murder
100	**Photomania**	pathological desire for light
101	**Phyllomania**	excessive or abnormal production of leaves
102	**Phytomania**	obsession with collecting plants
103	**Planomania**	abnormal desire to wander and disobey social norms
104	**Plutomania**	mania for money
105	**Polemomania**	mania for war
106	**Politicomania**	mania for politics
107	**Polkamania**	craze for polka dancing
108	**Polymania**	mania affecting several different mental faculties
109	**Poriomania**	abnormal compulsion to wander
110	**Pornomania**	obsession with pornography
111	**Potichomania**	craze for imitating Oriental porcelain
112	**Potomania**	abnormal desire to drink alcohol
113	**Pseudomania**	irrational predilection for lying
114	**Pteridomania**	passion for ferns
115	**Pyromania**	craze for starting fires
116	**Rhinotillexomania**	compulsive nose picking
117	**Rinkomania**	obsession with skating
118	**Satyromania**	abnormally great male sexual desire; satyriasis
119	**Scribbleomania**	obsession with scribbling
120	**Sebastomania**	religious insanity
121	**Sitiomania**	morbid aversion to food
122	**Sophomania**	delusion that one is incredibly intelligent
123	**Squandermania**	irrational propensity for spending money wastefully
124	**Stampomania**	obsession with stamp-collecting
125	**Syphilomania**	pathological belief that one is afflicted with syphilis
126	**Technomania**	craze for technology
127	**Teutomania**	obsession with Teutonic or German things
128	**Thanatomania**	belief that one has been affected by death magic, and resulting illness
129	**Theatromania**	craze for going to plays
130	**Theomania**	belief that one is a god
131	**Timbromania**	craze for stamp collecting

SN	Words	Definition
132	**Tomomania**	irrational predilection for performing surgery
133	**Toxicomania**	morbid craving for poisons
134	**Trichotillomania**	neurosis where patient pulls out own hair
135	**Tulipomania**	obsession with tulips
136	**Typhomania**	delirious state resulting from typhus fever
137	**Typomania**	craze for printing one's lucubrations
138	**Uranomania**	obsession with the idea of divinity
139	**Verbomania**	craze for words
140	**Xenomania**	inordinate attachment to foreign things
141	**Zoomania**	insane fondness for animals

SN	Words	Definition
1	**Ailurophile**	a person who likes cats, a cat lover
2	**Anglophile**	an admirer of England and English things
3	**Astrophile**	person interested in astronomy
4	**Audiophile**	a person who loves accurately reproduced recorded sound
5	**Autophile**	a person who loves solitude, being alone
6	**Bibliophile**	somea person who loves and usually collects books
7	**Ceraunophile**	a person who loves lightning and thunder
8	**Chionophile**	a person who finds comfort in cold weathers
9	**Clinophile**	a lover of reclining, lying in bed
10	**Coimetrophile**	a person who loves cemeteries
11	**Cynophile**	a person who loves canines, a dog lover
12	**Dendrophile**	a person who loves forests and trees
13	**Discophile**	a person who loves and studies sound recordings
14	**Electrophile**	substance having an affinity for electrons or negative charge
15	**Ergophile**	a person who loves work
16	**Europhile**	a person who loves Europe
17	**Francophile**	a person who loves France or the French
18	**Gallophile**	a person who loves France or the French
19	**Gynotikolobomassophile**	a person who nibbles on women's earlobes
20	**Heliophile**	a lover of the sun
21	**Hippophile**	lover of horses
22	**Homophile**	a person who prefers the company of the same sex; a homosexual
23	**Limnophile**	a person who loves lakes
24	**Logophile**	a lover of words
25	**Logophile**	a person who is a lover of words
26	**Lyophile**	easily dispersed in a suitable medium
27	**Negrophile**	a person who is sympathetic towards black people
28	**Neophile**	a person who loves novelty and trends
29	**Nyctophile**	a person who loves night, darkness
30	**Oenophile**	a person who is fond of or loves wine
31	**Palaeophile**	antiquarian
32	**Pedophile**	an adult who is sexually attracted to children
33	**Photophile**	a person who finds comfort in natural light
34	**Pluviophile**	a lover of rain; someone who finds joy and peace of mind during rainy days
35	**Pogonophile**	a person who loves beards
36	**Psammophile**	sand-loving plant
37	**Retrophile**	a person who loves artifacts and aesthetics from the past
38	**Rheophile**	living or thriving in running water
39	**Russophile**	a person who admires Russia or the Russians

SN	Words	Definition
40	**Selenophile**	a person who loves the moon
41	**Sinophile**	a person who admires china or the Chinese
42	**Slavophile**	a person who admires the slavs
43	**Spermophile**	member of family of seed-loving rodents
44	**Stigmatophile**	a person who is obsessed with tattoos, piercings
45	**Technophile**	a person who is fond of technology
46	**Thalassophile**	a lover of the sea, someone who loves the sea, ocean
47	**Theophile**	a person who loves or is loved by god
48	**Tobaccophile**	a person who loves tobacco
49	**Turophile**	cheese lover
50	**Typhlophile**	a person who is kind to the blind

SN	Words	Definition
1	**Aborticide**	killing of a fetus; abortion
2	**Acaricide**	killer of mites and ticks
3	**Algicide**	killer of algae
4	**Amicicide**	murder of a friend
5	**Aphicide**	killer of aphids (very small insects)
6	**Avicide**	killing of birds
7	**Bacillicide**	killer of bacteria
8	**Bactericide**	killer of bacteria
9	**Biocide**	killing living material
10	**Bovicide**	slaughter of cattle; one who kills cattle
11	**Ceticide**	killing of whales and other cetaceans
12	**Cimicide**	substance used to kill bed-bugs
13	**Deicide**	destruction or killing of a god
14	**Ecocide**	destruction of the environment
15	**Episcopicide**	killing of bishops
16	**Famicide**	one who destroys another's reputation; slanderer
17	**Felicide**	killing of a cat
18	**Femicide**	killing of a woman
19	**Feticide**	killing of a fetus
20	**Filicide**	killing of one's own child
21	**Floricide**	killing or killer of flowers
22	**Foeticide**	killing a fetus
23	**Formicide**	substance that kills ants
24	**Fratricide**	killing of one's brother
25	**Fungicide**	killing of fungus
26	**Genocide**	killing of a race or ethnic group
27	**Germicide**	substance that kills germs
28	**Giganticide**	killing of a giant
29	**Gynaecide**	killing of women
30	**Herbicide**	killing of plants
31	**Hereticide**	killing of heretics
32	**Homicide**	killing of a human being
33	**Infanticide**	killing of an infant
34	**Insecticide**	killing of insects
35	**Larvicide**	killing of larvae
36	**Liberticide**	destruction of liberty
37	**Lupicide**	killing of a wolf
38	**Mariticide**	killing or killer of one's husband
39	**Matricide**	killing of one's mother
40	**Menticide**	reduction of mind by psychological pressure
41	**Microbicide**	killing or killer of microbes
42	**Miticide**	agent which kills mites
43	**Molluscicide**	killing of mollusks
44	**Muscicide**	substance for killing flies

SN	Words	Definition
45	**Neonaticide**	killing or killer of a newborn infant
46	**Ovicide**	killing insect eggs
47	**Ovicide**	sheep-killing
48	**Parasiticide**	killing of parasites
49	**Parasuicide**	apparent attempted suicide without the actual intention of killing oneself
50	**Parenticide**	killing or killer of one's parents
51	**Parricide**	killing of parents or a parent-like close relative
52	**Patricide**	killing of one's father
53	**Perdricide**	killer of partridges
54	**Pesticide**	killing of pests
55	**Prolicide**	killing of offspring; killing of the human race
56	**Pulicide**	flea-killer
57	**Raticide**	substance or person who kills rats
58	**Regicide**	killing of a monarch
59	**Rodenticide**	killing of rodents
60	**Senicide**	killing of old men
61	**Serpenticide**	killing or killer of a snake
62	**Siblicide**	killing or killer of a sibling
63	**Silvicide**	substance that kills trees
64	**Sororicide**	killing of one's own sister
65	**Speciocide**	destruction of an entire species
66	**Spermicide**	killing of sperm
67	**Sporicide**	killing of spores
68	**Suicide**	killing of oneself
69	**Taeniacide**	killing of tapeworms
70	**Tauricide**	killing or killer of a bull
71	**Trypanocide**	killing of trypanosomes
72	**Tyrannicide**	killing or killer of a tyrant
73	**Urbicide**	destruction of a city
74	**Ursicide**	killing or killer of a bear
75	**Utricide**	one who stabs an inflated skin vessel instead of killing someone
76	**Uxoricide**	killing of one's own wife
77	**Vaticide**	killing or killer of a prophet
78	**Verbicide**	destroying the meaning of a word
79	**Vermicide**	killing of worms
80	**Vespacide**	substance or person who kills wasps
81	**Viricide**	killing of viruses; killing of men or of husbands
82	**Virucide**	killing of viruses
83	**Vulpicide**	killing of a fox
84	**Weedicide**	something that kills weeds

SN	Words	Definition
1	**Denarian**	a person between 10 and 19 years old
2	**Vicenarian**	a person between 20 and 29 years old
3	**Tricenarian**	a person between 30 and 39 years old
4	**Quadragenarian**	a person between 40 and 49 years old
5	**Quinquagenarian**	a person between 50 and 59 years old
6	**Sexagenarian**	a person between 60 and 69 years old
7	**Septuagenarian**	a person between 70 and 79 years old
8	**Octogenarian**	a person between 80 and 89 years old
9	**Nonagenarian**	a person between 90 and 99 years old
10	**Centenarian**	a person between 100 and 109 years old
11	**Supercentenarian**	a person 110 years old or older
12	**Methuselah**	a Person who is very old

SN	Words	Definition
1	**Dyssomnia**	a difficulty in falling asleep, or in remaining sleeping
2	**Hypersomnia**	excessive sleepiness.
3	**Hyposomnia**	inadequate sleep
4	**Insomnia**	the condition of being unable to sleep
5	**Parasomnia**	any of several sleep disorders
6	**Semisomnia**	a chronic state of low-grade exhaustion caused by too little or fitful sleep.
7	**Sexsomnia**	a form of non-rapid eye movement parasomnia that causes people to engage in various sexual acts while they are asleep.
8	**Somnambulism**	walking in sleep
9	**Somnambulist**	someone who walks about in sleep
10	**Somnial**	of or pertaining to sleep or dreams.
11	**Somniloquism**	talking in sleep
12	**Somniloquist**	someone who talks while asleep
13	**Somnolence**	the state of being almost asleep

SN	Word	Definition
1	Abattoir	a place where animals are slaughtered for the market
2	Apiary	a place where bees are kept
3	Aquarium	a tank for fishes
4	Archives	a place where government records are kept
5	Arena	a place for wrestling
6	Arsenal	a place for ammunition and weapons
7	Asylum	a place for lunatics, and political refugees
8	Aviary	a place where birds are kept
9	Burrow	the dwelling place of an animal underground
10	Cache	a place where ammunition is hidden
11	Cage	a place for birds
12	Caravan	the house or shelter of a gipsy
13	Casino	a place with gambling tables etc.
14	Cemetery	a graveyard where the dead are buried
15	Chalet	the house or shelter of a swiss peasant
16	Cloakroom	a place for luggage at a railway station
17	Convent	a residence for nuns
18	Crèche	a nursery where children of working parent are cared for while their parents are at work
19	Crematorium	a cremation ground where the last funeral rites are performed
20	Decanter	an ornamental glass bottle for holding wine or other alcoholic drinks
21	Den	the home of a lion
22	Dispensary	a place where medicines are compounded
23	Dormitory	the sleeping rooms in a college or public institution
24	Dovecot	a house or box in which live pigeons or doves
25	Dowar	the house or shelter of an Arab
26	Drey	a squirrel's home
27	Elysium	a paradise with perfect bliss
28	Eyrie, Aerie	a nest of a bird of prey
29	Granary	a place for storing grain
30	Gymnasium	a place where athletic exercises are performed
31	Hangar	a place for housing aeroplanes
32	Hive	a place for bees
33	Hutch	a wooden box with a front of wire for rabbits
34	Igloo	the house or shelter of an eskimo
35	Infirmary	a home for old persons
36	Insectarium	a place for keeping or breeding insects
37	Kabitka	the house or shelter of a kirghis
38	Kennel	a house of shelter for a dog
39	Lair / Den	the resting place of a wild animal
40	Menagerie	a place for wild animals and birds
41	Mint	a place where money is coined

SN	Word	Definition
42	**Monastery**	a residence for monks or priests
43	**Morgue**	a place where dead bodies are kept for identification
44	**Mortuary**	a place where dead bodies are kept for post mortem
45	**Orchard**	a place where fruit trees are grown
46	**Orphanage**	a place where orphans are housed
47	**Pen, Byre**	a house or shelter for a cow
48	**Portfolio**	a portable case for holding papers, drawing etc.
49	**Reservoir**	a place where water is collected and stored
50	**Resort**	a place frequented for reasons of pleasure or health
51	**Sanatorium**	a place for the sick to recover health
52	**Scullery**	a place where plates, dishes, pots and other cooking utensils are washed up
53	**Sheath, Scabbard**	a case in which the blade of sword is kept
54	**Stable**	a house of shelter for a horse
55	**Sty**	a place where pigs are kept
56	**Tannery**	a place where leather is tanned
57	**Wardrobe**	a place for clothes
58	**Wigwam, Tepee**	the house or shelter of an American Indian

SN	Words	Definition
1	**Acarology**	study of mites
2	**Accidence**	grammar book; science of inflections in grammar
3	**Aceology**	therapeutics
4	**Acology**	study of medical remedies
5	**Acoustics**	science of sound
6	**Adenology**	study of glands
7	**Aedoeology**	science of generative organs
8	**Aerobiology**	study of airborne organisms
9	**Aerodonetics**	science or study of gliding
10	**Aerodynamics**	dynamics of gases; science of movement in a flow of air or gas
11	**Aerolithology**	study of aerolites; meteorites
12	**Aerology**	study of the atmosphere
13	**Aeronautics**	study of navigation through air or space
14	**Aerophilately**	collecting of air-mail stamps
15	**Aerostatics**	science of air pressure; art of ballooning
16	**Agonistics**	art and theory of prize-fighting
17	**Agriology**	the comparative study of primitive peoples
18	**Agrobiology**	study of plant nutrition; soil yields
19	**Agrology**	study of agricultural soils
20	**Agronomics**	study of productivity of land
21	**Agrostology**	science or study of grasses
22	**Alethiology**	study of truth
23	**Algedonics**	science of pleasure and pain
24	**Algology**	study of algae
25	**Anaesthesiology**	study of anaesthetics
26	**Anaglyptics**	art of carving in bas-relief
27	**Anagraphy**	art of constructing catalogues
28	**Anatomy**	study of the structure of the body
29	**Andragogy**	science of teaching adults
30	**Anemology**	study of winds
31	**Angelology**	study of angels
32	**Angiology**	study of blood flow and lymphatic system
33	**Anthropobiology**	study of human biology
34	**Anthropology**	study of human cultures
35	**Aphnology**	science of wealth
36	**Apiology**	study of bees
37	**Arachnology**	study of spiders
38	**Archaeology**	study of human material remains
39	**Archelogy**	the study of first principles
40	**Archology**	science of the origins of government
41	**Arctophily**	study of teddy bears
42	**Areology**	study of Mars
43	**Aretaics**	the science of virtue
44	**Aristology**	the science or art of dining

SN	Words	Definition
45	**Arthrology**	study of joints
46	**Astacology**	the science of crayfish
47	**Astheniology**	study of diseases of weakening and aging
48	**Astrogeology**	study of extraterrestrial geology
49	**Astrology**	study of influence of stars on people
50	**Astrometeorology**	study of effect of stars on climate
51	**Astronomy**	study of celestial bodies
52	**Astrophysics**	study of behaviour of interstellar matter
53	**Astroseismology**	study of star oscillations
54	**Atmology**	the science of aqueous vapour
55	**Audiology**	study of hearing
56	**Autecology**	study of ecology of one species
57	**Autology**	scientific study of oneself
58	**Auxology**	science of growth
59	**Avionics**	the science of electronic devices for aircraft
60	**Axiology**	the science of the ultimate nature of values
61	**Bacteriology**	study of bacteria
62	**Balneology**	the science of the therapeutic use of baths
63	**Barodynamics**	science of the support and mechanics of bridges
64	**Barology**	study of gravitation
65	**Batology**	the study of brambles
66	**Bibliology**	study of books
67	**Bibliotics**	study of documents to determine authenticity
68	**Bioecology**	study of interaction of life in the environment
69	**Biology**	study of life
70	**Biometrics**	study of biological measurement
71	**Bionomics**	study of organisms interacting in their environments
72	**Botany**	study of plants
73	**Bromatology**	study of food
74	**Brontology**	scientific study of thunder
75	**Bryology**	the study of mosses and liverworts
76	**Cacogenics**	study of racial degeneration
77	**Caliology**	study of bird's nests
78	**Calorifics**	study of heat
79	**Cambistry**	science of international exchange
80	**Campanology**	the art of bell ringing
81	**Carcinology**	study of crabs and other crustaceans
82	**Cardiology**	study of the heart
83	**Caricology**	study of sedges
84	**Carpology**	study of fruit
85	**Cartography**	the science of making maps and globes
86	**Cartophily**	the hobby of collecting cigarette cards
87	**Castrametation**	the art of designing a camp
88	**Catacoustics**	science of echoes or reflected sounds

SN	Words	Definition
89	Catalactics	science of commercial exchange
90	Catechectics	the art of teaching by question and answer
91	Cetology	study of whales and dolphins
92	Chalcography	the art of engraving on copper or brass
93	Chalcotriptics	art of taking rubbings from ornamental brasses
94	Chaology	the study of chaos or chaos theory
95	Characterology	study of development of character
96	Chemistry	study of properties of substances
97	Chirocosmetics	beautifying the hands; art of manicure
98	Chirography	study of handwriting or penmanship
99	Chirology	study of the hands
100	Chiropody	medical science of feet
101	Chorology	science of the geographic description of anything
102	Chrematistics	the study of wealth; political economy
103	Chronobiology	study of biological rhythms
104	Chrysology	study of precious metals
105	Ciselure	the art of chasing metal
106	Climatology	study of climate
107	Clinology	study of aging or individual decline after maturity
108	Codicology	study of manuscripts
109	Coleopterology	study of beetles and weevils
110	Cometology	study of comets
111	Conchology	study of shells
112	Coprology	study of pornography
113	Cosmetology	study of cosmetics
114	Cosmology	study of the universe
115	Craniology	study of the skull
116	Criminology	study of crime; criminals
117	Cryobiology	study of life under cold conditions
118	Cryptology	study of codes
119	Cryptozoology	study of animals for whose existence there is no conclusive proof
120	Ctetology	study of the inheritance of acquired characteristics
121	Cynology	scientific study of dogs
122	Cytology	study of living cells
123	Dactyliology	study of rings
124	Dactylography	the study of fingerprints
125	Dactylology	study of sign language
126	Deltiology	the collection and study of picture postcards
127	Demology	study of human behaviour
128	Demonology	study of demons
129	Dendrochronology	study of tree rings
130	Dendrology	study of trees
131	Deontology	the theory or study of moral obligation

SN	Words	Definition
132	**Dermatoglyphics**	the study of skin patterns and fingerprints
133	**Dermatology**	study of skin
134	**Desmology**	study of ligaments
135	**Diabology**	study of devils
136	**Diagraphics**	art of making diagrams or drawings
137	**Dialectology**	study of dialects
138	**Dioptrics**	study of light refraction
139	**Diplomatics**	science of deciphering ancient writings and texts
140	**Diplomatology**	study of diplomats
141	**Docimology**	the art of assaying
142	**Dosiology**	the study of doses
143	**Dramaturgy**	art of producing and staging dramatic works
144	**Dysgenics**	the study of racial degeneration
145	**Dysteleology**	study of purposeless organs
146	**Ecclesiology**	study of church affairs
147	**Eccrinology**	study of excretion
148	**Ecology**	study of environment
149	**Economics**	study of material wealth
150	**Edaphology**	study of soils
151	**Egyptology**	study of ancient Egypt
152	**Ekistics**	study of human settlement
153	**Electrochemistry**	study of relations between electricity and chemicals
154	**Electrology**	study of electricity
155	**Electrostatics**	study of static electricity
156	**Embryology**	study of embryos
157	**Emetology**	study of vomiting
158	**Emmenology**	the study of menstruation
159	**Endemiology**	study of local diseases
160	**Endocrinology**	study of glands
161	**Enigmatology**	study of enigmas
162	**Entomology**	study of insects
163	**Entozoology**	study of parasites that live inside larger organisms
164	**Enzymology**	study of enzymes
165	**Ephebiatrics**	branch of medicine dealing with adolescence
166	**Epidemiology**	study of diseases; epidemics
167	**Epileptology**	study of epilepsy
168	**Epistemology**	study of grounds of knowledge
169	**Eremology**	study of deserts
170	**Ergology**	study of effects of work on humans
171	**Ergonomics**	study of people at work
172	**Escapology**	study of freeing oneself from constraints
173	**Eschatology**	study of death; final matters
174	**Ethnogeny**	study of origins of races or ethnic groups
175	**Ethnology**	study of cultures

SN	Words	Definition
176	**Ethnomethodology**	study of everyday communication
177	**Ethnomusicology**	study of comparative musical systems
178	**Ethology**	study of natural or biological character
179	**Ethonomics**	study of economic and ethical principles of a society
180	**Etiology**	the science of causes; especially of disease
181	**Etymology**	study of origins of words
182	**Euthenics**	science concerned with improving living conditions
183	**Exobiology**	study of extraterrestrial life
184	**Floristry**	the art of cultivating and selling flowers
185	**Fluviology**	study of watercourses
186	**Folkloristics**	study of folklore and fables
187	**Futurology**	study of future
188	**Garbology**	study of garbage
189	**Gastroenterology**	study of stomach; intestines
190	**Gastronomy**	study of fine dining
191	**Gemmology**	study of gems and jewels
192	**Genealogy**	study of descent of families
193	**Genesiology**	study of reproduction and heredity
194	**Genethlialogy**	the art of casting horoscopes
195	**Geochemistry**	study of chemistry of the earth's crust
196	**Geochronology**	study of measuring geological time
197	**Geogeny**	science of the formation of the earth's crust
198	**Geogony**	study of formation of the earth
199	**Geography**	study of surface of the earth and its inhabitants
200	**Geology**	study of earth's crust
201	**Geomorphogeny**	study of the origins of land forms
202	**Geoponics**	study of agriculture
203	**Geotechnics**	study of increasing habitability of the earth
204	**Geratology**	study of decadence and decay
205	**Gerocomy**	study of old age
206	**Gerontology**	study of the elderly; aging
207	**Gigantology**	study of giants
208	**Glaciology**	study of ice ages and glaciation
209	**Glossology**	study of language; study of the tongue
210	**Glyptography**	the art of engraving on gems
211	**Glyptology**	study of gem engravings
212	**Gnomonics**	the art of measuring time using sundials
213	**Gnosiology**	study of knowledge; philosophy of knowledge
214	**Gnotobiology**	study of life in germ-free conditions
215	**Graminology**	study of grasses
216	**Grammatology**	study of systems of writing
217	**Graphemics**	study of systems of representing speech in writing
218	**Graphology**	study of handwriting
219	**Gromatics**	science of surveying

SN	Words	Definition
220	**Gynaecology**	study of women's physiology
221	**Gyrostatics**	the study of rotating bodies
222	**Haemataulics**	study of movement of blood through blood vessels
223	**Hagiology**	study of saints
224	**Halieutics**	study of fishing
225	**Hamartiology**	study of sin
226	**Harmonics**	study of musical acoustics
227	**Hedonics**	part of ethics or psychology dealing with pleasure
228	**Helcology**	study of ulcers
229	**Heliology**	science of the sun
230	**Helioseismology**	study of sun's interior by observing its surface oscillations
231	**Helminthology**	study of worms
232	**Hematology**	study of blood
233	**Heortology**	study of religious feasts
234	**Hepatology**	study of liver
235	**Heraldry**	study of coats of arms
236	**Heresiology**	study of heresies
237	**Herpetology**	study of reptiles and amphibians
238	**Hierology**	science of sacred matters
239	**Hippiatrics**	study of diseases of horses
240	**Hippology**	the study of horses
241	**Histology**	study of the tissues of organisms
242	**Histopathology**	study of changes in tissue due to disease
243	**Historiography**	study of writing history
244	**Historiology**	study of history
245	**Homiletics**	the art of preaching
246	**Hoplology**	the study of weapons
247	**Horography**	art of constructing sundials or clocks
248	**Horology**	science of time measurement
249	**Horticulture**	study of gardening
250	**Hydrobiology**	study of aquatic organisms
251	**Hydrodynamics**	study of movement in liquids
252	**Hydrogeology**	study of ground water
253	**Hydrography**	study of investigating bodies of water
254	**Hydrokinetics**	study of motion of fluids
255	**Hydrology**	study of water resources
256	**Hydrometeorology**	study of atmospheric moisture
257	**Hydropathy**	study of treating diseases with water
258	**Hyetology**	science of rainfall
259	**Hygiastics**	science of health and hygiene
260	**Hygienics**	study of sanitation; health
261	**Hygiology**	hygienics; study of cleanliness
262	**Hygrology**	study of humidity
263	**Hygrometry**	science of humidity

SN	Words	Definition
264	Hymnography	study of writing hymns
265	Hymnology	study of hymns
266	Hypnology	study of sleep; study of hypnosis
267	Hypsography	science of measuring heights
268	Iamatology	study of remedies
269	Iatrology	treatise or text on medical topics; study of medicine
270	Iatromathematics	archaic practice of medicine in conjunction with astrology
271	Ichnography	art of drawing ground plans; a ground plan
272	Ichnology	science of fossilized footprints
273	Ichthyology	study of fish
274	Iconography	study of drawing symbols
275	Iconology	study of icons; symbols
276	Ideogeny	study of origins of ideas
277	Ideology	science of ideas; system of ideas used to justify behaviour
278	Idiomology	study of idiom, jargon or dialect
279	Idiopsychology	psychology of one's own mind
280	Immunogenetics	study of genetic characteristics of immunity
281	Immunology	study of immunity
282	Immunopathology	study of immunity to disease
283	Insectology	study of insects
284	Irenology	the study of peace
285	Iridology	study of the iris; diagnosis of disease based on the iris of the eye
286	Kalology	study of beauty
287	Karyology	study of cell nuclei
288	Kidology	study of kidding
289	Kinematics	study of motion
290	Kinesics	study of gestural communication
291	Kinesiology	study of human movement and posture
292	Kinetics	study of forces producing or changing motion
293	Koniology	study of atmospheric pollutants and dust
294	Ktenology	science of putting people to death
295	Kymatology	study of wave motion
296	Labeorphily	collection and study of beer bottle labels
297	Larithmics	study of population statistics
298	Laryngology	study of larynx
299	Lepidopterology	study of butterflies and moths
300	Leprology	study of leprosy
301	Lexicology	study of words and their meanings
302	Lexigraphy	art of definition of words
303	Lichenology	study of lichens
304	Limacology	study of slugs
305	Limnobiology	study of freshwater ecosystems

SN	Words	Definition
306	**Limnology**	study of bodies of fresh water
307	**Linguistics**	study of language
308	**Lithology**	study of rocks
309	**Liturgiology**	study of liturgical forms and church rituals
310	**Loimology**	study of plagues and epidemics
311	**Loxodromy**	study of sailing along rhumb-lines
312	**Magirics**	art of cookery
313	**Magnanerie**	art of raising silkworms
314	**Magnetics**	study of magnetism
315	**Malacology**	study of molluscs
316	**Malariology**	study of malaria
317	**Mammalogy**	study of mammals
318	**Manège**	the art of horsemanship
319	**Mariology**	study of the Virgin Mary
320	**Martyrology**	study of martyrs
321	**Mastology**	study of mammals
322	**Mathematics**	study of magnitude, number, and forms
323	**Mazology**	mammalogy; study of mammals
324	**Mechanics**	study of action of force on bodies
325	**Meconology**	study of or treatise concerning opium
326	**Melittology**	study of bees
327	**Mereology**	study of part-whole relationships
328	**Mesology**	ecology
329	**Metallogeny**	study of the origin and distribution of metal deposits
330	**Metallography**	study of the structure and constitution of metals
331	**Metallurgy**	study of alloying and treating metals
332	**Metaphysics**	study of principles of nature and thought
333	**Metapolitics**	study of politics in theory or abstract
334	**Metapsychology**	study of nature of the mind
335	**Meteoritics**	the study of meteors
336	**Meteorology**	study of weather
337	**Metrics**	study of versification
338	**Metrology**	science of weights and measures
339	**Microanatomy**	study of microscopic tissues
340	**Microbiology**	study of microscopic organisms
341	**Microclimatology**	study of local climates
342	**Micrology**	study or discussion of trivialities
343	**Micropalaeontology**	study of microscopic fossils
344	**Microphytology**	study of very small plant life
345	**Microscopy**	study of minute objects
346	**Mineralogy**	study of minerals
347	**Molinology**	study of mills and milling
348	**Momilogy**	study of mummies
349	**Morphology**	study of forms and the development of structures

SN	Words	Definition
350	**Muscology**	the study of mosses
351	**Museology**	the study of museums
352	**Musicology**	study of music
353	**Mycology**	study of funguses
354	**Myology**	study of muscles
355	**Myrmecology**	study of ants
356	**Mythology**	study of myths; fables; tales
357	**Naology**	study of church or temple architecture
358	**Nasology**	study of the nose
359	**Nautics**	art of navigation
360	**Nematology**	the study of nematodes
361	**Neonatology**	study of newborn babies
362	**Neossology**	study of nestling birds
363	**Nephology**	study of clouds
364	**Nephrology**	study of the kidneys
365	**Neurobiology**	study of anatomy of the nervous system
366	**Neurology**	study of nervous system
367	**Neuropsychology**	study of relation between brain and behaviour
368	**Neurypnology**	study of hypnotism
369	**Neutrosophy**	study of the origin and nature of philosophical neutralities
370	**Nidology**	study of nests
371	**Nomology**	the science of the laws; especially of the mind
372	**Noology**	science of the intellect
373	**Nosology**	study of diseases
374	**Nostology**	study of senility
375	**Notaphily**	collecting of bank-notes and cheques
376	**Numerology**	study of numbers
377	**Numismatics**	study of coins
378	**Nymphology**	study of nymphs
379	**Obstetrics**	study of midwifery
380	**Oceanography**	study of oceans
381	**Oceanology**	study of oceans
382	**Odology**	science of the hypothetical mystical force of od
383	**Odontology**	study of teeth
384	**Oenology**	study of wines
385	**Oikology**	science of housekeeping
386	**Olfactology**	study of the sense of smell
387	**Ombrology**	study of rain
388	**Oncology**	study of tumours
389	**Oneirology**	study of dreams
390	**Onomasiology**	study of nomenclature
391	**Onomastics**	study of proper names
392	**Ontology**	science of pure being; the nature of things

SN	Words	Definition
393	**Oology**	study of eggs
394	**Ophiology**	study of snakes
395	**Ophthalmology**	study of eye diseases
396	**Optics**	study of light
397	**Optology**	study of sight
398	**Optometry**	science of examining the eyes
399	**Orchidology**	study of orchids
400	**Ornithology**	study of birds
401	**Orology**	study of mountains
402	**Orthoepy**	study of correct pronunciation
403	**Orthography**	study of spelling
404	**Orthopterology**	study of cockroaches
405	**Oryctology**	mineralogy or paleontology
406	**Osmics**	scientific study of smells
407	**Osmology**	study of smells and olfactory processes
408	**Osphresiology**	study of the sense of smell
409	**Osteology**	study of bones
410	**Otology**	study of the ear
411	**Otorhinolaryngology**	study of ear, nose and throat
412	**Paedology**	study of children
413	**Paedotrophy**	art of rearing children
414	**Paidonosology**	study of children's diseases; pediatrics
415	**Palaeoanthropology**	study of early humans
416	**Palaeobiology**	study of fossil plants and animals
417	**Palaeoclimatology**	study of ancient climates
418	**Palaeolimnology**	study of ancient fish
419	**Palaeolimnology**	study of ancient lakes
420	**Palaeontology**	study of fossils
421	**Palaeopedology**	study of early soils
422	**Paleobotany**	study of ancient plants
423	**Paleo-Osteology**	study of ancient bones
424	**Palynology**	study of pollen
425	**Papyrology**	study of paper
426	**Parapsychology**	study of unexplained mental phenomena
427	**Parasitology**	study of parasites
428	**Paroemiology**	study of proverbs
429	**Parthenology**	study of virgins
430	**Pataphysics**	the science of imaginary solutions
431	**Pathology**	study of disease
432	**Patrology**	study of early Christianity
433	**Pedagogics**	study of teaching
434	**Pedology**	study of soils
435	**Pelology**	study of mud
436	**Penology**	study of crime and punishment

SN	Words	Definition
437	**Periodontics**	study of gums
438	**Peristerophily**	pigeon-collecting
439	**Pestology**	science of pests
440	**Petrology**	study of rocks
441	**Pharmacognosy**	study of drugs of animal and plant origin
442	**Pharmacology**	study of drugs
443	**Pharology**	study of lighthouses
444	**Pharyngology**	study of the throat
445	**Phenology**	study of organisms as affected by climate
446	**Phenomenology**	study of phenomena
447	**Philately**	study of postage stamps
448	**Philematology**	the act or study of kissing
449	**Phillumeny**	collecting of matchbox labels
450	**Philology**	study of ancient texts; historical linguistics
451	**Philosophy**	science of knowledge or wisdom
452	**Phoniatrics**	study and correction of speech defects
453	**Phonology**	study of speech sounds
454	**Photobiology**	study of effects of light on organisms
455	**Phraseology**	study of phrases
456	**Phrenology**	study of bumps on the head
457	**Phycology**	study of algae and seaweeds
458	**Physics**	study of properties of matter and energy
459	**Physiology**	study of processes of life
460	**Phytology**	study of plants; botany
461	**Piscatology**	study of fishes
462	**Pisteology**	science or study of faith
463	**Planetology**	study of planets
464	**Plutology**	political economy; study of wealth
465	**Pneumatics**	study of mechanics of gases
466	**Podiatry**	study and treatment of disorders of the foot; chiropody
467	**Podology**	study of the feet
468	**Polemology**	study of war
469	**Pomology**	study of fruit-growing
470	**Posology**	science of quantity or dosage
471	**Potamology**	study of rivers
472	**Praxeology**	study of practical or efficient activity
473	**Primatology**	study of primates
474	**Proctology**	study of rectum
475	**Prosody**	study of versification
476	**Protistology**	study of protists
477	**Proxemics**	study of man's need for personal space
478	**Psalligraphy**	the art of paper-cutting to make pictures
479	**Psephology**	study of election results and voting trends
480	**Pseudology**	art or science of lying

SN	Words	Definition
481	**Pseudoptics**	study of optical illusions
482	**Psychobiology**	study of biology of the mind
483	**Psychogenetics**	study of internal or mental states
484	**Psychognosy**	study of mentality, personality or character
485	**Psychology**	study of mind
486	**Psychopathology**	study of mental illness
487	**Psychophysics**	study of link between mental and physical processes
488	**Pteridology**	study of ferns
489	**Pterylology**	study of distribution of feathers on birds
490	**Pyretology**	study of fevers
491	**Pyrgology**	study of towers
492	**Pyroballogy**	study of artillery
493	**Pyrography**	study of woodburning
494	**Quinology**	study of quinine
495	**Raciology**	study of racial differences
496	**Radiology**	study of X-rays and their medical applications
497	**Reflexology**	study of reflexes
498	**Rhabdology**	knowledge or learning concerning divining rods
499	**Rhabdology**	art of calculating using numbering rods
500	**Rheology**	science of the deformation or flow of matter
501	**Rheumatology**	study of rheumatism
502	**Rhinology**	study of the nose
503	**Rhochrematics**	science of inventory management and the movement of products
504	**Runology**	study of runes
505	**Sarcology**	study of fleshy parts of the body
506	**Satanology**	study of the devil
507	**Scatology**	study of excrement or obscene literature
508	**Schematonics**	art of using gesture to express tones
509	**Sciagraphy**	art of shading
510	**Scripophily**	collection of bond and share certificates
511	**Sedimentology**	study of sediment
512	**Seismology**	study of earthquakes
513	**Selenodesy**	study of the shape and features of the moon
514	**Selenology**	study of the moon
515	**Semantics**	study of meaning
516	**Semantology**	science of meanings of words
517	**Semasiology**	study of meaning; semantics
518	**Semiology**	study of signs and signals
519	**Semiotics**	study of signs and symbols
520	**Serology**	study of serums
521	**Sexology**	study of sexual behaviour
522	**Siderography**	art of engraving on steel
523	**Sigillography**	study of seals

SN	Words	Definition
524	**Significs**	science of meaning
525	**Silvics**	study of tree's life
526	**Sindonology**	study of the shroud of Turin
527	**Sinology**	study of China
528	**Sitology**	dietetics
529	**Sociobiology**	study of biological basis of human behaviour
530	**Sociology**	study of society
531	**Somatology**	science of the properties of matter
532	**Sophiology**	science of ideas
533	**Soteriology**	study of theological salvation
534	**Spectrology**	study of ghosts
535	**Spectroscopy**	study of spectra
536	**Speleology**	study and exploration of caves
537	**Spermology**	study of seeds
538	**Sphagnology**	study of peat moss
539	**Sphragistics**	study of seals and signets
540	**Sphygmology**	study of the pulse
541	**Splanchnology**	study of the entrails or viscera
542	**Spongology**	study of sponges
543	**Stasiology**	study of political parties
544	**Statics**	study of bodies and forces in equilibrium
545	**Stemmatology**	study of relationships between texts
546	**Stoichiology**	science of elements of animal tissues
547	**Stomatology**	study of the mouth
548	**Storiology**	study of folk tales
549	**Stratigraphy**	study of geological layers or strata
550	**Stratography**	art of leading an army
551	**Stylometry**	studying literature by means of statistical analysis
552	**Suicidology**	study of suicide
553	**Symbology**	study of symbols
554	**Symptomatology**	study of symptoms of illness
555	**Synecology**	study of ecological communities
556	**Synectics**	study of processes of invention
557	**Syntax**	study of sentence structure
558	**Syphilology**	study of syphilis
559	**Systematology**	study of systems
560	**Taxidermy**	art of curing and stuffing animals
561	**Tectonics**	science of structure of objects, buildings and landforms
562	**Tegestology**	study and collecting of beer mats
563	**Teleology**	study of final causes; analysis in terms of purpose
564	**Telmatology**	study of swamps
565	**Teratology**	study of monsters, freaks or malformations etc
566	**Teuthology**	study of cephalopods
567	**Textology**	study of the production of texts

SN	Words	Definition
568	**Thalassography**	science of the sea
569	**Thanatology**	study of death and its customs
570	**Thaumatology**	study of miracles
571	**Theology**	study of religion; religious doctrine
572	**Theriatrics**	veterinary medicine
573	**Theriogenology**	study of animals' reproductive systems
574	**Thermodynamics**	study of relation of heat to motion
575	**Thermokinematics**	study of motion of heat
576	**Thermology**	study of heat
577	**Therology**	study of wild mammals
578	**Thremmatology**	science of breeding domestic animals and plants
579	**Threpsology**	science of nutrition
580	**Tidology**	study of tides
581	**Timbrology**	study of postage stamps
582	**Tocology**	obstetrics; midwifery
583	**Tonetics**	study of pronunciation
584	**Topology**	study of places and their natural features
585	**Toponymics**	study of place-names
586	**Toreutics**	study of artistic work in metal
587	**Toxicology**	study of poisons
588	**Toxophily**	love of archery; archery; study of archery
589	**Traumatology**	study of wounds and their effects
590	**Tribology**	study of friction and wear between surfaces
591	**Trichology**	study of hair and its disorders
592	**Trophology**	study of nutrition
593	**Tsiganology**	study of gypsies
594	**Turnery**	art of turning in a lathe
595	**Typhlology**	study of blindness and the blind
596	**Typography**	art of printing or using type
597	**Typology**	study of types of things
598	**Ufology**	study of alien spacecraft
599	**Uranography**	descriptive astronomy and mapping
600	**Uranology**	study of the heavens; astronomy
601	**Urbanology**	study of cities
602	**Urenology**	study of rust molds
603	**Urology**	study of urine; urinary tract
604	**Venereology**	study of venereal disease
605	**Vermeology**	study of worms
606	**Vexillology**	study of flags
607	**Victimology**	study of victims
608	**Vinology**	scientific study of vines and winemaking
609	**Virology**	study of viruses
610	**Vitrics**	glassy materials; glassware; study of glassware
611	**Volcanology**	study of volcanoes

SN	Words	Definition
612	**Vulcanology**	study of volcanoes
613	**Xylography**	art of engraving on wood
614	**Xylology**	study of wood
615	**Zenography**	study of the planet Jupiter
616	**Zoiatrics**	veterinary surgery
617	**Zooarchaeology**	study of animal remains of archaeological sites
618	**Zoochemistry**	chemistry of animals
619	**Zoogeography**	study of geographic distribution of animals
620	**Zoogeology**	study of fossil animal remains
621	**Zoology**	study of animals
622	**Zoonomy**	animal physiology
623	**Zoonosology**	study of animal diseases
624	**Zoopathology**	study of animal diseases
625	**Zoophysics**	physics of animal bodies
626	**Zoophysiology**	study of physiology of animals
627	**Zoophytology**	study of plant-like animals
628	**Zoosemiotics**	study of animal communication
629	**Zootaxy**	science of classifying animals
630	**Zootechnics**	science of breeding animals
631	**Zygology**	science of joining and fastening
632	**Zymology**	science of fermentation
633	**Zymurgy**	branch of chemistry dealing with brewing and distilling

SN	Words	Definition
1	**Acoustography**	an imaging process that employs a sensor to convert ultrasound into an image in near real-time, analogous to an X-ray
2	**Acrography**	a method of relief etching on wood, metal, or stone by means of a coating of compressed chalk
3	**Angiography**	roentgenographic examination of blood vessels after injection of a radiopaque contrast medium; produces an angiogram
4	**Arteriography**	roentgenographic examination of arteries
5	**Autobiography**	a biography of yourself
6	**Autography**	ariting done with one's own hand.
7	**Autoradiography**	producing a radiograph by means of the radiation emitted from the specimen being photographed
8	**Bibliography**	a list of writings with time and place of publication (such as the writings of a single author or the works referred to in preparing a document etc.)
9	**Biogeography**	dealing with the geographical distribution of animals and plants
10	**Biography**	an account of the series of events making up a person's life
11	**Cacography**	poor handwriting
12	**Calligraphy**	beautiful handwriting
13	**Cardiography**	diagnostic procedure consisting of recording the activity of the heart electronically with a cardiograph (and producing a cardiogram)
14	**Cartography**	the making of maps and charts
15	**Chirography**	beautiful handwriting
16	**Cholangiography**	roentgenographic examination of the bile ducts after a contrast medium has been injected
17	**Choreography**	a notation used by choreographers
18	**Chorography**	the systematic description and mapping of particular regions
19	**Chromatography**	a process used for separating mixtures by virtue of differences in absorbency
20	**Cinematography**	the act of making a film
21	**Cosmography**	a representation of the earth or the heavens
22	**Cryptography**	act of writing in code or cipher
23	**Crystallography**	the branch of science that studies the formation and structure of crystals
24	**Demography**	the branch of sociology that studies the characteristics of human populations
25	**Encephalography**	roentgenography of the brain after spinal fluid has been replaced by a gas (usually oxygen); produces an encephalogram

SN	Words	Definition
26	**Epigraphy**	the study of ancient inscriptions
27	**Ethnography**	the branch of anthropology that provides scientific description of individual human societies
28	**Geography**	study of the earth's surface; includes people's responses to topography and climate and soil and vegetation
29	**Hagiography**	a biography that idealizes or idolizes the person (especially a person who is a saint)
30	**Historiography**	the writing of history
31	**Holography**	the branch of optics that deals with the use of coherent light from a laser in order to make a hologram that can then be used to create a three dimensional image
32	**Hydrography**	the science of the measurement and description and mapping of the surface waters of the earth with special reference to navigation
33	**Iconography**	the images and symbolic representations that are traditionally associated with a person or a subject
34	**Ideography**	the use of ideograms in writing
35	**Lexicography**	the act of writing dictionaries
36	**Lithography**	the act of making a lithographic print
37	**Lymphography**	roentgenographic examination of lymph nodes and lymph vessels after injection of a radiopaque contrast medium; produces a lymphangiogram
38	**Mammography**	a diagnostic procedure to detect breast tumors by the use of X rays
39	**Oceanography**	the branch of science dealing with physical and biological aspects of the oceans
40	**Orography**	the science of mountains
41	**Orthography**	a method of representing the sounds of a language by written or printed symbols
42	**Paleogeography**	the study of the geography of ancient times or ancient epochs
43	**Paleography**	the study of ancient forms of writing (and the deciphering of them)
44	**Photography**	the occupation of taking and printing photographs or making movies
45	**Physiography**	the study of physical features of the earth's surface
46	**Planography**	the process of printing from a surface on which the printing areas are not raised but are ink receptive (as opposed to ink repellent)
47	**Polarography**	an electrochemical method of chemical analysis
48	**Pornography**	creative activity (writing or pictures or films etc.) of no literary or artistic value other than to stimulate sexual desire

SN	Words	Definition
49	**Radiography**	photography that uses other kinds of radiation than visible light
50	**Radiotelegraphy**	the use of radio to send telegraphic messages (usually by Morse code)
51	**Roentgenography**	radiography that uses X rays to produce a roentgenogram
52	**Seismography**	the measurement of tremors and shocks and undulatory movements of earthquakes
53	**Serigraphy**	the act of making a print by the silkscreen method
54	**Sonography**	using the reflections of high frequency sound waves to construct an image of a body organ (a sonogram); commonly used to observe fetal growth or study bodily organs
55	**Stenography**	the act or art of writing in shorthand
56	**Stratigraphy**	the branch of geology that studies the arrangement and succession of strata
57	**Telegraphy**	communicating at a distance by electric transmission over wire
58	**Telephotography**	photography using a telephoto lens
59	**Thermography**	diagnostic technique using a thermograph to record the heat produced by different parts of the body; used to study blood flow and to detect tumors
60	**Tomography**	(medicine) obtaining pictures of the interior of the body
61	**Topography**	the configuration of a surface and the relations among its man made and natural features
62	**Typography**	the craft of composing type and printing from it
63	**Ultrasonography**	using the reflections of high frequency sound waves to construct an image of a body organ (a sonogram); commonly used to observe fetal growth or study bodily organs
64	**Venography**	roentgenographic examination of veins
65	**Xerography**	forming an image by the action of light on a specially coated charged plate; the latent image is developed with powders that adhere only to electrically charged areas
66	**Xeroradiography**	radiography using X rays and xerographic (rather than roentgenographic) techniques

SN	Words	Definition
1	**Acracy**	government by none; anarchy
2	**Adhocracy**	government in an unstructured fashion; an unstructured organization
3	**Albocracy**	government by white people
4	**Anarchy**	government by none
5	**Androcracy**	government by men
6	**Anemocracy**	government by the wind
7	**Angelocracy**	government by angels
8	**Antarchy**	opposition to government; anarchy
9	**Argentocracy**	government by money
10	**Aristarchy**	government by the best
11	**Aristocracy**	government by the nobility
12	**Arithmocracy**	government by simple majority
13	**Autarchy**	government by an absolute ruler
14	**Autocracy**	government by one individual
15	**Barbarocracy**	government by barbarians
16	**Beerocracy**	government by brewers or brewing interests
17	**Bestiocracy**	rule by beasts
18	**Biarchy**	government by two people; diarchy
19	**Binarchy**	government by two people; diarchy
20	**Bureaucracy**	government by civil servants
21	**Cannonarchy**	government by superior firepower or by cannons
22	**Capelocracy**	government by shopkeepers
23	**Chiliarchy**	government by one thousand people
24	**Chirocracy**	government by physical force
25	**Chromatocracy**	government by rulers of a particular skin colour
26	**Chrysoaristocracy**	government by the wealthy; plutocracy
27	**Chrysocracy**	government by the wealthy; plutocracy
28	**Corpocracy**	government by corporate bureaucrats
29	**Cosmarchy**	rulership over the entire world, esp. by the devil
30	**Cottonocracy**	government by those involved in the cotton trade
31	**Cryptarchy**	secret rulership
32	**Decadarchy**	government by ten individuals; decarchy
33	**Decarchy**	government by ten individuals
34	**Demarchy**	government by the people; popular government
35	**Democracy**	government by the people
36	**Demonarchy**	government by a demon
37	**Demonocracy**	government by demons or evil forces
38	**Despotocracy**	government by despots or tyrants
39	**Diabolocracy**	government by the Devil
40	**Diarchy**	government by two people
41	**Dinarchy**	government by two people; diarchy
42	**Dodecarchy**	government by twelve people
43	**Doulocracy**	government by slaves

482

SN	Words	Definition
44	**Duarchy**	government by two people; diarchy
45	**Dulocracy**	government by slaves; doulocracy
46	**Dyarchy**	government by two people; diarchy
47	**Ecclesiarchy**	government by clerics or ecclesiastical authorities
48	**Endarchy**	centralised government
49	**Ergatocracy**	government by the workers or the working class
50	**Ethnarchy**	government over an ethnic group
51	**Ethnocracy**	government by an ethnic group or race
52	**Exarchy**	government by bishops
53	**Foolocracy**	government by fools
54	**Gerontocracy**	government by the aged
55	**Gunarchy**	government by women; gynarchy
56	**Gymnasiarchy**	government over a school or academy
57	**Gynaecocracy**	government by women; gynarchy
58	**Gynarchy**	government by women
59	**Gynocracy**	government by women; gynarchy
60	**Hagiarchy**	government by saints or holy persons
61	**Hagiocracy**	government by holy men
62	**Hamarchy**	government by a cooperative body of parts
63	**Hecatarchy**	government by one hundred people; hecatontarchy
64	**Hecatontarchy**	government by one hundred people
65	**Hendecarchy**	government by eleven people
66	**Heptarchy**	government by seven people
67	**Heroarchy**	government by heroes
68	**Hetaerocracy**	government by paramours
69	**Heterarchy**	government by a foreign ruler
70	**Hierarchy**	government by a ranked body; government by priests
71	**Hierocracy**	government by priests or religious ministers
72	**Hipparchy**	rule or control of horses
73	**Hoplarchy**	government by the military
74	**Hyperanarchy**	condition of extreme anarchy
75	**Hyperarchy**	excessive government
76	**Iatrarchy**	government by physicians
77	**Idiocracy**	personal rule; self-rule
78	**Infantocracy**	government by an infant
79	**Isocracy**	equal political power
80	**Jesuitocracy**	government by Jesuits
81	**Juntocracy**	government by a junta
82	**Kakistocracy**	government by the worst
83	**Kleptocracy**	government by thieves
84	**Kritarchy**	government by judges
85	**Landocracy**	government by the propertied class; timocracy
86	**Logocracy**	government of words
87	**Matriarchy**	government by women or mothers

SN	Words	Definition
88	**Meritocracy**	government by the meritorious
89	**Merocracy**	government by a part of the citizenry
90	**Mesocracy**	government by the middle classes
91	**Metrocracy**	government by mothers or women; matriarchy
92	**Millionocracy**	government by millionaires
93	**Millocracy**	government by mill owners
94	**Mobocracy**	government by mobs or crowds
95	**Monarchy**	government by one individual
96	**Moneyocracy**	government by the monied classes
97	**Monocracy**	government by one individual
98	**Myriarchy**	government by ten thousand individuals
99	**Narcokleptocracy**	government by those who profit from trade in illegal drugs
100	**Navarchy**	rulership over the seas
101	**Neocracy**	government by new or inexperienced rulers
102	**Nomocracy**	government based on legal system; rule of law
103	**Ochlocracy**	government by mobs
104	**Octarchy**	government by eight people
105	**Oligarchy**	government by the few
106	**Paedarchy**	government by children
107	**Paedocracy**	government by children; paedarchy
108	**Panarchy**	universal rule or dominion
109	**Pantarchy**	government by all the people; world government
110	**Pantisocracy**	government by all equally
111	**Paparchy**	government by the pope
112	**Papyrocracy**	government by newspapers or literature
113	**Parsonarchy**	government by parsons
114	**Partocracy**	government by a single unopposed political party
115	**Patriarchy**	government by men or fathers
116	**Pedantocracy**	government by pedants or strict rule-bound scholars
117	**Pentarchy**	government by five individuals
118	**Phallocracy**	government by men
119	**Philosophocracy**	government by philosophers
120	**Phylarchy**	government by a specific class or tribe
121	**Physiocracy**	government according to natural laws or principles
122	**Pigmentocracy**	government by those of one skin colour
123	**Plantocracy**	government by plantation owners
124	**Plousiocracy**	government by the wealthy; plutocracy
125	**Plutarchy**	government by the wealthy; plutocracy
126	**Plutocracy**	government by the wealthy
127	**Polarchy**	government by many people; polyarchy
128	**Policeocracy**	government by police
129	**Pollarchy**	government by the multitude or a mob; ochlocracy
130	**Polyarchy**	government by many people

SN	Words	Definition
131	**Polycracy**	government by many rulers; polyarchy
132	**Popocracy**	government by populists
133	**Pornocracy**	government by harlots
134	**Prophetocracy**	government by a prophet
135	**Psephocracy**	government resulting from election by ballot
136	**Ptochocracy**	government by beggars or paupers; wholesale pauperization
137	**Punditocracy**	government by political pundits
138	**Quangocracy**	rule of quasi-autonomous non-governmental organizations
139	**Rotocracy**	government by those who control rotten boroughs
140	**Septarchy**	government by seven rulers; heptarchy
141	**Shopocracy**	government by shopkeepers
142	**Slavocracy**	government by slave-owners
143	**Snobocracy**	government by snobs
144	**Sociocracy**	government by society as a whole
145	**Squarsonocracy**	government by landholding clergymen
146	**Squatterarchy**	government by squatters; squattocracy
147	**Squattocracy**	government by squatters
148	**Squirearchy**	government by squires
149	**Squirocracy**	government by squires; squirearchy
150	**Statocracy**	government by the state alone, without ecclesiastical influence
151	**Stratarchy**	rulership over an army
152	**Stratocracy**	military rule or despotism
153	**Strumpetocracy**	government by strumpets
154	**Synarchy**	joint sovereignty
155	**Technocracy**	government by technical experts
156	**Tetradarchy**	government by four people; tetrarchy
157	**Tetrarchy**	government by four people
158	**Thalassiarchy**	sovereignty of the seas; thalassocracy
159	**Thalassocracy**	sovereignty of the seas
160	**Thearchy**	rule by a god or gods; body of divine rulers
161	**Theatrocracy**	goverment by gathered assemblies of citizens
162	**Theocracy**	government by priests or by religious law
163	**Timarchy**	government by the propertied class; timocracy
164	**Timocracy**	government by the propertied class
165	**Triarchy**	government by three people
166	**Tritheocracy**	government by three gods
167	**Whiggarchy**	government by Whigs
168	**Xenocracy**	government by a body of foreigners

SN	Words	Definition
1	**Aischrolatry**	worship of filth, dirt, or smut
2	**Allotheism**	belief in or worship of strange gods
3	**Angelolatry**	worship of or belief in angels
4	**Anthropolatry**	worship of human beings
5	**Arborolatry**	worship of trees
6	**Archaeolatry**	worship of archaic things or old customs
7	**Astrolatry**	worship of stars
8	**Autolatry**	self-worship
9	**Bardolatry**	excessive devotion to or worship of Shakespeare
10	**Bibliolatry**	worship of the Bible or other books
11	**Christolatry**	worship of Christ
12	**Cosmolatry**	worship of the world
13	**Cynolatry**	worship of dogs
14	**Demonolatry**	worship of or devotion to demons
15	**Dendrolatry**	worship of trees
16	**Ecclesiolatry**	excessive devotion to church tradition and form
17	**Epeolatry**	worship of words
18	**Episcopolatry**	worship of bishops
19	**Gamidolatry**	worship of marriage
20	**Gastrolatry**	gluttony; excessive love of food
21	**Geolatry**	earth-worship
22	**Grammatolatry**	worship of letters and words
23	**Gyniolatry**	deep respect or devotion for women
24	**Hagiolatry**	worship or reverence for saints
25	**Heliolatry**	sun worship
26	**Hierolatry**	worship of saints or sacred things
27	**Hygeiolatry**	excessive devotion to health
28	**Ichthyolatry**	the worship of fish
29	**Iconolatry**	image-worship
30	**Ideolatry**	worship of ideas
31	**Idiolatry**	self-worship; egotism
32	**Idolatry**	worship of idols
33	**Ignicolist**	fire-worshipper
34	**Litholatry**	stone-worship
35	**Lordolatry**	worship of nobility
36	**Mariolatry**	worship of the virgin mother
37	**Martyrolatry**	excessive devotion to martyrs
38	**Mechanolatry**	worship of machines
39	**Monolatry**	worship of one god without excluding belief in others
40	**Necrolatry**	worship of the dead
41	**Neolatry**	worship of novelty
42	**Onolatry**	worship of asses or donkeys
43	**Ophiolatry**	worship of snakes
44	**Ophism**	snake-worship

SN	Words	Definition
45	**Pandemonism**	worship of spirits dwelling in all forms of nature
46	**Parthenolatry**	worship of the Virgin Mary
47	**Patriolatry**	excessive devotion or worship of one's native country
48	**Physiolatry**	nature-worship
49	**Planetolatry**	worship of the planets
50	**Plutolatry**	worship of wealth
51	**Poetolatry**	worship of poets
52	**Pseudolatry**	false worship
53	**Pyrolatry**	fire-worship
54	**Selenolatry**	worship of the moon
55	**Statolatry**	worship of the state
56	**Staurolatry**	worship of the cross or crucifix
57	**Symbolatry**	undue worship of symbols
58	**Thaumatolatry**	worship of miracles or wonders
59	**Theriolatry**	animal-worship
60	**Zoolatry**	excessive devotion to animals or pets

SN	Words	Definition
1	**Absorptiometer**	instrument for measuring solubility of gases in liquids
2	**Accelerometer**	instrument for measuring acceleration or vibrations
3	**Acetimeter**	instrument for measuring strength of vinegar
4	**Acidimeter**	instrument for measuring concentration of acids
5	**Actinograph**	instrument used to calculate time of photographic exposure
6	**Actinometer**	instrument for measuring incident radiation
7	**Aerometer**	instrument for measuring weight or density of gas
8	**Aethrioscope**	instrument for measuring temperature variations due to sky conditions
9	**Alcoholometer**	instrument for measuring proportion of alcohol in solutions
10	**Alcovinometer**	instrument to measure strength of wine
11	**Algometer**	instrument for measuring sensitivity to pain
12	**Alkalimeter**	instrument for measuring strength of alkalines
13	**Altimeter**	instrument for measuring altitude
14	**Ammeter**	instrument for measuring electrical current
15	**Anemograph**	instrument for measuring pressure and velocity of wind
16	**Anemometer**	instrument for measuring wind velocity
17	**Areometer**	instrument used for measuring specific gravity
18	**Arthroscope**	instrument for examining interior of a joint
19	**Atmometer**	instrument for measuring evaporating capacity of air
20	**Audiometer**	instrument for measuring acuity of hearing
21	**Auriscope**	instrument for examining the ear
22	**Auxanometer**	instrument for measuring growth of plants
23	**Auxometer**	instrument for measuring magnifying power
24	**Ballistocardiograph**	instrument for detecting body movements caused by heartbeat
25	**Barograph**	instrument for recording air pressure
26	**Barometer**	instrument for measuring air pressure
27	**Baroscope**	weather-glass
28	**Bathymeter**	instrument for recording contours of deep oceans
29	**Bathythermograph**	instrument for recording water temperature as compared to depth
30	**Bolometer**	instrument for measuring radiant energy or infrared light
31	**Bronchoscope**	instrument for examining the windpipe
32	**Calorimeter**	instrument for measuring absorbed or evolved heat
33	**Cardiograph**	instrument for recording movements of the heart
34	**Cathetometer**	instrument for measuring short vertical distances
35	**Ceilometer**	instrument for measuring height of cloud ceiling above earth
36	**Ceraunograph**	instrument for recording thunder and lightning
37	**Chlorometer**	instrument for measuring amount of chlorine in a solution
38	**Chromatograph**	instrument for performing chromatographic separations
39	**Chromatoptometer**	instrument measuring eyes' sensitivity to colour

SN	Words	Definition
40	**Chronograph**	instrument for recording the moment of an event
41	**Chronometer**	instrument for measuring time
42	**Chronoscope**	instrument for measuring very short time intervals
43	**Clinometer**	instrument used to measure slopes and elevations
44	**Coercimeter**	instrument for measuring coercive force
45	**Colonoscope**	instrument for viewing the colon
46	**Colorimeter**	instrument for measuring and determining colour
47	**Colposcope**	instrument for viewing the neck of the uterus
48	**Coronagraph**	instrument for viewing the corona of the sun
49	**Coulombmeter**	instrument for measuring electric charge
50	**Coulometer**	instrument measuring amount of substance released in electrolysis
51	**Craniometer**	instrument for measuring the skull
52	**Cratometer**	instrument for measuring power of magnification
53	**Crescograph**	instrument for measuring the growth of plants
54	**Cryometer**	instrument for measuring low temperatures
55	**Cryoscope**	instrument for determining freezing points of substances
56	**Cyanometer**	instrument for measuring blueness of the sky or ocean
57	**Cyclograph**	instrument for describing arcs of circles without compasses
58	**Cyclometer**	instrument for measuring revolutions of a wheel
59	**Cymograph**	instrument for tracing the outline of mouldings
60	**Cymometer**	instrument for measuring frequency of electrical waves
61	**Cystoscope**	instrument for examining the bladder
62	**Cytometer**	instrument for counting cells
63	**Decelerometer**	instrument for measuring deceleration
64	**Declinometer**	instrument for measuring magnetic declination
65	**Dendrometer**	instrument for measuring trees
66	**Densimeter**	instrument for measuring closeness of grain of a substance
67	**Densitometer**	instrument for measuring optical or photographic density
68	**Diagometer**	instrument for measuring electrical conductivity
69	**Diagraph**	instrument for enlarging or projecting drawings
70	**Diaphanometer**	instrument for measuring the transparency of air
71	**Dichroscope**	instrument for examining crystals for dichroism
72	**Diffractometer**	instrument for determining structure of crystal through light diffraction
73	**Dilatometer**	instrument for measuring expansion
74	**Dioptometer**	instrument for measuring focus or refraction of the eyes
75	**Dipleidoscope**	instrument for measuring moment when an object passes a meridian
76	**Diplograph**	instrument for writing two lines of text at once
77	**Dosimeter**	instrument for measuring dose of radiation
78	**Dromometer**	instrument for measuring speed
79	**Drosometer**	instrument for measuring dew

SN	Words	Definition
80	**Durometer**	instrument for measuring hardness of substances
81	**Dynamograph**	instrument for recording mechanical forces
82	**Dynamometer**	instrument for measuring mechanical force
83	**Ebullioscope**	instrument for measuring boiling point of liquids
84	**Effusiometer**	instrument for comparing molecular weights of gases
85	**Eidograph**	instrument for copying drawings
86	**Elatrometer**	instrument for measuring gaseous pressure
87	**Electrocardiograph**	instrument for recording unusual electrical fluctuations of the heart
88	**Electrodynamometer**	instrument for measuring electrical current
89	**Electroencephalograph**	instrument for measuring the brain's electrical impulses
90	**Electrograph**	instrument for recording electrical potential
91	**Electrometer**	instrument for measuring electrical potential
92	**Electromyograph**	instrument for diagnosing neuromuscular disorders
93	**Electroretinograph**	instrument for measuring electrical activity in the retina
94	**Electroscope**	instrument for detecting electrical charges in the body
95	**Ellipsograph**	instrument for describing ellipses
96	**Encephalograph**	instrument for recording brain images
97	**Endoscope**	instrument for visualizing interior of a hollow organ
98	**Endosmometer**	instrument for measuring osmosis into a solution
99	**Epidiascope**	instrument for projecting images of objects
100	**Episcope**	instrument for projecting images of opaque objects
101	**Ergograph**	instrument for measuring and recording muscular work
102	**Ergometer**	instrument for measuring work performed
103	**Eriometer**	instrument for measuring very small diameters
104	**Eudiometer**	instrument for measuring air purity
105	**Evaporimeter**	instrument for measuring rate of evaporation
106	**Extensometer**	instrument for measuring deformation in object due to forces applied
107	**Fathometer**	instrument for measuring underwater depth using sound
108	**Fiberscope**	instrument using fibre-optics to examine inaccessible areas
109	**Floriscope**	instrument for inspecting flowers
110	**Flowmeter**	instrument for measuring properties of flowing liquids
111	**Fluorimeter**	instrument for measuring fluorescence
112	**Fluoroscope**	instrument using x-rays to examine internal structure of opaque object
113	**Focimeter**	instrument for measuring focal length of a lens
114	**Galactometer**	instrument for measuring specific gravity of milk
115	**Galvanometer**	instrument for measuring electrical current

SN	Words	Definition
116	**Galvanoscope**	instrument for detecting presence and direction of electric current
117	**Gasometer**	instrument for holding and measuring gases
118	**Gastroscope**	instrument for examining interior of the stomach
119	**Geothermometer**	instrument for measuring subterranean temperatures
120	**Goniometer**	instrument for measuring angles between faces
121	**Gradiometer**	instrument for measuring gradient of a physical quantity
122	**Gravimeter**	instrument for measuring variations in gravitational fields
123	**Gyrograph**	instrument for counting a wheel's revolutions
124	**Haptometer**	instrument measuring sensitivity to touch
125	**Harmonograph**	instrument drawing curves representing vibrations
126	**Harmonometer**	instrument measuring harmonic relations of sounds
127	**Helicograph**	instrument for drawing spirals on a plane
128	**Heliograph**	instrument for measuring intensity of sunlight
129	**Heliometer**	instrument for measuring apparent diameter of the sun
130	**Helioscope**	instrument for observing sun without injury to the eyes
131	**Hemacytometer**	instrument for counting blood cells
132	**Hippometer**	instrument to measure height of horses
133	**Hodoscope**	instrument for tracing paths of ionizing particles
134	**Hydrometer**	instrument for measuring specific gravity of liquids
135	**Hydroscope**	instrument for viewing under water
136	**Hydrotimeter**	instrument for measuring water hardness
137	**Hyetograph**	instrument for recording rainfall
138	**Hyetometer**	instrument for measuring rainfall
139	**Hyetometrograph**	instrument for recording rainfall
140	**Hygrograph**	instrument for recording variations in atmospheric humidity
141	**Hygrometer**	instrument for measuring air moisture
142	**Hygroscope**	instrument for displaying changes in air humidity
143	**Hypsometer**	instrument for measuring height of trees through triangulation
144	**Iconometer**	instrument for finding size of object by measuring its image
145	**Idiometer**	instrument for measuring motion of observer in relation to transit of the heavens
146	**Inclinometer**	instrument for measuring inclination to the horizontal of an axis
147	**Interferometer**	instrument for analysing spectra of light
148	**Iriscope**	instrument for exhibiting the prismatic colours

SN	Words	Definition
149	**Katathermometer**	instrument for measuring the cooling power of air
150	**Katharometer**	instrument measuring changes in composition of gases
151	**Keratometer**	instrument for measuring curvature of the cornea
152	**Keraunograph**	instrument for recording distant thunderstorms
153	**Kinetoscope**	instrument for producing curves by combination of circular movements
154	**Konimeter**	instrument measuring amount of dust in air
155	**Koniscope**	instrument for measuring dust in air
156	**Kymograph**	instrument for recording fluid pressure
157	**Labidometer**	instrument for measuring size of the head of a fetus
158	**Lactometer**	instrument for testing relative density of milk
159	**Lactoscope**	instrument for measuring purity or richness of milk
160	**Lanameter**	instrument for measuring quality of wool
161	**Laparoscope**	instrument for viewing interior of peritoneal cavity
162	**Laryngoscope**	instrument for examining interior of the larynx
163	**Leptometer**	instrument for measuring oil viscosity
164	**Loxodograph**	device used to record ship's travels
165	**Lucimeter**	instrument for measuring light intensity
166	**Luxmeter**	instrument for measuring illumination
167	**Lysimeter**	instrument for measuring percolation of water through soil
168	**Magnetograph**	instrument for recording measurements of magnetic fields
169	**Magnetometer**	instrument for measuring intensity of magnetic fields
170	**Manometer**	instrument for measuring pressure of a liquid or gas
171	**Marigraph**	instrument for recording tide levels
172	**Mecometer**	instrument for measuring length
173	**Megameter**	instrument for determining longitude by observing stars
174	**Megascope**	instrument for projecting an enlarged image
175	**Mekometer**	range-finder
176	**Meldometer**	instrument for measuring melting points of substances
177	**Meteorograph**	instrument recording a variety of meteorological observations
178	**Methanometer**	instrument for detecting presence of methane
179	**Microbarograph**	instrument for recording minute changes in atmospheric pressure
180	**Microcalorimeter**	instrument for measuring tiny quantities of heat
181	**Micrograph**	instrument used to write on a very small scale
182	**Micrometer**	instrument for measuring very small distances
183	**Micronometer**	instrument for measuring short periods of time
184	**Microscope**	instrument for magnifying small objects

SN	Words	Definition
185	**Microseismograph**	instrument for recording small or distant earthquakes
186	**Microseismometer**	instrument for measuring small or distant earthquakes
187	**Mileometer**	instrument for recording distance travelled in miles
188	**Milliammeter**	instrument for recording very small electrical currents
189	**Myograph**	instrument for recording muscular contractions
190	**Myringoscope**	instrument for viewing the eardrum
191	**Nephelometer**	instrument for measuring cloudiness
192	**Nephograph**	instrument for photographing clouds
193	**Nephoscope**	instrument for observing direction and velocity of clouds
194	**Nitrometer**	instrument for measuring nitrogen and its compounds
195	**Odograph**	odometer; instrument for measuring distance travelled
196	**Odometer**	instrument for measuring distance travelled
197	**Odontograph**	instrument for obtaining curves for gear-teeth
198	**Oenometer**	instrument for measuring alcoholic strength of wine
199	**Ohmmeter**	instrument for measuring electrical resistance
200	**Oleometer**	instrument for measuring amount of oil in a substance
201	**Olfactometer**	instrument measuring intensity of odour of a substance
202	**Ombrometer**	rain-gauge
203	**Oncometer**	instrument measuring change in size of internal organs
204	**Oncosimeter**	instrument measuring variations in density of molten metal
205	**Ondograph**	instrument measuring change in wave formations of electricity
206	**Oometer**	instrument for measuring eggs
207	**Opacimeter**	instrument for measuring opacity
208	**Opeidoscope**	instrument for illustrating sound by means of light
209	**Ophthalmometer**	instrument for measuring the eye
210	**Ophthalmoscope**	instrument for viewing the interior of the eye
211	**Opisometer**	instrument for measuring curved lines
212	**Opsiometer**	instrument for testing vision
213	**Optometer**	instrument for testing vision
214	**Orchidometer**	instrument for measuring the size of the testicles
215	**Oscillograph**	instrument for recording alternating current wave forms
216	**Oscillometer**	instrument for measuring ship's rollings

SN	Words	Definition
217	**Oscilloscope**	instrument for detecting electrical fluctuations
218	**Osmometer**	instrument for measuring osmotic pressure
219	**Otoscope**	instrument for examining the ear
220	**Pachymeter**	instrument for measuring small thicknesses
221	**Pallograph**	instrument measuring ship's vibration
222	**Pantochronometer**	combined sundial and compass
223	**Pantograph**	instrument for copying drawing to a different scale
224	**Passimeter**	instrument for issuing automatic tickets
225	**Pedometer**	instrument for measuring distance travelled on foot
226	**Peirameter**	instrument measuring resistance of road surfaces to wheel movement
227	**Pelvimeter**	instrument for measuring the pelvis
228	**Penetrometer**	instrument for measuring firmness or consistency of substances
229	**Permeameter**	instrument for measuring permeability
230	**Phacometer**	instrument for measuring lenses
231	**Phaometer**	old instrument for measuring light intensity
232	**Pharmacometer**	instrument for measuring drugs
233	**Pharyngoscope**	instrument for inspecting the pharynx
234	**Phonautograph**	instrument for recording sound vibrations
235	**Phonendoscope**	device which amplifies small sounds
236	**Phonometer**	instrument for measuring sound levels
237	**Phorometer**	instrument used to correct abnormalities in eye muscles
238	**Photometer**	instrument for measuring light intensity
239	**Photopolarimeter**	instrument for measuring intensity and polarization of reflected light
240	**Phototachometer**	instrument for measuring the speed of light
241	**Phototelegraph**	instrument for transmitting drawings telegraphically
242	**Phthongometer**	instrument measuring intensity of vowel sounds
243	**Piezometer**	instrument for measuring pressure or compressibility
244	**Pitchometer**	instrument for measuring angles of ship's propeller blades
245	**Planigraph**	instrument for copying drawings at a different scale
246	**Planimeter**	instrument for measuring area of plane figures
247	**Platometer**	instrument for measuring area; planimeter
248	**Plegometer**	instrument for measuring the strength of a blow
249	**Plemyrameter**	instrument for measuring variations in water level
250	**Plethysmograph**	instrument for measuring change in body part size due to blood flow
251	**Pluviograph**	self-registering rain gauge
252	**Pluviometer**	rain-meter
253	**Pneometer**	instrument that measures respiration
254	**Pneumatometer**	instrument for measuring quantity of air breathed

SN	Words	Definition
255	**Pneumograph**	instrument for measuring and recording respiration
256	**Polarimeter**	instrument for measuring polarised light
257	**Polariscope**	instrument for detecting polarized light
258	**Polygraph**	instrument for measuring small changes in pulse and respiration
259	**Porometer**	instrument for measuring degree of porosity
260	**Poroscope**	instrument for investigating porosity
261	**Potentiometer**	instrument for measuring electromotive forces
262	**Potometer**	instrument measuring rate at which plants absorb water
263	**Prisoptometer**	instrument for measuring degree of astigmatism
264	**Proctoscope**	instrument for examining the rectum
265	**Psophometer**	instrument measuring audible interference of electrical current
266	**Psychograph**	instrument that supposedly records spirit messages
267	**Psychrometer**	instrument for measuring air moisture or temperature
268	**Psychrometer**	instrument for measuring dryness of the atmosphere
269	**Pulsimeter**	instrument for measuring the pulse
270	**Pycnometer**	instrument for measuring specific gravity or density
271	**Pyknometer**	instrument for measuring specific gravities
272	**Pyranometer**	instrument measuring solar radiation from the sky's whole hemisphere
273	**Pyrgeometer**	instrument for measuring radiation from earth
274	**Pyrheliometer**	instrument for measuring heating effect of sun
275	**Pyrometer**	instrument for measuring very high temperatures
276	**Pyroscope**	instrument for measuring intensity of radiant heat
277	**Qualimeter**	apparatus for measuring penetrating power of X-ray beams
278	**Quantimeter**	apparatus for measuring quantity of X-rays
279	**Quantometer**	instrument for measuring proportions of elements in metallic samples
280	**Rachiometer**	instrument for measuring the spine
281	**Radarscope**	instrument for detecting radar signals
282	**Radiogoniometer**	instrument for finding direction through radio signals
283	**Radiometeorograph**	instrument for measuring atmospheric conditions at high altitude
284	**Radiometer**	instrument measuring radiation energy
285	**Radioscope**	instrument for viewing objects using X-rays
286	**Ratemeter**	instrument for measuring counting rate of electronic counters
287	**Recipiangle**	old instrument with two arms used for measuring angles

SN	Words	Definition
288	**Reflectometer**	instrument for measuring reflectance of radiant energy
289	**Refractometer**	instrument measuring refraction of light
290	**Respirometer**	instrument for measuring and studying respiration
291	**Retinoscope**	instrument for measuring and viewing the retina
292	**Rheometer**	instrument that measures current
293	**Rhinoscope**	instrument for examining the nose
294	**Rhythmometer**	instrument for measuring speed of rhythms
295	**Riometer**	instrument for measuring absorbed cosmic radio waves
296	**Rotameter**	old instrument for measuring length of curved lines
297	**Rotameter**	instrument consisting of glass tube with free float for measuring liquid flow
298	**Saccharimeter**	instrument for measuring amount of sugar in a solution
299	**Salinometer**	instrument for measuring amount of salt in a solution
300	**Scintillometer**	instrument measuring scintillation of star
301	**Scintilloscope**	instrument for measuring gamma rays emitted by a radioactive body
302	**Sclerometer**	instrument measuring hardness
303	**Scoliometer**	instrument measuring curvature
304	**Scotograph**	instrument for writing without seeing
305	**Scotoscope**	instrument for detecting objects in darkness
306	**Seismograph**	instrument for recording earthquakes
307	**Seismometer**	instrument for measuring earthquake intensity
308	**Seismoscope**	instrument for detecting earthquakes
309	**Selenoscope**	instrument for viewing the moon
310	**Sensitometer**	instrument for measuring sensitivity of photographic material
311	**Sepometer**	instrument for measuring septic matter in the air
312	**Serimeter**	instrument for testing quality of silk
313	**Shuftiscope**	instrument used to explore interior of dysentery case
314	**Siccimeter**	instrument for measuring liquid evaporation
315	**Sideroscope**	instrument using magnets to detect presence of iron
316	**Sigmoidoscope**	instrument for examining the interior of the rectum and sigmoid colon
317	**Sillometer**	instrument measuring speed of ship
318	**Skiascope**	instrument for measuring eye's refraction from movement of shadows
319	**Snooperscope**	instrument for viewing infrared radiation
320	**Solarimeter**	instrument for measuring solar radiation
321	**Sonograph**	instrument for recording and analysing sound

SN	Words	Definition
322	**Spectrofluorimeter**	instrument for measuring and recording fluorescence spectra
323	**Spectrograph**	instrument for viewing a spectrum
324	**Spectroheliograph**	instrument for taking pictures of the sun
325	**Spectroheliokinematograph**	camera for taking pictures of the sun
326	**Spectrohelioscope**	instrument for viewing solar disc in light of a single wavelength
327	**Spectrometer**	instrument measuring wavelengths of light of a spectrum
328	**Spectrophotometer**	instrument for measuring speed of different parts of light spectrum
329	**Spectroscope**	instrument for forming spectra by dispersing rays of light
330	**Speedometer**	instrument for measuring velocity
331	**Spherometer**	instrument measuring curvature
332	**Sphygmograph**	instrument for recording pulse
333	**Sphygmomanometer**	instrument for measuring arterial blood pressure
334	**Sphygmometer**	instrument for measuring arterial blood pressure
335	**Sphygmoscope**	instrument for making arterial pulsations visible
336	**Spinthariscope**	instrument for visually detecting alpha particles
337	**Spirograph**	instrument recording movements of breathing
338	**Spirometer**	instrument measuring lung capacity
339	**Stactometer**	pipette with hollow bulb for counting drops
340	**Stadiometer**	instrument for measuring the length of a curved line
341	**Stagmometer**	instrument for measuring number of drops in volume of liquid
342	**Stalagmometer**	instrument for measuring surface tension by drops
343	**Statoscope**	instrument for measuring small changes in atmospheric pressure
344	**Stauroscope**	instrument for studying structure of crystals with polarised light
345	**Stenometer**	instrument for measuring distances
346	**Stereometer**	instrument for measuring specific gravity
347	**Stereoscope**	instrument for viewing special three-dimensional photographs
348	**Stethometer**	instrument measuring chest expansion during breathing
349	**Stethoscope**	instrument for detecting sounds produced by the body
350	**Strabismometer**	instrument measuring degree of squinting
351	**Strabometer**	instrument for measuring strabismus in the eyes
352	**Stroboscope**	instrument for studying motion using flashes of light
353	**Stylometer**	instrument for measuring columns

SN	Words	Definition
354	**Swingometer**	instrument for measuring swing in votes during an election
355	**Sympiesometer**	instrument for measuring pressure of a current
356	**Synchroscope**	instrument for detecting whether two moving parts are synchronized
357	**Tacheometer**	instrument for rapidly measuring survey points on a map
358	**Tachistoscope**	instrument for rapidly showing images on a screen to test perception
359	**Tachograph**	instrument for recording speed of rotation
360	**Tachometer**	instrument for measuring speed of rotation
361	**Taseometer**	instrument for measuring stress in a structure
362	**Tasimeter**	instrument for measuring changes in pressure
363	**Taximeter**	instrument for measuring fee for hired vehicle
364	**Telemeter**	instrument for measuring strain or distance from observer
365	**Telescope**	instrument for viewing objects at great distances
366	**Telespectroscope**	instrument for analysing radiation omitted by distant bodies
367	**Telestereoscope**	instrument for viewing distant objects stereoscopically
368	**Tellurometer**	instrument using microwaves to measure distance
369	**Tenderometer**	instrument for measuring tenderness of fruits and vegetables
370	**Tensimeter**	instrument for measuring vapour pressure
371	**Tensiometer**	instrument for measuring tension
372	**Thalassometer**	instrument for measuring tides
373	**Thermograph**	instrument for recording changes in temperature
374	**Thermometer**	instrument for measuring temperature
375	**Thermometrograph**	instrument for recording changes in temperature
376	**Thermoscope**	instrument indicating change in temperature
377	**Thoracoscope**	instrument for viewing the thorax and chest wall
378	**Tiltmeter**	instrument for measuring tilting of earth's surface
379	**Tocodynamometer**	instrument for measuring uterine contractions during childbirth
380	**Tomograph**	instrument for viewing section of an object using X-rays
381	**Tonometer**	instrument measuring pitch of musical tones
382	**Topophone**	instrument to determine direction and distance of a fog-horn
383	**Torsiograph**	instrument for recording torsional vibrations on an object
384	**Transmissometer**	instrument for measuring transmission of light through a fluid

SN	Words	Definition
385	**Trechometer**	instrument for determining distance travelled; odometer
386	**Tremograph**	instrument for recording involuntary muscular motion
387	**Tribometer**	instrument measuring friction
388	**Trigonometer**	instrument for solving triangles
389	**Trocheameter**	instrument counting wheel's revolutions
390	**Tromometer**	instrument for measuring slight earthquake shocks
391	**Tropometer**	instrument measuring rotation
392	**Turbidimeter**	instrument for measuring turbidity of liquids
393	**Turgometer**	instrument for measuring turgidity
394	**Typhlograph**	instrument to help the blind write clearly
395	**Udometer**	instrument for measuring rainfall
396	**Ultramicroscope**	instrument for viewing extremely small objects
397	**Urethroscope**	instrument for viewing the interior of the urethra
398	**Urinometer**	instrument for measuring specific gravity of urine
399	**Vaporimeter**	instrument for measuring vapour pressure
400	**Variometer**	instrument for measuring magnetic declination
401	**Velocimeter**	instrument for measuring velocity
402	**Velometer**	instrument for measuring speed of air
403	**Viameter**	instrument for measuring revolutions of a wheel
404	**Vibrograph**	instrument for recording vibrations
405	**Vibrometer**	instrument for measuring vibrations
406	**Viscometer**	instrument for measuring viscosity
407	**Visometer**	instrument for measuring focal length of the eye
408	**Voltameter**	instrument for measuring electrical current indirectly
409	**Voltmeter**	instrument for measuring electrical potential
410	**Volumenometer**	instrument for measuring volume of a solid
411	**Volumeter**	instrument for measuring volume of a liquid or gas
412	**Wattmeter**	instrument for measuring electrical power
413	**Wavemeter**	instrument for measuring wavelengths
414	**Weatherometer**	instrument for measuring weather-resisting properties of paint
415	**Xanthometer**	instrument for measuring colour of sea or lake water
416	**Xylometer**	instrument measuring specific gravity of wood
417	**Zymometer**	instrument for measuring fermentation
418	**Zymosimeter**	instrument for measuring fermentation

SN	Words	Definition
1	**Ballad**	A poem or song narrating a story in short stanzas. Traditional ballads are typically of unknown authorship, having been passed on orally from one generation to the next
2	**Concrete**	Poetry in which the meaning or effect is conveyed partly or wholly by visual means, using patterns of words or letters and other typographical devices
3	**Couplet**	Two lines of poetry that rhyme
4	**Elegy**	This is a particular type of lyric that is written to mourn the passing of something or someone.
5	**Epic**	This is a very, very long poem that tells a story. Epic poems are narrative poems that are long enough to be in a book of their own, rather than an anthology
6	**Epigram**	These are very short, witty poems that make a pithy pronouncement about something. Usually they are written as a couplet.
7	**Epitaphs**	Epitaphs are poems about the dead that are written to be on a tombstone; this means they are usually very short.
8	**Euphony**	Sounds that are very pleasant to the ear. The opposite of cacophony
9	**Idyll**	A short poem which depicts the rustic life of people
10	**Metaphor**	A direct comparison between two dissimilar items. She is a monster is a metaphor comparing a girl to a monster.
11	**Metonymy**	This is a type of metaphor in which a reference point is substituted for the thing to which reference is actually made. The pen is mightier than the sword
12	**Novel**	A fictitious prose narrative of book length, typically representing character and action with some degree of realism
13	**Octave**	Eight lines of poetry that have a rhyme scheme
14	**Ode**	This is a very serious form of the lyric; it is written about a serious topic and is very dignified, if not stately, in tone and style
15	**Oxymoron**	An oxymoron is a pair of single word opposites placed side by side for dramatic effect. A contradiction in terms. For example, "cold fire" or "sick health" or "jumbo shrimp".
16	**Paradox**	A large oxymoron. An apparently contradictory statement that, despite the contradiction, has an element of truth in it. Wordsworth's "the child is the father of the man" is a paradoxical statement.
17	**Parody**	A parody is a mockery of another piece of literature; it copies the style and voice, and sometimes language of the original for comedic effect

SN	Words	Definition
18	**Pastoral**	A pastoral is a poem that is set in the countryside. It often presents an unrealistic, idealistic notion of country living: happy shepherds, lovely shepherdesses, contented flocks of sheep, sunny meadows, and gentle weather
19	**Personification**	A comparison between a non-human item and a human so that the non-human item is given human characteristics.
20	**Quatrain**	Four lines of poetry that have a rhyme scheme
21	**Satire**	A style of writing that has the goal of mocking or scorning an individual, an institution, or society as a whole.
22	**Sestet**	Six lines of poetry that have a rhyme scheme
23	**Simile**	A comparison between two dissimilar items using "like" or "as" to make the comparison. The stars are like diamonds in the sky is a simile, comparing stars to diamonds.
24	**Sonnet**	A fourteen-line lyric written in iambic pentameter

SN	Words	Origin	Definition
1	**ab initio**	*Latin*	from the beginning
2	**ad hoc**	*Latin*	made or done for a particular purpose
3	**ad infinitum**	*Latin*	endlessly; forever
4	**ad interim**	*Latin*	for the meantime
5	**ad nauseam**	*Latin*	to a tiresomely excessive degree
6	**a fortiori**	*Latin*	more conclusively
7	**annus mirabilis**	*Latin*	a remarkable or auspicious year
8	**a posteriori**	*Latin*	based on reasoning from known facts or past events rather than on assumptions or predictions
9	**a priori**	*Latin*	based on deduction rather than experience
10	**bona fide**	*Latin*	genuine; real
11	**carpe diem**	*Latin*	make the most of the present time
12	**caveat emptor**	*Latin*	the buyer is responsible for checking the quality of goods before purchasing them
13	**compos mentis**	*Latin*	sane; in full control of one's mind
14	**cui bono?**	*Latin*	who stands to gain?
15	**de facto**	*Latin*	in fact, whether by right or not
16	**dei gratia**	*Latin*	by the grace of God
17	**de jure**	*Latin*	rightful; by right
18	**deo gratias**	*Latin*	thanks be to God
19	**deo volente**	*Latin*	God willing
20	**de profundis**	*Latin*	expressing one's deepest feelings
21	**deus ex machina**	*Latin*	an unexpected event that saves an apparently hopeless situation
22	**dramatis personae**	*Latin*	the characters in a play
23	**ex gratia**	*Latin*	(with reference to payment) done from a sense of moral obligation rather than because of any legal requirement
24	**ex officio**	*Latin*	by virtue of one's position or status
25	**in absentia**	*Latin*	while not present
26	**in camera**	*Latin*	in private
27	**in extremis**	*Latin*	in an extremely difficult situation; at the point of death
28	**in loco parentis**	*Latin*	in the place of a parent
29	**in medias res**	*Latin*	in or into the middle of things
30	**in propria persona**	*Latin*	in his or her own person
31	**in situ**	*Latin*	in the original or appropriate position
32	**inter alia**	*Latin*	among other things
33	**in toto**	*Latin*	as a whole
34	**ipso facto**	*Latin*	by that very fact or act
35	**locum tenens**	*Latin*	a temporary deputy or stand-in

SN	Words	Origin	Definition
36	**locus classicus**	Latin	the best known or most authoritative passage on a subject
37	**magnum opus**	Latin	the most important work of an artist, writer, etc.
38	**mea culpa**	Latin	an acknowledgement that something is one's fault
39	**memento mori**	Latin	something kept as a reminder that death is inevitable
40	**modus operandi**	Latin	a way of doing something
41	**modus vivendi**	Latin	an arrangement that allows conflicting parties to coexist peacefully
42	**ne plus ultra**	Latin	the best example of something
43	**nil desperandum**	Latin	do not despair
44	**nolens volens**	Latin	whether one wants or likes something or not
45	**non sequitur**	Latin	a conclusion or statement that does not logically follow from the previous statement
46	**per annum**	Latin	for each year
47	**per capita**	Latin	for each person
48	**per se**	Latin	by or in itself or themselves
49	**persona non grata**	Latin	a person who is not welcome somewhere
50	**prima facie**	Latin	accepted as so until proved otherwise
51	**primus inter pares**	Latin	the senior or representative member of a group
52	**pro rata**	Latin	proportional; proportionally
53	**proxime accessit**	Latin	the person who comes second in an examination or is runner-up for an award
54	**quid pro quo**	Latin	a favour or advantage given in return for something
55	**reductio ad absurdum**	Latin	a method of disproving a premise by showing that its logical conclusion is absurd
56	**sine die**	Latin	no appointed date for resumption
57	**sine qua non**	Latin	a thing that is absolutely essential
58	**sub judice**	Latin	being considered by a court of law and therefore not to be publicly discussed elsewhere
59	**sub rosa**	Latin	happening or done in secret
60	**sui generis**	Latin	unique
61	**terra firma**	Latin	dry land; the ground
62	**terra incognita**	Latin	unknown territory
63	**via media**	Latin	a compromise
64	**victor ludorum**	Latin	the overall champion in a sports competition
65	**vox populi**	Latin	public opinion
66	**a cappella**	Italian	sung without instrumental accompaniment
67	**al dente**	Italian	(of food, typically pasta) cooked so as to be still firm when bitten
68	**alfresco**	Italian	in the open air
69	**cognoscenti**	Italian	people who are well informed about something
70	**cosa nostra**	Italian	a US criminal organization related to the Mafia

SN	Words	Origin	Definition
71	**dolce far niente**	*Italian*	pleasant idleness
72	**dolce vita**	*Italian*	a life of pleasure and luxury
73	**papabile**	*Italian*	worthy or eligible to be elected pope
74	**pococurante**	*Italian*	careless or nonchalant
75	**sotto voce**	*Italian*	in a quiet voice
76	**blitzkrieg**	*German*	an intense, violent military campaign intended to bring about a swift victory
77	**doppelgänger**	*German*	an apparition or double of a living person
78	**katzenjammer**	*German*	a hangover or a severe headache accompanying a hangover
79	**unheimlich**	*German*	uncanny or weird
80	**verboten**	*German*	forbidden
81	**zeitgeist**	*German*	the characteristic spirit or mood of a particular historical period
82	**à deux**	*French*	for or involving two people
83	**agent provocateur**	*French*	a person who tempts a suspected criminal to commit a crime so that they can be caught and convicted
84	**à huis clos**	*French*	in private
85	**amour propre**	*French*	self-respect
86	**au courant**	*French*	well informed; up to date
87	**au fait**	*French*	having a good or detailed knowledge
88	**au fond**	*French*	basically; in essence
89	**au naturel**	*French*	in the most simple or natural way
90	**beau geste**	*French*	a noble and generous act
91	**beau idéal**	*French*	the highest standard of excellence
92	**beau monde**	*French*	fashionable society
93	**beaux arts**	*French*	the fine arts
94	**bête noire**	*French*	a person or thing one particularly dislikes
95	**belles-lettres**	*French*	literary works written and read for their elegant style
96	**billet-doux**	*French*	a love letter
97	**bon mot**	*French*	a clever or witty remark
98	**bon vivant**	*French*	a person with a sociable and luxurious lifestyle
99	**brasserie**	*French*	an informal or inexpensive restaurant
100	**carte blanche**	*French*	complete freedom to act as one wishes
101	**cause célèbre**	*French*	a controversial issue attracting much public attention
102	**c'est la guerre**	*French*	used as an expression of resigned acceptance
103	**chacun à son gout**	*French*	everyone to their own taste
104	**chef-d'œuvre**	*French*	a masterpiece
105	**cherchez la femme**	*French*	there is certain to be a woman at the bottom of a problem or mystery
106	**comme il faut**	*French*	correct in behaviour or etiquette

SN	Words	Origin	Definition
107	**cordon sanitaire**	*French*	a guarded line placed around an area infected by disease to prevent anyone from leaving
108	**coup de foudre**	*French*	love at first sight
109	**coup de grâce**	*French*	a blow by which a mortally wounded person or thing is mercifully killed
110	**coup de main**	*French*	a sudden surprise attack
111	**coup d'état**	*French*	a sudden violent seizure of power
112	**cri de cœur**	*French*	a passionate appeal or protest
113	**déjà vu**	*French*	the sense of having experienced the present situation before
114	**de nos jours**	*French*	contemporary
115	**de rigueur**	*French*	obligatory; required by etiquette or current fashion
116	**dernier cri**	*French*	the very latest fashion
117	**de trop**	*French*	not wanted; superfluous
118	**double entendre**	*French*	a word or phrase with two possible interpretations
119	**embarras de richesse**	*French*	more options or resources than one knows what to do with
120	**éminence grise**	*French*	a person who has power or influence without holding an official position
121	**en famille**	*French*	with one's family; in an informal way
122	**enfant terrible**	*French*	a person whose behaviour is unconventional or controversial
123	**en masse**	*French*	all together
124	**en passant**	*French*	by the way
125	**entente cordiale**	*French*	a friendly understanding between states
126	**entre nous**	*French*	between ourselves
127	**esprit de corps**	*French*	a feeling of pride and loyalty uniting the members of a group
128	**fait accompli**	*French*	a thing that has been done or decided and cannot now be altered
129	**faute de mieux**	*French*	for want of a better alternative
130	**faux pas**	*French*	an embarrassing blunder or indiscretion
131	**femme fatale**	*French*	a seductive woman
132	**fête champêtre**	*French*	an outdoor entertainment; a garden party
133	**fin de siècle**	*French*	relating to the end of a century
134	**force majeure**	*French*	superior strength
135	**folie de grandeur**	*French*	delusions of grandeur
136	**gîte**	*French*	a small furnished holiday house in France
137	**grande dame**	*French*	a woman who is influential within a particular sphere
138	**haute couture**	*French*	the designing and making of clothes by leading fashion houses
139	**haute cuisine**	*French*	high-quality cooking
140	**haut monde**	*French*	fashionable society

SN	Words	Origin	Definition
141	**hors de combat**	French	out of action due to injury or damage
142	**ideé fixe**	French	an obsession
143	**je ne sais quoi**	French	a quality that is hard to describe
144	**jeu d'esprit**	French	a light-hearted display of wit
145	**jeunesse dorée**	French	wealthy, fashionable young people
146	**joie de vivre**	French	exuberant enjoyment of life
147	**laissez-faire**	French	a non-interventionist policy
148	**manqué**	French	having failed to become what one might have been
149	**ménage à trois**	French	an arrangement in which a married couple and the lover of one of them live together
150	**mot juste**	French	the most appropriate word or expression
151	**noblesse oblige**	French	privilege entails responsibility
152	**nouveau riche**	French	people who have recently become rich and who display their wealth ostentatiously
153	**objet d'art**	French	a small decorative or artistic object
154	**on dit**	French	a piece of gossip
155	**par excellence**	French	better or more than all others of the same kind
156	**parti pris**	French	a preconceived view; a bias
157	**pièce de résistance**	French	the most important or impressive item
158	**pied-à-terre**	French	a small flat or house kept for occasional use
159	**pis aller**	French	a last resort
160	**plat du jour**	French	a special dish prepared by a restaurant on a particular day
161	**plus ça change**	French	used to express resigned acknowledgement of the fact that certain things never change
162	**raison d'être**	French	the most important reason for someone or something's existence
163	**roman-à-clef**	French	a novel in which real people or events appear with invented names
164	**sangfroid**	French	the ability to stay calm in difficult circumstances
165	**savoir faire**	French	the ability to act appropriately in social situations
166	**soi-disant**	French	self-styled; so-called
167	**table d'hôte**	French	a restaurant meal offered at a fixed price, with few if any choices
168	**tant mieux**	French	so much the better
169	**tant pis**	French	so much the worse; too bad
170	**tête-à-tête**	French	a private conversation
171	**tour de force**	French	a thing accomplished with great skill
172	**tout de suite**	French	at once
173	**vis-à-vis**	French	in relation to; as compared with

Root word	Meanings	Examples
a	without	**Abyss** - without bottom **Achromatic** - without color **Anhydrous** - without water **Amoral** - without moral sense **Asexual** - without sexual feelings or associations
a	on	**Afire** - on fire **Ashore** - on the shore **Aside -** on the side
ab	not	**Abnormal** - not normal **Absent** - not present **Aberration** - a departure from normal **Abstinence** - not indulging in alcohol or sex
acro	height, tip, beginning	**Acrobat** - a high walker **Acronym** - a word formed from the first (capital) letters of a word **Acrophobia** - fear of height **Acropolis** - a citadel in ancient greek city built on a hill
aer/o	air	**Aerate** - to let air reach something **Aerial** - relating to the air **Aerospace** - the air space **Aeronaut** - someone who operates an aircraft **Aerodynamics** - the branch of mechanics that deals with the motion of gases (especially air) and their effects on bodies in the flow
Agog	leading	**Demagogue** - an orator who appeals to the passions and prejudices of his audience **Pedagogue** - someone who educates young people **Pedagogy** - the activities of educating or instructing **Synagogue** - the place of worship for a jewish congregation
agr/i/o	farming	**Agriculture** - management of the land **Agribusiness** - making money by utilizing land **Agrarian** - relating to the management of land
aholic /oholic	obsession for	**Workaholic** - obsession for work **Shopaholic** - obsession for shopping **Alcoholic** - obsession for alcohol
alg/o	pain	**Neuralgia** - pain caused by a nerve **Analgesic** - a drug that makes one pain free **Nostalgia** - aching for the familiar

Root word	Meanings	Examples
ambi, amphi	both, on both sides, around	**Ambidextrous** - able to use both hands equally **Ambient** - completely enveloping **Ambiguous** - having more than one meaning **Ambivalence** - conflicting or opposite feelings toward a person or thing
ambul	walk, move	**Amble** - to walk in a slow relaxed manner **Ambulant** - walking or moving around **Ambulance** - a vehicle that moves a patient
ami/o	love	**Amiable** - friendly and lovable **Amity** - friendly and peaceful relations **Amorous** - showing romantic love
andr/o	man, male	**Androgynous** - being both male and female **Android** - resembling a human **Misandry** - hatred towards men
anim	life, spirit	**Animal** - a living organism **Animate** - to make alive **Equanimity** - of balanced spirit
ann/enn	year	**Anniversary** - a date observed once a year **Annual** - happening once a year **Millennium** - 1,000 years
ante	before, in front	**Antecede** - to come before something in time **Antemeridian** - before noon **Anteroom** - a small room before the main room
anthrop/o	human	**Anthropology** - the study of mankind **Anthropomorphism** - giving human form to non-human things **Philanthropy** - the love to mankind
anti	against, opposite of	**Antibody** - a substance that destroys micro-organisms **Antiseptic** - preventing infection **Antisocial** - opposing social norm
aqu/a	water	**Aquarium** - a water container for fish **Aquatic** - relating to water **Aqueduct** - a pipeline for water
arbor	tree	**Arborist** - someone working with trees **Arbor** - a shady area formed by trees **Arborous** - having many trees
arch/i	chief, most important, rule	**Archbishop** - the highest ranking bishop **Archenemy** - chief or worst enemy **Matriarch** - a female who rules a group **Patriarch** - a male who rules a group **Monarch** - a king or queen

Root word	Meanings	Examples
arch/a/i	primitive, ancient	**Archaeology** - the study of ancient cultures **Archaic** - belonging to an earlier period **Archive** - a collection of historical materials
arthr/o	joint	**Arthroscope** - a tool to see inside a joint **Arthritis** - inflammation of a joint **Arthropod** - invertebrates
art	skill	**Artifact** - object made by a person's skill **Artisan** - a person skilled in a craft **Artist** - a person who creates skillfully
astro, aster	star, stars, outer space	**Astronaut** - a person traveling to the stars **Astronomer** - someone who studies the stars **A star**-shaped sign used as a reference tool star-shaped sign used as a reference tool
aud/i/io	hear	**Audible** - loud enough to be heard **Audience** - people who listen to a program **Audiovisual** - relating to sound and vision
auto	self, same, one	**Autocrat** - a person who governs with absolute power **Autograph** - a person's own signature **Automatic** - moving by itself
avi/a	bird	**Aviary** - a large enclosure for birds **Aviatrix** - a female airplane pilot **Aviation** - the art of designing or operating aircraft
bar/o	pressure, weight	**Baric** - pertaining to pressure, esp. of the atmosphere **Millibar** - metric unit, equal to 1/1000th of a bar **Baryon** - heavy elementary particle
bell/i	war	**Bellicose** - warlike **Belligerent** - hostile, ready to fight **Rebel** - person who opposes and fights
bene	good, well	**Benefactor** - person who gives money to a cause **Beneficial** - producing a good effect **Benevolent** - showing kindness or goodwill
bi/n	two, twice, once in every two	**Biannual** - happening twice a year **Binoculars** - optical device with two lenses **Bilateral** - of or involving two sides
bibli/o	book	**Bibliography** - a list of books used as sources **Bibliomania** - an extreme love of books **Bibliophile** - a person who loves books
bio	life, living matter	**Biography**- a life story written by another person **Biology** - the science of life **Biosphere** - earth's surface inhabited by living things
cand	glowing, iridescent	**Candid**- free from bias, prejudice, or malice **Candle**- something that gives light **Incandescent**- white, glowing, or luminous with intense heat

Root word	Meanings	Examples
cardi/o	heart	**Cardiac** - relating to the heart **Cardiogenic** - resulting from heart disease **Cardiologist** - a heart doctor
carn/i	flesh, meat	**Carnivorous** - flesh-eating **Carnal** - pertaining to the body or flesh **Incarnate** - given bodily form
cata	intensive, completely	**Cataclysm** - a flood or other disaster **Catalog** - a complete listing **Catastrophe** - turning for the worst, a substantial disaster
caust, caut	to burn	**Cauterize** - to burn with a hot instrument **Caustic** - capable of burning or eating away **Holocaust** - total devastation, especially by fire
cede, ceed, cess	go, yield	**Exceed** - to go beyond the limits **Recede** - to go back **Accessible** - easily entered, approached, or obtained
cent/i	hundred, hundredth	**Centennial** - the 100th anniversary **Centimeter** - 1/100 of a meter **Century** - 100 years
centr/o/i	center	**Egocentric** - self-centered **Eccentric** - not having a common center **Centrifugal** - moving outward from a center
cerebr/o	brain	**Cerebral** - pertaining to the brain **Cerebrate** - to use the brain **Cerebrospinal** - pertaining to the brain and the spinal cord
chrom/o, chromat/o, chros	color, pigment	**Achromatic** - without color **Chromium** - a blue-white metallic chemical element **Chromatics** - the study of color
chron/o	time	**Chronic** - lasting for a long time **Chronological** - arranging events in time order **Synchronize** - happening at the same time
cide, cise	cut, kill	**Homicide** - murder **Insecticide** - a chemical used to kill insects **Incisor** - a sharp tooth for cutting food
circum, circle	around, about	**Circumnavigate** - to sail around **Circumscribe** - to draw around **Circumspect** - looking around
co	with, together, joint	**Coauthor** - writer who collaborates with another author **Coeducation** - educating males and females together **Cohousing** - planning your neighborhood in an intentional neighborly fashion

Root word	Meanings	Examples
col	together, jointly	**Collaborate** - to work together **Collision** - smashing together **Colloquial** - words formed by everday interaction
com	together, common	**Commemorate** - to memorize together **Composition** - an arrangement or putting together of parts **Commune** - living together while owning things in common
cogn/i	know	**Cognition** - process of acquiring knowledge **Incognito** - disguised so no one knows you **Recognize** - to discover that one knows
con	with, jointly	**Concur** - to agree with someone **Contemporary** - of the same time period as others **Convention** - a gathering of people with a common interest
contra/o	against, opposite	**Contradict** - to argue against **Contrary** - not in agreement **Controversy** - disagreement
corp/o	body	**Corporation** - a company recognized by law as a single body **Corpse** - a dead body **Corporal** - pertaining to the body
cosm/o	universe	**Cosmonaut** - a russian astronaut **Cosmos** - the universe **Microcosm** - a miniature universe
counter	opposite, contrary, opposing	**Counteract** - to oppose the effects of an action **Countermand** - to cancel a previous order **Counteroffensive** - attack against an attack
cracy	rule, government, power	**Aristocracy** - government by nobility **Bureaucracy** - government by state officials **Theocracy** - government by gods
cranio	skull	**Craniology** - the study of skull characteristics **Cranium** - skull of vertebrates **Cranial** - pertaining to the skull
cred	believe	**Credence** - belief that something is true or valid **Credulous** - believing things too easily **Incredible** - unbelievable
crypto	hidden, secret	**Cryptic** - of hidden meaning **Cryptography** - science of secret codes **Encrypt** - encode into secret code
de	reduce, away, down, remove	**Decelerate** - to slow down **Dethrone** - to remove from power **Debug** - to remove bugs

Root word	Meanings	Examples
dec/a, deka	ten	**Decade** - 10 years **Decathlon** - athletic contest that includes 10 disciplines in which each participant competes **December** - formerly the 10th month of the roman calendar
deci	one tenth	**Deciliter** - a tenth of a liter **Decimate** - reduce dramatically **Decibel** - one tenth of the sound volume unit bel
dem/o	people	**Democracy** - government of the people **Demographic** - the study of people **Epidemic** - spreading among people in a region
demi	half, less than	**Demitasse** - a small cup of coffee **Demimonde** - someone of little respected life style **Demi god** - half god
dendr/o/i	tree	**Philodendron** - a climbing plant that grows on trees **Dendrochronology** - dating events by studying growth rings in trees **Dendriform** - in the shape of a tree
dent, dont	tooth	**Dental** - relating to teeth **Dentist** - a doctor for the teeth **Dentures** - a set of false teeth
derm/a	skin	**Dermatologist** - a doctor for the skin **Pachyderm** - a class of animals with very thick skin **Dermatitis** - inflammation of the skin
di/plo	two, twice	**Dichromatic** - displaying two colors **Diploma** - a certificate, literally "a letter folded double" **Dilemma** - a situation that requires a choice between two alternative
domin	master	**Dominate** - to be the master of; domineering **Domineering** - excessively controlling **Predominate** - to have more power than others
du/o	two, twice	**Duplicate** - make an identical copy **Duet** - a musical composition for two voices or instruments **Duo** - a pair normally thought of as being together
dys	abnormal, bad	**Dyspepsia** - abnormal digestion **Dystopia** - an imaginary place of total misery **Dyslexia** - impairment of the ability to handle words
ectomy	surgical removal of	**Appendectomy** - a surgical operation to remove the appendix **Hysterectomy** - a surgical operation to remove all or part of the uterus

Root word	Meanings	Examples
ego	self	**Egoistic** - self-centered **Alter ego** - a higher aspect of oneself **Egomania** - excessive preoccupation with oneself
endo	within, inside	**Endotherm** - a creature that can keep its inside temperature fairly constant **Endocrine** - relating to glands that secrete directly into the blood or lymph **Endogamy** - the custom to marry within one's clan, tribe etc.
enn/i, anni	years	**Bicentennial** - of or relating to an age or period of 200 years **Centennial** - of or relating to an age or period of 100 years **Perennial** -lasting through many years
ep/i	on, upon, over, at, after,	**Epidemic** - the rapid spread of something negative **Epilogue** - a short speech delivered after a play **Epicenter** - the center of an earthquake
equ/i	equal, equally	**Equidistant** - an equal distance from two points **Equanimity** - calm temperament, evenness of temper **Equation** - a statement of equality.
erg/o	work	**Ergonomics** - study of the working environment **Energy** - the power to accomplish work **Energetics** - science that looks at energy and its transformation.
esth/aesth	feeling, sensation, beauty	**Esthetician** - someone who beautifies **Aesthetic** - pertaining to a sense of beauty **Kinesthesia** - the sensation of bodily movement.
ethno	race, people	**Ethnic** - pertaining to a defined group of people **Ethnocentric** - focusing on the ethnicity of people **Ethnology** - the science of people and races.
eu	good, well	**Euphemism** - replacing an offensive word with an inoffensive one **Euphonious** - having a pleasant sound **Euphoria** - feeling of well-being.
ex	from, out,	**Excavate** - to dig out **Exhale** - to breathe out **Extract** - to pull out.
extra, extro	outside, beyond	**Extraordinary** - beyond ordinary **Extraterrestrial** - outside the earth **Extrovert** - an outgoing person.
fid	faith	**Confide** - place trust in someone **Fiduciary** - a trustee **Fidelity** - faithfulness

Root word	Meanings	Examples
flor/a, fleur	flower	**Florist** - someone working with flowers **Floral** - flowerlike **Flora** - the plant life of a particular time or area
fore	in front of, previous, earlier	**Forebear** - ancestor **Forebode** - to give an advance warning of something bad **Forecast** - a preview of events to be.
gamy	marriage, union	**Monogamy** - the practice of marrying one person at a time **Polygamy** - the practice or custom of having more than one wife or husband at the same time
gastr/o	stomach	**Gastric** - pertaining to the stomach **Gastronomy** - serving the stomach by providing good food **Gastritis** - inflammation of the stomach.
gen/o/e/	birth,	**Genealogy** - the study of the history of a family **Generation** - all the people born at approximately the
geo	earth, soil, global	**Geography** - study of the earth's surface **Geology** - study of the structure of the earth **Geoponics** - soil based agriculture.
ger	old age	**Geriatrics** - medicine pertaining to the elderly **Gerontocracy** - the rule of the elders **Gerontology** - the science of aging.
giga	a billion	**Gigabyte** - unit of computer storage space **Gigahertz** - unit of frequency (one billion hz/sec) **Gigawatt** - unit of electric power (one billion watts)
gon	angle	**Decagon** - a polygon with 1 angles **Diagonal** - a slanting line running across a space **Octagon** - a geometrical figure with 8 angles.
gram	letter, written	**Diagram** - a simple drawing **Grammar** - rules of how to write words in sentences **Telegram** - a message sent by telegraph.
graph/y	writing, recording, written	**Graphology** - the study of handwritings **Autograph** - written with one's own hand **Seismograph** - a machine noting strength and duration of earthquakes
gyn/o/e	woman, female	**Gynecology** - the science of female reproductive health **Gynephobia** - fear of women **Gynecoid** - resembling a woman.
gress, grad/e/i	to step, to go	**Digression** - a departure from the main issue, subject, etc. **Progress** - movement forward or onward **Gradual** - step by step.

Root word	Meanings	Examples
hect/o, hecat	hundred	**Hectoliter** - 100 liters **Hectare** - metric unit equaling 100 ares or 10,000 square meters **Hectometer** - 100 meters.
helic/o	spiral, circular	**Helicopter** - an aircraft with horizontal rotating wing **Helix** - a spiral form **Helicon** - a circular tuba.
heli/o	sun	**Heliotropism** - movement or growth in relating to the sun **Heliograph** - apparatus used to send message with the help of sunlight **Helianthus** - genus of plants including sunflowers.
hemi	half, partial	**Hemicycle** - a semicircular structure **Hemisphere** - one half of the earth **Hemistich** - half a line of poetry.
hem/o/a	blood	**Hemorrhage** - clotting of the blood **Hemorrhoids** - swelling of the blood vessels **Hemoglobin** - red blood particle.
hepa	liver	**Hepatitis** - inflammation of the liver **Hepatoma** - a tumor of the liver **Hepatotoxic** - toxic and damaging to the liver.
hept/a	seven	**Heptagon** - a shape with seven angles and seven sides **Heptateuch** - the first seven books of the old testament **Heptameter** - a line of verse consisting of seven metrical feet.
herbi	grass, plant	**Herbicide** - any chemical used to kill unwanted plants, etc. **Herbivorous** - plant-eating **Herbal** - relating to plants.
hetero	different, other	**Heterogeneous** - made up of unrelated parts **Heteronyms** - words with same spelling but different meanings **Heterodox** - not conforming to traditional beliefs.
hex/a	six	**Hexagon** - a shape with six angles/sides **Hexameter** - a verse measured in six **Hexapod** - having six legs.
homo, homeo	like, alike, same	**Homogeneous** - of the same nature or kind **Homonym** - sounding alike **Homeopath** - a therapy that is based on treating "same with same"

Root word	Meanings	Examples
hydr/o	liquid, water	**Hydrate** - to add water to **Hydrophobia** - intense fear of water **Hydroponics** - growing plants in liquid nutrient solution **Hydraulic** - operated by force created by a liquid.
hyper	too much, over, excessive, beyond	**Hyperactive** - very restless **Hypercritical** - too critical **Hypertension** - above normal pressure.
hyp/o	under	**Hypoglycemia** - an abnormally low level of sugar in the blood **Hypothermia** - abnormally low body temperature **Hypothesis** - a theory that is unproven but used under the assumption that it is true.
iatr/o	medical care	**Geriatrics** - medical care of the elderly **Pediatrician** - a doctor who treats children **Podiatry** - medical care for feet.
icon/o	image	**Icon** - an (often religious) image, in modern usage a simplified graphic of high symbolic content **Iconology** - science of symbols and icons **Iconoclast** - someone who destroys religious images and traditional beliefs.
idio	peculiar, personal, distinct	**Idiomatic** - peculiar to a particular language **Idiosyncracy** - a physical or mental characteristic typical or a particular person **Idiot** - someone who is distinctly foolish or stupid.
il, im, in	not, without	**Illegal** - not legal **Impossible** - not possible **Inappropriate** - not appropriate
imag	likeness	**Image** - a likeness of someone **Imaginative** - able to think up new ideas or images **Imagine** - to form a picture or likeness in the mind.
infra	beneath, below	**Infrastructure** - underlying framework of a system **Infrared** - below the regular light spectrum.
inter	between, among, jointly	**International** - involving two or more countries **Intersection** - place where roads come together **Intercept** - to stop or interrupt the course of.
intra, intro	within, inside	**Intrastate** - existing in one state **Intravenous** - inside or into a vein **Introvert** - shy person who keeps within him/herself.
ir	not	**Irredeemable** - not redeemable **Irreformable** - not reformable **Irrational** - not rational.

Root word	Meanings	Examples
iso	equal	**Isobar** - a line on a map connecting points of equal barometric pressure **Isometric** - having equality of measure **Isothermal** - having equal or constant temperature.
ject	throw	**Eject** - to throw someone/something out **Interject** - to throw a remark into a discussion **Project** - to cast or throw something.
jud	law	**Judgment** - a decision of a court of law **Judicial** - having to do with judges or courts of law **Judiciary** - a system of courts of law. **Disjunction** - a disconnection **Junction** - a place where two things join.
juven	young	**Juvenile** - youthful or childish **Rejuvenate** - to bring back to youthful strength or appearance.
kilo	thousand	**Kilometer** - 1,000 meters **Kilograms** - 1,000 grams.
kine/t /mat	motion, division	**Kinetics** - study of the force of motion **Psychokinesis or telekinesis** - the ability to move objects with your mind **Cinematography** - motion picture making.
lab	work	**Collaborate** - to work with a person **Elaborate** - to work out the details **Laborious** - requiring a lot of hard work.
lact/o	milk	**Lactate** - to give milk, nurse **Lactose** - the sugar contained in milk **Lactic acid.**
liber	free	**Liberate** - to set free **Libertine** - a person with a free, wild lifestyle **Liberty** - freedom.
lingu	language, tongue	**Linguist** - one who studies languages **Multilingual** - able to communicate in multiple languages **Linguine** - long, flat "tongue-shaped" pasta.
lip/o	fat	**Liposuction** - the mechanical removal of fat reserves in the tissue **Lipase** - enzyme that breaks down fat **Lipoid** - resembling fat.
loc	place	**Dislocate** - to put something out of its usual place **Location** - a place **Relocate** - to move to a new place.

Root word	Meanings	Examples
log/o	word, doctrine, discourse	**Logic** - correct reasoning **Monologue** - a long speech by one speaker **Analogy** - similarity, especially between things otherwise dissimilar.
loqu, locu	speak	**Eloquent** - speaking beautifully and forcefully **Loquacious** - very talkative **Elocution** - art of public speaking.
lumin	light	**Illuminate** - to fill with light **Lumen** - unit measuring light.
lun/a/i	moon	**Lunar** - relating to the moon **Lunarscape** - the surface of the moon **Lunatic** - insane (as if driven mad by the moon).
macro	large, great	**Macroevolution** - large scale evolution **Macromolecule** - a large molecule **Macroeconomics** - study of the overall forces of economy.
magn/a/i	great, large	**Magnify** - make larger **Magnificent** - grand **Magnate** - a powerful person, especially in business or industry.
mal/e	bad, ill, wrong	**Malcontent** - wrong content **Malaria** - "bad air", infectious disease thought to originate from the "bad air" of the swamps, but caused by the bite of an infected mosquito **Malicious** - showing strong ill will.
man/i/u	hand	**Maneuver** - to move by hand **Manual** - done with the hands **Manuscript** - a book written by hand.
mania	madness, insanity, excessive desire	**Bibliomania** - a crazy love of books **Egomania** - a mad love of oneself **Maniac** - an insane person.
mar/i	sea	**Marina** - a harbor for pleasure boats **Maritime** - relating to the sea **Submarine** - an undersea boat **Aquamarine** - color of sea water.
mater, matr/i	mother	**Maternal** - relating to motherhood **Maternity** - the state of being a mother **Matriarch** - a woman head of a household.
max	greatest	**Maximal** - the best or greatest possible **Maximize** - to make as great as possible **Maximum** - the greatest amount.
medi	middle	**Medieval** - pertaining to the middle ages **Medium** - in the middle **Mediocre** - only of medium (inferior) quality.

Root word	Meanings	Examples
mega	great, large, million	**Megalopolis** - an area with many nearby cities **Megaphone** - a device that projects a loud voice **Megastructure** - huge building or other structure.
melan/o	black	**Melancholy** - a state of dark emotions **Melanoma** - malignant dark tumor of the skin **Melodrama** - a dark, pathetic drama.
memor/i	remember	**Commemorate** - to honor the memory of, as by a ceremony **Memorial** - related to remembering a person or event **Memory** - an ability to retain knowledge or an individual's stock of retained knowledge
meta	change, after, beyond, between	**Metaphysics** - study of nature and reality **Metamorphosis** - a complete change of form **Metastasis** - the transmission of disease to other parts of the body.
meter, metr/y	measure	**Audiometer**- an instrument that measures hearing acuteness **Chronometer**- an instrument that measures time **Metric** - measured.
micro	very small, short, minute	**Microbe** - a very small living thing **Microchip** - a tiny wafer with an integrated circuit **Microscope** - a device to see very small things.
mid	middle	**Midriff** - the area between the chest and the waist **Midterm** - middle of a term in school **Midway** - halfway between.
migr	move	**Immigrant** - a person who moves to a new country to settle **Migrant** - person who moves from place to place **Migration** - the process of moving.
milli	onethousandth	**Millimeter** - one thousandth of a meter **Millibar** - one thousandth of a bar **Milliliter** - one thousandth of a liter.
min/i	small, less	**Mini** - something that is very small **Minuscule** - extremely tiny **Minutiae** - very small or trivial details.
mis/o	bad, badly, wrong, wrongly, to hate	**Misbehave** - to behave badly **Misprint** - an error in printing **Misnomer** - an error in naming a person or thing.
miss, mit	send, let go	**Dismiss** - to send someone away **Missile** - a weapon sent into the air **Emit** - to send something out **Admittance** - entry.

Root word	Meanings	Examples
mob	move	**Immobilize** - to stop from moving **Mobile** - able to move freely **Mobility** - the quality of being able to move.
mon/o	one, single, alone	**Monochromat** - having one color **Monologue** - a speech spoken by one person **Monotheism** - belief in one god.
mot, mov	move	**Motion** - the act of moving **Motivate** - to move someone to action **Promote** - to move someone forward **Removable** - able to be taken or carried away.
morph/o	form	**Metamorphosis** - complete change of form **Endorphins** - chemical in the brain able to transform pain **Amorphous** - without distinct shape or form.
mort	death	**Immortal** - living forever, unable to die **Mortal** - certain to die **Mortician** - an undertaker.
multi	many, more than one or two	**Multicolored** - having many colors **Multimedia** - using a range of media **Multitasking** - doing many things at once.
mut	change	**Immutable** - not changing **Mutant** - an organism that has undergone change **Mutate** - to undergo a change.
my/o	muscle	**Myocardium** - the middle muscle of the heart **Myasthenia** - muscle fatigue or weakness **Myosin** - common protein in muscle tissue.
narr	tell	**Narrate** - to tell a story **Narrative** - a story **Narrator** - a person who tells a story.
nat	born	**Innate** - included since birth **Natal** - relating to birth **Natural** - gotten at birth, not afterward.
nav	ship	**Circumnavigate** - to sail around a place **Naval** - relating to a navy or warships **Navigate** - to sail a ship through a place.
necr/o	dead, death	**Necrophil** - loving death **Necrosis** - the death of tissue due to disease or injury **Necrology** - a list of persons who have recently died.
neg	no	**Negate** - to say it didn't happen **Negative** - meaning "no" **Renege** - to go back on a promise.

Root word	Meanings	Examples
neo	new, recent	**Neoclassic** - a revival of classic form, neocolonialism - the indirect ("new") economical and political control of a region by a more powerful foreign power **Neonatal** - a newborn child, especially the first few weeks.
nephr/o	kidney	**Nephritis** - inflammation of the kidneys **Nephrotomy** - surgical incision of a kidney **Nephron** - a single, excretory unit in the kidney.
neur/o	nerve	**Neuralgia** - pain along a nerve **Neurologist** - doctor specializing in the nerves **Neurotic** - mental disorder that usually does not include an impaired perception of reality.
nom/in	name	**Misnomer** - an error in naming a person or thing **Nominal** - being something in name only but not in reality **Nominate** - to name for election or appointment, to designate.
non	no, not, without	**Nondescript** - with no special characteristics **Nonfiction** - true, real, not made-up **Nonsense** - without sense.
noun, nunc	declare	**Announce** - to declare in public **Denounce** - to proclaim harsh criticism **Enunciate** - to speak or declare something clearly.
nov	new	**Innovate** - to introduce a new way **Novelty** - something new **Novice** - a person who is new at a job **Renovate** - to make something like new again.
numer	number	**Enumerate** - to name a number of items on a list **Numerology** - the study of magical uses of numbers **Numerous** - a large number.
ob, op	in the way, against	**Object** - to be against something **Obscure** - hard to understand **Opposition** - the act of resistance or action against.
oct/a/o	eight	**Octagon** - a figure with 8 sides and 8 angles **Octogenarian** - person in his or her 80s **Octopus** - sea animal with 8 arms.
ocu	eye	**Binoculars** - lens device for seeing distances **Monocula** - relating to one eye **Oculist** - an eye doctor.
odor	smell, scent	**Deodorant** - a substance that helps prevent body odor **Malodorous** - having a terribly bad smell **Odoriferous**- something that bears or diffuses a scent

Root word	Meanings	Examples
ology	study of, science of	**Anthropology** - the study of human societies and cultures and their development **Archaeology** - the study of human history and prehistory through the excavation of sites **Biology** - the study of living organisms
omni	all	**Omnipotent** - with all the power **Omniscient** - knowing all things **Omnivorous** - eating all foods
ortho	straight	**Orthodontist** - a dentist that straightens teeth **Orthopedic** - a doctor concerned with the proper alignment of the bones **Orthography** - the correct way of writing.
osteo	bone	**Osteoarthritis** - inflammation caused by degeneration of the joints **Osteopathy** - therapy that uses among others manipulation of the skeleton to restore health **Osteology** - the study of bones.
over	excessive	**Overconfident** - more confident than is appropriate **Overstock** - more supplies than is desirable **Overexcited** - ,more excited than one should be.
pale/o	ancient	**Paleontology** - study of ancient fossils **Paleography** - the study of ancient forms of writing **Paleolithic** - period of the stone age.
pan	all, any, everyone	**Panacea** - a cure for all diseases or problems **Panorama** - an all-around view **Pantheism** - the worship of all gods **Pandemic** - affecting all.
para	beside, beyond, abnormal, assistant	**Parasite** - an organism that lives on and off another living being **Parallel** - alongside and always an equal distance apart **Paragraph** - a portion of a writtenn document that presents a distinct idea.
pater, patr/i	father	**Paternal** - relating to fathers **Paternity** - fatherhood **Patriarch** - a man who rules a group.
path	feeling, emotion	**Antipathy** - a feeling of great dislike **Apathy** - a lack of feeling or interest **Empathy** - ability to understand another's feelings.
ped/i/e	foot, feet	**Pedal** - a lever pushed by the foot **Pedestrian** - one who walks **Pedicure** - cosmetic treatment of feet and toes.

Root word	Meanings	Examples
pent/a	five	**Pentagon** - shape having 5 angles and 5 sides, pentagram - a five-pointed star formerly used as a symbolic figure in magic **Pentathlon** - an athletic contest that includes five events.
pept, peps	digestion	**Dyspepsia** - abnormal digestion **Peptic** - aiding digestion **Pepsin** - a digestive enzyme.
per	through, throughout	**Permanent** - lasting throughout all time **Permeate** - to spread throughout **Persist** - to continue for a long time **Perennial** - lasting through many years.
peri	around, enclosing	**Periodontal** - pertaining to bone and tissue around a tooth **Peripheral** - lying outside of the center **Perimeter** - the outer boundary of an area.
phag/e	to eat	**Esophagus** - muscular tube that carries food to the stomach **Anthropophagy or sarcophagy** - cannibalism **Xylophagous** - feeding on wood.
phil/o	love, friend	**Philanthropist** - one who loves humanity **Philology** - the love of words **Philosophy** - the love of wisdom **Bibliophil** - loving books. **Pyrophile** - the love of fire or fireworks **Audiophile** - the love of high-fidelity sound reproduction
phobia	abnormal fear of	**Acrophobia** - abnormal fear of heights **Claustrophobia** - abnormal fear of closed or narrow spaces **Xenophobia** - abnormal fear of against people from other countries
phon/o /e/y	sound	**Cacophony** - loud, unpleasant sounds **Microphone** - a device that records and amplifies sound **Phonetic** - relating to human speech sounds.
phot/o	light	**Photogenic** - caused by light **Photograph** - image made on light-sensitive film **Photon** - the smallest possible unit of light.
phyll/o	leaf	**Chlorophyll** - a group of green pigments found in leaves **Phyllotaxis** - the arrangement of leaves on a stem **Phyllite** - a rock that forms sheets, similar to slate.

Root word	Meanings	Examples
phys	nature, medicine, the body	**Physical** - relating to the body **Physician** - a doctor **Physique** - nature and shape of one's body.
phyt/o/e	plant, to grow	**Epiphyte** - a plant growing independently on the surface of another **Hydrophyte** - a plant that grows only in water **Neophyte** - a beginner, especially a person recently converted to a new belief.
pneum/o	breathing, lung, air, spirit	**Pneumonia** - inflammation of the lungs **Pneumatic** - using the force of air **Dyspnea** - difficulty in breathing.
pod/e	foot	**Podiatrist** - a doctor for the feet **Podium** - a small platform to stand on **Tripod** - a stand or frame with 3 legs.
poly	many, more than one	**Polychrome** - with many colors **Polyglot** - a person fluent in many languages **Polygon** - shape with 3 or more straight sides.
pop	people	**Popular** - appealing to a lot of people **Population** - all of the people who live in a particular area **Populist** - a supporter of the rights of people.
port	carry	**Export** - to carry goods out of a place to another **Portable** - able to be carried **Porter** - a person who carries luggage.
post	after, behind	**Posthumous** - after someone's death **Postpone** - to delay something **Postscript** - an addition to an place where someone is.
pre	earlier, before, in front of	**Preamble** - a part in front of a formal document **Prepare** - to get ready in advance **Prediction** - a statement foretelling the future.
pro	before, in front of, for, forward	**Prognosis** - a prediction of what will happen **Prologue** - a passage before the main part **Prophet** - a person who foretells the future.
prot/o	primitive, first, chief	**Prototype** - the first of a kind **Proton** - on of the very basic parts of an atom **Protocol** - a first draft from which a document is prepared.
pseud/o	wrong,false	**Pseudonym** - a fictitious name **Pseudoscience** - theories presumed without proof of a scientific nature **Pseudopregnancy** - a false pregnancy.

Root word	Meanings	Examples
psych/o	mind, mental	**Psyche** - the human spirit or soul **Psychic** - relating to the human mind or someone who has supernatural mental abilities **Psychology** - the study of the mind.
pugn/a, pung	to fight	**Pugnacious** - having a quarrelsome or aggressive nature **Repugnant** - distasteful, offensive or revolting **Pungent** - piercing.
pul	urge	**Compulsion** - a very strong urge **Expulsion** - to someone out **Impulsive** - having a spontaneous urge to do something.
purg	clean	**Purge** - remove anything undesirable **Purgatory** - according to roman catholics a place where souls must clean themselves of sin **Expurgate** - remove objectionable passages from a publication.
pyr/o	fire, heat	**Pyrotechnics** - the art of making fireworks **Pyrometer** - a thermometer for measuring high temperature **Pyretic** - relating to or producing fever.
quad/r/ri	four	**Quadrant** - open space with buildings on 4 sides **Quadrennium** - period of 4 years **Quadruped** - a 4- footed animal.
quart	fourth	**Quarter** - one fourth **Quart** - a fourth of a gallon **Quartet** - a musical composition or group involving 4 voices or instruments.
quin/t	five, fifth	**Quintett** - a composition for 5 voices or instruments **Quintessence** - pure essence, based on the ancient philosophy that there was a fifth element that was present in all things **Quintuple** - fivefold.
radic, radix	root	**Eradicate** - pull out at the roots **Radical** - fundamental, looking at things from a drastic point of view **Radish** - an edible root of the mustard family.
radio	radiation, ray	**Radioactive** - emitting radiation **Radiologist** - someone diagnosing or treating via radiation.
ram/i	branch	**Ramification** - the resulting consequence of a decision **Ramify** - to spread or branch out **Ramus** - a branchlike part.

Root word	Meanings	Examples
re	again, back, backward	**Rebound** -to spring back again **Rewind** - to wind something backward **Reaction: a response** **Recognize** - to identify someone or something seen before
retro	backward, back	**Retroactive** - relating to something in the past **Retrogress** - to go back to an earlier condition **Retrospect** - the remembering of past events.
rhin/o	nose	**Rhinoceros** - a species of animals with a big horn on the snout **Rhinoplasty** - surgery of the nose **Rhinovirus** - viruses that are causing the common cold.
rhod/o	red	**Rhododendron** - a flower with red/pink flowers **Rhodium** - an element which produces a red solution **Rhodopsin** - a purple pigment in the retina that is needed for vision.
rupt	break, burst	**Bankrupt** - unable to pay because you're "broke" **Interrupt** - to break into a conversation or event, to disturb **Rupture** - a break in something.
san	health	**Sane** - mentally healthy **Sanitary** - relating to cleanliness and health **Sanitation** - maintenance of public health and cleanliness.
scend	climb, go	**Ascend** - to climb upward **Crescendo** - a climbing up of the volume of music **Descend** - to go or climb down.
sci	know	**Conscience** - sense of knowing right from wrong **Conscious** - knowing what is happening **Omniscient** - knowing everything.
scop/e/y	see, examine, observe	**Microscope** - a device used to see tiny things **Periscope** - a seeing instrument on a submarine **Telescope** - a device used to see over a distance.
scrib, script	write, written	**Inscribe** - to write letters or words on a surface **Scribe** - a person who writes out documents **Describe** - to represent with words or pictures.
se	apart	**Secede** - to formally break away from **Seclude** - to keep away from **Serum** - a liquid isolated out of another.
sect	cut	**Dissect** - to cut apart piece by piece **Intersection** - the place or point where two things cross each other **Bisect** - to cut into two equal parts.

Root word	Meanings	Examples
semi	half, partial	**Semiannual** - every half year **Semicircle** - half a circle **Semiconscious** - partly conscious **Semiannual** - every half of a year.
sept/i	seven	**September** - this used to be the seventh month in the roman calendar **Septet** - a group of seven musicians **Septuagenarian** - a person in his/her seventies.
sol	alone	**Desolate** - lonely, dismal, gloomy **Solitary** - done alone, by yourself **Solo** - a performance done by one person alone.
sol	sun	**Solar** - involving the sun **Parasol** - umbrella protecting from the sun **Solarium** - a room where one is exposed to sun light.
somn/I	sleep	**Insomnia** - inability to fall asleep **Somniloquy** - talking in your sleep **Somnolent** - feeling sleepy.
son	sound	**Consonant** - a speech sound **Sonorous** - producing loud, full, rich sounds **Supersonic** - faster than sound **Unison** - as one voice.
soph	wise	**Philosopher** - a wise person **Sophisticated** - wise about the ways of the world **Sophism** - a clever but misleading argument.
spec/t, spic	see, look	**Circumspect** - cautious, looking all around **Retrospective** - a looking back at past things **Spectator** - a person who sees an event.
spir	breathe	**Inspire** - to stimulate or animate **Transpire** - to give of vapor with waste product through the skin or a membrane **Spirit** - invisible life force.
sta	stand	**Stable** - standing steady and firm **Stagnant** - standing still, not moving **Stationary** - at a standstill, fixed.
stell	star	**Constellation** - a group of stars that forms a pattern **Interstellar** - between the stars **Stellar** - relating to stars.
struct	build	**Construct** - to build **Destruction** - the act of destroying something that was built **Structure** - something built **Infrastructure** - underlying framework of a system.

Root word	Meanings	Examples
sub	under, lower than, inferior to	**Submarine** - an underwater boat **Submerge** - to put underwater **Substandard** - inferior to accepted standards.
sum	highest	**Sum** - the combined total of everything **Summation** - the total, highest amount **Summit** - the highest point or top
super	higher in quality or quantity	**Super bowl** - the final annual football game **Superior** - above average, better in quality **Supersonic** - faster than the speed of sound.
tact, tang	touch	**Contact** - a state in which two things touch **Tactile** - relating to the sense of touch **Tangible** - able to be touched **Intact** - with nothing missing.
tel/e/o	far, distant, complete	**Telephone** - a device to talk to a distant person **Telescope** - a device to view distant objects **Television** - a device to receive pictures from afar **Telecommuting** - working remotely, bridging the distance via virtual devices.
temp/or	time	**Contemporary** - existing at the same time **Temporal** - relating to time **Temporary** - lasting for a limited time.
ter, trit	rub	**Attrition** - the act of rubbing together or wearing down **Detritus** - a product of disintegration or wearing away **Trite** - used or occurring so often as to have lost interest, freshness, or force
term/ina	end, limit	**Determine** - to find something out at the end of an investigation **Terminate** - to end **Exterminate** - to destroy or get rid of completely.
terr/a/i	land, earth	**Extraterrestrial** - existing outside the earth **Terrain** - ground or land **Territory** - an area of land.
tetra	four	**Tetrapod** - having 4 legs **Tetrarchy** - government by 4 rulers **Tetrose** - a monosaccharide with four carbon atoms.
the/o	god	**Monotheism** - belief in one god **Polytheism** - worshiping more than one god **Theology** - the study of religion, god, etc.
therm/o	heat	**Thermal** - relating to heat **Thermos** - an insulated jar that keeps heat in **Thermostat** - a device that controls heat.

Root word	Meanings	Examples
tort	twist	**Contortion** - a twisted shape or position **Distort** - to alter the shape or condition of **Retort** - reply in a manner that is supposed to change the effect of something previously said.
tox	poison	**Detoxification** - the process of removing poisons **Toxic** - poisonous **Toxicology** - the study of poisons **Intoxicated** - influenced by drugs.
tract	pull, drag	**Attract** - to pull objects nearer **Distract** - to drag attention away from something **Tractor** - a motor vehicle that pulls things.
trans	across, beyond, through	**Transcontinental** - across the continent **Transfer** - to move from one place to another **Transport** - to carry something across a space.
tri	three, once in every three, third	**Triangle** - a figure with 3 sides and 3 angles **Triathlon** - an athletic contest with 3 events **Tricycle** - a 3-wheel vehicle with pedals.
ultra	beyond, extreme, more than	**Ultrahigh** - extremely high **Ultramodern** - more modern than anything else **Ultrasonic** - sound waves beyond human hearing.
un	not, opposite of, lacking	**Unabridged** - not shortened **Unfair** - opposite of fair **Unfriendly** - lacking friendliness.
uni	one, single	**Unicycle** - a vehicle with one wheel **Unilateral** - decided by only one person or nation **Unique** - the only one of its kind **Unison** - as one voice.
urb	city	**Suburb** - residential area on the edge of a city **Urban** - relating to a city **Urbanology** - the study of city life.
vac	empty	**Evacuate** - to empty a dangerous place **Vacant** - empty, not occupied **Vacation** - a time without work.
ven/t	come	**Circumvent** - to go around or bypass restrictions **Convention** - a gathering or assembly of people with a common interest **Intervene** - to come between.
ver/I	truth	**Veracious** - truthful, honest **Veracity** - the truth **Verify** - to make sure that something is true.
verb	word	**Verbalize** - to put into words **Adverb** - a word relating to a verb **Proverb** - a short saying that expresses a well-known truth.

Root word	Meanings	Examples
vers, vert	turn	**Reverse** - to turn around **Introvert** - being turned towards the inside **Version** - a variation of an original **Controversy** - a conversation in which positions are turned against each other.
vince, vic	conquer	**Convince** - to win someone over **Invincible** - not able to be conquered **Victory** - the conquest of an enemy.
viv, vit	live, life	**Revival** - the act of bringing back to life **Vital** - pertaining to live **Vivacious** - high-spirited and full of life.
voc/i	voice, call	**Advocate** - to speak in favor of **Equivocate** - to use misleading language that could be interpreted two different ways **Vocalize** - to produce with your voice.
vor, vour	eat	**Carnivorous** - meat-eating **Voracious** - desiring or eating food in great quantities **Devour** - to eat quickly.
xen/o	foreign	**Xenophobic** - afraid of foreigners **Xenogenesis** - the creation of offspring that is completely different from either parent **Xenophile** - attracted to foreigners.
xer/o/I	dry	**Xerophyte** - a plant that grows in dry climate **Xerography** - a dry photocopying process **Xeric** - requiring small amounts of moisture.

OWS Questions asked in SSC GD Constable 2022

SN	Phrases	One Word
1	The possible results of an action	Ramification
2	study of chemistry in a medieval fashion	Alchemy
3	A perfect society in which people work well with each other and are happy	Utopia
4	The situation in which a disease is spread by touching someone or something	Contagion
5	The study of ancient writings and scriptures	Palaeography
6	study of stars	Astronomy

Idioms / Phrases Questions asked in SSC GD Constable 2022

SN	Idioms / Phrases	Meaning
1	Face the music	To face the unpleasant consequences of one's actions
2	Royal road	Achieving something trouble free
3	Public enemy number one	Someone who is the greatest threat to a group or community
4	Silver tongue	Speaking with an eloquent expression to convince people
5	in the doldrums	In low spirits and despair
6	Where the shoe pinches	Where the difficulty lies
7	a thorn in the flesh	annoying and irritating
8	showed a clean pair of heels	ran away
9	Bag and baggage	With all belongings
10	Bed of roses	A pleasant condition of life
11	After one's own heart	Having likes and dislikes similar to one's own
12	take stock of	surveys
13	The whys and wherefores	Underlying reason
14	At your beck and call	To have absolute control over someone
15	A night owl	A person who prefers to be awake late at night
16	In dire straits	Very bad situation
17	a Herculean effort	a difficult task
18	made a hash of	made a mess of
19	Steal someone's thunder	To take the credit for something someone else did
20	Go the extra mile	Do much more than required
21	Flash in the pan	Something that looks promising in the beginning but fails to deliver anything in the end
22	a snake in the grass	A deceitful person
23	To call in question	Challenge
24	going for a song	Incredibly inexpensive
25	Light at the end of tunnel	Something that signals the end of a difficult situation
26	Fit as a fiddle	In good health
27	Take it with a grain of salt	To understand that something is likely to be untrue
28	Wild goose chase	To do something pointless
29	An axe to grind	Personal and selfish reason
30	Get the picture	To understand what's happening
31	Wear your heart on your sleeve	Expressing emotions very openly

32	To add fuel to fire	To make a bad situation worse
33	Up a creek without a paddle	In a troublesome and serious situation
34	An ox on their tongue	Bribed to remain silent
35	at the eleventh hour	at the last minute
36	Get a second wind	Have renewed energy after having been tired
37	spick and span	clean and organised
38	On the fence	Halting between two options
39	Add fuel to the flames	Making a bad situation even worse
40	To put a spoke in one's wheel	To thwart someone in execution of one's design
41	Hang in there	Don't give up
42	Bite off more than you can chew	Take on a task that you cannot finish
43	Lose your marbles	To become insane
44	Blow one's own trumpet	To praise oneself
45	cries over split milk	regrets uselessly
46	after a fashion	to only a certain extent
47	A herculean task	A tough job
48	hand in glove	To be in close association
49	Bounce something off someone	Discuss ideas with someone to get their views
50	The best thing since sliced bread	A really good invention
51	To be in the doldrums	To be in low and dull spirits
52	let the cat out of the bag	revealed the secret
53	In the blink of an eye	Happen fast and instantaneously
54	An arm and a leg	Very expensive
55	Miss the boat	Fail to take advantage of an opportunity
56	Rain on someone's parade	To spoil and ruin a happy moment
57	Raining cats and dogs	A very heavy downpour
58	Level playing field	A fair competition
59	Spick and span	To be neat and clean
60	Blaze the trail	Be first to do something important
61	Keep a straight face	Look serious though you want to laugh
62	At the drop of a hat	Do something immediately without hesitation
63	on the cards	Probable
64	In the fast lane	In great excitement
65	Penny wise and pound foolish	Careful in trivial matters but wasteful in large
66	Out of the woods	Not in danger
67	Hit the sack	To go to bed in order to sleep
68	break the bank	To be very expensive
69	On the ball	Aware of any changes or developments and quick to react to them
70	Gate-crasher	A person who enters an event without any invitation
71	Bear a grudge	To feel angry against somebody for a past incident
72	Bone to pick	Having a complaint that needs to be discussed
73	hangs in the balance	remains undecided

74	promised the earth	Promised an impossible thing
75	by hook or by crook	By one or the other means
76	to grease the palm of	To bribe
77	beating around the bush	speaking vaguely to avoid talking about it
78	an open book	straightforward and honest
79	Beside oneself	Feeling overwhelming fear or worry
80	has a bee in her bonnet	talks incessantly
81	Hold your horses	Be patient
82	Throw caution to the wind	Ignore the risk
83	Lay hands on	To touch or grasp someone, often with the threat of violence
84	child's play	easy task
85	Wrangle for an ass's shadow	Argue over petty issues
86	Snake in the grass	Treacherous person
87	Risk life and limb	In danger of death or serious injury
88	take a leaf out of your book	Imitate or emulate someone in a particular way
89	Bury the hatchet	To end a quarrel
90	Chew someone out	To scold someone
91	burning question	most important issue to be discussed
92	The pot calling the kettle black	People are guilty of the very fault they identify in others
93	Explore all avenues	Try out every possibility to get a result
94	Spinning one's wheels	To make a lot of effort without achieving anything
95	Keep an eye on	Observe continually and carefully
96	took heart	felt encouraged
97	not fit to hold a candle to	cannot to be compared with
98	Done for	Ruined
99	It takes two to tango	A conflict where both people are at fault
100	Called for	To require something
101	Back to square one	Having to start all over again
102	Spill the beans	Tell something that should be kept secret
103	Grease someone's palm	To bribe one discreetly
104	A man of means	A wealthy man with lots of money and assets
105	go cold turkey	Quite addictive or dangerous behaviour
106	Without any question	Beyond a doubt
107	Sow wild oats	Engaging in rebelliousness or promiscuity
108	Let the cat out of the bag	To reveal a secret accidentally
109	Pull yourself together	Calm down
110	not turn a hair	To show no outward emotion
111	Fish out of water	Not feeling comfortable in a new environment
112	full of wisdom	an old head on young shoulders
113	pulling someone's leg	teasing and making fun of people
114	gift of gab	gift of speaking
115	Will-o-the-wisp	An unrealistic or unattainable goal

116	Better the devil you know than the devil you don't	It is easier to be in a known bad situation than being in an unknown worse situation
117	Like oil and water	Two people who are different from each other
118	White elephant	Something that costs a lot of money but has no useful purpose
119	Be riding high	To be very successful
120	A vicious cycle	When one problem causes another problem
121	at sea	perplexed
122	go back to the drawing board	start it over again
123	Be in seventh heaven	To be extremely happy
124	a wry face	A disappointed look
125	To go through fire and water	To face many challenges
126	Taste of your own medicine	Have the same bad treatment that you have given to others
127	Has bigger fish to fry	Has more important work to do
128	A cakewalk	An easy task or victory
129	Forty winks	To take a short nap
130	A Penelope's web	An endless job
131	Once in a blue moon	Very rarely
132	rock the boat	Upset the balance
133	Heart in your mouth	Feeling extremely nervous
134	Head over heels	To be madly in love
135	missed the boat	missed out an opportunity
136	A slap on the wrist	A small punishment
137	bite the bullet	To accept a difficult or unpleasant situation
138	Armed to the teeth	Carrying a lot of weapons
139	In the long run	In the end
140	Judas kiss	Deceitful pretence of friendship
141	a clean slate	Situation in which you can start again
142	Pour out one's heart	To express openly
143	A chip on one's shoulder	An attitude that leads one to become easily angered
144	beat around the bush	to talk around a subject without getting to the point

SN	Word - Synonym
	Synonym Questions asked in SSC GD Constable 2022
1	Queer - Strange
2	Competent - Capable
3	Fascinating - Interesting
4	Splendid - Spectacular
5	Hesitation - Reluctance
6	Colossal - Immense
7	Blend - Fusion
8	Lassitude - Weariness
9	Nepotism - Favouritism
10	Conceal - Hide
11	Bankrupt - Insolvent
12	Sumptuous - Lavish
13	Rejuvenate - Refreshen
14	Lustre - Shine
15	Deadly - Fatal
16	Abundant - Ample
17	Blast - Blow Up
18	Colloquial - Conversational
19	Drowsy - Sleepy
20	Procure - Obtain
21	Fair - Unbiased
22	Conviction - Belief
23	Prosperity - Richness
24	Funny - Humorous
25	Benevolent - Gracious
26	Compact - Dense
27	Ideal - Excellent
28	Orifice - Opening
29	Deceive - Cheat
30	Omnipresent - Universal
31	Awkward - Unskilful
32	Earn - Receive
33	Consistent - Constant
34	Pamper - Coddle
35	Auspicious - Fortunate
36	Admonition - Counsel
37	Exciting - Electrifying
38	Conquer - Defeat
39	Constant - Steady
40	Valid - Logical
41	Peak - Zenith
42	Obliterate - Erase
43	Fair - Reasonable
44	Hypocrisy - Trickery
45	Objective - Purpose
46	Elaborate - Intricate
47	Arrogant - Haughty
48	Secure - Safe
49	Baffle - Amaze
50	Endeavours - Efforts
51	Introvert - Shy
52	Austere - Strict
53	An Important - A Significant
54	Aghast - Horrified
55	Liberty - Freedom
56	Benefit - Advantage
57	Perturbed - Disturbed
58	Firewall - Bulwark
59	Dazzling - Brilliant
60	Yields - Produces
61	Cocoon - Encasement
62	Dodge - Cheat
63	Palpable - Detectable
64	Exterminate - Eradicate
65	Manifest - Apparent
66	Narrow - Cramped
67	Courage - Valour
68	Timid - Fearful
69	Declining - Decreasing
70	Acquired - Obtained
71	Contagion - Transmission
72	Negative - Adverse
73	Static - Inert
74	Futile - Unsuccessful
75	Titan - Giant
76	Annoy - Irritate
77	Despise - Dislike
78	Brazen - Bold
79	Sombre - Doleful
80	Paramount - Central
81	Imminent - Approaching
82	Anger - Fury
83	Privilege - Honour
84	Cherish - Admire
85	Startled - Frightened
86	Doubtful - Dilemma
87	Attain - Achieve
88	Incompetent - Inefficient
89	Cheerless - Gloomy
90	Despair - Misery
91	Liberate - Free
92	False - Untrue
93	Attacked - Assaulted
94	Enmity - Hostility
95	Sailor - Mariner
96	Hallway - Aisle
97	Sanctions - Permissions
98	Forbore - Refrain
99	Admitted - Acknowledged
100	Affliction - Bane
101	Eligible - Qualified
102	Ample - Sufficient
103	Frozen - Icy
104	Immune - Resistant
105	Perilous - Dangerous

106	Wealth - Riches		160	Solitary - Single
107	Proficient - Skilful		161	Single - Fair
108	Enough - Sufficient		162	Rogue - Ruffian
109	Stroll - Saunter		163	Vacate - Depart
110	Solitude - Seclusion		164	Confuse - Puzzle
111	Sedulous - Diligent		165	Deficient - Insufficient
112	Brave - Daring		166	Culpable - Guilty
113	Handy - Useful		167	Deceive - Trick
114	Earned - Gained		168	Decay - Degeneration
115	Indebted - Thankful		169	Antagonist - Adversary
116	Nasty - Despicable		170	Glowing - Dazzling
117	Obstinate - Adamant		171	Fleeting - Brief
118	Casual - Regular		172	False - Untrue
119	Beautiful - Pretty		173	Brusque - Abrupt
120	Heyday - Prime		174	Gloomy - Cloudy
121	Annoyance - Anger		175	Slack - Inactive
122	Stratified - Laminated		176	Accomplish - Achieve
123	Gloomy - Unhappy		177	Baffle - Confuse
124	Strict - Austere		178	Tomb - Grave
125	Adversity - Misfortune		179	Ample - Abundant
126	Bargain - Deal		180	Swindle - Fraud
127	Toying - Playing		181	Insufficient - Lacked
128	Burgled - Looted		182	Calamity - Disaster
129	Mean - Greedy		183	Wily - Crafty
130	Pious - Devout		184	Adversity - Hardships
131	Built Up - Gained		185	Amputate - Sever
132	Debonair - Charming		186	Disclose - Revealed
133	Curious - Inquisitive		187	Graphic - Vivid
134	Destroyed - Ruined		188	Leap - Hop
135	Despise - Hate		189	Judicious - Thoughtful
136	Noble - Dignified		190	Paused - Halted
137	Reckon - Think		191	Propel - Move
138	Commerce - Trade		192	Grandeur - Magnificence
139	Leave - Exit		193	Frantic - Violent
140	Look - See		194	Surrender - Yield
141	Glimpse - Glance		195	Capitulate - Surrender
142	Alight - Descend		196	Stimulate - Energises
143	Grief - Anguish		197	Impress - Influence
144	Rigid - Stiff		198	Gigantic - Huge
145	Counsel - Advice		199	Supreme - Paramount
146	Plead - Beseech		200	Confined - Limited
147	Daunt - Discourage		201	Bliss - Joy
148	Entrap - Entrap		202	Scared - Frightened
149	Hearth - Fireside		203	Cordial - Warm
150	Ruthless - Merciless			
151	Blunt - Dull			
152	Esteem - Respect			
153	Respect - Stubborn			
154	Salty - Saline			
155	Early - Beforehand			
156	Obstruct - Block			
157	Compulsion - Obligation			
158	Serpentine - Zigzag			
159	Progress - Betterment			

Antonym Questions asked in SSC GD Constable 2022

SN	Word - Antonym
1	Lively - Gloomy
2	Empty - Overfed
3	Perplex - Simplify
4	Dignify - Condemn
5	Cranky - Cheerful
6	Symbolise - Hide
7	Native - Foreign
8	Dream - Reality
9	Unfathomable - Comprehensible
10	Truth - Falsity
11	Cruel - Kind
12	Boor - Gentleman
13	Steadfast - Dishonest
14	Anxious - Unconcerned
15	Absurd - Reasonable
16	Solitary - Gregarious
17	Captivity - Liberty
18	Acceptance - Rejection
19	Timid - Bold
20	Liability - Asset
21	Rancid - Fresh
22	Fatuity - Sapience
23	Neglect - Remember
24	Just - Unfair
25	Apparent - Hidden
26	Ancestor - Descendant
27	Insipid - Tasty
28	Autonomy - Dependency
29	Feeble - Sturdy
30	Compassionate - Cruel
31	Sweet - Sour
32	Inferior - Superior
33	Neglected - Attended
34	Benign - Wicked
35	Retain - Forget
36	Generous - Selfish
37	Hope - Despair
38	Curtail - Amplify
39	Exaggerated - Understate
40	Outgoing - Introverted
41	Eager - Indifferent
42	Invincible - Vulnerable
43	Freedom - Bondage
44	Verbose - Brief
45	Lucid - Dark
46	Smart - Shabby
47	Derogatory - Appreciative
48	Flexible - Obstinate
49	Esteem - Condemn
50	Revive - Destroy
51	Attend - Miss
52	Accepted - Rejected
53	Gratification - Dissatisfaction
54	Divulgence - Repudiation
55	Ready - Unresponsive
56	Frugality - Luxury
57	Significant - Paltry
58	Confident - Cowardly
59	Transient - Permanent
60	Exhaust - Restore
61	Dominate - Surrender
62	Amused - Bored
63	Comical - Serious
64	Brittle - Resilient
65	Applaud - Denounce
66	Borrowed - Lent
67	Sublime - Ordinary
68	Huge - Minute
69	Put Forth - Conceal
70	Accurate - Unreliable
71	Disdain - Respect
72	Feeble - Strong
73	Cease - Commence
74	Generous - Stingy
75	Barren - Fertile
76	Doleful - Joyous
77	Cynical - Optimistic
78	Nadir - Zenith
79	Sensitive - Numb
80	Camouflage - Reveal
81	Scintillating - Dark
82	Austere - Genial
83	Sluggish - Active
84	Betray - Protect
85	Salient - Negligible
86	Quiet - Commotion
87	Restore - Destroy
88	After - Before
89	Courtesy - Crudeness
90	Steady - Wavering
91	Realm - Sky
92	Repulsive - Innocuous
93	Tedious - Exciting
94	Shabby - Respectable
95	Drenched - Fresh
96	Bleak - Cordial
97	Ponderous - Graceful
98	Alienate - Reconcile
99	Feeble - Powerful
100	Vicinity - Remote
101	Jaded - Renewed
102	Gather - Spread
103	Fragile - Healthy
104	Negotiate - Disagree
105	Recede - Advance

106	Distasteful - Delicious		160	Encircle - Exclude
107	Obedient - Disobedient		161	Misfortune - Blessing
108	Horrible - Pleasant		162	Compact - Expand
109	Subordinate - Superior		163	Polite - Rude
110	Jovial - Gloomy		164	Criticise - Praise
111	Benevolence - Cruelty		165	Causes - Consequences
112	Sustain - Obstruct		166	Pure - Tainted
113	Last - Foremost		167	Presumable - Improbable
114	Cramped - Extensive		168	Scanty - Abundant
115	Hasty - Cautious		169	Gratitude - Thanklessness
116	Profound - Shallow		170	Mandatory - Optional
117	Celebrate - Disgrace		171	Abolish - Construct
118	Subjugate - Liberate		172	Worthless - Productive
119	Frail - Strong		173	Diminish - Grow
120	Obvious - Ambiguous		174	Naïve - Sophisticated
121	Enormous - Negligible		175	Cruel - Sympathetic
122	Quietness - Agitation		176	Malice - Goodwill
123	Miser - Spendthrift		177	Destroyed - Restored
124	Eradicate - Conserve		178	Tasty - Insipid
125	Vanquish - Surrender		179	Officious - Timid
126	Convivial - Antisocial		180	Captured - Released
127	Centre - Outskirts		181	Agree - Refuse
128	Honest - Corrupt		182	Dense - Sparse
129	Witty - Stupid		183	Perfume - Stench
130	Cluster - Individual		184	Prosperity - Failure
131	Succinct - Lengthy		185	Escalate - Diminish
132	Erudite - Ignorant		186	Follow - Predate
133	Calmed - Agitated		187	Common - Rare
134	Obvious - Cryptic		188	Hostility - Friendship
135	Spendthrift - Miser		189	Annoying - Delightful
136	Accuse - Defend		190	Rival - Comrade
137	Grumble - Praise		191	Influence - Deter
138	Extravagant - Frugal		192	Servile - Dominant
139	Sage - Foolish		193	Rustic - Urbane
140	Blunt - Sharp		194	Follow - Lead
141	Hyper - Tranquil		195	Prompt - Delayed
142	Endurance - Indolence		196	Relevant - Insignificant
143	Savage - Tame		197	Dismal - Intelligent
144	Blank - Filled		198	Savage - Civilised
145	Banal - Novel		199	Silent - Noisy
146	Protest - Support		200	Reluctant - Willing
147	Local - Foreign		201	Hesitate - Resolve
148	Object to - Approve of		202	Evasive - Truthful
149	Lovely - Lousy		203	Capture - Liberate
150	Dispel - Integrate		204	Courteous - Discourteous
151	Arrogant - Humble		205	Busy - Idle
152	Honest - Corrupt		206	Enormous - Tiny
153	Propagate - Deplete		207	Frankness - Deception
154	Initial - Terminal		208	Candid - Tactful
155	Latent - Obvious		209	Progressive - Conservative
156	Rare - Usual			
157	Humility - Pride			
158	Flatter - Insult			
159	Alert - Distracted			

SN	Correct Spelling						
Spelling Questions asked in SSC GD Constable 2022		47	Height	97	Consonant	147	Phlegm
		48	Enthusiastic	98	Similar	148	Illustrious
		49	Explanation	99	Treasure	149	Mathematics
		50	Pesticides	100	Vaccination	150	Celestial
1	Naturally	51	Flowers	101	Deceive	151	Triumphant
2	Laundry	52	Reduced	102	Deposit	152	Abundant
3	Maintenance	53	Blame	103	Decision	153	Engineer
4	Jeweller	54	Phenomenon	104	Definite	154	Ecstasy
5	Sentence	55	Dampness	105	License	155	Pioneer
6	Artificial	56	Slaughter	106	Exclusive	156	Demolish
7	Tendency	57	Anthropology	107	Lament	157	Discursive
8	Matrimony	58	Accountable	108	Juggle	158	Discard
9	Potable	59	Miraculous	109	Necessity	159	Jeopardy
10	Meticulous	60	Vision	110	Weather	160	Unanimous
11	Erroneous	61	Sculptor	111	Modest	161	Cautious
12	Enterprising	62	Succeed	112	Knowledge	162	Intelligent
13	Frequent	63	Separate	113	Geometry	163	Irrational
14	Ferocious	64	Suitable	114	Contradict	164	Excessive
15	Collide	65	Nutrient	115	Auspicious	165	Hierarchical
16	Coherent	66	Permanent	116	Arrogant	166	Pathetic
17	Bureaucracy	67	Pancake	117	Technique	167	Troublesome
18	Doubtful	68	Modern	118	Garrulous	168	Cognizant
19	Wilful	69	Passage	119	Simultaneous	169	Manufacturer
20	Powerful	70	Pasion	120	Reluctant	170	Separate
21	Grateful	71	Neurological	121	Supersede	171	Ravishing
22	Slice	72	List	122	Etiquette	172	Inadvertent
23	Dribbling	73	Approximate	123	Flimsy	173	Irresponsible
24	Solvent	74	Catalogue	124	Intercede	174	Capacious
25	Temperament	75	Blink	125	Fractural	175	Receipt
26	Ignorance	76	Spoil	126	Historiography	176	Thankful
27	Harass	77	Lapse	127	Antagonistic	177	Merciful
28	Occasion	78	Argue	128	Periphery	178	Plentiful
29	Misspell	79	Kindergarten	129	Abbreviations	179	Dutiful
30	Cauliflower	80	Swindle	130	Adjudicate	180	Miniature
31	Orthopaedic	81	Grammar	131	Luggage	181	Millennium
32	Task	82	Imaginary	132	Electricity	182	Condolence
33	Speed	83	Cowardice	133	Eccentricity	183	Irrelevant
34	Salt	84	Statutory	134	Extreme	184	Flabbergasted
35	Brand	85	Brandish	135	Excite	185	Vacuum
36	Chronological	86	Treachery	136	Enduring	186	Breakage
37	Stakeholder	87	Accretion	137	Agony	187	Wreckage
38	Permanent	88	Entrepreneur	138	Health	188	Drainage
39	Longitude	89	Quickly	139	Mantel	189	Marriage
40	Maladjusted	90	Bravely	140	Secede	190	Arrived
41	Loneliness	91	Slowly	141	Seismic	191	Allergy
42	Compassion	92	Happily	142	Relevance	192	Fabulous
43	Efficient	93	Viceregal	143	Titillate	193	Furnish
44	Mortality	94	Dalmatian	144	Psalm	194	Attain
45	Futuristic	95	Venerate	145	Intermittence	195	Cherish
46	Curriculum	96	Retinal	146	Cholera	196	Mice

197	Wisdom	247	Vacuum	297	Manipulate	347	Contagious
198	Calendar	248	Trendy	298	Instigate	348	Irreparable
199	Convertible	249	Domicile	299	Philosophy	349	Teetotaller
200	Cancellation	250	Vacillate	300	Horrendous	350	Unanimously
201	Credible	251	Unique	301	Passive	351	Artisan
202	Conscious	252	Flora	302	Pharmaceutical	352	Technician
203	Tremendous	253	Fiona	303	Reverberation	353	Plumber
204	Bankruptcies	254	Regina	304	Occupation	354	Electrician
205	Appearance	255	Interpretation	305	Hallucination		
206	Classified	256	Amplification	306	Constipation		
207	Caterpillar	257	Theoretical	307	Alternative		
208	Persist	258	Administration	308	Renewable		
209	Conceive	259	Reluctant	309	Venomous		
210	Repair	260	Ordinary	310	Pyramid		
211	Strict	261	Cautious	311	Strategies		
212	Collector	262	Slippery	312	Effective		
213	Magistrate	263	Aboveboard	313	Innovative		
214	Administration	264	Telepathy	314	Interventions		
215	Circumference	265	Refrigeration	315	Maintenance		
216	Passengers	266	Bewilderment	316	Defrauded		
217	Snatching	267	Strangulate	317	Continuation		
218	Bas	268	Falcon	318	Discrimination		
219	Monkeys	269	Talon	319	Acclaim		
220	Adopt	270	Parlour	320	Opportunity		
221	Reasonable	271	Tailor	321	Convenience		
222	Unconscious	272	Neigh	322	Calendar		
223	Pester	273	Mischievous	323	Reckon		
224	Orientation	274	Gaiety	324	Subservient		
225	Exaggerate	275	Inoculate	325	Subvert		
226	Reference	276	Circular	326	Rebuke		
227	Perceive	277	Perceive	327	Incompetent		
228	Vacuous	278	Mischief	328	Rubber		
229	Malicious	279	Achieve	329	Robber		
230	Repugnant	280	Receive	330	Radar		
231	Spiteful	281	Quotable	331	Rather		
232	Debatable	282	Volunteer	332	Applicable		
233	Rotational	283	Raisin	333	Success		
234	Magnificent	284	Pamphlet	334	Stepping		
235	Regions	285	Wrapped	335	Failure		
236	Issue	286	Messenger	336	Stone		
237	Significantly	287	Disciplines	337	Kaleidoscope		
238	Geospatial	288	Discussions	338	Align		
239	Unaffected	289	Interactive	339	Fantastic		
240	Minimal	290	Requirements	340	Mirror		
241	Supervision	291	Avoidance	341	Secretly		
242	Dynamics	292	Correction	342	Reckless		
243	Conscientious	293	Preference	343	Palpable		
244	Extinguish	294	Tolerance	344	Endeavor		
245	Moan	295	Anticipate	345	Rubbish		
246	Definite	296	Calculate	346	Physiotherapist		

SN	Select the most appropriate homonym of the given word.	Answer
	Homonyms Questions asked in SSC GD Constable 2022	
1	This nation is _______ to each of its citizens. 1) fare 2) fair 3) feel 4) fur	**fair**
2	He confessed about his affairs as the _______ made him sleepless. 1) gilled 2) gild 3) guild 4) guilt	**guilt**
3	What _______ of a movie is this? 1) kind 2) can 3) keen 4) con	**kind**
4	What she _______ is that he is a _______ person. 1) grown, groaned 2) mean, meant 3) growing, grown 4) meant, mean	**meant, mean**
5	The authorities _______ the unregistered companies. 1) sees 2) seize 3) seas 4) cease	**seize**
6	If you want to _______ the world, you should be the one to take the first step. 1) change (switch) 2) change (alter) 3) change (loose money) 4) change (transfer)	**change (alter)**
7	At a particular _______ of life, the body goes through some unnecessary changes. 1) Stage (a raised platform) 2) Plane 3) Plain 4) Stage (step)	**Stage (step)**
8	Select the most appropriate homonym of the given word. Blue 1) Blew 2) Bellow 3) Below 4) Blow	**Blew**
9	The Prime Minister _______ the nation asking for the _______ of the traitors. 1) meant, mean 2) addressed, address 3) mean, meant 4) address, addressed	**addressed, address**
10	I think he is the _______ person for this job. 1) right 2) write 3) rite 4) wright	**right**
11	In order to keep _______ I jog for 45 minutes daily. 1) fitt 2) feat 3) feet 4) fit	**fit**
12	Due to the attack his vital organs _______ functioning. 1) ceased 2) seized 3) sized 4) seas	**ceased**
13	He was supposed to _______ this work. 1) dew 2) doux 3) due 4) do	**do**
14	Select the most appropriate homonym of the given word. Idol 1) eye lid 2) doll 3) dull 4) Idle	**Idle**
15	These products _______ for a long time. 1) last 2) lust 3) lost 4) least	**last**
16	The annual extraction of this _______ costs around $10,000,000. 1) or 2) ore 3) o'er 4) arc	**ore**
17	The construction _______ was far from his home. 1) sight 2) site 3) cite 4) cyte	**site**
18	He planned a weeklong _______ down the Nile. 1) cruise 2) crews 3) cruse 4) crus	**cruise**
19	"Where is my _______ ?" cried the boatman. 1) oar 2) or 3) o'er 4) oat	**oar**
20	The river _______ provide a reserve _______ for minerals that enrich the soil's fertility. 1) banks, bank 2) right, right 3) band, band 4) quail, quail	**banks, bank**
21	I had to keep very _______ when the photographer was taking my picture. 1) still 2) lid 3) chum 4) shrill	**still**
22	The sales of _______, _______ by 20% on Valentine's Day. 1) roses, rose 2) pear, pair 3) dates, dated 4) roll, rolled	**roses, rose**
23	Select the most appropriate homonym of the given word. Flea 1) Flee 2) Flew 3) Fly 4) Fleece	**Flee**

OWS Questions asked in SSC CGL T-2 2022

SN	Phrases	One Word
1	The science and art of growing vegetables, fruits and flowers	Horticulture
2	One who is a boot licker and flatterer	Sycophant
3	Wilful destruction	Sabotage
4	A person who admires himself or herself too much, especially their appearance	Narcissist
5	Photographers who follow celebrities to get their pictures to sell them	Paparazzi
6	Someone who is reserved and shy.	Introvert
7	The one who loves mankind	Philanthropist
8	An arched structure in a garden having climbing plants	Pergola

Idioms / Phrases Questions asked in SSC CGL T-2 2022

SN	Idioms / Phrases	Meaning
1	chip off the old block	Similar to one's parents in behaviour
2	Achilles' Heel	Vulnerable point
3	escaped by the skin of his teeth.	Barely managed to escape
4	at a stone's throw	at a close distance
5	running around in circles.	To be very active but with few results
6	Catch 22 situation	A difficult situation in which the solution to a problem is impossible
7	with a pinch of salt	Doubt the truth or value of something
8	Water under the bridge	Past events that are not important anymore

Synonyms asked in SSC CGL T-2 2022

SN	Word - Synonym
1	Unacknowledged - Unidentified
2	Vogue - Fashion
3	Threshold - Dawn
4	Advised - Prescribed
5	Fruition - Accomplishment

Antonyms asked in SSC CGL T-2 2022

SN	Word - Antonym
1	Often - Seldom
2	Insolvent - Affluent
3	Colossal - Tiny
4	Stern - Lenient
5	Clandestine - Overt
6	Placid - Angry
7	Sneered - Lauded
8	Stable - Mutable

Spelling asked in SSC CGL T-2 2022

SN	Correct Spelling	SN	Correct Spelling
1	Descendant	12	Gravely
2	Deceased	13	Grandeur
3	Decimate	14	Monuments
4	Descent	15	Deadline
5	Attempt	16	Intricate
6	Philosophy	17	Succeeded
7	Think	18	Earlier
8	Systematic	19	Irregular
9	Greave	20	Academic
10	Groan	21	Review
11	Guarantee	22	Affiliated

Homonyms Questions asked in SSC CGL T-2 2022

SN	Select the most appropriate homonym to fill in the blank.	Answer
1	The farmers grow ______ in their fields. 1) mays 2) mase 3) maze 4) maize	**maize**
2	______ knowledge in this field is really profound. 1) There 2) Dare 3) They're 4) Their	**Their**
3	Which ______ does the minister take to reach the Assembly? 1) root 2) rot 3) riot 4) route	**route**
4	The wind ______ so powerfully that the door closed. 1) blow 2) blues 3) blue 4) blew	**blew**
5	The athlete's ______ was badly injured due to a fall on the track. 1) toad 2) tow 3) to 4) toe	**toe**

Join Us:

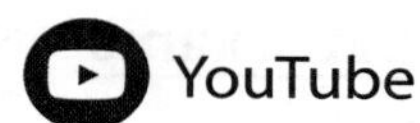 YouTube

https://bit.ly/Qm_YT

 Facebook

https://bit.ly/Qm_fb

 Telegram

https://bit.ly/Qm_tele

 Twitter

https://bit.ly/Qm_Tw

 Instagram

https://bit.ly/Qm_insta